T0238782

Boosting

Foundations and Algorithms

Adaptive Computation and Machine Learning

Thomas Dietterich, Editor

Christopher Bishop, David Heckerman, Michael Jordan, and Michael Kearns, Associate Editors

A complete list of the books published in this series may be found at the back of the book.

Boosting

Foundations and Algorithms

Robert E. Schapire
Yoav Freund

The MIT Press
Cambridge, Massachusetts
London, England

First MIT Press paperback edition, 2014

© 2012 Massachusetts Institute of Technology

All rights reserved. No part of this book may be reproduced in any form by any electronic or mechanical means (including photocopying, recording, or information storage and retrieval) without permission in writing from the publisher.

This book was set in Times Roman by Westchester Book Composition.

Library of Congress Cataloging-in-Publication Data

Schapire, Robert E.
Boosting : foundations and algorithms / Robert E. Schapire and Yoav Freund.
   p.   cm.—(Adaptive computation and machine learning series)
Includes bibliographical references and index.
ISBN 978-0-262-01718-3 (hardcover : alk. paper), 978-0-262-52603-6 (pb.)
1. Boosting (Algorithms) 2. Supervised learning (Machine learning) I. Freund, Yoav. II. Title.
Q325.75.S33 2012
006.3'1—dc23
2011038972

To our families

On the cover: A randomized depiction of the potential function $\Phi_t(s)$ used in the boost-by-majority algorithm, as given in equation (13.30). Each pixel, identified with an integer pair (t, s), was randomly colored blue with probability $\Phi_t(s)$, and was otherwise colored yellow (with colors inverted where lettering appears). The round t runs horizontally from $T = 1225$ at the far left down to 0 at the far right, and position s runs vertically from -225 at the top to 35 at the bottom. An edge of $\gamma = 0.06$ was used. [Cover design by Molly Seamans and the authors.]

Contents

Series Foreword

The goal of building systems that can adapt to their environments and learn from their experience has attracted researchers from many fields, including computer science, engineering, mathematics, physics, neuroscience, and cognitive science. Out of this research has come a wide variety of learning techniques that are transforming many industrial and scientific fields. Recently, several research communities have converged on a common set of issues surrounding supervised, unsupervised, and reinforcement learning problems. The MIT Press Series on Adaptive Computation and Machine Learning seeks to unify the many diverse strands of machine learning research and to foster high quality research and innovative applications.

The MIT Press is extremely pleased to publish this contribution by Robert Schapire and Yoav Freund. The development of boosting algorithms by Schapire, Freund, and their collaborators over the last twenty years has had an immense impact on machine learning, statistics, and data mining. Originally developed to address a fundamental theoretical question, boosting has become a standard tool for solving a wide variety of problems in machine learning and optimization. The book offers a definitive, yet highly accessible, treatment of boosting. It explains the theory underlying the basic algorithm as well as presenting extensions to confidence-rated prediction, multi-class classification, and ranking. This book will serve as a valuable reference for researchers and as a focused introduction to machine learning for undergraduate and beginning graduate students interested in understanding this elegant approach to machine learning.

Preface

This book is about boosting, an approach to machine learning based on the idea of creating a highly accurate prediction rule by combining many relatively weak and inaccurate rules. A remarkably rich theory has evolved around boosting, with connections to a wide range of topics including statistics, game theory, convex optimization, and information geometry. In addition, AdaBoost and other boosting algorithms have enjoyed practical success with applications, for instance, in biology, vision, and speech processing. At various times in its history, boosting has been the subject of controversy for the mystery and paradox that it seems to present.

In writing this book, we have aimed to reach nearly anyone with an interest in boosting (as well as an appropriate, but relatively minimal, technical background), whether students or advanced researchers, whether trained in computer science, statistics, or some other field. We specifically hope that the book will be useful as an educational tool, and have therefore included exercises in every chapter. Although centered on boosting, the book introduces a variety of topics relevant to machine learning generally, as well as to related fields such as game theory and information theory.

The main prerequisite for this book is an elementary background in probability. We also assume familiarity with calculus and linear algebra at a basic, undergraduate level. An appendix provides background on some more advanced mathematical concepts which are used mainly in later chapters. The central notions of machine learning, boosting, and so on are all presented from the ground up.

Research on boosting has spread across multiple publications and disciplines over a period of many years. This book attempts to bring together, organize, extend, and simplify a significant chunk of this work. Some of this research is our own or with co-authors, but a very large part of what we present—including a few of the chapters almost in their entirety—is based on the contributions of the many other excellent researchers who work in this area. Credit for such previously published work is given in the bibliographic notes at the end of every chapter. Although most of the material in this book has appeared elsewhere, the majority of chapters also include new results that have never before been published.

The focus of this book is on foundations and algorithms, but also on applications. Following a general introduction to machine learning algorithms and their analysis, the book explores in part I the core theory of boosting, particularly its ability to generalize (that is, make accurate predictions on new data). This includes an analysis of boosting's training error, as well as bounds on the generalization error based both on direct methods and on the margins theory. Next, part II systematically explores some of the other myriad theoretical viewpoints that have helped to explain and understand boosting, including the game-theoretic interpretation, the view of AdaBoost as a greedy procedure for minimizing a loss function, and an understanding of boosting as an iterative-projection algorithm with connections to information geometry and convex optimization. Part III focuses on practical extensions of AdaBoost based on the use of confidence-rated weak hypotheses, and for multiclass and ranking problems. Finally, some advanced theoretical topics are covered in part IV, including the statistical consistency of AdaBoost, optimal boosting, and boosting algorithms which operate in continuous time. Although the book is organized around theory and algorithms, most of the chapters include specific applications and practical illustrations.

Readers with particular interests, or those organizing a course, might choose one of a number of natural tracks through this book. For a more theoretical treatment, part III could be omitted. A track focused on the practical application of boosting might omit chapters 4, 6, and 8, and all of part IV. A statistical approach might emphasize chapters 7 and 12 while omitting chapters 4, 6, 8, 13, and 14. Some of the proofs included in this book are somewhat involved and technical, and can certainly be skipped or skimmed. A rough depiction of how the chapters depend on each other is shown in figure P.1.

This book benefited tremendously from comments and criticisms we received from numerous individuals. We are especially grateful to ten students who read an earlier draft of the book as part of a Princeton graduate seminar course: Jonathan Chang, Sean Gerrish, Sina Jafarpour, Berk Kapicioglu, Indraneel Mukherjee, Gungor Polatkan, Alexander

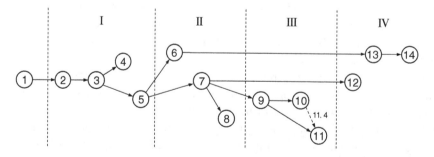

Figure P.1
An approximate depiction of how the chapters of this book depend on each other. Each edge $u \rightarrow v$ represents a suggestion that chapter u be read before chapter v. (The dashed edge indicates that section 11.4 depends on chapter 10, but the other sections of chapter 11 do not.)

Schwing, Umar Syed, Yongxin (Taylor) Xi, and Zhen (James) Xiang. Their close reading and numerous suggestions, both in and out of class, were extraordinarily helpful and led to significant improvements in content and presentation in every one of the chapters.

Thanks also to Peter Bartlett, Vladimir Koltchinskii, Saharon Rosset, Yoram Singer, and other anonymous reviewers of this book for their time and their many constructive suggestions and criticisms. An incomplete list of the many, many others who provided help, comments, ideas, and insights includes: Shivani Agarwal, Jordan Boyd-Graber, Olivier Chapelle, Kamalika Chaudhuri, Michael Collins, Edgar Dobriban, Miro Dudík, Dave Helmbold, Ludmila Kuncheva, John Langford, Phil Long, Taesup Moon, Lev Reyzin, Ron Rivest, Cynthia Rudin, Rocco Servedio, Matus Telgarsky, Paul Viola, and Manfred Warmuth. Our apologies to others who were surely, though certainly not intentionally, omitted from this list.

We are grateful to our past and present employers for supporting this work: AT&T Labs; Columbia Center for Computational Learning Systems; Princeton University; University of California, San Diego; and Yahoo! Research. Support for this research was also generously provided by the National Science Foundation under awards 0325463, 0325500, 0513552, 0812598, and 1016029.

Thanks to all of our collaborators and colleagues whose research appears in this book, and who kindly allowed us to include specific materials, especially figures, as cited and acknowledged with gratitude in the appropriate chapters. We are grateful to Katherine Almeida, Ada Brunstein, Jim DeWolf, Marc Lowenthal, Molly Seamans and everyone at MIT Press for their tireless assistance in preparing and publishing this book. Thanks also to the various editors at other publishers we considered, and to all those who helped with some occasionally thorny copyright issues, particularly Laurinda Alcorn and Frank Politano.

Finally, we are grateful for the love, support, encouragement, and patience provided by our families: Roberta, Jeni, and Zak; Laurie, Talia, and Rafi; and by our parents: Hans and Libby, Ora and Rafi.

1 Introduction and Overview

How is it that a committee of blockheads can somehow arrive at highly reasoned decisions, despite the weak judgment of the individual members? How can the shaky separate views of a panel of dolts be combined into a single opinion that is very likely to be correct? That this possibility of garnering wisdom from a council of fools can be harnessed and used to advantage may seem far-fetched and implausible, especially in real life. Nevertheless, this unlikely strategy turns out to form the basis of *boosting*, an approach to machine learning that is the topic of this book. Indeed, at its core, boosting solves hard machine-learning problems by forming a very smart committee of grossly incompetent but carefully selected members.

To see how this might work in the context of machine learning, consider the problem of filtering out spam, or junk email. Spam is a modern-day nuisance, and one that is ideally handled by highly accurate filters that can identify and remove spam from the flow of legitimate email. Thus, to build a spam filter, the main problem is to create a method by which a computer can automatically categorize email as spam (junk) or ham (legitimate). The machine learning approach to this problem prescribes that we begin by gathering a collection of examples of the two classes, that is, a collection of email messages which have been labeled, presumably by a human, as spam or ham. The purpose of the machine learning algorithm is to automatically produce from such data a prediction rule that can be used to reliably classify new examples (email messages) as spam or ham.

For any of us who has ever been bombarded with spam, rules for identifying spam or ham will immediately come to mind. For instance, if it contains the word *Viagra*, then it is probably spam. Or, as another example, email from one's spouse is quite likely to be ham. Such individual rules of thumb are far from complete as a means of separating spam from ham. A rule that classifies all email containing *Viagra* as spam, and all other email as ham, will very often be wrong. On the other hand, such a rule is undoubtedly telling us something useful and nontrivial, and its accuracy, however poor, will nonetheless be significantly better than simply guessing entirely at random as to whether each email is spam or ham.

Intuitively, finding these weak rules of thumb should be relatively easy—so easy, in fact, that one might reasonably envision a kind of automatic "weak learning" program that, given any set of email examples, could effectively search for a simple prediction rule that may be rough and rather inaccurate, but that nonetheless provides some nontrivial guidance in separating the given examples as spam or ham. Furthermore, by calling such a weak learning program repeatedly on various subsets of our dataset, it would be possible to extract a collection of rules of thumb. The main idea of boosting is to somehow combine these weak and inaccurate rules of thumb into a single "committee" whose overall predictions will be quite accurate.

In order to use these rules of thumb to maximum advantage, there are two critical problems that we face: First, how should we choose the collections of email examples presented to the weak learning program so as to extract rules of thumb that will be the most useful? And second, once we have collected many rules of thumb, how can they be combined into a single, highly accurate prediction rule? For the latter question, a reasonable approach is simply for the combined rule to take a vote of the predictions of the rules of thumb. For the first question, we will advocate an approach in which the weak learning program is forced to focus its attention on the "hardest" examples, that is, the ones for which the previously chosen rules of thumb were most apt to give incorrect predictions.

Boosting refers to a general and provably effective method of producing a very accurate prediction rule by combining rough and moderately inaccurate rules of thumb in a manner similar to that suggested above. This book presents in detail much of the recent work on boosting, focusing especially on the *AdaBoost* algorithm, which has undergone intense theoretical study and empirical testing. In this first chapter, we introduce AdaBoost and some of the key concepts required for its study. We also give a brief overview of the entire book.

See the appendix for a description of the notation used here and throughout the book, as well as some brief, mathematical background.

1.1 Classification Problems and Machine Learning

This book focuses primarily on *classification* problems in which the goal is to categorize objects into one of a relatively small set of classes. For instance, an optical character recognition (OCR) system must classify images of letters into the categories A, B, C, etc. Medical diagnosis is another example of a classification problem in which the goal is to diagnose a patient. In other words, given the symptoms manifested by the patient, our goal is to categorize him or her as a sufferer or non-sufferer of a particular disease. The spam-filtering example is also a classification problem in which we attempt to categorize emails as spam or ham.

We focus especially on a machine-learning approach to classification problems. Machine learning studies the design of automatic methods for making predictions about the future based on past experiences. In the context of classification problems, machine-learning methods attempt to learn to predict the correct classifications of unseen examples through the careful examination of examples which were previously labeled with their correct classifications, usually by a human.

We refer to the objects to be classified as *instances*. Thus, an instance is a description of some kind which is used to derive a predicted classification. In the OCR example, the instances are the images of letters. In the medical-diagnosis example, the instances are descriptions of a patient's symptoms. The space of all possible instances is called the *instance space* or *domain*, and is denoted by $\mathcal{X}$. A *(labeled) example* is an instance together with an associated *label* indicating its correct classification. Instances are also sometimes referred to as (unlabeled) examples.

During training, a *learning algorithm* receives as input a *training set* of labeled examples called the *training examples*. The output of the learning algorithm is a prediction rule called a *classifier* or *hypothesis*. A classifier can itself be thought of as a computer program which takes as input a new unlabeled instance and outputs a predicted classification; so, in mathematical terms, a classifier is a function that maps instances to labels. In this book, we use the terms *classifier* and *hypothesis* fairly interchangeably, with the former emphasizing a prediction rule's use in classifying new examples, and the latter emphasizing the fact that the rule has been (or could be) generated as the result of some learning process. Other terms that have been used in the literature include *rule, prediction rule, classification rule, predictor,* and *model*.

To assess the quality of a given classifier, we measure its error rate, that is, the frequency with which it makes incorrect classifications. To do this, we need a *test set*, a separate set of *test examples*. The classifier is evaluated on each of the test instances, and its predictions are compared against the correct classifications of the test examples. The fraction of examples on which incorrect classifications were made is called the *test error* of the classifier. Similarly, the fraction of mistakes on the training set is called the *training error*. The fraction of correct predictions is called the (test or training) *accuracy*.

Of course, the classifier's performance on the training set is not of much interest since our purpose is to build a classifier that works well on unseen data. On the other hand, if there is no relationship at all between the training set and the test set, then the learning problem is unsolvable; the future can be predicted only if it resembles the past. Therefore, in designing and studying learning algorithms, we generally assume that the training and test examples are taken from the *same* random source. That is, we assume that the examples are chosen randomly from some fixed but unknown distribution $\mathcal{D}$ over the space of labeled examples and, moreover, that the training and test examples are generated by the *same* distribution. The *generalization error* of a classifier measures the probability of misclassifying a random example from this distribution $\mathcal{D}$; equivalently, the generalization error is the expected test error of the classifier on any test set generated by $\mathcal{D}$. The goal of learning can now be stated succinctly as producing a classifier with low generalization error.

To illustrate these concepts, consider the problem of diagnosing a patient with coronary artery disease. For this problem, an instance consists of a description of the patient including items such as sex, age, cholesterol level, chest pain type (if any), blood pressure, and results of various medical tests. The label or class associated with each instance is a diagnosis provided by a doctor as to whether or not the patient described actually suffers from the disease. During training, a learning algorithm is provided with a set of labeled examples and attempts to produce a classifier for predicting if new patients suffer from the disease. The goal is to produce a classifier that is as accurate as possible. Later, in section 1.2.3, we describe experiments using a publicly available dataset for this problem.

1.2 Boosting

We can now make some of the informal notions about boosting described above more precise. Boosting assumes the availability of a *base* or *weak learning algorithm* which, given labeled training examples, produces a *base* or *weak classifier*. The goal of boosting is to improve the performance of the weak learning algorithm while treating it as a "black box" which can be called repeatedly, like a subroutine, but whose innards cannot be observed or manipulated. We wish to make only the most minimal assumptions about this learning algorithm. Perhaps the least we can assume is that the weak classifiers are not entirely trivial in the sense that their error rates are at least a little bit better than a classifier whose every prediction is a random guess. Thus, like the rules of thumb in the spam-filtering example, the weak classifiers can be rough and moderately inaccurate, but not entirely trivial and uninformative. This assumption, that the base learner produces a weak hypothesis that is at least slightly better than random guessing on the examples on which it was trained, is called the *weak learning assumption*, and it is central to the study of boosting.

As with the words *classifier* and *hypothesis*, we use the terms *base* and *weak* roughly interchangeably, with *weak* emphasizing mediocrity in performance and *base* connoting use as a building block.

Like any learning algorithm, a boosting algorithm takes as input a set of training examples $(x_1, y_1), \ldots, (x_m, y_m)$ where each x_i is an instance from $\mathcal{X}$, and each y_i is the associated label or class. For now, and indeed for most of this book, we assume the simplest case in which there are only two classes, -1 and $+1$, although we do explore extensions to multiclass problems in chapter 10.

A boosting algorithm's only means of learning from the data is through calls to the base learning algorithm. However, if the base learner is simply called repeatedly, always with the same set of training data, we cannot expect anything interesting to happen; instead, we expect the same, or nearly the same, base classifier to be produced over and over again, so that little is gained over running the base learner just once. This shows that the boosting algorithm, if it is to improve on the base learner, must in some way manipulate the data that it feeds to it.

Indeed, the key idea behind boosting is to choose training sets for the base learner in such a fashion as to force it to infer something new about the data each time it is called. This can be accomplished by choosing training sets on which we can reasonably expect the performance of the preceding base classifiers to be very poor—even poorer than their regular weak performance. If this can be accomplished, then we can expect the base learner to output a new base classifier which is significantly different from its predecessors. This is because, although we think of the base learner as a weak and mediocre learning algorithm, we nevertheless expect it to output classifiers that make nontrivial predictions.

We are now ready to describe in detail the boosting algorithm AdaBoost, which incorporates these ideas, and whose pseudocode is shown as algorithm 1.1. AdaBoost proceeds in *rounds* or iterative calls to the base learner. For choosing the training sets provided to the base learner on each round, AdaBoost maintains a *distribution* over the training examples. The distribution used on the t-th round is denoted D_t, and the weight it assigns to training example i is denoted $D_t(i)$. Intuitively, this weight is a measure of the importance of correctly classifying example i on the current round. Initially, all weights are set equally, but on each round, the weights of incorrectly classified examples are increased so that, effectively, hard examples get successively higher weight, forcing the base learner to focus its attention on them.

Algorithm 1.1
The boosting algorithm AdaBoost

Given: $(x_1, y_1), \ldots, (x_m, y_m)$ where $x_i \in \mathcal{X}$, $y_i \in \{-1, +1\}$.
Initialize: $D_1(i) = 1/m$ for $i = 1, \ldots, m$.
For $t = 1, \ldots, T$:

- Train weak learner using distribution D_t.
- Get weak hypothesis $h_t : \mathcal{X} \to \{-1, +1\}$.
- Aim: select h_t to minimalize the weighted error:

$$\epsilon_t \doteq \mathbf{Pr}_{i \sim D_t}[h_t(x_i) \neq y_i].$$

- Choose $\alpha_t = \dfrac{1}{2} \ln\left(\dfrac{1 - \epsilon_t}{\epsilon_t}\right)$.
- Update, for $i = 1, \ldots, m$:

$$D_{t+1}(i) = \frac{D_t(i)}{Z_t} \times \begin{cases} e^{-\alpha_t} & \text{if } h_t(x_i) = y_i \\ e^{\alpha_t} & \text{if } h_t(x_i) \neq y_i \end{cases}$$

$$= \frac{D_t(i) \exp(-\alpha_t y_i h_t(x_i))}{Z_t},$$

where Z_t is a normalization factor (chosen so that D_{t+1} will be a distribution).

Output the final hypothesis:

$$H(x) = \text{sign}\left(\sum_{t=1}^{T} \alpha_t h_t(x)\right).$$

The base learner's job is to find a base classifier $h_t : \mathcal{X} \to \{-1, +1\}$ appropriate for the distribution D_t. Consistent with the earlier discussion, the quality of a base classifier is measured by its error *weighted* by the distribution D_t:

$$\epsilon_t \doteq \mathbf{Pr}_{i \sim D_t}[h_t(x_i) \neq y_i] = \sum_{i : h_t(x_i) \neq y_i} D_t(i).$$

Here, $\mathbf{Pr}_{i \sim D_t}[\cdot]$ denotes probability with respect to the random selection of an example (as specified by its index i) according to distribution D_t. Thus, the weighted error ϵ_t is the chance of h_t misclassifying a random example if selected according to D_t. Equivalently, it is the sum of the weights of the misclassified examples. Notice that the error is measured with respect to the same distribution D_t on which the base classifier was trained.

The weak learner attempts to choose a weak hypothesis h_t with low weighted error ϵ_t. In this setting, however, we do not expect that this error will be especially small in an absolute sense, but only in a more general and relative sense; in particular, we expect it to be only a bit better than random, and typically far from zero. To emphasize this looseness in what we require of the weak learner, we say that the weak learner's aim is to *minimalize* the weighted error, using this word to signify a vaguer and less stringent diminishment than that connoted by *minimize*.

If a classifier makes each of its predictions entirely at random, choosing each predicted label to be -1 or $+1$ with equal probability, then its probability of misclassifying any given example will be exactly $\frac{1}{2}$. Therefore, the error of this classifier will always be $\frac{1}{2}$, regardless of the data on which the error is measured. Thus, a weak hypothesis with weighted error ϵ_t equal to $\frac{1}{2}$ can be obtained trivially by formulating each prediction as a random guess. The weak learning assumption then, for our present purposes, amounts to an assumption that the error of each weak classifier is bounded away from $\frac{1}{2}$, so that each ϵ_t is at most $\frac{1}{2} - \gamma$ for some small positive constant γ. In this way, each weak hypothesis is assumed to be slightly better than random guessing by some small amount, as measured by its error. (This assumption will be refined considerably in section 2.3.)

As for the weights $D_t(i)$ that AdaBoost calculates on the training examples, in practice, there are several ways in which these can be used by the base learner. In some cases, the base learner can use these weights directly. In other cases, an unweighted training set is generated for the base learner by selecting examples at random from the original training set. The probability of selecting an example in this case is set to be proportional to the weight of the example. These methods are discussed in more detail in section 3.4.

Returning to the spam-filtering example, the instances x_i correspond to email messages, and the labels y_i give the correct classification as spam or ham. The base classifiers are the rules of thumb provided by the weak learning program where the subcollections on which it is run are chosen randomly according to the distribution D_t.

Once the base classifier h_t has been received, AdaBoost chooses a parameter α_t as in algorithm 1.1. Intuitively, α_t measures the importance that is assigned to h_t. The precise choice of α_t is unimportant for our present purposes; the rationale for this particular choice will become apparent in chapter 3. For now, it is enough to observe that $\alpha_t > 0$ if $\epsilon_t < \frac{1}{2}$, and that α_t gets larger as ϵ_t gets smaller. Thus, the more accurate the base classifier h_t, the more importance we assign to it.

The distribution D_t is next updated using the rule shown in the algorithm. First, all of the weights are multiplied either by $e^{-\alpha_t} < 1$ for examples correctly classified by h_t, or by $e^{\alpha_t} > 1$ for incorrectly classified examples. Equivalently, since we are using labels and predictions in $\{-1, +1\}$, this update can be expressed more succinctly as a scaling of each example i by $\exp(-\alpha_t y_i h_t(x_i))$. Next, the resulting set of values is renormalized by dividing through by the factor Z_t to ensure that the new distribution D_{t+1} does indeed sum to 1. The effect of this rule is to increase the weights of examples misclassified by h_t, and to decrease the weights of correctly classified examples. Thus, the weight tends to concentrate on "hard" examples. Actually, to be more precise, AdaBoost chooses a new distribution D_{t+1} on which the last base classifier h_t is sure to do extremely poorly: It can be shown by a simple computation that the error of h_t with respect to distribution D_{t+1} is exactly $\frac{1}{2}$, that is, exactly the trivial error rate achievable through simple random guessing (see exercise 1.1). In this way, as discussed above, AdaBoost tries on each round to force the base learner to learn something new about the data.

After many calls to the base learner, AdaBoost combines the many base classifiers into a single *combined* or *final classifier* H. This is accomplished by a simple weighted vote of the base classifiers. That is, given a new instance x, the combined classifier evaluates all of the base classifiers, and predicts with the weighted majority of the base classifiers' predicted classifications. Here, the vote of the t-th base classifier h_t is weighted by the previously chosen parameter α_t. The resulting formula for H's prediction is as shown in the algorithm.

1.2.1 A Toy Example

To illustrate how AdaBoost works, let us look at the tiny toy learning problem shown in figure 1.1. Here, the instances are points in the plane which are labeled + or −. In this case, there are $m = 10$ training examples, as shown in the figure; five are positive and five are negative.

Let us suppose that our base learner finds classifiers defined by vertical or horizontal lines through the plane. For instance, such a base classifier defined by a vertical line might classify all points to the right of the line as positive, and all points to the left as negative. It can be checked that no base classifier of this form correctly classifies more than seven of the ten training examples, meaning that none has an unweighted training error below 30%. On each round t, we suppose that the base learner always finds the base hypothesis of this form that has *minimum* weighted error with respect to the distribution D_t (breaking ties arbitrarily). We will see in this example how, using such a base learner for finding such weak base classifiers, AdaBoost is able to construct a combined classifier that correctly classifies all of the training examples in only $T = 3$ boosting rounds.

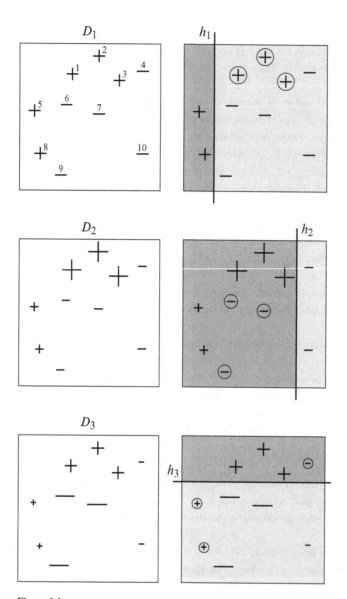

Figure 1.1
An illustration of how AdaBoost behaves on a tiny toy problem with $m = 10$ examples. Each row depicts one round, for $t = 1, 2, 3$. The left box in each row represents the distribution D_t, with the size of each example scaled in proportion to its weight under that distribution. Each box on the right shows the weak hypothesis h_t, where darker shading indicates the region of the domain predicted to be positive. Examples that are misclassified by h_t have been circled.

Table 1.1
The numerical calculations corresponding to the toy example in figure 1.1

	1	2	3	4	5	6	7	8	9	10	
$D_1(i)$	0.10	0.10	0.10	0.10	0.10	0.10	0.10	0.10	0.10	0.10	$\epsilon_1 = 0.30, \alpha_1 \approx 0.42$
$e^{-\alpha_1 y_i h_1(x_i)}$	1.53	1.53	1.53	0.65	0.65	0.65	0.65	0.65	0.65	0.65	
$D_1(i)\, e^{-\alpha_1 y_i h_1(x_i)}$	0.15	0.15	0.15	0.07	0.07	0.07	0.07	0.07	0.07	0.07	$Z_1 \approx 0.92$
$D_2(i)$	0.17	0.17	0.17	0.07	0.07	0.07	0.07	0.07	0.07	0.07	$\epsilon_2 \approx 0.21, \alpha_2 \approx 0.65$
$e^{-\alpha_2 y_i h_2(x_i)}$	0.52	0.52	0.52	0.52	0.52	1.91	1.91	0.52	1.91	0.52	
$D_2(i)\, e^{-\alpha_2 y_i h_2(x_i)}$	0.09	0.09	0.09	0.04	0.04	0.14	0.14	0.04	0.14	0.04	$Z_2 \approx 0.82$
$D_3(i)$	0.11	0.11	0.11	0.05	0.05	0.17	0.17	0.05	0.17	0.05	$\epsilon_3 \approx 0.14, \alpha_3 \approx 0.92$
$e^{-\alpha_3 y_i h_3(x_i)}$	0.40	0.40	0.40	2.52	2.52	0.40	0.40	2.52	0.40	0.40	
$D_3(i)\, e^{-\alpha_3 y_i h_3(x_i)}$	0.04	0.04	0.04	0.11	0.11	0.07	0.07	0.11	0.07	0.02	$Z_3 \approx 0.69$

Calculations are shown for the ten examples as numbered in the figure. Examples on which hypothesis h_t makes a mistake are indicated by underlined figures in the rows marked D_t.

On round 1, AdaBoost assigns equal weight to all of the examples, as is indicated in the figure by drawing all examples in the box marked D_1 to be of the same size. Given examples with these weights, the base learner chooses the base hypothesis indicated by h_1 in the figure, which classifies points as positive if and only if they lie to the left of this line. This hypothesis incorrectly classifies three points—namely, the three circled positive points—so its error ϵ_1 is 0.30. Plugging into the formula of algorithm 1.1 gives $\alpha_1 \approx 0.42$.

In constructing D_2, the weights of the three points misclassified by h_1 are increased while the weights of all other points are decreased. This is indicated by the sizes of the points in the box marked D_2. See also table 1.1, which shows the numerical calculations involved in running AdaBoost on this toy example.

On round 2, the base learner chooses the line marked h_2. This base classifier correctly classifies the three relatively high-weight points missed by h_1, though at the expense of missing three other comparatively low-weight points which were correctly classified by h_1. Under distribution D_2, these three points have weight only around 0.07, so the error of h_2 with respect to D_2 is $\epsilon_2 \approx 0.21$, giving $\alpha_2 \approx 0.65$. In constructing D_3, the weights of these three misclassified points are increased while the weights of the other points are decreased.

On round 3, classifier h_3 is chosen. This classifier misses none of the points misclassified by h_1 and h_2 since these points have relatively high weight under D_3. Instead, it misclassifies three points which, because they were not misclassified by h_1 or h_2, are of very low weight under D_3. On round 3, $\epsilon_3 \approx 0.14$ and $\alpha_3 \approx 0.92$.

Note that our earlier remark that the error of each hypothesis h_t is exactly $\frac{1}{2}$ on the new distribution D_{t+1} can be verified numerically in this case from table 1.1 (modulo small discrepancies due to rounding).

The combined classifier H is a weighted vote of h_1, h_2, and h_3 as shown in figure 1.2, where the weights on the respective classifiers are α_1, α_2, and α_3. Although each of the composite weak classifiers misclassifies three of the ten examples, the combined classifier,

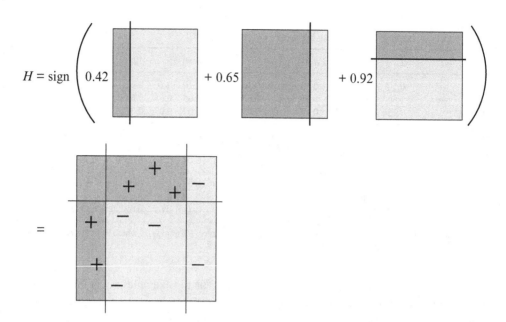

Figure 1.2
The combined classifier for the toy example of figure 1.1 is computed as the sign of the weighted sum of the three weak hypotheses, $\alpha_1 h_1 + \alpha_2 h_2 + \alpha_3 h_3$, as shown at the top. This is equivalent to the classifier shown at the bottom. (As in figure 1.1, the regions that a classifier predicts positive are indicated using darker shading.)

as shown in the figure, correctly classifies *all* of the training examples. For instance, the classification of the negative example in the upper right corner (instance #4), which is classified negative by h_1 and h_2 but positive by h_3, is

$$\text{sign}(-\alpha_1 - \alpha_2 + \alpha_3) = \text{sign}(-0.15) = -1.$$

One might reasonably ask if such a rapid reduction in training error is typical for Ada-Boost. The answer turns out to be yes in the following sense: Given the weak learning assumption (that is, that the error of each weak classifier ϵ_t is at most $\frac{1}{2} - \gamma$ for some $\gamma > 0$), we can prove that the training error of the combined classifier drops exponentially fast as a function of the number of weak classifiers combined. Although this fact, which is proved in chapter 3, says nothing directly about generalization error, it does suggest that boosting, which is so effective at driving down the training error, may also be effective at producing a combined classifier with low generalization error. And indeed, in chapter 4 and 5, we prove various theorems about the generalization error of AdaBoost's combined classifier.

Note also that although we depend on the weak learning assumption to prove these results, AdaBoost does not need to know the "edge" γ referred to above, but rather adjusts and adapts to errors ϵ_t which may vary considerably, reflecting the varying levels of performance among the base classifiers. It is in this sense that AdaBoost is an *adaptive boosting* algorithm—which is exactly what the name stands for.[1] Moreover, this adaptiveness is one of the key qualities that make AdaBoost practical.

1.2.2 Experimental Performance

Experimentally, on data arising from many real-world applications, AdaBoost also turns out to be highly effective. To get a sense of AdaBoost's performance overall, we can compare it with other methods on a broad variety of publicly available benchmark datasets, an important methodology in machine learning since different algorithms can exhibit relative strengths that vary substantially from one dataset to the next. Here, we consider two base learning algorithms: one that produces quite weak and simple base classifiers called decision stumps; and the other, called C4.5, that is an established and already highly effective program for learning decision trees, which are generally more complex but also quite a bit more accurate than decision stumps. Both of these base classifiers are described further in sections 1.2.3 and 1.3.

Boosting algorithms work by improving the accuracy of the base learning algorithm. Figure 1.3 shows this effect on 27 benchmark datasets. In each scatterplot, each point shows the test error rate of boosting (x-coordinate) versus that of the base learner (y-coordinate) on a single benchmark. All error rates have been averaged over multiple runs and multiple random splits of the given data into training and testing sets. In these experiments, boosting was run for $T = 100$ rounds.

To "read" such a scatterplot, note that a point lands above the line $y = x$ if and only if boosting shows improvement over the base learner. Thus, we see that when using the relatively strong base learner C4.5, an algorithm that is very effective in its own right, AdaBoost is often able to provide quite a significant boost in performance. Even more dramatic is the improvement effected when using the rather weak decision stumps as base classifiers. In fact, this improvement is so substantial that boosting stumps is often even better than C4.5, as can be seen in figure 1.4. On the other hand, overall, boosting C4.5 seems to give more accurate results than boosting stumps.

In short, empirically, AdaBoost appears to be highly effective as a learning tool for generalizing beyond the training set. How can we explain this capacity to extrapolate beyond the observed training data? Attempting to answer this question is a primary objective of this book.

1.2.3 A Medical-Diagnosis Example

As a more detailed example, let us return to the heart-disease dataset described briefly in section 1.1. To apply boosting on this dataset, we first need to choose the base learner and base

---

1. This is also why *AdaBoost*, which is short for "adaptive boosting," is pronounced *ADD-uh-boost*, similar to *adaptation*.

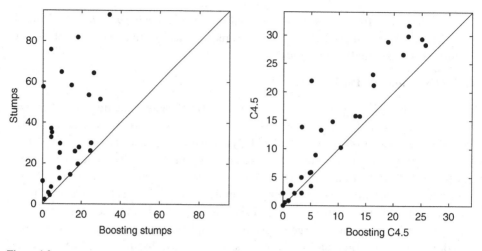

Figure 1.3
Comparison of two base learning algorithms—decision stumps and C4.5—with and without boosting. Each point in each scatterplot shows the test error rate of the two competing algorithms on one of 27 benchmark learning problems. The x-coordinate of each point gives the test error rate (in percent) using boosting, and the y-coordinate gives the error rate without boosting when using decision stumps (left plot) or C4.5 (right plot). All error rates have been averaged over multiple runs.

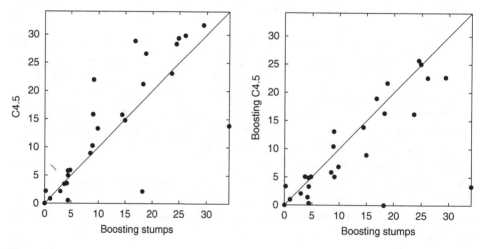

Figure 1.4
Comparison of boosting using decision stumps as the base learner versus unboosted C4.5 (left plot) and boosted C4.5 (right plot).

classifiers. Here we have many options, but perhaps the simplest rules of thumb are those which test on a single attribute describing the patient. For instance, such a rule might state:

If the patient's cholesterol is at least 228.5, then predict that the patient has heart disease; otherwise, predict that the patient is healthy.

In the experiments we are about to describe, we used base classifiers of just this form, which are the *decision stumps* alluded to in section 1.2.2. (In fact, the weak classifiers used in the toy example of section 1.2.1 are also decision stumps.) It turns out, as will be seen in section 3.4.2, that a base learner which does an exhaustive search for the best decision stump can be implemented very efficiently (where, as before, "best" means the one having lowest weighted training error with respect to a given distribution D_t over training examples). Table 1.2 shows the first six base classifiers produced by this base learner when AdaBoost is applied to this entire dataset.

To measure performance on such a small dataset, we can divide the data randomly into disjoint training and test sets. Because the test set for such a split is very small, we repeat this many times, using a standard technique called cross validation. We then take the averages of the training and test errors for the various splits of the data. Figure 1.5 shows these average error rates for this dataset as a function of the number of base classifiers combined. Boosting steadily drives down the training error. The test error also drops quickly, reaching a low point of 15.3% after only three rounds, a rather significant improvement over using just one of the base classifiers, the best of which has a test error of 28.0%. However, after reaching this low point, the test error begins to *increase* again, so that after 100 rounds, the test error is up to 18.8%, and after 1000 rounds, up to 22.0%.

This deterioration in performance with continued training is an example of an important and ubiquitous phenomenon called *overfitting*. As the number of base classifiers becomes larger and larger, the combined classifier becomes more and more complex, leading somehow to a deterioration of test-error performance. Overfitting, which has been observed in many machine-learning settings and which has also received considerable theoretical study, is consistent with the intuition that a simpler explanation of the data is better than a more

Table 1.2
The first six base classifiers found when using AdaBoost on the heart-disease dataset

Round	If	Then Predict	Else Predict
1	thalamus normal	healthy	sick
2	number of major vessels colored by fluoroscopy > 0	sick	healthy
3	chest pain type is asymptomatic	sick	healthy
4	ST depression induced by exercise relative to rest ≥ 0.75	sick	healthy
5	cholesterol ≥ 228.5	sick	healthy
6	resting electrocardiographic results are normal	healthy	sick

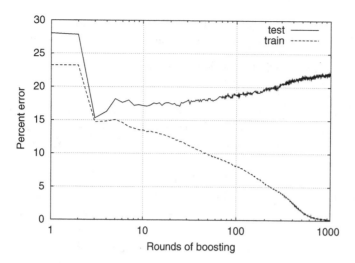

Figure 1.5
The training and test percent error rates obtained using boosting on the heart-disease dataset. Results are averaged over multiple train-test splits of the data.

complicated one, a notion sometimes called "Occam's razor." With more rounds of boosting, the combined classifier grows in size and complexity, apparently overwhelming good performance on the training set. This general connection between simplicity and accuracy is explored in chapter 2. For boosting, exactly the kind of behavior observed in figure 1.5 is predicted by the analysis in chapter 4.

Overfitting is a significant problem because it means that we have to be very careful about when to stop boosting. If we stop too soon or too late, our performance on the test set may suffer significantly, as can be seen in this example. Moreover, performance on the training set provides little guidance about when to stop training since the training error typically continues to drop even as overfitting gets worse and worse.

1.3   Resistance to Overfitting and the Margins Theory

This last example describes a case in which boosting was used with very weak base classifiers. This is one possible use of boosting, namely, in conjunction with a very simple but truly mediocre weak learning algorithm. A rather different use of boosting is instead to boost the accuracy of a learning algorithm that is already quite good.

This is the approach taken in the next example. Here, rather than a very weak base learner, we used the well-known and highly developed machine-learning algorithm C4.5 as the base learner. As mentioned earlier, C4.5 produces classifiers called *decision trees*. Figure 1.6 shows an example of a decision tree. The nodes are identified with tests having a small

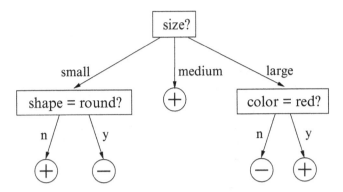

Figure 1.6
An example of a decision tree.

number of outcomes corresponding to the outgoing edges of the node. The leaves are identified with predicted labels. To classify an example, a path is traversed through the tree from the root to a leaf. The path is determined by the outcomes of the tests that are encountered along the way, and the predicted classification is determined by the leaf that is ultimately reached. For instance, in the figure, a large, square, blue item would be classified − while a medium, round, red item would be classified +.

We tested boosting using C4.5 as the base learner on a benchmark dataset in which the goal is to identify images of handwritten characters as letters of the alphabet. The features used are derived from the raw pixel images, including such items as the average of the x-coordinates of the pixels that are turned on. The dataset consists of 16,000 training examples and 4000 test examples.

Figure 1.7 shows training and test error rates for AdaBoost's combined classifier on this dataset as a function of the number of decision trees (base classifiers) combined. A single decision tree produced by C4.5 on this dataset has a test error rate of 13.8%. In this example, boosting very quickly drives down the training error; in fact, after only five rounds the training error is zero, so that all training examples are correctly classified. Note that there is no reason why boosting cannot proceed beyond this point. Although the training error of the *combined* classifier is zero, the individual *base* classifiers continue to incur significant weighted error—around 5–6%—on the distributions on which they are trained, so that ϵ_t remains in this range, even for large t. This permits AdaBoost to proceed with the reweighting of training examples and the continued training of base classifiers.

The test performance of boosting on this dataset is extremely good, far better than a single decision tree. And surprisingly, unlike the earlier example, the test error on this dataset never increases, even after 1000 trees have been combined—by which point, the combined classifier involves more than two million decision nodes. Even after the training error hits zero, the test error continues to drop, from 8.4% on round 5 down to 3.1% on round 1000.

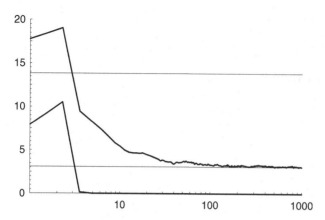

Figure 1.7
The training and test percent error rates obtained using boosting on an OCR dataset with C4.5 as the base learner. The top and bottom curves are test and training error, respectively. The top horizontal line shows the test error rate using just C4.5. The bottom line shows the final test error rate of AdaBoost after 1000 rounds. (Reprinted with permission of the Institute of Mathematical Statistics.)

This pronounced lack of overfitting seems to flatly contradict our earlier intuition that simpler is better. Surely, a combination of five trees is much, much simpler than a combination of 1000 trees (about 200 times simpler, in terms of raw size), and both perform equally well on the training set (perfectly, in fact). So how can it be that the far larger and more complex combined classifier performs so much better on the test set? This would appear to be a paradox.

One superficially plausible explanation is that the α_t's are converging rapidly to zero, so that the number of base classifiers being combined is effectively bounded. However, as noted above, the ϵ_t's remain around 5–6% in this case, well below $\frac{1}{2}$, which means that the weights α_t on the individual base classifiers are also bounded well above zero, so that the combined classifier is constantly growing and evolving with each round of boosting.

Such resistance to overfitting is typical of boosting, although, as we have seen in section 1.2.3, boosting certainly *can* overfit. This resistance is one of the properties that make it such an attractive learning algorithm. But how can we understand this behavior?

In chapter 5, we present a theoretical explanation of how, why, and when AdaBoost works and, in particular, of why it often does not overfit. Briefly, the main idea is the following. The description above of AdaBoost's performance on the training set took into account only the training error, which is already zero after just five rounds. However, training error tells only part of the story, in that it reports just the number of examples that are correctly or incorrectly classified. Instead, to understand AdaBoost, we also need to consider how *confident* the predictions being made by the algorithm are. We will see that such confidence can be measured by a quantity called the *margin*. According to this explanation, although the training error—that is, whether or not the predictions are correct—is not changing after round 5, the confidence in those predictions is increasing dramatically with additional rounds of boosting. And it is this increase in confidence which accounts for the better generalization performance.

This theory, for which we present both empirical and theoretical evidence, not only explains the lack of overfitting but also provides a detailed framework for fundamentally understanding the conditions under which AdaBoost can fail or succeed.

1.4 Foundations and Algorithms

The core analysis outlined above forms part I of this book, a largely mathematical study of AdaBoost's capacity to minimize both the training and the generalization error. Here, our focus is on understanding how, why, and when AdaBoost is effective as a learning algorithm.

This analysis, including the margins theory, is paramount in our study of boosting; however, it is hardly the end of the story. Indeed, although it is an enticingly simple algorithm, AdaBoost turns out to be understandable from a striking number of disparate theoretical perspectives. Taken together, these provide a remarkably rich and encompassing illumination of the algorithm, in addition to practical generalizations and variations along multiple dimensions. Part II of the book explores three of these fundamental perspectives.

In the first of these, the interaction between a boosting algorithm and a weak learning algorithm is viewed as a game between these two players—a game not only in the informal, everyday sense but also in the mathematical sense studied in the field of game theory. In fact, it turns out that AdaBoost is a special case of a more general algorithm for playing any game in a repeated fashion. This perspective, presented in chapter 6, helps us to understand numerous properties of the algorithm, such as its limiting behavior, in broader, game-theoretic terms. We will see that notions that are central to boosting, such as margins and the weak learning assumption, have very natural game-theoretic interpretations. Indeed, the very idea of boosting turns out to be intimately entwined with one of the most fundamental theorems of game theory. This view also unifies AdaBoost with another branch of learning known as online learning.

AdaBoost can be further understood as an algorithm for optimizing a particular objective function measuring the fit of a model to the available data. In this way, AdaBoost can be seen as an instance of a more general approach that can be applied to a broader range of statistical learning problems, as we describe in chapter 7. This view further leads to a unification of AdaBoost with the more established statistical method called logistic regression, and suggests how AdaBoost's predictions can be used to estimate the probability of a particular example being positive or negative.

From yet another vantage point, which turns out to be "dual" to the one given in chapter 7, AdaBoost can be interpreted in a kind of abstract, geometric framework. Here, the fundamental operation is projection of a point onto a subspace. In this case, the "points" are in fact the distributions D_t computed by AdaBoost, which exist in a kind of "information geometric" space—one based on notions from information theory—rather than the usual Euclidean geometry. As discussed in chapter 8, this view leads to a deeper understanding of AdaBoost's dynamics and underlying mathematical structure, and yields proofs of fundamental convergence properties.

Part III of this book focuses on practical, algorithmic extensions of AdaBoost. In the basic form shown in algorithm 1.1, AdaBoost is intended for the simplest learning setting in which the goal is binary classification, that is, classification problems with only two possible classes or categories. To apply AdaBoost to a much broader range of real-world learning problems, the algorithm must be extended along multiple dimensions.

In chapter 9, we describe an extension to AdaBoost in which the base classifiers themselves are permitted to output predictions that vary in their self-rated level of confidence. In practical terms, this modification of boosting leads to a dramatic speedup in learning time. Moreover, within this framework we derive two algorithms designed to produce classifiers that are not only accurate, but also understandable in form to humans.

Chapter 10 extends AdaBoost to the case in which there are more than two possible classes, as is very commonly the case in actual applications. For instance, if recognizing digits, there are ten classes, one for each digit. As will be seen, it turns out that there are quite a number of methods for modifying AdaBoost for this purpose, and we will see how a great many of these can be studied in a unified framework.

Chapter 11 extends AdaBoost to ranking problems, that is, problems in which the goal is to learn to rank a set of objects. For instance, the goal might be to rank credit card transactions according to the likelihood of each one being fraudulent, so that those at the top of the ranking can be investigated.

Finally, in part IV, we study a number of advanced theoretical topics.

The first of these provides an alternative approach for the understanding of AdaBoost's generalization capabilities, which explicitly takes into consideration intrinsic randomness or "noise" in the data that may prevent perfect generalization by *any* classifier. In such a setting, we show in chapter 12 that the accuracy of AdaBoost will nevertheless converge to that of the best possible classifier, under appropriate assumptions. However, we also show that without these assumptions, AdaBoost's performance can be rather poor when the data is noisy.

AdaBoost can be understood in many ways, but at its foundation, it is a boosting algorithm in the original technical meaning of the word, a provable method for driving down the error of the combined classifier by combining a number of weak classifiers. In fact, for this specific problem, AdaBoost is not the best possible; rather, there is another algorithm called "boost-by-majority" that is optimal in a very strong sense, as we will see in chapter 13. However, this latter algorithm is not practical because it is not adaptive in the sense described in section 1.2.1. Nevertheless, as we show in chapter 14, this algorithm can be made adaptive by taking a kind of limit in which the discrete time steps in the usual boosting framework are replaced by a *continuous* sequence of time steps. This leads to the "BrownBoost" algorithm, which has certain properties that suggest greater tolerance to noise, and from which AdaBoost can be derived in the "zero-noise" limit.

Although this book is about foundations and algorithms, we also provide numerous examples illustrating how the theory we develop can be applied practically. Indeed, as seen earlier in this chapter, AdaBoost has many practical advantages. It is fast, simple, and easy to program. It has no parameters to tune (except for the number of rounds T). It requires no prior knowledge about the base learner, and so can be flexibly combined with any method for finding base classifiers. Finally, it comes with a set of theoretical guarantees, given sufficient data and a base learner that can reliably provide only moderately accurate base classifiers. This is a shift in mind-set for the learning-system designer: instead of trying to design a learning algorithm that is accurate over the entire space, we can instead focus on finding weak learning algorithms that only need to be better than random.

On the other hand, some caveats are certainly in order. The actual performance of boosting on a particular problem is clearly dependent on the data and the base learner. Consistent with the theory outlined above and discussed in detail in this book, boosting can fail to perform well, given insufficient data, overly complex base classifiers, or base classifiers that are too weak. Boosting seems to be especially susceptible to noise, as we discuss in section 12.3. Nonetheless, as seen in section 1.2.2, on a wide range of real-world learning problems, boosting's performance overall is quite good.

To illustrate its empirical performance and application, throughout this book we give examples of its use on practical problems such as human-face detection, topic identification, language understanding in spoken-dialogue systems, and natural-language parsing.

Summary

In this chapter, we have given an introduction to machine learning, classification problems, and boosting, particularly AdaBoost and its variants, which are the focus of this book. We have presented examples of boosting's empirical performance, as well as an overview of some of the highlights of its rich and varied theory. In the chapters ahead, we explore the foundations of boosting from many vantage points, and develop key principles in the design of boosting algorithms, while also giving examples of their application to practical problems.

Bibliographic Notes

Boosting has its roots in a theoretical framework for studying machine learning called the PAC model, proposed by Valiant [221], which we discuss in more detail in section 2.3. Working in this framework, Kearns and Valiant [133] posed the question of whether a weak learning algorithm that performs just slightly better than random guessing can be boosted into one with arbitrarily high accuracy. Schapire [199] came up with the first provable polynomial-time boosting algorithm in 1989. A year later, Freund [88] developed a much more efficient boosting algorithm called boost-by-majority that is essentially optimal (see chapter 13). The first experiments with these early boosting algorithms were carried out by Drucker, Schapire, and Simard [72] on an OCR task. However, both algorithms were largely impractical because of their nonadaptiveness. AdaBoost, the first adaptive boosting algorithm, was introduced in 1995 by Freund and Schapire [95].

There are many fine textbooks which provide a broader treatment of machine learning, a field that overlaps considerably with statistics, pattern recognition, and data mining. See, for instance, [7, 22, 67, 73, 120, 134, 166, 171, 223, 224]. For alternative surveys of boosting and related methods for combining classifiers, see refs. [40, 69, 146, 170, 214].

The medical-diagnosis data used in section 1.2.3 was collected from the Cleveland Clinic Foundation by Detrano et al. [66]. The letter recognition dataset used in section 1.3 was created by Frey and Slate [97]. The C4.5 decision-tree learning algorithm used in sections 1.2.2 and 1.3 is due to Quinlan [184], and is similar to the CART algorithm of Breiman et al. [39].

Drucker and Cortes [71] and Jackson and Craven [126] were the first to test AdaBoost experimentally. The experiments in section 1.2.2 were originally reported by Freund and Schapire [93] from which the right plot of figure 1.3 and left plot of figure 1.4 were adapted. AdaBoost's resistance to overfitting was noticed early on by Drucker and Cortes [71], as well as by Breiman [35] and Quinlan [183]. The experiments in section 1.3, including figure 1.7, are taken from Schapire et al. [202]. There have been numerous other systematic experimental studies of AdaBoost, such as [15, 68, 162, 209], as well as Caruana and Niculescu-Mizil's [42] large-scale comparison of several learning algorithms, including AdaBoost.

Exercises

1.1 Show that the error of h_t on distribution D_{t+1} is exactly $\frac{1}{2}$, that is,

$$\mathbf{Pr}_{i \sim D_{t+1}}[h_t(x_i) \neq y_i] = \frac{1}{2}.$$

1.2 For each of the following cases, explain how AdaBoost, as given in algorithm 1.1, will treat a weak hypothesis h_t with weighted error ϵ_t. Also, in each case, explain how this behavior makes sense.

a. $\epsilon_t = \frac{1}{2}$.

b. $\epsilon_t > \frac{1}{2}$.

c. $\epsilon_t = 0$.

1.3 In figure 1.7, the training error and test error of the combined classifier H are seen to increase significantly on the second round. Give a plausible explanation why we might expect these error rates to be higher after two rounds than after only one.

I CORE ANALYSIS

2 Foundations of Machine Learning

Soon we will embark on a theoretical study of AdaBoost in order to understand its properties, particularly its ability as a learning algorithm to generalize, that is, to make accurate predictions on data not seen during training. Before this will be possible, however, it will be necessary to take a step back to outline our approach to the more general problem of machine learning, including some fundamental general-purpose tools that will be invaluable in our analysis of AdaBoost.

We study the basic problem of inferring from a set of training examples a classification rule whose predictions are highly accurate on freshly observed test data. On first encounter, it may seem questionable whether this kind of learning should even be possible. After all, why should there be any connection between the training and test examples, and why should it be possible to generalize from a relatively small number of training examples to a potentially vast universe of test examples? Although such objections have indeed often been the subject of philosophical debate, in this chapter we will identify an idealized but realistic model of the inference problem in which this kind of learning can be proved to be entirely feasible when certain conditions are satisfied. In particular, we will see that if we can find a *simple* rule that fits the training data well, and if the training set is not too small, then this rule will in fact generalize well, providing accurate predictions on previously unseen test examples. This is the basis of the approach presented in this chapter, and we will often use the general analysis on which it is founded to guide us in understanding how, why, and when learning is possible.

We also outline in this chapter a mathematical framework for studying machine learning, one in which a precise formulation of the boosting problem can be clearly and naturally expressed.

Note that, unlike the rest of the book, this chapter omits nearly all of the proofs of the main results since these have largely all appeared in various texts and articles. See the bibliographic notes at the end of the chapter for references.

Table 2.1
A sample dataset

Instances	1.2	2.8	8.0	3.3	5.0	4.5	7.4	5.6	3.8	6.6	6.1	1.7
Labels	−	−	+	−	−	−	+	+	−	+	+	−

Each column is a labeled example. For instance, the third example is the instance $x = 8.0$ with corresponding label $y = +1$.

2.1 A Direct Approach to Machine Learning

We start with an introduction to our approach to machine learning. This will lead to the identification of criteria that are sufficient to assure generalization, laying the intuitive groundwork for the formal treatment that follows.

2.1.1 Conditions Sufficient for Learning

As described in chapter 1, a learning algorithm takes as input a labeled sequence of training examples $(x_1, y_1), \ldots, (x_m, y_m)$, and must use these to formulate a hypothesis for classifying new instances. As before, and for most of the book, we assume that there are only two possible labels, so that each $y_i \in \{-1, +1\}$. As is customary, we routinely refer to the training examples as comprising a training *set*, or a data*set*, even though they actually form a tuple (in which the same example may appear more than once) rather than a set. Likewise for the test set.

Let us begin with an example in which the instances x_i are simply real numbers, and in which the training set looks something like the one in table 2.1. Given such a dataset, how might we formulate a prediction rule? After examining these examples, most of us would eventually notice that the larger examples, above some cutoff, are positive, and the smaller examples are negative. This would lead most people to choose a rule based on the observed cutoff behavior exhibited by this data; in other words, they would eventually choose a threshold rule that predicts all instances x above some threshold ν are $+1$, and all instances below ν are -1; that is,

$$h(x) = \begin{cases} +1 & \text{if } x \geq \nu \\ -1 & \text{otherwise} \end{cases} \tag{2.1}$$

for some choice of ν, such as 5.3, or any other value between 5.0 (the largest negative example) and 5.6 (the smallest positive example). Such a rule—which is essentially the same in form as the decision stumps used in section 1.2.3—seems so obvious and irresistibly attractive because it has the two properties that people instinctively seem to prefer: First of all, it is *consistent* with the given data, meaning that it predicts the correct labels on all of the given training examples. And second, the rule is *simple*.

This preference for simple explanations, as noted in chapter 1, is often referred to as *Occam's razor*, a central tenet, for instance, of mathematics and most areas of scientific

Table 2.2
A slightly different sample dataset

Instances	1.2	2.8	8.0	3.3	5.0	4.5	7.4	5.6	3.8	6.6	6.1	1.7
Labels	−	−	+	−	−	−	+	+	+	−	+	−

inquiry. However, unlike consistency, simplicity is not at all simple to define, and seems vague, even mystical, although most of us feel that we recognize it when we see it. The notion of simplicity is closely related to our prior expectations: We expect the data to be explainable by a simple rule, and conversely, we usually consider a rule to be simple if it matches our expectations. One of the triumphs of modern research on learning has been the development of quantitative measures of simplicity and its role in generalization, as we will see shortly.

When faced with a harder dataset, such as the slightly modified version in table 2.2, it is not so immediate how to find a simple and consistent rule. On the one hand, we might choose a simple threshold rule as before, but since none are consistent with this dataset, we will inevitably be forced to accept a small number of mistakes on the training set itself. Alternatively, we might choose a considerably more complex rule that *is* consistent, such as this one:

$$
h(x) = \begin{cases}
-1 & \text{if } x < 3.4 \\
+1 & \text{if } 3.4 \le x < 4.0 \\
-1 & \text{if } 4.0 \le x < 5.2 \\
+1 & \text{if } 5.2 \le x < 6.3 \\
-1 & \text{if } 6.3 \le x < 7.1 \\
+1 & \text{if } x \ge 7.1.
\end{cases}
\tag{2.2}
$$

Thus, we face a trade-off between simplicity and fit to the data, one that will require balance and compromise.

Generally, then, we see that a natural approach to learning is to seek a hypothesis satisfying two basic criteria:

1. It fits the data well.
2. It is simple.

As indicated in the example above, however, these two criteria are often in conflict: We can typically fit the data better at the cost of choosing a more complex hypothesis, and conversely, simpler hypotheses are prone to give a poorer fit to the data. This trade-off is quite general, and is at the heart of the most central issue in the study of machine learning.

This issue must be faced at some point in the design of every learning algorithm, since we must eventually make an explicit or implicit decision about the form of the hypotheses that will be used. The form that is chosen reflects an assumption about what we expect in the data, and it is the *form* that determines simplicity or complexity. For instance, we might choose to use threshold rules of the form given in equation (2.1), or we might instead use rules of a much freer form, as in equation (2.2). In principle, the more we know about a particular learning problem, the simpler (and more restrictive) the form of the hypotheses that can be used.

We measure how well a particular hypothesis h fits the training data by its *training* (or *empirical*) *error*, that is, the fraction of the m training examples that it misclassifies, denoted

$$\widehat{\text{err}}(h) \doteq \frac{1}{m} \sum_{i=1}^{m} \mathbf{1}\{h(x_i) \neq y_i\},$$

where $\mathbf{1}\{\cdot\}$ is an indicator function that is 1 if its argument is true, and 0 otherwise. Although we seek a simple classifier h with low training error, the ultimate goal of learning is to find a rule that is highly accurate as measured on a separate test set. We generally assume that both the training examples and the test examples are generated from the same distribution $\mathcal{D}$ on labeled pairs (x, y). With respect to this true distribution, the expected test error of a hypothesis h is called the *true* or *generalization error*; it is the same as the probability of misclassifying a single example (x, y) chosen at random from $\mathcal{D}$, and is denoted

$$\text{err}(h) \doteq \mathbf{Pr}_{(x,y)\sim\mathcal{D}}[h(x) \neq y]. \tag{2.3}$$

Of course, a learning algorithm does not have the means to directly measure the generalization error $\text{err}(h)$ that it aims to minimize. Instead, it must use the training error $\widehat{\text{err}}(h)$ as an estimate of or proxy for the generalization error. If working with a single hypothesis h, then the training error will be a reasonable estimate of the generalization error, which it equals in expectation; in this sense, it is an *unbiased* estimator. Generally, however, a learning algorithm will work with a large space of hypotheses, and will choose the hypothesis from this space with (approximately) minimum training error. Unfortunately, the training error of a hypothesis selected in this fashion will not be unbiased, but instead will almost certainly underestimate its true error. This is because, in selecting the hypothesis with minimum training error, the algorithm favors hypotheses whose training errors are, by chance, much lower than their true errors.

To get an intuition for this effect, imagine an experiment in which each student in a class is asked to predict the outcomes of ten coin flips. Clearly, any individual student will, in expectation, correctly predict just half of the flips. However, in a class of perhaps 50 students, it is highly likely that one student will be very lucky and will correctly predict eight or even nine of the coin flips. This student will appear to possess remarkable powers of clairvoyance, when in fact it was only chance that made the student's true prediction accuracy of 50% appear to be much higher. The larger the class, the greater this effect will be: At an extreme, for a very large class of over a thousand students, we will expect there to be one student who perfectly predicts all ten coin flips.

In the learning setting, for the same reasons, it is quite likely that the apparently good performance of the best hypothesis on the training set will in part be the result of having fitted spurious patterns that appeared in the training data entirely by chance. Inevitably, this will cause the training error to be lower than the true error for the chosen hypothesis. Moreover, the amount of this bias depends directly on the simplicity or complexity of the hypotheses considered—the more complex, and thus the less restrictive, the form of the hypotheses, the larger the space from which they are selected and the greater the bias, just as in the example above. On the other hand, we will see that the bias can be controlled when a sufficiently large training set is available.

Finding the hypothesis with minimal or nearly minimal training error can often be accomplished through an exhaustive or heuristic search, even when working with an infinitely large space of hypotheses. As an example, consider our sample dataset in table 2.2 when using threshold rules as in equation (2.1). Figure 2.1 shows a plot of the training error $\widehat{err}(h)$ of such rules as a function of the threshold v. As can be seen from the figure, even though the set of potential classifiers of this form is uncountably infinite, a training set of m examples partitions the classifiers into $m + 1$ subsets such that all of the rules in any single subset make the same predictions on the training examples, and thus have the same empirical error. (For instance, the threshold rule defined by setting the threshold v to be 3.9 makes exactly the same predictions on all m of the examples as if we instead set v to be 4.2.) As a result, we can find a classifier that minimizes the training error by first sorting the data according to the instance values x_i, and then computing the training error for all possible values of the threshold v in a single scan through the sorted examples. In this case, we would find that the minimum training error is attained when v is between 5.0 and 5.6. (More details of this method will be given in section 3.4.2.)

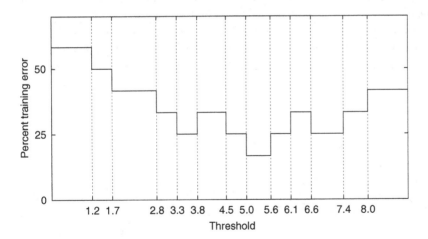

Figure 2.1
The empirical error, on the data in table 2.2, of a threshold rule of the form given in equation (2.1), plotted as a function of the threshold v.

In general, balancing simplicity against fit to the training data is key to many practical learning algorithms. For instance, decision-tree algorithms (see section 1.3) typically grow a large tree that fits the data very well (usually too well), and then heavily prune the tree so as to limit its overall complexity as measured by its gross size.

2.1.2 Comparison to an Alternative Approach

As a brief aside, we take a moment to contrast the approach we are following with a well-studied alternative. When faced with data as in tables 2.1 and 2.2, we may in some cases have additional information available to us. For instance, maybe we know that each example i corresponds to a person where x_i represents the person's height and y_i represents the person's gender (say $+1$ means male and -1 means female); in other words, the problem is to learn to predict a person's gender from his or her height. This information leads to some natural assumptions. Specifically, we might assume that height among men is normally distributed, and likewise among women, where naturally the means μ_+ and μ_- will be different, with $\mu_+ > \mu_-$. We might further assume equal variance σ^2 for these two normal distributions, and that the two classes (genders) occur with equal probability.

These assumptions suggest a different way of proceeding. Our goal is still to classify instances whose label is unknown, but now, if we know the values of the means μ_+ and μ_-, we can easily calculate the best possible classifier, which in this case simply predicts, for a given instance (height) x, with the mean that is closest; in other words, $+1$ if $x \geq (\mu_+ + \mu_-)/2$, and -1 otherwise. (See figure 2.2.) Note that this classifier has the form of a threshold rule as in equation (2.1), although our rationale for using such a rule here is rather different. If the distribution parameters μ_+ and μ_- are unknown, they can be estimated from training data, and then used to classify test examples in the same way.

This is sometimes called a *generative* approach since we attempt to model how the data is being generated. In contrast, the approach we outlined in section 2.1.1 is often said to be *discriminative*, since the emphasis is on directly discriminating between the two classes.

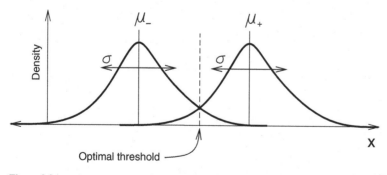

Figure 2.2
A classification problem in which both classes are normally distributed with equal variances but different means.

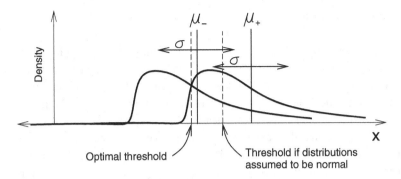

Figure 2.3
A classification problem in which both classes have the same skewed, nonnormal distribution but with different means.

When the assumptions we have made above about the data are valid, good generalization is assured in this simple case. Most importantly, such a guarantee of good performance is dependent on the data actually being generated by two normal distributions. If this assumption does not hold, then the performance of the resulting classifier can become arbitrarily poor, as can be seen in figure 2.3. There, because the two distributions are far from normal, the threshold between positives and negatives that is found by incorrectly assuming normality ends up being well away from optimal, regardless of how much training data is provided.

Normality assumptions lead naturally to the use of threshold rules as in equation (2.1), but we see in this example that an over-dependence on this assumption can yield poor performance. On the other hand, a discriminative approach to this problem in which the best threshold rule is selected based on its training error would be very likely to perform well, since the optimal classifier is a simple threshold here as well. So because the discriminative approach is not based on distributional assumptions, it also can be more robust.

Moreover, if our only goal is to produce a good classifier, then estimating the distribution parameters of each class is entirely irrelevant to the task at hand. We do not care what the means of the distributions are, or even whether or not the distributions are normal. The only thing we care about in classification is which label y is more likely to correspond to any given instance x.

The generative approach can provide a powerful and convenient framework for incorporating into the learning process information that may be available about how the data is generated. However, its performance may be sensitive to the validity of those assumptions. The discriminative approach, on the other hand, attempts more directly to find a good hypothesis by searching for a simple rule that makes accurate predictions on the training data without regard to underlying distributional assumptions. In this latter approach, preconceptions about the data are used to guide how we choose the form of the rules considered, but actual performance may be relatively robust.

2.2   General Methods of Analysis

We return now to the development of general methods for analyzing the generalization error of classifiers generated by learning algorithms. This is the essence of proving an algorithm's effectiveness. As we have discussed, success in learning depends intuitively on finding a classifier (1) that fits the training data well, that is, has low training error, and (2) that is simple. A third prerequisite, of course, is that the learner be provided with a sufficiently large training set. We will see that the generalization error depends on these same three interacting factors in a way that can be formalized in precise terms. On the other hand, the analysis we present does not in any way depend on the form of the distribution of data; for instance, we make no assumptions of normality. This reflects the general robustness of this approach which is largely immune to changes in the underlying distribution.

We begin by analyzing the generalization error of a single hypothesis and then move on to analyze families of hypotheses. Along the way, we will develop several different techniques for measuring the central notion of simplicity and complexity.

2.2.1   A Single Hypothesis

To start, consider a single, fixed hypothesis h. Earlier, we discussed how the training error is used as a proxy for the true error. This motivates us to ask how much the training error $\widehat{\text{err}}(h)$ can differ from the true error $\text{err}(h)$ as a function of the number of training examples m. Note first that there is always a chance that the selected training set will be highly unrepresentative, so that the training error will be a very poor estimate of the true error. This means that it is impossible to give a guarantee that holds with absolute certainty. Instead, we seek bounds that hold true *with high probability* over the choice of the random training set.

In fact, the problem can be seen to be equivalent to one involving coin flipping. When a training example (x_i, y_i) is selected at random, the probability that $h(x_i) \neq y_i$ is exactly $p = \text{err}(h)$, an event that we can identify with a flipped, biased coin coming up heads. In this way, the training set can be viewed as a sequence of m coin flips, each of which is heads with probability p. The problem then is to determine the probability that the fraction $\hat{p}$ of heads in the actual observed sequence of coin flips—that is, the training error—will be significantly different from p. We can explicitly write down the probability, say, of getting at most $(p - \varepsilon)m$ heads, which is exactly

$$\sum_{i=0}^{\lfloor (p-\varepsilon)m \rfloor} \binom{m}{i} p^i (1 - p)^{m-i}. \tag{2.4}$$

This is a rather unwieldy expression, but fortunately there exist a number of tools for bounding it. Foremost among these is the family of *Chernoff bounds*, including *Hoeffding's inequality*, one of the simplest and most widely used, which can be stated as follows:

Theorem 2.1 Let $X_1, \ldots, X_m$ be independent random variables such that $X_i \in [0, 1]$. Denote their average value by $A_m = \frac{1}{m} \sum_{i=1}^{m} X_i$. Then for any $\varepsilon > 0$ we have

$$\Pr[A_m \geq \mathbf{E}[A_m] + \varepsilon] \leq e^{-2m\varepsilon^2} \tag{2.5}$$

and

$$\Pr[A_m \leq \mathbf{E}[A_m] - \varepsilon] \leq e^{-2m\varepsilon^2}. \tag{2.6}$$

Hoeffding's inequality applies to averages of arbitrary bounded and independent random variables. In the coin flipping example, we can take $X_i = 1$ (heads) with probability p and $X_i = 0$ (tails) with probability $1 - p$. Then A_m is equal to $\hat{p}$, the fraction of heads observed in a sequence of m flips; its expected value $\mathbf{E}[A_m]$ is p; and equation (2.6) tells us that the chance of at most $(p - \varepsilon)m$ heads, written explicitly in equation (2.4), is at most $e^{-2m\varepsilon^2}$.

In the learning setting, we can define the random variable X_i to be 1 if $h(x_i) \neq y_i$ and 0 otherwise. This means that the average value A_m is exactly $\widehat{\mathrm{err}}(h)$, the training error of h, and that $\mathbf{E}[A_m]$ is exactly the generalization error $\mathrm{err}(h)$. Thus, theorem 2.1, using equation (2.6), implies that the probability of a training sample of size m for which

$$\mathrm{err}(h) \geq \widehat{\mathrm{err}}(h) + \varepsilon$$

is at most $e^{-2m\varepsilon^2}$. Said differently, given m random examples, and for any $\delta > 0$, we can deduce that with probability at least $1 - \delta$, the following upper bound holds on the generalization error of h:

$$\mathrm{err}(h) \leq \widehat{\mathrm{err}}(h) + \sqrt{\frac{\ln(1/\delta)}{2m}}.$$

This follows by setting $\delta = e^{-2m\varepsilon^2}$ and solving for ε. This means, in quantifiable terms, that if h has low training error on a good-size training set, then we can be quite confident that h's true error is also low.

Using equation (2.5) gives a corresponding lower bound on $\mathrm{err}(h)$. We can combine these using the *union bound*, which states simply that

$$\Pr[a \vee b] \leq \Pr[a] + \Pr[b]$$

for any two events a and b. Together, the two bounds imply that the chance that

$$|\mathrm{err}(h) - \widehat{\mathrm{err}}(h)| \geq \varepsilon$$

is at most $2e^{-2m\varepsilon^2}$, or that

$$|\mathrm{err}(h) - \widehat{\mathrm{err}}(h)| \leq \sqrt{\frac{\ln(2/\delta)}{2m}}$$

with probability at least $1 - \delta$.

As with most of the results in this chapter, we do not prove theorem 2.1. However, we note as an aside that the standard technique for proving Chernoff bounds is closely related to the method we use in chapter 3 to analyze AdaBoost's training error. Indeed, as will be seen in section 3.3, a special case of Hoeffding's inequality follows as a direct corollary of our analysis of AdaBoost.

2.2.2   Finite Hypothesis Spaces

Thus, we can bound the difference between the training error and the true error of a *single*, fixed classifier. To apply this to a learning algorithm, it might seem tempting to use the same argument to estimate the error of the single hypothesis that is chosen by the algorithm by minimizing the training error—after all, this is still only one hypothesis that we care about. However, such reasoning would be entirely fallacious. Informally, the problem is that in such an argument, the training errors are used twice—first to choose the seemingly best hypothesis, and then to estimate its true error. Said differently, the reasoning in section 2.2.1 requires that we select the single hypothesis h *before* the training set is randomly chosen. The argument is invalid if h is itself a random variable that depends on the training set as it would be if selected to minimize the training error. Moreover, we have already argued informally in section 2.1.1 that the hypothesis that appears best on the training set is very likely to have a true error that is significantly higher, whereas, for a single hypothesis, the training error is an unbiased estimate of the true error; this is another indication of the fallacy of such an argument.

Despite these difficulties, we will see now how we can analyze the error of the classifier produced by a learning algorithm, even if it is found by minimizing the training error. The intuitive arguments outlined in section 2.1.1 indicate that such a bound will depend on the form of the hypotheses being used, since this form defines how simple or complex they are. Saying that a hypothesis has a particular form is abstractly equivalent to saying that it belongs to some set of hypotheses $\mathcal{H}$, since we can define $\mathcal{H}$ tautologically to be the set of all hypotheses of the chosen form. For instance, $\mathcal{H}$ might be the set of all threshold rules, as in equation (2.1). We call $\mathcal{H}$ the *hypothesis class* or *hypothesis space*.

Generally, our approach will be to show that the training error of *every* hypothesis $h \in \mathcal{H}$ is close to its true error with high probability, leading to so-called *uniform error* or *uniform convergence* bounds. This condition will ensure that the hypothesis with minimum training error also has nearly minimal true error among all hypotheses in the class. For if

$$|\mathrm{err}(h) - \widehat{\mathrm{err}}(h)| \leq \varepsilon \tag{2.7}$$

holds for all $h \in \mathcal{H}$, and if $\hat{h}$ minimizes the training error $\widehat{\mathrm{err}}(h)$, and h^* minimizes the true error $\mathrm{err}(h)$, then $\hat{h}$ also approximately minimizes the true error, since

$$\mathrm{err}(\hat{h}) \leq \widehat{\mathrm{err}}(\hat{h}) + \varepsilon$$

$$= \min_{h \in \mathcal{H}} \widehat{\mathrm{err}}(h) + \varepsilon.$$

$$\le \widehat{\mathrm{err}}(h^*) + \varepsilon$$

$$\le (\mathrm{err}(h^*) + \varepsilon) + \varepsilon$$

$$= \min_{h \in \mathcal{H}} \mathrm{err}(h) + 2\varepsilon. \tag{2.8}$$

(We assumed that the minima above exist, as will be the case, for instance, if $\mathcal{H}$ is finite; it is straightforward to modify the argument if they do not.)

Although we assumed a two-sided bound as in equation (2.7), we will henceforth restrict our attention primarily to proving one-sided bounds of the form

$$\mathrm{err}(h) \le \widehat{\mathrm{err}}(h) + \varepsilon \tag{2.9}$$

for all $h \in \mathcal{H}$. We do this for simplicity of presentation, but also for the reason that we typically are interested only in upper bounds on generalization error. This is because, first of all, there is no harm done if the learning algorithm manages to get lucky in picking a hypothesis whose generalization error is significantly *lower* than its training error. But more importantly, this case almost never occurs: Since the learning algorithm is biased toward choosing hypotheses that already have low training error, the generalization error is quite unlikely to be even lower. In fact, a closer look at the argument in equation (2.8) reveals that only one-sided uniform error bounds, as in equation (2.9), were actually used. (We did use the fact that $\widehat{\mathrm{err}}(h^*) \le \mathrm{err}(h^*) + \varepsilon$, but this does not require the use of a *uniform* bound since it involves only the single, fixed hypothesis h^*.)

To prove that such uniform bounds hold with high probability, the simplest case is when $\mathcal{H}$ is finite, so that the hypothesis h is selected from a finite set of hypotheses that is fixed before observing the training set. In this case, we can use a simple argument based on the union bound: If we fix any *single* hypothesis $h \in \mathcal{H}$, then, as in section 2.2.1, we can use theorem 2.1 to bound the probability of choosing a training set for which $\mathrm{err}(h) - \widehat{\mathrm{err}}(h) \ge \varepsilon$; this will be at most $e^{-2m\varepsilon^2}$. By the union bound, the chance that this happens for *any* hypothesis in $\mathcal{H}$ can be upper bounded simply by summing this probability bound over all the hypotheses in $\mathcal{H}$, which gives $|\mathcal{H}|e^{-2m\varepsilon^2}$. Thus, we obtain the following:

Theorem 2.2   Let $\mathcal{H}$ be a finite space of hypotheses, and assume that a random training set of size m is chosen. Then for any $\varepsilon > 0$,

$$\mathbf{Pr}[\exists h \in \mathcal{H} : \mathrm{err}(h) \ge \widehat{\mathrm{err}}(h) + \varepsilon] \le |\mathcal{H}|e^{-2m\varepsilon^2}.$$

Thus, with probability at least $1 - \delta$,

$$\mathrm{err}(h) \le \widehat{\mathrm{err}}(h) + \sqrt{\frac{\ln |\mathcal{H}| + \ln(1/\delta)}{2m}} \tag{2.10}$$

for all $h \in \mathcal{H}$.

The second bound, equation (2.10), on the generalization performance of any hypothesis h captures in a single formula the three factors noted earlier which determine the success of a learning algorithm. With regard to the training error $\widehat{\text{err}}(h)$, the first of these factors, we see that the formula is consistent with the intuition that better fit to the training data implies better generalization. The second factor is the number of training examples m, where again the bound captures quantitatively the unarguable notion that having more data is better. Finally, the formula contains a term that depends on the form of the hypotheses being used, that is, on the class $\mathcal{H}$ from which they are chosen. Note that if hypotheses in $\mathcal{H}$ are written down in some way, then the number of bits needed to give each hypothesis $h \in \mathcal{H}$ a unique name is about $\lg |\mathcal{H}|$. Thus, we can think of $\ln |\mathcal{H}|$—the term appearing in the formula, which is off by only a constant from $\lg |\mathcal{H}|$—as roughly the "description length" of the hypotheses being used, rather a natural measure of $\mathcal{H}$'s complexity, the third factor affecting generalization performance. In this way, the formula is consistent with Occam's razor, the notion that, all else being equal, simpler hypotheses perform better than more complex ones.

2.2.3 Infinite Hypothesis Spaces

We next consider infinitely large hypothesis spaces. The results of section 2.2.2 are useless in such cases—for instance, when using threshold rules of the form given in equation (2.1), where there are infinitely many choices for the threshold ν, and thus infinitely many hypotheses of this form. However, this hypothesis space has an important property that was noted in section 2.1: Any training set of m (distinct) examples partitions the infinitely large space into just $m + 1$ equivalence classes such that the predictions of any two hypotheses in the same equivalence class are identical on all m points. Said differently, the number of distinct labelings of the m training points that can be produced by hypotheses in $\mathcal{H}$ is at most $m + 1$. See figure 2.4 for an example.

Thus, in this case, although there are infinitely many hypotheses in $\mathcal{H}$, there are, in a sense, effectively only $m + 1$ hypotheses of any relevance with respect to a fixed set of m examples. It would be tempting indeed to regard $m + 1$ as the "effective" size of the hypothesis space, and then to attempt to apply theorem 2.2 with $|\mathcal{H}|$ replaced by $m + 1$. This would give very reasonable bounds. Unfortunately, such an argument would be flawed because the finite set of effective hypotheses that is induced in this way *depends on the training data*, so that the argument suggested earlier for proving theorem 2.2 using the union bound cannot be applied. Nevertheless, using more sophisticated arguments, it turns out to be possible to prove that this alluring idea actually works so that, modulo some adjusting of the constants, $|\mathcal{H}|$ can be replaced in theorem 2.2 with the "effective" size of $\mathcal{H}$ as measured by the number of labelings of $\mathcal{H}$ on a finite sample.

To make these ideas formal, for any hypothesis class $\mathcal{H}$ over $\mathcal{X}$ and for any finite sample $S = \langle x_1, \ldots, x_m \rangle$, we define the set of *dichotomies* or *behaviors* $\Pi_{\mathcal{H}}(S)$ to be all possible labelings of S by functions in $\mathcal{H}$. That is,

$$\Pi_{\mathcal{H}}(S) \doteq \left\{ \langle h(x_1), \ldots, h(x_m) \rangle : h \in \mathcal{H} \right\}.$$

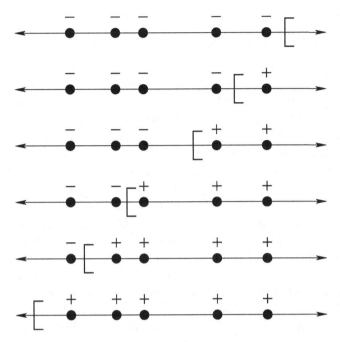

Figure 2.4
Five points on the real line, and a listing of all six possible labelings of the points using threshold functions of the form shown in equation (2.1). On each line, the left bracket [shows a sample threshold ν realizing the given labeling.

We also define the *growth function* $\Pi_{\mathcal{H}}(m)$ which measures the maximum number of dichotomies for any sample S of size m:

$$\Pi_{\mathcal{H}}(m) \doteq \max_{S \in \mathcal{X}^m} |\Pi_{\mathcal{H}}(S)|.$$

For instance, when $\mathcal{H}$ is the class of threshold functions, $\Pi_{\mathcal{H}}(m) = m + 1$, as we have already seen.

We can now state a more general result than theorem 2.2 that is applicable to both finite and infinite hypothesis spaces. Ignoring constants, this theorem has replaced $|\mathcal{H}|$ with the growth function $\Pi_{\mathcal{H}}(m)$.

Theorem 2.3 Let $\mathcal{H}$ be any[1] space of hypotheses, and assume that a random training set of size m is chosen. Then for any $\varepsilon > 0$,

$$\mathbf{Pr}[\exists h \in \mathcal{H} : \mathrm{err}(h) \geq \widehat{\mathrm{err}}(h) + \varepsilon] \leq 8\Pi_{\mathcal{H}}(m)e^{-m\varepsilon^2/32}.$$

Thus, with probability at least $1 - \delta$,

---

1. To be strictly formal, we have to restrict the class $\mathcal{H}$ to be measurable with respect to an appropriate probability space. Here, and throughout this book, we ignore this finer point, which we implicitly assume to hold.

$$\text{err}(h) \le \widehat{\text{err}}(h) + \sqrt{\frac{32(\ln \Pi_{\mathcal{H}}(m) + \ln(8/\delta))}{m}} \tag{2.11}$$

for all $h \in \mathcal{H}$.

So our attention naturally turns to the growth function $\Pi_{\mathcal{H}}(m)$. In "nice" cases, such as for threshold functions, the growth function is only polynomial in m, that is, $O(m^d)$ for some constant d that depends on $\mathcal{H}$. In such a case, $\ln \Pi_{\mathcal{H}}(m)$ is roughly $d \ln m$ so that the term on the far right of equation (2.11), as a function of the training set size m, approaches zero at the favorable rate $O(\sqrt{(\ln m)/m})$.

However, the growth function need not always be polynomial. For instance, consider the class of all hypotheses that are defined to be $+1$ on some finite but unrestricted set of intervals of the real line and -1 on the complement (where instances here are points on the line). An example of a hypothesis in this class is given by the classifier in equation (2.2), which is $+1$ on the intervals $[3.4, 4.0)$, $[5.2, 6.3)$, and $[7.1, \infty)$, and -1 on all other points. This hypothesis space is so rich that for *any* labeling of any set of distinct training points, there always exists a consistent classifier which can be constructed simply by choosing sufficiently small intervals around each of the positively labeled instances. Thus, the number of dichotomies for any set of m distinct points is exactly 2^m, the worst possible value of the growth function. In such a case, $\ln \Pi_{\mathcal{H}}(m) = m \ln 2$, so the bound in theorem 2.3 is useless, being of order $\theta(1)$. On the other hand, the very richness that makes it so easy to find a hypothesis consistent with any training set also strongly suggests that the generalization capabilities of such hypotheses will be very weak indeed.

So we have seen one case in which $\Pi_{\mathcal{H}}(m)$ is polynomial, and another in which it is 2^m for all m. It is a remarkable fact of combinatorics that these are the *only* two behaviors that are possible for the growth function, no matter what the space $\mathcal{H}$ may be. Moreover, as we will soon see, statistically tractable learning turns out to correspond exactly to the former case, with the exponent of the polynomial acting as a natural measure of the complexity of the class $\mathcal{H}$.

To characterize this exponent, we now define some key combinatorial concepts. First, when all 2^m possible labelings of a sample S of size m can be realized by hypotheses in $\mathcal{H}$, we say that S is *shattered* by $\mathcal{H}$. Thus, S is shattered by $\mathcal{H}$ if $|\Pi_{\mathcal{H}}(S)| = 2^m$. Further, we define the *Vapnik-Chervonenkis (VC) dimension* of $\mathcal{H}$ to be the size of the largest sample S shattered by $\mathcal{H}$. If arbitrarily large finite samples can be shattered by $\mathcal{H}$, then the VC-dimension is ∞.

For instance, for threshold functions as in equation (2.1), the VC-dimension is 1 since a single point can be labeled $+1$ or -1 by such rules (which means the VC-dimension is at least 1), but no pair of points can be shattered, since if the leftmost point is labeled $+1$, the rightmost point must also be labeled $+1$ (thus, the VC-dimension is strictly less than 2). For the unions-of-intervals example above, we saw that any set of distinct points is shattered, so the VC-dimension is ∞ in this case.

Indeed, when the VC-dimension is infinite, $\Pi_{\mathcal{H}}(m) = 2^m$ by definition. On the other hand, when the VC-dimension is a finite number d, the growth function turns out to be polynomial, specifically, $O(m^d)$. This follows from a beautiful combinatorial fact known as Sauer's lemma:

Lemma 2.4 (Sauer's lemma) *If $\mathcal{H}$ is a hypothesis class of VC-dimension $d < \infty$, then for all m*

$$\Pi_{\mathcal{H}}(m) \le \sum_{i=0}^{d} \binom{m}{i}.$$

(We follow the convention that $\binom{n}{k} = 0$ if $k < 0$ or $k > n$.) For $m \le d$, this bound is equal to 2^m (and indeed, by d's definition, the bound matches $\Pi_{\mathcal{H}}(m)$ in this case). For $m \ge d \ge 1$, the following bound is often useful:

$$\sum_{i=0}^{d} \binom{m}{i} \le \left(\frac{em}{d}\right)^d \tag{2.12}$$

(where, as usual, e is the base of the natural logarithm).

We can plug this bound immediately into theorem 2.3 to obtain the following:

Theorem 2.5 Let $\mathcal{H}$ be a hypothesis space of VC-dimension $d < \infty$, and assume that a random training set of size m is chosen where $m \ge d \ge 1$. Then for any $\varepsilon > 0$,

$$\mathbf{Pr}[\exists h \in \mathcal{H} : \mathrm{err}(h) \ge \widehat{\mathrm{err}}(h) + \varepsilon] \le 8 \left(\frac{em}{d}\right)^d e^{-m\varepsilon^2/32}.$$

Thus, with probability at least $1 - \delta$,

$$\mathrm{err}(h) \le \widehat{\mathrm{err}}(h) + O\left(\sqrt{\frac{d \ln(m/d) + \ln(1/\delta)}{m}}\right) \tag{2.13}$$

for all $h \in \mathcal{H}$.

As before, this second bound on the generalization error captures the three factors discussed earlier. However, the complexity of $\mathcal{H}$, which was earlier measured by $\ln|\mathcal{H}|$, now is measured instead by the VC-dimension d. This is an important result because it shows that limiting the VC-dimension of a hypothesis class can be used as a general tool for avoiding overfitting.

The VC-dimension may not at first seem intuitive as a measure of complexity. However, it can be shown that the VC-dimension can also be used to provide a general lower bound on the number of examples needed for learning. Thus, in this sense, VC-dimension fully characterizes the (statistical) complexity of learning. Moreover, VC-dimension is related to our earlier complexity measure in that it can never exceed $\lg|\mathcal{H}|$ (see exercise 2.2).

In addition, VC-dimension turns out often (but not always!) to be equal to the number of parameters defining hypotheses in $\mathcal{H}$. For instance, suppose that examples are points $\mathbf{x}$ in $\mathbb{R}^n$, and that hypotheses in $\mathcal{H}$ are *linear threshold functions* of the form

$$h(\mathbf{x}) = \begin{cases} +1 & \text{if } \mathbf{w} \cdot \mathbf{x} > 0 \\ -1 & \text{else} \end{cases}$$

for some weight vector $\mathbf{w} \in \mathbb{R}^n$. Then it can be shown (see lemma 4.1) that the VC-dimension of this class is exactly n, which matches the number of parameters, that is, the number of dimensions in the vector $\mathbf{w}$ that defines each hypothesis in $\mathcal{H}$.

2.2.4 A More Abstract Formulation

The framework above, particularly theorem 2.3, can be stated in more abstract terms that we will sometimes find easier to work with. However, the reader may wish to skip this technical section and come back to it when needed later in the book.

Briefly, let $\mathcal{Z}$ be any set, let $\mathcal{A}$ be a family of subsets of $\mathcal{Z}$, and let $\mathcal{D}$ be a distribution over $\mathcal{Z}$. We consider the problem of estimating from a random sample $S = \langle z_1, \ldots, z_m \rangle$ the probability of each set $A \in \mathcal{A}$. As usual, $\mathbf{Pr}_{z \sim \mathcal{D}}[\cdot]$ denotes probability when z is chosen at random according to the distribution $\mathcal{D}$, and we let $\mathbf{Pr}_{z \sim S}[\cdot]$ denote empirical probability, that is, probability when z is chosen uniformly at random from among the m sample points $z_1, \ldots, z_m$. We wish to show that $\mathbf{Pr}_{z \sim S}[z \in A]$, the empirical probability of any set A, is likely to be close to its true probability $\mathbf{Pr}_{z \sim \mathcal{D}}[z \in A]$, and we want this to be true simultaneously for *every* set $A \in \mathcal{A}$. For a single, fixed set A, this can be shown using Hoeffding's inequality (theorem 2.1). Likewise, if $\mathcal{A}$ is finite, then it can be shown by an application of the union bound. But when $\mathcal{A}$ is infinite, we need to generalize the machinery developed in section 2.2.3.

For any finite sample S as above, we consider the restriction of $\mathcal{A}$ to S, denoted $\Pi_{\mathcal{A}}(S)$, that is, the intersection of S (treated as a set) with each set $A \in \mathcal{A}$:

$$\Pi_{\mathcal{A}}(S) \doteq \{\{z_1, \ldots, z_m\} \cap A : A \in \mathcal{A}\}.$$

Analogous to $\Pi_{\mathcal{H}}(S)$, this collection can be viewed as the set of all "in-out behaviors" of sets $A \in \mathcal{A}$ on the points in S. As before, the growth function is the maximum cardinality of this set over all samples S of size m:

$$\Pi_{\mathcal{A}}(m) \doteq \max_{S \in \mathcal{Z}^m} |\Pi_{\mathcal{A}}(S)|.$$

With these definitions, theorem 2.3 becomes:

Theorem 2.6 Let $\mathcal{A}$ be a family of subsets of $\mathcal{Z}$, and suppose that a random sample S of m points is chosen independently from $\mathcal{Z}$, each point selected according to the same distribution $\mathcal{D}$. Then for any $\varepsilon > 0$,

$$\mathbf{Pr}[\exists A \in \mathcal{A} : \mathbf{Pr}_{z \sim \mathcal{D}}[z \in A] \geq \mathbf{Pr}_{z \sim S}[z \in A] + \varepsilon] \leq 8\Pi_{\mathcal{A}}(m)e^{-m\varepsilon^2/32}.$$

Thus, with probability at least $1 - \delta$,

$$\mathbf{Pr}_{z \sim \mathcal{D}}[z \in A] \leq \mathbf{Pr}_{z \sim S}[z \in A] + \sqrt{\frac{32(\ln \Pi_{\mathcal{A}}(m) + \ln(8/\delta))}{m}}$$

for all $A \in \mathcal{A}$.

To obtain the formulation given in section 2.2.3 as a special case, we first let $\mathcal{Z} \doteq \mathcal{X} \times \{-1, +1\}$, the space of all possible labeled examples. Then, for a given hypothesis space $\mathcal{H}$, we define a family $\mathcal{A}$ of subsets A_h, one for each $h \in \mathcal{H}$, where A_h is the set of examples on which h makes a mistake. That is,

$$\mathcal{A} \doteq \{A_h : h \in \mathcal{H}\}, \tag{2.14}$$

and

$$A_h \doteq \{(x, y) \in \mathcal{Z} : h(x) \neq y\}.$$

Then it can be verified with these definitions that

$$\Pi_{\mathcal{H}}(m) = \Pi_{\mathcal{A}}(m) \tag{2.15}$$

and that theorem 2.6 yields exactly theorem 2.3. (See exercise 2.9.)

2.2.5   Consistent Hypotheses

We have seen that, when possible, it is sometimes desirable for a learning algorithm to produce a hypothesis that is *consistent* with the training data so that it makes no mistakes at all on the training set. Of course, our preceding analyses hold; this is just a special case in which $\widehat{\mathrm{err}}(h) = 0$. However, the bounds obtained in this fashion are particularly loose, giving bounds on the order of $1/\sqrt{m}$. In fact, for consistent hypotheses, it turns out that the square roots on all of our convergence bounds can generally be removed (with some adjusting of constants), giving the far faster convergence rate of just $1/m$ (ignoring log terms).

To get an intuitive feeling for why this is so, consider again the problem of estimating the bias p of a coin, as in section 2.2.1. It turns out that a coin with bias p close to 0 or 1 is much easier to estimate (in the sense of requiring fewer samples) than one with bias close to $\frac{1}{2}$. This is reflected in the bounds that can be proved. According to Hoeffding's inequality (theorem 2.1), if $\hat{p}$ is the observed fraction of heads in m flips, then

$$p \leq \hat{p} + \sqrt{\frac{\ln(1/\delta)}{2m}} \tag{2.16}$$

with probability at least $1 - \delta$. In other words, the true probability p is within $O(1/\sqrt{m})$ of its estimate $\hat{p}$.

Now let us consider what happens when $\hat{p} = 0$, that is, when there are no heads in the observed sequence, corresponding to the case of a hypothesis that is consistent with the entire training set. The probability of getting *no* heads in m flips is exactly $(1-p)^m \leq e^{-pm}$. This means that if $p \geq \ln(1/\delta)/m$, then $\hat{p}$ will be zero with probability at most δ. Turning this statement around implies that when $\hat{p} = 0$, we can conclude that

$$p < \frac{\ln(1/\delta)}{m}$$

with probability at least $1 - \delta$. Note that this estimate is $O(1/m)$ rather than $O(1/\sqrt{m})$ as in equation (2.16).

This style of argument can be applied in the learning setting as well, yielding results such as those summarized in the following theorem:

Theorem 2.7 Let $\mathcal{H}$ be a space of hypotheses, and assume that a random training set S of size m is chosen.

If $\mathcal{H}$ is finite, then with probability at least $1 - \delta$,

$$\mathrm{err}(h) \leq \frac{\ln|\mathcal{H}| + \ln(1/\delta)}{m} \tag{2.17}$$

for every $h \in \mathcal{H}$ that is consistent with S.

More generally, for any (finite or infinite) $\mathcal{H}$, with probability at least $1 - \delta$,

$$\mathrm{err}(h) \leq \frac{2\lg \Pi_{\mathcal{H}}(2m) + 2\lg(2/\delta)}{m} \tag{2.18}$$

for every $h \in \mathcal{H}$ that is consistent with S. If $\mathcal{H}$ has VC-dimension d, where $m \geq d \geq 1$, then with probability at least $1 - \delta$,

$$\mathrm{err}(h) \leq \frac{2d\lg(2em/d) + 2\lg(2/\delta)}{m} \tag{2.19}$$

for every $h \in \mathcal{H}$ that is consistent with S.

This theorem gives high-probability bounds on the true error of all consistent hypotheses. Each of the three bounds in equations (2.17), (2.18), and (2.19) states that, with probability at least $1 - \delta$, $\mathrm{err}(h) \leq \varepsilon$ for every $h \in \mathcal{H}$ that is consistent with S (for values of ε as given in the theorem). In other words, using slightly different phrasing, each bound says that with probability at least $1 - \delta$, for every $h \in \mathcal{H}$, if h is consistent with S, then $\mathrm{err}(h) \leq \varepsilon$. Or, formalizing these results in more precise, mathematical terms, the bounds state that with probability at least $1 - \delta$, the random variable

$$\sup\{\mathrm{err}(h) \mid h \in \mathcal{H} \text{ is consistent with } S\}$$

is at most ε.

2.2.6   Compression-Based Bounds

We have described two general techniques for analyzing a learning algorithm, one based simply on counting the number of hypotheses in the class $\mathcal{H}$, and the other based on $\mathcal{H}$'s VC-dimension. In this section, we briefly describe a third approach.

It has already been noted that $\lg |\mathcal{H}|$, our first complexity measure, is closely related to the number of bits needed to describe each hypothesis $h \in \mathcal{H}$. Thus, from this perspective, the learning algorithm must find a relatively short description that can be used to reconstruct labels for the training examples. This idea depends on the description being in bits, and thus on $\mathcal{H}$ being finite.

Nevertheless, even when $\mathcal{H}$ is infinite, it will often be the case that the hypotheses produced by a particular algorithm can be given a short description, not in bits but in terms of *training examples* themselves. For instance, for the class of threshold functions as in equation (2.1), each classifier is defined by the threshold ν. Moreover, as we have seen, the behavior of such classifiers is equivalent with respect to a particular training set for all thresholds ν lying between two adjacent data points. Thus, a learning algorithm can choose ν to be one of those data points, and, in so doing, produces a classifier that can be described by just one of the training examples. (Alternatively, if it seems more natural, the learner can take ν to be the midpoint between two adjacent data points. This hypothesis can be described by two of the training examples.)

We call such an algorithm whose hypotheses can be represented by κ of the training examples a *compression scheme of size κ*. Thus, formally, such an algorithm is associated with a function $\mathcal{K}$ that maps κ-tuples of labeled examples to hypotheses h in some space $\mathcal{H}$. Given training examples $(x_1, y_1), \ldots, (x_m, y_m)$, such an algorithm chooses some indices $i_1, \ldots, i_\kappa \in \{1, \ldots, m\}$, and outputs the hypothesis

$$h = \mathcal{K}((x_{i_1}, y_{i_1}), \ldots, (x_{i_\kappa}, y_{i_\kappa}))$$

determined by the corresponding examples.

For such algorithms, which arise quite often and quite naturally, bounds on the generalization error can be derived in much the same way as for the case of finite $\mathcal{H}$. In particular, the following can be proved:

Theorem 2.8   Suppose a learning algorithm based on a compression scheme of size κ is provided with a random training set of size m. Then with probability at least $1 - \delta$, the hypothesis h produced by this algorithm satisfies

$$\mathrm{err}(h) \leq \left(\frac{m}{m - \kappa} \right) \widehat{\mathrm{err}}(h) + \sqrt{\frac{\kappa \ln m + \ln(1/\delta)}{2(m - \kappa)}}.$$

Furthermore, with probability at least $1 - \delta$, any consistent hypothesis h produced by this algorithm satisfies

$$\mathrm{err}(h) \le \frac{\kappa \ln m + \ln(1/\delta)}{m - \kappa}.$$

Thus, for such algorithms it is the size κ of the compression scheme that acts as a complexity term.

2.2.7 Discussion

We have explored three general methods for analyzing learning algorithms. The techniques are closely related, differing primarily in the complexity measure employed. These bounds are extremely useful in understanding the *qualitative* behavior of learning algorithms. As we have discussed already, the bounds describe the dependence of the generalization error on the training error, the number of examples, and the complexity of the chosen hypothesis. Furthermore, these bounds are quite helpful in understanding the important and ubiquitous phenomenon of overfitting. Disregarding δ and log factors, each of the bounds in theorems 2.2, 2.5 and 2.8 have the form

$$\mathrm{err}(h) \le \widehat{\mathrm{err}}(h) + \tilde{O}\left(\sqrt{\frac{C_{\mathcal{H}}}{m}}\right) \tag{2.20}$$

where $C_{\mathcal{H}}$ is some measure of the complexity of $\mathcal{H}$. As the complexity of the hypotheses used is permitted to increase, the training error tends to decrease, causing the first term in equation (2.20) to decrease. However, this also causes the second term to increase. The result is an idealized "learning curve" like the one in figure 2.5, which pretty well matches the kind of overfitting behavior often observed in practice.

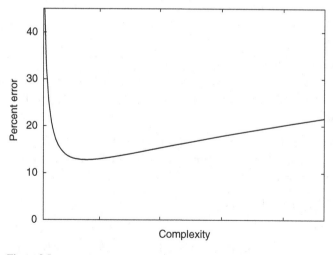

Figure 2.5
An idealized plot of the generalization error of a classifier with varying complexity, as predicted by a bound of the form in equation (2.20).

On the other hand, these bounds are usually too loose to be applied *quantitatively* on actual learning problems. In most cases, the bounds suggest that, with the amount of training data available, only very simple hypothesis classes can be used, while in actual practice, quite large hypothesis classes are used regularly with good results. The problem is that the bounds are overly pessimistic, holding as they do for *all* distributions, including those "worst-case" distributions which make learning as difficult as possible. Thus, while the uniform nature of the bounds is an unquestionable strength that lends generality and robustness to the results, this same uniformity can also be a weakness in the sense that the results may better characterize the theoretical worst case than the actual case encountered in practice.

One way to tighten the bounds may be to take into account additional quantities that can be measured on the training set. Bounds of the type given in the theorems above take into account only the training error $\widehat{\mathrm{err}}(h)$, but other quantities can be considered. For instance, chapter 5 describes bounds on the generalization error of boosting algorithms which depend on properties of the *margin distribution* of the training set.

2.3 A Foundation for the Study of Boosting Algorithms

We next introduce an idealized framework for the mathematical study of machine learning, one that admits absolute guarantees on performance. As we will see, this model of learning will allow us to define the concept of boosting in precise terms, and will thus provide a foundation for the development and analysis of boosting algorithms.

2.3.1 Absolute Guarantees on Performance

As just discussed, the mode of analysis studied in section 2.2 is very general and quite agnostic in the sense that we have made no assumptions about the form of the distribution $\mathcal{D}$ generating the labeled examples (x, y). On the one hand, this generality has made it possible to state results that are applicable in a very broad range of settings without the need for prior assumptions about the data distribution. On the other hand, this same generality has also precluded us from providing *absolute* guarantees on performance. Rather, the bounds that we have discussed tell us that the generalization error will be small *if* during training we can place our hands on a simple hypothesis with low training error on a sufficiently large training set. The bounds do not tell us when it will be possible to obtain a hypothesis that has, say, 99% generalization accuracy. This can only be deduced, according to the bounds, *after* the training error has been observed.

Even as the training set becomes extremely large, the bounds do not guarantee low generalization error. Indeed, such guarantees are impossible in such generality since the distribution $\mathcal{D}$ may be such that the label y is intrinsically unpredictable. For instance, since we assume nothing about $\mathcal{D}$, it is possible that y is equally likely to be $+1$ or -1, independent of x; in such an extreme case, no amount of training or computation can result in a hypothesis with generalization error less than 50%. Thus, to develop a mathematical model of learning which admits absolute guarantees on the generalization error, we must accept additional assumptions about the form of the generating distribution $\mathcal{D}$.

As a first step, we suppose for now that the goal is to learn a classifier with nearly perfect accuracy. We have just seen that this is not always possible, and indeed, realistically, is almost never attainable in practice. Nevertheless, achieving the highest possible accuracy is the ultimate goal of learning, and as such, understanding theoretically when near perfect accuracy can be achieved is a fundamental question.

As we have seen, when there is intrinsic randomness in the labels y themselves, so that y is not strictly determined by x, there is no way to find a hypothesis h which can predict y perfectly for any x, since such a hypothesis does not exist. Thus, the first necessary assumption in our model is that there exists a functional relationship between the instances x and the labels y; in other words, we assume that there exists a *target function*

$$c : \mathcal{X} \to \{-1, +1\}$$

such that, for any x, the associated label y is equal to $c(x)$ with probability 1. That is,

$$\mathbf{Pr}_{(x,y)\sim\mathcal{D}}[y = c(x) \mid x] = 1.$$

This is equivalent to simply regarding $\mathcal{D}$ as a distribution over $\mathcal{X}$ and assuming that examples are of the form $(x, c(x))$, so that each example x is deterministically assigned the label $c(x)$.

Even with such deterministic labeling of the data, learning may be impossible. For instance, if the target function c is an entirely arbitrary function over $\mathcal{X}$, then no finite training set can provide any connection to examples not seen during training; therefore, we cannot hope to find a hypothesis that makes accurate predictions, other than on the examples seen during training. Thus, for generalization to be plausible, we also must make assumptions about the nature of the target function so that there can exist some relationship between the labels of the training data and those on test examples. We can summarize any such knowledge about c by assuming that c comes from some known class of functions $\mathcal{C}$, called the *target (function) class*.

So our problem of understanding the circumstances under which nearly perfect learning is possible can be rephrased as that of determining for which classes $\mathcal{C}$—embodying our assumptions about the target c—such learning is achievable. Here, again, our goal is to learn a hypothesis h with nearly perfect accuracy, that is, with generalization error below ϵ for any specified value of $\epsilon > 0$, though naturally more data will need to be allowed for smaller values of ϵ. Moreover, to avoid further assumptions, we ask that learning be possible for any distribution $\mathcal{D}$ over the instance space $\mathcal{X}$, and for any target function $c \in \mathcal{C}$. Finally, since there is always the possibility that a highly unrepresentative random training sample will be selected, we allow learning to fail entirely with probability $\delta > 0$, where δ should be controllable in a manner similar to ϵ.

So this notion of learning requires that, with high probability over the choice of the random sample, a hypothesis h be found that is nearly perfect, or approximately correct, hence the name *probably approximately correct (PAC) learnability*. To distinguish from what is to follow, we also call this *strong learnability*. Formally, then, a class $\mathcal{C}$ is *strongly PAC learnable* if there exists a learning algorithm A such that for any distribution $\mathcal{D}$ over the instance space $\mathcal{X}$, and for any $c \in \mathcal{C}$ and for any positive values of ϵ and δ, algorithm A takes as input $m = m(\epsilon, \delta)$ examples $(x_1, c(x_1)), \ldots, (x_m, c(x_m))$ where x_i is chosen independently at random according to $\mathcal{D}$, and produces a hypothesis h such that

$$\mathbf{Pr}[\mathrm{err}(h) > \epsilon] \leq \delta.$$

Here, $\mathrm{err}(h)$ is the generalization error of h with respect to distribution $\mathcal{D}$, and the probability is over the random selection of training examples $x_1, \ldots, x_m$. Note that the training set size m can depend on ϵ and δ, and we typically require these to be polynomial in $1/\epsilon$ and $1/\delta$. Further, the sample size will usually also depend on properties of the class $\mathcal{C}$.

When computability is not an issue, we can immediately apply the results of section 2.2.5 to obtain quite general PAC results. In particular, for any class $\mathcal{C}$, consider an algorithm A that, given any sample, selects h to be any function in $\mathcal{C}$ that is consistent with the observed data. By assumption, such a hypothesis h must exist (although the computational considerations of finding it might be prohibitive). Thus, in this case our hypothesis space $\mathcal{H}$ is identical to $\mathcal{C}$. When $\mathcal{C}$ is finite, applying theorem 2.7, we thus immediately get that with probability at least $1 - \delta$,

$$\mathrm{err}(h) \leq \frac{\ln |\mathcal{C}| + \ln(1/\delta)}{m}.$$

Setting the right-hand side equal to ϵ, this means that A is PAC (so that $\mathrm{err}(h) \leq \epsilon$ with probability at least $1 - \delta$) when given a sample of size

$$m = \left\lceil \frac{\ln |\mathcal{C}| + \ln(1/\delta)}{\epsilon} \right\rceil.$$

Similarly, for $\mathcal{C}$ infinite, the algorithm can be shown to be PAC for some sample size that depends on the VC-dimension of $\mathcal{C}$ (provided it is finite).

Thus, our generalization bounds indicate generally that only a moderate-size sample is statistically adequate for PAC learning. What remains is the problem of finding an efficient learning algorithm, an issue that cannot be ignored in the real world. Therefore, we often add an efficiency requirement that the learning algorithm A compute h in polynomial time. Characterizing *efficient* PAC learnability turns out to be much more difficult and involved. Indeed, computational tractability has very often been found to be far more limiting and constraining in the design of learning systems than any statistical considerations. In other words, it is often the case that a learning problem cannot be solved, even when more than enough data has been provided to ensure statistical generalization, solely because the associated computational problem is intractable. (For instance, it is known that this is the case when C is the class of all polynomial-size formulas constructed using the usual operations (AND, OR, and NOT) over n Boolean variables.)

2.3.2 Weak Learnability and Boosting Algorithms

As indicated above, requiring nearly perfect generalization is usually unrealistic, sometimes for statistical reasons and often for purely computational reasons. What happens if we drop this overly stringent requirement? In other words, rather than requiring a generalization error below, say, 1%, what if we were content with error below 10%? or 25%? In the most extreme case, what if our goal is merely to find a hypothesis whose error is just slightly below the trivial baseline of 50%, which is attainable simply by guessing every label at random? Surely, learning must become easier when (far) less-than-perfect accuracy is deemed sufficient.

Learning with such a weak demand on accuracy is called *weak learning*. In terms of its definition, the problem is only a slight modification of PAC learning in which we drop the requirement that the learning algorithm achieve error at most ϵ for *every* $\epsilon > 0$. Rather, we only make this requirement for some *fixed* ϵ, say $\epsilon = \frac{1}{2} - \gamma$, for some fixed but small "edge" $\gamma > 0$. Formally, then, a target class C is *weakly PAC learnable* if for some $\gamma > 0$, there exists a learning algorithm A such that for any distribution $\mathcal{D}$ over the instance space $\mathcal{X}$, and for any $c \in C$ and for any positive value of δ, algorithm A takes as input $m = m(\delta)$ examples $(x_1, c(x_1)), \ldots, (x_m, c(x_m))$, where x_i is chosen independently at random according to $\mathcal{D}$, and produces a hypothesis h such that

$$\mathbf{Pr}\left[\text{err}(h) > \tfrac{1}{2} - \gamma\right] \leq \delta.$$

Weak learnability arises as a natural relaxation of the overly demanding strong learning model. Indeed, on its face one might be concerned that the model is now too weak, accepting as it does any hypothesis that is even slightly better than random guessing. Surely, it would seem, there must be many examples of classes that are weakly learnable (with accuracy only 51%) but not strongly learnable (to accuracy 99%).

This intuition—which turns out to be entirely incorrect—points to a fundamental question: Are the strong and weak learning models equivalent? In other words, is it the case that there exist classes that are weakly but not strongly learnable? Or is it the case that any class that can be weakly learned can also be strongly learned? Boosting arose as an answer to exactly this theoretical question. The existence of boosting algorithms proves that the models are equivalent by showing constructively that any weak learning algorithm can be converted into a strong learning algorithm. Indeed, it is exactly this property that defines boosting in its true technical sense.

Formally, a *boosting algorithm* B is given access to a weak learning algorithm A for C which, when provided with $m_0(\delta)$ examples, is guaranteed to produce a weak hypothesis

h with err$(h) \leq \frac{1}{2} - \gamma$ with probability at least $1 - \delta$. In addition, like any PAC algorithm, B is provided with $\epsilon > 0$, $\delta > 0$, and m labeled examples $(x_1, c(x_1)), \ldots, (x_m, c(x_m))$ for some $c \in \mathcal{C}$ (where $\mathcal{C}$ need not be known to B). Using its access to A, the boosting algorithm must produce its own (strong) hypothesis H such that

$$\mathbf{Pr}[\mathrm{err}(H) > \epsilon] \leq \delta. \tag{2.21}$$

Further, there should only be a polynomial blowup in complexity. In other words, B's sample size m should only be polynomial in $1/\epsilon$, $1/\delta$, $1/\gamma$ and m_0, and similarly, B's running time should be polynomially related to A's (as well as the other parameters). Clearly, applying such an algorithm to a weak learning algorithm for some class $\mathcal{C}$ demonstrates, by definition, that the class is strongly learnable as well. AdaBoost is indeed a boosting algorithm in this technical sense, as will be discussed in section 4.3.

That strong and weak learnability are equivalent implies that learning, as we have defined it, is an "all or nothing" phenomenon in the sense that for every class $\mathcal{C}$, either $\mathcal{C}$ is learnable with nearly perfect accuracy for every distribution, or $\mathcal{C}$ cannot be learned in even the most minimal way on every distribution. There is nothing in between these two extremes.

2.3.3 Approaches to the Analysis of Boosting Algorithms

In this chapter, we have explored two modes of analysis. In the first, the generalization error of a selected hypothesis is bounded in terms of measurable empirical statistics, most commonly its training error. No explicit assumptions are made about the data, and as a result, good generalization depends on an implicit assumption that a hypothesis with low training error can be found. In the second style of analysis, additional assumptions are made about the underlying data generation process, admitting absolute bounds on generalization. In the same way, boosting algorithms can be analyzed using either approach.

Every learning algorithm depends explicitly or implicitly upon assumptions, since learning is quite impossible otherwise. Boosting algorithms are built upon the assumption of weak learnability, the premise that a method already exists for finding poor though not entirely trivial classifiers. In its original form, the boosting question begins by assuming that a given class $\mathcal{C}$ is weakly PAC learnable as defined above. With such an assumption, as we have seen, it is possible to prove strong absolute guarantees on the PAC learnability of $\mathcal{C}$, ensuring near perfect generalization.

However, in practical settings, this assumption may be too onerous, requiring that the labels be deterministic according to a target function from a known class $\mathcal{C}$, that weak learning hold for every distribution, and that the edge γ be known ahead of time. Practically, these requirements can be very difficult to check or guarantee. As we now discuss, there are many ways in which these assumptions can be weakened, and most (but not all) of the book is founded on such relaxed versions of the weak learning assumption.

To begin, for the sake of generality we can usually drop any explicit assumptions about the data, returning to the more agnostic framework seen earlier in the chapter in which labeled examples (x, y) are generated by an arbitrary distribution $\mathcal{D}$ with no functional dependence assumed for the labels y. In this case, as in chapter 1, the training set consists simply of labeled pairs $(x_1, y_1), \dots, (x_m, y_m)$.

Furthermore, rather than the far-reaching assumption of weak PAC learnability described above, we can instead assume only that the weak hypotheses found by the given weak learning algorithm A have weighted *training* error bounded away from $\frac{1}{2}$. This leads to a different and weaker notion of weak learnability that is particular to the actual training set. Specifically, we say that the *empirical γ-weak learning assumption* holds if for any distribution D on the indices $\{1, \dots, m\}$ of the training examples, the weak learning algorithm A is able to find a hypothesis h with weighted *training* error at most $\frac{1}{2} - \gamma$:

$$\mathbf{Pr}_{i \sim D}[h(x_i) \neq y_i] \leq \tfrac{1}{2} - \gamma.$$

Thus, empirical weak learnability is defined with respect to distributions defined on a particular training set with particular labels, while weak PAC learnability is defined with respect to any distribution on the entire domain $\mathcal{X}$, and any labeling consistent with one of the targets in the class $\mathcal{C}$. These two notions are clearly related, but are also quite distinct. Even so, when clear from context, we often use shortened terminology, such as "weak learning assumption" and "weakly learnable," omitting "PAC" or "empirical."

This condition can be weakened still further. Rather than assuming that the weak learner A can achieve a training error of $\frac{1}{2} - \gamma$ on *every* distribution on the training set, we can assume only that this happens on the *particular* distributions on which it is actually trained during boosting. In the notation of algorithm 1.1 (p. 5), this means, for AdaBoost, simply that $\epsilon_t \leq \frac{1}{2} - \gamma$ for all t, for some $\gamma > 0$. This property clearly follows from the empirical γ-weak learning assumption, and also follows from the weak PAC learnability assumption, as will be seen in section 4.3. Furthermore, in comparison to what was earlier assumed regarding the weak PAC learnability of a known class $\mathcal{C}$, this assumption is quite benign, and can be verified immediately in an actual learning setting.

We can even go one step farther and drop the assumption that the edge γ is known; as discussed in chapter 1, this is the defining property of a boosting algorithm that is *adaptive*, such as AdaBoost.

In the resulting fully relaxed framework, no assumptions at all are made about the data, analogous to the agnostic approach taken earlier in the chapter. Rather, generalization performance is analyzed in terms of the weighted training errors ϵ_t, as well as other relevant parameters, such as the complexity of the weak hypotheses. Although the ϵ_t's are not explicitly assumed to be bounded below $\frac{1}{2}$, when this is the case, such bounds should imply high generalization accuracy. Since it is the most general and practical, we will mostly follow this mode of analysis, particularly in chapters 4 and 5, where bounds of just this form are proved.

Summary

This chapter has reviewed some fundamental results at the foundation of theoretical machine learning, tools we will use extensively in later chapters in the analysis of boosting algorithms. These general results formalize our intuition of the requirements for learning: sufficient data, low training error, and simplicity, the last of these being measurable in various ways, including description length, VC-dimension, and degree of compressibility. This understanding also captures the essential problem of learning, namely, the careful balancing of the trade-off between fit to training data and simplicity. Finally, we looked at the formal PAC learning framework and the notion of weak learnability from which arises the basic question of the existence of boosting algorithms.

With this foundation, we can begin our analysis of AdaBoost.

Bibliographic Notes

The overall approach to machine learning that we have adopted in this chapter, particularly in sections 2.1 and 2.2, was initially pioneered in the groundbreaking work of Vapnik and Chervonenkis [225, 226]. For a more complete treatment, see, for instance, the books by Vapnik [222, 223, 224], and by Devroye, Györfi, and Lugosi [67]. The approach and analysis described in sections 2.2.3 and 2.2.4, including theorems 2.3, 2.5, and 2.6, lemma 2.4, and the VC-dimension as applied in this setting, are all due to Vapnik and Chervonenkis [225]. However, the constants that appear in their versions of these theorems are slightly different from what we have given here, which are based instead on theorem 12.5 of Devroye, Györfi, and Lugosi [67]. This latter source includes an overview of some of the other versions that have been proved, some of which have better constants. Also, lemma 2.4 was proved independently by Sauer [198]. A short proof of equation (2.12) is given by Kearns and Vazirani [134]. Examples of lower bounds on learning in terms of the VC-dimension include the work of Ehrenfeucht et al. [80] and Gentile and Helmbold [107]. Hoeffding's inequality (theorem 2.1) is due to Hoeffding [123]. Regarding theorem 2.7, equation (2.17) was proved by Vapnik and Chervonenkis [226], and later by Blumer et al. [27]. Equation (2.18) was proved by Blumer et al. [28].

Further background on the generative (or Bayesian) approach described in section 2.1.2 can be found, for instance, in Duda, Hart, and Stork [73], and Bishop [22].

The approach given in section 2.2.6, including theorem 2.8, is due to Littlestone and Warmuth [154], and Floyd and Warmuth [85]. The minimum description length principle, though not discussed in this book, is the foundation for another, related approach to learning and statistics which is also based on compression—see, for instance, Grünwald's book [112].

The PAC learning model of section 2.3.1 was proposed by Valiant [221]. Further background can be found in Kearns and Vazirani's book [134]. The notion of weak PAC learning in section 2.3.2 was first considered by Kearns and Valiant [133]. This latter work also contains examples of learning problems which are computationally intractable even when provided with a statistically adequate amount of data, as mentioned in section 2.3.1.

Some of the exercises in this chapter are based on material from [28, 154, 198, 221, 225].

Exercises

2.1 For any hypothesis space $\mathcal{H}$, let $\hat{h}$ minimize the training error, and let h^* minimize the generalization error:

$$\hat{h} \doteq \arg\min_{h \in \mathcal{H}} \widehat{\text{err}}(h)$$

$$h^* \doteq \arg\min_{h \in \mathcal{H}} \text{err}(h).$$

Note that $\hat{h}$ depends implicitly on the training set. Prove that

$$\mathbf{E}\left[\widehat{\text{err}}(\hat{h})\right] \leq \text{err}(h^*) \leq \mathbf{E}\left[\text{err}(\hat{h})\right]$$

(where expectation is with respect to the choice of the random training examples).

2.2 Show that the VC-dimension of any finite hypothesis space $\mathcal{H}$ is at most $\lg|\mathcal{H}|$. Also, show that this bound is tight; that is, for every $d \geq 1$, give an example of a hypothesis space $\mathcal{H}$ with VC-dimension equal to d for which $d = \lg|\mathcal{H}|$.

2.3 Let $\mathcal{X} = \{0, 1\}^n$, and let $\mathcal{C}$ be the space of Boolean monomials, that is, functions of the form

$$c(\mathbf{x}) = \begin{cases} +1 & \text{if } \prod_{j \in R} x_j = 1 \\ -1 & \text{else} \end{cases}$$

for some $R \subseteq \{1, \ldots, n\}$. In other words, $c(\mathbf{x}) = +1$ if and only if all of the variables $x_j = 1$, for all $j \in R$. Show that $\mathcal{C}$ is efficiently PAC learnable. That is, describe an efficient (polynomial-time) algorithm for finding a monomial consistent with any dataset (assuming one exists), and show that the PAC criterion (equation (2.21)) holds for a sample of size polynomial in $1/\epsilon$, $1/\delta$, and n.

2.4 Let $\mathcal{X} = \mathbb{R}^n$, and let $\mathcal{H}$ be the space of hypotheses defined by *axis-aligned rectangles*, that is, functions of the form

$$h(\mathbf{x}) = \begin{cases} +1 & \text{if } a_j \leq x_j \leq b_j \text{ for all } j = 1, \ldots, n \\ -1 & \text{else} \end{cases}$$

for some $a_1, \ldots, a_n, b_1, \ldots, b_n \in \mathbb{R}$. Compute exactly the VC-dimension of $\mathcal{H}$.

2.5 Let $\mathcal{X} = \mathbb{R}^n$, and let $\mathcal{C}$ be the space of functions defined by axis-aligned rectangles, as in exercise 2.4. Show that $\mathcal{C}$ is efficiently PAC learnable (as in exercise 2.3), using a compression scheme.

2.6 Let $\mathcal{X} = \mathbb{R}$, and let $\mathcal{C}$ be the space of functions defined by unions of at most n intervals, that is, functions of the form

$$c(x) = \begin{cases} +1 & \text{if } x \in [a_1, b_1] \cup \cdots \cup [a_n, b_n] \\ -1 & \text{else} \end{cases}$$

for some $a_1, \ldots, a_n, b_1, \ldots, b_n \in \mathbb{R}$.

a. Compute the VC-dimension of $\mathcal{C}$ exactly.

b. Use the result from part (a) to show that $\mathcal{C}$ is efficiently PAC learnable (as in exercise 2.3).

2.7 Show that Sauer's lemma (lemma 2.4) is tight. That is, for every $d \geq 1$, give an example of a space $\mathcal{H}$ with VC-dimension equal to d such that for each m,

$$\Pi_{\mathcal{H}}(m) = \sum_{i=0}^{d} \binom{m}{i}.$$

2.8 Let $\mathcal{H}$ be a countably infinite space of hypotheses. Let $g : \mathcal{H} \to (0, 1]$ be any function such that

$$\sum_{h \in \mathcal{H}} g(h) \leq 1.$$

Although g may look a bit like a probability distribution, it is just a function—any function—whose positive values happen to add up to a number not bigger than 1. Assume a random training set of size m has been chosen.

a. Prove that, with probability at least $1 - \delta$,

$$\text{err}(h) \leq \widehat{\text{err}}(h) + \sqrt{\frac{\ln(1/g(h)) + \ln(1/\delta)}{2m}}$$

for all $h \in \mathcal{H}$.

b. Suppose hypotheses in $\mathcal{H}$ are represented by bit strings and that $|h|$ denotes the number of bits needed to represent h. Show how to choose g to prove that, with probability at least $1 - \delta$,

$$\text{err}(h) \leq \widehat{\text{err}}(h) + O\left(\sqrt{\frac{|h| + \ln(1/\delta)}{m}}\right)$$

for all $h \in \mathcal{H}$.

c. How does the bound in part (b) reflect the intuitive trade-off between fit to data and simplicity?

2.9 Show that theorems 2.3 and 2.6 are equivalent. That is:

a. For $\mathcal{A}$ constructed as in equation (2.14), verify equation (2.15), and show that theorem 2.6 yields exactly theorem 2.3.

b. For a general family $\mathcal{A}$ of subsets, show that theorem 2.3 can be used to prove theorem 2.6.

2.10 Let the domain be $\mathcal{X}_n = \mathbb{R}^n$, and let $\mathcal{H}_n$ be the space of all decision stumps of the (simplified) form

$$h(\mathbf{x}) = \begin{cases} c_0 & \text{if } x_k \leq \nu \\ c_1 & \text{if } x_k > \nu \end{cases}$$

for some $c_0, c_1 \in \{-1, +1\}$, $k \in \{1, \ldots, n\}$, and $\nu \in \mathbb{R}$. (In section 3.4.2, we will consider decision stumps in greater generality.)

a. Show that $\Pi_{\mathcal{H}_n}(m) \leq 2nm$.

b. Show that there exist positive constants a and b such that for all $n \geq 1$, the VC-dimension of $\mathcal{H}_n$ is at most $a + b \ln n$.

3 Using AdaBoost to Minimize Training Error

In this chapter, we study how AdaBoost can be used to minimize the training error, that is, the number of mistakes on the training set itself. As discussed in chapter 1, we will prove that AdaBoost drives the training error down very fast as a function of the error rates of the weak classifiers, even if they all have error rates that are close (but not too close) to the trivial error rate of 50% achievable by simple random guessing. This is AdaBoost's most basic theoretical property.

Note that our approach is deliberately vague with regard to the weak learning algorithm, that is, the source of the weak hypotheses. As discussed in section 2.3.3, our analysis depends only on an assumption of empirical weak learnability. Such an agnostic approach has the important advantage of generality and flexibility: By leaving the weak learner unspecified, we are able to derive a boosting algorithm and an analysis that are immediately applicable to any choice of weak learning algorithm. However, in practice, we must at some point choose or design an appropriate algorithm for this purpose, one that achieves better-than-guessing accuracy on any given distribution over the training set. This chapter therefore includes a discussion of some of the practical approaches that can be used here.

We also look at general conditions that guarantee weak learnability. And as an aside, we dwell briefly on the close relationship between the simple proof technique used to analyze AdaBoost's training error and those commonly used to prove Chernoff bounds, such as theorem 2.1.

One may wonder why it is worthwhile to study the training error at all since our prime interest is in the generalization error. However, as was seen in chapter 2, fitting the training data, typically by minimizing the training error, is one of the main conditions for successful learning. Of course, for now, we are ignoring the other main condition for learning, that of simplicity, an issue that will be addressed in later chapters in our upcoming analysis of the generalization error. Moreover, for that analysis, we will see that the present study of the training error will turn out to be very helpful.

3.1   A Bound on AdaBoost's Training Error

We begin by proving a fundamental bound on AdaBoost's training error. In proving this main theorem, we make no assumptions about the training set and how it was generated, nor about the weak learner. The theorem simply gives a bound on the training error in terms of the error rates of the weak hypotheses.

In the simple version of AdaBoost shown as algorithm 1.1 (p. 5), D_1 is initialized to the uniform distribution over the training set. Here, however, we give a slightly more general proof applicable to an arbitrary initialization of D_1. The resulting proof provides an upper bound on the *weighted* fraction of examples misclassified by H, where each example i is weighted by $D_1(i)$. A bound on the ordinary, unweighted training error, when D_1 is initialized as in algorithm 1.1, follows immediately as a special case.

Theorem 3.1   Given the notation of algorithm 1.1, let $\gamma_t \doteq \frac{1}{2} - \epsilon_t$, and let D_1 be an arbitrary initial distribution over the training set. Then the weighted training error of the combined classifier H with respect to D_1 is bounded as

$$\mathbf{Pr}_{i \sim D_1}[H(x_i) \neq y_i] \leq \prod_{t=1}^{T} \sqrt{1 - 4\gamma_t^2} \leq \exp\left(-2\sum_{t=1}^{T} \gamma_t^2\right).$$

Note that because $\epsilon_t = \frac{1}{2} - \gamma_t$, the *edge* γ_t measures how much better than the random-guessing error rate of $\frac{1}{2}$ is the error rate of the t-th weak classifier h_t. As an illustration of the theorem, suppose all of the γ_t's are at least 10% so that no h_t has error rate above 40%. Then the theorem implies that the training error of the combined classifier is at most

$$\left(\sqrt{1 - 4(0.1)^2}\right)^T \approx (0.98)^T.$$

In other words, the training error drops *exponentially fast* as a function of the number of base classifiers combined. More discussion of this property follows below.

Here is the informal idea behind the theorem: On every round, AdaBoost increases the weights (under distribution D_t) of the misclassified examples. Moreover, because the final classifier H is a (weighted) majority vote of the weak classifiers, if some example is misclassified by H, then it must have been misclassified by most of the weak classifiers as well. This means that it must have had its weight increased on many rounds, so that its weight under the final distribution D_{T+1} must be large. However, because D_{T+1} is a distribution (with weights that sum to 1), there can be only a few examples with large weights, that is, where H makes an incorrect prediction. Therefore, the training error of H must be small.

We now give a formal argument.

Proof   Let

$$F(x) \doteq \sum_{t=1}^{T} \alpha_t h_t(x). \tag{3.1}$$

Unraveling the recurrence in algorithm 1.1 that defines D_{t+1} in terms of D_t gives

$$D_{T+1}(i) = D_1(i) \times \frac{e^{-y_i \alpha_1 h_1(x_i)}}{Z_1} \times \cdots \times \frac{e^{-y_i \alpha_T h_T(x_i)}}{Z_T}$$

$$= \frac{D_1(i) \exp\left(-y_i \sum_{t=1}^{T} \alpha_t h_t(x_i)\right)}{\prod_{t=1}^{T} Z_t}$$

$$= \frac{D_1(i) \exp\left(-y_i F(x_i)\right)}{\prod_{t=1}^{T} Z_t}. \tag{3.2}$$

Since $H(x) = \text{sign}(F(x))$, if $H(x) \neq y$, then $yF(x) \leq 0$, which implies that $e^{-yF(x)} \geq 1$. That is, $1\{H(x) \neq y\} \leq e^{-yF(x)}$. Therefore, the (weighted) training error is

$$\mathbf{Pr}_{i \sim D_1}[H(x_i) \neq y_i] = \sum_{i=1}^{m} D_1(i) \, 1\{H(x_i) \neq y_i\}$$

$$\leq \sum_{i=1}^{m} D_1(i) \exp\left(-y_i F(x_i)\right) \tag{3.3}$$

$$= \sum_{i=1}^{m} D_{T+1}(i) \prod_{t=1}^{T} Z_t \tag{3.4}$$

$$= \prod_{t=1}^{T} Z_t \tag{3.5}$$

where equation (3.4) uses equation (3.2), and equation (3.5) uses the fact that D_{T+1} is a distribution (which sums to 1). Finally, by our choice of α_t, we have that

$$Z_t = \sum_{i=1}^{m} D_t(i) e^{-\alpha_t y_i h_t(x_i)}$$

$$= \sum_{i:y_i = h_t(x_i)} D_t(i) e^{-\alpha_t} + \sum_{i:y_i \neq h_t(x_i)} D_t(i) e^{\alpha_t} \tag{3.6}$$

$$= e^{-\alpha_t} (1 - \epsilon_t) + e^{\alpha_t} \epsilon_t \tag{3.7}$$

$$= e^{-\alpha_t} \left(\frac{1}{2} + \gamma_t\right) + e^{\alpha_t} \left(\frac{1}{2} - \gamma_t\right) \tag{3.8}$$

$$= \sqrt{1 - 4\gamma_t^2}. \tag{3.9}$$

Here, equation (3.6) uses the fact that both y_i and $h_t(x_i)$ are $\{-1, +1\}$-valued; equation (3.7) follows from the definition of ϵ_t; and equation (3.9) uses the definition of α_t, which, as we will discuss shortly, was chosen specifically to minimize equation (3.7).

Plugging into equation (3.5) gives the first bound of the theorem. For the second bound, we simply apply the approximation $1 + x \leq e^x$ for all real x.   ∎

From the proof, it is apparent where AdaBoost's choice of α_t comes from: The proof shows that the training error is upper bounded by $\prod_t Z_t$. To minimize this expression, we can minimize each Z_t separately. Expanding Z_t gives equation (3.7), which can be minimized over choices of α_t using simple calculus giving the choice of α_t used in algorithm 1.1. Note that α_t is being chosen *greedily* on each round t without consideration of how that choice will affect future rounds.

As discussed above, theorem 3.1 assures a rapid drop in training error when each weak classifier is assumed to have error bounded away from $\frac{1}{2}$. This assumption, that $\epsilon_t \leq \frac{1}{2} - \gamma$ for some $\gamma > 0$ on every round t, is a slight relaxation of the empirical γ-weak learning assumption, as discussed in section 2.3.3. When this condition holds, theorem 3.1 implies that the combined classifier will have training error at most

$$\left(\sqrt{1 - 4\gamma^2}\right)^T \leq e^{-2\gamma^2 T},$$

an exponentially decreasing function of T for any $\gamma > 0$. Although the bound on training error is easier to understand in light of the weak-learnability condition, it is important to remember that AdaBoost and its analysis do *not* require this condition. AdaBoost, being adaptive, does not need to assume an a priori lower bound on the γ_t's, and the analysis takes into account all of the γ_t's. If some γ_t's are large, then the progress (in terms of reducing the bound on the training error) will be that much greater.

Although the bound implies an exponential drop in training error, the bound itself is nevertheless rather loose. For instance, figure 3.1 shows a plot of the training error of the combined classifier compared to the theoretical upper bound as a function of the number of rounds of boosting for the heart-disease dataset described in section 1.2.3. The figure also shows the training errors ϵ_t of the base classifiers h_t with respect to the distributions D_t on which they were trained.

3.2 A Sufficient Condition for Weak Learnability

The assumption of empirical γ-weak learnability is fundamental to the study of boosting, and theorem 3.1 proves that this assumption is sufficient to ensure that AdaBoost will drive down the training error very quickly. But when does this assumption actually hold? Is it possible that this assumption is actually vacuous, in other words, that there are no natural situations in which it holds? What's more, our formulation of weak learnability is somewhat cumbersome, depending as it does on the weighted training error of base hypotheses with respect to virtually any distribution over the training set.

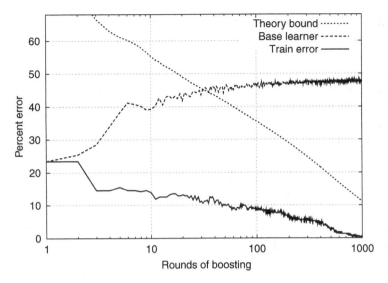

Figure 3.1
The training percent error rate and theoretical upper bound on the training error rate of the combined classifier
obtained by using boosting on the entire heart-disease dataset from section 1.2.3. The error rates ϵ_t of the base
classifiers on their respective weighted training sets are also plotted.

In this section, we provide a simple condition that itself implies the assumption of empirical weak learnability. As we will see, this condition is only in terms of the functional
relationship between the instances and their labels, and does not involve distributions over
examples. Although we show only the sufficiency of the condition, later, in section 5.4.3,
we will discuss the necessity of the condition as well, thus providing a fairly complete characterization of weak learnability (but one that ignores issues of computational efficiency).

Let all the weak hypotheses belong to some class of hypotheses $\mathcal{H}$. Since we are ignoring
computational issues, we simply seek a sufficient condition for there always to exist a weak
hypothesis in $\mathcal{H}$ that is significantly better than random for any distribution.

Suppose our training sample S is such that for some weak hypotheses $g_1, \dots, g_k$ from
the given space $\mathcal{H}$, and for some nonnegative coefficients $a_1, \dots, a_k$ with $\sum_{j=1}^{k} a_j = 1$,
and for some $\theta > 0$, it holds that

$$y_i \sum_{j=1}^{k} a_j g_j(x_i) \geq \theta \tag{3.10}$$

for each example (x_i, y_i) in S. This condition implies that y_i can be computed by a weighted
majority vote of the weak hypotheses since equation (3.10) implies that

$$y_i = \text{sign}\left(\sum_{j=1}^{k} a_j g_j(x_i)\right). \tag{3.11}$$

However, the condition in equation (3.10) is a bit stronger; whereas equation (3.11) specifies that barely a weighted majority of the predictions be correct on each example, equation (3.10) demands that *significantly more* than a bare weighted majority be correct. When the condition in equation (3.10) holds for all i, we say that the sample S is *linearly separable with margin θ*. (Margins will be discussed in far more detail in chapter 5.)

In fact, when this condition holds, the assumption of empirical weak learnability holds as well. For suppose that D is any distribution over S. Then, taking expectations of both sides of equation (3.10) and applying linearity of expectations gives

$$\sum_{j=1}^{k} a_j \mathbf{E}_{i \sim D}\left[y_i g_j(x_i) \right] = \mathbf{E}_{i \sim D}\left[y_i \sum_{j=1}^{k} a_j g_j(x_i) \right] \geq \theta.$$

Since the a_j's constitute a distribution, this means that there exists j (and thus a corresponding weak hypothesis $g_j \in \mathcal{H}$) such that

$$\mathbf{E}_{i \sim D}\left[y_i g_j(x_i) \right] \geq \theta.$$

In general, we have that

$$\mathbf{E}_{i \sim D}\left[y_i g_j(x_i) \right] = 1 \cdot \mathbf{Pr}_{i \sim D}\left[y_i = g_j(x_i) \right] + (-1) \cdot \mathbf{Pr}_{i \sim D}\left[y_i \neq g_j(x_i) \right]$$

$$= 1 - 2 \mathbf{Pr}_{i \sim D}\left[y_i \neq g_j(x_i) \right],$$

so the weighted error of g_j is

$$\mathbf{Pr}_{i \sim D}\left[y_i \neq g_j(x_i) \right] = \frac{1 - \mathbf{E}_{i \sim D}\left[y_i g_j(x_i) \right]}{2}$$

$$\leq \frac{1}{2} - \frac{\theta}{2}.$$

Thus, this argument shows that if the sample is linearly separable with margin 2γ, then for every distribution over the sample, there exists a base hypothesis in the space $\mathcal{H}$ with weighted error at most $\frac{1}{2} - \gamma$. Such a hypothesis would surely be found by an *exhaustive weak learning algorithm*, meaning a (possibly prohibitively inefficient) base learning algorithm that conducts a brute-force search for the *best* (that is, minimum weighted training error) weak hypothesis in $\mathcal{H}$. This means that when computational costs are not an issue, linear separability with positive margin 2γ is a sufficient condition that guarantees γ-weak learnability.

This assumption of linear separability can be shown to hold in various natural settings. As a simple example, suppose each instance $\mathbf{x}_i$ is a vector in $\mathbb{R}^n$, and that the label y_i is $+1$ for points $\mathbf{x}_i$ falling inside some hyper-rectangle

$$[a_1, b_1] \times \cdots \times [a_n, b_n],$$

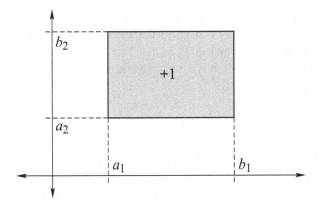

Figure 3.2
A sample target that is +1 inside the two-dimensional rectangle $[a_1, b_1] \times [a_2, b_2]$, and −1 outside.

and −1 otherwise. (See figure 3.2 for an example in $n = 2$ dimensions.) Let

$$f(\mathbf{x}) \doteq \frac{1}{4n-1} \left[\sum_{j=1}^{n} \left(\mathbf{1}^*\{x_j \geq a_j\} + \mathbf{1}^*\{x_j \leq b_j\} \right) - (2n-1) \right] \tag{3.12}$$

where $\mathbf{1}^*\{\cdot\}$ is +1 if its argument holds true, and −1 otherwise. Then it can be argued that

$$y_i f(\mathbf{x}_i) \geq \frac{1}{4n-1}$$

for all i since the inner sum of equation (3.12) will be equal to $2n$ if $\mathbf{x}_i$ is in the defining hyper-rectangle, and will be at most $2n - 2$ otherwise. Noting that f has been written as a convex combination (or average) of decision stumps (over features matching the dimensions of the instances, and including the "constant" stump that always predicts +1 or always −1), this shows that our linear separability assumption holds, and thus that the weak learning assumption holds as well when using decision stumps. (See section 3.4.2 for more detail on decision stumps.)

Theorem 3.1 already provides us with the beginnings of a converse to what was shown above. As noted earlier, if the γ-weak learning assumption holds for some $\gamma > 0$, then the number of mistakes of the combined classifier is at most $e^{-2\gamma^2 T}$ (taking D_1 to be uniform). Thus, if

$$T > \frac{\ln m}{2\gamma^2}$$

so that $e^{-2\gamma^2 T} < 1/m$, then the training error of the combined classifier, which is always an integer multiple of $1/m$, must in fact be zero. Moreover, this final classifier has the form of a weighted majority vote. This means that, under the weak learning assumption, theorem 3.1 implies that equation (3.11) must hold for some choice of base classifiers and corresponding coefficients as witnessed by AdaBoost's own combined classifier. This is clearly weaker than equation (3.10), as noted earlier. Nevertheless, it is a start, and in section 5.4.2 we will have the necessary tools to prove the full converse.

3.3   Relation to Chernoff Bounds

As remarked in section 2.2.1, the proof technique used to prove theorem 3.1 is closely related to a standard technique for proving Chernoff bounds, such as Hoeffding's inequality (theorem 2.1). To bring out this connection, we show, as a brief, somewhat whimsical digression, how a special case of Hoeffding's inequality can be derived as an immediate corollary of theorem 3.1. Let $X_1, \ldots, X_n$ be independent, identically distributed random variables such that

$$
X_t = \begin{cases} 1 & \text{with probability } \frac{1}{2} + \gamma \\ 0 & \text{with probability } \frac{1}{2} - \gamma \end{cases}
$$

for some $\gamma > 0$. What is the probability that at most half of the X_t's are 1? That is, we seek the probability that

$$
\frac{1}{n} \sum_{t=1}^{n} X_t \leq \frac{1}{2}. \tag{3.13}
$$

According to theorem 2.1, this probability is at most $e^{-2n\gamma^2}$ since, in the notation of that theorem, $\mathbf{E}[A_n] = \frac{1}{2} + \gamma$.

This same result can be derived using our analysis of AdaBoost's training error by contriving an artificially defined training set. In particular, let the instances in the "training set" S be $\{0, 1\}^n$, that is, all n-bit sequences $\mathbf{x}$ corresponding to outcomes of $X_1, \ldots, X_n$. Each example in S is defined to have label $y = +1$. Let the initial distribution D_1 be defined to match the process generating these random variables so that

$$
D_1(\mathbf{x}) = \mathbf{Pr}[X_1 = x_1, \ldots, X_n = x_n] = \prod_{t=1}^{n} \left[\left(\tfrac{1}{2} + \gamma \right)^{x_t} \left(\tfrac{1}{2} - \gamma \right)^{1-x_t} \right].
$$

(Here, we abuse notation slightly so that the distributions D_t are defined directly over instances in S rather than over the *indices* of those examples.) Now let the number of rounds T be equal to n, and define the t-th "weak hypothesis" h_t to be

$$
h_t(\mathbf{x}) = \begin{cases} +1 & \text{if } x_t = 1 \\ -1 & \text{if } x_t = 0. \end{cases}
$$

With these definitions, it can be shown (exercise 3.4) that

$$\epsilon_t = \mathbf{Pr}_{\mathbf{x} \sim D_t}[h_t(\mathbf{x}) \neq +1] = \tfrac{1}{2} - \gamma. \tag{3.14}$$

This follows from the independence of the predictions of the h_t's under distribution D_1, as well as from the multiplicative nature of the updates to the distributions created by AdaBoost. This means that all the α_t's are equal to the same positive constant

$$\alpha_t = \alpha = \frac{1}{2} \ln \left(\frac{\frac{1}{2} + \gamma}{\frac{1}{2} - \gamma} \right),$$

so the combined classifier $H(\mathbf{x})$ is a simple (unweighted) majority vote of the h_t's, which is $+1$ if and only if

$$\sum_{t=1}^{n} h_t(\mathbf{x}) > 0,$$

or, equivalently,

$$\frac{1}{n} \sum_{t=1}^{n} x_t > \frac{1}{2}.$$

Thus, applying theorem 3.1, we have that the probability of equation (3.13) is equal to

$$\mathbf{Pr}_{\mathbf{x} \sim D_1} \left[\frac{1}{n} \sum_{t=1}^{n} x_t \leq \frac{1}{2} \right] = \mathbf{Pr}_{\mathbf{x} \sim D_1}[H(\mathbf{x}) \neq +1]$$

$$\leq \left(1 - 4\gamma^2 \right)^{n/2} \leq e^{-2n\gamma^2}.$$

Again, the fact that we get the identical bound as when we apply Hoeffding's inequality directly is not a coincidence, but a consequence of the similar proof techniques used. Moreover, direct generalizations of AdaBoost and theorem 3.1, such as those discussed in section 5.4.2, can be used to prove theorem 2.1 in full generality (see exercise 5.4), as well as some of its extensions, such as Azuma's lemma for non-independent random variables called martingales. That our analysis of AdaBoost applies even when the weak hypotheses are not independent (or martingales) suggests that AdaBoost's mechanism is somehow forcing them to behave as if they actually were independent.

Thus, AdaBoost is a kind of analogue of Hoeffding's inequality for the boosting setting. Hoeffding's inequality is an approximation of the tail of the binomial distribution (equation (2.4)). So what is the analogous boosting algorithm corresponding to the *exact* binomial tail? There is no apparent reason why this strange question should have a meaningful answer. But it does, in the form of the boost-by-majority algorithm presented in chapter 13, which provides an "exact" form of boosting, and one whose corresponding bounds involve exact tails of the binomial distribution, rather than Chernoff-style approximations to it.

3.4 Using and Designing Base Learning Algorithms

AdaBoost, like all boosting algorithms, is an inherently incomplete learning method since it is, by its nature, a "meta-algorithm," one which is meant to be built on top of, or in combination with, some unspecified base learning algorithm. In this section, we explore some general approaches in the use and choice of the base learning algorithm.

The job of the base learner is to produce base hypotheses h_t. As input, the algorithm accepts a training set

$$S = \langle (x_1, y_1), \ldots, (x_m, y_m) \rangle \tag{3.15}$$

and a set of weights D_t. Its criterion for measuring the goodness of any candidate hypothesis h is the weighted training error

$$\epsilon_t \doteq \mathbf{Pr}_{i \sim D_t}[h(x_i) \neq y_i] . \tag{3.16}$$

In other words, it seeks a base hypothesis h_t that minimizes ϵ_t, or at least one for which ϵ_t is somewhat smaller than $\frac{1}{2}$. Theorem 3.1 shows that this is sufficient to drive down AdaBoost's training error very quickly. Moreover, in later chapters we will see that the weighted training errors ϵ_t of the base classifiers are also directly related to AdaBoost's generalization error.

In what follows, we simplify notation by dropping subscripts so that $D = D_t$, $h = h_t$, and so on.

3.4.1 Using the Example Weights

The objective that the base learner seeks to minimize is nearly identical to the ordinary training error, except that training examples now have varying weights. So the first question we need to address is how these weights should be used. Here, there are two main approaches. The first is to use the given distribution D to generate an ordinary, unweighted training sample simply by randomly selecting a sequence of examples S' according to D. In other words,

$$S' = \langle (x_{i_1}, y_{i_1}), \ldots, (x_{i_{m'}}, y_{i_{m'}}) \rangle,$$

where each i_j is selected[1] independently at random according to D. This unweighted sample can then be fed to a base learning algorithm but one that need not be concerned with

---

1. To select a point i from a distribution D, given access to a standard (pseudo)random number generator, we first precompute in linear time the cumulative distribution $0 = C_0 \leq C_1 \leq \ldots \leq C_m = 1$ where

$$C_i = C_{i-1} + D(i) = \sum_{j=1}^{i} D(j).$$

weighted samples. Thus, this approach, called *boosting by resampling*, is often useful when the chosen base learner cannot easily be modified to handle the given weights directly.

If m', the size of S', is sufficiently large, then the unweighted training error with respect to S' will be a reasonable estimate of the weighted training error on S with respect to D—modulo the issues discussed at length in chapter 2 regarding the complexity of base classifiers and how that complexity relates to the tendency of the error on a sample to diverge from its true error when the sampled error is minimized. Typically, m' is chosen to be equal to m, though sometimes there are reasons to choose larger or smaller values. For instance, using a sample size m' that is significantly smaller than m can sometimes afford a computational speedup. And although boosting by resampling introduces an additional layer of indirection away from the goal of error minimization, this injection of randomness can sometimes be beneficial to the learning process by providing a smoothing effect that can counter the part of the error due to the base learner's variable behavior. A related method called "bagging," which we discuss in section 5.5, works on essentially this same principle.

Of course, in boosting by resampling, the base learner only minimizes an approximation of the weighted training error. An alternative approach is to modify the base learning algorithm to directly utilize the given example weights so that the weighted training error is minimized explicitly. We will see examples shortly. This approach, called *boosting by reweighting*, has the advantage of being direct and exact, and of avoiding all issues of imprecision in estimating the best base hypothesis.

3.4.2   Designing an Algorithm

In the design of the base learner itself, there are again, broadly speaking, two general approaches. The first is to select an existing, off-the-shelf learning algorithm. Boosting is designed for use with any learning algorithm, so there is no reason not to use boosting to improve the performance of an algorithm that may already be pretty good. Thus, for the base learner, we can use standard and well-studied algorithms such as decision trees (see section 1.3) or neural networks. Some of these may expect an unweighted sample, but this is not a problem if boosting by resampling is used. Even if boosting by reweighting is used, many of these algorithms can be modified to handle example weights. For instance, a standard decision tree algorithm may select a node for placement at the root of the tree that maximizes some measure of "purity," such as entropy or the Gini index. Such measures can usually be modified sensibly to take example weights into consideration (this is very natural for something like entropy which is defined for any distribution).

The other broad approach is to design a base learner that finds very simple base hypotheses, ones that, in the spirit of boosting, are expected to be only a bit better than random

---

Next, we select r uniformly at random from $[0, 1)$ and let i be the unique integer in $\{1, \ldots, m\}$ for which $r \in [C_{i-1}, C_i)$. This i can be found using binary search in $O(\log m)$ time. Moreover, it can be verified that such a random i is distributed exactly according to D.

guessing. A typical choice would be to use *decision stumps* for this purpose. These are single-level decision trees (hence the name), exactly like the ones used in section 1.2.3, where numerous examples are given. Finding the best decision stump for a given weighted training set—the one that minimizes equation (3.16)—can generally be computed very fast. We illustrate this here as a concrete example of a frequently used base learner.

As in the example in section 1.2.3, we assume that our instances are described by a given set of *features* or *attributes* $f_1, \ldots, f_n$. For instance, if each instance x is a person, then a feature $f_k(x)$ might encode the person x's height, or the person's gender, or the person's eye color, and so on. There may be a variety of types of features, such as *binary features* with values in $\{0, 1\}$; *discrete* (or *categorical*) *features* with values taken from an unordered, finite set; and *continuous features*, taking values in $\mathbb{R}$. A particular decision stump is associated with a single feature, but the exact form will depend on the type of the feature.

Given a dataset S as in equation (3.15), and given a distribution D over S, our goal now in designing a decision-stump base learner is to find the best decision stump with respect to S and D. We do this by efficiently searching, eventually considering all possible decision stumps. The "outer loop" of this search considers each of the features f_k in turn, finding the best decision stump associated with that feature, and finally selecting the best stump overall. Since this is straightforward, let us fix a particular feature f_k, and focus on the "inner loop," that is, the problem of finding the best stump associated with this one feature.

If f_k is binary, then the decision stump can vary only in the predictions made for each branch of the split. Thus, it will have the form

$$h(x) = \begin{cases} c_0 & \text{if } f_k(x) = 0 \\ c_1 & \text{if } f_k(x) = 1, \end{cases} \tag{3.17}$$

and we only need to choose the best values of c_0 and c_1 from $\{-1, +1\}$. This could be done by trying all four possibilities, but there is a more generalizable approach. For $j \in \{0, 1\}$ and $b \in \{-1, +1\}$, let

$$W_b^j \doteq \sum_{i: f_k(x_i) = j \wedge y_i = b} D(i) = \mathbf{Pr}_{i \sim D}[f_k(x_i) = j \wedge y_i = b] \tag{3.18}$$

be the weighted fraction of examples with label b and for which the feature f_k is equal to j. We also use the shorthand W_+^j and W_-^j for W_{+1}^j and W_{-1}^j, respectively. Then the weighted error of h as in equation (3.17) can be computed to be

$$W_{-c_0}^0 + W_{-c_1}^1. \tag{3.19}$$

This is because if $f_k(x) = 0$, then $h(x) = c_0$, so the weight of examples with labels different from $h(x)$ is the first term of equation (3.19), and similarly for the case $f_k(x) = 1$. Equation (3.19) is minimized over c_0 and c_1 if

$$c_j = \begin{cases} +1 & \text{if } W_-^j < W_+^j \\ -1 & \text{if } W_-^j > W_+^j \end{cases} \tag{3.20}$$

(and with c_j chosen arbitrarily if $W_-^j = W_+^j$). Plugging into equation (3.19) gives that the weighted error of h for this optimal setting is

$$\min\{W_-^0, W_+^0\} + \min\{W_-^1, W_+^1\}.$$

Now suppose f_k is discrete with values in some finite set, say $\{1, \ldots, J\}$. We might consider stumps making a J-way split, that is, of the form

$$h(x) = \begin{cases} c_1 & \text{if } f_k(x) = 1 \\ \vdots \\ c_J & \text{if } f_k(x) = J. \end{cases} \tag{3.21}$$

Directly generalizing the argument above, we let W_b^j be defined as in equation (3.18) for $j = 1, \ldots, J$. Note that all of these can be computed in a single pass through the data in $O(m)$ time. Then the optimal setting of c_j is still exactly as in equation (3.20), giving a stump whose weighted error is

$$\sum_{j=1}^{J} \min\{W_-^j, W_+^j\}. \tag{3.22}$$

Alternatively, we might wish to use simpler stumps making a binary split of the form

$$h(x) = \begin{cases} c_0 & \text{if } f_k(x) = r \\ c_1 & \text{else} \end{cases}$$

for some choice of c_0 and $c_1 \in \{-1, +1\}$, and $r \in \{1, \ldots, J\}$. Again, all $4J$ choices could be tried exhaustively, but a more efficient approach would be first to compute the W_b^j's as above in linear time, as well as

$$W_b \doteq \sum_{j=1}^{J} W_b^j.$$

Then, by arguments similar to those above, the best choices of c_0 and c_1 for a particular choice of r will have a weighted training error of

$$\min\{W_-^r, W_+^r\} + \min\{W_- - W_-^r, \; W_+ - W_+^r\}.$$

Thus, the best choice of r can be found quickly in $O(J)$ time to be the one minimizing this expression, and then the best choice of c_0 and c_1 can be determined using an expression analogous to equation (3.20).

The case where f_k is continuous is the most challenging. Here, we consider decision stumps of the form

$$h(x) = \begin{cases} c_0 & \text{if } f_k(x) \le v \\ c_1 & \text{if } f_k(x) > v \end{cases} \tag{3.23}$$

for some real-valued threshold v. For a fixed choice of v, we are essentially in the binary case from above. We can compute

$$W_b^0 \doteq \mathbf{Pr}_{i \sim D}[f_k(x_i) \le v \wedge y_i = b]$$

$$W_b^1 \doteq \mathbf{Pr}_{i \sim D}[f_k(x_i) > v \wedge y_i = b]$$

and then set c_0 and c_1 as before. However, it appears that in addition to the four possible settings of c_0 and c_1, we also need to consider an infinite number of settings of v. Nevertheless, similar to arguments used in section 2.2.3, we can take advantage of the fact that any finite set S of m examples will divide the space of possible thresholds $v \in \mathbb{R}$ into just $m + 1$ equivalence classes, so that the behavior of a stump of the form above on the sample S will be the same for any two choices of v selected from the same equivalence class. More concretely, suppose S has been sorted by f_k so that

$$f_k(x_1) \le f_k(x_2) \le \cdots \le f_k(x_m).$$

Then, in searching for the best stump of the form above, it suffices to consider just one threshold value v from each of the intervals $[f_k(x_i), f_k(x_{i+1}))$ for $i = 1, \ldots, m - 1$, as well as $[-\infty, f_k(x_1))$ and $[f_k(x_m), +\infty]$.

So there are essentially $4(m + 1)$ choices of c_0, c_1, and v to consider. Exhaustively computing the weighted training error of each would take $O(m^2)$ time. However, if the examples have been presorted by f_k, then the best decision stump can be found in only $O(m)$ time. This can be done by scanning through the examples, considering each threshold equivalence class in turn, and incrementally updating the W_b^j's as each example is passed. Pseudocode is shown as algorithm 3.1, for the special case in which no two examples have the same value of f_k. To see why this algorithm works, the main point to observe is that, following each iteration $i = 1, \ldots, m - 1$, the W_b^j's are set correctly for a decision stump defined by any $v \in [f_k(x_i), f_k(x_{i+1}))$, from which the correctness of the other computations follows directly. (If the f_k values are not all distinct, the algorithm can be modified so that, on rounds in which $f_k(x_i) = f_k(x_{i+1})$, only the W_b^j's are updated and all other computations are skipped.)

Note that with sufficient memory, for each feature, the examples need to be presorted only once (*not* on every round), requiring time $O(m \log m)$.

3.4.3 An Application to Face Detection

The methods outlined above are intended to be general-purpose. Sometimes, however, the base learning algorithm can be specially tailored to the application at hand, often to great

Algorithm 3.1
Finding a decision stump for a single continuous feature

Given: $(x_1, y_1), \ldots, (x_m, y_m)$
        real-valued feature f_k with $f_k(x_1) < \cdots < f_k(x_m)$
        distribution D over $\{1, \ldots, m\}$.
Goal: find stump for f_k with minimum weighted training error.
Initialize:

- $W_b^0 \leftarrow 0$, $W_b^1 \leftarrow \sum_{i:y_i=b} D(i)$ for $b \in \{-1, +1\}$.
- $\epsilon_{best} \leftarrow \min\{W_-^1, W_+^1\}$.
- Pick $\nu \in [-\infty, f_k(x_1))$, and compute c_0 and c_1 as in equation (3.20).

For $i = 1, \ldots, m$:

- $W_{y_i}^0 \leftarrow W_{y_i}^0 + D(i)$.

- $W_{y_i}^1 \leftarrow W_{y_i}^1 - D(i)$.

- $\epsilon \leftarrow \min\{W_-^0, W_+^0\} + \min\{W_-^1, W_+^1\}$.

- If $\epsilon < \epsilon_{best}$:

  - $\epsilon_{best} \leftarrow \epsilon$.

  - Pick $\nu \in \begin{cases} [f_k(x_i), f_k(x_{i+1})) & \text{if } i < m \\ [f_k(x_m), +\infty) & \text{if } i = m. \end{cases}$

  - Recompute c_0 and c_1 as in equation (3.20).

Output: h as in equation (3.23) for the current final values of c_0, c_1, and ν.

---

benefit. Indeed, the choice of base learning algorithm affords our greatest opportunity for incorporating prior expert knowledge about a specific problem into the boosting process. A beautiful example of this is given in the application of boosting to face detection. Visually detecting all instances of some object type, such as human faces, in photographs, movies, and other digital images is a fundamental problem in computer vision.

As a first step in applying boosting to this challenge, we need to transform what is really a search task (looking for faces) into a classification problem. To do so, we can regard our instances as small subimages of size, say, 24×24 pixels, each of which would be considered positive if and only if it captures a full frontal shot of a face at a standard scale. An example

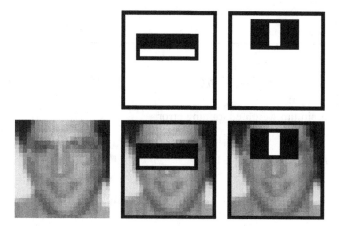

Figure 3.3
The features selected on the first two rounds of boosting, shown in isolation in the top row and as overlays on the sample face at left in the bottom row. (Copyright ©2001 IEEE. Reprinted, with permission, from [227].)

is shown on the left of figure 3.3. Clearly, an accurate classifier for such subimages can be used to detect all faces in an image simply by scanning the entire image and reporting the presence of a face anywhere that it registers a positive instance. Faces of varying sizes can be found by repeating this process at various scales. Needless to say, such an exhaustive process demands that a very fast classifier be used in the innermost loop.

The next major design decision is the choice of weak classifier and weak learning algorithm. The boosting paradigm allows us to choose weak classifiers that are very simple, even if they are individually rather inaccurate; potentially, such simple classifiers can have the additional advantage of being very fast to evaluate. At somewhat of an extreme, we can use weak classifiers which merely detect rectangular patterns of relative light and darkness in the image. Examples are shown in the top row of figure 3.3. The one on the left is sensitive to a dark region over a light region at the specified location of the image; the one on the right is similarly sensitive to dark regions surrounding a light region. In more precise terms, such a pattern defines a real-valued feature that is equal to the sum of the intensities of all the pixels in the black rectangle(s) minus the sum of the intensities of all the pixels in the white rectangle(s). Such a feature can be used to define a decision stump, as described in section 3.4.2, that makes its predictions based on whether the feature value for a particular image is above or below some threshold.

During training, we can consider features defined by all possible patterns of a small number of types, such as the four given in figure 3.4. Each one of these types defines a large number of patterns, each of which is identified with a feature. For instance, the one on the left defines all possible patterns consisting of a white rectangle directly above a black rectangle of equal size. In 24×24 pixel images, the four types of figure 3.4 define some 45,396 features.

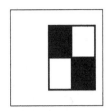

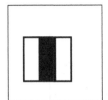

Figure 3.4
The four pattern types used to define features.

Figure 3.5
The faces detected by the final classifier obtained using boosting on some sample test images. (Copyright ©2001 IEEE. Reprinted, with permission, from [227].)

Having defined this large set of real-valued features, we can apply AdaBoost using the weak learning algorithm given in section 3.4.2 to find the best decision stump. Figure 3.3 in fact shows the two features found on the first two rounds of boosting. The first apparently exploits the tendency of the eyes to appear darker than the upper cheeks, while the second exploits a similar tendency for the eyes to appear darker than the bridge of the nose. Clearly, such weak detectors will individually do a very poor job of identifying faces.

However, when combined with boosting in this fashion, the performance of AdaBoost's final classifier is extremely good. For instance, after 200 rounds of boosting, on one test dataset, the final classifier was able to detect 95% of the faces while reporting false positives at a rate of only 1 in 14,084. Detection results of the complete system are shown on some sample test images in figure 3.5.

In addition to its high accuracy, this approach to face detection can be made extremely fast. Naively, the features we have described require time proportional to the size of the rectangles involved. However, given a bit of precomputation, it becomes possible to evaluate any feature in *constant* time. To see this, we can first define the *integral image* $I(x, y)$ to be the sum of the intensities of all pixels above and to the left of position (x, y). This can be computed for all pixels (x, y) in a single pass over the image, beginning in the

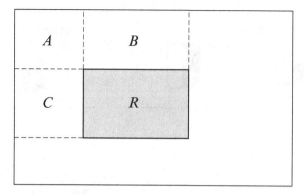

Figure 3.6
The sum of the pixels in any rectangle R can be computed in just four references to the integral image.

upper left corner. Once computed, the sum of all pixels of *any* rectangle can be computed in just four references to the integral image: For suppose we want the sum of pixels in the rectangle R in figure 3.6. This sum can be computed as

$$R = (A + B + C + R) - (A + C) - (A + B) + (A), \tag{3.24}$$

where, with slight abuse of notation, we use A, B, C, and R to stand both for the rectangles in the figure and for the sum of the pixels in each. Note that each of the four parenthesized terms in equation (3.24) can be looked up in the integral image by referencing, respectively, the bottom right, bottom left, top right, and top left corners of rectangle R. Thus, the sum of the pixels in any rectangle, and therefore also any feature, can be evaluated in a small and constant number of references to the integral image. This means that these features can be evaluated very quickly, dramatically speeding up both training and evaluation on test examples.

Evaluation can be made even faster by using a cascading technique in which relatively small and rough classifiers are trained which are good enough to quickly eliminate the vast majority of background images as non-faces. The entire system is so fast that it can be used, for instance, to find all faces in video in real time at 15 frames per second.

Summary

In summary, in this chapter we have proved a bound on the training error obtained by AdaBoost, and we have seen that this error drops exponentially fast as a function of the number of rounds of boosting, given the weak learning assumption. We have also proved a general sufficient condition for the weak learning assumption to hold, and have looked at how to choose or design a weak learning algorithm. Next, we turn to the central issue of generalization beyond the training data.

Bibliographic Notes

The bound on the training error given in theorem 3.1 is due to Freund and Schapire [95].

The connection between linear separability with positive margin and weak learnability given in section 3.2 was first spelled out explicitly by Rätsch and Warmuth [187] using the game-theoretic view of boosting that will be presented in chapter 6. See also more recent work by Shalev-Shwartz and Singer [211].

For a comparison with the technique used in section 3.3 to prove a Chernoff bound, see the proof in Hoeffding's paper [123].

Prior to the advent of AdaBoost, Holte [125] studied "1-rules," which are quite similar to decision stumps, and found that such very simple rules can by themselves provide surprisingly high accuracy. The algorithm described in section 3.4.2 for finding the best decision stump is adapted from standard techniques for constructing decision trees [39, 184].

The face detection system of section 3.4.3 is due to Viola and Jones [227, 228]. Figures 3.4 and 3.6 were adapted from these sources, and figures 3.3 and 3.5 are reprinted directly from [227].

Some of the exercises in this chapter are based on material from [88, 95, 108, 194, 199].

Exercises

3.1 Show that the AdaBoost update in algorithm 1.1 for computing D_{t+1} from D_t can be rewritten in the following equivalent form, for $i = 1, \ldots, m$:

$$D_{t+1}(i) = \frac{D_t(i)}{1 + 2 y_i h_t(x_i) \gamma_t}.$$

3.2 Consider the following "mini" boosting algorithm which runs for exactly three rounds:

- Given training data as in AdaBoost (algorithm 1.1), let D_1, h_1, ϵ_1, and D_2, h_2, ϵ_2 be computed exactly as in AdaBoost on the first two rounds.

- Compute, for $i = 1, \ldots, m$:

$$D_3(i) = \begin{cases} D_1(i)/\mathcal{Z} & \text{if } h_1(x_i) \neq h_2(x_i) \\ 0 & \text{else} \end{cases}$$

  where $\mathcal{Z}$ is a normalization factor (chosen so that D_3 will be a distribution).

- Get weak hypothesis h_3.

- Output the final hypothesis:

  $$H(x) = \text{sign}\left(h_1(x) + h_2(x) + h_3(x)\right).$$

We will see that this three-round procedure can effect a small but significant boost in accuracy.

Let $\gamma_t \doteq \frac{1}{2} - \epsilon_t$ be the edge on round t, and assume $0 < \gamma_t < \frac{1}{2}$ for $t = 1, 2, 3$. Let

$$b \doteq \mathbf{Pr}_{i \sim D_2}[h_1(x_i) \neq y_i \wedge h_2(x_i) \neq y_i],$$

that is, b is the probability with respect to D_2 that both h_1 and h_2 are incorrect.

a. In terms of $\gamma_1, \gamma_2, \gamma_3$, and b, write *exact* expressions for each of the following:

  i. $\mathbf{Pr}_{i \sim D_1}[h_1(x_i) \neq y_i \wedge h_2(x_i) \neq y_i]$.

  ii. $\mathbf{Pr}_{i \sim D_1}[h_1(x_i) \neq y_i \wedge h_2(x_i) = y_i]$.

  iii. $\mathbf{Pr}_{i \sim D_1}[h_1(x_i) = y_i \wedge h_2(x_i) \neq y_i]$.

  iv. $\mathbf{Pr}_{i \sim D_1}[h_1(x_i) \neq h_2(x_i) \wedge h_3(x_i) \neq y_i]$.

  v. $\mathbf{Pr}_{i \sim D_1}[H(x_i) \neq y_i]$.

  [*Hint:* Use exercises 1.1 and 3.1.]

b. Suppose $\gamma = \min\{\gamma_1, \gamma_2, \gamma_3\}$. Show that the training error of the final classifier H is at most

$$\frac{1}{2} - \frac{3}{2}\gamma + 2\gamma^3,$$

and show that this quantity is strictly less than $\frac{1}{2} - \gamma$, the (worst) error of the weak hypotheses. Thus, the accuracy receives a small boost (which, we remark, can be amplified by applying this technique recursively).

3.3 Consider a variant of AdaBoost in which the combined classifier H is replaced by a classifier $\tilde{H}$ whose predictions are *randomized*; specifically, suppose, for any x, that $\tilde{H}$ predicts $+1$ with probability

$$\mathbf{Pr}_{\tilde{H}}\left[\tilde{H}(x) = +1\right] = \frac{e^{F(x)}}{e^{F(x)} + e^{-F(x)}},$$

and otherwise predicts -1, where F is as given in equation (3.1). Prove a bound on the training error of $\tilde{H}$ that is half the bound for H in theorem 3.1; that is, show that

$$\mathbf{Pr}_{i \sim D_1, \tilde{H}}\left[\tilde{H}(x_i) \neq y_i\right] \leq \frac{1}{2}\prod_{t=1}^{T}\sqrt{1 - 4\gamma_t^2}$$

(where probability is computed with respect to both the choice of i according to D_1 and the randomization of $\tilde{H}$'s predictions).

3.4 Prove equation (3.14).

3.5 Suppose the weak learning condition is guaranteed to hold so that $\epsilon_t \leq \frac{1}{2} - \gamma$ for some $\gamma > 0$ which is *known* before boosting begins. Describe a modified version of AdaBoost whose final classifier is a simple (unweighted) majority vote, and show that its training error is at most $(1 - 4\gamma^2)^{T/2}$.

3.6 Let $\mathcal{X}_n = \{0, 1\}^n$, and let $\mathcal{G}_n$ be a class of Boolean functions $g : \mathcal{X}_n \to \{-1, +1\}$. Let $\mathcal{M}_{n,k}$ be the class of all Boolean functions that can be written as a simple majority vote of k (not necessarily distinct) functions in $\mathcal{G}_n$, where k is odd:

$$\mathcal{M}_{n,k} \doteq \left\{ f : x \mapsto \text{sign}\left(\sum_{j=1}^{k} g_j(x) \right) \ \middle| \ g_1, \ldots, g_k \in \mathcal{G}_n \right\}.$$

In this problem we will see, roughly speaking, that if f can be written as a majority vote of polynomially many functions in $\mathcal{G}_n$, then under any distribution, f can be approximated by some function in $\mathcal{G}_n$. But if f cannot be so written as a majority vote, then there exists some "hard" distribution under which f cannot be approximated by *any* function in $\mathcal{G}_n$.

a. Show that if $f \in \mathcal{M}_{n,k}$, then for all distributions D on $\mathcal{X}_n$, there exists a function $g \in \mathcal{G}_n$ for which

$$\mathbf{Pr}_{x \sim D}[f(x) \neq g(x)] \leq \frac{1}{2} - \frac{1}{2k}.$$

b. Show that if $f \notin \mathcal{M}_{n,k}$ then there exists a distribution D on $\mathcal{X}_n$ such that

$$\mathbf{Pr}_{x \sim D}[f(x) \neq g(x)] > \frac{1}{2} - \sqrt{\frac{n \ln 2}{2k}}$$

for every $g \in \mathcal{G}_n$. [*Hint:* Use boosting.]

4 Direct Bounds on the Generalization Error

In chapter 3, we proved a bound on the training error of AdaBoost. However, as has already been pointed out, what we really care about in learning is how well we can generalize to data not seen during training. Indeed, an algorithm that drives down the training error does not necessarily qualify as a boosting algorithm. Rather, as discussed in section 2.3, a boosting algorithm is one that can drive the *generalization error* arbitrarily close to zero; in other words, it is a learning algorithm that makes nearly perfect predictions on data *not* seen during training, provided the algorithm is supplied with a reasonable number of training examples and access to a weak learning algorithm that can consistently find weak hypotheses that are slightly better than random.

In fact, there are numerous ways of analyzing AdaBoost's generalization error, several of which will be explored in this book. In this chapter, we present the first of these methods, focusing on the direct application of the general techniques outlined in chapter 2, and basing our analyses on the structural form of the final classifier as a combination of base hypotheses. This will be enough to prove that AdaBoost is indeed a boosting algorithm. However, we will also see that the bound we derive on the generalization error predicts that AdaBoost will overfit, a prediction that often turns out to be false in actual experiments. This deficiency in the analysis will be addressed in chapter 5, where a margins-based analysis is presented.

4.1 Using VC Theory to Bound the Generalization Error

We begin with an analysis based directly on the form of the hypotheses output by AdaBoost.

4.1.1 Basic Assumptions

In proving a bound on the training error in chapter 3, we did not need to make any assumptions about the data. The (x_i, y_i) pairs were entirely arbitrary, as were the weak hypotheses h_t. Theorem 3.1 held regardless, without any assumptions. In turning now to the study of generalization error, we can no longer afford this luxury, and must accept additional assumptions. This is because, as discussed in chapter 2, if there is no relationship between the data observed during training and the data encountered during testing, then we cannot possibly hope to do well in the test phase. Therefore, as in chapter 2, we assume that all examples, during both training and testing, are generated at random according to the same (unknown) distribution $\mathcal{D}$ over $\mathcal{X} \times \{-1, +1\}$. As before, our goal is to find a classifier h with low generalization error

$$\text{err}(h) \doteq \mathbf{Pr}_{(x,y)\sim\mathcal{D}}[h(x) \neq y] \,,$$

that is, low probability of misclassifying a new example (x, y) chosen at random from the same distribution $\mathcal{D}$ that generated each of the training examples $(x_1, y_1), \ldots, (x_m, y_m)$. We assume this probabilistic framework throughout all of our analyses of AdaBoost's generalization error.

As discussed in chapters 1 and 2, learning is all about fitting the data well, but not overfitting it. As in science, we want to "explain" our observations (the data) using the "simplest" explanation (classifier) possible. A boosting algorithm has no direct control over the base classifiers h_t that are selected on each round. If these base classifiers are already of an extremely complex form that overfits the data, then the boosting algorithm is immediately doomed to suffer overfitting as well. Therefore, in order to derive a meaningful bound on the generalization error, we also must assume something about the complexity or expressiveness of the base classifiers. Said differently, our generalization error bounds for AdaBoost will inevitably depend on some measure of the complexity of the base classifiers.

To be more precise, we assume that all base classifiers are selected from some space of classifiers $\mathcal{H}$. For instance, this might be the space of all decision stumps, or the space of all decision trees (perhaps of bounded size). As in section 2.2.2, when $\mathcal{H}$ is finite in cardinality, we can measure its complexity by $\lg |\mathcal{H}|$, which can be interpreted as the number of bits needed to specify one of its members. When $\mathcal{H}$ is infinite, we instead use the VC-dimension of $\mathcal{H}$, a combinatorial measure which, as seen in section 2.2.3, is appropriate for measuring the difficulty of learning a class of functions. Thus, we expect our bounds to depend on one of these two complexity measures.

Having proved in section 3.1 a bound on the training error, in this chapter we derive bounds on the generalization error by proving a bound on the magnitude of the difference between the generalization error and the training error. This is essentially the mode of analysis presented in chapter 2. There, we saw that for a particular classifier h, the training error $\widehat{\text{err}}(h)$ can be regarded as an empirical estimate of the generalization error, an estimate that gets better and better with more data. However, in learning, we generally select the classifier h based on the training data, and usually from among those classifiers with the lowest training error. Such a process for selecting h typically leads to a significant gap between the training and generalization errors. Moreover, because we do not know which classifier h will be chosen prior to the choice of training examples, we must bound the difference $\text{err}(h) - \widehat{\text{err}}(h)$ for *all* h which might potentially be generated by the learning algorithm. Here, we apply to boosting the powerful tools developed in section 2.2 for proving such general results.

4.1.2 The Form and Complexity of AdaBoost's Classifiers

As above, $\mathcal{H}$ is the base classifier space from which all of the h_t's are selected. Let $\mathcal{C}_T$ be the space of *combined* classifiers that might potentially be generated by AdaBoost if run for T rounds. Such a combined classifier H computes a weighted majority vote of T base classifiers so that

$$H(x) = \text{sign}\left(\sum_{t=1}^{T} \alpha_t h_t(x)\right) \tag{4.1}$$

for some real numbers $\alpha_1, \ldots, \alpha_T$, and some base classifiers $h_1, \ldots, h_T$ in $\mathcal{H}$. Expressed differently, we can write H in the form

$$H(x) = \sigma(h_1(x), \ldots, h_T(x))$$

where $\sigma : \mathbb{R}^T \to \{-1, 0, +1\}$ is some linear threshold function of the form

$$\sigma(\mathbf{x}) = \text{sign}(\mathbf{w} \cdot \mathbf{x}) \tag{4.2}$$

for some $\mathbf{w} \in \mathbb{R}^T$. Let Σ_T be the space of all such linear threshold functions. Then $\mathcal{C}_T$ is simply the space of linear threshold functions defined over T hypotheses from $\mathcal{H}$. That is,

$$\mathcal{C}_T = \{x \mapsto \sigma(h_1(x), \ldots, h_T(x)) : \sigma \in \Sigma_T; h_1, \ldots, h_T \in \mathcal{H}\}.$$

Our goal, then, is to show that the training error $\widehat{\text{err}}(h)$ is a good estimate of $\text{err}(h)$ for all $h \in \mathcal{C}_T$. We saw in section 2.2 that this can be proved by counting the number of functions in $\mathcal{C}_T$. Unfortunately, since Σ_T is infinite (each linear threshold function being defined by a vector $\mathbf{w} \in \mathbb{R}^T$), $\mathcal{C}_T$ is as well. However, we also saw that it suffices to count the number of possible behaviors or dichotomies that can be realized by functions in $\mathcal{C}_T$ on a finite set of points. We make this computation in the lemmas below.

Technically, to apply the formalism from section 2.2, the combined classifier must output predictions in $\{-1, +1\}$, not $\{-1, 0, +1\}$. Therefore, in this chapter only, we redefine the sign function in equations (4.1) and (4.2) to have range $\{-1, +1\}$ simply by redefining $\text{sign}(0)$ to be -1, rather than 0 as it is defined in the rest of the book. There are other ways of handling this technical annoyance which avoid this bit of inelegance, but this is perhaps the most straightforward (see exercise 4.1).

In section 2.2.3, we noted that Σ_n, the space of linear threshold functions over $\mathbb{R}^n$, has VC-dimension n, a property that we exploit below. Here we give a proof.

Lemma 4.1 The space Σ_n of linear threshold functions over $\mathbb{R}^n$ has VC-dimension n.

Proof   Let $\mathbf{e}_i \in \mathbb{R}^n$ be a basis vector with a 1 in dimension i and 0 in all other dimensions. Then $\mathbf{e}_1, \ldots, \mathbf{e}_n$ is shattered by Σ_n. For if $y_1, \ldots, y_n$ is any set of labels in $\{-1, +1\}$, then $\mathbf{w} = \langle y_1, \ldots, y_n \rangle$ realizes the corresponding dichotomy since

$$\text{sign}(\mathbf{w} \cdot \mathbf{e}_i) = y_i.$$

Thus, the VC-dimension of Σ_n is at least n.

By way of reaching a contradiction, suppose now that there exists a set of $n + 1$ points $\mathbf{x}_1, \ldots, \mathbf{x}_{n+1} \in \mathbb{R}^n$ which are shattered by Σ_n. Then, being $n + 1$ points in n-dimensional space, there must exist real numbers $\beta_1, \ldots, \beta_{n+1}$, not all zero, such that

$$\sum_{i=1}^{n+1} \beta_i \mathbf{x}_i = \mathbf{0}.$$

Assume without loss of generality that $\beta_{n+1} > 0$. Since these points are shattered by Σ_n, there exists $\mathbf{w} \in \mathbb{R}^n$ such that

$$\text{sign}(\mathbf{w} \cdot \mathbf{x}_{n+1}) = +1, \tag{4.3}$$

and such that

$$\text{sign}(\mathbf{w} \cdot \mathbf{x}_i) = \begin{cases} +1 & \text{if } \beta_i > 0 \\ -1 & \text{if } \beta_i \leq 0 \end{cases} \tag{4.4}$$

for $i = 1, \ldots, n$. Then equation (4.3) says that $\mathbf{w} \cdot \mathbf{x}_{n+1} > 0$, while equation (4.4) implies that $\beta_i(\mathbf{w} \cdot \mathbf{x}_i) \geq 0$ for $i = 1, \ldots, n$. This gives the following contradiction:

$$0 = \mathbf{w} \cdot \mathbf{0}$$
$$= \mathbf{w} \cdot \sum_{i=1}^{n+1} \beta_i \mathbf{x}_i$$
$$= \sum_{i=1}^{n} \beta_i(\mathbf{w} \cdot \mathbf{x}_i) + \beta_{n+1}(\mathbf{w} \cdot \mathbf{x}_{n+1})$$
$$> 0.$$

Thus, the VC-dimension of Σ_n is at most n.   ∎

4.1.3   Finite Base Hypothesis Spaces

We are now ready to count the number of dichotomies induced by classifiers in $\mathcal{C}_T$ on any sample S. For simplicity, we focus mainly on the case where the base hypothesis space $\mathcal{H}$ is finite.

Lemma 4.2 Assume $\mathcal{H}$ is finite. Let $m \geq T \geq 1$. For any set S of m points, the number of dichotomies realizable by $\mathcal{C}_T$ is bounded as follows:

$$\left|\Pi_{\mathcal{C}_T}(S)\right| \leq \Pi_{\mathcal{C}_T}(m) \leq \left(\frac{em}{T}\right)^T |\mathcal{H}|^T.$$

Proof Let $S = \langle x_1, \ldots, x_m \rangle$. Consider a specific *fixed* sequence of base hypotheses $h_1, \ldots, h_T \in \mathcal{H}$. With respect to these, we create a modified sample $S' \doteq \langle \mathbf{x}'_1, \ldots, \mathbf{x}'_m \rangle$ where we define

$$\mathbf{x}'_i \doteq \langle h_1(x_i), \ldots, h_T(x_i) \rangle$$

to be the vector $\mathbb{R}^T$ obtained by applying $h_1, \ldots, h_T$ to x_i.

Since Σ_T has VC-dimension equal to T by lemma 4.1, we have by Sauer's lemma (lemma 2.4) and equation (2.12) applied to S' that

$$\left|\Pi_{\Sigma_T}(S')\right| \leq \left(\frac{em}{T}\right)^T. \tag{4.5}$$

That is, for *fixed* $h_1, \ldots, h_T$, the number of dichotomies defined by functions of the form

$$\sigma(h_1(x), \ldots, h_T(x))$$

for $\sigma \in \Sigma_T$ is bounded as in equation (4.5). Since the number of choices for $h_1, \ldots, h_T$ is equal to $|\mathcal{H}|^T$, and since for each one of these, the number of dichotomies is as in equation (4.5), we thus obtain the bound stated in the lemma. ∎

We can now directly apply theorems 2.3 and 2.7 to obtain the following theorem, which provides general bounds on the generalization error of AdaBoost or, for that matter, of any combined classifier H formed by taking a weighted majority vote of base classifiers. In line with the results and intuitions of chapter 2, the bound is in terms of the training error $\widehat{\mathrm{err}}(H)$, the sample size m, and two terms which effectively stand in for the complexity of H, namely, the number of rounds T, and $\lg |\mathcal{H}|$, a measure of the complexity of the base classifiers. These are intuitive measures of H's complexity since they roughly correspond to the overall size of H, which consists of T base classifiers, each of size (in bits) $\lg |\mathcal{H}|$.

Theorem 4.3 Suppose AdaBoost is run for T rounds on $m \geq T$ random examples, using base classifiers from a finite space $\mathcal{H}$. Then, with probability at least $1 - \delta$ (over the choice of the random sample), the combined classifier H satisfies

$$\mathrm{err}(H) \leq \widehat{\mathrm{err}}(H) + \sqrt{\frac{32[T \ln(em|\mathcal{H}|/T) + \ln(8/\delta)]}{m}}.$$

Furthermore, with probability at least $1 - \delta$, if H is consistent with the training set (so that $\widehat{\mathrm{err}}(H) = 0$), then

$$\mathrm{err}(H) \leq \frac{2T \lg(2em|\mathcal{H}|/T) + 2\lg(2/\delta)}{m}.$$

Proof This is simply a matter of plugging the bound from lemma 4.2 into theorems 2.3 and 2.7. ∎

It is now possible to prove that the empirical weak learning assumption is enough to guarantee that AdaBoost will achieve arbitrarily low generalization error, given sufficient data. This is almost but not quite equivalent to saying that AdaBoost is a boosting algorithm in the technical sense given in section 2.3, an issue we discuss in section 4.3. Nevertheless, corollary 4.4 provides practical conditions under which AdaBoost is guaranteed to give nearly perfect generalization.

Corollary 4.4 Assume, in addition to the assumptions of theorem 4.3, that each base classifier has weighted error $\epsilon_t \leq \frac{1}{2} - \gamma$ for some $\gamma > 0$. Let the number of rounds T be equal to the smallest integer exceeding $(\ln m)/(2\gamma^2)$. Then, with probability at least $1 - \delta$, the generalization error of the combined classifier H will be at most

$$O\left(\frac{1}{m}\left[\frac{(\ln m)(\ln m + \ln |\mathcal{H}|)}{\gamma^2} + \ln\left(\frac{1}{\delta}\right)\right]\right).$$

Proof By theorem 3.1, the training error of the combined classifier is at most $e^{-2\gamma^2 T} < 1/m$. Since there are m examples, this means that the training error must actually be zero. Applying the second part of theorem 4.3 gives the result. ∎

Note that, in terms of the sample size m, this bound converges to zero at the rate $O((\ln m)^2/m)$, and therefore can be made smaller than ϵ, for any $\epsilon > 0$, for a setting of m that is polynomial in the relevant parameters: $1/\gamma$, $1/\epsilon$, $1/\delta$, and $\ln |\mathcal{H}|$.

Corollary 4.4 gives us a bound on the generalization error when AdaBoost is stopped just when the theoretical bound on the training error reaches zero. What happens on other rounds? Combining theorems 3.1 and 4.3, we get a bound on the generalization error of the form

$$e^{-2\gamma^2 T} + O\left(\sqrt{\frac{T \ln(m|\mathcal{H}|/T) + \ln(1/\delta)}{m}}\right). \tag{4.6}$$

This function is plotted in figure 4.1. When T is small, the first term dominates and we see an exponential drop in the bound. However, as T becomes large, the second term dominates, leading to a substantial increase in the bound. In other words, the bound predicts classic overfitting behavior. This would seem to make sense since, as T grows, the number of base classifiers comprising the combined classifier steadily increases, suggesting an increase in the size and complexity of the combined classifier. Switching to the second bound of theorem 4.3 once H is consistent does not help much since this bound also increases without limit as a function of T, suggesting that it is best to stop running AdaBoost the moment the training error reaches zero (if not sooner). Indeed, such overfitting behavior is sometimes observed with AdaBoost, as was seen in section 1.2.3. However, we also saw in section 1.3

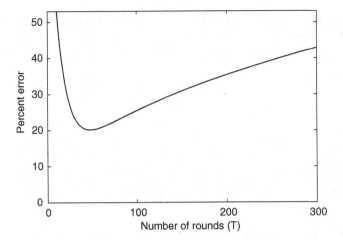

Figure 4.1
A plot of the bound on the generalization error given in equation (4.6) as a function of the number of rounds T, using the constants from theorem 4.3 with $\gamma = 0.2$, $m = 10^6$, $\ln |\mathcal{H}| = 10$, and $\delta = 0.05$.

that AdaBoost is often resistant to overfitting, and that there can be significant benefit in running AdaBoost long after consistency on the training set is reached. These phenomena cannot be explained by the analysis given above. We take up an alternative explanation of AdaBoost's behavior in chapter 5.

4.1.4   Infinite Base Classifier Spaces

Theorem 4.3 was proved for the case that the space of base classifiers $\mathcal{H}$ is finite. If $\mathcal{H}$ is infinite, a similar argument can be made using its VC-dimension d. Essentially, this is just a matter of adjusting our calculation of $\Pi_{\mathcal{C}_T}(m)$ in lemma 4.2.

Lemma 4.5   Assume $\mathcal{H}$ has finite VC-dimension $d \geq 1$. Let $m \geq \max\{d, T\}$. For any set S of m points, the number of dichotomies realizable by $\mathcal{C}_T$ is bounded as follows:

$$\left|\Pi_{\mathcal{C}_T}(S)\right| \leq \Pi_{\mathcal{C}_T}(m) \leq \left(\frac{em}{T}\right)^T \left(\frac{em}{d}\right)^{dT}.$$

Proof   Let $S = \langle x_1, \ldots, x_m \rangle$. We know that $\mathcal{H}$ can realize only a finite set of dichotomies on S. Let $\mathcal{H}'$ be a subset of $\mathcal{H}$ containing exactly one "representative" for each such dichotomy. In other words, for every $h \in \mathcal{H}$ there exists exactly one $h' \in \mathcal{H}'$ such that $h(x_i) = h'(x_i)$ for every example x_i appearing in S. By definition and Sauer's lemma (lemma 2.4), together with equation (2.12),

$$|\mathcal{H}'| = |\Pi_{\mathcal{H}}(S)| \leq \left(\frac{em}{d}\right)^d.$$

Since every function in $\mathcal{H}$, with regard to its behavior on S, is represented in $\mathcal{H}'$, choosing a set of functions $h_1, \ldots, h_T \in \mathcal{H}$ as in the proof of lemma 4.2 is equivalent to choosing functions from $\mathcal{H}'$. Thus, the number of such choices is $|\mathcal{H}'|^T$. Therefore, by the argument used to prove lemma 4.2,

$$
\begin{aligned}
\left|\Pi_{\mathcal{C}_T}(S)\right| &\leq \left(\frac{em}{T}\right)^T |\mathcal{H}'|^T \\
&\leq \left(\frac{em}{T}\right)^T \left(\frac{em}{d}\right)^{dT}.
\end{aligned}
$$
∎

The modification of theorem 4.3 and corollary 4.4 using lemma 4.5 is straightforward. Essentially, we end up with bounds in which $\ln |\mathcal{H}|$ is replaced by d, plus some additional log factors.

Theorem 4.6 Suppose AdaBoost is run for T rounds on m random examples, using base classifiers from a space $\mathcal{H}$ of finite VC-dimension $d \geq 1$. Assume $m \geq \max\{d, T\}$. Then with probability at least $1 - \delta$ (over the choice of the random sample), the combined classifier H satisfies

$$
\text{err}(H) \leq \widehat{\text{err}}(H) + \sqrt{\frac{32[T(\ln(em/T) + d\ln(em/d)) + \ln(8/\delta)]}{m}}.
$$

Furthermore, with probability at least $1 - \delta$, if H is consistent with the training set (so that $\widehat{\text{err}}(H) = 0$), then

$$
\text{err}(H) \leq \frac{2T(\lg(2em/T) + d\lg(2em/d)) + 2\lg(2/\delta)}{m}.
$$

Corollary 4.7 Assume, in addition to the assumptions of theorem 4.6, that each base classifier has weighted error $\epsilon_t \leq \frac{1}{2} - \gamma$ for some $\gamma > 0$. Let the number of rounds T be equal to the smallest integer exceeding $(\ln m)/(2\gamma^2)$. Then, with probability at least $1 - \delta$, the generalization error of the combined classifier H will be at most

$$
O\left(\frac{1}{m}\left[\frac{\ln m}{\gamma^2}\left(\ln m + d\ln\left(\frac{m}{d}\right)\right) + \ln\left(\frac{1}{\delta}\right)\right]\right).
$$

Thus, summarizing, theorems 4.3 and 4.6 show that, ignoring log factors,

$$
\text{err}(H) \leq \widehat{\text{err}}(H) + \tilde{O}\left(\sqrt{\frac{T \cdot C_{\mathcal{H}}}{m}}\right)
$$

where $C_{\mathcal{H}}$ is some measure of the complexity of the base hypothesis space $\mathcal{H}$. Likewise, if H is consistent, the bounds state that

$$\mathrm{err}(H) \le \tilde{O}\left(\frac{T \cdot C_{\mathcal{H}}}{m}\right).$$

As in the generalization bounds of section 2.2, these combine fit to data, complexity, and training set size, where now we measure the overall complexity of the combination of T base hypotheses by $T \cdot C_{\mathcal{H}}$.

Corollaries 4.4 and 4.7 show that when the complexity $C_{\mathcal{H}}$ is finite and fixed, the generalization error rapidly approaches zero, given the empirical weak learning assumption.

4.2 Compression-Based Bounds

So far, we have seen how AdaBoost can be analyzed in terms of the complexity of the base hypotheses. Thus, we have focused on the hypotheses *output* by the base learning algorithm. In this section, we will explore the opposing idea of instead analyzing AdaBoost based on the *input* to the base learning algorithm, in particular, the number of examples used by the base learner. This curious mode of analysis turns out to be very natural for boosting. In addition to providing generalization bounds, this approach will allow us to prove the general equivalence of strong and weak learnability by showing that AdaBoost, when appropriately configured, is a true boosting algorithm. Moreover, in studying AdaBoost from this perspective, we will highlight the remarkable property that in boosting, only a tiny fraction of the training set is ever used by the weak learning algorithm—the vast majority of the examples are never even seen by the weak learner. Indeed, it is exactly this property that forms the basis for this analysis.

4.2.1 The Idea

We assume throughout this section that boosting by resampling is employed. In other words, as described in section 3.4.1, we assume on each round t that the weak learner is trained on an *unweighted* sample selected at random by resampling with replacement from the entire training set according to the current distribution D_t. (Thus, these results are not directly applicable when boosting by reweighting is used instead.) We further assume that the unweighted sample generated on each round consists of a fixed size $m' = m_0$, not dependent (or at least not heavily dependent) on the overall sample size m. This is not unreasonable since the weak learner is aiming for a fixed accuracy $\frac{1}{2} - \gamma$, and therefore should require only a fixed sample size.

We also assume explicitly that the weak learning algorithm does not employ randomization, so that it can be regarded as a fixed, deterministic mapping from a sequence of m_0 unweighted examples to a hypothesis h. Under this assumption, any weak hypothesis produced by the weak learner can be represented rather trivially by the very sequence of m_0 examples on which it was trained.

Moreover, if we were to suppose momentarily that AdaBoost has been modified to output a combined classifier that is a simple (unweighted) majority vote, then this combined classifier can similarly be represented by the Tm_0 examples on which its T weak hypotheses were trained. In other words, under this scheme a sequence of Tm_0 examples represents the combined classifier which is a majority vote of weak hypotheses that can be computed simply by breaking the sequence into T blocks of m_0 examples, each of which is then converted into a weak hypothesis by running the weak learning algorithm on it.

Thus AdaBoost, under the assumptions above, is in fact a compression scheme of size $\kappa = Tm_0$ as described in section 2.2.6. In other words, because the combined classifier can be represented by Tm_0 of the training examples, and because m_0 is fixed, and consistency with the training set can be achieved for $T \ll m$, we can immediately apply theorem 2.8 to obtain a bound on the generalization error. Such an analysis is based solely on these properties, without any consideration of the form of the base hypotheses used.

But how can we apply this idea to AdaBoost, which in fact outputs a *weighted* majority vote? We can use the same idea above to represent the weak hypotheses by a sequence of examples, but how can we represent the real-valued weights $\alpha_1, \ldots, \alpha_T$? To answer this, we provide a general *hybrid* approach that combines the compression-based analysis of section 2.2.6 with the VC theory presented in section 2.2.3.

4.2.2 Hybrid Compression Schemes

In a standard compression scheme, as described in section 2.2.6, the learning algorithm outputs a hypothesis h that can itself be represented by a sequence of training examples. In a *hybrid compression scheme* of size κ, the hypothesis is instead selected from a *class* of hypotheses $\mathcal{F}$ where the *class* (rather than the hypothesis itself) can be represented by a sequence of κ training examples. Thus, a hybrid compression scheme is defined by a size κ and a mapping $\mathcal{K}$ from κ-tuples of labeled examples to *sets* of hypotheses. Given a training set $(x_1, y_1), \ldots, (x_m, y_m)$, the associated learning algorithm first chooses indices $i_1, \ldots, i_\kappa \in \{1, \ldots, m\}$, thus specifying a class

$$\mathcal{F} = \mathcal{K}((x_{i_1}, y_{i_1}), \ldots, (x_{i_\kappa}, y_{i_\kappa})). \tag{4.7}$$

The algorithm then chooses and outputs one hypothesis $h \in \mathcal{F}$ from this class.

Note that a standard compression scheme is simply a special case in which $\mathcal{F}$ is always a singleton.

AdaBoost is an example of a hybrid compression scheme for the setting above. We have already seen that the T weak hypotheses $h_1, \ldots, h_T$ can be represented by a sequence of $\kappa = Tm_0$ training examples. Then the resulting class $\mathcal{F}$ from which the final hypothesis H is selected consists of all linear threshold functions (that is, weighted majority vote classifiers) over the selected, fixed set of weak hypotheses $h_1, \ldots, h_T$:

$$\mathcal{F} = \left\{ H : x \mapsto \mathrm{sign}\left(\sum_{t=1}^{T} \alpha_t h_t(x) \right) \;\middle|\; \alpha_1, \ldots, \alpha_T \in \mathbb{R} \right\}. \tag{4.8}$$

By combining theorem 2.7 with theorem 2.8, we obtain a general result for hybrid compression schemes that depends both on the size κ and on the complexity of the class $\mathcal{F}$ selected by the scheme. For simplicity, we focus only on the consistent case, although the same technique can certainly be generalized.

Theorem 4.8 Suppose a learning algorithm based on a hybrid compression scheme of size κ with an associated function $\mathcal{K}$ as in equation (4.7) is provided with a random training set S of size m. Suppose further that for every κ-tuple, the resulting class $\mathcal{F}$ has VC-dimension at most $d \geq 1$. Assume $m \geq d + \kappa$. Then, with probability at least $1 - \delta$, any hypothesis h produced by this algorithm that is consistent with S must satisfy

$$\mathrm{err}(h) \leq \frac{2d \lg(2e(m - \kappa)/d) + 2\kappa \lg m + 2\lg(2/\delta)}{m - \kappa}. \tag{4.9}$$

Proof Let ε be equal to the quantity on the right-hand side of equation (4.9).

First, let us fix the indices $i_1, \ldots, i_\kappa$, and let $I = \{i_1, \ldots, i_\kappa\}$. Once the examples $(x_{i_1}, y_{i_1}), \ldots, (x_{i_\kappa}, y_{i_\kappa})$ with indices in this set have been selected, this also fixes the class $\mathcal{F}$ as in equation (4.7), Moreover, because the training examples are assumed to be independent, the training points not in I, that is, $S' = \langle (x_i, y_i) \rangle_{i \notin I}$, are also independent of the class $\mathcal{F}$. Thus, we can apply theorem 2.7, specifically equation (2.19), where we regard $\mathcal{F}$ as the hypothesis space and S' as a training set of size $m - |I| \geq m - \kappa$, and where we replace δ by δ/m^κ. Then, since $\mathcal{F}$ has VC-dimension at most d, with probability at least $1 - \delta/m^\kappa$, this result implies that $\mathrm{err}(h) \leq \varepsilon$ for every $h \in \mathcal{F}$ that is consistent with S', and therefore also for every $h \in \mathcal{F}$ that is consistent with the entire sample S. This holds true for any particular selection of examples $(x_{i_1}, y_{i_1}), \ldots, (x_{i_\kappa}, y_{i_\kappa})$, which means that it also holds true if these examples are selected at random.

Thus we have argued that for any fixed choice of indices $i_1, \ldots, i_\kappa$, with probability at least $1 - \delta/m^\kappa$, $\mathrm{err}(h) \leq \varepsilon$ for any consistent $h \in \mathcal{F}$. Therefore, by the union bound, since there are m^κ choices for these indices, this result holds for *all* sequences of indices with probability at least $1 - \delta$, implying the result. ∎

4.2.3 Application to AdaBoost

We can apply this result immediately to AdaBoost, where we already have discussed the appropriate hybrid compression scheme. Here, the class $\mathcal{F}$ consists of all linear threshold functions over a fixed set of T weak hypotheses as in equation (4.8). This class cannot have VC-dimension greater than that of linear threshold functions over points in $\mathbb{R}^T$, a class that we showed in lemma 4.1 has VC-dimension exactly T. Thus, in constructing this scheme for AdaBoost, we have proved the following:

Theorem 4.9 Suppose AdaBoost is run for T rounds on m random examples. Assume each weak hypothesis is trained using a deterministic weak learning algorithm on m_0 unweighted examples selected using resampling, and assume $m \geq (m_0 + 1)T$. Then, with probability at least $1 - \delta$ (over the choice of the random sample), if the combined classifier H is consistent with the entire training set, then

$$\text{err}(H) \leq \frac{2T \lg(2e(m - Tm_0)/T) + 2Tm_0 \lg m + 2 \lg(2/\delta)}{m - Tm_0}.$$

Proof Just plug $\kappa = Tm_0$ and $d = T$ into theorem 4.8.   ∎

When we add the weak learning assumption, we get the following corollary analogous to corollary 4.4.

Corollary 4.10 Assume, in addition to the assumptions of theorem 4.9, that each base classifier has weighted error $\epsilon_t \leq \frac{1}{2} - \gamma$ for some $\gamma > 0$. Let the number of rounds T be equal to the smallest integer exceeding $(\ln m)/(2\gamma^2)$. Then, with probability at least $1 - \delta$, the generalization error of the combined classifier H will be at most

$$O\left(\frac{1}{m}\left[\frac{m_0(\ln m)^2}{\gamma^2} + \ln\left(\frac{1}{\delta}\right)\right]\right) \tag{4.10}$$

(where, for purposes of $O(\cdot)$ notation, we assume $Tm_0 \leq cm$ for some constant $c < 1$).

In both these bounds m_0, the number of examples used to train the weak learner, is acting as a complexity measure rather than some measure based on the weak hypotheses that it outputs. Otherwise, the bounds have essentially the same form as in section 4.1.

4.3 The Equivalence of Strong and Weak Learnability

Finally, we are ready to prove that AdaBoost is a boosting algorithm in the technical sense, and that strong and weak learnability are equivalent in the PAC model described in section 2.3. Note that corollaries 4.4 and 4.7 do not quite prove this since their bounds depend on a measure of the complexity of the weak hypotheses. Thus, they implicitly require that the sample size m be sufficiently large relative to this complexity measure. This goes beyond a bare assumption of weak learnability. A compression-based analysis, however, allows us to sidestep this difficulty.

Theorem 4.11 A target class $\mathcal{C}$ is (efficiently) weakly PAC learnable if and only if it is (efficiently) strongly PAC learnable.

Proof That strong learning implies weak learning is trivial. To prove the converse, we apply AdaBoost to a given weak learning algorithm. Here are the details.

Suppose $\mathcal{C}$ is weakly PAC learnable. Then there exists a constant $\gamma > 0$, and an algorithm A such that for any distribution $\mathcal{D}$ over the instance space $\mathcal{X}$, and for any $c \in \mathcal{C}$, A takes as input m_0 random examples $(x_1, c(x_1)), \ldots, (x_{m_0}, c(x_{m_0}))$ and, with probability at least $\frac{1}{2}$, outputs a hypothesis with $\text{err}(h) \le \frac{1}{2} - \gamma$. Note that here we have weakened the requirement for A even further than the definition given in section 2.3 by requiring only that A succeed with probability at least $\frac{1}{2}$, effectively fixing δ in the earlier definition to this constant.

We assume A is deterministic. If it is not, there are general constructions that can be used here for converting a randomized PAC algorithm into a deterministic one; however, these go beyond the scope of this book.

To construct a strong PAC learning algorithm, we apply AdaBoost with A as the weak learning algorithm. Given m examples from some unknown target $c \in \mathcal{C}$, and given $\delta > 0$, we run AdaBoost for T rounds where T is the smallest integer exceeding $(\ln m)/(2\gamma^2)$. On each round t, we use boosting by resampling to select a sample of size m_0 according to distribution D_t. This sample is fed to the weak learning algorithm A, which produces a weak hypothesis h_t. If the error of h_t on D_t is bigger than $\frac{1}{2} - \gamma$, that is, if it is *not* the case that

$$\mathbf{Pr}_{i \sim D_t}[h_t(x_i) \ne c(x_i)] \le \tfrac{1}{2} - \gamma, \tag{4.11}$$

then h_t is discarded and the process is repeated until h_t satisfying equation (4.11) is found. If no such h_t is found after $L \doteq \lceil \lg(2T/\delta) \rceil$ attempts, then boosting fails.

What is the probability of such failure? The weak learning algorithm's training set on round t consists of m_0 examples selected from distribution D_t, so from A's perspective, D_t is the "true" distribution. Therefore, according to our assumptions regarding this algorithm, the probability that its hypothesis h_t will have weighted error greater than $\frac{1}{2} - \gamma$ on this "true" distribution is at most $\frac{1}{2}$. Thus, the chance of failure on all L (independent) attempts is at most

$$2^{-L} \le \frac{\delta}{2T}.$$

Therefore, the chance of failure on any of the T rounds is at most $\delta/2$ by the union bound.

When no such failures occur, each hypothesis h_t will have weighted error $\epsilon_t \le \frac{1}{2} - \gamma$, so that corollary 4.10 can be applied where we replace δ with $\delta/2$ so that the overall probability of failure either in the search for weak hypotheses or in the choice of the training set is at most δ (again, by the union bound).

Thus, with probability at least $1 - \delta$, AdaBoost produces a combined classifier H with error at most as given in equation (4.10). This bound can be made smaller than any $\epsilon > 0$ by choosing m to be a suitable polynomial in m_0, $1/\gamma$, $1/\epsilon$, and $1/\delta$. Thus, the class $\mathcal{C}$ is strongly learnable in the PAC model. Furthermore, if A is efficient (that is, polynomial-time), then AdaBoost, as we have described it, will be as well since the overall running time is polynomial in m, $1/\delta$, $1/\gamma$, and the running time of the weak learner A itself. ∎

Note that in the construction used in this proof, only a total of

$$Tm_0 = O\left(\frac{m_0 \ln m}{\gamma^2}\right)$$

examples are used by the weak learning algorithm in the computation of the weak hypotheses comprising the combined classifier. (Even if we count runs in which the weak learner fails to provide an adequate weak hypothesis, this number goes up by only a small factor.) Since we regard m_0 and γ as fixed, this means that only a vanishingly small fraction of the training set—just $O(\ln m)$ of the m examples—are ever even presented as input to the weak learner. All the work of boosting apparently goes into the careful selection of this tiny sliver of the dataset.

Furthermore, our analysis provides bounds not only for boosting but also for learning in a much more general sense. For instance, the proof of theorem 4.11 gave a construction in which the generalization error of AdaBoost was shown to drop at the rate

$$O\left(\frac{(\ln m)^2}{m}\right) \tag{4.12}$$

as a function of m (for T chosen as above). But this same construction also shows that *any* PAC learning algorithm A can be converted into one with such behavior. To make such a conversion, we simply hardwire A's parameters, say, to $\epsilon = \frac{1}{4}$ and $\delta = \frac{1}{2}$. Then the resulting algorithm will be a weak learning algorithm which, when combined with AdaBoost, will have the same rate of generalization as in equation (4.12). Thus, if a class is (efficiently) learnable at all, then it is (efficiently) learnable at the learning rate given in equation (4.12). This kind of argument is applicable to other measures of performance as well.

Summary

In summary, we have described several modes of analysis applicable to AdaBoost. Each of these has measured the complexity of the combined classifier in terms of its gross size, that is, the number of base hypotheses being combined, and some varying measure of the complexity of the base hypotheses themselves. We have seen that AdaBoost's generalization error can be made very small if the weak hypotheses are a bit better than random, and thus, that strong and weak PAC learnability, which seem superficially to be so different, actually turn out to be equivalent. However, all of our analyses have predicted overfitting, which is only sometimes a problem for AdaBoost. In chapter 5, we present a rather different analysis that appears to better match AdaBoost's behavior in many practical cases.

Bibliographic Notes

The style of analysis presented in section 4.1 was applied to AdaBoost by Freund and Schapire [95], and is based directly on the work of Baum and Haussler [16]. Lemma 4.1 was proved (in a more general setting) by Dudley [77]. See Anthony and Bartlett's book [8] for further background.

The hybrid compression schemes of section 4.2 are based on the standard compression schemes of Littlestone and Warmuth [154] and Floyd and Warmuth [85]. The propensity of boosting algorithms to compress a dataset was noted by Schapire [199], and was first used as a basis for analyzing their generalization error by Freund [88].

The equivalence of strong and weak learnability shown in section 4.3 was first proved by Schapire [199], and later by Freund [88], though using boosting algorithms which preceded AdaBoost. Both of these works also proved general resource requirements for PAC learning.

The fact noted in the proof of theorem 4.11 that a randomized PAC learning algorithm can be converted into one that is deterministic was proved by Haussler et al. [121].

Some of the exercises in this chapter are based on material from [16, 77, 85, 88, 199].

Exercises

4.1 In the development given in section 4.1, we found it necessary to redefine $\text{sign}(0)$ to be -1, rather than 0, so that the combined classifier H would have range $\{-1, +1\}$ rather than $\{-1, 0, +1\}$ (with predictions of 0 always counting as a mistake). Show how to modify the proofs leading to theorems 4.3 and 4.6 when $\text{sign}(0)$ is instead defined to be 0. [*Hint:* Apply the results of section 2.2.4 to an appropriate family of subsets of $\mathcal{X} \times \{-1, +1\}$.]

4.2 Let Σ'_n be the space of all functions mapping $\mathbb{R}^n$ to $\{-1, +1\}$ of the form

$$\mathbf{x} \mapsto \text{sign}(\mathbf{w} \cdot \mathbf{x} + b)$$

for some $\mathbf{w} \in \mathbb{R}^n$ and $b \in \mathbb{R}$ (where we continue to define $\text{sign}(0)$ to be -1). These are sometimes called *affine threshold functions*, and differ from linear threshold functions only in the "bias term" b. Find the VC-dimension of Σ'_n exactly.

4.3 A *feedforward network*, as in the example in figure 4.2, is defined by a directed acyclic graph on a set of *input nodes* $x_1, \ldots, x_n$, and *computation nodes* $u_1, \ldots, u_N$. The input nodes have no incoming edges. One of the computation nodes is called the *output node*, and has no outgoing edges. Each computation node u_k is associated with a function $f_k :$ $\mathbb{R}^{n_k} \to \{-1, +1\}$, where n_k is u_k's indegree (number of ingoing edges). On input $\mathbf{x} \in \mathbb{R}^n$, the network computes its output $g(\mathbf{x})$ in a natural, feedforward fashion. For instance, given input $\mathbf{x} = \langle x_1, x_2, x_3 \rangle$, the network in figure 4.2 computes $g(\mathbf{x})$ as follows:

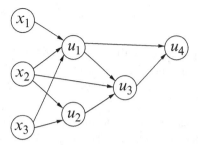

Figure 4.2
An example feedforward network with $n = 3$ input nodes, x_1, x_2, x_3; $N = 4$ computation nodes, u_1, u_2, u_3, u_4; and $W = 10$ edges. The output node is u_4.

$$u_1 = f_1(x_1, x_2, x_3)$$

$$u_2 = f_2(x_2, x_3)$$

$$u_3 = f_3(u_1, x_2, u_2)$$

$$u_4 = f_4(u_1, u_3)$$

$$g(\mathbf{x}) = u_4.$$

(Here, we slightly abuse notation, writing x_j and u_k both for nodes of the network and for the input/computed values associated with these nodes.) The number of edges in the graph is denoted W.

In what follows, we regard the underlying graph as fixed, but allow the functions f_k to vary, or to be learned from data. In particular, let $\mathcal{F}_1, \ldots, \mathcal{F}_N$ be spaces of functions. As explained above, every choice of functions $f_1, \ldots, f_N$ induces an overall function $g : \mathbb{R}^n \to \{-1, +1\}$ for the network. We let $\mathcal{G}$ denote the space of all such functions when f_k is chosen from $\mathcal{F}_k$ for $k = 1, \ldots, N$.

a. Prove that

$$\Pi_{\mathcal{G}}(m) \leq \prod_{k=1}^{N} \Pi_{\mathcal{F}_k}(m).$$

b. Let d_k be the VC-dimension of $\mathcal{F}_k$, and let $d \doteq \sum_{k=1}^{N} d_k$. Assume $m \geq d_k \geq 1$ for all k. Prove that

$$\Pi_{\mathcal{G}}(m) \leq \left(\frac{emN}{d}\right)^d.$$

[*Hint:* Use Jensen's inequality (equation (A.4)).]

c. In a typical *neural network* or *multilayer perceptron*, the functions f_k are affine threshold functions as in exercise 4.2, so that $\mathcal{F}_k = \Sigma'_{n_k}$. For this case, give an exact expression for d in terms of N, n, and W. Conclude by deriving a bound, analogous to theorems 4.3 and 4.6, on the generalization error of every $g \in \mathcal{G}$ which holds with probability at least $1 - \delta$ for $m \geq d$, and which is expressed in terms of $\widehat{err}(g)$, N, n, W, m, and δ. Also give a bound for when g is consistent.

4.4 This exercise relates the size of compression schemes to VC dimension. Assume throughout that all training examples are labeled according to some unknown target c in a known class $\mathcal{C}$ of VC-dimension $d \geq 1$. Assume also the existence of a (deterministic) algorithm A which, given any dataset S, outputs some $h \in \mathcal{C}$ consistent with S. You need not consider issues of efficiency.

a. Suppose B is a (standard) compression scheme of size κ which, when given $m \geq d$ training examples labeled as above, always produces a hypothesis h that is consistent with the given data. Being a compression scheme, each such hypothesis h can be represented by κ of the training examples. Prove that $\kappa \geq d/(1 + \lg d)$. [*Hint:* By counting the number of possible inputs and outputs for B on a shattered training set, show that, when κ is too small, there must exist two distinct labelings of the shattered set that are mapped to the same hypothesis, leading to a contradiction.]

b. Show that there exists a compression scheme B with the same properties as in part (a) whose size κ (when $m \geq d$) is at most $Cd \ln m$, for some absolute constant C. (We here allow the size κ to depend moderately on the sample size m.) [*Hint:* First show how A can be used as a weak learning algorithm requiring a sample of size $O(d)$. Then apply boosting.]

4.5 Support-vector machines, which will be discussed in section 5.6, produce classifiers of the form

$$h(x) = \text{sign}\left(\sum_{i=1}^{m} b_i g(x_i, x)\right)$$

for some $b_1, \ldots, b_m \in \mathbb{R}$, where $x_1, \ldots, x_m$ are the training examples, and where $g : \mathcal{X} \times \mathcal{X} \to \mathbb{R}$ is a *fixed* function. We say such a classifier is κ-*sparse* if at most κ of the b_i's are nonzero. Show that, with probability at least $1 - \delta$, every classifier of this form which is κ-sparse and which is consistent with a random training set of size m has generalization error at most

$$O\left(\frac{\kappa \ln m + \ln(1/\delta)}{m - \kappa}\right).$$

Give explicit constants.

5 The Margins Explanation for Boosting's Effectiveness

In chapter 4, we proved bounds on the generalization error of AdaBoost that all predicted classic overfitting. This prediction seemed reasonable and intuitive, given the apparently increasing complexity of AdaBoost's combined classifier with additional rounds of boosting. Although such overfitting is possible, we saw in section 1.3 that AdaBoost sometimes does *not* overfit. There, we gave an example in which a combined classifier of 1000 decision trees far outperforms on test data one consisting of only five trees, even though both perform perfectly on the training set. Indeed, extensive experiments indicate that AdaBoost generally tends to be quite resistant to overfitting. How can we account for this phenomenon? Why is the theory developed in chapter 4 inadequate? How can a combined classifier as huge and complex as the one above—consisting of 1000 trees and roughly two million decision nodes—perform so well on test data?

In this chapter, we find a way out of this seeming paradox. We develop an alternative theory for analyzing AdaBoost's generalization error that provides a qualitative explanation for its lack of overfitting, as well as specific predictions about the conditions under which boosting can fail. The concept at the core of the new approach is the notion of *confidence*, the idea that a classifier can be more sure of some predictions than of others, and that differences in confidence have consequences for generalization. Confidence was entirely ignored in chapter 4, where our analysis took into consideration only the number of incorrect classifications on the training set, rather than the sureness of the predictions. By explicitly taking confidence into account, our new analysis will give bounds that make very different predictions about how AdaBoost works and when to expect overfitting.

To quantify confidence formally, we introduce a measure called the *margin*. Our analysis then follows a two-part argument. First, we show that larger margins on the training set guarantee better generalization performance (or, more precisely, an improvement in a provable upper bound on the generalization error). And second, we show that AdaBoost provably tends to increase the margins on the training set, even after the training error is zero. Thus, we show that with continued training, AdaBoost tends to become more confident in its own predictions, and that the greater the confidence in a prediction, the more likely it is to be correct. Note that in this analysis, the number of rounds of boosting, which is proportional to the overall size of the final classifier, has little or no impact on generalization, which is instead controlled by the margins; since these are likely to increase with further rounds, this theory predicts an absence of overfitting under identifiable circumstances.

The methods that we use to prove both parts of the analysis outlined above build directly on those developed in the preceding chapters. In addition, we also introduce another general and very powerful technique based on a different measure of hypothesis complexity called Rademacher complexity.

The view of AdaBoost as a margin-maximizing algorithm suggests that it may be possible to derive a better algorithm by modifying AdaBoost to maximize the margins more aggressively. Later in this chapter, we consider how this might be done, as well as some of the subtle difficulties that are involved. We also discuss AdaBoost's connection to other large-margin learning algorithms, particularly support-vector machines.

The margins explanation of boosting contrasts not only with the kind of analysis seen in chapter 4, but also with a competing explanation based on bias-variance theory and the notion that AdaBoost's strong performance is principally due to its "averaging" or "smoothing" effect on the predictions of an "unstable" base learning algorithm. We discuss further in this chapter why these explanations, though possibly relevant to related methods, are ultimately inadequate for AdaBoost.

Finally, we explore some practical applications of margins and their interpretation as a measure of confidence.

5.1   Margin as a Measure of Confidence

The basis of our analysis is the *margin*, a quantitative measure of the confidence of a prediction made by the combined classifier. Recall that the combined classifier has the form

$$H(x) = \text{sign}(F(x))$$

where

$$F(x) \doteq \sum_{t=1}^{T} \alpha_t h_t(x).$$

It will be convenient to normalize the nonnegative weights α_t on the base classifiers. Let

$$a_t \doteq \frac{\alpha_t}{\sum_{t'=1}^{T} \alpha_{t'}}, \tag{5.1}$$

and let

$$f(x) \doteq \sum_{t=1}^{T} a_t h_t(x) = \frac{F(x)}{\sum_{t=1}^{T} \alpha_t}. \tag{5.2}$$

Then $\sum_{t=1}^{T} a_t = 1$, and since multiplying by a positive constant does not change the sign of $F(x)$, we can write

$$H(x) = \text{sign}(f(x)). \tag{5.3}$$

For a given labeled example (x, y), we can now define the *margin* simply to be $yf(x)$. For clarity, this quantity is sometimes referred to as the *normalized margin* to distinguish it from the *unnormalized margin* $yF(x)$ obtained by omitting the normalization step above. Later, we will be interested in both quantities, although their properties are quite distinct. We will often use the shorter term *margin* when the context is sufficient to prevent confusion. In particular, throughout this chapter, this term will refer exclusively to the normalized margin.

Recall that the base classifiers h_t have range $\{-1, +1\}$, and that labels y also are in $\{-1, +1\}$. Because the weights a_t are normalized, this implies that f has range $[-1, +1]$, and so the margin also is in $[-1, +1]$. Furthermore, $y = H(x)$ if and only if y has the same sign as $f(x)$, that is, if and only if the margin of (x, y) is positive. Thus, the sign of the margin indicates whether or not the example is correctly classified by the combined classifier.

As has been noted before, the combined classifier H is simply a weighted majority vote of the predictions of the base classifiers in which the vote of h_t is given weight a_t. An equivalent way of thinking about the margin is as the difference between the weight of the base classifiers predicting the correct label y and the weight of those predicting the incorrect label $-y$. When this vote is very close, so that the predicted label $H(x)$ is based on a narrow majority, the margin will be small in magnitude and, intuitively, we will have little confidence in the prediction. On the other hand, when the prediction $H(x)$ is based on a clear and substantial majority of the base classifiers, the margin will be correspondingly large lending greater confidence in the predicted label. Thus, the magnitude of the margin (or, equivalently, of $f(x)$) is a reasonable measure of confidence. These interpretations of the range of values of the margin can be diagrammed as in figure 5.1.

We can visualize the effect AdaBoost has on the margins of the training examples by plotting their distribution. In particular, we can create a plot showing, for each $\theta \in [-1, +1]$, the fraction of training examples with margin at most θ. For such a cumulative distribution curve, the bulk of the distribution lies where the curve rises the most steeply. Figure 5.2 shows such a *margin distribution graph* for the same dataset used to create figure 1.7 (p. 16),

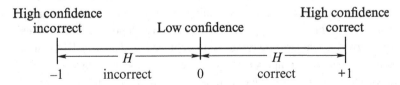

Figure 5.1
An example's margin is in the range $[-1, +1]$ with a positive sign if and only if the combined classifier H is correct. Its magnitude measures the confidence in the combined classifier's prediction.

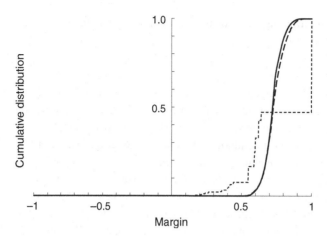

Figure 5.2
The margin distribution graph for boosting C4.5 on the letter dataset showing the cumulative distribution of margins of the training instances after 5, 100, and 1000 iterations, indicated by short-dashed, long-dashed (mostly hidden), and solid curves, respectively. (Reprinted with permission of the Institute of Mathematical Statistics.)

showing the margin distribution after 5, 100, and 1000 rounds of boosting. Whereas nothing at all is happening to the training error, these curves expose dramatic changes happening on the margin distribution. For instance, after five rounds, although the training error is zero (so that no examples have negative margin), a rather substantial fraction of the training examples (7.7%) have margin below 0.5. By round 100, all of these examples have been swept to the right so that not a single example has margin below 0.5, and nearly all have margin above 0.6. (On the other hand, many with margin 1.0 have slipped back to the 0.6–0.8 range.) In line with this trend, the minimum margin of any training example has increased from 0.14 at round 5 to 0.52 at round 100, and 0.55 at round 1000.

Thus, this example is indicative of the powerful effect AdaBoost has on the margins, aggressively pushing up those examples with small or negative margin. Moreover, in comparison with figure 1.7, we see that this overall increase in the margins appears to be correlated with better performance on the test set.

Indeed, as will be seen, AdaBoost can be analyzed theoretically along exactly these lines. We will first prove a bound on the generalization error of AdaBoost—or any other voting method—that depends only on the margins of the training examples, and *not* on the number of rounds of boosting. Thus, this bound predicts that AdaBoost will not overfit regardless of how long it is run, provided that large margins can be achieved (and provided, of course, that the base classifiers are not too complex relative to the size of the training set).

The second part of the analysis is to prove that, as observed empirically in figure 5.2, AdaBoost generally tends to increase the margins of all training examples. All of this will be made precise shortly.

5.2   A Margins-Based Analysis of the Generalization Error

We begin our analysis with a proof of a generalization-error bound in terms of the training-set margins.

5.2.1   Intuition

Let us first try to provide a bit of intuition behind the proof. AdaBoost's combined classifier is a (weighted) majority vote over a possibly very large "committee" of voting base classifiers. Similarly, real-world political elections also may be held with tens or hundreds of millions of voters. Even so, the outcome of such an election can often be predicted by taking a survey, that is, by randomly polling a relatively tiny subset of the electorate, usually around a thousand voters, regardless of the size of the entire electorate. This approach works provided that the election is not too close, that is, provided one candidate has a substantial lead over his or her opponent. This notion of closeness is exactly what is measured by the margin.

In the same manner, the overall prediction of even a very large combined classifier can be determined by sampling randomly among its base classifiers. The majority vote of these "polled" base classifiers will usually be the same as the entire committee represented by the combined classifier, provided that the margin of the overall vote is large. And the larger the margin, the fewer the base classifiers that need to be polled.

So if most examples have large margins, then the combined classifier can be approximated by a much smaller combination of base classifiers, allowing us to use techniques, like those in chapter 4, which are applicable to such classifiers composed of a relatively small number of base classifiers. Thus, the idea is to show that any combined classifier that attains large margins, even a very big one, must be close to a fairly small classifier, and then to use more direct techniques on this simpler approximating set of classifiers.

We now give a more formal treatment. As in chapter 4, we assume that all base classifiers belong to some space $\mathcal{H}$. For simplicity, we assume without loss of generality that $\mathcal{H}$ is closed under negation so that $-h \in \mathcal{H}$ whenever $h \in \mathcal{H}$. (This allows us to avoid considering negative weights on the base classifiers.) We define the *convex hull* $\mathrm{co}(\mathcal{H})$ of $\mathcal{H}$ as the set of all mappings that can be generated by taking a weighted average of classifiers from $\mathcal{H}$:

$$\mathrm{co}(\mathcal{H}) \doteq \left\{ f : x \mapsto \sum_{t=1}^{T} a_t h_t(x) \;\middle|\; a_1, \ldots, a_T \geq 0; \sum_{t=1}^{T} a_t = 1; h_1, \ldots, h_T \in \mathcal{H}; T \geq 1 \right\}.$$

$$(5.4)$$

Note that the function f generated by AdaBoost as in equation (5.2) is a member of this set.

As usual, $\mathcal{D}$ is the true distribution from which all examples are generated, and $S = \langle (x_1, y_1), \ldots, (x_m, y_m) \rangle$ is the training set. We will sometimes be interested in computing probabilities or expectations with respect to an example (x, y) chosen randomly according to distribution $\mathcal{D}$, which we denote by $\mathbf{Pr}_{\mathcal{D}}[\cdot]$ or $\mathbf{E}_{\mathcal{D}}[\cdot]$. We also will sometimes consider the choice of (x, y) from the empirical distribution, that is, selected uniformly at random from the training set S. In this case, we use the notation $\mathbf{Pr}_S[\cdot]$ and $\mathbf{E}_S[\cdot]$. For instance, $\mathbf{Pr}_{\mathcal{D}}[H(x) \neq y]$ is the true generalization error of H, and

$$\mathbf{Pr}_S[H(x) \neq y] \doteq \frac{1}{m} \sum_{i=1}^{m} \mathbf{1}\{H(x_i) \neq y_i\}$$

is the training error. Recalling that H makes a mistake if and only if the margin $yf(x)$ is not positive, we can write H's generalization error equivalently as $\mathbf{Pr}_{\mathcal{D}}[yf(x) \leq 0]$, and similarly for the training error.

Theorems 5.1 and 5.5, the main results of this section, state that with high probability, the generalization error of any majority vote classifier can be bounded in terms of the number of training examples with margin below a threshold θ, plus an additional term which depends on the number of training examples, some "complexity" measure of $\mathcal{H}$, and the threshold θ (preventing us from choosing θ too close to zero). As in chapters 2 and 4, when $\mathcal{H}$ is finite, complexity is measured by $\log |\mathcal{H}|$; when $\mathcal{H}$ is infinite, its VC-dimension is used instead.

5.2.2 Finite Base Hypothesis Spaces

We begin with the simpler case that the space $\mathcal{H}$ of base classifiers is finite.

Theorem 5.1 Let $\mathcal{D}$ be a distribution over $\mathcal{X} \times \{-1, +1\}$, and let S be a sample of m examples chosen independently at random according to $\mathcal{D}$. Assume that the base classifier space $\mathcal{H}$ is finite, and let $\delta > 0$. Then with probability at least $1 - \delta$ over the random choice of the training set S, every weighted average function $f \in \text{co}(\mathcal{H})$ satisfies the following bound:

$$\mathbf{Pr}_{\mathcal{D}}[yf(x) \leq 0] \leq \mathbf{Pr}_S[yf(x) \leq \theta] + O\left(\sqrt{\frac{\log |\mathcal{H}|}{m\theta^2} \cdot \log\left(\frac{m\theta^2}{\log |\mathcal{H}|}\right) + \frac{\log(1/\delta)}{m}}\right)$$

for all $\theta > \sqrt{(\ln |\mathcal{H}|)/(4m)}$.

The term on the left is the generalization error, as noted above. The first term on the right is the fraction of training examples with margin below some threshold θ. This term will be small if most training examples have large margin (i.e., larger than θ). The second term on the right is an additional term that becomes small as the size of the training set m gets larger, provided the complexity of the base classifiers is controlled for θ bounded away from zero. This bound is analogous to the sorts of bounds seen in chapter 2, such as theorems 2.2 and 2.5, which quantify how the generalization error depends upon fit to the training set and complexity of the hypotheses used. Here, however, fit to the data is measured by the number of examples with small margin (at most θ), rather than the training error and, importantly, only the complexity of the *base* classifiers enters the bound—the number of nonzero terms comprising f, that is, the number of rounds T in the boosting context, does not appear anywhere in the bound.

Such an analysis is entirely consistent with the behavior observed in the example discussed in section 5.1, where no degradation in performance was observed with further rounds of boosting. Rather, performance improved with continued boosting in a manner apparently correlated with a general increase in the margins of the training examples. The overfitting behavior seen in section 1.2.3 is also qualitatively consistent with this analysis; in that case, it seems that a relatively small sample size and generally small margins together have doomed the performance beyond just a few rounds of boosting.

Proof   For the sake of the proof, we define $\mathcal{A}_n$ to be the set of *unweighted* averages over n elements from $\mathcal{H}$:

$$
\mathcal{A}_n \doteq \left\{ f : x \mapsto \frac{1}{n} \sum_{j=1}^{n} h_j(x) \,\middle|\, h_1, \ldots, h_n \in \mathcal{H} \right\}.
$$

Note that the same $h \in \mathcal{H}$ may appear multiple times in such an average.

As outlined above, the main idea of the proof is to approximate any weighted average function $f \in \mathrm{co}(\mathcal{H})$ by randomly polling its constituents. Any such function has the form given in equations (5.2) and (5.4). Note that the weights a_t on the base classifiers naturally define a probability distribution over $\mathcal{H}$ according to which individual base classifiers can be sampled randomly. Going a step further, we can imagine an experiment in which n base classifiers $\tilde{h}_1, \ldots, \tilde{h}_n$ from $\mathcal{H}$ are selected independently at random. Thus, each $\tilde{h}_j$ is selected independently at random from $\mathcal{H}$ where we choose $\tilde{h}_j$ to be equal to h_t with probability a_t. We can then form their unweighted average

$$
\tilde{f}(x) \doteq \frac{1}{n} \sum_{j=1}^{n} \tilde{h}_j(x), \tag{5.5}
$$

which is clearly a member of $\mathcal{A}_n$. It is this function $\tilde{f}$ that we use to approximate f.

We assume throughout this proof that $\tilde{f}$ is selected in this random manner, denoting probability and expectations with respect to its random selection by $\mathbf{Pr}_{\tilde{f}}[\cdot]$ and $\mathbf{E}_{\tilde{f}}[\cdot]$. The particular choice of n will come later.

Here is an informal outline of the proof, which has two main parts. First, we will show that $\tilde{f}$ is typically a good approximation of f in the sense that, for "most" examples (x, y),

$$
\left| yf(x) - y\tilde{f}(x) \right| \le \frac{\theta}{2}.
$$

Thus, if $yf(x) \le 0$, then it is likely that $y\tilde{f}(x) \le \theta/2$, which means that

$$\mathbf{Pr}_D[yf(x) \le 0] \lesssim \mathbf{Pr}_D\left[y\tilde{f}(x) \le \frac{\theta}{2}\right], \tag{5.6}$$

where we use $\lesssim$ to indicate approximate inequality in a strictly informal sense. A similar argument will show that

$$\mathbf{Pr}_S\left[y\tilde{f}(x) \le \frac{\theta}{2}\right] \lesssim \mathbf{Pr}_S[yf(x) \le \theta]. \tag{5.7}$$

The second key ingredient of the proof is an argument that the margins of functions in $\mathcal{A}_n$ have statistics on the training set that are similar to those on the true distribution $\mathcal{D}$. In particular, we show that, with high probability, the empirical probability of a small margin is close to its true probability for all $\tilde{f} \in \mathcal{A}_n$. That is,

$$\mathbf{Pr}_D\left[y\tilde{f}(x) \le \frac{\theta}{2}\right] \lesssim \mathbf{Pr}_S\left[y\tilde{f}(x) \le \frac{\theta}{2}\right]. \tag{5.8}$$

Combining equations (5.6), (5.7), and (5.8) will give

$$\mathbf{Pr}_D[yf(x) \le 0] \lesssim \mathbf{Pr}_D\left[y\tilde{f}(x) \le \frac{\theta}{2}\right] \lesssim \mathbf{Pr}_S\left[y\tilde{f}(x) \le \frac{\theta}{2}\right] \lesssim \mathbf{Pr}_S[yf(x) \le \theta],$$

proving the theorem.

We now proceed to the details. Our first observation is that, for fixed x, if n is sufficiently large, then $\tilde{f}(x)$ will be close to its expectation, which by construction turns out to be $f(x)$. Specifically, we have:

Lemma 5.2 For fixed x, $\theta > 0$, and $n \ge 1$,

$$\mathbf{Pr}_{\tilde{f}}\left[\left|\tilde{f}(x) - f(x)\right| \ge \frac{\theta}{2}\right] \le 2e^{-n\theta^2/8} \doteq \beta_{n,\theta}.$$

Proof With x fixed, $\tilde{h}_j(x)$ is a random variable with range $\{-1, +1\}$. Since $\tilde{h}_j = h_t$ with probability a_t, its expected value is

$$\mathbf{E}_{\tilde{f}}\left[\tilde{h}_j(x)\right] = \sum_{t=1}^{T} a_t h_t(x) = f(x),$$

and so, by equation (5.5), $\mathbf{E}_{\tilde{f}}\left[\tilde{f}(x)\right] = f(x)$ as well. Thus, with minor rescaling, we can apply Hoeffding's inequality (theorem 2.1) to this set of independent random variables $\tilde{h}_1(x), \dots, \tilde{h}_n(x)$ to obtain

$$\mathbf{Pr}_{\tilde{f}}\left[\left|\tilde{f}(x) - f(x)\right| \ge \frac{\theta}{2}\right] \le \beta_{n,\theta}. \qquad \blacksquare$$

The next lemma shows further that the margin for f, $yf(x)$, will be close to the margin for $\tilde{f}$, $y\tilde{f}(x)$, "on average" if the pair (x, y) is chosen at random from an arbitrary distribution P. Below, $\mathbf{Pr}_P[\cdot]$ and $\mathbf{E}_P[\cdot]$ denote probability and expectation over the random choice of (x, y) from P, respectively.

The proof uses *marginalization*, the principle that if X and Y are random variables, then the probability of any event a can be computed as the expected probability of the event when one of the variables is held fixed:

$$\mathbf{Pr}_{X,Y}[a] = \mathbf{E}_X[\mathbf{Pr}_Y[a|X]].$$

Lemma 5.3 Suppose P is any distribution over pairs (x, y). Then for $\theta > 0$ and $n \geq 1$,

$$\mathbf{Pr}_{P,\tilde{f}}\left[\left|yf(x) - y\tilde{f}(x)\right| \geq \frac{\theta}{2}\right] \leq \beta_{n,\theta}.$$

Proof Using marginalization and lemma 5.2, we have that

$$\mathbf{Pr}_{P,\tilde{f}}\left[\left|yf(x) - y\tilde{f}(x)\right| \geq \frac{\theta}{2}\right] = \mathbf{Pr}_{P,\tilde{f}}\left[\left|f(x) - \tilde{f}(x)\right| \geq \frac{\theta}{2}\right]$$

$$= \mathbf{E}_P\left[\mathbf{Pr}_{\tilde{f}}\left[\left|f(x) - \tilde{f}(x)\right| \geq \frac{\theta}{2}\right]\right]$$

$$\leq \mathbf{E}_P\left[\beta_{n,\theta}\right] = \beta_{n,\theta}. \qquad \blacksquare$$

Thus, $\tilde{f}$ is a good approximation of f. In particular, we can now prove equation (5.6) in more precise terms. Specifically, lemma 5.3, applied to distribution $\mathcal{D}$, gives that

$$\mathbf{Pr}_{\mathcal{D}}[yf(x) \leq 0] = \mathbf{Pr}_{\mathcal{D},\tilde{f}}[yf(x) \leq 0]$$

$$\leq \mathbf{Pr}_{\mathcal{D},\tilde{f}}\left[y\tilde{f}(x) \leq \frac{\theta}{2}\right] + \mathbf{Pr}_{\mathcal{D},\tilde{f}}\left[yf(x) \leq 0, y\tilde{f}(x) > \frac{\theta}{2}\right] \qquad (5.9)$$

$$\leq \mathbf{Pr}_{\mathcal{D},\tilde{f}}\left[y\tilde{f}(x) \leq \frac{\theta}{2}\right] + \mathbf{Pr}_{\mathcal{D},\tilde{f}}\left[\left|yf(x) - y\tilde{f}(x)\right| > \frac{\theta}{2}\right]$$

$$\leq \mathbf{Pr}_{\mathcal{D},\tilde{f}}\left[y\tilde{f}(x) \leq \frac{\theta}{2}\right] + \beta_{n,\theta}. \qquad (5.10)$$

Here, equation (5.9) uses the simple fact that for any two events a and b,

$$\mathbf{Pr}[a] = \mathbf{Pr}[a, b] + \mathbf{Pr}[a, \neg b] \leq \mathbf{Pr}[b] + \mathbf{Pr}[a, \neg b]. \qquad (5.11)$$

Equation (5.7) follows from a similar derivation that again uses equation (5.11) and lemma 5.3 now applied instead to the empirical distribution:

$$\mathbf{Pr}_{S,\tilde{f}}\left[y\tilde{f}(x) \leq \frac{\theta}{2}\right] \leq \mathbf{Pr}_{S,\tilde{f}}[yf(x) \leq \theta] + \mathbf{Pr}_{S,\tilde{f}}\left[y\tilde{f}(x) \leq \frac{\theta}{2}, yf(x) > \theta\right]$$

$$\leq \mathbf{Pr}_{S,\tilde{f}}[yf(x) \leq \theta] + \mathbf{Pr}_{S,\tilde{f}}\left[\left|yf(x) - y\tilde{f}(x)\right| > \frac{\theta}{2}\right]$$

$$\leq \mathbf{Pr}_{S}[yf(x) \leq \theta] + \beta_{n,\theta}. \tag{5.12}$$

We move on now to the second part of the proof, in which we show that equation (5.8) holds for all $\tilde{f} \in \mathcal{A}_n$ with high probability.

Lemma 5.4 Let

$$\varepsilon_n \doteq \sqrt{\frac{\ln\left[n(n+1)^2|\mathcal{H}|^n/\delta\right]}{2m}}.$$

Then, with probability at least $1 - \delta$ (where the probability is taken over the choice of the random training set S), for all $n \geq 1$, for all $\tilde{f} \in \mathcal{A}_n$, and for all $\theta \geq 0$,

$$\mathbf{Pr}_{\mathcal{D}}\left[y\tilde{f}(x) \leq \frac{\theta}{2}\right] \leq \mathbf{Pr}_{S}\left[y\tilde{f}(x) \leq \frac{\theta}{2}\right] + \varepsilon_n. \tag{5.13}$$

Proof Let $p_{\tilde{f},\theta} = \mathbf{Pr}_{\mathcal{D}}\left[y\tilde{f}(x) \leq \theta/2\right]$, and let $\hat{p}_{\tilde{f},\theta} = \mathbf{Pr}_{S}\left[y\tilde{f}(x) \leq \theta/2\right]$. Consider first a particular *fixed* choice of n, $\tilde{f}$, and θ. Let B_i be a Bernoulli random variable that is 1 if $y_i\tilde{f}(x_i) \leq \theta/2$, and 0 otherwise. Note that here the underlying random process is the choice of the random sample S. Then

$$\hat{p}_{\tilde{f},\theta} = \frac{1}{m}\sum_{i=1}^{m} B_i,$$

and

$$p_{\tilde{f},\theta} = \mathbf{E}[B_i] = \mathbf{E}\left[\hat{p}_{\tilde{f},\theta}\right].$$

Thus, by Hoeffding's inequality (theorem 2.1),

$$\mathbf{Pr}\left[p_{\tilde{f},\theta} \geq \hat{p}_{\tilde{f},\theta} + \varepsilon_n\right] = \mathbf{Pr}\left[\hat{p}_{\tilde{f},\theta} \leq \mathbf{E}\left[\hat{p}_{\tilde{f},\theta}\right] - \varepsilon_n\right] \leq e^{-2\varepsilon_n^2 m}, \tag{5.14}$$

which means that equation (5.13) holds for fixed $\tilde{f}$ and θ with high probability. We next use the union bound to show that it also holds for all $\tilde{f}$ and θ simultaneously with high probability.

Note that $y\tilde{f}(x) \leq \theta/2$ if and only if

$$y\sum_{j=1}^{n}\tilde{h}_j(x) \leq \frac{n\theta}{2}$$

(by definition of $\tilde{f}$), which in turn holds if and only if

$$y \sum_{j=1}^{n} \tilde{h}_j(x) \leq \left\lfloor \frac{n\theta}{2} \right\rfloor,$$

since the term on the left is an integer. Thus, $p_{\tilde{f},\theta} = p_{\tilde{f},\bar{\theta}}$ and $\hat{p}_{\tilde{f},\theta} = \hat{p}_{\tilde{f},\bar{\theta}}$, where $\bar{\theta}$ is chosen so that

$$\frac{n\bar{\theta}}{2} = \left\lfloor \frac{n\theta}{2} \right\rfloor,$$

that is, from the set

$$\Theta_n \doteq \left\{ \frac{2i}{n} : i = 0, 1, \ldots, n \right\}.$$

(There is never a need to consider $\theta > 2$ since $y\tilde{f}(x) \in [-1, +1]$.) Thus, for fixed n, the chance that $p_{\tilde{f},\theta} \geq \hat{p}_{\tilde{f},\theta} + \varepsilon_n$ for any $\tilde{f} \in \mathcal{A}_n$ and any $\theta \geq 0$ is

$$\mathbf{Pr}\left[\exists \tilde{f} \in \mathcal{A}_n, \theta \geq 0 : p_{\tilde{f},\theta} \geq \hat{p}_{\tilde{f},\theta} + \varepsilon_n\right] = \mathbf{Pr}\left[\exists \tilde{f} \in \mathcal{A}_n, \theta \in \Theta_n : p_{\tilde{f},\theta} \geq \hat{p}_{\tilde{f},\theta} + \varepsilon_n\right]$$

$$\leq |\mathcal{A}_n| \cdot |\Theta_n| \cdot e^{-2\varepsilon_n^2 m} \tag{5.15}$$

$$\leq |\mathcal{H}|^n \cdot (n+1) \cdot e^{-2\varepsilon_n^2 m} \tag{5.16}$$

$$= \frac{\delta}{n(n+1)}. \tag{5.17}$$

Equation (5.15) uses equation (5.14) and the union bound. Equation (5.16) is simple counting. And equation (5.17) follows from our choice of ε_n.

Applying the union bound one last time, we have that the probability of this happening for any $n \geq 1$ is at most

$$\sum_{n=1}^{\infty} \frac{\delta}{n(n+1)} = \delta. \qquad \blacksquare$$

We can now complete the proof of theorem 5.1. We assume that we are in the "good" case in which equation (5.13) holds for all $n \geq 1$, for all $\tilde{f} \in \mathcal{A}_n$, and for all $\theta \geq 0$ (as will happen with probability at least $1 - \delta$, by lemma 5.4). Using marginalization (twice), this implies that

$$\mathbf{Pr}_{\mathcal{D},\tilde{f}}\left[y\tilde{f}(x) \leq \frac{\theta}{2}\right] = \mathbf{E}_{\tilde{f}}\left[\mathbf{Pr}_{\mathcal{D}}\left[y\tilde{f}(x) \leq \frac{\theta}{2}\right]\right]$$

$$\leq \mathbf{E}_{\tilde{f}}\left[\mathbf{Pr}_{S}\left[y\tilde{f}(x) \leq \frac{\theta}{2}\right] + \varepsilon_n\right]$$

$$= \mathbf{Pr}_{S,\tilde{f}}\left[y\tilde{f}(x) \leq \frac{\theta}{2}\right] + \varepsilon_n. \tag{5.18}$$

Thus, pulling everything together—specifically, equations (5.10), (5.18), and (5.12)—we have, with probability at least $1 - \delta$, for every $f \in \text{co}(\mathcal{H})$, for every $n \geq 1$, and for every $\theta > 0$,

$$\mathbf{Pr}_{\mathcal{D}}[yf(x) \leq 0] \leq \mathbf{Pr}_{\mathcal{D}, \tilde{f}}\left[y\tilde{f}(x) \leq \frac{\theta}{2}\right] + \beta_{n,\theta}$$

$$\leq \mathbf{Pr}_{S, \tilde{f}}\left[y\tilde{f}(x) \leq \frac{\theta}{2}\right] + \varepsilon_n + \beta_{n,\theta}$$

$$\leq \mathbf{Pr}_S[yf(x) \leq \theta] + \beta_{n,\theta} + \varepsilon_n + \beta_{n,\theta}$$

$$= \mathbf{Pr}_S[yf(x) \leq \theta] + 4e^{-n\theta^2/8} + \sqrt{\frac{\ln\left[n(n+1)^2|\mathcal{H}|^n/\delta\right]}{2m}}.$$

The bound in the statement of the theorem can now be obtained by setting

$$n = \left\lceil \frac{4}{\theta^2} \ln\left(\frac{4m\theta^2}{\ln|\mathcal{H}|}\right)\right\rceil. \qquad\blacksquare$$

5.2.3 Infinite Base Hypothesis Spaces

Theorem 5.1 applies only to the case of a finite base classifier space $\mathcal{H}$. When this space is infinite, we instead use its VC-dimension as a measure of complexity, giving the following analogue of theorem 5.1:

Theorem 5.5 Let $\mathcal{D}$ be a distribution over $\mathcal{X} \times \{-1, +1\}$, and let S be a sample of m examples chosen independently at random according to $\mathcal{D}$. Suppose the base-classifier space $\mathcal{H}$ has VC-dimension d, and let $\delta > 0$. Assume that $m \geq d \geq 1$. Then, with probability at least $1 - \delta$ over the random choice of the training set S, every weighted average function $f \in \text{co}(\mathcal{H})$ satisfies the following bound:

$$\mathbf{Pr}_{\mathcal{D}}[yf(x) \leq 0] \leq \mathbf{Pr}_S[yf(x) \leq \theta] + O\left(\sqrt{\frac{d \log(m/d) \log(m\theta^2/d)}{m\theta^2}} + \frac{\log(1/\delta)}{m}\right)$$

for all $\theta > \sqrt{8d \ln(em/d)/m}$.

Proof This theorem can be proved exactly like theorem 5.1, except that lemma 5.4 needs to be modified as follows:

Lemma 5.6 Let

$$\varepsilon_n \doteq \sqrt{\frac{32[\ln(n(n+1)^2) + dn \ln(em/d) + \ln(8/\delta)]}{m}}.$$

Then, with probability at least $1 - \delta$ (over the choice of the random training set), for all $n \geq 1$, for all $\tilde{f} \in \mathcal{A}_n$ and for all $\theta \geq 0$,

$$\mathbf{Pr}_{\mathcal{D}}\left[y\tilde{f}(x) \leq \frac{\theta}{2}\right] \leq \mathbf{Pr}_S\left[y\tilde{f}(x) \leq \frac{\theta}{2}\right] + \varepsilon_n. \tag{5.19}$$

Proof   To prove the lemma, we make use of theorem 2.6 rather than the union bound. To do so, we construct a family of subsets of the space $\mathcal{Z} = \mathcal{X} \times \{-1, +1\}$ of instance-label pairs. For any $\tilde{f} \in \mathcal{A}_n$ and $\theta \geq 0$, let

$$B_{\tilde{f}, \theta} \doteq \left\{(x, y) \in \mathcal{Z} : y\tilde{f}(x) \leq \theta/2\right\}$$

be the set of pairs whose margin with respect to $\tilde{f}$ is at most $\theta/2$. Then let $\mathcal{B}_n$ be the collection of all such subsets:

$$\mathcal{B}_n \doteq \left\{B_{\tilde{f}, \theta} : \tilde{f} \in \mathcal{A}_n, \theta \geq 0\right\}.$$

To apply theorem 2.6 to this collection, we first count the number of in-out behaviors realizable by sets in $\mathcal{B}_n$ on a finite set of m points, that is, $\Pi_{\mathcal{B}_n}(m)$. Let $x_1, \ldots, x_m \in \mathcal{X}$ and $y_1, \ldots, y_m \in \{-1, +1\}$. Since the VC-dimension of $\mathcal{H}$ is d, Sauer's lemma (lemma 2.4) and equation (2.12) give that the number of labelings of the x_i's by hypotheses in $\mathcal{H}$ is

$$|\{\langle h(x_1), \ldots, h(x_m)\rangle : h \in \mathcal{H}\}| \leq \sum_{i=0}^{d}\binom{m}{i} \leq \left(\frac{em}{d}\right)^d$$

for $m \geq d \geq 1$. This implies that the number of margin behaviors associated with functions $\tilde{f} \in \mathcal{A}_n$ is

$$\left|\left\{\langle y_1\tilde{f}(x_1), \ldots, y_m\tilde{f}(x_m)\rangle : \tilde{f} \in \mathcal{A}_n\right\}\right| \leq \left(\frac{em}{d}\right)^{dn},$$

since each $\tilde{f} \in \mathcal{A}_n$ is composed of n functions from $\mathcal{H}$. Since we need consider only $n + 1$ distinct values of θ (that is, only $\theta \in \Theta_n$ as in the proof of lemma 5.4), it follows that

$$\Pi_{\mathcal{B}_n}(m) \leq (n + 1)\left(\frac{em}{d}\right)^{dn}.$$

Applying theorem 2.6 now gives that, for $n \geq 1$, with probability at least $1 - \delta/(n(n + 1))$, for all $B_{\tilde{f}, \theta} \in \mathcal{B}_n$,

$$\mathbf{Pr}_{z \sim \mathcal{D}}\left[z \in B_{\tilde{f}, \theta}\right] \leq \mathbf{Pr}_{z \sim S}\left[z \in B_{\tilde{f}, \theta}\right] + \varepsilon_n$$

for the choice of ε_n given in the lemma. This is equivalent to equation (5.19). Thus, by the union bound, this same statement holds for all $n \geq 1$ simultaneously with probability at least $1 - \delta$, proving the lemma.   ∎

The rest of the proof of theorem 5.5 is the same as before until it is time to plug in our new choice of ε_n giving, with probability at least $1 - \delta$,

$$\mathbf{Pr}_{\mathcal{D}}[yf(x) \leq 0] \leq \mathbf{Pr}_S[yf(x) \leq \theta] + 4e^{-n\theta^2/8}$$

$$+ \sqrt{\frac{32[\ln(n(n+1)^2) + dn\ln(em/d) + \ln(8/\delta)]}{m}}$$

for all $f \in co(\mathcal{H})$, $n \geq 1$, and $\theta > 0$. Setting

$$n = \left\lceil \frac{4}{\theta^2} \ln\left(\frac{m\theta^2}{8d\ln(em/d)}\right) \right\rceil$$

gives the bound stated in the theorem.   ∎

We have focused our attention on the general case in which some of the training examples may have small margins below some value θ of interest. This has led to an additional term in the bounds in theorems 5.1 and 5.5 of the form $\tilde{O}\left(1/\sqrt{m}\right)$ as a function of m. However, just as we saw in section 2.2.5 that better rates of convergence are possible with consistent hypotheses, for the same reasons given in that section, these theorems can be similarly modified to give much better bounds on the order of $\tilde{O}\left(1/m\right)$ when *all* training examples have margin above θ so that $\mathbf{Pr}_S[yf(x) \leq \theta] = 0$.

5.3 Analysis Based on Rademacher Complexity

Before continuing forward, we pause to outline an alternative method of analysis that is perhaps more abstract mathematically but is very general and powerful. We sketch only the main ideas, and omit most of the proofs. (See the bibliographic notes for further reading.)

We have already explored a number of techniques for measuring the complexity of a space of classifiers. Here we introduce yet another measure, which is at the core of this approach. Intuitively, a space $\mathcal{H}$ is especially "rich" or "expressive" if we find it easy to fit any dataset using classifiers in $\mathcal{H}$. We have routinely measured how well a hypothesis h fits a dataset $(x_1, y_1), \ldots, (x_m, y_m)$ by its training error, a measure that is essentially equivalent to the correlation of the predictions $h(x_i)$ with the labels y_i, that is,

$$\frac{1}{m}\sum_{i=1}^{m} y_i h(x_i).$$

The hypothesis $h \in \mathcal{H}$ that has the best fit then has correlation

$$\max_{h \in \mathcal{H}} \frac{1}{m}\sum_{i=1}^{m} y_i h(x_i).$$

This gives a measure of how well the space $\mathcal{H}$ as a whole fits the data.

Suppose now that the labels y_i are chosen *at random* without regard to the x_i's. In other words, suppose we replace each y_i by a random variable σ_i that is -1 or $+1$ with equal probability, independent of everything else. Thus, the σ_i's represent labels that are pure noise. We can measure how well the space $\mathcal{H}$ can fit this noise in expectation by

$$\mathbf{E}_\sigma \left[\max_{h \in \mathcal{H}} \frac{1}{m} \sum_{i=1}^m \sigma_i h(x_i) \right], \tag{5.20}$$

where we write $\mathbf{E}_\sigma[\cdot]$ for expectation with respect to the choice of the σ_i's. Returning to our earlier intuition, if $\mathcal{H}$ is a rich class, it should have an easier time fitting even random noise, so that equation (5.20) will be large; conversely, for a more restricted class, we expect equation (5.20) to be small. This suggests that this expression may be a reasonable measure of $\mathcal{H}$'s complexity.

This notion generalizes immediately to families of real-valued functions, not just classifiers. In abstract terms, let $\mathcal{Z}$ be any space and $\mathcal{F}$ any family of functions $f : \mathcal{Z} \to \mathbb{R}$. Let $S = \langle z_1, \ldots, z_m \rangle$ be a sequence of points in $\mathcal{Z}$. Then the *Rademacher complexity* of $\mathcal{F}$ with respect to S, which is the focus of this section, is defined to be[1]

$$R_S(\mathcal{F}) \doteq \mathbf{E}_\sigma \left[\sup_{f \in \mathcal{F}} \frac{1}{m} \sum_{i=1}^m \sigma_i f(z_i) \right]. \tag{5.21}$$

Note that equation (5.20) is the Rademacher complexity of $\mathcal{H}$ with respect to $\langle x_1, \ldots, x_m \rangle$ obtained by taking $\mathcal{F} = \mathcal{H}$ and $\mathcal{Z} = \mathcal{X}$.

Like the complexity measures introduced in section 2.2, the primary purpose of Rademacher complexity is in bounding the difference between empirical and true probabilities or expectations. In particular, the following very general result can be proved.

Theorem 5.7 Let $\mathcal{F}$ be any family of functions $f : \mathcal{Z} \to [-1, +1]$. Let S be a random sequence of m points chosen independently from $\mathcal{Z}$ according to some distribution $\mathcal{D}$. Then with probability at least $1 - \delta$,

$$\mathbf{E}_{z \sim \mathcal{D}}[f(z)] \le \mathbf{E}_{z \sim S}[f(z)] + 2R_S(\mathcal{F}) + \sqrt{\frac{2 \ln(2/\delta)}{m}}$$

for all $f \in \mathcal{F}$.

---

1. Rademacher complexity is commonly defined instead to be $\mathbf{E}_\sigma \left[\sup_{f \in \mathcal{F}} \frac{1}{m} \left| \sum_{i=1}^m \sigma_i f(z_i) \right| \right]$. We use the "one-sided" version given in equation (5.21) because it turns out to be simpler and more convenient for our purposes.

(As in section 2.2.4, $\mathbf{E}_{z\sim\mathcal{D}}[\cdot]$ and $\mathbf{E}_{z\sim S}[\cdot]$ denote expectation with respect to the true and empirical distributions, respectively.) Note that the Rademacher complexity that appears here is relative to the sample S. Alternative results can be obtained based on either expected or worst-case complexity.

Thus, proving uniform convergence results, according to this theorem, reduces to computing Rademacher complexity. We briefly outline three techniques that are useful for this purpose. When combined with theorem 5.7, these will be sufficient to give a complete analysis of margin-based voting classifiers.

First, in the special case given above in which $\mathcal{H}$ is a space of binary classifiers and $\mathcal{Z} = \mathcal{X}$, Rademacher complexity can be immediately related to the other complexity measures we have been using. In particular, if $\mathcal{H}$ is finite, then it can be shown (see exercise 6.4) that

$$R_S(\mathcal{H}) \le \sqrt{\frac{2\ln|\mathcal{H}|}{m}} \tag{5.22}$$

(where m is the size of S, throughout). And in general, for any $\mathcal{H}$,

$$R_S(\mathcal{H}) \le \sqrt{\frac{2\ln|\Pi_{\mathcal{H}}(S)|}{m}}$$

where $\Pi_{\mathcal{H}}(S)$ is the set of dichotomies realized by $\mathcal{H}$ on S, as in section 2.2.3. By Sauer's lemma (lemma 2.4) and equation (2.12), this implies that if $\mathcal{H}$ has VC-dimension d, then

$$R_S(\mathcal{H}) \le \sqrt{\frac{2d\ln(em/d)}{m}} \tag{5.23}$$

for $m \ge d \ge 1$. Thus, in a sense, Rademacher complexity subsumes both $\lg|\mathcal{H}|$ and VC-dimension as a complexity measure, and yields results that are at least as general. For instance, theorems 2.2 and 2.5 can now be derived as corollaries of theorem 5.7 (possibly with some adjustment of constants).

In studying voting classifiers, we have been especially interested in the convex hull $\mathrm{co}(\mathcal{H})$ of a space of base classifiers $\mathcal{H}$, as defined in equation (5.4). Remarkably, the Rademacher complexity of the convex hull, despite being a much larger space, is always the same as that of the original space $\mathcal{H}$. That is,

$$R_S(\mathrm{co}(\mathcal{H})) = R_S(\mathcal{H}). \tag{5.24}$$

This follows immediately from the definition of Rademacher complexity given in equation (5.21) since, for any values of the σ_i's and x_i's, the maximum of

$$\sum_{i=1}^{m} \sigma_i f(x_i)$$

over functions f in $\mathrm{co}(\mathcal{H})$ will be realized "at a corner," that is, at an f that is actually equal to one of the classifiers h in the original space $\mathcal{H}$. This property makes Rademacher complexity particularly well suited to the study of voting classifiers, as we will soon see.

Finally, we consider what happens to the Rademacher complexity when all of the functions in a class $\mathcal{F}$ undergo the same transformation. Specifically, let $\phi : \mathbb{R} \to \mathbb{R}$ be any *Lipschitz function*, that is, a function such that, for some constant $L_\phi > 0$ called the *Lipschitz constant*, we have that

$$|\phi(u) - \phi(v)| \leq L_\phi \cdot |u - v|$$

for all $u, v \in \mathbb{R}$. Let $\phi \circ \mathcal{F}$ be the result of composing ϕ with all functions in $\mathcal{F}$:

$$\phi \circ \mathcal{F} \doteq \{z \mapsto \phi(f(z)) \mid f \in \mathcal{F}\}.$$

Then it can be shown (see exercise 5.5) that the Rademacher complexity of the transformed class scales that of the original class by at most L_ϕ. That is,

$$R_S(\phi \circ \mathcal{F}) \leq L_\phi \cdot R_S(\mathcal{F}). \tag{5.25}$$

With these general tools, we can now derive a margins-based analysis that is similar to (actually, slightly better than) the one given in section 5.2.

Let $\mathcal{H}$ be our space of base classifiers, and let $\mathcal{M}$ be the space of all "margin functions" of the form $yf(x)$ where f is any convex combination of base classifiers:

$$\mathcal{M} \doteq \{(x, y) \mapsto yf(x) \mid f \in \mathrm{co}(\mathcal{H})\}.$$

Note that

$$R_S(\mathcal{M}) = R_S(\mathrm{co}(\mathcal{H})) \tag{5.26}$$

since the labels y_i are "absorbed" by the σ_i's and so become irrelevant under the definition of Rademacher complexity given in equation (5.21).

For any $\theta > 0$, let ϕ be the piecewise-linear function

$$\phi(u) \doteq \begin{cases} 1 & \text{if } u \leq 0 \\ 1 - u/\theta & \text{if } 0 \leq u \leq \theta \\ 0 & \text{if } u \geq \theta. \end{cases} \tag{5.27}$$

See figure 5.3. This function is Lipschitz with $L_\phi = 1/\theta$.

We apply theorem 5.7 to the class $\phi \circ \mathcal{M}$. Working through definitions, for a sample of size m, this gives that with probability at least $1 - \delta$,

$$\mathbf{E}_{\mathcal{D}}[\phi(yf(x))] \leq \mathbf{E}_S[\phi(yf(x))] + 2R_S(\phi \circ \mathcal{M}) + \sqrt{\frac{2\ln(2/\delta)}{m}} \tag{5.28}$$

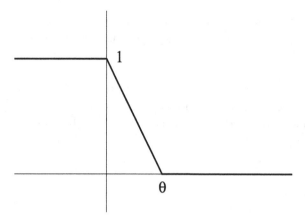

Figure 5.3
A plot of the piecewise-linear function ϕ given in equation (5.27).

for all $f \in \mathrm{co}(\mathcal{H})$. Using, in order, equations (5.25), (5.26), (5.24), and (5.23), we can compute the Rademacher complexity that appears in this expression to be

$$R_S(\phi \circ \mathcal{M}) \le L_\phi \cdot R_S(\mathcal{M})$$

$$= L_\phi \cdot R_S(\mathrm{co}(\mathcal{H}))$$

$$= L_\phi \cdot R_S(\mathcal{H})$$

$$\le \frac{1}{\theta} \cdot \sqrt{\frac{2d \ln(em/d)}{m}} \tag{5.29}$$

where d is the VC-dimension of $\mathcal{H}$, and assuming $m \ge d \ge 1$. (Alternatively, a bound in terms of $\ln |\mathcal{H}|$ could be obtained using equation (5.22).)

Note that

$$\mathbf{1}\{u \le 0\} \; \le \; \phi(u) \; \le \; \mathbf{1}\{u \le \theta\},$$

as is evident from figure 5.3, so that

$$\mathbf{Pr}_{\mathcal{D}}[yf(x) \le 0] = \mathbf{E}_{\mathcal{D}}[\mathbf{1}\{yf(x) \le 0\}] \le \mathbf{E}_{\mathcal{D}}[\phi(yf(x))]$$

and

$$\mathbf{E}_S[\phi(yf(x))] \le \mathbf{E}_S[\mathbf{1}\{yf(x) \le \theta\}] = \mathbf{Pr}_S[yf(x) \le \theta].$$

Therefore, combining with equations (5.28) and (5.29) gives

$$\mathbf{Pr}_{\mathcal{D}}[yf(x) \le 0] \le \mathbf{Pr}_S[yf(x) \le \theta] + \frac{2}{\theta} \cdot \sqrt{\frac{2d \ln(em/d)}{m}} + \sqrt{\frac{2 \ln(2/\delta)}{m}}$$

for all $f \in \text{co}(\mathcal{H})$, with probability at least $1 - \delta$. This is essentially the same as theorem 5.5 (actually, a bit better).

5.4 The Effect of Boosting on Margin Distributions

The analyses given in sections 5.2 and 5.3 apply to any voting classifier, not just those produced by boosting. In this section, we give theoretical evidence that AdaBoost is especially suited to the task of maximizing the number of training examples with large margin. Informally, this is because, at every round, AdaBoost puts the most weight on the examples with the smallest margins.

5.4.1 Bounding AdaBoost's Margins

In theorem 3.1, we proved that if the empirical γ-weak learning assumption holds or, more specifically, if the weighted training errors ϵ_t of the weak classifiers are all bounded below $\frac{1}{2} - \gamma$, then the training error of the combined classifier—that is, the fraction of training examples with margin below zero—decreases exponentially fast with the number of weak classifiers that are combined. Here, we extend this proof to give a more general bound on the fraction of training examples with margin below θ, for any $\theta \geq 0$. The resulting bound is in terms of the edges γ_t of the weak hypotheses, as well as θ, and shows that, under the same weak learning condition, if θ is not too large, then the fraction of training examples with margin below θ also decreases to zero exponentially fast with the number of rounds of boosting.

Note that theorem 3.1 is a special case of this theorem in which we set $\theta = 0$.

Theorem 5.8 Given the notation of algorithm 1.1 (p. 5), let $\gamma_t \doteq \frac{1}{2} - \epsilon_t$. Then the fraction of training examples with margin at most θ is at most

$$\prod_{t=1}^{T} \sqrt{(1 + 2\gamma_t)^{1+\theta}(1 - 2\gamma_t)^{1-\theta}}.$$

Proof Let f be as defined in equation (5.2). Note that $yf(x) \leq \theta$ if and only if

$$y \sum_{t=1}^{T} \alpha_t h_t(x) \leq \theta \sum_{t=1}^{T} \alpha_t,$$

which in turn holds if and only if

$$\exp\left(-y \sum_{t=1}^{T} \alpha_t h_t(x) + \theta \sum_{t=1}^{T} \alpha_t\right) \geq 1.$$

Thus,

$$\mathbf{1}\{yf(x) \le \theta\} \le \exp\left(-y \sum_{t=1}^{T} \alpha_t h_t(x) + \theta \sum_{t=1}^{T} \alpha_t\right).$$

Therefore, the fraction of training examples with margin at most θ is

$$\mathbf{Pr}_S[yf(x) \le \theta] = \frac{1}{m} \sum_{i=1}^{m} \mathbf{1}\{y_i f(x_i) \le \theta\}$$

$$\le \frac{1}{m} \sum_{i=1}^{m} \exp\left(-y_i \sum_{t=1}^{T} \alpha_t h_t(x_i) + \theta \sum_{t=1}^{T} \alpha_t\right)$$

$$= \frac{\exp\left(\theta \sum_{t=1}^{T} \alpha_t\right)}{m} \sum_{i=1}^{m} \exp\left(-y_i \sum_{t=1}^{T} \alpha_t h_t(x_i)\right)$$

$$= \exp\left(\theta \sum_{t=1}^{T} \alpha_t\right)\left(\prod_{t=1}^{T} Z_t\right) \tag{5.30}$$

where the last equality follows from the identical derivation used in the proof of theorem 3.1. Plugging in the values of α_t and Z_t from equation (3.9) gives the theorem. ∎

To get a feeling for this bound, consider what happens when, for all t, $\epsilon_t \le \frac{1}{2} - \gamma$ for some $\gamma > 0$. Given this assumption, we can simplify the upper bound in theorem 5.8 to

$$\left(\sqrt{(1-2\gamma)^{1-\theta}(1+2\gamma)^{1+\theta}}\right)^T.$$

When the expression inside the parentheses is strictly smaller than 1, that is, when

$$\sqrt{(1-2\gamma)^{1-\theta}(1+2\gamma)^{1+\theta}} < 1, \tag{5.31}$$

this bound implies that the fraction of training examples with $yf(x) \le \theta$ decreases to zero exponentially fast with T, and must actually be equal to zero at some point since this fraction must always be a multiple of $1/m$. Moreover, by solving for θ, we see that equation (5.31) holds if and only if

$$\theta < \Upsilon(\gamma)$$

where

$$\Upsilon(\gamma) \doteq \frac{-\ln(1-4\gamma^2)}{\ln\left(\frac{1+2\gamma}{1-2\gamma}\right)}. \tag{5.32}$$

This function is plotted in figure 5.4, where it can be seen that $\gamma \le \Upsilon(\gamma) \le 2\gamma$ for $0 \le \gamma \le \frac{1}{2}$, and that $\Upsilon(\gamma)$ is close to γ when γ is small. So, to rephrase, we have shown that

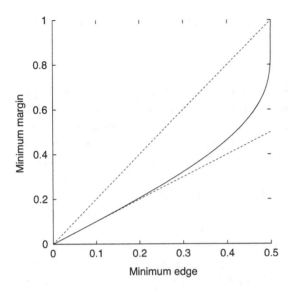

Figure 5.4
A plot of the minimum margin $\Upsilon(\gamma)$ guaranteed for AdaBoost as a function of the minimum edge γ. Also plotted are the linear lower and upper bounds, γ and 2γ.

if every weak hypothesis has edge at least γ (as will happen when the empirical γ-weak learning assumption holds), then in the limit of a large number of rounds T, all examples will eventually have margin at least $\Upsilon(\gamma) \geq \gamma$. In this sense, $\Upsilon(\gamma)$ bounds the minimum margin as a function of the minimum edge.

Thus, when the weak classifiers are consistently better than random guessing, the margins of the training examples are guaranteed to be large after a sufficient number of boosting iterations. Moreover, we see that there is a direct relationship at work here: The higher the edges γ_t of the weak classifiers, the higher the margins that will be attained by Ada-Boost's combined classifier. This tight connection between edges and margins, which arose in section 3.2, turns out to be rooted in the game-theoretic view of boosting which will be explored in chapter 6.

This also suggests that stronger base classifiers, such as decision trees, which produce higher accuracy prediction rules, and therefore larger edges, will also yield larger margins and less overfitting, exactly as observed in the example in section 5.1. Conversely, weaker base classifiers, such as decision stumps, tend to produce smaller edges, and therefore also smaller margins, as can be seen, for instance, in the margin distributions shown in figure 5.5 on a benchmark dataset using stumps (see further discussion of this figure below). On the other hand, stronger base classifiers generally have higher complexity than weaker ones, and this complexity, according both to intuition and to the bounds in theorems 5.1 and 5.5, is likely to be a detriment to performance. Thus, we are again faced with the fundamental trade-off between complexity (of the base classifiers) and fit to the data (as measured by their edges).

5.4.2 More Aggressive Margin Maximization

Theorem 5.8 shows that, under the empirical γ-weak learning assumption, all training examples will eventually have margin at least $\Upsilon(\gamma) \geq \gamma$. This is encouraging since the analysis in section 5.2 suggests that larger margins are conducive to better generalization. However, this turns out not to be the best that can be done. Although in practice AdaBoost often seems to achieve the largest possible minimum margin (that is, the smallest of the margins of the training examples), theoretically it can be shown that $\Upsilon(\gamma)$ is the best general bound that can be proved on the minimum margin attained by AdaBoost under the γ-weak learning assumption (see exercise 5.1). In contrast, it turns out that other methods can achieve a margin of 2γ, which is roughly twice as large as $\Upsilon(\gamma)$ when γ is small.

In fact, the proof of theorem 5.8 can be used to derive variations of AdaBoost for more directly maximizing the number of training examples with margin above some prespecified level θ. AdaBoost, as was seen in the proof of theorem 3.1, was derived for the purpose of minimizing the usual training error $\mathbf{Pr}_S[yf(x) \leq 0]$. Suppose instead that our goal is to minimize $\mathbf{Pr}_S[yf(x) \leq \theta]$ for a chosen value of θ. Then equation (5.30) combined with equation (3.8) tells us generally that

$$\mathbf{Pr}_S[yf(x) \leq \theta] \leq \prod_{t=1}^{T} \left[e^{(\theta-1)\alpha_t} \left(\tfrac{1}{2} + \gamma_t \right) + e^{(\theta+1)\alpha_t} \left(\tfrac{1}{2} - \gamma_t \right) \right]. \tag{5.33}$$

Rather than choosing α_t as in AdaBoost, we can instead select α_t to minimize equation (5.33) directly. Doing so gives

$$\alpha_t = \frac{1}{2} \ln \left(\frac{1 + 2\gamma_t}{1 - 2\gamma_t} \right) - \frac{1}{2} \ln \left(\frac{1 + \theta}{1 - \theta} \right), \tag{5.34}$$

which is smaller than the AdaBoost choice by the additive constant appearing as the right-most term of this expression. Assuming each $\alpha_t \geq 0$ (which is equivalent to assuming $\gamma_t \geq \theta/2$), we can plug this choice into equation (5.33), which gives a bound that can be written succinctly as

$$\mathbf{Pr}_S[yf(x) \leq \theta] \leq \exp \left(-\sum_{t=1}^{T} \mathrm{RE}_b \left(\frac{1}{2} + \frac{\theta}{2} \ \| \ \frac{1}{2} + \gamma_t \right) \right). \tag{5.35}$$

Here, $\mathrm{RE}_b (p \ \| \ q)$, for $p, q \in [0, 1]$, is the *(binary) relative entropy*:

$$\mathrm{RE}_b (p \ \| \ q) = p \ln \left(\frac{p}{q} \right) + (1 - p) \ln \left(\frac{1 - p}{1 - q} \right), \tag{5.36}$$

which is really just a special case of the more general relative entropy encountered in section 6.2.3 applied to Bernoulli distributions $(p, 1 - p)$ and $(q, 1 - q)$. As in the general case, binary relative entropy is always nonnegative, and is equal to zero if and only if $p = q$. Furthermore, it is increasing in q for $q \geq p$. See section 8.1.2 for further background.

So if θ is chosen ahead of time, and if the γ-weak learning assumption holds for some $\gamma > \theta/2$, then the fraction of training examples with margin at most θ will be no more than

$$\exp\left(-T \cdot \mathrm{RE}_b\left(\frac{1}{2} + \frac{\theta}{2} \;\|\; \frac{1}{2} + \gamma\right)\right),$$

which tends to zero exponentially fast in the number of rounds T. Thus, when T is sufficiently large, all of the training examples will have margin at least θ. If γ is known ahead of time, then θ can be chosen to be slightly smaller than 2γ. This shows that, with additional information regarding the edges, AdaBoost can be modified so that all training examples will have margins arbitrarily close to 2γ, roughly twice the bound that we derived from theorem 5.8 for (unmodified) AdaBoost, and also the best bound attainable by any algorithm, as will be discussed in section 5.4.3.

When γ is not known ahead of time, methods have been developed, such as arc-gv and AdaBoost$_\nu^*$, for adjusting θ dynamically so as to achieve the same bound on the margins without such prior information (see exercise 5.3). In this fashion, AdaBoost can be modified so that the minimum margin provably converges to the largest value possible. Theorems 5.1 and 5.5, which say roughly that larger margins are better, suggest that this should benefit the algorithm's performance. However, in practice such methods often fail to give improvement, apparently for two reasons. First, by attempting to more aggressively maximize the minimum margin, the base learning algorithm is often forced to return base classifiers of higher complexity so that the complexity terms ($\lg |\mathcal{H}|$ or d) appearing in these theorems will effectively be larger, counteracting improvements in the margin. This can especially be a problem with very flexible base classifiers, such as decision trees, which can vary considerably in complexity based on overall size and depth.

For instance, this can be seen in table 5.1, which shows the results of running AdaBoost and arc-gv on five benchmark datasets using the decision-tree algorithm CART as base learner. Arc-gv consistently gives larger minimum margins than AdaBoost, but also gives consistently higher test error. Although an attempt was made in these experiments to control complexity by forcing CART always to return trees with a fixed number of nodes, a more careful examination of the results shows that when run with arc-gv, CART is likely to produce deeper, skinnier trees which, it can be argued, tend to be more specialized in their predictions and thus more prone to overfitting.

Even when the base-classifier complexity can be controlled (for instance, by using decision stumps), there may be a second reason for a lack of improvement. Although such methods may succeed at increasing the *minimum* margin among all training examples, this increase may come at the expense of the vast majority of the other training examples,

Table 5.1
Test errors (in percent), minimum margins, and average tree depths, averaged over ten trials, for AdaBoost and arc-gv, run for 500 rounds using CART decision trees pruned to 16-leaf nodes as weak classifiers

	Test Error		Minimum Margin		Tree Depth	
	arc-gv	AdaBoost	arc-gv	AdaBoost	arc-gv	AdaBoost
breast cancer	3.04	2.46	0.64	0.61	9.71	7.86
ionosphere	7.69	3.46	0.97	0.77	8.89	7.23
ocr 17	1.76	0.96	0.95	0.88	7.47	7.41
ocr 49	2.38	2.04	0.53	0.49	7.39	6.70
splice	3.45	3.18	0.46	0.42	7.12	6.67

so that although the minimum margin increases, the bulk of the margin distribution actually decreases. Note that the bounds in theorems 5.1 and 5.5 depend on the *entire* margin distribution, not just the minimum margin.

For instance, figure 5.5 shows the margin distributions produced when running AdaBoost and arc-gv using decision stumps as the weak hypotheses on one of the benchmark datasets. Arc-gv does indeed achieve higher *minimum* margin (-0.01 for arc-gv versus -0.06 for AdaBoost), but, as the figure shows, the bulk of the training examples have substantially higher margin for AdaBoost.

5.4.3   A Necessary and Sufficient Condition for Weak Learnability

In section 3.2, we gave a sufficient condition for the empirical γ-weak learning assumption to hold, namely, that the training data be linearly separable with margin 2γ, meaning that there exists some linear threshold function (that is, some combined classifier) under which every training example has margin at least 2γ. Now we have the tools to prove the exact converse, and to show that this condition is both sufficient and necessary. Suppose the empirical γ-weak learning assumption holds. Then the argument above shows that modified AdaBoost, for any $\theta < 2\gamma$, will find a combined classifier under which all training examples have margin at least θ, in other words, witnessing that the data is linearly separable with margin θ. Since θ can be made arbitrarily close to 2γ, this essentially proves the converse. Thus, there exists a combined classifier for which every training example has margin at least 2γ if and only if for every distribution over the training set there exists a weak hypothesis with edge at least γ.

Furthermore, we can define a natural notion of *optimal margin*, meaning the largest value θ^* such that for some combined classifier, every training example has margin at least θ^*. And we can define a corresponding notion of *optimal edge*, meaning the largest value γ^* such that for every distribution, there is some weak hypothesis with edge at least γ^*. (Like the other concepts in this section, both of these are defined with respect to a particular dataset and hypothesis space.) Then the equivalence outlined above implies further that the optimal edge is equal to some value γ^* if and only if the optimal margin is $2\gamma^*$.

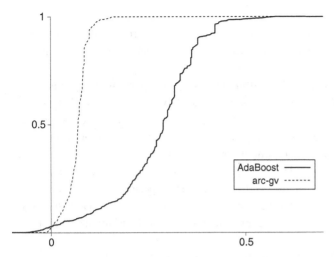

Figure 5.5
Cumulative margins for AdaBoost and arc-gv for the breast cancer dataset after 100 rounds of boosting on decision
stumps.

Here, we again encounter the inseparable relationship between edges and margins.
Understood more deeply, this equivalence between margins and edges, and between linear
separability and the empirical weak learning assumption, turns out to be a direct consequence
of fundamental results of game theory, as will be seen in chapter 6.

5.5   Bias, Variance, and Stability

In this chapter, we have presented an explanation of AdaBoost's successes and failures in
terms of the margins theory. One of the main alternative explanations for the improvements
achieved by voting classifiers is based instead on separating the expected generalization
error of a classifier into a *bias* term and a *variance* term. While the details of these definitions
differ from author to author, they are all attempts to capture the following quantities: The
bias term measures the *persistent* error of the learning algorithm, the error that would remain
even if we had an infinite number of independently trained classifiers. The variance term
measures the error that is due to *fluctuations* that are a part of generating a single classifier.
The idea is that by averaging over many classifiers, one can reduce the variance term and
in that way reduce the expected error. In this section, we discuss a few of the strengths
and weaknesses of bias-variance theory as an explanation for the performance of voting
methods, especially boosting.

The origins of bias-variance analysis are in quadratic regression where performance is
measured using the squared error (see chapter 7). Averaging several independently trained

regression functions will never increase the expected error. This encouraging fact is nicely reflected in the bias-variance separation of the expected quadratic error. Both bias and variance are always nonnegative, and averaging decreases the variance term without changing the bias term.

One would naturally hope that this beautiful analysis would carry over from quadratic regression to classification. Unfortunately, taking the majority vote over several classification rules can sometimes result in an *increase* in the expected classification error (and we will shortly see an example of how voting can make things worse). This simple observation suggests that it may be inherently more difficult or even impossible to find a bias-variance decomposition for classification as natural and satisfying as in quadratic regression. This difficulty is reflected in the myriad definitions that have been proposed for bias and variance.

The principle of variance reduction is the basis of other voting methods, notably *bagging*. This is a procedure quite similar to boosting, but one in which the distributions D_t are fixed for all iterations to be uniform over the training set, and resampling, as in section 3.4.1, is always employed so that the base classifiers are each trained on so-called *bootstrap samples* of the data. That is, on each round t, the base learner is trained on a dataset consisting of m examples, each selected uniformly at random from the original dataset (with replacement, of course). Thus, some examples will be included more than once in a given dataset, while more than a third, on average, will be omitted entirely.

The notion of variance certainly seems to be helpful in understanding bagging; empirically, bagging appears to be most effective for learning algorithms with large variance which are unstable in the sense that small changes in the data can cause large changes in the learned classifier. In fact, variance has sometimes been *defined* to be the amount of decrease in error effected by bagging a large number of base classifiers under idealized conditions. This ideal situation is one in which the bootstrap samples used in bagging faithfully approximate truly independent samples. However, this assumption can fail to hold in practice, in which case bagging may not perform as well as expected, even when variance dominates the error of the base learning algorithm.

It has been argued that boosting is also primarily a variance-reducing procedure. Some of the evidence for this comes from the observed effectiveness of boosting when used with decision-tree learning algorithms like C4.5 or CART, algorithms known empirically to have high variance. As the error of these algorithms is mostly due to variance, it is not surprising that the reduction in the error is primarily due to a reduction in the variance. However, boosting can also be highly effective when used with learning algorithms whose error tends to be dominated by bias rather than variance. Indeed, boosting is intended for use with quite weak base learning algorithms, such as decision stumps, which often have high bias and low variance.

To illustrate this point, table 5.2 shows the results of running boosting and bagging on three artificial datasets on training sets of size 300. For the base learning algorithm, both the decision-tree algorithm C4.5 (section 1.3) and decision stumps (section 3.4.2) were used.

Table 5.2
Results of bias-variance experiments using boosting and bagging on three synthetic datasets

| | | Kong & Dietterich Definitions | | | | | | Breiman Definitions | | | | | |
| | | Stumps | | | C4.5 | | | Stumps | | | C4.5 | | |
Name		—	Boost	Bag	—	Boost	Bag	—	Boost	Bag	—	Boost	Bag
twonorm	bias	2.5	0.6	2.0	0.5	0.2	0.5	1.3	0.3	1.1	0.3	0.1	0.3
	variance	28.5	2.3	17.3	18.7	1.8	5.4	29.6	2.6	18.2	19.0	1.9	5.6
	error	33.3	5.3	21.7	21.6	4.4	8.3	33.3	5.3	21.7	21.6	4.4	8.3
threenorm	bias	24.5	6.3	21.6	4.7	2.9	5.0	14.2	4.1	13.8	2.6	1.9	3.1
	variance	6.9	5.1	4.8	16.7	5.2	6.8	17.2	7.3	12.6	18.8	6.3	8.6
	error	41.9	22.0	36.9	31.9	18.6	22.3	41.9	22.0	36.9	31.9	18.6	22.3
ringnorm	bias	46.9	4.1	46.9	2.0	0.7	1.7	32.3	2.7	37.6	1.1	0.4	1.1
	variance	−7.9	6.6	−7.1	15.5	2.3	6.3	6.7	8.0	2.2	16.4	2.6	6.9
	error	40.6	12.2	41.4	19.0	4.5	9.5	40.6	12.2	41.4	19.0	4.5	9.5

For each dataset and each learning method, bias, variance, and generalization error rate were estimated, then reported in percent, using two sets of definitions for bias and variance. Both C4.5 and decision stumps were used as base learning algorithms. Columns headed with a dash indicate that the base learning algorithm was run by itself.

Bias, variance, and average generalization error were estimated by rerunning each algorithm many times. Two different definitions of bias and variance were used, one due to Kong and Dieterich, and the other due to Breiman. (See the bibliographic notes for references with details.)

Clearly, these experiments show that boosting is doing more than reducing variance. For instance, on the "ringnorm" dataset, boosting decreases the overall error of the stump algorithm from 40.6% to 12.2%, but *increases* the variance from -7.9% to 6.6% using Kong and Dieterich's definitions, or from 6.7% to 8.0% using Breiman's definitions. The decrease in error is instead due to a very substantial drop in the bias.

The view of boosting as mainly a variance-reducing procedure predicts that boosting will fail when combined with a "stable" learning algorithm with low variance. This is clearly false, as the experiments above demonstrate. The theory presented in this chapter suggests a different characterization of the cases in which boosting might fail. Theorems 5.1 and 5.5, together with theorem 5.8, predict that boosting can perform poorly only when either (1) there is insufficient training data relative to the complexity of the base classifiers, or (2) the training errors of the base classifiers (the ϵ_t's in theorem 5.8) become too large too quickly.

Moreover, although bagging was originally introduced as a method based on variance reduction, it too can be analyzed using the part of the margins theory developed in section 5.2 since this theory is generally applicable to any voting method, including bagging. Such an analysis would, as usual, be in terms of the margin distribution, as well as base-classifier complexity and training set size, and would not depend on the number of rounds of bagging. In the case of bagging, the margin of a training example is simply a measure of the fraction of selected base classifiers that correctly classify it, a quantity that must converge after a large number of rounds to the probability of a base classifier, randomly generated according to the bootstrap process, correctly classifying it. Thus, this analysis predicts little or no overfitting, while providing nonasymptotic bounds on performance in terms of intuitive quantities. As an example, figure 5.6 shows the learning curves and margin distribution when bagging is used instead of boosting with the same base learner and dataset as in section 5.1, for comparison with figures 1.7 and 5.2. As is typical, bagging's margin distribution has a qualitatively different form than boosting's, but nevertheless shows that a fairly small fraction of the examples have low margin (though not as few as with boosting, in this case).

The bias-variance interpretation of boosting and other voting methods is closely related to an intuition that averaging (or really voting) many classifiers is sure to lead to better predictions than the individual base classifiers, just as one expects that the average of many estimates (say, of the bias of a coin) will be better than the individual estimates. This view is supported by a supposition that a combined classifier formed by voting does not have higher complexity than the base classifiers. Unfortunately, these intuitions do not hold true in general for classification problems. A majority-vote classifier may be substantially more complex and prone to overfitting than its constituent classifiers, which might be very simple.

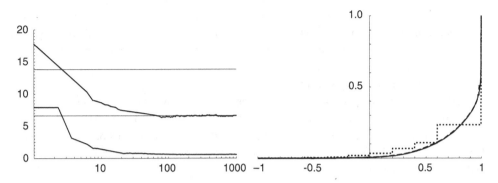

Figure 5.6
Results of running bagging on C4.5 on the letter dataset. The figure on the left shows the test (top) and training (bottom) percent error rates for bagging as a function of the number of rounds. The figure on the right shows the margin distribution graph. See the analogous figures 1.7 and 5.2 for further description. (Reprinted with permission of the Institute of Mathematical Statistics.)

As an example, suppose we use base classifiers that are delta-functions which predict $+1$ on a single point in the input space and -1 everywhere else, or vice versa (-1 on one point and $+1$ elsewhere), or that are constant functions predicting -1 everywhere or $+1$ everywhere. For any training set of size m, assuming the same instance never appears twice with different labels, and for any distribution D over this set, there must always exist a delta-function with error (with respect to D) at most

$$\frac{1}{2} - \frac{1}{2m}.$$

This is because one training example (x_i, y_i) must have probability at least $1/m$ under D, so an appropriately constructed delta-function will classify x_i correctly, as well as at least half of the probability mass of the remaining examples. Thus, the empirical γ-weak learning assumption holds for $\gamma = 1/(2m)$, which implies that, by theorem 3.1, AdaBoost will eventually construct a combined classifier that correctly classifies all m training examples.

As discussed in chapter 2, the very fact that we can easily fit such a rule to *any* training set implies that we do not expect the rule to be very good on new test examples outside of the training set. In other words, the complexity of these voting rules is too large, relative to the size of the sample, to make them useful. In fact, exactly this argument shows that their VC-dimension is infinite. Note that this complexity is entirely the result of voting. Each one of the delta-functions is very simple (the VC-dimension of this class is exactly 3), and would likely underfit most datasets. By voting many such simple rules, we end up with a combined classifier that is instead overly complex, one that would certainly overfit nearly any dataset.

Our analysis shows that AdaBoost controls the complexity of the combined classifier by striving for one with large margins. Indeed, when large margins can be attained, theorems 5.1 and 5.5 show that AdaBoost will perform as if the complexity of the combined classifier is on the same order as that of the *base* classifiers, so that the penalty for forming a majority vote of a large number of these is minimized.

AdaBoost's predicted poor performance in the example above is entirely consistent with our margin-based analysis; if AdaBoost is run for a long time, as noted earlier, all of the training examples will be correctly classified, but only with tiny margins of size $O(1/m)$, far too small to predict good generalization performance. (To be meaningful, theorems 5.1 and 5.5 require margins of size at least $\Omega(1/\sqrt{m})$.)

5.6   Relation to Support-Vector Machines

Boosting is not the only classification method that seems to operate on the principle of (approximate) margin maximization. In particular, *support-vector machines (SVMs)*, which are based explicitly on this principle, are currently very popular due to their effectiveness for general machine-learning tasks. Although boosting and SVMs are both learning methods based on maximization of quantities referred to loosely as "margins," we will see in this section how they differ significantly in important respects.

5.6.1   Brief Overview of SVMs

Since a full treatment of SVMs is well beyond the scope of this book, we give only an overview of the main ingredients of this approach.

Let us for now suppose that the instances **x** being classified are actually points in Euclidean space $\mathbb{R}^n$. Thus, the learner is given $(\mathbf{x}_1, y_1), \ldots, (\mathbf{x}_m, y_m)$ where $\mathbf{x}_i \in \mathbb{R}^n$ and $y_i \in \{-1, +1\}$. For instance, we might be given the examples in figure 5.7, where $n = 2$. Already we see an important difference from boosting: SVMs are based on a strongly geometrical view of the data.

Given such data, the first idea of SVMs is to find a linear classifier, or linear threshold function, that correctly labels the data. In general, if there is even one, then there are likely to be many such linear classifiers. Rather than choosing one arbitrarily, in SVMs, we choose the hyperplane which separates the positive examples from the negative examples, and is maximally far from the closest data point. For instance, in figure 5.7 we might find a hyperplane (in this case, a line) like the one shown so as to maximize the indicated separation distance. Thus, not only do we want to correctly classify the training points, we also want those training points to be as far from the dividing boundary as possible.

More formally, a separating hyperplane is given by the equation[2] $\mathbf{w} \cdot \mathbf{x} = 0$, where **w**, without loss of generality, has unit length ($\|\mathbf{w}\|_2 = 1$). An instance **x** is classified by such a

---

2. We have simplified our discussion by assuming that the hyperplane passes through the origin.

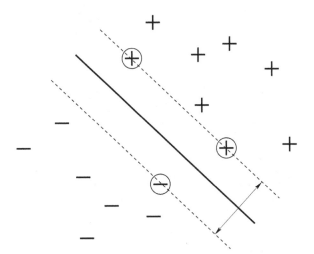

Figure 5.7
Sample data in two dimensions, and the separating hyperplane (a line in this case) that might be found by SVMs in this case. The *support vectors*, the examples closest to the hyperplane, have been circled.

hyperplane according to which side it falls on, that is, using the prediction rule

$\text{sign}(\mathbf{w} \cdot \mathbf{x})$.

With respect to the hyperplane defined by $\mathbf{w}$, the (signed) distance of an example from the separating hyperplane is called the *margin*. As we will see, it is related to, but distinct from, the margin used in boosting. The margin of example $(\mathbf{x}, y)$ can be computed to be $y(\mathbf{w} \cdot \mathbf{x})$. The margin of an entire training set is the minimum of the margins of the individual training examples, that is, $\min_i y_i(\mathbf{w} \cdot \mathbf{x}_i)$. The idea then is to find the hyperplane $\mathbf{w}$ that maximizes this minimum margin.

Of course, it is well known that linear threshold functions are limited in their expressiveness, especially in low dimensions. Nevertheless, data that starts out being linearly inseparable in its original low-dimensional space may become separable if mapped into a higher-dimensional space.

For instance, the data in figure 5.8 is clearly linearly inseparable. However, suppose we map these two-dimensional points $\mathbf{x} = \langle x_1, x_2 \rangle$ into $\mathbb{R}^6$ by the map

$$\mathbf{h}(\mathbf{x}) = \mathbf{h}(x_1, x_2) \doteq \langle 1, x_1, x_2, x_1 x_2, x_1^2, x_2^2 \rangle.$$

Then a linear hyperplane defined on these mapped points has the form

$$\mathbf{w} \cdot \mathbf{h}(\mathbf{x}) = w_1 + w_2 x_1 + w_3 x_2 + w_4 x_1 x_2 + w_5 x_1^2 + w_6 x_2^2 = 0$$

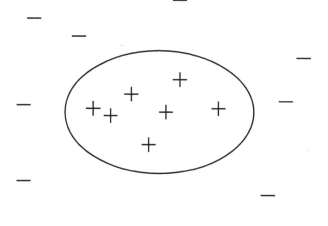

Figure 5.8
Data in two dimensions that cannot be linearly separated, but can be separated using an ellipse or, equivalently, a hyperplane following projection into six dimensions.

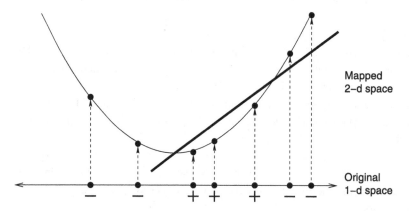

Figure 5.9
In their original, one-dimensional space, the seven points comprising this dataset are evidently linearly inseparable. However, when each point x is mapped to the two-dimensional vector $\langle x, x^2 \rangle$, that is, onto the parabola shown in the figure, the data now becomes linearly separable.

for scalars $w_1, \ldots, w_6$. In other words, a linear hyperplane in the mapped space can be used to represent any conic section in the original space, including, for instance, the ellipse in figure 5.8, which clearly does separate the positive and negative examples. An even simpler example is shown in figure 5.9.

Thus, in general, the instances $\mathbf{x} \in \mathbb{R}^n$ may be mapped to a higher-dimensional space $\mathbb{R}^N$ using a map $\mathbf{h}$, simply by replacing all appearances of $\mathbf{x}$ in the algorithm with $\mathbf{h}(\mathbf{x})$. In this example, $n = 2$ dimensions were mapped to $N = 6$. In practice, however, points starting out in a reasonable number of dimensions (say, 100) can easily end up being mapped into an extremely large number of dimensions (perhaps in the billions, or worse), so this would seem to be a very expensive computational operation.

Fortunately, in many cases a remarkable technique based on *kernels* can be applied to make for computational feasibility. It turns out that the only operation that is needed to implement SVMs is inner product between pairs of (mapped) points, that is, $\mathbf{h}(\mathbf{x}) \cdot \mathbf{h}(\mathbf{z})$. This sometimes can be done very efficiently. For instance, we can modify the example above slightly so that

$$\mathbf{h}(\mathbf{x}) = \mathbf{h}(x_1, x_2) \doteq \langle 1, \sqrt{2}x_1, \sqrt{2}x_2, \sqrt{2}x_1x_2, x_1^2, x_2^2 \rangle.$$

The insertion of a few constants does not change the expressiveness of the linear threshold functions that can be computed using this mapping, but now it can be verified that

$$\mathbf{h}(\mathbf{x}) \cdot \mathbf{h}(\mathbf{z}) = 1 + 2x_1z_1 + 2x_2z_2 + 2x_1x_2z_1z_2 + x_1^2z_1^2 + x_2^2z_2^2$$

$$= (1 + \mathbf{x} \cdot \mathbf{z})^2. \tag{5.37}$$

Thus, the inner product of mapped points can be computed *without ever expanding explicitly* into the higher-dimensional space, but rather simply by taking inner product in the *original* low-dimensional space, adding 1, and squaring.

The function on the right-hand side of equation (5.37) is called a *kernel function*, and there are many other such functions which make it possible to implement SVMs even when mapping into very high-dimensional spaces. The computational savings effected by this trick can be tremendous. For instance, generalizing the example above, if we wanted to add all terms up to degree k (rather than degree 2, as above), so that we are mapping from n dimensions to $O(n^k)$ dimensions, we can compute inner products in this very high-dimensional space using a kernel identical to the one in equation (5.37), but with the exponent 2 replaced by k; this kernel can be computed in $O(n + \ln k)$ time. Using kernels to quickly compute inner products in very high-dimensional spaces is the second key ingredient of SVMs.

Many types of kernels have been developed; the polynomial kernels above are just one example. In fact, kernels can even be defined on objects other than vectors, such as strings and trees. Because the original objects need not be vectors, we therefore revert in the following to writing instances as the more generic x rather than $\mathbf{x}$.

Although the computational difficulty of mapping to a very high-dimensional space can sometimes be made tractable, there remains the statistical "curse of dimensionality," which suggests that generalization based on high-dimensional data (relative to the number of training examples) is likely to be poor. Indeed, the VC-dimension of general linear threshold functions in $\mathbb{R}^N$ is equal to N (see lemma 4.1), suggesting that the number of training examples must be on the same order as the number of dimensions. However, the VC-dimension of linear threshold functions with large margin may be much lower. In particular, suppose without loss of generality that all examples are mapped inside a unit ball so that $\|\mathbf{h}(x)\|_2 \leq 1$. Then it can be shown that the VC-dimension of linear threshold functions with margin $\gamma > 0$ is at most $1/\gamma^2$, regardless of the number of dimensions. This suggests that generalization may be possible even in extremely high-dimensional spaces, provided it is possible to achieve large margins.

5.6.2 Comparison to Boosting

When using a mapping function $\mathbf{h}$ as above, the linear classifier produced by SVMs has the form

$$\text{sign}(\mathbf{w} \cdot \mathbf{h}(x)).$$

AdaBoost, on the other hand, computes a final classifier of the form given in equation (5.3):

$$\text{sign}\left(\sum_{t=1}^{T} a_t h_t(x)\right),$$

where the a_t's, as in equation (5.1), are nonnegative and sum to 1. In fact, with a little bit more notation, these can be seen to be of exactly the same form as in SVMs. For simplicity, let us assume that the base-classifier space $\mathcal{H}$ is finite, and consists of the functions $\hbar_1, \ldots, \hbar_N$. Then we can define a vector

$$\mathbf{h}(x) \doteq \langle \hbar_1(x), \ldots, \hbar_N(x) \rangle.$$

Although $\mathcal{H}$ is finite, it will typically be huge, so $\mathbf{h}(x)$ is an extremely high-dimensional vector. On each round t of boosting, one coordinate j_t of this vector is selected corresponding to the chosen base classifier $h_t = \hbar_{j_t}$. By setting

$$w_j = \sum_{t:j_t=j} a_t$$

for $j = 1, \ldots, N$, we can also define a weight vector $\mathbf{w} \in \mathbb{R}^N$ in terms of the a_t's so that

$$\mathbf{w} \cdot \mathbf{h}(x) = \sum_{t=1}^{T} a_t h_t(x).$$

Thus, AdaBoost's final classifier now has the identical form as SVMs, both being linear threshold functions, though over rather different spaces. This representation also emphasizes the fact that AdaBoost, like SVMs, employs a mapping $\mathbf{h}$ into a very high-dimensional space; indeed, as already noted, the number of dimensions of the mapped space is equal to the cardinality of the *entire* space of base classifiers—typically, an extremely large space.

As noted earlier, SVMs and boosting can both be understood and analyzed as methods for maximizing some notion of margin. However, the precise forms of margin used for the two methods are different in subtle but important ways. The margin used in SVMs for an example (x, y) is defined to be $y(\mathbf{w} \cdot \mathbf{h}(x))$. The margin used in boosting would appear to be identical:

$$yf(x) = y \sum_{t=1}^{T} a_t h_t(x) = y(\mathbf{w} \cdot \mathbf{h}(x)).$$

However, there is a major difference not revealed by the notation. In analyzing SVMs, we assumed that $\mathbf{w}$ has unit Euclidean length (so that $\|\mathbf{w}\|_2 = 1$) and, moreover, that $\mathbf{h}$ maps into the unit ball so that $\|\mathbf{h}(x)\|_2 \le 1$ for all x. In contrast, for boosting we found it natural to normalize the weights a_t so that $\sum_{t=1}^{T} |a_t| = 1$, that is, so that $\|\mathbf{w}\|_1 = 1$. Further, the coordinates of the mapping $\mathbf{h}$ correspond to base classifiers, each with range $\{-1, +1\}$. Thus,

$$\max_j |\hbar_j(x)| = 1$$

or, more succinctly, $\|\mathbf{h}(x)\|_\infty = 1$ for all x. (See appendix A.2 for more about ℓ_p-norms.)

Thus, both definitions of margin assume that the weight vector $\mathbf{w}$ and the map $\mathbf{h}$ are bounded, but using different norms. The SVM approach, being intrinsically geometrical, uses Euclidean norms, while boosting utilizes the ℓ_1- and ℓ_∞-norms.

This choice of norms can make a big difference. For instance, suppose all the components of $\mathbf{h}(x)$ have range $\{-1, +1\}$, and that the weight vector $\mathbf{w}$ assigns unit weights to k of the N coordinates (where k is odd), and zero weight to all others. In other words, $\text{sign}(\mathbf{w} \cdot \mathbf{h}(x))$ is computing a simple majority vote of k of the dimensions or base classifiers. Although overly simplistic, this is suggestive of learning problems in which only a subset of a very large number of features/dimensions/base classifiers are actually relevant to what is being learned. Normalizing appropriately, we see that the boosting (ℓ_1/ℓ_∞) margin of this classifier is $1/k$, which is reasonable if k is not too large. Also, this margin is independent of the number of dimensions N. On the other hand, the SVM (ℓ_2/ℓ_2) margin would be $1/\sqrt{kN}$, which could be far worse if N is very large. Other examples in which the SVM margin is far superior can also be constructed.

There is another important difference between boosting and SVMs. Both aim to find a linear classifier in a very high-dimensional space. However, computationally they are quite different in how they manage to do this: SVMs use the method of kernels to perform computations in the high-dimensional space, while boosting relies on a base learning algorithm that explores the high-dimensional space one coordinate at a time.

Finally, we point out that the SVM approach is predicated on explicitly maximizing the *minimum* margin (although some variants relax this objective somewhat). AdaBoost, as discussed in section 5.4, does not provably maximize the minimum margin, but only tends to increase the overall distribution of margins, a property that empirically seems sometimes to be advantageous.

5.7 Practical Applications of Margins

Although we have focused largely on their theoretical utility, in practical terms margins can be quite useful as a reasonable measure of confidence. In this section, we describe two applications of this principle.

5.7.1 Rejecting Low-Confidence Predictions for Higher Accuracy

As previously discussed, the larger the magnitude of the margin, the greater our confidence in the predictions of the combined classifier. Intuitively, and also in line with our earlier theoretical development, we expect such high-confidence examples to have a correspondingly greater chance of being correctly classified. Moreover, note that the absolute margin—that is, $|yf(x)| = |f(x)|$—can be computed without knowledge of the label y. As we will see, these properties can be very useful in applications that demand high accuracy predictions, even if they are limited to only a part of the domain, since such settings require the use of a classifier that "knows what it knows" (or does not know).

For example, consider a classifier that is used as part of a spoken-dialogue system to categorize verbal utterances according to their meaning (see section 10.3). Knowing that a particular classification was made with high confidence means that it can be relied upon by the rest of the system. On the other hand, a low-confidence classification can be handled accordingly, for instance, by asking the user to repeat a response or to provide further information. Likewise, a classifier designed for the automatic categorization of news articles by major topic can be used and trusted when producing high-confidence predictions, while articles classified with low confidence can be handed off to a human for manual annotation. In other tasks, like spam filtering, we may instead want to treat all low-confidence predictions as ham so that only email messages that are predicted spam with high confidence are filtered out, thus minimizing the number of legitimate emails mistaken for spam.

In general, we might select a threshold so that all predictions with absolute margin above this value are trusted for their "high" confidence, while those with "low" confidence, below the chosen threshold, are rejected, for instance, in one of the ways described above. The particular threshold value can be chosen based on performance on held-out data not used

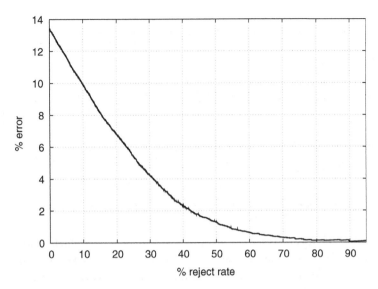

Figure 5.10
The trade-off between error and reject rate on the census dataset. One point is plotted for every possible margin threshold with the *x*-coordinate indicating the fraction of test examples rejected (that is, with absolute margin below threshold), and the *y*-coordinate giving the error as measured over the part of the test set not rejected (with margin above threshold).

for training, taking into account the requirements of the application. Naturally, the more examples rejected, the higher the accuracy on the examples that remain.

Figure 5.10 shows this trade-off on actual data. In this case, the instances are persons from a 1994 US Census database, each described by age, education, marital status, and so on. The problem is to predict whether or not a given individual's income exceeds \$50,000. In this experiment, AdaBoost was run on 10,000 training examples using decision stumps for 1000 rounds. (Also, real-valued weak hypotheses were employed, as described in chapter 9.)

On the entire test set of 20,000 examples, the overall test error was 13.4%. However, as the figure shows, a much lower error can be attained by rejecting a fraction of the test data. For instance, when the 20% of the test set with smallest absolute margins are rejected, the error on the remaining 80% drops by about half to 6.8%. A test error below 2% can be achieved at the cost of rejecting about 43% of the test examples. Thus, quite high accuracy can be attained on an identifiable and nonnegligible fraction of the dataset.

5.7.2   Active Learning

We turn next to a second application of margins. Throughout this book, we have taken for granted an adequate supply of labeled examples. In many applications, however, although there may well be an abundance of *un*labeled examples, we may find that reliable labels

Algorithm 5.1
An active learning method based on AdaBoost, using the absolute margin as a measure of confidence

---

Given: large set of unlabeled examples
       limited annotation resources.
Initialize: choose an initial set of random examples for labeling.
Repeat:

- Train AdaBoost on all examples labeled so far.
- Obtain (normalized) final hypothesis $f(x)$ as in equation (5.2).
- Choose the k unlabeled examples x with minimum $|f(x)|$ for labeling.

---

are rather scarce due to the difficulty, expense, or time involved in obtaining human annotations. For example, in a vision task like face detection (section 3.4.3), it is not hard to gather thousands or millions of images, for instance, off the Internet. However, manually identifying all of the faces (and non-faces) in a large collection of images can be exceedingly slow and tedious. Likewise, in the kind of spoken-dialogue task mentioned earlier, obtaining recordings of utterances is relatively cheap; the expense is in annotating those recordings according to their proper categorization.

In such a setting where we have a large number of unlabeled examples but limited resources for obtaining labels, it makes sense to carefully and selectively choose which examples will be labeled, an approach known as *active learning*. Ideally, we would like to choose examples whose labels will be most "informative" and most helpful in driving the learning process forward. These are generally difficult notions to quantify and measure, especially without knowledge of the true labels. Nevertheless, intuitively, examples with low-confidence predictions are likely to have these properties: If we are very unsure of the correct label for a given example, then whatever that label turns out to be will be new information that can move learning forward. So the idea is to iteratively train a classifier using a growing pool of labeled examples where, on each iteration, the unlabeled examples we are least confident about are selected for labeling.

In boosting, as we have discussed at length, the absolute margin $|f(x)|$ can be used as a measure of confidence. Putting these ideas together leads to a procedure like algorithm 5.1. This simple approach to active learning can be surprisingly effective.

For instance, this approach has been applied to the spoken-dialogue task mentioned above and described in detail in section 10.3. Figure 5.11 shows how actively selecting examples for labeling in the manner described above compares with choosing the examples at random on each iteration. In these experiments, an initial set of 1000 examples was chosen for labeling, and $k = 500$ examples were added on each iteration. Decision stumps were used as described in section 10.3, and boosting was run for 500 rounds. These experiments

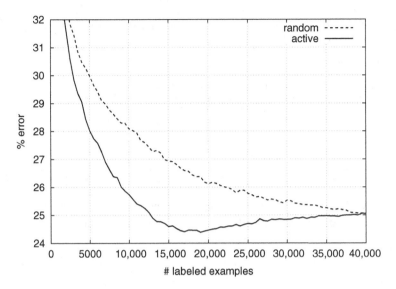

Figure 5.11
A comparison of the percent test error achieved on a spoken-dialogue task for an increasing number of labeled examples selected from a fixed pool using either active learning or random selection.

were repeated ten times and the results were averaged. In each case, examples were selected from a training pool of 40,000 examples, initially all unlabeled.[3]

In terms of labeling effort, figure 5.11 shows that the savings can be tremendous. For example, as shown in table 5.3, to obtain a test error rate of 25%, some 40,000 randomly selected examples must be labeled (that is, the entire training set), while only 13,000 actively selected examples suffice—more than a threefold savings.

In these controlled experiments, a fixed set of 40,000 examples was used for training so that the performance of both active and random selection must finally converge to the same point. This means that the latter part of the active-learning curve reflects the addition of less informative examples added later in the process, once all the other examples have been labeled, and suggests that even greater improvements in performance may be possible with larger pools of unlabeled examples. (In some applications, where a steady stream of unlabeled examples arrives every day, the supply is virtually infinite.) Furthermore, it is interesting that on this dataset, using only about half the data, if chosen selectively, gives better results than using the entire dataset: With 19,000 labeled examples, active learning gives a test error of 24.4% compared to 25.0% using the entire set of 40,000 examples.

---

3. Since this dataset is multiclass and multi-label, a modified definition of margin was used, namely, the difference of the "scores" predicted by the final classifier for the top two labels. Also, "one-error" was used instead of classification error. See chapter 10.

Table 5.3
The number of rounds needed to achieve various test error rates for the experimental results in figure 5.11, as well as the percentage labeling effort reduced by active learning

	First Reached		
% error	Random	Active	% Label Savings
27.0	14,500	7,000	51.7
26.0	22,000	9,000	59.1
25.0	40,000	13,000	67.5
24.5	–	16,000	–

Apparently, the examples labeled toward the end of the process not only are uninformative, but actually seem to have a "disinformative" effect, perhaps due to mislabeling.

Summary

We have explored in this chapter a theory for understanding AdaBoost's generalization capabilities in terms of its propensity to maximize the margins of the training examples. Specifically, the theory provides that AdaBoost's generalization performance is largely a function of the number of training examples, the complexity of the base classifiers, and the margins of the training examples. These margins in turn are intimately related to the edges of the base classifiers. The theory gives an explanation of why AdaBoost often does not overfit, as well as qualitative predictions of the conditions under which the algorithm can fail.

The margins theory seems to provide a more complete explanation for AdaBoost's behavior than bias-variance analysis does, and links AdaBoost with SVMs, another margins-based learning method. Unfortunately, attempts to directly apply insights from the theory as a means of improving AdaBoost have met with mixed success for a number of reasons. Even so, margins are practically useful as a natural measure of confidence.

In the following chapters, we turn to some alternative interpretations of the AdaBoost algorithm itself.

Bibliographic Notes

The margins explanation for the effectiveness of AdaBoost and other voting methods, as presented in sections 5.1 and 5.2 (including figure 5.2), is due to Schapire et al. [202]. Their analysis, in turn, was based significantly on a related result of Bartlett [11] for neural networks. An improved bound for the case in which all examples have margin above θ (as in the last paragraph of section 5.2) was proved by Breiman [36]. See also the refined analysis of Wang et al. [230] based on the notion of an "equilibrium margin."

The use of Rademacher complexity as a tool in the analysis of voting methods, as in section 5.3, was introduced by Koltchinskii and Panchenko [139]. An excellent review of these methods, including proofs and references, is given by Boucheron, Bousquet, and Lugosi [30].

Theorem 5.8 was proved by Schapire et al. [202]. The bound $\Upsilon(\gamma)$ derived in section 5.4.1 on the asymptotic minimum margin is due to Rätsch and Warmuth [187]. This bound was shown to be tight by Rudin, Schapire, and Daubechies [196]. That AdaBoost need not always achieve the largest possible minimum margin, even when using an exhaustive weak learner, was first proved by Rudin, Daubechies, and Schapire [194].

The modified version of AdaBoost given by the choice of α_t in equation (5.34) was initially studied by Rätsch et al. [186] and Breiman [36], and later by Rätsch and Warmuth [187], who called the resulting algorithm AdaBoost$_\rho$, and who gave an analysis similar to the one in section 5.4.2. The algorithms arc-gv and AdaBoost$_\nu^*$, which provably maximize the minimum margin, are due to Breiman [36] and Rätsch and Warmuth [187], respectively. Other algorithms with this property have also been given by Grove and Schuurmans [111], Rudin, Schapire, and Daubechies [196], and Shalev-Shwartz and Singer [211]. A different approach for directly optimizing the margins (though not necessarily the minimum margin) is given by Mason, Bartlett, and Baxter [167].

Breiman [36] conducted experiments with arc-gv which showed that it tends to achieve higher margins than AdaBoost, but also slightly higher test errors. Results of a similar flavor were also obtained by Grove and Schuurmans [111]. The experiments reported in table 5.1 and figure 5.5, as well as the explanation given of Breiman's findings, are due to Reyzin and Schapire [188].

As noted in chapter 3, the connection between optimal margins and optimal edges, as in section 5.4.3, was first made explicit by Rätsch and Warmuth [187].

Bagging, as discussed in section 5.5, is due to Breiman [34], who also proposed a bias-variance explanation for both bagging's and boosting's effectiveness [35]. The definitions of bias and variance used here are due to Breiman [35] and Kong and Dietterich [140], although others have been proposed [138, 217]. The main arguments and results of this section, including table 5.2 (adapted) and figure 5.6, are taken from Schapire et al. [202]. The synthetic datasets used in table 5.2 are from Breiman [35]. Bagging is closely related to Breiman's random forests [37], another highly effective method for combining decision trees.

Support-vector machines were pioneered by Boser, Guyon, and Vapnik [29] and Cortes and Vapnik [56]. See also, for instance, the books by Cristianini and Shawe-Taylor [58], and Schölkopf and Smola [208]. The comparison with boosting given in section 5.6 is taken from Schapire et al. [202].

The census dataset used in section 5.7.1 originated with the U.S. Census Bureau and was prepared by Terran Lane and Ronny Kohavi.

Research on active learning dates to the work of Cohn, Atlas, and Ladner [51], and Lewis and Catlett [151]. The use of boosting for active learning, essentially along the lines of the method used in section 5.7.2, is due to Abe and Mamitsuka [1]. The experiments and results appearing in this section (including figure 5.11, adapted) are taken from Tur, Schapire, and Hakkani-Tür [220]; see also Tur, Hakkani-Tür, and Schapire [219]. The observation that less data can be more effective when using active learning was previously noted in another context by Schohn and Cohn [207].

Some of the exercises in this chapter are based on material from [10, 13, 26, 150, 187, 196].

Exercises

5.1 Suppose AdaBoost is run for an unterminating number of rounds. In addition to our usual notation, let

$$F_T(x) \doteq \sum_{t=1}^{T} \alpha_t h_t(x) \text{ and } s_T \doteq \sum_{t=1}^{T} \alpha_t.$$

We assume without loss of generality that each $\alpha_t \geq 0$. Let the minimum (normalized) margin on round t be denoted

$$\theta_t \doteq \min_i \frac{y_i F_t(x_i)}{s_t}.$$

Finally, we define the *smooth margin* on round t to be

$$g_t \doteq \frac{-\ln\left(\frac{1}{m}\sum_{i=1}^{m} e^{-y_i F_t(x_i)}\right)}{s_t}.$$

a. Prove that

$$\theta_t \leq g_t \leq \theta_t + \frac{\ln m}{s_t}.$$

Thus, if s_t gets large, then g_t gets very close to θ_t.

b. Prove that g_T is a weighted average of the values $\Upsilon(\gamma_t)$, specifically,

$$g_T = \frac{\sum_{t=1}^{T} \alpha_t \Upsilon(\gamma_t)}{s_T}.$$

c. Let $0 < \gamma_{\min} < \gamma_{\max} < \frac{1}{2}$. Show that if the edges γ_t eventually all lie in the narrow range $[\gamma_{\min}, \gamma_{\max}]$, then the smooth margins g_t—and therefore also the minimum margins θ_t—must similarly converge to the narrow range $[\Upsilon(\gamma_{\min}), \Upsilon(\gamma_{\max})]$. More precisely, suppose for some $t_0 > 0$ that $\gamma_{\min} \leq \gamma_t \leq \gamma_{\max}$ for all $t \geq t_0$. Prove that

$$\liminf_{t \to \infty} \theta_t = \liminf_{t \to \infty} g_t \geq \Upsilon(\gamma_{\min}),$$

and that

$$\limsup_{t \to \infty} \theta_t = \limsup_{t \to \infty} g_t \leq \Upsilon(\gamma_{\max}).$$

(See appendix A.4 for definitions.)

d. Prove that if the edges γ_t converge (as $t \to \infty$) to some value $\gamma \in (0, \frac{1}{2})$, then the minimum margins θ_t converge to $\Upsilon(\gamma)$.

5.2 Prove the following properties of binary relative entropy:

a. $\text{RE}_b (p \parallel q)$ is convex in q (for any fixed p), and convex in p (for any fixed q). (Refer to appendix A.7 for definitions.)

b. $\text{RE}_b (p \parallel q) \geq 2(p - q)^2$ for all $p, q \in [0, 1]$. [*Hint:* Use Taylor's theorem (theorem A.1).]

5.3 Suppose the γ^*-weak learning assumption holds for some $\gamma^* > 0$ that is *not* known ahead of time. In this case, the algorithm *AdaBoost*$_v^*$ can be used to efficiently find a combined classifier with minimum margin arbitrarily close to $2\gamma^*$, that is, with margin at least $\theta \doteq 2\gamma^* - v$ on all training examples, where $v > 0$ is a given accuracy parameter. This algorithm proceeds exactly like AdaBoost (algorithm 1.1 (p. 5)), except that α_t is computed on round t as follows:

- $\gamma_t = \frac{1}{2} - \epsilon_t$. (Note that $\gamma_t \geq \gamma^*$ by assumption.)
- $\hat{\gamma}_t = \min\{\gamma_1, \ldots, \gamma_t\}$.
- $\hat{\theta}_t = 2\hat{\gamma}_t - v$.
- $\alpha_t = \dfrac{1}{2} \ln \left(\dfrac{1 + 2\gamma_t}{1 - 2\gamma_t} \right) - \dfrac{1}{2} \ln \left(\dfrac{1 + \hat{\theta}_t}{1 - \hat{\theta}_t} \right).$

a. Prove that after T rounds, the fraction of training examples with margin below θ is at most

$$\exp \left(-\sum_{t=1}^{T} \text{RE}_b \left(\frac{1}{2} + \frac{\hat{\theta}_t}{2} \;\middle\|\; \frac{1}{2} + \gamma_t \right) \right).$$

b. Show that if $T > 2(\ln m)/v^2$, then the margin on *all* training examples is at least θ.

5.4 Let $X_1, \ldots, X_n$ be independent Bernoulli random variables with

$$X_i = \begin{cases} 1 & \text{with probability } p \\ 0 & \text{with probability } 1 - p. \end{cases}$$

Let $A_n \doteq \frac{1}{n} \sum_{i=1}^{n} X_i$.

a. Generalize the technique of section 3.3 to prove that if $q \leq p$, then

$$\mathbf{Pr}[A_n \leq q] \leq \exp\left(-n \cdot \mathrm{RE}_b\left(q \parallel p\right)\right)$$

$$\leq e^{-2n(q-p)^2}.$$

b. By reducing to the previous case in part (a), state and prove bounds analogous to those in (a) on $\mathbf{Pr}[A_n \geq q]$.

5.5 This exercise develops a proof of equation (5.25). As in section 5.3, let $\mathcal{F}$ be a family of real-valued functions on $\mathcal{Z}$, and let $S = \langle z_1, \ldots, z_m \rangle$ be a sequence of points in $\mathcal{Z}$.

a. Suppose $\phi(u) \doteq au + b$ for all u, where $a \geq 0$ and $b \in \mathbb{R}$. Find $R_S(\phi \circ \mathcal{F})$ exactly in terms of a, b, and $R_S(\mathcal{F})$.

b. Now let $\phi : \mathbb{R} \to \mathbb{R}$ be any *contraction*, that is, a Lipschitz function with Lipschitz constant $L_\phi = 1$. Let $U \subseteq \mathbb{R}^2$ be any set of pairs of real numbers. Prove that

$$\mathbf{E}_\sigma\left[\sup_{(u,v) \in U} (u + \sigma\phi(v))\right] \leq \mathbf{E}_\sigma\left[\sup_{(u,v) \in U} (u + \sigma v)\right]$$

where expectation is with respect to a uniformly random choice of $\sigma \in \{-1, +1\}$. [*Hint:* First show that for all $u_1, v_1, u_2, v_2 \in \mathbb{R}$, $(u_1 + \phi(v_1)) + (u_2 - \phi(v_2)) \leq \max\{(u_1 + v_1) + (u_2 - v_2), (u_1 - v_1) + (u_2 + v_2)\}$.]

c. Use part (b) to prove that if ϕ is a contraction, then $R_S(\phi \circ \mathcal{F}) \leq R_S(\mathcal{F})$.

d. Conclude that if ϕ is a Lipschitz function with Lipschitz constant $L_\phi > 0$, then $R_S(\phi \circ \mathcal{F}) \leq L_\phi \cdot R_S(\mathcal{F})$.

5.6 This exercise derives a generalization error bound for margin-based classifiers which use ℓ_2/ℓ_2-norms, such as SVMs. Let $\mathcal{X}$ be the unit ball in $\mathbb{R}^n$:

$$\mathcal{X} \doteq \left\{\mathbf{x} \in \mathbb{R}^n : \|\mathbf{x}\|_2 \leq 1\right\}.$$

Thus, each of the m random training examples in S is a pair $(\mathbf{x}_i, y_i)$ in $\mathcal{X} \times \{-1, +1\}$. Let $\mathcal{F}$ be the set of all possible margin functions defined by unit-length weight vectors $\mathbf{w}$:

$$\mathcal{F} \doteq \left\{(\mathbf{x}, y) \mapsto y(\mathbf{w} \cdot \mathbf{x}) \mid \mathbf{w} \in \mathbb{R}^n, \|\mathbf{w}\|_2 = 1\right\}.$$

a. Prove that $\mathcal{F}$'s Rademacher complexity is

$$R_S(\mathcal{F}) \leq \frac{1}{\sqrt{m}}.$$

[*Hint:* First show that $R_S(\mathcal{F}) = \frac{1}{m}\mathbf{E}_\sigma\left[\left\|\sum_{i=1}^m \sigma_i \mathbf{x}_i\right\|_2\right]$, and then apply Jensen's inequality (equation (A.4)).]

b. For any $\theta > 0$, show that with probability at least $1 - \delta$, for all weight vectors $\mathbf{w} \in \mathbb{R}^n$ with $\|\mathbf{w}\|_2 = 1$,

$$\mathbf{Pr}_{\mathcal{D}}[y(\mathbf{w} \cdot \mathbf{x}) \leq 0] \leq \mathbf{Pr}_S[y(\mathbf{w} \cdot \mathbf{x}) \leq \theta] + O\left(\frac{1}{\theta\sqrt{m}} + \sqrt{\frac{\ln(1/\delta)}{m}}\right).$$

Give explicit constants.

5.7 Suppose, as in the example given in section 5.5, that we are using delta-functions and constant functions for base classifiers. Give an example of a random data source such that for any training set of any (finite) size $m \geq 1$, there always exists a (weighted) majority-vote classifier (defined over these base classifiers) whose training error is zero but whose generalization error is 100%.

5.8 Suppose we are using simplified decision stumps, as in exercise 2.10, as base classifiers. Assume that the same instance x can never appear in the training set with opposite labels.

a. When the number of dimensions $n = 1$, prove or disprove that for every training set, there must always exist a weighted majority-vote classifier defined over decision stumps that is consistent (that is, whose training error is zero).

b. Prove or disprove the same statement for $n \geq 2$.

5.9 Let the domain $\mathcal{X}$ be the unit sphere $\mathcal{S}$ in $\mathbb{R}^n$, that is,

$$\mathcal{S} \doteq \left\{\mathbf{x} \in \mathbb{R}^n : \|\mathbf{x}\|_2 = 1\right\}.$$

Given training data $(\mathbf{x}_1, y_1), \ldots, (\mathbf{x}_m, y_m)$ in $\mathcal{S} \times \{-1, +1\}$, suppose there exists an unknown weight vector $\mathbf{w}^* \in \mathcal{S}$ such that $y_i(\mathbf{w}^* \cdot \mathbf{x}_i) \geq \gamma$ for all i, where $\gamma \geq 0$ is known. Thus, the data is linearly separable with positive margin, but using ℓ_2/ℓ_2-norms rather than ℓ_1/ℓ_∞.

Consider the following weak learning algorithm for a given distribution D over the data:

- Choose $\mathbf{w}$ uniformly at random from $\mathcal{S}$, and let $h_{\mathbf{w}}(\mathbf{x}) \doteq \text{sign}(\mathbf{w} \cdot \mathbf{x})$.
- If $\text{err}_D(h_{\mathbf{w}}) \doteq \mathbf{Pr}_{i \sim D}[h_{\mathbf{w}}(\mathbf{x}_i) \neq y_i]$ is at most $1/2 - \gamma/4$, then halt and output $h_{\mathbf{w}}$.
- Otherwise, repeat.

If this procedure halts, then clearly it has succeeded in finding a weak classifier $h_{\mathbf{w}}$ with edge $\gamma/4$. But in principle, it could take a very long time (or forever) for it to halt. We will see that this is unlikely to happen when γ is not too small.

For parts (a) and (b), fix a particular example $(\mathbf{x}_i, y_i)$.

a. Show that the angle between $\mathbf{w}^*$ and $y_i\mathbf{x}_i$ is at most $\pi/2 - \gamma$. (You can use the inequality $\sin\theta \leq \theta$ for $\theta \geq 0$.)

b. Conditional on $\mathbf{w}$ being chosen so that $\mathbf{w} \cdot \mathbf{w}^* \geq 0$, show that the probability that $h_{\mathbf{w}}(\mathbf{x}_i) \neq y_i$ is at most $1/2 - \gamma/\pi$. That is, show that

$$\mathbf{Pr_w}\big[h_\mathbf{w}(\mathbf{x}_i) \neq y_i \mid \mathbf{w} \cdot \mathbf{w}^* \geq 0\big] \leq \frac{1}{2} - \frac{\gamma}{\pi}$$

where $\mathbf{Pr_w}[\cdot]$ denotes probability with respect to the random choice of $\mathbf{w}$. [*Hint:* Consider the projection $\overline{\mathbf{w}}$ of $\mathbf{w}$ into the two-dimensional plane defined by $\mathbf{w}^*$ and $y_i\mathbf{x}_i$. Start by arguing that its direction, $\overline{\mathbf{w}}/\|\overline{\mathbf{w}}\|_2$, is uniformly distributed on the unit circle in this plane.]

c. For some absolute constant $c > 0$, show that

$$\mathbf{Pr_w}\left[\mathrm{err}_D(h_\mathbf{w}) \leq \frac{1}{2} - \frac{\gamma}{4}\right] \geq c\gamma,$$

and therefore that the above procedure, in expectation, will halt in $O(1/\gamma)$ iterations for any distribution D.

II FUNDAMENTAL PERSPECTIVES

6 Game Theory, Online Learning, and Boosting

Having studied methods of analyzing boosting's training and generalization errors, we turn now to some of the other ways that boosting can be thought about, understood, and interpreted. We begin with the fundamental and beautiful connection between boosting and game theory. Using mathematical abstractions, *game theory* studies ordinary games, such as chess and checkers, but more generally the field also attempts to model all forms of interactions between people, animals, corporations, nations, software agents, and so on. In boosting, there is a natural interaction between two agents, the boosting algorithm and the weak learning algorithm. As we will see, these two agents are in fact playing a game repeatedly in a standard game-theoretic fashion. Moreover, we will see that some of the key concepts of boosting, including margin, edge, and the weak learning assumption, all have direct and natural interpretations in the game-theoretic context. Indeed, the principle that boosting should be possible at all, given the weak learning assumption, is very closely related to von Neumann's famous minmax theorem, the fundamental theorem of zero-sum games. Moreover, the learning framework presented in this chapter allows us to give a very simple proof of this classic theorem.

AdaBoost and its simplified variants turn out to be special cases of a more general algorithm for playing general repeated games. We devote much of this chapter to a description of this general game-playing algorithm. Later, we will see how boosting can be achieved and understood as a special case for an appropriately chosen game. Moreover, by reversing the roles of the two players, we will see that a solution is obtained for a different learning problem, namely, the well-studied online prediction model in which a learning agent predicts the classifications of a sequence of instances while attempting to minimize the number of prediction mistakes. Thus, an extremely tight connection between boosting and online learning is revealed by placing them both in a general game-theoretic context.

We end the chapter with an application to a classic game that involves an element of "mind-reading."

6.1 Game Theory

We begin with a review of basic game theory. We study two-person games in *normal form*. Such a game is defined by a matrix $\mathbf{M}$. There are two players, the row player and the column player. To play the game, the row player chooses a row i and, simultaneously, the column player chooses a column j. The selected entry $\mathbf{M}(i, j)$ is the *loss* suffered by the row player. (Although it is common in game theory for the players' purpose to be specified in terms of a "gain" or "reward" to be maximized, we use an equivalent, if gloomier, formulation based on "loss" for the sake of consistency with the rest of the book.)

As an example, the loss matrix for the children's game[1] Rock-Paper-Scissors is given by:

	Rock	Paper	Scissors
Rock	$\frac{1}{2}$	1	0
Paper	0	$\frac{1}{2}$	1
Scissors	1	0	$\frac{1}{2}$

For instance, if the row player plays Paper and the column player plays Scissors, then the row player loses, suffering a loss of 1.

The row player's goal is to minimize its loss, and we will generally focus mainly on this player's perspective of the game. Often, the goal of the column player is to maximize this loss, in which case the game is said to be *zero-sum*, so named because the column player's loss can be viewed as the negative of the row player's, so that the losses of the two players always add up to exactly zero. Most of our results are given in the context of a zero-sum game. However, the results also apply when no assumptions are made about the goal or strategy of the column player, who might possibly have some other purpose in mind. We return to this point below.

6.1.1 Randomized Play

As just described, each player chooses a single row or column. Usually, this choice of play is allowed to be randomized. That is, the row player chooses a distribution P over the rows of $\mathbf{M}$, and (simultaneously) the column player chooses a distribution Q over columns. The two distributions P and Q define the random choice of row or column. The row player's expected loss is then easily computed as

$$\mathbf{M}(P, Q) \doteq \sum_{i,j} P(i)\mathbf{M}(i, j)Q(j) = P^{\top}\mathbf{M}Q,$$

---

1. In this game, each of two children simultaneously throw down hand signals indicating Rock, Paper, or Scissors. If one plays Scissors, for instance, and the other plays Paper, then the former wins since "Scissors cut Paper." Similarly, Paper beats Rock, and Rock beats Scissors. A tie occurs if the same object is chosen by both children.

where we sometimes, as in this expression, regard P and Q as (column) vectors. For ease of notation, we denote this quantity by $\mathbf{M}(P, Q)$, as above, and refer to it simply as the loss (rather than the expected loss). In addition, if the row player chooses a distribution P but the column player chooses a single column j, then the (expected) loss is $\sum_i P(i)\mathbf{M}(i, j)$, which we denote by $\mathbf{M}(P, j)$. The notation $\mathbf{M}(i, Q)$ is defined analogously.

Individual (deterministically chosen) rows i and columns j are called *pure strategies*. Randomized plays defined by distributions P and Q over rows and columns are called *mixed strategies*. The number of rows of the matrix $\mathbf{M}$ will be denoted by m.

6.1.2 Sequential Play

Until now, we have assumed that the players choose their (pure or mixed) strategies simultaneously. Suppose now that play instead is sequential. That is, suppose that the column player chooses its strategy Q *after* the row player has chosen and announced its strategy P. Assume further that the column player's goal is to maximize the row player's loss (that is, that the game is zero-sum). Then, given knowledge of P, such a "worst-case" or "adversarial" column player will choose Q to maximize $\mathbf{M}(P, Q)$; that is, if the row player plays mixed strategy P, then its loss will be

$$\max_Q \; \mathbf{M}(P, Q). \tag{6.1}$$

(It is understood here and throughout the chapter that $\max_Q$ denotes maximum over all probability distributions over columns; similarly, $\min_P$ will always denote minimum over all probability distributions over rows. These extrema exist because the set of distributions over a finite space is compact.)

Equation (6.1) can be viewed as a function of P that specifies what the loss will be for the row player if it chooses to play that particular strategy. Knowing this, the row player should choose P to minimize this expression. Doing so will result in a loss for the row player of exactly

$$\min_P \max_Q \mathbf{M}(P, Q). \tag{6.2}$$

Thus, this quantity represents the loss that will be suffered when the row player plays first, followed by the column player, and assuming both play optimally. Note that the order of the minmax in equation (6.2) matches the order of play (although, of course, the minimum and maximum would be evaluated mathematically from the inside out).

A mixed strategy P^* realizing the minimum in equation (6.2) is called a *minmax strategy*, and is optimal in this particular setting.

If now we reverse the order of play so that the column player plays first and the row player can choose its play with the benefit of knowing the column player's chosen strategy Q, then by a symmetric argument, the loss of the row player will be

$$\max_Q \min_P \mathbf{M}(P, Q).$$

A strategy Q^* realizing the maximum is called a *maxmin strategy*.

Note that because

$$\mathbf{M}(P, Q) = \sum_{j=1}^{n} \mathbf{M}(P, j) Q(j),$$

the maximum over distributions Q in equation (6.1) will always be realized when Q is concentrated on a single column j. In other words, for any P,

$$\max_Q \mathbf{M}(P, Q) = \max_j \mathbf{M}(P, j), \tag{6.3}$$

and similarly, for any Q,

$$\min_P \mathbf{M}(P, Q) = \min_i \mathbf{M}(i, Q) \tag{6.4}$$

(where $\min_i$ and $\max_j$ will always denote minimum over all rows i or maximum over all columns j). On the other hand, the minmax strategy P^*, which realizes the minimum in equation (6.2), will not, in general, be a pure strategy (likewise for Q^*).

6.1.3 The Minmax Theorem

Intuitively, we expect the player that chooses its strategy last to have the advantage since it plays knowing its opponent's strategy exactly—at least, we expect there to be no disadvantage in playing second. Thus, we expect the row player's loss to be no greater when playing second than when playing first, so that

$$\max_Q \min_P \mathbf{M}(P, Q) \leq \min_P \max_Q \mathbf{M}(P, Q). \tag{6.5}$$

Indeed, this is true in general. We might go on naively to conjecture that there is a real advantage to playing last in some games, so that, at least in some cases, the inequality in equation (6.5) is strict. Surprisingly, it turns out not to matter which player plays first. Von Neumann's well-known *minmax theorem* states that the outcome is the same in either case, so that

$$\max_Q \min_P \mathbf{M}(P, Q) = \min_P \max_Q \mathbf{M}(P, Q) \tag{6.6}$$

for every matrix $\mathbf{M}$. The common value v of the two sides of the equality is called the *value* of the game $\mathbf{M}$. A proof of the minmax theorem will be given in section 6.2.4.

In words, equation (6.6) means that the row player has a (minmax) strategy P^* such that, regardless of the strategy Q played by the column player, even if chosen with knowledge of P^*, the loss suffered $\mathbf{M}(P^*, Q)$ will be *at most v*. Moreover, P^* is optimal in the sense that by playing Q^*, the column player can force a loss of *at least* v for any strategy P played by the row player, including P^*. The (maxmin) strategy Q^* is symmetrically optimal.

For instance, for Rock-Paper-Scissors, the optimal minmax strategy is to play each of the three possible moves with equal probability $\frac{1}{3}$. Regardless of what the opponent does, the expected loss for this strategy will always be exactly $\frac{1}{2}$, the value of this game. In this case, playing any other (mixed) strategy, if known to an optimal opponent, will result in a strictly higher loss.

Thus, classical game theory says that, given a (zero-sum) game $\mathbf{M}$, one should play using a minmax strategy. Computing such a strategy, a problem called *solving the game*, can be accomplished using linear programming, that is, using standard techniques for maximizing a linear function subject to linear inequality constraints (see exercise 6.9). However, there are a number of problems with this approach. For instance,

- $\mathbf{M}$ may be unknown;
- $\mathbf{M}$ may be so large that computing a minmax strategy using linear programming becomes infeasible;
- the column player may not be truly adversarial, and may behave in a manner that admits loss significantly smaller than the game value v.

Regarding the last point, consider again the example of Rock-Paper-Scissors. Suppose, as happened on one episode of *The Simpsons*, that Bart is playing against his sister Lisa. Lisa thinks, "Poor predictable Bart, always takes Rock," while Bart thinks, "Good old Rock, nothing beats that." If Lisa were to follow the supposedly "optimal" minmax strategy given above, she would still suffer loss of $\frac{1}{2}$, and would miss an obvious opportunity to beat Bart every single time by always playing Paper. This is because a minmax strategy is intended for use against a fully adversarial opponent (in this case, one much smarter than Bart), and will perform suboptimally if played against a suboptimal opponent.

6.2 Learning in Repeated Game Playing

If playing a game only once, we cannot hope to overcome a lack of prior knowledge about either the game $\mathbf{M}$ or the opponent's intentions and abilities. However, in *repeated* play, in which the same game is played over and over against the same opponent, one can hope to *learn* to play the game well against the particular opponent being faced. This is the main topic of this section.

6.2.1 The Learning Model

We begin by formalizing a model of repeated play. To simplify the presentation, we assume for the remainder of this chapter that all of the losses appearing in the matrix $\mathbf{M}$ are in the range $[0, 1]$. This does not at all limit the generality of the results since any matrix, having only a finite number of entries, can be shifted and scaled to satisfy this assumption without fundamentally altering the game.

To emphasize the roles of the two players, we here refer to the row player as the *learner*, and the column player as the *environment*. As before, $\mathbf{M}$ is a game matrix, possibly unknown to the learner. This game is played repeatedly in a sequence of *rounds*. On round $t = 1, \ldots, T$

1. the learner chooses mixed strategy P_t;
2. the environment chooses mixed strategy Q_t (which may be chosen with knowledge of P_t);
3. the learner is permitted to observe the loss $\mathbf{M}(i, Q_t)$ for each row i; this is the loss it would have suffered had it played using pure strategy i;
4. the learner suffers loss $\mathbf{M}(P_t, Q_t)$.

The basic goal of the learner is to minimize its total *cumulative loss*:

$$\sum_{t=1}^{T} \mathbf{M}(P_t, Q_t). \tag{6.7}$$

If the environment is adversarial, then a related goal is to approximate the performance of the optimal, minmax strategy P^*. However, for more benign environments, the goal may be to suffer the minimum loss possible, which may be much better than the value of the game. Thus, the goal of the learner is to do almost as well as the best strategy against the actual sequence of plays $Q_1, \ldots, Q_T$ which were chosen by the environment. That is, the learner's goal is to suffer cumulative loss which is "not much worse" than the cumulative loss of the *best* (fixed) strategy *in hindsight*, namely,

$$\min_{P} \sum_{t=1}^{T} \mathbf{M}(P, Q_t). \tag{6.8}$$

6.2.2 The Basic Algorithm

We now describe an algorithm for achieving this goal in repeated play, which we call *MW* for "multiplicative weights." The learning algorithm MW starts with some initial mixed strategy P_1 which it uses for the first round of the game. After each round t, the learner computes a new mixed strategy P_{t+1} by a simple multiplicative rule:

$$P_{t+1}(i) = \frac{P_t(i) \exp(-\eta \mathbf{M}(i, Q_t))}{Z_t} \tag{6.9}$$

where Z_t is a normalization factor

$$Z_t = \sum_{i=1}^{m} P_t(i) \exp(-\eta \mathbf{M}(i, Q_t)),$$ (6.10)

and $\eta > 0$ is a parameter of the algorithm. This is a very intuitive rule which increases the chance of playing strategies in the future that had low loss on the preceding round (that is, for which $\mathbf{M}(i, Q_t)$ is small), while similarly decreasing the chance of playing strategies with high loss. Later, we discuss the choice of P_1 and η.

6.2.3 Analysis

The main theorem concerning this algorithm is given next. Roughly speaking, this general theorem gives a bound on the learner's cumulative loss (equation (6.7)) in terms of the cumulative loss of the best strategy in hindsight (equation (6.8)), plus an additional term which will be shown later to be relatively insignificant for large T. As we will see, this result will have many implications.

The theorem and its proof make use of a measure of distance (or "divergence") between two probability distributions P and P' over $\{1, \ldots, m\}$ called *relative entropy*, also known as *Kullback-Leibler divergence*:

$$\mathrm{RE}\left(P \parallel P'\right) \doteq \sum_{i=1}^{m} P(i) \ln\left(\frac{P(i)}{P'(i)}\right).$$ (6.11)

This measure, though not a metric, is always nonnegative, and is equal to zero if and only if $P = P'$. See section 8.1.2 for further background.

Theorem 6.1 For any matrix $\mathbf{M}$ with m rows and entries in $[0, 1]$, and for any sequence of mixed strategies $Q_1, \ldots, Q_T$ played by the environment, the sequence of mixed strategies $P_1, \ldots, P_T$ produced by algorithm MW with parameter η satisfies

$$\sum_{t=1}^{T} \mathbf{M}(P_t, Q_t) \leq \min_{P} \left[a_\eta \sum_{t=1}^{T} \mathbf{M}(P, Q_t) + c_\eta \mathrm{RE}\left(P \parallel P_1\right) \right]$$

where

$$a_\eta = \frac{\eta}{1 - e^{-\eta}} \qquad c_\eta = \frac{1}{1 - e^{-\eta}}.$$

Our proof uses a kind of "amortized analysis" in which relative entropy is used as a "potential" function, or measure of progress. The heart of the proof is in the following lemma, which bounds the change in potential before and after a single round. Note that the potential is measured relative to an arbitrary *reference distribution* $\tilde{P}$, which can be thought of as the "best" distribution, although the analysis actually applies simultaneously to all possible choices of $\tilde{P}$. In words, the lemma shows that whenever the learner suffers significant loss relative to $\tilde{P}$, the potential must drop substantially. Since the potential can never become negative, this will allow us to bound the learner's cumulative loss relative to that of $\tilde{P}$.

Lemma 6.2 For any iteration t where MW is used with parameter η, and for any mixed strategy $\tilde{P}$,

$$\mathrm{RE}\left(\tilde{P} \parallel P_{t+1}\right) - \mathrm{RE}\left(\tilde{P} \parallel P_t\right) \leq \eta \mathbf{M}(\tilde{P}, Q_t) + \ln\left(1 - (1 - e^{-\eta})\mathbf{M}(P_t, Q_t)\right).$$

Proof We have the following sequence of equalities and inequalities:

$$\mathrm{RE}\left(\tilde{P} \parallel P_{t+1}\right) - \mathrm{RE}\left(\tilde{P} \parallel P_t\right)$$

$$= \sum_{i=1}^m \tilde{P}(i) \ln\left(\frac{\tilde{P}(i)}{P_{t+1}(i)}\right) - \sum_{i=1}^m \tilde{P}(i) \ln\left(\frac{\tilde{P}(i)}{P_t(i)}\right) \tag{6.12}$$

$$= \sum_{i=1}^m \tilde{P}(i) \ln\left(\frac{P_t(i)}{P_{t+1}(i)}\right)$$

$$= \sum_{i=1}^m \tilde{P}(i) \ln\left(\frac{Z_t}{\exp(-\eta\mathbf{M}(i, Q_t))}\right) \tag{6.13}$$

$$= \eta \sum_{i=1}^m \tilde{P}(i)\mathbf{M}(i, Q_t) + \ln Z_t$$

$$= \eta \sum_{i=1}^m \tilde{P}(i)\mathbf{M}(i, Q_t) + \ln\left[\sum_{i=1}^m P_t(i) \exp(-\eta\mathbf{M}(i, Q_t))\right] \tag{6.14}$$

$$\leq \eta \mathbf{M}(\tilde{P}, Q_t) + \ln\left[\sum_{i=1}^m P_t(i)\left(1 - (1 - e^{-\eta})\mathbf{M}(i, Q_t)\right)\right] \tag{6.15}$$

$$= \eta \mathbf{M}(\tilde{P}, Q_t) + \ln\left[1 - (1 - e^{-\eta})\mathbf{M}(P_t, Q_t)\right].$$

Equation (6.12) is simply the definition of relative entropy. Equation (6.13) follows from the update rule of MW given in equation (6.9). Equation (6.14) uses the definition of Z_t in equation (6.10). And equation (6.15) uses the fact that, by convexity of e^x, for $q \in [0, 1]$,

$$e^{-\eta q} = \exp(q(-\eta) + (1 - q) \cdot 0) \leq qe^{-\eta} + (1 - q)e^0 = 1 - (1 - e^{-\eta})q. \qquad \blacksquare$$

Proof of Theorem 6.1 Let $\tilde{P}$ be any mixed row strategy. We first simplify the last term in the inequality of lemma 6.2 by using the fact that $\ln(1 - x) \leq -x$ for any $x < 1$, which implies that

$$\mathrm{RE}\left(\tilde{P} \ \| \ P_{t+1}\right) - \mathrm{RE}\left(\tilde{P} \ \| \ P_t\right) \leq \eta \mathbf{M}(\tilde{P}, Q_t) - (1 - e^{-\eta})\mathbf{M}(P_t, Q_t).$$

Summing this inequality over $t = 1, \ldots, T$, we get

$$\mathrm{RE}\left(\tilde{P} \ \| \ P_{T+1}\right) - \mathrm{RE}\left(\tilde{P} \ \| \ P_1\right) \leq \eta \sum_{t=1}^{T} \mathbf{M}(\tilde{P}, Q_t) - (1 - e^{-\eta}) \sum_{t=1}^{T} \mathbf{M}(P_t, Q_t).$$

Rearranging the inequality and noting that $\mathrm{RE}\left(\tilde{P} \ \| \ P_{T+1}\right) \geq 0$ gives

$$(1 - e^{-\eta}) \sum_{t=1}^{T} \mathbf{M}(P_t, Q_t) \leq \eta \sum_{t=1}^{T} \mathbf{M}(\tilde{P}, Q_t) + \mathrm{RE}\left(\tilde{P} \ \| \ P_1\right) - \mathrm{RE}\left(\tilde{P} \ \| \ P_{T+1}\right)$$

$$\leq \eta \sum_{t=1}^{T} \mathbf{M}(\tilde{P}, Q_t) + \mathrm{RE}\left(\tilde{P} \ \| \ P_1\right).$$

Since $\tilde{P}$ was chosen arbitrarily, this gives the statement of the theorem. ∎

In order to use MW, we need to choose the initial distribution P_1 and the parameter η. We start with the choice of P_1. In general, the closer P_1 is to a good mixed strategy $\tilde{P}$, the better the bound on the total loss of MW. However, even if we have no prior knowledge about the good mixed strategies, we can achieve reasonable performance by using the uniform distribution over the rows as the initial strategy. This gives us a performance bound that holds uniformly for all games with m rows. Note that there is *no* explicit dependence in this bound on the number of columns and only logarithmic dependence on the number of rows. Later, we exploit both these properties in the applications that follow.

Corollary 6.3 If MW is used with P_1 set to the uniform distribution, then its total loss is bounded by

$$\sum_{t=1}^{T} \mathbf{M}(P_t, Q_t) \leq a_\eta \min_P \sum_{t=1}^{T} \mathbf{M}(P, Q_t) + c_\eta \ln m$$

where a_η and c_η are as defined in theorem 6.1.

Proof If $P_1(i) = 1/m$ for all i, then $\mathrm{RE}\left(P \ \| \ P_1\right) \leq \ln m$ for all P. ∎

Next we discuss the choice of the parameter η. As η approaches zero, a_η approaches 1 from above while c_η increases to infinity. On the other hand, if we fix η and let the number of rounds T increase, then the second term $c_\eta \ln m$ becomes negligible (since it is fixed) relative to T. Thus, by choosing η as a function of T which approaches 0 for $T \to \infty$, the learner can ensure that its average per-trial loss will not be much worse than the loss of the best strategy. This is formalized in the following corollary:

Corollary 6.4 Under the conditions of theorem 6.1 and with η set to

$$\ln\left(1+\sqrt{\frac{2\ln m}{T}}\right),$$

the average per-trial loss suffered by the learner is

$$\frac{1}{T}\sum_{t=1}^{T}\mathbf{M}(P_t, Q_t) \leq \min_{P}\frac{1}{T}\sum_{t=1}^{T}\mathbf{M}(P, Q_t)+\Delta_T$$

where

$$\Delta_T \doteq \sqrt{\frac{2\ln m}{T}}+\frac{\ln m}{T}=O\left(\sqrt{\frac{\ln m}{T}}\right).$$

Proof By corollary 6.3,

$$\sum_{t=1}^{T}\mathbf{M}(P_t, Q_t) \leq \min_{P}\sum_{t=1}^{T}\mathbf{M}(P, Q_t)+(a_\eta-1)T+c_\eta\ln m \tag{6.16}$$

$$= \min_{P}\sum_{t=1}^{T}\mathbf{M}(P, Q_t)+\left[\left(\frac{\eta}{1-e^{-\eta}}-1\right)T+\frac{\ln m}{1-e^{-\eta}}\right]$$

$$\leq \min_{P}\sum_{t=1}^{T}\mathbf{M}(P, Q_t)+\left[\left(\frac{e^\eta-e^{-\eta}}{2(1-e^{-\eta})}-1\right)T+\frac{\ln m}{1-e^{-\eta}}\right]. \tag{6.17}$$

In equation (6.16), we used our assumption that the losses in $\mathbf{M}$ are bounded in $[0, 1]$, which implies that the loss in any sequence of T plays cannot exceed T. In equation (6.17), we used the approximation $\eta \leq (e^\eta-e^{-\eta})/2$, which holds for any $\eta \geq 0$ since, by Taylor series expansion,

$$\frac{e^\eta-e^{-\eta}}{2}=\eta+\frac{\eta^3}{3!}+\frac{\eta^5}{5!}+\cdots \geq \eta.$$

Minimizing the bracketed expression on the right-hand side of equation (6.17) gives the stated choice of η. Plugging in this choice gives the stated bound. ∎

Since $\Delta_T \to 0$ as $T \to \infty$, we see that the amount by which the average per-trial loss of the learner exceeds that of the best mixed strategy can be made arbitrarily small for large T. In other words, even with no prior knowledge of $\mathbf{M}$ or the environment, the learner plays almost as well online as if it knew ahead of time both the matrix $\mathbf{M}$ and the exact sequence of plays of the environment $Q_1, \ldots, Q_T$ (assuming the learner is restricted to using a fixed, mixed strategy for the entire sequence).

Note that in the analysis we made no assumptions at all about the environment. Theorem 6.1 guarantees that the learner's cumulative loss is not much larger than that of *any* fixed mixed strategy. As shown in the next corollary, this implies that the loss cannot be much larger than the game value. However, this is a considerable weakening of the general result: If the environment is nonadversarial, there might be a better row strategy, in which case the algorithm is guaranteed to be almost as good as this better strategy.

Corollary 6.5 Under the conditions of corollary 6.4,

$$\frac{1}{T}\sum_{t=1}^{T}\mathbf{M}(P_t, Q_t) \leq v + \Delta_T$$

where v is the value of the game $\mathbf{M}$.

Proof Let P^* be a minmax strategy for $\mathbf{M}$ so that for all column strategies Q, $\mathbf{M}(P^*, Q) \leq v$. Then, by corollary 6.4,

$$\frac{1}{T}\sum_{t=1}^{T}\mathbf{M}(P_t, Q_t) \leq \frac{1}{T}\sum_{t=1}^{T}\mathbf{M}(P^*, Q_t) + \Delta_T \leq v + \Delta_T. \qquad \blacksquare$$

6.2.4 Proof of the Minmax theorem

More interestingly, corollary 6.4 can be used to derive a very simple proof of von Neumann's minmax theorem as discussed in section 6.1.3. To prove this theorem, we need to show that

$$\min_{P}\max_{Q}\mathbf{M}(P, Q) = \max_{Q}\min_{P}\mathbf{M}(P, Q).$$

Proving that

$$\min_{P}\max_{Q}\mathbf{M}(P, Q) \geq \max_{Q}\min_{P}\mathbf{M}(P, Q), \tag{6.18}$$

as suggested earlier, is straightforward: For any $\tilde{P}$ and any Q, $\mathbf{M}(\tilde{P}, Q) \geq \min_P \mathbf{M}(P, Q)$. Thus, $\max_Q \mathbf{M}(\tilde{P}, Q) \geq \max_Q \min_P \mathbf{M}(P, Q)$. Since this holds for all $\tilde{P}$, we get equation (6.18). So the hard part of proving the minmax theorem is showing that

$$\min_{P}\max_{Q}\mathbf{M}(P, Q) \leq \max_{Q}\min_{P}\mathbf{M}(P, Q). \tag{6.19}$$

Suppose that we run algorithm MW (with η set as in corollary 6.4) against a maximally adversarial environment which always chooses strategies that maximize the learner's loss. That is, on each round t, the environment chooses

$$Q_t = \arg\max_{Q}\mathbf{M}(P_t, Q). \tag{6.20}$$

Let $\overline{P}$ and $\overline{Q}$ be the average of the strategies played by each side:

$$\overline{P} \doteq \frac{1}{T}\sum_{t=1}^{T}P_t \qquad \overline{Q} \doteq \frac{1}{T}\sum_{t=1}^{T}Q_t. \qquad\qquad (6.21)$$

Clearly, $\overline{P}$ and $\overline{Q}$ are probability distributions.

Then we have

$$\min_{P}\max_{Q} P^{\top}\mathbf{M}Q \le \max_{Q} \overline{P}^{\top}\mathbf{M}Q$$

$$= \max_{Q} \frac{1}{T}\sum_{t=1}^{T}P_t{}^{\top}\mathbf{M}Q \qquad \text{by definition of } \overline{P}$$

$$\le \frac{1}{T}\sum_{t=1}^{T}\max_{Q} P_t{}^{\top}\mathbf{M}Q$$

$$= \frac{1}{T}\sum_{t=1}^{T}P_t{}^{\top}\mathbf{M}Q_t \qquad \text{by definition of } Q_t$$

$$\le \min_{P} \frac{1}{T}\sum_{t=1}^{T}P^{\top}\mathbf{M}Q_t + \Delta_T \quad \text{by corollary 6.4}$$

$$= \min_{P} P^{\top}\mathbf{M}\overline{Q} + \Delta_T \qquad \text{by definition of } \overline{Q}$$

$$\le \max_{Q}\min_{P} P^{\top}\mathbf{M}Q + \Delta_T.$$

Since Δ_T can be made arbitrarily close to zero, this proves equation (6.19) and the minmax theorem.

6.2.5 Approximately Solving a Game

Aside from yielding a proof for a famous theorem that by now has many proofs, the preceding derivation shows that algorithm MW can be used to find an approximate minmax or maxmin strategy, that is, for approximately solving the game $\mathbf{M}$.

Skipping the first inequality of the sequence of equalities and inequalities given above, we see that

$$\max_{Q}\mathbf{M}(\overline{P}, Q) \le \max_{Q}\min_{P}\mathbf{M}(P, Q) + \Delta_T = v + \Delta_T.$$

Thus, the mixed strategy $\overline{P}$ is an *approximate minmax strategy* in the sense that for all column strategies Q, $\mathbf{M}(\overline{P}, Q)$ does not exceed the game value v by more than Δ_T. Since Δ_T can be made arbitrarily small, this approximation can be made arbitrarily tight.

Similarly, ignoring the last inequality of this derivation, we have that

$$\min_P \mathbf{M}(P, \overline{Q}) \ge v - \Delta_T,$$

so $\overline{Q}$ also is an *approximate maxmin strategy*. Furthermore, by equation (6.3), Q_t satisfying equation (6.20) can always be chosen to be a pure strategy (that is, a mixed strategy concentrated on a single column of $\mathbf{M}$). Therefore, the approximate maxmin strategy $\overline{Q}$ has the additional favorable property of being *sparse* in the sense that at most T of its entries will be nonzero.

Viewing MW as a method for approximately solving a game will be central to our derivation of a boosting algorithm in section 6.4.

6.3 Online Prediction

So far in this book, we have considered only learning in a "batch" setting in which the learner is provided with a random batch of training examples, and must formulate a single hypothesis that is then used for making predictions on new random test examples. Once training is complete, no further changes are made to the chosen prediction rule.

In contrast, in the *online prediction model*, the learner instead observes a sequence of examples and predicts their labels one at a time. Thus, at each of a series of time steps $t = 1, \ldots, T$, the learner is presented with an instance x_t, predicts the label for x_t, and then immediately gets to observe the correct label for x_t. A mistake occurs if the predicted and correct labels disagree. The learner's goal is to minimize the total number of mistakes made.

As a concrete example of where online learning might be appropriate, suppose we wish to predict stock market behavior over the course of some time period. Each morning, based on current market conditions, we predict whether or not some market indicator will go up or down that day. Then each evening, we find out whether that morning's prediction was right or not. Our goal is to learn over time how to make accurate predictions so that the total number of mistakes will be small.

There are important differences between the online and batch models. In the batch model, there is a strict division between the training phase and the testing phase. In the online model, training and testing occur together all at the same time since every example acts both as a test of what was learned in the past and as a training example for improving our predictions in the future.

A second key difference relates to the generation of examples. In the batch setting, we always assumed all examples to be random, independently and identically distributed. In the online model, *no* assumptions are made about the generation of examples. The sequence of examples is entirely arbitrary, and may even be under the control of an adversary who is deliberately trying to ruin the learner's performance.

The labels also might be adversarially chosen, in which case there is no way to limit the number of mistakes that might be forced on the learner. To provide meaningful results in such a setting, we therefore seek learning algorithms that perform well relative to the best fixed prediction rule or hypothesis in some possibly very large class of hypotheses. Thus, if there is any one hypothesis in this class that makes accurate predictions, then our learning algorithm should do so as well.

Historically, the game-playing algorithm MW presented above was a direct generalization of an online prediction algorithm called the *Weighted Majority Algorithm*. It is not surprising, therefore, that an online prediction algorithm can be derived from the more general game-playing algorithm by an appropriate choice of game **M**. In this section, we make this connection explicit as a step toward exposing the fundamental link that exists between online learning and boosting under the common umbrella of game theory.

To formalize the learning problem, let X be a finite set of instances, and let $\mathcal{H}$ be a finite space of hypotheses $h : X \rightarrow \{-1, +1\}$. These represent the fixed set of prediction rules against which the performance of the learning algorithm is to be compared. Let $c : X \rightarrow \{-1, +1\}$ be an unknown *target*, not necessarily in $\mathcal{H}$, defining the true and correct labels of each instance. This target may be entirely arbitrary. Even so, here we are implicitly introducing the mild assumption that the same instance never appears twice with different labels; this assumption is entirely unnecessary (see exercise 6.7), but it does simplify the presentation.

Learning takes place in a sequence of rounds. On round $t = 1, \ldots, T$:

1. the learner observes an instance $x_t \in X$, selected arbitrarily;
2. the learner makes a randomized prediction $\hat{y}_t \in \{-1, +1\}$ of the label associated with x_t;
3. the learner observes the correct label $c(x_t)$.

The expected number of mistakes made by the learner is

$$\mathbf{E}\left[\sum_{t=1}^{T} \mathbf{1}\{\hat{y}_t \neq c(x_t)\}\right] = \sum_{t=1}^{T} \mathbf{Pr}\left[\hat{y}_t \neq c(x_t)\right]. \tag{6.22}$$

Note that all expectations and probabilities in this context are taken with respect to the learner's own randomization, *not* the presentation of examples and labels which need not be random in any way. The number of mistakes made by any fixed hypothesis h is equal to

$$\sum_{t=1}^{T} \mathbf{1}\{h(x_t) \neq c(x_t)\}.$$

The goal of the learner is to minimize the expected number of mistakes made by the learner relative to the number of mistakes made by the *best* hypothesis in the space $\mathcal{H}$, determined in hindsight, that is,

$$\min_{h \in \mathcal{H}} \sum_{t=1}^{T} \mathbf{1}\{h(x_t) \neq c(x_t)\}.$$

Thus, we ask that the learner perform well whenever the target c is "close" to any one of the hypotheses in $\mathcal{H}$.

It is straightforward now to *reduce* the online prediction problem to a special case of the repeated game problem, that is, to show how an algorithm for repeated game-playing can be used as a "subroutine" to solve the online prediction problem. In this reduction, the environment's choice of a column will correspond to the choice of an instance $x \in X$ that is presented to the learner on a given iteration, while the learner's choice of a row will correspond to choosing a specific hypothesis $h \in \mathcal{H}$ which is then used to predict the label $h(x)$. More specifically, we define a game matrix that has $|\mathcal{H}|$ rows, indexed by $h \in \mathcal{H}$, and $|X|$ columns, indexed by $x \in X$. The matrix entry associated with hypothesis (row) h and instance (column) x is defined to be

$$\mathbf{M}(h, x) \doteq \mathbf{1}\{h(x) \neq c(x)\} = \begin{cases} 1 & \text{if } h(x) \neq c(x) \\ 0 & \text{otherwise.} \end{cases}$$

Thus, $\mathbf{M}(h, x)$ is 1 if and only if h disagrees with the target c on instance x. We call this the *mistake matrix*.

To derive an online learning algorithm, we apply MW to the mistake matrix $\mathbf{M}$. The reduction, shown schematically in figure 6.1, creates an intermediary between MW and the online prediction problem. On each round, P_t from MW and the selected instance x_t are used to compute a prediction $\hat{y}_t$. Then, after receiving $c(x_t)$, the matrix values $\mathbf{M}(\cdot, Q_t)$ can be computed and passed to MW for a suitable choice of Q_t.

More precisely, the distribution P_1 is first initialized by MW to be uniform over the hypotheses in $\mathcal{H}$. Next, on each round $t = 1, \dots, T$, the online learning algorithm based on this reduction does the following:

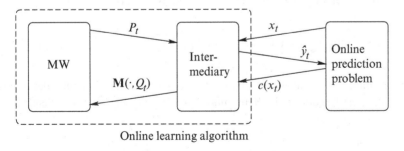

Online learning algorithm

Figure 6.1
A schematic diagram of the reduction showing how MW can be used in the context of online prediction.

1. receives instance $x_t \in X$;
2. chooses $h_t \in \mathcal{H}$ randomly according to the distribution P_t computed by MW;
3. predicts $\hat{y}_t = h_t(x_t)$;
4. receives $c(x_t)$;
5. lets Q_t be the pure strategy concentrated on x_t, and computes

$$\mathbf{M}(h, Q_t) = \mathbf{M}(h, x_t) = \mathbf{1}\{h(x_t) \neq c(x_t)\}$$

   for all $h \in \mathcal{H}$;
6. computes distribution P_{t+1} using algorithm MW; this reduces to the following update rule for all $h \in \mathcal{H}$:

$$P_{t+1}(h) = \frac{P_t(h)}{Z_t} \times \begin{cases} e^{-\eta} & \text{if } h(x_t) \neq c(x_t) \\ 1 & \text{otherwise} \end{cases}$$

   where Z_t is a normalization factor.

For the analysis, note that

$$
\begin{aligned}
\mathbf{M}(P_t, x_t) &= \sum_{h \in \mathcal{H}} P_t(h)\mathbf{M}(h, x_t) \\
&= \mathbf{Pr}_{h \sim P_t}[h(x_t) \neq c(x_t)] \\
&= \mathbf{Pr}[\hat{y}_t \neq c(x_t)].
\end{aligned}
\tag{6.23}
$$

By a direct application of corollary 6.4 (for an appropriate choice of η), we have

$$\sum_{t=1}^{T} \mathbf{M}(P_t, x_t) \leq \min_{h \in \mathcal{H}} \sum_{t=1}^{T} \mathbf{M}(h, x_t) + O\left(\sqrt{T \ln |\mathcal{H}|}\right).$$

Rewriting using the definition of $\mathbf{M}$ and equations (6.22) and (6.23) gives

$$\mathbf{E}\left[\sum_{t=1}^{T} \mathbf{1}\{\hat{y}_t \neq c(x_t)\}\right] \leq \min_{h \in \mathcal{H}} \sum_{t=1}^{T} \mathbf{1}\{h(x_t) \neq c(x_t)\} + O\left(\sqrt{T \ln |\mathcal{H}|}\right). \tag{6.24}$$

Thus, the expected number of mistakes made by the learner cannot exceed the number of mistakes made by the best hypothesis in $\mathcal{H}$ by more than $O\left(\sqrt{T \ln |\mathcal{H}|}\right)$. Equivalently, dividing both sides by T, we have

$$\mathbf{E}\left[\frac{1}{T}\sum_{t=1}^{T} \mathbf{1}\{\hat{y}_t \neq c(x_t)\}\right] \leq \min_{h \in \mathcal{H}} \frac{1}{T}\sum_{t=1}^{T} \mathbf{1}\{h(x_t) \neq c(x_t)\} + O\left(\sqrt{\frac{\ln |\mathcal{H}|}{T}}\right).$$

Since the last term vanishes as T becomes large, this says that the proportion of rounds where a mistake is made by the algorithm becomes very close to the best possible among all $h \in \mathcal{H}$.

These results can be straightforwardly generalized in many ways, for instance, to any bounded "loss" function (such as square loss rather than 0–1 mistake loss), or to a setting in which the learner attempts to achieve performance comparable to that of the best among a (possibly changing) set of "experts" rather than a fixed set of hypotheses.

6.4 Boosting

Finally, we come to boosting, which we study here in a simplified form. We will see now how boosting is a special case of the general game-playing setup of this chapter, and how this view leads not only to a (re-)derivation of an algorithm for boosting, but also to new insights into the very nature of the boosting problem.

As in section 6.3, let X be a space of instances (typically, in this setting, the training set), $\mathcal{H}$ a space of (weak) hypotheses, and c some unknown target or labeling function, used here, again, for simplicity of presentation. We assume the availability of a weak learning algorithm such that, for some $\gamma > 0$, and for any distribution D over the set X, the algorithm is able to find a hypothesis $h \in \mathcal{H}$ with error at most $\frac{1}{2} - \gamma$ with respect to the distribution D; this is the empirical γ-weak learning assumption of section 2.3.3.

To review, in boosting, the weak learning algorithm is run many times on many distributions, and the selected weak hypotheses are combined into a final hypothesis whose error should be small, or even zero. Thus, boosting proceeds in rounds. On round $t = 1, \ldots, T$:

1. the booster constructs a distribution D_t on X which is passed to the weak learner;

2. the weak learner produces a hypothesis $h_t \in \mathcal{H}$ with error at most $\frac{1}{2} - \gamma$:

$$\mathbf{Pr}_{x \sim D_t}[h_t(x) \neq c(x)] \leq \tfrac{1}{2} - \gamma.$$

After T rounds, the weak hypotheses $h_1, \ldots, h_T$ are combined into a final hypothesis H. As we know, the important issues for designing a boosting algorithm are (1) how to choose distributions D_t, and (2) how to combine the h_t's into a final hypothesis.

6.4.1 Boosting and the Minmax Theorem

Before deriving our boosting algorithm, let us step back for a moment to consider the relationship between the mistake matrix $\mathbf{M}$ used in section 6.3 and the minmax theorem. This relationship will turn out to be highly relevant to the design and understanding of the boosting algorithm that will follow.

Recall that the mistake matrix $\mathbf{M}$ has rows and columns indexed by hypotheses and instances, respectively, and that $\mathbf{M}(h, x) = 1$ if $h(x) \neq c(x)$ and is 0 otherwise. Assuming empirical γ-weak learnability as above, what does the minmax theorem say about $\mathbf{M}$? Suppose that the value of $\mathbf{M}$ is v. Then, together with equations (6.3) and (6.4), the minmax theorem tells us that

$$
\min_{P} \max_{x \in X} \mathbf{M}(P, x) = \min_{P} \max_{Q} \mathbf{M}(P, Q)
$$

$$
= v
$$

$$
= \max_{Q} \min_{P} \mathbf{M}(P, Q)
$$

$$
= \max_{Q} \min_{h \in \mathcal{H}} \mathbf{M}(h, Q). \tag{6.25}
$$

Note that, by $\mathbf{M}$'s definition,

$$
\mathbf{M}(h, Q) = \mathbf{Pr}_{x \sim Q}[h(x) \neq c(x)].
$$

Therefore, the right-hand part of equation (6.25) says that there exists a distribution Q^* on X such that for every hypothesis h, $\mathbf{M}(h, Q^*) = \mathbf{Pr}_{x \sim Q^*}[h(x) \neq c(x)] \geq v$. However, because we assume γ-weak learnability, there must exist a hypothesis h such that

$$
\mathbf{Pr}_{x \sim Q^*}[h(x) \neq c(x)] \leq \tfrac{1}{2} - \gamma.
$$

Combining these facts gives that $v \leq \tfrac{1}{2} - \gamma$.

On the other hand, the left part of equation (6.25) implies that there exists a distribution P^* over the hypothesis space $\mathcal{H}$ such that for every $x \in X$,

$$
\mathbf{Pr}_{h \sim P^*}[h(x) \neq c(x)] = \mathbf{M}(P^*, x) \leq v \leq \tfrac{1}{2} - \gamma < \tfrac{1}{2}. \tag{6.26}
$$

In words, this says that every instance x is misclassified by less than $\tfrac{1}{2}$ of the hypotheses, as weighted by P^*. That is, a weighted majority-vote classifier defined over $\mathcal{H}$, in which each hypothesis $h \in \mathcal{H}$ is assigned weight $P^*(h)$, will correctly classify all of the instances x; in symbols,

$$
c(x) = \mathrm{sign}\left(\sum_{h \in \mathcal{H}} P^*(h)\, h(x)\right)
$$

for all $x \in X$. Thus, the weak learning assumption, together with the minmax theorem, implies that the target c must be functionally equivalent (on X) to some weighted majority of hypotheses in $\mathcal{H}$.

This reasoning tells us something even stronger about the *margins* for this weighted majority vote. Recall from chapter 5 that the margin of an example is the difference between the weighted fraction of hypotheses voting for the correct label and the weighted fraction voting for an incorrect label. In this case, by equation (6.26), that difference will be at least

$$
\left(\tfrac{1}{2} + \gamma\right) - \left(\tfrac{1}{2} - \gamma\right) = 2\gamma.
$$

That is, the minimum margin over all examples will be at least 2γ. This is essentially the same result as in section 5.4.3, where it was argued that empirical γ-weak learnability implies (and is in fact equivalent to) linear separability with margin 2γ, an important example of the tight relationship between edges and margins. Now, within a game-theoretic context, we can see that they are both manifestations of the value of a very natural game, and that their close connection is a direct and immediate consequence of the minmax theorem.

6.4.2 Idea for Boosting

So the assumption of empirical γ-weak learnability implies that the target c can be computed exactly as a weighted majority of hypotheses in $\mathcal{H}$. Moreover, the weights used in this function (defined by distribution P^* above) are not just any old weights, but rather are a minmax strategy for the game $\mathbf{M}$. This is the basis of our boosting algorithm, namely, the idea of fitting the target labels c by approximating the weights P^* of this function. Since these weights are a minmax strategy of the game $\mathbf{M}$, our hope is to apply the method described in section 6.2 for approximately solving a game using the MW algorithm.

The problem is that the resulting algorithm does not fit the boosting model if applied to the mistake matrix $\mathbf{M}$. Recall that on each round, algorithm MW computes a distribution over the rows of the game matrix (hypotheses, in the case of matrix $\mathbf{M}$). However, in the boosting model, we want to compute on each round a distribution over instances (columns of $\mathbf{M}$).

Since we have an algorithm which computes distributions over rows, but need one that computes distributions over columns, the obvious solution is to reverse the roles of rows and columns. This is exactly the approach that we follow. That is, rather than using game $\mathbf{M}$ directly, we construct the *dual* of $\mathbf{M}$, which is the identical game except that the roles of the row and column players have been switched.

Constructing the dual $\mathbf{M}'$ of a game $\mathbf{M}$ is straightforward. First, we need to reverse row and column, so we take the transpose $\mathbf{M}^\top$. This, however, is not enough since the column player of $\mathbf{M}$ wants to maximize the outcome, but the row player of $\mathbf{M}'$ wants to minimize the outcome (loss). Therefore, we also need to reverse the meaning of minimum and maximum, which is easily done by negating the matrix, yielding $-\mathbf{M}^\top$. Finally, to adhere to our convention of losses being in the range $[0, 1]$, we add the constant 1 to every outcome, which has no effect on the game. Thus, the dual $\mathbf{M}'$ of $\mathbf{M}$ is simply

$$\mathbf{M}' = \mathbf{1} - \mathbf{M}^\top \tag{6.27}$$

where $\mathbf{1}$ is an all 1's matrix of the appropriate dimensions.

In the case of the mistake matrix $\mathbf{M}$, the dual now has $|X|$ rows and $|\mathcal{H}|$ columns indexed by instances and hypotheses, respectively, and each entry is

$$\mathbf{M}'(x, h) \doteq 1 - \mathbf{M}(h, x) = \mathbf{1}\{h(x) = c(x)\} = \begin{cases} 1 & \text{if } h(x) = c(x) \\ 0 & \text{otherwise.} \end{cases}$$

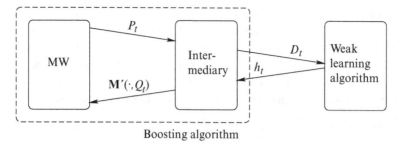

Figure 6.2
A schematic diagram of the reduction showing how MW can be used to derive a boosting algorithm.

Note that any minmax strategy of the game $\mathbf{M}$ becomes a maxmin strategy of the game $\mathbf{M}'$. Therefore, whereas previously we were interested in finding an approximate minmax strategy of $\mathbf{M}$, we are now interested in finding an approximate maxmin strategy of $\mathbf{M}'$.

We can now apply algorithm MW to game matrix $\mathbf{M}'$ since, by the results of section 6.2.5, this will lead to the construction of an approximate maxmin strategy. As shown in figure 6.2, the reduction now creates an intermediary between MW and the weak learning algorithm, on each round using the distribution P_t received from MW to compute D_t, then using the hypothesis h_t received in response from the weak learner to compute $\mathbf{M}'(\cdot, Q_t)$ for an appropriate choice of Q_t. In more detailed terms, the reduction proceeds as follows: The distribution P_1 is initialized as in MW, that is, uniform over X. Then on each round of boosting $t = 1, \dots, T$, under this reduction the boosting algorithm does the following:

1. sets $D_t = P_t$ and passes D_t to the weak learning algorithm;

2. receives from the weak learner a hypothesis h_t satisfying

$$\mathbf{Pr}_{x \sim D_t}[h_t(x) = c(x)] \geq \tfrac{1}{2} + \gamma;$$

3. lets Q_t be the pure strategy concentrated on h_t, and computes

$$\mathbf{M}'(x, Q_t) = \mathbf{M}'(x, h_t) = \mathbf{1}\{h_t(x) = c(x)\}$$

for all $x \in X$;

4. computes the new distribution P_{t+1} using algorithm MW; that is, for all $x \in X$,

$$P_{t+1}(x) = \frac{P_t(x)}{Z_t} \times \begin{cases} e^{-\eta} & \text{if } h_t(x) = c(x) \\ 1 & \text{otherwise} \end{cases}$$

where Z_t is a normalization factor.

Our goal, again, is to find an approximate maxmin strategy of $\mathbf{M}'$ using the method of approximately solving a game given in section 6.2.5. According to that method, on each round t, Q_t may be a pure strategy h_t, and should be chosen to maximize

$$\mathbf{M}'(P_t, h_t) = \sum_x P_t(x)\mathbf{M}'(x, h_t) = \mathbf{Pr}_{x \sim P_t}[h_t(x) = c(x)].$$

In other words, h_t should have maximum accuracy with respect to distribution P_t. This is exactly the goal of the weak learner. (Although it is not guaranteed to succeed in finding the *best* h_t, finding one of accuracy $\frac{1}{2} + \gamma$ turns out to be sufficient for our purposes.)

So the weak learner aims to maximize the weighted accuracy of the weak hypotheses, as is natural, but in this game-theoretic setting, the goal of the booster is exactly the opposite, namely, to choose distributions D_t which make it as hard as possible for the weak learner to find an accurate hypothesis. Thus, although we have said informally that boosting focuses on hard examples, we see now that it would be more accurate to say that boosting focuses on finding the hardest *distribution* over examples.

Finally, the method from section 6.2.5 suggests that $\overline{Q} = \frac{1}{T}\sum_{t=1}^{T} Q_t$ is an approximate maxmin strategy, and we know that the target c is equivalent to a majority of the hypotheses if weighted by a maxmin strategy of $\mathbf{M}'$. Since Q_t is, in our case, concentrated on pure strategy (hypothesis) h_t, this leads us to choose a final hypothesis H which is the (simple) majority of $h_1, \ldots, h_T$:

$$H(x) = \text{sign}\left(\sum_{t=1}^{T} h_t(x)\right).$$

Note that as a side effect,

$$\overline{P} = \frac{1}{T}\sum_{t=1}^{T} P_t = \frac{1}{T}\sum_{t=1}^{T} D_t$$

will likewise converge to an approximate minmax solution of $\mathbf{M}'$. Thus, the (average of the) distributions D_t computed by boosting also have a natural game-theoretic interpretation.

6.4.3 Analysis

Indeed, the resulting boosting procedure will compute a final hypothesis H that is functionally equivalent to c for sufficiently large T. We show in this section how this follows from corollary 6.4.

As noted earlier, for all t, by our assumption of γ-weak learnability,

$$\mathbf{M}'(P_t, h_t) = \mathbf{Pr}_{x \sim P_t}[h_t(x) = c(x)] \geq \frac{1}{2} + \gamma.$$

By corollary 6.4, for an appropriate choice of η, this implies that

$$\frac{1}{2} + \gamma \leq \frac{1}{T}\sum_{t=1}^{T} \mathbf{M}'(P_t, h_t) \leq \min_{x \in X} \frac{1}{T}\sum_{t=1}^{T} \mathbf{M}'(x, h_t) + \Delta_T, \tag{6.28}$$

and so, for all x,

$$\frac{1}{T}\sum_{t=1}^{T}\mathbf{M}'(x,h_t) \geq \frac{1}{2}+\gamma-\Delta_T > \frac{1}{2} \tag{6.29}$$

where the last inequality holds for sufficiently large T (specifically, when $\Delta_T < \gamma$). Note that by definition of $\mathbf{M}'$, $\sum_{t=1}^{T}\mathbf{M}'(x,h_t)$ is exactly the number of hypotheses h_t which agree with c on instance x. Therefore, in words, equation (6.29) says that more than half the hypotheses h_t are correct on x. This means, by definition of H, that $H(x)=c(x)$ for all x.

For the above to hold, we need only that $\Delta_T < \gamma$, which will be the case for $T = \Omega((\ln|X|)/\gamma^2)$. Moreover, by the same argument as in section 6.4.2 applied to equation (6.29), we see that every x will have margin at least $2\gamma-2\Delta_T$. Thus, as T gets large and Δ_T approaches zero, a minimum margin of at least 2γ is obtained asymptotically. Together with the discussion in section 5.4.3, this shows that the optimal margin is achieved asymptotically, assuming that the "best" (minimum weighted error) weak hypothesis h_t is chosen on every round.

When the game-playing subroutine MW is "compiled out," and when η is replaced by 2α (for cosmetic compatibility with earlier notation), the result of our reduction is a simplified version of AdaBoost (algorithm 1.1 (p. 5)) in which all of the α_t's are set equal to the fixed parameter α. We refer to this simplified algorithm as α-Boost, although it has sometimes also been called ε-boosting or ε-AdaBoost.

The analysis above shows that α-Boost converges to the maximum margin combined classifier when α and T are chosen together in concert according to the dictates of corollary 6.4, suggesting that T must be delicately tuned as a function of α (or vice versa). In fact, a slightly different analysis shows that the same result holds true if α is simply chosen to be "very small" and the algorithm is then run for a "long time" (with no danger of running for too long). In particular, instead of using corollary 6.4 in equation (6.28), we can apply corollary 6.3. This gives

$$\frac{1}{2}+\gamma \leq \frac{1}{T}\sum_{t=1}^{T}\mathbf{M}'(P_t,h_t) \leq a_\eta \min_{x\in X}\frac{1}{T}\sum_{t=1}^{T}\mathbf{M}'(x,h_t)+\frac{c_\eta\ln m}{T}$$

where $\eta=2\alpha$. Rearranging gives

$$\min_{x\in X}\frac{1}{T}\sum_{t=1}^{T}\mathbf{M}'(x,h_t) \geq \frac{1}{a_\eta}\left[\left(\frac{1}{2}+\gamma\right)-\frac{c_\eta\ln m}{T}\right]$$

$$=\left(\frac{1}{2}+\gamma\right)-\left(1-\frac{1-e^{-2\alpha}}{2\alpha}\right)\left(\frac{1}{2}+\gamma\right)-\frac{\ln m}{2\alpha T}$$

$$\geq \left(\frac{1}{2}+\gamma\right) - \alpha\left(\frac{1}{2}+\gamma\right) - \frac{\ln m}{2\alpha T}$$

where the last inequality uses the Taylor approximation $e^{-z} \leq 1 - z + z^2/2$ for all $z \geq 0$. Thus, by similar arguments as before, all examples x will have margin at least

$$2\gamma - \alpha(1 + 2\gamma) - \frac{\ln m}{\alpha T}.$$

When T is very large, the rightmost term becomes negligible, so that asymptotically the margins come within $\alpha(1 + 2\gamma) \leq 2\alpha$ of 2γ, the best possible margin for the given γ-weak learning assumption (see section 5.4.3). Thus, this argument shows that a combined classifier can be found with a minimum margin that is arbitrarily close to optimal by using an appropriately small choice of α, followed by a long run of the algorithm (with specific rates of convergence as given above).

So, as an alternative to AdaBoost or the variants given in section 5.4.2, we see that the simpler algorithm α-Boost can be used for maximizing the minimum margin. However, in addition to the caveats of section 5.4.2, we expect this procedure in practice to be slow since α must be small, and T must be correspondingly large.

6.5 Application to a "Mind-Reading" Game

We end this chapter with a brief description of an application of these ideas to a simple game called *penny-matching*, or *odds and evens*. One player is designated the "evens" player and the other is "odds." On every round of play, they both choose and then simultaneously reveal a single bit, either $+$ or $-$ (which we sometimes identify with $+1$ and -1). If the two bits match, then the evens player wins; otherwise, the odds player wins. The game is typically played for multiple rounds.

As in Rock-Paper-Scissors, the penny-matching game incorporates elements of a mind-reading contest in the sense that each player attempts to predict what the other player will do, and to act accordingly, while simultaneously trying to behave unpredictably. Of course, the players can in principle choose their bits entirely at random (which would be the minmax strategy for the game); however, unless provided with an external source of randomness, such as an actual coin or a computer, humans turn out to be very bad at behaving in a truly random fashion (we will see some empirical evidence for this below). Moreover, players who can successfully discern their opponent's intentions will have a much better chance of winning.

In the 1950s, David Hagelbarger and later Claude Shannon created learning machines to play this game against a human in an early exploration of how to make "intelligent" computing devices. In those days, this meant literally building a machine—figure 6.3 shows a schematic diagram of Hagelbarger's, which he called a "sequence extrapolating robot."

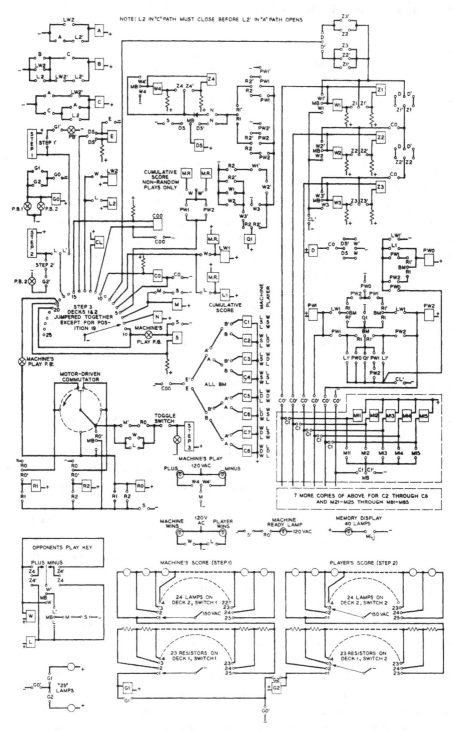

Figure 6.3
(Caption on facing page)

(Shannon referred to his as a "mind-reading (?) machine" (*sic*).) Both their designs were very simple, keeping track of how the human behaved in similar circumstances, and then acting accordingly based on this history. On each round, their machines would consider the current "state of play" and how the human had previously behaved when this identical state had been encountered, then formulating a prediction of the human's next play accordingly. In their machines, the notion of state of play was limited to what had happened on the last two rounds, specifically, whether the human won or lost the last round; whether the human won or lost the time before that; and whether the human played differently or the same on the last two rounds.

Here, we describe a more sophisticated approach to playing this game based on the online prediction framework of section 6.3. As we have discussed, the essential problem in this game is that of predicting what one's opponent will do next. Moreover, these predictions must be made in an online fashion. And regarding the "data" as random in this adversarial setting seems entirely unreasonable. Given these attributes of the problem, the online learning model seems to be especially well suited.

Recall that in online prediction, on each round t the learner receives an instance x_t, formulates a prediction $\hat{y}_t$, and observes an outcome, or label $c(x_t)$, which we henceforth denote by y_t. The learner's goal is to minimize the number of mistakes, that is, rounds in which $\hat{y}_t \neq y_t$. To cast the penny-matching game in these terms, we first identify the learner with the "evens" player, whose goal is to match the human opponent's bits. On round t, we identify y_t with the human's chosen bit on that round, and we take the learner's prediction $\hat{y}_t$ to be its own chosen bit. Then the learner loses the round if and only if $\hat{y}_t \neq y_t$. In other words, in this setup minimizing mistakes in online prediction is the same as minimizing the number of rounds lost in penny-matching.

As presented in section 6.3, given an instance x_t, an online learning algorithm formulates its own prediction $\hat{y}_t$ based on the predictions $h(x_t)$ made by the rules h in a space $\mathcal{H}$. In the current setting, we take the instance x_t to be the entire history up to (but not including) round t; specifically, this means all of the plays made by both players on the first $t-1$ rounds. Given this history, each prediction rule h makes its own prediction of what the human will do next.

The algorithm presented in section 6.3 gives a technique for combining the predictions of the rules in $\mathcal{H}$ so that the composite predictions $\hat{y}_t$ will be almost as good as those of the best rule in the space.

So all that remains is to choose a set $\mathcal{H}$ of predictors. Our bounds suggest that $\mathcal{H}$ can be rather large, and we only need to anticipate that one of the rules will be good. Clearly, there are many sorts of predictors we might imagine, and here we describe just one of many possible approaches.

Figure 6.3
The circuit design of Hagelbarger's machine for playing penny-matching. (Copyright ©1956 IRE (now IEEE). Reprinted, with permission, from *IRE Transactions on Electronic Computers*, EC-5(1):1–7, March 1956.)

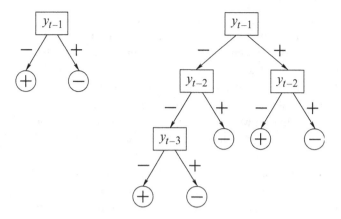

Figure 6.4
Two example context trees for predicting the human's next bit y_t based on those previously played, $y_1, \ldots, y_{t-1}$.
The trees are evaluated as in section 1.3, which in this case means working our way backward through the history
of played bits until a leaf node is reached that provides the tree's prediction for the current context.

As was done by Hagelbarger and Shannon, it seems especially natural to consider predictors that take into account the recent past. For instance, suppose the human tends to alternate
between plays of $-$ and $+$ leading to runs like this:

$$- + - + - + - + - + - + - \cdots$$

Such a pattern can be captured by a rule that says if the last bit was $-$, then predict $+$ for the
current round; and if the last bit was $+$, then predict $-$. This simple rule can be represented
by a decision tree like the stubby one on the left of figure 6.4, where the nodes indicate
the bit to be tested to determine which branch to follow, and the leaves provide the rule's
prediction for the next bit.

Suppose now that the human instead tends to create more complicated patterns like this
one:

$$+ + - - - + + - - - + + - - - \cdots$$

This pattern can be similarly captured by a decision tree as shown on the right of figure 6.4.
For instance, the tree tells us, in part, that if the last bit was $+$ and the one before that was
$-$, then the next bit should be predicted $+$. But if the last two bits were $-$, then, according
to this rule, we need to look one more bit back to arrive at a prediction,

Note that although we have motivated these rules with simple patterns like the ones
above, such rules need not give perfect predictions to be useful in our setting. It is enough
that they capture general tendencies that enable them to make predictions that are better
than random.

Such decision trees are called *context trees* since each prediction is formulated based on
the context of the recent past and we work our way back in time until the rule has enough

information to make a prediction. The trees we have considered so far take into account only how the human has played, but in general we may also wish to consider other aspects of the recent past, such as who won the round, and whether or not the human's predictions changed from one round to the next. Indeed, rules based on Hagelbarger and Shannon's "state of play" could be put into the form of such a tree as well.

So the idea is to identify the rules used by our online prediction algorithm with such context trees. This leads, of course, to the question of *which* trees to include in our rule space. To answer this, we begin by fixing an order in which the past is probed. For instance, the trees above, on round t, first test the last bit y_{t-1} played by the human, then the preceding bit y_{t-2}, then y_{t-3}, and so on. This means that all the trees we consider will test the value of y_{t-1} at the root, then all nodes at the next level down will test y_{t-2}, and so on. The point is that the tests associated with particular nodes are fixed and the same for all trees in the family. (Although we focus on there being just a single, fixed ordering of the tests, these methods can immediately be generalized to the case in which there are instead a small number of orderings considered, each defining its own family of trees.)

Subject to this restriction on the ordering of the tests, we can now consider including in $\mathcal{H}$ *all possible* context trees, meaning all possible topologies, or ways of cutting off the tree, and all possible ways of labeling the leaves. For instance, figure 6.4 shows two possible trees that are consistent with the specific restrictions we described above. In general, there will be an exponential number of such trees since there are exponentially many tree topologies and exponentially many leaf labelings to consider. As previously mentioned, this huge number of rules is not necessarily a problem in terms of performance since the bounds (such as in equation (6.24)) are only logarithmic in $|\mathcal{H}|$. Moreover, it is not implausible to expect at least one such rule to capture the kinds of patterns typically selected by humans.

On the other hand, computationally, having a very large number of rules is prohibitively expensive since a naive implementation of this algorithm requires space and time-per-round that are linear in $|\mathcal{H}|$. Nevertheless, for this particular well-structured family of rules, it turns out that the online learning algorithm of section 6.3 can be implemented extremely efficiently in terms of both time and space. This is because the required tree-based computations collapse into a form in which a kind of dynamic programming can be applied.

These ideas were implemented into a "mind-reading game" that is publicly available on the Internet (`seed.ucsd.edu/~mindreader`) in which the computer and the human play against one another until one player has won a hundred rounds.

Figure 6.5 shows a histogram of the final scores for 11,882 games recorded between March 2006 and June 2008. The score is the number of rounds won by the human minus the number won by the computer (so it is positive if and only if the human won the entire game). The figure shows that the computer usually wins, and often by a wide margin. In fact, the computer won 86.6% of these games. The average score of all the games was -41.0 with a median of -42, meaning that on half the games, the human had won 58 or fewer rounds by the time the computer had won 100. Of course, a purely random player

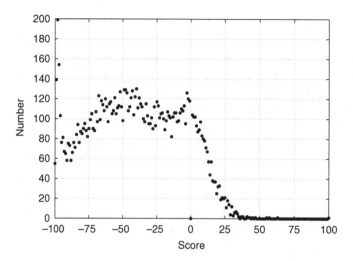

Figure 6.5
A histogram of the number of games played (out of 11,882) for each possible final score between −100 and 100, where the score is the number of rounds won by the human minus the number won by the computer, so games with negative scores were won by the computer. (No games had a score of zero since ties are not possible under the rules of this game.)

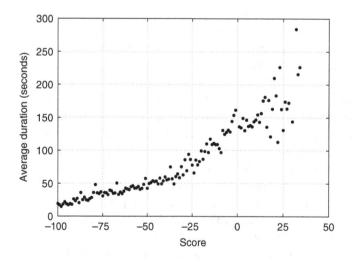

Figure 6.6
A plot of the average duration (in seconds) of the game compared with the final score of the game. For every possible score, a point is plotted whose x-value is the score and whose y-value is the average of the durations of all games which ended with that particular final score. (No point was plotted for scores with fewer than five such games. Also, to mitigate the effect of outliers, the few games that lasted more than ten minutes were treated as if they had lasted exactly ten minutes.)

would do much better than humans against the computer, necessarily winning 50% of the games, and achieving an average and median score of zero (in expectation).

A curious phenomenon revealed by this data is shown in figure 6.6. Apparently, the faster humans play, the more likely they are to lose. Presumably, this is because faster play tends to be more predictable, often leading to rhythmic and patterned key banging that the learning algorithm can quickly pick up on.

Summary

We have seen in this chapter how AdaBoost (or at least a simplified variant) can be viewed as a special case of a more general algorithm for solving games through repeated play. This has allowed us to understand AdaBoost more deeply, showing, for instance, that:

1. the weights on the weak hypotheses in the combined classifier must converge to an approximate maxmin strategy for the (dual) mistake-matrix game associated with boosting;

2. the (average of the) distributions D_t over examples must converge to an approximate minmax strategy for this same game;

3. the notions of edge and margin are intimately connected via the minmax theorem.

Moreover, we have seen how online learning is the dual problem of boosting.

Bibliographic Notes

Our development of basic game theory in section 6.1 is standard. Further background can be found in any of a number of introductory texts, such as [103, 174, 179, 180]. The minmax theorem of section 6.1.3 is due to von Neumann [175].

The algorithm and its analysis, and the proof of the minmax theorem appearing in section 6.2, are all taken from Freund and Schapire [94, 96], whose work is a direct generalization of Littlestone and Warmuth's [155]. Algorithms with this same "no-regret" property (also called "Hannan consistency" or "universal consistency"), whose loss is guaranteed to be not much worse than that of the best fixed strategy, date back to the 1950s with the work of Hannan [117] and Blackwell [23, 24]. Other methods include those of Foster and Vohra [86], and Hart and Mas-Colell [118], as well as Fudenberg and Levine [101], whose method of "exponential fictitious play" strongly resembles the Weighted Majority Algorithm.

The online prediction model studied in section 6.3 was first considered by Littlestone and Warmuth [155] and Vovk [229], although its roots connect it with work in numerous other fields, such as game theory and data compression. The Weighted Majority Algorithm and its analysis, as presented here, are originally due to Littlestone and Warmuth [155]. Its rederivation is due to Freund and Schapire [94]. Better bounds than those presented here for the online prediction problem were obtained by Cesa-Bianchi et al. [45], and Vovk [229].

For further background on no-regret algorithms and online learning, see Cesa-Bianchi and Lugosi's excellent book [47]. A somewhat different perspective on learning and game theory is given in Fudenberg and Levine's book [102].

The connection between boosting and game playing described in section 6.4 is due to Freund and Schapire [94]. However, from the very beginning, AdaBoost was linked with online learning, having been originally derived directly from a generalization of the Weighted Majority Algorithm called "Hedge" [95].

The α-Boost algorithm of section 6.4.3, in which all of the α_t's are held fixed to a small constant α, was suggested by Friedman [100]. The convergence and margin-maximizing properties of this algorithm were studied by Rosset, Zhu, and Hastie [192], and by Zhang and Yu [236]. The proof given here is similar to the one given by Xi et al. [233].

Any game can be solved using linear programming, and, conversely, it is known that the solution of any linear program can be obtained by solving an appropriate zero-sum game [62]. This equivalence also points to the close relationship between boosting and linear programming; indeed, the problem of finding the maximum-margin classifier can be formulated as a linear program. This connection is studied in depth by Grove and Schuurmans [111] and Demiriz, Bennett, and Shawe-Taylor [65].

A method for combining online learning and boosting—specifically, for running AdaBoost in an online fashion—is given by Oza and Russell [181].

Early machines for learning to play penny-matching, as in section 6.5, were invented by Hagelbarger [115] and later by Shannon [213]. Figure 6.3 is reprinted from the former. The technique of combining the predictions of all possible context trees is due to Helmbold and Schapire [122], in a direct adaptation of Willems, Shtarkov, and Tjalkens's method for weighting context trees [231]. The Internet implementation was created by the authors with Anup Doshi.

The episode of *The Simpsons* quoted in section 6.1.3 first aired on April 15, 1993 (episode #9F16).

Some of the exercises in this chapter are based on material from [62, 96, 153].

Exercises

In the exercises below, assume all game matrices have entries only in [0, 1], except where noted otherwise.

6.1 Show that the minmax theorem (equation (6.6)) is false when working with pure strategies. In other words, give an example of a game $\mathbf{M}$ for which

$$\min_i \max_j \mathbf{M}(i, j) \neq \max_j \min_i \mathbf{M}(i, j).$$

6.2 Suppose MW is used to play against itself on an $m \times n$ game matrix $\mathbf{M}$. That is, on each round, the row player selects its mixed strategy P_t using MW, and the column player selects Q_t using another copy of MW applied to the dual matrix $\mathbf{M}'$ (equation (6.27)). Use corollary 6.4, applied to these two copies of MW, to give an alternative proof of the minmax theorem. Also, show that $\overline{P}$ and $\overline{Q}$, as defined in equation (6.21), are approximate minmax and maxmin strategies.

6.3 What is the relationship between the value v of a game $\mathbf{M}$ and the value v' of its dual $\mathbf{M}'$ (equation (6.27))? In particular, if $\mathbf{M}$ is *symmetric* (that is, equal to its dual), what must its value be? Justify your answers.

6.4 Let $S = \langle x_1, \ldots, x_m \rangle$ be any sequence of m distinct points in $\mathcal{X}$. Referring to the definitions in section 5.3, prove that

$$R_S(\mathcal{H}) \leq O\left(\sqrt{\frac{\ln |\mathcal{H}|}{m}}\right) \tag{6.30}$$

by applying the analysis in section 6.3 to an appropriately constructed presentation of examples and labels. (Equation (6.30) is the same as equation (5.22), but with possibly weaker constants.) [*Hint:* Consider choosing all labels uniformly at random.]

6.5 The vMW algorithm is a variant of MW in which the parameter η varies from round to round. Let $u \in [0, 1]$ be a given "estimate" of the value of the game $\mathbf{M}$. The vMW algorithm starts with an arbitrary initial strategy P_1. On each round t, the new mixed strategy P_{t+1} is computed from P_t as in equation (6.9), but with η replaced by η_t where

$$\eta_t \doteq \max\left\{0, \ln\left(\frac{(1-u)\ell_t}{u(1-\ell_t)}\right)\right\},$$

and where $\ell_t \doteq \mathbf{M}(P_t, Q_t)$. Let

$$\hat{Q} \doteq \frac{\sum_{t=1}^{T} \eta_t Q_t}{\sum_{t=1}^{T} \eta_t}.$$

For parts (a) and (b), assume $\ell_t \geq u$ for all t.

a. For any mixed strategy $\tilde{P}$, show that if $\mathbf{M}(\tilde{P}, \hat{Q}) \leq u$, then

$$\mathrm{RE}\left(\tilde{P} \parallel P_{T+1}\right) - \mathrm{RE}\left(\tilde{P} \parallel P_1\right) \leq -\sum_{t=1}^{T} \mathrm{RE}_b\left(u \parallel \ell_t\right).$$

b. Show that

$$\mathbf{Pr}_{i \sim P_1}\left[\mathbf{M}(i, \hat{Q}) \leq u\right] = \sum_{i : \mathbf{M}(i, \hat{Q}) \leq u} P_1(i) \leq \exp\left(-\sum_{t=1}^{T} \mathrm{RE}_b\left(u \parallel \ell_t\right)\right).$$

c. Suppose the value v of the game is at most u, and suppose vMW is run with P_1 chosen to be the uniform distribution. For all $\varepsilon > 0$, show that the number of rounds t on which $\ell_t \geq u + \varepsilon$ cannot exceed

$$\frac{\ln m}{\mathrm{RE}_b\left(u \parallel u + \varepsilon\right)}.$$

d. Show how AdaBoost can be derived from vMW, and how its analysis in theorem 3.1 follows as a special case of part (b). (You can assume that $\epsilon_t \leq \frac{1}{2}$ on every round of AdaBoost.)

e. Likewise, show how the version of AdaBoost given in section 5.4.2 with α_t set as in equation (5.34) can be derived from vMW, and how the bound in equation (5.35) follows as a special case of part (b). (Assume $\gamma_t \geq \theta/2$ on every round t.)

f. Explain in precise terms, using the language of boosting, the implications of part (c) for the boosting algorithms considered in parts (d) and (e).

6.6 In the online learning framework of section 6.3, suppose the target c is linearly separable with margin θ. That is, suppose there exists a weight vector $\mathbf{w}$ on the classifiers in $\mathcal{H}$ such that $\|\mathbf{w}\|_1 = 1$, and for all $x \in X$,

$$c(x) \left(\sum_{h \in \mathcal{H}} w_h h(x) \right) \geq \theta$$

where $\theta > 0$ is known (but $\mathbf{w}$ is not). Derive and analyze an online algorithm that makes its predictions on each round using a (deterministic) weighted majority vote of the classifiers in $\mathcal{H}$, and that makes at most

$$O\left(\frac{\ln |\mathcal{H}|}{\theta^2} \right)$$

mistakes on any sequence of examples. Give explicit constants. [*Hint:* Use exercise 6.5.]

6.7 In the online learning framework of section 6.3, we assumed that each instance x_t is labeled by $c(x_t)$, where c is some unknown target function. This means that the same instance x cannot appear twice with different labels. Suppose we remove this assumption so that the "correct" label associated with each instance x_t is now allowed to be an arbitrary value $y_t \in \{-1, +1\}$. For this relaxed setting, show that the bound in equation (6.24), with $c(x_t)$ replaced by y_t, holds for an appropriate modification of the algorithm given in section 6.3.

6.8 In the modified online learning setting of exercise 6.7, suppose that the instance space X is not too large, and that $\mathcal{H}$ is chosen to be all possible binary functions on X, that is, all functions $h : X \to \{-1, +1\}$. Since $|\mathcal{H}| = 2^{|X|}$, a naive implementation of the (modified) algorithm of section 6.3 would require time and space that are exponential in $|X|$. Devise an alternative algorithm which (1) is equivalent in terms of its input-output behavior (so that it makes identical (randomized) predictions when given identical observations), but (2) whose space requirements are only linear in $|X|$, and whose per-round time requirements are even better. Show that your algorithm has both these properties.

6.9 This exercise explores a kind of equivalence that exists between linear programming and solving zero-sum games. A *linear program* is an optimization problem in which the goal is to maximize a linear objective function subject to linear inequality constraints. Thus, the problem has the following form:

maximize: $\mathbf{c} \cdot \mathbf{x}$

subject to: $\mathbf{A}\mathbf{x} \le \mathbf{b}$ and $\mathbf{x} \ge \mathbf{0}$.   (6.31)

Here, our aim is to solve for $\mathbf{x} \in \mathbb{R}^n$ given $\mathbf{A} \in \mathbb{R}^{m \times n}$, $\mathbf{b} \in \mathbb{R}^m$, and $\mathbf{c} \in \mathbb{R}^n$. Also, in this exercise we use inequality between vectors to mean componentwise inequality (that is, $\mathbf{u} \ge \mathbf{v}$ if and only if $u_i \ge v_i$ for all i).

a. Show that the problem of solving a game, that is, finding a minmax strategy P^*, can be formulated as a linear program.

Every linear program in its *primal form*, as in program (6.31), has a corresponding *dual program* over dual variables $\mathbf{y} \in \mathbb{R}^m$:

minimize: $\mathbf{b} \cdot \mathbf{y}$

subject to: $\mathbf{A}^\top \mathbf{y} \ge \mathbf{c}$ and $\mathbf{y} \ge \mathbf{0}$.   (6.32)

b. What is the dual of the linear program that was found in part (a)? In game-theoretic terms, what is the meaning of its solution?

Returning to the general linear program above and its dual (programs (6.31) and (6.32)), a vector $\mathbf{x} \in \mathbb{R}^n$ is said to be *feasible* if $\mathbf{A}\mathbf{x} \le \mathbf{b}$ and $\mathbf{x} \ge \mathbf{0}$; likewise, $\mathbf{y} \in \mathbb{R}^m$ is feasible if $\mathbf{A}^\top \mathbf{y} \ge \mathbf{c}$ and $\mathbf{y} \ge \mathbf{0}$.

c. Show that if $\mathbf{x}$ and $\mathbf{y}$ are both feasible, then $\mathbf{c} \cdot \mathbf{x} \le \mathbf{b} \cdot \mathbf{y}$. Further, if $\mathbf{x}$ and $\mathbf{y}$ are feasible and $\mathbf{c} \cdot \mathbf{x} = \mathbf{b} \cdot \mathbf{y}$, show that $\mathbf{x}$ and $\mathbf{y}$ are solutions of the primal and dual problems, respectively. [*Hint:* Consider $\mathbf{y}^\top \mathbf{A}\mathbf{x}$.]

Consider the $(m+n+1) \times (m+n+1)$ game matrix

$$\mathbf{M} \doteq \begin{pmatrix} \mathbf{0} & \mathbf{A}^\top & -\mathbf{c} \\ -\mathbf{A} & \mathbf{0} & \mathbf{b} \\ \mathbf{c}^\top & -\mathbf{b}^\top & \mathbf{0} \end{pmatrix}.$$

Here, entries of $\mathbf{M}$ that are matrices or vectors stand for entire blocks of entries, and each $\mathbf{0}$ is a matrix composed of 0's of the appropriate size. (Note that here we have dropped our convention of requiring that all entries of $\mathbf{M}$ be in $[0, 1]$.)

d. What is the value of the game $\mathbf{M}$?

e. Let P^* be a minmax solution of the game $\mathbf{M}$ which, being a vector in $\mathbb{R}^{m+n+1}$, can be written in the form

$$\begin{pmatrix} \mathbf{x} \\ \mathbf{y} \\ z \end{pmatrix}$$

where $\mathbf{x} \in \mathbb{R}^n$, $\mathbf{y} \in \mathbb{R}^m$, and $z \in \mathbb{R}$. Show that if $z \neq 0$, then $\mathbf{x}/z$ and $\mathbf{y}/z$ are solutions of the primal and dual problems, respectively.

7 Loss Minimization and Generalizations of Boosting

In recent years many, if not most, statistical and machine learning methods have been based in one way or another on the optimization of an *objective* or *loss function*. For instance, in the simplest form of linear regression, given examples $(\mathbf{x}_1, y_1), \ldots, (\mathbf{x}_m, y_m)$, where $\mathbf{x}_i \in \mathbb{R}^n$ and $y_i \in \mathbb{R}$, one seeks to find a weight vector $\mathbf{w}$ such that $\mathbf{w} \cdot \mathbf{x}_i$ will be a good approximation of y_i. More precisely, the goal is to find $\mathbf{w} \in \mathbb{R}^n$ minimizing the average (or sum) of the squared errors:

$$L(\mathbf{w}) = \frac{1}{m} \sum_{i=1}^{m} (\mathbf{w} \cdot \mathbf{x}_i - y_i)^2.$$

Here, the squared error of each example $(\mathbf{w} \cdot \mathbf{x}_i - y_i)^2$ is the loss function—in this case, the *square* or *quadratic loss*—and the goal is to minimize the average of the losses over all m examples. A host of other techniques, including neural networks, support-vector machines, maximum likelihood, logistic regression, and many more, can be viewed similarly as optimization of some objective function defined over a set of real-valued parameters.

This approach of defining and then optimizing a specific optimization function has many advantages. First of all, this approach allows us to make the goal of the learning method clear and explicit. This clarity can help tremendously in understanding what a learning method is doing, and in proving properties of the method, for instance, that an iterative procedure eventually converges to something useful. A second major benefit is the decoupling of the objective of learning (minimization of some function) from the particular numerical method that is applied to reach this goal. This means, for instance, that fast, general-purpose numerical methods can be developed and applied to a range of learning objectives. Finally, objective functions can often be easily modified to fit new learning challenges; a number of examples are given in this chapter.

All this leads to the question of whether AdaBoost, too, like so many other modern learning methods, is in fact a procedure for optimizing some associated objective function. Certainly, AdaBoost was not designed with this purpose in mind. Nevertheless, as will be seen in this chapter, there is indeed a loss function, called the exponential loss, that Ada-Boost turns out to greedily minimize. This realization is helpful in a number of ways. First, the fact that AdaBoost is minimizing this particular loss function helps us to understand the algorithm, and is useful in extending the algorithm, for instance, as a tool for estimating conditional probabilities. Second, the AdaBoost algorithm itself can be viewed as a particular technique for minimizing this loss function. This understanding means that AdaBoost can be generalized to handle loss functions other than exponential loss, thus admitting the derivation of boosting-like procedures for other purposes, such as regression (prediction of real-valued labels).

As an important example, these insights help to expose the close connection between Ada-Boost and logistic regression, one of the oldest and most widely used statistical approaches for learning to classify discretely labeled data. As we will see, the exponential loss function associated with AdaBoost is related to the loss function for logistic regression. More-over, AdaBoost can be almost trivially modified to minimize logistic regression's loss function. This view also helps us to see how the predictions made by AdaBoost can be used to estimate the *probability* of a particular example being labeled $+1$ or -1, rather than the classification problem of predicting the most likely label, which we have focused on through most of this book. Finally, this view provides a unified framework in which AdaBoost and logistic regression can be regarded as sibling algorithms in the context of convex optimization and information geometry, topics that will be explored further in chapter 8.

Although the interpretation of AdaBoost as a method for optimizing a particular objective function is very useful, a certain note of caution is in order. It is indisputable that AdaBoost minimizes exponential loss. Nevertheless, this does not mean that AdaBoost's effectiveness comes as a direct consequence of this property. Indeed, we will see that other methods for minimizing the same loss associated with AdaBoost can perform arbitrarily poorly. This means that AdaBoost's effectiveness must in some way follow from the particular dynamics of the algorithm—not just *what* it is minimizing, but *how* it is doing it.

This chapter also studies *regularization*, a commonly used "smoothing" technique for avoiding overfitting by bounding the magnitude of the weights computed on the base classifiers. Regularization and boosting turn out to be linked fundamentally. In particular, we will see that the behavior of α-Boost (a variant of AdaBoost encountered in section 6.4.3), when run for a limited number of rounds, can be regarded as a reasonable approximation of a particular form of regularization. In other words, stopping boosting after fewer rounds can be viewed in this sense as a method of regularization which may be appropriate when working with limited or especially noisy data that might otherwise lead to overfitting. Further, when applied in its weakest form, we will see that regularization produces classifiers with margin-maximizing properties similar to those at the core of our understanding of AdaBoost, as seen in chapter 5.

As further examples of how the general techniques presented in this chapter can be applied, we show in closing how two practical learning scenarios which arise naturally as a result of limitations in the availability of data might be handled through the careful design of an appropriate loss function.

7.1 AdaBoost's Loss Function

So what is the loss function that is naturally associated with AdaBoost? For most of this book, the emphasis has been on minimizing the probability of making an incorrect prediction. That is, the loss of interest for a classifier H on labeled example (x, y) has been the *classification loss* or *0-1 loss*

$$\mathbf{1}\{H(x) \neq y\},$$

which is equal to 1 if the classifier H misclassifies (x, y), and 0 otherwise. Indeed, chapter 3 focused on deriving bounds on AdaBoost's training error

$$\frac{1}{m} \sum_{i=1}^{m} \mathbf{1}\{H(x_i) \neq y_i\} \tag{7.1}$$

where $(x_1, y_1), \ldots, (x_m, y_m)$ is the given training set, and where, as before, H is the combined classifier of the form

$$H(x) = \text{sign}(F(x)),$$

and

$$F(x) \doteq \sum_{t=1}^{T} \alpha_t h_t(x) \tag{7.2}$$

is the linear combination of weak classifiers computed by AdaBoost.

So is AdaBoost a method for minimizing the objective function in equation (7.1)? The answer is "no," in the sense that it can be shown that AdaBoost will not necessarily find the combined classifier of the form above that minimizes equation (7.1). In fact, this problem turns out to be NP-complete, meaning that no polynomial-time algorithm is believed to exist for it. Moreover, on close inspection of the proof of theorem 3.1, we can see that at least with regard to the choice of α_t's, the algorithm was not optimized for the purpose of minimizing the training error in equation (7.1) per se, but rather an *upper bound* on the training error.

This is brought out most clearly in equation (3.3) of the proof of theorem 3.1 (where, throughout the current discussion, we fix D_1 to the uniform distribution). There, we upper bounded the training error

Algorithm 7.1
A greedy algorithm for minimizing exponential loss

Given: $(x_1, y_1), \ldots, (x_m, y_m)$ where $x_i \in \mathcal{X}$, $y_i \in \{-1, +1\}$.
Initialize: $F_0 \equiv 0$.
For $t = 1, \ldots, T$:

- Choose $h_t \in \mathcal{H}$, $\alpha_t \in \mathbb{R}$ to minimize

$$\frac{1}{m} \sum_{i=1}^{m} \exp(-y_i(F_{t-1}(x_i) + \alpha_t h_t(x_i)))$$

  (over all choices of α_t and h_t).

- Update:

$$F_t = F_{t-1} + \alpha_t h_t.$$

Output F_T.

$$\frac{1}{m} \sum_{i=1}^{m} \mathbf{1}\{\text{sign}(F(x_i)) \neq y_i\} = \frac{1}{m} \sum_{i=1}^{m} \mathbf{1}\{y_i F(x_i) \leq 0\}$$

by the *exponential loss*

$$\frac{1}{m} \sum_{i=1}^{m} e^{-y_i F(x_i)}, \tag{7.3}$$

using the bound $\mathbf{1}\{x \leq 0\} \leq e^{-x}$. This is the only step where an inequality was used in that proof; all other steps, including, for instance, the greedy choice of α_t, involved strict equalities. Thus, in a nutshell, AdaBoost's training error was first upper bounded by the exponential loss in equation (7.3), which in turn is greedily minimized by the algorithm.

We claim that AdaBoost is in fact a greedy procedure for minimizing equation (7.3). More precisely, consider algorithm 7.1, which iteratively constructs a linear combination $F = F_T$ of the form given in equation (7.2), on each round choosing α_t and h_t so as to cause the greatest decrease in the exponential loss of equation (7.3). We claim that this greedy procedure is equivalent to AdaBoost, making the same choices of α_t and h_t if given the same data and base hypothesis space (and assuming throughout that we are using an exhaustive weak learner that always chooses h_t to minimize the weighted training error ϵ_t over all $h_t \in \mathcal{H}$). The proof of this is embedded in the proof of theorem 3.1. Note first that, using the notation from theorem 3.1, equation (3.2) of that proof shows that on any round t, and for all examples i,

$$\frac{1}{m}e^{-y_i F_{t-1}(x_i)} = D_t(i)\left(\prod_{t'=1}^{t-1} Z_{t'}\right). \tag{7.4}$$

This implies that

$$\frac{1}{m}\sum_{i=1}^{m} e^{-y_i F_t(x_i)} = \frac{1}{m}\sum_{i=1}^{m} \exp(-y_i(F_{t-1}(x_i) + \alpha_t h_t(x_i)))$$

$$= \sum_{i=1}^{m} D_t(i)\left(\prod_{t'=1}^{t-1} Z_{t'}\right)e^{-y_i \alpha_t h_t(x_i)}$$

$$\propto \sum_{i=1}^{m} D_t(i)e^{-y_i \alpha_t h_t(x_i)} \doteq Z_t$$

(where $f \propto g$ here means that f is equal to g times a positive constant that does not depend on α_t or h_t). Thus, minimizing the exponential loss on round t as in algorithm 7.1 is equivalent to minimizing the normalization factor Z_t. Moreover, in equation (3.7) we showed that for a given h_t with weighted error ϵ_t,

$$Z_t = e^{-\alpha_t}(1 - \epsilon_t) + e^{\alpha_t}\epsilon_t,$$

an expression that is minimized for exactly the choice of α_t used by AdaBoost. Thus, for a given h_t, α_t greedily minimizes the exponential loss for round t. Furthermore, plugging in this minimizing choice of α_t gives

$$Z_t = 2\sqrt{\epsilon_t(1 - \epsilon_t)}, \tag{7.5}$$

which is monotonically increasing for $0 \le \epsilon_t \le \frac{1}{2}$, and decreasing for $\frac{1}{2} \le \epsilon_t \le 1$ (see figure 7.1). Thus, the combination of α_t and h_t that minimizes exponential loss for round t is found by choosing α_t as above after first choosing h_t with weighted error ϵ_t as far from $\frac{1}{2}$ as possible; or, alternatively, assuming that $-h$ can be chosen whenever h can be, this is the same as choosing ϵ_t as close to zero as possible. This, of course, is exactly what AdaBoost is doing, in concert with the weak learner.

7.2 Coordinate Descent

When put into slightly different terms, we will see in this section that this basic algorithmic technique turns out to be a numerical method called coordinate descent, which can immediately be applied to other objective functions.

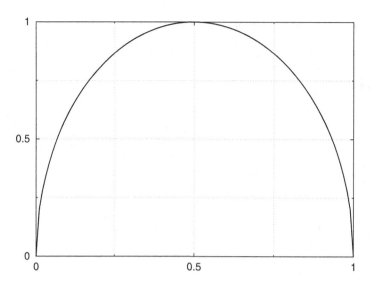

Figure 7.1
A plot of the function $Z(\epsilon) = 2\sqrt{\epsilon(1 - \epsilon)}$, as in equation (7.5).

7.2.1   Generalizing AdaBoost

Suppose for simplicity that we are working over a finite space $\mathcal{H}$ of N base hypotheses. Because the space is finite, we can list all of its N members explicitly so that

$$\mathcal{H} = \{\hbar_1, \ldots, \hbar_N\}.$$

To be clear about the notation, $\hbar_j$ represents the j-th weak hypothesis under an arbitrary but fixed indexing of all the weak hypotheses in $\mathcal{H}$, while h_t, as used in AdaBoost (algorithm 1.1 (p. 5) or, equivalently, algorithm 7.1), represents the weak hypothesis from $\mathcal{H}$ that was selected on round t. Note that N, though assumed to be finite, is typically extremely large.

We know that AdaBoost seeks a linear combination of $\mathcal{H}$ as in equation (7.2). Since each h_t is equal to some $\hbar_j \in \mathcal{H}$, such a combination can be re-expressed in the new notation as

$$F_\lambda(x) \doteq \sum_{j=1}^{N} \lambda_j \hbar_j(x) \tag{7.6}$$

for some set of weights λ. Further, the exponential loss function to be minimized can be written as

$$L(\lambda_1, \ldots, \lambda_N) \doteq \frac{1}{m} \sum_{i=1}^{m} \exp(-y_i F_\lambda(x_i))$$

Algorithm 7.2
A generic greedy coordinate descent algorithm

Goal: minimization of $L(\lambda_1, \ldots, \lambda_N)$.

Initialize: $\lambda_j \leftarrow 0$ for $j = 1, \ldots, N$.

For $t = 1, \ldots, T$:

- Let j, α minimize $L(\lambda_1, \ldots, \lambda_{j-1}, \lambda_j + \alpha, \lambda_{j+1}, \ldots, \lambda_N)$
  over $j \in \{1, \ldots, N\}, \alpha \in \mathbb{R}$.

- $\lambda_j \leftarrow \lambda_j + \alpha$.

Output $\lambda_1, \ldots, \lambda_N$.

$$= \frac{1}{m} \sum_{i=1}^{m} \exp\left(-y_i \sum_{j=1}^{N} \lambda_j \hbar_j(x_i)\right). \tag{7.7}$$

As we have seen, AdaBoost behaves as though the goal were minimization of this loss, which we have here expressed as a real-valued function L over N real-valued parameters, or weights, $\lambda_1, \ldots, \lambda_N$. The method that it uses is to select, on each round t, a weak classifier $h_t \in \mathcal{H}$ and a real number α_t, and then to add a new term $\alpha_t h_t$ to F_{t-1} as in the update step of algorithm 7.1. Since h_t is in $\mathcal{H}$, it must be the same as some $\hbar_j$, so choosing h_t is equivalent to choosing one of the weights λ_j. Further, adding $\alpha_t h_t$ to F_{t-1} is then equivalent to adding α_t to λ_j, that is, applying the update

$$\lambda_j \leftarrow \lambda_j + \alpha_t.$$

Thus, on each round, AdaBoost adjusts just *one* of the weights λ_j. Moreover, the argument given in section 7.1 shows that both the weight λ_j and the adjustment α_t are chosen so as to cause the greatest decrease in the loss function L.

In this sense, AdaBoost can be regarded as a *coordinate descent* method which seeks to minimize its objective function L by iteratively descending along just one coordinate direction at a time. Generic pseudocode for coordinate descent is given as algorithm 7.2. This is in contrast, say, to ordinary gradient descent, which we discuss in section 7.3, and which adjusts *all* of the weights $\lambda_1, \ldots, \lambda_N$ simultaneously on every iteration. When the size N of the weak-classifier space $\mathcal{H}$ is very large (as is typically the case), a sequential update procedure like coordinate descent may make more sense since it leads to a sparse solution, that is, one in which the vast majority of the λ_j's remain equal to zero. This has clear computational benefits since many computations can be carried out without regard to the base hypotheses that have zero weight; indeed, it is for this reason that AdaBoost's running time does not depend at all on the total number of base hypotheses in $\mathcal{H}$ (although the weak learner's running time might). There may also be statistical benefits, as was seen in section 4.1, where we proved generalization bounds that depended directly on T, the number of nonzero weights, but only logarithmically on $N = |\mathcal{H}|$, the total number of weights.

One still needs to search, on each round, for the best single weight to update, but in many cases this search, at least approximately, can be carried out efficiently. For instance, in AdaBoost this amounts to the familiar search for a base classifier with minimum weighted error, and can be carried out using any standard learning algorithm.

7.2.2 Convergence

The exponential loss function L in equation (7.7) can be shown to be convex in the parameters $\lambda_1, \ldots, \lambda_N$ (see appendix A.7). This is a very nice property because it means that a search procedure like coordinate descent cannot get stuck in local minima since there are none. If the algorithm reaches a point λ at which no adjustment along a coordinate direction leads to a lower value of L, then it must be that the partial derivative $\partial L / \partial \lambda_j$ along any coordinate λ_j is equal to zero. This implies that the *gradient*

$$\nabla L \doteq \left\langle \frac{\partial L}{\partial \lambda_1}, \ldots, \frac{\partial L}{\partial \lambda_N} \right\rangle$$

is also equal to zero, which, since L is convex, is enough to conclude that a global minimum has been reached.

These facts, however, are not in themselves sufficient to conclude that such a global minimum will ever be reached. In fact, even though L is convex and nonnegative, it is entirely possible for it not to attain a global minimum at *any* finite value of λ. Instead, its minimum might be attained only when some or all of the λ_j's have grown to infinity in a particular direction. For instance, for an appropriate choice of data, the function L could be

$$L(\lambda_1, \lambda_2) = \tfrac{1}{3} \left(e^{\lambda_1 - \lambda_2} + e^{\lambda_2 - \lambda_1} + e^{-\lambda_1 - \lambda_2} \right).$$

The first two terms together are minimized when $\lambda_1 = \lambda_2$, and the third term is minimized when $\lambda_1 + \lambda_2 \to +\infty$. Thus, the minimum of L in this case is attained when we fix $\lambda_1 = \lambda_2$, and the two weights together grow to infinity at the same pace.

Despite these difficulties, it will be proved in chapter 8 that coordinate descent—that is, AdaBoost—does indeed converge asymptotically to the global minimum of the exponential loss.

7.2.3 Other Loss Functions

Clearly, this coordinate-descent approach to function minimization can be applied to other objective functions as well. To be easy to implement, effective, and efficient, the objective function L must be amenable to an efficient search for the best coordinate to adjust, and the amount of adjustment must also be easy to compute. Moreover, to avoid local minima, convexity and smoothness of the function L appear to be useful qualities.

For example, all of the same ideas can be applied to a quadratic loss function in place of the exponential loss. Thus, given data $(x_1, y_1), \ldots, (x_m, y_m)$, where $y_i \in \mathbb{R}$, and given a space of real-valued functions $\mathcal{H} = \{\hbar_1, \ldots, \hbar_N\}$, the goal is to find a linear combination

$$F_\lambda = \sum_{j=1}^{N} \lambda_j \hbar_j$$

with low square loss

$$L(\lambda_1, \ldots, \lambda_N) \doteq \frac{1}{m} \sum_{i=1}^{m} (F_\lambda(x_i) - y_i)^2.$$

This is standard linear regression, but we imagine here that the cardinality N of $\mathcal{H}$ is enormous—for instance, $\mathcal{H}$ might be the space of all decision trees, a truly vast space of functions. Applying coordinate descent in this case leads to a procedure like algorithm 7.1, but with the exponential loss appearing in that algorithm replaced by

$$\frac{1}{m} \sum_{i=1}^{m} (F_{t-1}(x_i) + \alpha_t h_t(x_i) - y_i)^2.$$

For a given choice of h_t, it can be shown, using straightforward calculus, that the minimizing value of α_t is

$$\alpha_t = \sum_{i=1}^{m} r_i \frac{h_t(x_i)}{\|h_t\|_2^2} \tag{7.8}$$

where r_i is the "residual"

$$r_i \doteq y_i - F_{t-1}(x_i), \tag{7.9}$$

and

$$\|h_t\|_2 = \sqrt{\sum_{i=1}^{m} h_t(x_i)^2}.$$

For this choice of α_t, the change in L is

$$-\frac{1}{m}\left(\sum_{i=1}^{m} r_i \frac{h_t(x_i)}{\|h_t\|_2}\right)^2. \qquad (7.10)$$

Thus, h_t should be chosen to maximize (the absolute value of) equation (7.10). This is equivalent, up to a possible sign change in h_t, to saying that h_t should be chosen to minimize

$$\frac{1}{m}\sum_{i=1}^{m}\left(\frac{h_t(x_i)}{\|h_t\|_2}-r_i\right)^2,$$

that is, its ℓ_2-distance to the residuals (after normalizing).

7.3   Loss Minimization Cannot Explain Generalization

From the foregoing, it might seem tempting to conclude that AdaBoost's effectiveness as a learning algorithm is derived from the choice of loss function that it apparently aims to minimize—in other words, that AdaBoost works *only because* it minimizes exponential loss. If this were true, then it would follow that a still better algorithm could be designed using more powerful and sophisticated approaches to optimization than AdaBoost's comparatively meek approach.

However, it is critical to keep in mind that minimization of exponential loss by itself is *not* sufficient to guarantee low generalization error. On the contrary, it is very much possible to minimize the exponential loss (using a procedure other than AdaBoost) while suffering quite substantial generalization error (relative, say, to AdaBoost). We make this point with both a theoretical argument and an empirical demonstration.

Beginning with the former, in the setup given above, our aim is to minimize equation (7.7). Suppose the data is linearly separable so that there exist $\lambda_1, \ldots, \lambda_N$ for which $y_i F_\lambda(x_i) > 0$ for all i. In this case, given any such set of parameters λ, we can trivially minimize equation (7.7) simply by multiplying λ by a large positive constant c, which is equivalent to multiplying F_λ by c so that

$$\frac{1}{m}\sum_{i=1}^{m}\exp\left(-y_i F_{c\lambda}(x_i)\right) = \frac{1}{m}\sum_{i=1}^{m}\exp\left(-y_i c F_\lambda(x_i)\right)$$

must converge to zero as $c \to \infty$. Of course, multiplying by $c > 0$ has no impact on the predictions $H(x) = \mathrm{sign}(F_\lambda(x))$. This means that the exponential loss, in the case of linearly separable data, can be minimized by *any* set of separating parameters λ multiplied by a large but inconsequential constant. Said differently, knowing that λ minimizes the exponential loss in this case tells us nothing about λ except that the combined classifier $H(x)$ has zero training error. Otherwise, λ is entirely unconstrained. The complexity, or VC-dimension, of such classifiers is roughly the number of base classifiers N (see lemma 4.1). Since VC-dimension provides both lower and upper bounds on the amount of data needed for learning, this implies that the performance can be quite poor in the typical case that N is very large.

In contrast, given the weak learning assumption, AdaBoost's generalization performance will be much better, on the order of $\log N$, as seen in chapter 5. This is because AdaBoost does not construct an arbitrary zero-training-error classifier, but rather one with large (normalized) margins, a property that does not follow from its status as a method for minimizing exponential loss.

To be more concrete, we consider empirically three different algorithms for minimizing exponential loss and how they compare on a specific dataset. In this experiment, the data was generated synthetically with each instance $\mathbf{x}$ a 10,000-dimensional $\{-1, +1\}$-valued vector, that is, a point in $\{-1, +1\}^{10,000}$. Each of the 1000 training and 10,000 test examples was generated uniformly at random from this space. The label y associated with an instance $\mathbf{x}$ was defined to be the majority vote of three designated coordinates of $\mathbf{x}$; that is,

$$y = \text{sign}(x_a + x_b + x_c)$$

for some fixed and distinct values a, b, and c. The weak hypotheses used were associated with coordinates. Thus, the weak-hypothesis space $\mathcal{H}$ included, for each of the 10,000 coordinates j, a weak hypothesis h of the form $h(\mathbf{x}) = x_j$ for all $\mathbf{x}$. (The negatives of these were also included.)

Three different algorithms were tested on this data. The first was ordinary AdaBoost using an exhaustive weak learner that, on each round, finds the minimum-weighted-error weak hypothesis. In the results below, we refer to this as *exhaustive AdaBoost*.

The second algorithm was *gradient descent* on the loss function given in equation (7.7). In this standard approach, we iteratively adjust $\boldsymbol{\lambda}$ by taking a series of steps, each in the direction that locally causes the quickest decrease in the loss L; this direction turns out to be the negative gradient. Thus, we begin at $\boldsymbol{\lambda} = \mathbf{0}$, and on each round we adjust $\boldsymbol{\lambda}$ using the update

$$\boldsymbol{\lambda} \leftarrow \boldsymbol{\lambda} - \alpha \nabla L(\boldsymbol{\lambda})$$

where α is a step size. In these experiments, $\alpha > 0$ was chosen on each round using a *line search* to find the value that (approximately) causes the greatest decrease in the loss in the given direction.

As we will see, gradient descent is much faster than AdaBoost at driving down the exponential loss (where, for the purposes of this discussion, speed is with reference to the number of rounds, not the overall computation time). A third algorithm that is much slower was also tested. This algorithm is actually the same as AdaBoost except that the weak learner does not actively search for the best, or even a good, weak hypothesis. Rather, on every round, the weak learner simply selects one weak hypothesis h uniformly at random from $\mathcal{H}$, returning either it or its negation $-h$, whichever has the lower weighted error (thus ensuring a weighted error no greater than $\frac{1}{2}$). We refer to this method as *random AdaBoost*.

All three algorithms are guaranteed to minimize the exponential loss (almost surely, in the case of random AdaBoost). But that does *not* mean that they will necessarily perform the same on actual data in terms of classification accuracy. It is true that the exponential loss function L in equation (7.7) is convex, and therefore that it can have no local minima. But that does not mean that the minimum is unique. For instance, the function

$$\frac{1}{2}\left(e^{\lambda_1 - \lambda_2} + e^{\lambda_2 - \lambda_1}\right)$$

is minimized at any values for which $\lambda_1 = \lambda_2$. In fact, in the typical case that N is very large, we expect the minimum of L to be realized at a rather large set of values λ. The fact that two algorithms both minimize L only guarantees that both solutions will be in this set, telling us essentially nothing about their relative accuracy.

The results of these experiments are shown in table 7.1. Regarding speed, the table shows that, as commented above, gradient descent is extremely fast at minimizing exponential loss, while random AdaBoost is unbearably slow, though eventually effective. Exhaustive AdaBoost is somewhere in between.

As for accuracy, the table shows that both gradient descent and random AdaBoost performed very poorly on this data, with test errors never dropping significantly below 40%. In contrast, exhaustive AdaBoost quickly achieved and maintained perfect test accuracy beginning after the third round.

Of course, this artificial example is not meant to show that exhaustive AdaBoost is always a better algorithm than the other two methods. Rather, the point is that AdaBoost's strong performance as a classification algorithm cannot be credited—at least not exclusively—to

Table 7.1
Results of the experiment described in section 7.3

Exp. Loss	% Test Error [# Rounds]					
	Exhaustive AdaBoost		Gradient Descent		Random AdaBoost	
10^{-10}	0.0	[94]	40.7	[5]	44.0	[24,464]
10^{-20}	0.0	[190]	40.8	[9]	41.6	[47,534]
10^{-40}	0.0	[382]	40.8	[21]	40.9	[94,479]
10^{-100}	0.0	[956]	40.8	[70]	40.3	[234,654]

The numbers in brackets are the number of rounds required for each algorithm to reach specified values of the exponential loss. The unbracketed numbers show the percent test error achieved by each algorithm at the point in its run where the exponential loss first dropped below the specified values. All results are averaged over ten random repetitions of the experiment.

its effect on the exponential loss. If this were the case, then any algorithm achieving equally low exponential loss should have equally low generalization error. But this is far from what we see in this example where exhaustive AdaBoost's very low exponential loss is matched by the competitors, but their test errors are not even close. Clearly, some other factor beyond its exponential loss must be at work to explain exhaustive AdaBoost's comparatively strong performance.

Indeed, these results are entirely consistent with the margins theory of chapter 5, which does have something direct to say about generalization error. That theory states that the generalization error can be bounded in terms of the number of training examples, the complexity of the base classifiers, and the distribution of the normalized margins on the training set. The first two of these are the same for all three methods tested. However, there were very significant differences in the margin distributions, which are shown in figure 7.2. As can be seen, exhaustive AdaBoost achieves very large margins of at least 0.33 on all of the training examples, in correlation with its excellent accuracy. In sharp contrast, both of the poorly performing competitors had margins below 0.07 on nearly all of the training examples (even lower for random AdaBoost).

Minimization of exponential loss is a fundamental property of AdaBoost, and one that opens the door for a range of practical generalizations of the algorithm. However, the examples in this section demonstrate that any understanding of AdaBoost's generalization

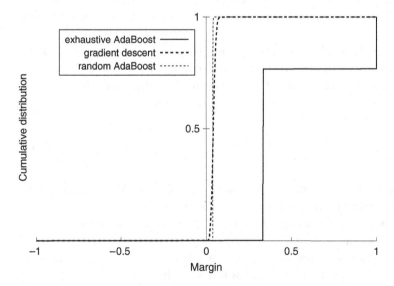

Figure 7.2
The distributions of margins achieved by three algorithms on synthetic data at the point where their exponential loss first dropped below 10^{-40}.

capabilities must in some way take into account the particular dynamics of the algorithm, not just the objective function but also what procedure is actually being used to minimize it.

7.4 Functional Gradient Descent

AdaBoost, as was seen in section 7.2, can be viewed as coordinate-descent minimization of a particular optimization function. This view is useful and general, but can be cumbersome to implement for other loss functions when the choice of best adjustment along the best coordinate is not straightforward to find. In this section, we give a second view of AdaBoost as an algorithm for optimization of an objective function, and we will see that this new view can also be generalized to other loss functions, but in a way that may overcome possible computational difficulties with the coordinate descent view. In fact, in many cases the choice of best base function to add on a given round will turn out to be a matter of finding a classifier with minimum error rate, just as in the case of boosting. Thus, this technique allows the minimization of many loss functions to be reduced to a sequence of ordinary classification problems.

7.4.1 A Different Generalization

In the coordinate descent view, we regarded our objective function, as in equation (7.7), as a function of a set of parameters $\lambda_1, \ldots, \lambda_N$ representing the weights over all of the base functions in the space $\mathcal{H}$. All optimizations then were carried out by manipulating these parameters.

The new view provides a rather different approach in which the focus is on entire *functions*, rather than on a set of parameters. In particular, our objective function $\mathcal{L}$ now takes as input another function F. In the case of the exponential loss associated with AdaBoost, this would be

$$\mathcal{L}(F) \doteq \frac{1}{m} \sum_{i=1}^{m} e^{-y_i F(x_i)}. \tag{7.11}$$

Thus, $\mathcal{L}$ is a *functional*, that is, a function whose input argument is itself a function, and the goal is to find F minimizing $\mathcal{L}$ (possibly with some constraints on F).

In fact, for the purpose of optimizing equation (7.11), we only care about the value of F at $x_1, \ldots, x_m$. Thus, we can think of $\mathcal{L}$ as a function of just the values $F(x_1), \ldots, F(x_m)$, which we can regard as m ordinary real variables. In other words, if we for the moment write $F(x_i)$ as f_i, then our goal can be viewed as that of minimizing

$$\mathcal{L}(f_1, \ldots, f_m) \doteq \frac{1}{m} \sum_{i=1}^{m} e^{-y_i f_i}.$$

In this way, $\mathcal{L}$ can be thought of as a real-valued function on $\mathbb{R}^m$.

How can we optimize such a function? As described in section 7.3, gradient descent is a standard approach, the idea being to iteratively take small steps in the direction of steepest descent, which is the negative gradient. Applying this idea here means repeatedly updating F by the rule

$$F \leftarrow F - \alpha \nabla \mathcal{L}(F) \tag{7.12}$$

where $\nabla \mathcal{L}(F)$ represents the gradient of $\mathcal{L}$ at F, and α is some small positive value, sometimes called the *learning rate*. If we view F only as a function of $x_1, \ldots, x_m$, then its gradient is the vector in $\mathbb{R}^m$,

$$\nabla \mathcal{L}(F) \doteq \left\langle \frac{\partial \mathcal{L}(F)}{\partial F(x_1)}, \ldots, \frac{\partial \mathcal{L}(F)}{\partial F(x_m)} \right\rangle,$$

and the gradient descent update in equation (7.12) is equivalent to

$$F(x_i) \leftarrow F(x_i) - \alpha \frac{\partial \mathcal{L}(F)}{\partial F(x_i)}$$

for $i = 1, \ldots, m$.

This technique is certainly simple. The problem is that it leaves F entirely unconstrained in form, and therefore makes overfitting a certainty. Indeed, as presented, this approach does not even specify meaningful predictions on test points not seen in training. Therefore, to constrain F, we impose the limitation that each update to F must come from some class of base functions $\mathcal{H}$. That is, any update to F must be of the form

$$F \leftarrow F + \alpha h \tag{7.13}$$

for some $\alpha > 0$ and some $h \in \mathcal{H}$. Thus, if each $h \in \mathcal{H}$ is defined over the entire domain (not just the training set), then F will be so defined as well, and hopefully will give meaningful and accurate predictions on test points if the functions in $\mathcal{H}$ are simple enough.

How should we select the function $h \in \mathcal{H}$ to add to F as in equation (7.13)? We have seen that moving in a negative gradient direction $-\nabla \mathcal{L}(F)$ may be sensible, but might not be feasible since updates must be in the direction of some $h \in \mathcal{H}$. What we can do, however, is to choose the base function $h \in \mathcal{H}$ that is *closest* in direction to the negative gradient. Ignoring issues of normalization, this can be done by choosing that $h \in \mathcal{H}$ which maximizes its inner product with the negative gradient (since inner product measures how much two vectors are aligned), that is, which maximizes

$$-\nabla \mathcal{L}(F) \cdot h = -\sum_{i=1}^{m} \frac{\partial \mathcal{L}(F)}{\partial F(x_i)} h(x_i). \tag{7.14}$$

Algorithm 7.3
AnyBoost, a generic functional gradient descent algorithm

Goal: minimization of $\mathcal{L}(F)$.
Initialize: $F_0 \equiv 0$.
For $t = 1, \ldots, T$:

- Select $h_t \in \mathcal{H}$ that maximizes $-\nabla\mathcal{L}(F_{t-1}) \cdot h_t$.
- Choose $\alpha_t > 0$.
- Update: $F_t = F_{t-1} + \alpha_t h_t$.

Output F_T.

Once h has been chosen, the function F can be updated as in equation (7.13) for some appropriate $\alpha > 0$. One possibility is simply to let α be a small positive constant. An alternative is to select α so that $\mathcal{L}$ (or some approximation of $\mathcal{L}$) is minimized by performing a one-dimensional line search.

The general approach that we have described here is called *functional gradient descent*. The resulting procedure, in a general form, is called *AnyBoost*, and is shown as algorithm 7.3.

In the AdaBoost case, the loss function is as given in equation (7.11). The partial derivatives are easily computed to be

$$\frac{\partial\mathcal{L}(F)}{\partial F(x_i)} = \frac{-y_i e^{-y_i F(x_i)}}{m}.$$

Thus, on round t, the goal is to find h_t maximizing

$$\frac{1}{m}\sum_{i=1}^{m} y_i h_t(x_i) e^{-y_i F_{t-1}(x_i)}, \tag{7.15}$$

which, in our standard AdaBoost notation, is proportional to

$$\sum_{i=1}^{m} D_t(i) y_i h_t(x_i) \tag{7.16}$$

by equation (7.4). Assuming h_t has range $\{-1, +1\}$, equation (7.16) can be shown to equal $1 - 2\epsilon_t$, where, as usual,

$$\epsilon_t \doteq \mathbf{Pr}_{i \sim D_t}[h_t(x_i) \neq y_i].$$

Thus, maximizing equation (7.15) is equivalent to minimizing the weighted error ϵ_t as in AdaBoost. As for the choice of α_t, we have already seen that AdaBoost chooses α_t to minimize exponential loss (see section 7.1). Thus, AdaBoost is a special case of the general functional gradient descent technique given as algorithm 7.3 (assuming exhaustive weak-hypothesis selection). A variant in which a small constant learning rate $\alpha > 0$ is used instead yields the α-Boost algorithm discussed in section 6.4.

Applying this framework to the square loss, as in section 7.2.3, gives a similar algorithm. In this case,

$$\mathcal{L}(F) \doteq \frac{1}{m} \sum_{i=1}^{m} (F(x_i) - y_i)^2$$

so that

$$\frac{\partial \mathcal{L}(F)}{\partial F(x_i)} = \frac{2}{m} (F(x_i) - y_i).$$

Thus, h_t should be chosen to maximize

$$\frac{2}{m} \sum_{i=1}^{m} h_t(x_i) r_i$$

where r_i is the residual as in equation (7.9). This is nearly the same optimization criterion for choosing h_t as in equation (7.10), but without explicit normalization. Such an h_t could be found, for instance, using a classification learning algorithm as explained in section 7.4.3. Once h_t is selected, the minimizing α_t can be chosen as in equation (7.8).

7.4.2 Relation to Coordinate Descent

The ease of working with the optimization problem that is central to the functional gradient descent approach (namely, maximization of equation (7.14)) is a key practical advantage over the coordinate descent view where we attempted to find a parameter λ_j whose adjustment would cause the greatest drop in the objective function. In fact, however, the two views are rather closely related, and the functional gradient descent view can be derived naturally as an approximation of coordinate descent. In particular, rather than selecting the very best coordinate, we might attempt a compromise between coordinate descent and gradient descent in which we instead select and update the coordinate in whose direction the *negative gradient* is largest. Such a variant of coordinate descent is sometimes called a Gauss-Southwell procedure. Thus, if the optimization function is $L(\lambda_1, \ldots, \lambda_N)$, then on each round of coordinate descent, we select the λ_j for which $-\partial L / \partial \lambda_j$ is largest. If in addition the objective function L can be written in the form

$$L(\lambda_1, \ldots, \lambda_N) = \mathcal{L}(F_\lambda),$$

where F_λ is as in equation (7.6), then by the chain rule from calculus (see appendix A.6), this is equivalent to adjusting that λ_j for which

$$-\frac{\partial L}{\partial \lambda_j} = -\sum_{i=1}^{m} \frac{\partial \mathcal{L}(F_\lambda)}{\partial F_\lambda(x_i)} \hbar_j(x_i)$$

is maximized. This, of course, is exactly what is done in functional gradient descent.

7.4.3   Using Classification and Regression for General Loss Functions

Generalizing what was done above for AdaBoost, we can show that the central problem of maximizing $-\nabla \mathcal{L}(F_{t-1}) \cdot h_t$ on each round of AnyBoost (algorithm 7.3) can be viewed as an ordinary classification problem if each h_t is constrained to have range $\{-1, +1\}$. To see this, let

$$\ell_i = -\frac{\partial \mathcal{L}(F_{t-1})}{\partial F(x_i)},$$

and let

$$\tilde{y}_i = \text{sign}(\ell_i)$$

$$d(i) = \frac{|\ell_i|}{\sum_{i=1}^{m} |\ell_i|}.$$

The problem then is to maximize

$$\sum_{i=1}^{m} \ell_i h_t(x_i) \propto \sum_{i=1}^{m} d(i) \tilde{y}_i h_t(x_i)$$

$$= 1 - 2 \sum_{i: \tilde{y}_i \neq h_t(x_i)} d(i)$$

$$= 1 - 2 \mathbf{Pr}_{i \sim d}[\tilde{y}_i \neq h_t(x_i)]$$

(where $f \propto g$ means that f is equal to g times a positive constant that does not depend on h_t). Thus, to maximize $\nabla \mathcal{L}(F_{t-1}) \cdot h_t$, we can create "pseudolabels" $\tilde{y}_i \in \{-1, +1\}$ as above, and assign a probability weight $d(i)$ to each example. The maximization problem then becomes equivalent to finding a classifier h_t having minimum weighted error with respect to the probability distribution defined by the weights $d(i)$ on a (pseudo) training set $(x_1, \tilde{y}_1), \ldots, (x_m, \tilde{y}_m)$. Note that these pseudolabels $\tilde{y}_i$ vary from round to round, and might or might not agree with any labels which might have been provided as part of the "real" dataset (although in AdaBoost's case, they always will). Thus, in this fashion, any optimization problem can in principle be reduced to a sequence of classification problems.

Alternatively, rather than seeking a function $h_t \in \mathcal{H}$ that is similar to the negative gradient $-\nabla \mathcal{L}(F_{t-1})$ by maximizing their inner product, we can instead try to minimize the Euclidean distance between them (where we continue to treat these functions as vectors in $\mathbb{R}^m$). That is, the idea is to modify algorithm 7.3 so that rather than maximizing $-\nabla \mathcal{L}(F_{t-1}) \cdot h_t$, we instead attempt to minimize

$$\|-\nabla \mathcal{L}(F_{t-1}) - h_t\|_2^2 = \sum_{i=1}^{m} \left(-\frac{\partial \mathcal{L}(F_{t-1})}{\partial F(x_i)} - h_t(x_i) \right)^2. \tag{7.17}$$

Finding such an h_t is itself a least-squares regression problem where the real-valued pseudolabels now are

$$\tilde{y}_i = -\frac{\partial \mathcal{L}(F_{t-1})}{\partial F(x_i)},$$

so that equation (7.17) becomes

$$\sum_{i=1}^{m} (\tilde{y}_i - h_t(x_i))^2.$$

In this formulation, it is natural to allow h_t to be real-valued and, moreover, to assume that it can be scaled by any constant (in other words, if h is in the class of allowable functions $\mathcal{H}$, then ch is assumed to be as well, for any scalar $c \in \mathbb{R}$). After h_t has been chosen, the weight α_t can be selected using the methods already discussed, such as a line search for the value that causes the greatest drop in loss. Thus, in this way, any loss-minimization problem can be reduced to a sequence of regression problems.

For instance, returning to the example of square loss discussed above, the pseudolabels are proportional to the residuals $\tilde{y}_i = (2/m)r_i$ so that, on each round, the problem is to find h_t that is close, in terms of squared difference, to the residuals (times an irrelevant constant). For this purpose, we might employ a decision-tree algorithm like CART designed, in part, for such regression problems. Once a tree is found, the value of α_t that effects the greatest decrease in square loss can be set as in equation (7.8). (On the other hand, in practice it is often necessary to limit the magnitude of the weights to avoid overfitting, for instance, using regularization, or by selecting α_t that is only a fraction of that given in equation (7.8).) In any case, the resulting combined hypothesis F_T will now be a weighted average of regression trees.

7.5   Logistic Regression and Conditional Probabilities

Next we study the close connection between AdaBoost and logistic regression, beginning with a brief description of the latter method. This will lead both to a boosting-like algorithm for logistic regression and to a technique for using AdaBoost to estimate conditional probabilities.

7.5.1   Logistic Regression

As usual, we assume that we are given data $(x_1, y_1), \ldots, (x_m, y_m)$ where $y_i \in \{-1, +1\}$. We also assume we are given a set of real-valued base functions, or what are sometimes called *features*, $\mathcal{H} = \{\hbar_1, \ldots, \hbar_N\}$. These play a role analogous to weak hypotheses in the context of boosting, and they are formally equivalent. Until now, we have generally taken these base functions/hypotheses to be binary ($\{-1, +1\}$-valued) classifiers, but most of the discussion that follows holds when they are real-valued instead. Boosting using real-valued base hypotheses is studied in greater detail in chapter 9.

In *logistic regression*, the goal is to estimate the *conditional probability* of the label y, given a particular example x, rather than merely to predict whether y is positive or negative. Further, we posit that this conditional probability has a particular parametric form, specifically, a sigmoid function of a linear combination of the features. That is, we posit that instance-label pairs (x, y) are generated randomly in such a way that the true conditional probability of a positive label is equal to

$$\mathbf{Pr}[y = +1 \mid x; \boldsymbol{\lambda}] = \sigma \left(\sum_{j=1}^{N} \lambda_j \hbar_j(x) \right) \tag{7.18}$$

for some setting of the parameters $\boldsymbol{\lambda} = \langle \lambda_1, \ldots, \lambda_N \rangle$, and where

$$\sigma(z) = \frac{1}{1 + e^{-z}} \tag{7.19}$$

is a sigmoid function with range $[0, 1]$. (See figure 7.3.) As before, let $F_{\boldsymbol{\lambda}}$ be as in equation (7.6). Note that $\sigma(z)$ is greater than, equal to, or smaller than $\frac{1}{2}$ when z is positive, zero, or negative (respectively). Thus, in words, this model is positing that a linear hyperplane in "feature space" (namely, $F_{\boldsymbol{\lambda}}(x) = 0$) separates the points which are more likely to be positive from those which are more likely to be negative. Furthermore, the closer the point is to this separating hyperplane, the more uncertain is its classification.

Note that the conditional probability of a negative label is

$$\mathbf{Pr}[y = -1 \mid x; \boldsymbol{\lambda}] = 1 - \sigma(F_{\boldsymbol{\lambda}}(x))$$

$$= \sigma(-F_{\boldsymbol{\lambda}}(x))$$

by straightforward algebra. Thus, for $y \in \{-1, +1\}$, we can write

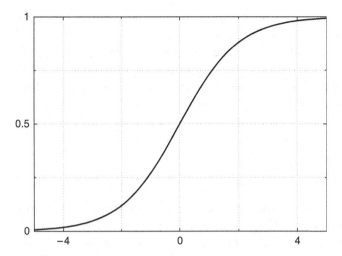

Figure 7.3
A plot of the sigmoid function $\sigma(z)$ given in equation (7.19).

$$\mathbf{Pr}[y \mid x; \lambda] = \sigma(y F_\lambda(x)).$$

How can we find the parameters λ so that we can estimate these conditional probabilities? A very standard statistical approach is to find the parameters which maximize the conditional likelihood of the data, that is, the probability of observing the given labels y_i, conditioned on the instances x_i. In our case, the conditional likelihood of example (x_i, y_i), for some setting of the parameters λ, is simply

$$\mathbf{Pr}[y_i \mid x_i; \lambda] = \sigma(y_i F_\lambda(x_i)).$$

Thus, assuming independence, the conditional likelihood of the entire dataset is

$$\prod_{i=1}^{m} \sigma(y_i F_\lambda(x_i)).$$

Maximizing this likelihood is equivalent to minimizing its negative logarithm, which is (after multiplying by $1/m$) equal to

$$-\frac{1}{m} \sum_{i=1}^{m} \ln \sigma(y_i F_\lambda(x_i)) = \frac{1}{m} \sum_{i=1}^{m} \ln \left(1 + e^{-y_i F_\lambda(x_i)}\right). \tag{7.20}$$

This is the loss function to be minimized by logistic regression, which we henceforth refer to as *logistic loss*. Once the parameters λ which minimize this loss have been found, conditional probabilities of the labels for a test instance x can be estimated as in equation (7.18).

Alternatively, a "hard" classification can be obtained as usual by thresholding, that is, by computing $\text{sign}(F_\lambda(x))$.

As discussed in section 7.2, AdaBoost minimizes the exponential loss given in equation (7.7). Since $\ln(1+x) \leq x$ for $x > -1$, it is clear that logistic loss is upper bounded by exponential loss. Moreover, if the natural logarithm in equation (7.20) is replaced by log base 2 (which is the same as multiplying by the constant $\log_2 e$), then logistic loss, like exponential loss, upper bounds the classification loss, that is, the training error

$$\frac{1}{m}\sum_{i=1}^{m} \mathbf{1}\{y_i F_\lambda(x_i) \leq 0\} = \frac{1}{m}\sum_{i=1}^{m} \mathbf{1}\{y_i \neq \text{sign}(F_\lambda(x_i))\}.$$

The relationship among these loss functions can be seen in figure 7.4. However, as we will see, the connection between exponential loss and logistic loss goes much deeper.

Both exponential and logistic loss give upper bounds on the classification error. Moreover, the two loss functions are very close when the (unnormalized) margin $z = y F_\lambda(x)$ is positive. However, they diverge tremendously when z is negative, with exponential loss growing exponentially, but logistic loss growing only linearly (since $\ln(1 + e^{-z}) \approx -z$ when z is large and negative). This suggests that logistic loss could be somewhat better behaved in some situations.

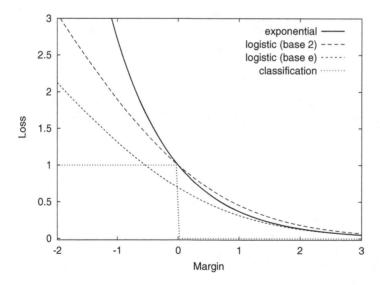

Figure 7.4
A plot of the exponential loss, the logistic loss (using both logarithm base 2 and logarithm base e), and classification loss. Each loss is plotted as a function of the unnormalized margin $y F(x)$.

7.5.2 Modifying AdaBoost for Logistic Loss

How, then, can we minimize the logistic loss function? Standard techniques, based, for instance, on gradient descent or Newton's method, are less effective when the number of base functions is very large. In this situation, a boosting-like approach may be appropriate.

In sections 7.2 and 7.4, we discussed techniques that generalize AdaBoost for minimizing an objective function, so it seems natural to try to apply these to logistic loss. The first of these approaches was coordinate descent, which entails repeatedly finding and adjusting the parameter λ_j that admits the greatest decrease in the objective function. Unfortunately, for logistic loss this turns out to be difficult analytically.

The other approach was functional gradient descent, in which, on each iteration, we select the base function that is closest to the negative functional gradient of the objective function. In this case, the functional of interest is

$$\mathcal{L}(F) = \sum_{i=1}^{m} \ln\left(1 + e^{-y_i F(x_i)}\right), \tag{7.21}$$

and its partial derivatives are

$$\frac{\partial \mathcal{L}(F)}{\partial F(x_i)} = \frac{-y_i}{1 + e^{y_i F(x_i)}}.$$

Thus, this approach prescribes iteratively adding to F a multiple of some base function $h \in \mathcal{H}$ that maximizes

$$\sum_{i=1}^{m} \frac{y_i h(x_i)}{1 + e^{y_i F(x_i)}}. \tag{7.22}$$

In other words, the idea is to weight example i by

$$\frac{1}{1 + e^{y_i F(x_i)}} \tag{7.23}$$

and then to find h most correlated with the labels y_i with respect to this set of weights. These weights are almost the same as for AdaBoost, where the weights

$$e^{-y_i F(x_i)} \tag{7.24}$$

are used instead. However, the weights in equation (7.24) may be highly unbounded, while the weights in equation (7.23) are likely to be much more moderate, always being bounded in the range [0, 1].

Thus, the functional gradient descent approach suggests how to choose a base function h on each round. However, the approach does not specify what multiple of h to add to F, that is, how to select α in the method's iterative update

$$F \leftarrow F + \alpha h. \tag{7.25}$$

Possibilities include a line search to select the α that causes the greatest decrease in $\mathcal{L}(F)$, or simply choosing α to be "suitably small." Neither approach seems to be easily amenable to an analytic treatment.

However, there is another approach that essentially reduces the problem, on each round, to the same sort of tractable minimization encountered for exponential loss. The idea is to derive an upper bound on the change in the loss which can be minimized as a proxy for the actual change in loss. In particular, consider an update as in equation (7.25) where $\alpha \in \mathbb{R}$ and $h \in \mathcal{H}$. We can compute and upper bound the change $\Delta \mathcal{L}$ in the logistic loss when the old F is replaced by $F + \alpha h$ as follows:

$$\Delta \mathcal{L} \doteq \mathcal{L}(F + \alpha h) - \mathcal{L}(F)$$

$$= \sum_{i=1}^{m} \ln\left(1 + e^{-y_i(F(x_i) + \alpha h(x_i))}\right) - \sum_{i=1}^{m} \ln\left(1 + e^{-y_i F(x_i)}\right) \tag{7.26}$$

$$= \sum_{i=1}^{m} \ln\left(\frac{1 + e^{-y_i(F(x_i) + \alpha h(x_i))}}{1 + e^{-y_i F(x_i)}}\right)$$

$$= \sum_{i=1}^{m} \ln\left(1 + \frac{e^{-y_i(F(x_i) + \alpha h(x_i))} - e^{-y_i F(x_i)}}{1 + e^{-y_i F(x_i)}}\right)$$

$$\leq \sum_{i=1}^{m} \frac{e^{-y_i(F(x_i) + \alpha h(x_i))} - e^{-y_i F(x_i)}}{1 + e^{-y_i F(x_i)}}$$

$$= \sum_{i=1}^{m} \frac{e^{-y_i \alpha h(x_i)} - 1}{1 + e^{y_i F(x_i)}} \tag{7.27}$$

where the inequality uses $\ln(1 + z) \leq z$ for $z > -1$, and each of the equalities follows from simple algebraic manipulations. The idea now is to choose α and h so as to minimize the upper bound in equation (7.27). Conveniently, this upper bound has exactly the same form as the objective that is minimized by AdaBoost on every round. In other words, minimizing equation (7.27) is equivalent to minimizing

$$\sum_{i=1}^{m} D(i) e^{-y_i \alpha h(x_i)}$$

where the weights $D(i)$ are equal (or proportional) to

Algorithm 7.4
AdaBoost.L, a variant of AdaBoost for minimizing logistic loss

---

Given: $(x_1, y_1), \ldots, (x_m, y_m)$ where $x_i \in \mathcal{X}$, $y_i \in \{-1, +1\}$.
Initialize: $F_0 \equiv 0$.
For $t = 1, \ldots, T$:

- $D_t(i) = \dfrac{1}{\mathcal{Z}_t} \cdot \dfrac{1}{1 + e^{y_i F_{t-1}(x_i)}}$ for $i = 1, \ldots, m$,

  where $\mathcal{Z}_t$ is a normalization factor.

- Choose $\alpha_t \in \mathbb{R}$ and $h_t \in \mathcal{H}$ to minimize (or approximately minimize if a heuristic search is used):

$$\sum_{i=1}^{m} D_t(i) e^{-y_i \alpha_t h_t(x_i)}.$$

- Update: $F_t = F_{t-1} + \alpha_t h_t$.

Output F_T.

$$\frac{1}{1 + e^{y_i F(x_i)}}.$$

As discussed in section 7.1, this is exactly the form minimized by AdaBoost where on each round $D(i)$ was instead chosen to be $e^{-y_i F(x_i)}$. Thus, as was the case for AdaBoost, if each h is binary, then the best h is the one with minimum weighted error ϵ with respect to D, and the best α is

$$\alpha = \frac{1}{2} \ln \left(\frac{1 - \epsilon}{\epsilon} \right).$$

Putting these ideas together leads to algorithm 7.4, called *AdaBoost.L*.[1] As noted earlier, this procedure is identical to AdaBoost, except that in AdaBoost, $D_t(i)$ is instead made proportional to $e^{-y_i F_{t-1}(x_i)}$. In particular, this means that the same weak learner can be used without any changes at all.

With this slight modification in the choice of D_t, it can be proved, using techniques to be developed in chapter 8, that this procedure asymptotically minimizes the logistic loss rather than the exponential loss (see exercise 8.6). But at this point, we can already get

---

1. This algorithm has sometimes also been called LogAdaBoost and LogitBoost, although the latter name is erroneous since the original LogitBoost algorithm also utilized a Newton-like search that is not incorporated into AdaBoost.L. (See exercises 7.8 and 7.9.)

some intuition as to why the procedure is effective, despite the fact that we are minimizing an upper bound on each round. Consider the derivative, with respect to α, of the upper bound in equation (7.27), compared with the derivative of the actual change in loss in equation (7.26). When evaluated at $\alpha = 0$, the two derivatives are equal to one another; specifically, they are both equal to the negative of equation (7.22). This means that if the bound in equation (7.27) is never negative for any α (so that no improvement is possible), then we must be at a minimum of this function so that its derivative is zero at $\alpha = 0$, which must also be the case for the derivative of the change in loss in equation (7.26). Therefore, if this is the case for all $h \in \mathcal{H}$, so that no progress is possible in the upper bound, then it must be that we have also reached a minimum of the logistic loss (which by convexity must be a global minimum).

Note that this approach is essentially the same as functional gradient descent, but with a particular specification in the choice of α_t. In particular, the weights $D_t(i)$ on examples are the same as for functional gradient descent, and if binary weak hypotheses are used, then the choice of h_t will be identical.

As noted earlier, the weights $D_t(i)$ used in algorithm 7.4 are far less drastic than those for AdaBoost, and in particular never leave the range $[0, 1]$. This may provide less sensitivity to outliers than with AdaBoost.

7.5.3 Estimating Conditional Probabilities

An apparent advantage of logistic regression is its ability to estimate the conditional probability of y for a given example x. In many contexts, such a capability can be extremely useful since it is so much more informative than an unqualified prediction of the most probable label. In this section, we will see that AdaBoost, which until now has been described strictly as a method for classification, also can be used to estimate conditional probabilities.

Earlier, we derived logistic regression by positing a particular form for these conditional probabilities, and then used this form to derive a loss function. It turns out that the opposite is possible. That is, beginning with the loss function, we can derive an estimate of conditional label probabilities, a technique that can be applied to exponential loss as well.

Let $\ell(z)$ denote the loss function for F on a single example (x, y) as a function of the unnormalized margin $z = yF(x)$. Thus, for logistic regression

$$\ell(z) = \ln(1 + e^{-z}), \tag{7.28}$$

and the goal is to find F minimizing

$$\frac{1}{m} \sum_{i=1}^{m} \ell(y_i F(x_i)). \tag{7.29}$$

This objective function can be regarded as an empirical proxy or estimate for the expected loss

$$\mathbf{E}_{(x,y)\sim\mathcal{D}}[\ell(yF(x))], \tag{7.30}$$

where expectation is over the choice of a random example (x, y) selected from the true distribution $\mathcal{D}$. In other words, we suppose that the ideal goal is minimization of this true *risk*, or expected loss, which in practice must be approximated empirically using a training set.

Let

$$\pi(x) = \mathbf{Pr}_y[y = +1 \mid x]$$

be the true conditional probability that x is positive. Let us suppose for the moment that $\pi(x)$ is known, and let us further suppose that the function F is allowed to be entirely arbitrary and unrestricted (rather than a linear combination of features). How should we choose F? The expectation in equation (7.30) can be rewritten by conditioning on x as

$$\mathbf{E}_x\big[\mathbf{E}_y[\ell(yF(x)) \mid x]\big] = \mathbf{E}_x[\pi(x)\ell(F(x)) + (1 - \pi(x))\ell(-F(x))].$$

Thus, the optimal choice of $F(x)$ can be made separately for each x and, in particular, should minimize

$$\pi(x)\ell(F(x)) + (1 - \pi(x))\ell(-F(x)).$$

Differentiating this expression with respect to $F(x)$, we see that the optimal $F(x)$ should satisfy

$$\pi(x)\ell'(F(x)) - (1 - \pi(x))\ell'(-F(x)) = 0, \tag{7.31}$$

where ℓ' is the derivative of ℓ. For the choice of ℓ given in equation (7.28), this happens to give

$$F(x) = \ln\left(\frac{\pi(x)}{1 - \pi(x)}\right).$$

More important for our purposes, this suggests that once an algorithm has computed a function F that approximately minimizes the logistic loss, we can transform $F(x)$ into an estimate of $\pi(x)$ using the inverse of this formula

$$\pi(x) = \frac{1}{1 + e^{-F(x)}}, \tag{7.32}$$

which of course is perfectly consistent with the original derivation of logistic regression given in section 7.5.1.

This same approach can be applied to other loss functions as well. Solving equation (7.31) in general for $\pi(x)$ gives

$$\pi(x) = \frac{1}{1 + \dfrac{\ell'(F(x))}{\ell'(-F(x))}}.$$

For exponential loss as used by AdaBoost, we have $\ell(z) = e^{-z}$. Plugging in gives

$$\pi(x) = \frac{1}{1 + e^{-2F(x)}}.$$ (7.33)

Thus, to convert the output of AdaBoost

$$F(x) = \sum_{t=1}^{T} \alpha_t h_t(x)$$

to a conditional probability, we can simply pass $F(x)$ through the sigmoid given in equation (7.33), a transformation that is almost identical to the one used by logistic regression in equation (7.32).

It is important to note that this approach is founded on two possibly dubious assumptions. First, we assumed that the empirical loss (or risk) in equation (7.29) is a reasonable estimate of the true risk (expected loss) in equation (7.30) for all functions F of interest. This may or may not hold, and indeed is likely to be especially suspect for unbounded loss functions like the logistic and exponential losses. Second, we assumed that the function F computed by logistic regression or AdaBoost is a minimum over *all* functions F without restriction, whereas, as we know, both algorithms compute a function F which is a linear combination of base functions or weak classifiers.

Figure 7.5 shows the result of applying this method to actual data, in this case, the census dataset described in section 5.7.1, using the same setup as before. After training, AdaBoost's combined hypothesis F was used as in equation (7.33) to produce an estimate $\pi(x)$ of the probability of each test example x being positive (income above \$50,000). To produce the *calibration curve* shown in the figure, the 20,000 test examples were sorted by their $\pi(x)$ values, then broken up into contiguous groups of 100 examples each. Each point on each plot corresponds to one such group where the x-coordinate gives the average of the probability estimates $\pi(x)$ for the instances in the group, and the y-coordinate is the fraction of truly positive instances in the group. Thus, if the probability estimates are accurate, then all points should be close to the line $y = x$. In particular, in this figure, with the large training set of size 10,000 that was used, we see that the probability estimates are quite accurate on test data. However, with smaller training sets, performance may degrade significantly for the reasons cited above.

7.6 Regularization

7.6.1 Avoiding Overfitting

Throughout this book, we have discussed the central importance of avoiding overfitting in learning. Certainly, this is important in classification, but when estimating conditional

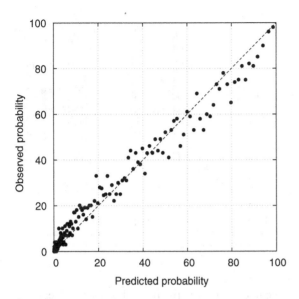

Figure 7.5
A calibration curve for the census dataset. Each point on the plot represents a single cluster of 100 test examples, grouped according to their estimated probability of being positive. The x-coordinate of each point is the average predicted percent probability of a positive label for examples in the group, according to the learned model. The y-coordinate is the actual percent positive in the group. Thus, ideal predictions will be close to the line $y = x$.

probabilities, it can be even more critical. This is because the latter task entails the actual numerical estimation of individual probabilities, while in classification it is enough merely to predict if the probability of an example being positive is larger or smaller than its probability of being negative. Thus, classification demands less of the learning algorithm, and is based on a criterion that can be considerably more forgiving.

The example in section 7.5.3 shows that AdaBoost can effectively estimate probabilities. However, far worse performance is possible when working with smaller training sets or much noisier data. An extreme example is shown in figure 7.6. Here, the artificially generated instances x are real numbers uniformly distributed on the interval $[-2, +2]$, and for any x, the label y is chosen to be $+1$ with probability 2^{-x^2}, and -1 otherwise. This conditional probability, as a function of x, is plotted on the left of the figure. On the right is plotted the estimated conditional probability function computed by running AdaBoost with decision stumps on 500 training examples for 10,000 rounds (and applying equation (7.33)). Clearly, these probability estimates are extremely poor, as are the corresponding classifications. The problem, of course, is excessive overfitting of the noise or randomness in the data.

To avoid overfitting, as we saw in chapter 2, it is necessary to balance how well the learned model fits the data against its complexity. In this example, we have not attempted to limit the complexity of the learned model. Although we might consider restricting the base classifier space $\mathcal{H}$ for this purpose, we here assume that this space has been given and

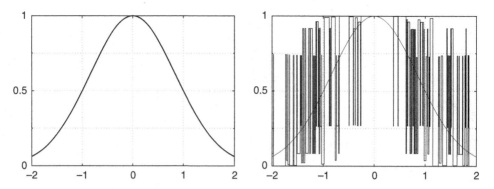

Figure 7.6
Left: A plot of the conditional probability that $y = +1$, given x, on the synthetic example described in section 7.6.1.
Right: The result of running AdaBoost with decision stumps on 500 examples generated in such manner. The
darker, jagged curve shows the conditional probability as estimated using equation (7.33), overlaid with the true
conditional probability.

is fixed so as to emphasize alternative techniques. (Furthermore, in this particular case $\mathcal{H}$
already has very low VC-dimension.) Instead, we focus on the weight vector $\boldsymbol{\lambda}$ computed by
AdaBoost as in the formulation given in section 7.2 since, with $\mathcal{H}$ fixed, $\boldsymbol{\lambda}$ entirely defines
the learned model.

Since it is a vector in $\mathbb{R}^N$, we can measure the complexity of $\boldsymbol{\lambda}$ naturally by its "size," for
instance, its Euclidean length $\|\boldsymbol{\lambda}\|_2$, or as measured using some other norm. Because of its
particular relevance to what follows, we focus specifically on the ℓ_1-norm as a complexity
measure:

$$\|\boldsymbol{\lambda}\|_1 \doteq \sum_{j=1}^{N} |\lambda_j|.$$

With such a measure in hand, we can explicitly limit complexity by seeking to minimize
loss as before, but now subject to a strict bound on the ℓ_1-norm. For exponential loss, this
leads to the following constrained optimization problem:

minimize: $L(\boldsymbol{\lambda})$

subject to: $\|\boldsymbol{\lambda}\|_1 \le B$ (7.34)

for some fixed parameter $B \ge 0$ where, throughout this section, $L(\boldsymbol{\lambda})$ is the exponential loss
as defined in equation (7.7). Alternatively, we might define an unconstrained optimization
problem that attempts to minimize a weighted combination of the loss and the ℓ_1-norm:

$$L(\boldsymbol{\lambda}) + \beta \|\boldsymbol{\lambda}\|_1$$ (7.35)

for some fixed parameter $\beta \geq 0$. These are both called *regularization* techniques. The two forms given here can be shown to be equivalent in the sense of yielding the same solutions for appropriate settings of the parameters B and β. Note that the minimization in equation (7.35) can be solved numerically, for instance, using coordinate descent as in section 7.2.

Naturally, other loss functions can be used in place of exponential loss, and other regularization terms can be used in place of $\|\boldsymbol{\lambda}\|_1$, such as $\|\boldsymbol{\lambda}\|_2^2$. A favorable property of ℓ_1-regularization, however, is its observed tendency to prefer sparse solutions, that is, vectors $\boldsymbol{\lambda}$ with relatively few nonzero components.

For classification, limiting the norm of $\boldsymbol{\lambda}$ would seem to be of no consequence since scaling $\boldsymbol{\lambda}$ by any positive constant has no effect on the predictions of a classifier of the form $\text{sign}(F_{\boldsymbol{\lambda}}(x))$. However, when combined with loss minimization as above, the effect can be significant for both classification and estimation of conditional probabilities. For instance, continuing the example above, figure 7.7 shows the estimated conditional probability functions that result from minimizing equation (7.35) for various settings of β. As the results on this toy problem illustrate, regularization effectively smooths out noise in the data, leading to much more sensible predictions. But as usual, there is a trade-off, and too much regularization can lead to overly smooth predictions; indeed, at an extreme, $\boldsymbol{\lambda}$ is forced to be $\mathbf{0}$, yielding meaningless probability estimates of $\frac{1}{2}$ on all instances.

7.6.2 A Connection to Boosting with Early Stopping

Regularization based on the ℓ_1-norm turns out to be closely connected to boosting algorithms. In particular, we will see that a simple variant of AdaBoost, when stopped after any number of rounds, can often be viewed as providing an approximate solution to the ℓ_1-regularized constrained optimization problem given in equation (7.34) for a corresponding choice of the parameter B.

To make this precise, for any $B \geq 0$, let $\boldsymbol{\lambda}_B^*$ denote any solution of equation (7.34). Then, as B varies, $\boldsymbol{\lambda}_B^*$ traces out a path or trajectory through $\mathbb{R}^N$. When N is small, we can visualize this trajectory as shown at the top of figure 7.8. In this example, data was taken from the heart-disease dataset described in section 1.2.3. However, for illustrative purposes, rather than using all possible decision stumps for base classifiers, we used only the six stumps shown in table 1.2, so that $N = 6$ in this case.[2] The figure shows all six components of $\boldsymbol{\lambda}_B^*$. Specifically, each curve marked j, for $j = 1, \ldots, 6$, is a plot of the j-th component $\lambda_{B,j}^*$ as a function of B. Thus, the figure depicts the entire trajectory. Notice how, as B is increased, nonzero components are added to $\boldsymbol{\lambda}_B^*$ just one or two at a time so that this solution vector tends to remain sparse as long as possible.

For comparison, we consider next the α-Boost variant of AdaBoost described in section 6.4.3. Recall that this is the same as AdaBoost (algorithm 1.1), except that on each

---

2. We also modified the predictions of these six stumps so that each predicts $+1$ (healthy) when its condition is satisfied, and -1 (sick) otherwise. Since the weights on the base classifiers can be positive or negative, this change is of no consequence.

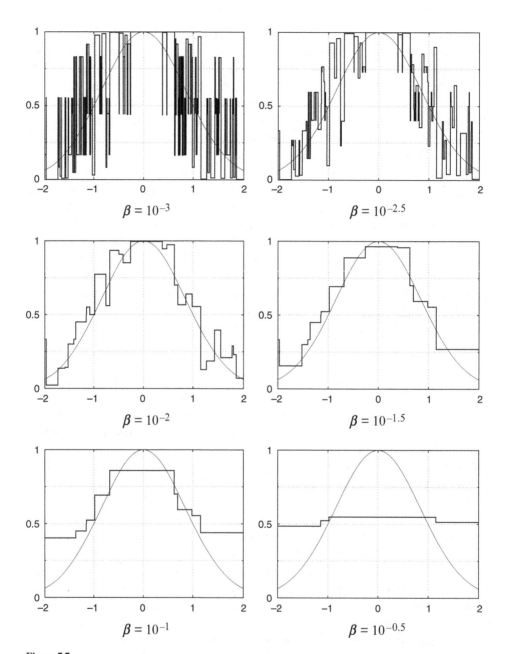

Figure 7.7
The result of minimizing the regularized exponential loss given in equation (7.35), for varying values of β on the same learning problem as in figure 7.6. The darker curves in each figure show the conditional probability as estimated using equation (7.33), overlaid with the true conditional probability.

round, α_t is set equal to some fixed constant α. This is also the same as coordinate descent (section 7.2) or AnyBoost (section 7.4) applied to exponential loss, but using a fixed learning rate α on each iteration. Here, we think of α as a tiny, but positive, constant. Throughout this discussion, we assume that an exhaustive weak learner is used and, furthermore, one which is permitted to choose either a base classifier $\hbar_j \in \mathcal{H}$ or its negation $-\hbar_j$, leading to an update to λ_j of α or $-\alpha$, respectively.

As above, we can plot the trajectory of λ_T, the weight vector that defines the combined classifier computed by α-Boost after T iterations. This is shown, for the same dataset, in the middle of figure 7.8. Each curve j is a plot of $\lambda_{T,j}$ as a function of time T, multiplied by the constant α, so that the resulting scale αT is equal to the cumulative sum of weight updates after T iterations. (Here, we used $\alpha = 10^{-6}$.)

Remarkably, the two plots at the top of figure 7.8—one for the trajectory of ℓ_1-regularization, and the other for α-Boost—are practically indistinguishable. This shows that, at least in this case, α-Boost, when run for T rounds, computes essentially the same solution vectors as when using ℓ_1-regularization with B set to αT. This also means, of course, that the predictions of the two methods will be nearly identical (for either classification or probability estimation). Thus, early stopping—that is, halting boosting after a limited number of rounds—is in this sense apparently equivalent to regularization.

In fact, this correspondence is known to hold much more generally under appropriate technical conditions. When these conditions do not hold, a variant of α-Boost can be used instead which is known to match the computation of ℓ_1-regularization in general. Although the details are beyond the scope of this book, we can provide some intuition as to why α-Boost's trajectory should be so similar to that of ℓ_1-regularization.

Suppose for some $B \geq 0$ that we have already computed the ℓ_1-regularized solution $\lambda = \lambda_B^*$ for equation (7.34), and that we now wish to compute the solution $\lambda' = \lambda_{B+\alpha}^*$ when B is incremented by α, for some tiny $\alpha > 0$. If we can do this repeatedly, then in principle we can trace out the entire trajectory, or at least a good approximation of it. Let us assume for this discussion that $\|\lambda\|_1 = B$, since if $\|\lambda\|_1 < B$, then it can be argued that λ is also a solution for any larger value of B as well (see exercise 7.10). Similarly, assume $\|\lambda'\|_1 = B + \alpha$. Let us define the difference vector $\delta \doteq \lambda' - \lambda$. Clearly, if we can find δ, then we can find $\lambda' = \lambda + \delta$ as well.

By the triangle inequality,

$$B + \alpha = \|\lambda'\|_1 = \|\lambda + \delta\|_1 \leq \|\lambda\|_1 + \|\delta\|_1 = B + \|\delta\|_1. \tag{7.36}$$

In general, equality need not hold here. However, if it happens that the signs of the components of λ and δ align in the right way so that $\lambda_j \delta_j \geq 0$ for all j, then equation (7.36) will indeed hold with equality, implying that $\|\delta\|_1 = \alpha$ in this case. This suggests the heuristic of seeking that δ with $\|\delta\|_1 = \alpha$ which minimizes $L(\lambda') = L(\lambda + \delta)$. When α is small, we have by a Taylor expansion that

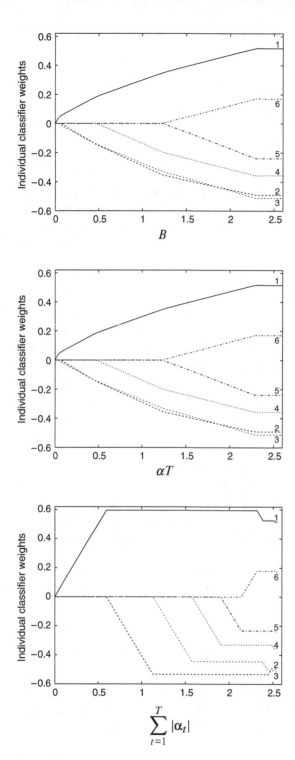

Figure 7.8
(Caption on facing page)

$$L(\lambda + \delta) \approx L(\lambda) + \nabla L(\lambda) \cdot \delta = L(\lambda) + \sum_{j=1}^{N} \frac{\partial L(\lambda)}{\partial \lambda_j} \cdot \delta_j.$$

Among all δ with $\|\delta\|_1 = \alpha$, the right-hand side is minimized when δ is a vector of all zeros, except for that single component j for which $\left|\partial L(\lambda)/\partial \lambda_j\right|$ is largest, which is set to $-\alpha \cdot \mathrm{sign}(\partial L(\lambda)/\partial \lambda_j)$.

In fact, the update we have just described for computing $\lambda' = \lambda + \delta$ from λ is *exactly* what α-Boost computes on each iteration by the arguments given in section 7.4. Thus, we have derived α-Boost as an approximate method for incrementally following the trajectory of ℓ_1-regularization. However, as noted above, the heuristic depends on the updates δ having the same component-wise signs as λ. Informally, this means that the updates applied to the weight λ_j associated with any base classifier $\hbar_j$ should always be of the same sign. It is when this condition holds, as in figure 7.8, that the trajectories will be the same. When it does not hold, when α-Boost occasionally takes a "backwards" step, the correspondence no longer holds exactly.

As a side note, we can compare these trajectories against that of AdaBoost as well. The bottom of figure 7.8 shows such a plot in which the vectors λ computed by AdaBoost are shown in a similar manner as before, but now as a function of the cumulative sum of weight updates $\sum_{t=1}^{T} |\alpha_t|$. Compared to the other plots, we can see some correspondence in behavior, but the resemblance is rather coarse and stylized. Thus, this small example suggests that the connection of AdaBoost to ℓ_1-regularization, if present, is rougher than for α-Boost.

7.6.3 A Connection to Margin Maximization

There is another connection between ℓ_1-regularization and boosting, specifically, to margin maximization, which was studied as a core property of AdaBoost in chapter 5. In particular, if the regularization is relaxed to the limit so that $B \to \infty$ in the optimization problem given in equation (7.34) (or, equivalently, if $\beta \to 0$ in minimizing equation (7.35)), then the solution vectors λ_B^* turn out asymptotically to maximize the margins of the training examples. This suggests that regularization may generalize well on classification problems as a result of margin-maximizing properties not unlike those of AdaBoost. However, this holds true only as the regularization is weakened to the point of apparently disappearing altogether. In such a regime, good performance cannot be attributed to the kind of smoothing associated with regularization that was discussed above.

Figure 7.8
The trajectories of the weight vectors λ computed on the heart-disease dataset of section 1.2.3, using only the six base classifiers from table 1.2 (p. 13). Trajectories are plotted for ℓ_1-regularized exponential loss as in equation (7.34) (top); α-Boost with $\alpha = 10^{-6}$ (middle); and AdaBoost (bottom). Each figure includes one curve for each of the six base classifiers from table 1.2, showing its associated weight as a function of the total weight added.

Note also the subtle distinction between $B \to \infty$ (or equivalently, $\beta \to 0$) and $B = \infty$ ($\beta = 0$). In the former case, regularization yields a maximum margin solution; in the latter case, in which we are minimizing unregularized exponential loss, the solution need not have any such properties (depending on the algorithm used to effect the minimization), as seen, for instance, in the example of section 7.3.

To make this margin-maximizing property precise, let us first define f_λ, for any $\lambda \neq \mathbf{0}$, to be a version of F_λ (equation (7.6)) in which the weights have been normalized:

$$f_\lambda(x) \doteq \frac{F_\lambda(x)}{\|\lambda\|_1} = \frac{\sum_{j=1}^N \lambda_j \hbar_j(x)}{\|\lambda\|_1}.$$

We assume that the data is linearly separable with positive margin $\theta > 0$, as defined in section 3.2. That is, we assume there exists a vector $\tilde{\lambda}$ for which every training example has margin at least θ, so that

$$y_i f_{\tilde{\lambda}}(x_i) \geq \theta \tag{7.37}$$

for all $i = 1, \dots, m$. Without loss of generality, we assume $\|\tilde{\lambda}\|_1 = 1$. To simplify notation, we also write F_B^* and f_B^* for $F_{\lambda_B^*}$ and $f_{\lambda_B^*}$, respectively.

We claim that as B is made large, the margins $y_i f_B^*(x_i)$ approach or exceed θ; specifically, we claim that

$$y_i f_B^*(x_i) \geq \theta - \frac{\ln m}{B}$$

for each of the m training examples i, provided $B > (\ln m)/\theta$. To see this, we start with the fact that λ_B^* minimizes the exponential loss L among all vectors of ℓ_1-norm at most B; thus, in particular,

$$L(\lambda_B^*) \leq L(B\tilde{\lambda}) \tag{7.38}$$

since $\|B\tilde{\lambda}\|_1 = B$. We can bound the right-hand side using equation (7.37):

$$mL(B\tilde{\lambda}) = \sum_{i=1}^m \exp\left(-y_i F_{B\tilde{\lambda}}(x_i)\right)$$

$$= \sum_{i=1}^m \exp\left(-y_i B f_{\tilde{\lambda}}(x_i)\right)$$

$$\leq m e^{-B\theta}.$$

Further, when $B > (\ln m)/\theta$, this is strictly less than 1. Combined with equation (7.38), this implies, for any i, that

$$\exp\left(-y_i F_B^*(x_i)\right) \le m L(\lambda_B^*) \le m e^{-B\theta} < 1$$

or, equivalently,

$$y_i \|\lambda_B^*\|_1 f_B^*(x_i) = y_i F_B^*(x_i) \ge B\theta - \ln m > 0.$$

Thus, as claimed,

$$y_i f_B^*(x_i) \ge \frac{B\theta - \ln m}{\|\lambda_B^*\|_1} \ge \theta - \frac{\ln m}{B}$$

since $\|\lambda_B^*\|_1 \le B$.

So very weak ℓ_1-regularization can be used to find a maximum margin classifier, as can other techniques discussed in section 5.4.2, as well as α-Boost with α very small, as seen in section 6.4.3. Indeed, the fact that both α-Boost and ℓ_1-regularization can be used for this purpose is entirely consistent with our earlier discussion linking the behavior of the two algorithms.

7.7 Applications to Data-Limited Learning

The tools developed in this chapter are quite general purpose, and can be used, through careful design of the loss function, for a range of learning problems. In this last section, we give two examples of how these methods can be applied practically, in both cases to problems that arise as a result of limitations in the availability of data.

7.7.1 Incorporating Prior Knowledge

Throughout this book, we have focused on highly data-driven learning algorithms which derive a hypothesis exclusively through the examination of the training set itself. This approach makes sense when data is abundant. However, in some applications, data may be severely limited. Nevertheless, there may be accessible human knowledge that, in principle, might compensate for the shortage of data.

For instance, in the development of a spoken-dialogue system of the sort described in section 10.3 and more briefly in section 5.7, training a classifier for categorizing spoken utterances requires considerable data. This is a problem, however, because often such a system must be deployed *before* enough data has been collected. Indeed, real data in the form of actual conversations with genuine customers cannot be easily collected until *after* the system has been deployed. The idea then is to use human-crafted knowledge to compensate for this initial dearth of data until enough can be collected following deployment.

In its standard form, boosting does not allow for the direct incorporation of such prior knowledge (other than implicit knowledge encoded in the choice of weak-learning algorithm). Here, we describe a modification of boosting that combines and balances human expertise with available training data. The aim is to allow the human's rough judgments to be refined, reinforced, and adjusted by the statistics of the training data, but in a manner that does not permit the data to entirely overwhelm human judgments.

The basic idea is to modify the loss function used by boosting so that the algorithm balances two terms, one measuring fit to the training data and the other measuring fit to a human-built model.

As usual, we assume we are given m training examples $(x_1, y_1), \ldots, (x_m, y_m)$ with $y_i \in \{-1, +1\}$. Now, however, we suppose that the number of examples m is rather limited. Our starting point is AdaBoost.L (algorithm 7.4), the boosting-style algorithm for logistic regression presented in section 7.5. We saw earlier that this algorithm is based on the loss function given in equation (7.21), which is the negative log conditional likelihood of the data when the conditional probability that an example x is positive is estimated by $\sigma(F(x))$, where σ is as defined in equation (7.19).

Into this data-driven approach we wish to incorporate prior knowledge. There are of course many forms and representations that "knowledge" can take. Here, we assume that a human "expert" has somehow constructed a function $\tilde{p}(x)$ that estimates, perhaps quite crudely, the conditional probability that any example x will be positive, that is, $\mathbf{Pr}_{\mathcal{D}}[y = +1 \mid x]$.

Given both a prior model and training data, we now have two possibly conflicting goals in constructing a hypothesis: (1) fit the data, and (2) fit the prior model. As before, we can measure fit to the data using log conditional likelihood as in equation (7.21). But how do we measure fit to the prior model? As just discussed, the learning algorithm seeks a model of the form $\sigma(F(x))$ which estimates the conditional distribution of labels for any example x. This is also the same conditional distribution being estimated by the prior model $\tilde{p}$. Thus, to measure the difference between the models, we can use the discrepancy between these conditional distributions. And since distributions are involved, it is natural to measure this discrepancy using relative entropy.

Thus, to measure fit to the prior model, for each example x_i we use the relative entropy between the prior model distribution given by $\tilde{p}(x_i)$ and the distribution over labels associated with our constructed logistic model $\sigma(F(x_i))$. These are then added over all of the training examples so that the overall fit of the constructed hypothesis to the prior model is computed by

$$\sum_{i=1}^{m} \mathrm{RE}_b \left(\tilde{p}(x_i) \parallel \sigma(F(x_i)) \right) \tag{7.39}$$

where $\mathrm{RE}_b (\cdot \parallel \cdot)$ is the binary relative entropy defined in equation (5.36).

So our goal now is to minimize equations (7.21) and (7.39). These can be combined, with the introduction of a parameter $\eta > 0$ measuring their relative importance, to arrive at the modified loss function

$$\sum_{i=1}^{m} \left[\ln\left(1 + \exp(-y_i F(x_i))\right) + \eta \text{RE}_b\left(\tilde{p}(x_i) \parallel \sigma(F(x_i))\right) \right].$$

This expression can be rewritten as

$$C + \sum_{i=1}^{m} \left[\ln\left(1 + e^{-y_i F(x_i)}\right) + \eta \tilde{p}(x_i) \ln\left(1 + e^{-F(x_i)}\right) + \eta(1 - \tilde{p}(x_i)) \ln\left(1 + e^{F(x_i)}\right) \right]$$

$$(7.40)$$

where C is a term that is independent of F, and so can be disregarded.

Note that this objective function has the same form as equation (7.21) over a larger set, and with the addition of nonnegative weights on each term. Therefore, to minimize equation (7.40), we apply the AdaBoost.L procedure to a larger weighted training set. This new set includes all of the original training examples (x_i, y_i), each with unit weight. In addition, for each training example (x_i, y_i), we create two new training examples $(x_i, +1)$ and $(x_i, -1)$ with weights $\eta \tilde{p}(x_i)$ and $\eta(1 - \tilde{p}(x_i))$, respectively. Thus, we triple the number of examples (although, by noticing that (x_i, y_i) occurs twice, we can get away with only doubling the training set). AdaBoost.L can be easily modified to incorporate these weights w_0 in the computation of D_t in algorithm 7.4, using instead

$$D_t(i) \propto \frac{w_0(i)}{1 + \exp\left(y_i F_{t-1}(x_i)\right)}$$

(where i ranges over all of the examples in the *new* training set).

One final modification that we make is to add a 0-th base function h_0 that is based on $\tilde{p}$, so as to incorporate $\tilde{p}$ from the start. In particular, we take

$$h_0(x) = \sigma^{-1}(\tilde{p}(x)) = \ln\left(\frac{\tilde{p}(x)}{1 - \tilde{p}(x)}\right)$$

and include h_0 in computing the final classifier F.

As a concrete example, this technique can be applied to classify the headlines of news articles from the Associated Press by topic. The dataset used here consists of 29,841 examples (of which only a subset were used for training) over 20 topics or classes. A multiclass extension of the approach above was used based on the kind of techniques developed in chapter 10.

Our framework permits prior knowledge of any kind, so long as it provides estimates, however rough, of the probability of any example belonging to any class. Here is one possible technique for creating such a rough model that was tested experimentally. First, a human with no expertise beyond ordinary knowledge of news events, and with access

Table 7.2
The keywords used for each class on the AP headlines dataset

Class	Keywords
japan	japan, tokyo, yen
bush	bush, george, president, election
israel	israel, jerusalem, peres, sharon, palestinian, israeli, arafat
britx	britain, british, england, english, london, thatcher
gulf	gulf, iraq, saudi, arab, iraqi, saddam, hussein, kuwait
german	german, germany, bonn, berlin, mark
weather	weather, rain, snow, cold, ice, sun, sunny, cloudy
dollargold	dollar, gold, price
hostages	hostages, ransom, holding, hostage
budget	budget, deficit, taxes
arts	art, painting, artist, music, entertainment, museum, theater
dukakis	dukakis, boston, taxes, governor
yugoslavia	yugoslavia
quayle	quayle, dan
ireland	ireland, ira, dublin
burma	burma
bonds	bond, bonds, yield, interest
nielsens	nielsens, rating, t v, tv
boxoffice	box office, movie
tickertalk	stock, bond, bonds, stocks, price, earnings

to the list of categories but not to the data itself, thought up a handful of keywords for each class. This list of keywords is shown in table 7.2. These keywords were produced through an entirely subjective process of free association with general knowledge of what the categories were about (and also the time period during which the data was collected), but no other information or access to the data.

Such a list of keywords can next be used to construct a simple and naive, but very rough, prior model. To do so, we posit that if a keyword w is present, then there is a 90% probability that the correct class is among those that list w as a keyword, and a 10% chance that it is one of the others. For instance, conditional on the presence of the keyword *price* in the headline, the naive prior model estimates that there would be a 90% probability of the correct class being "dollargold" or "tickertalk" (that is, a 45% chance for each one separately), and a 10% chance of one of the other 18 topics being the correct class (giving $10\%/18 \approx 0.6\%$ probability to each). If the keyword is absent, we posit that all classes are equally likely. These conditional probabilities can then be combined using very naive independence assumptions, together with simple probabilistic reasoning.

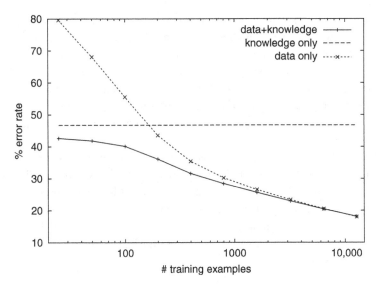

Figure 7.9
Comparison of test error rate using prior knowledge and data separately or together on the AP headlines dataset, measured as a function of the number of training examples. Results are averaged over ten runs, each with a different random partition of the data into training and testing.

Figure 7.9 shows the performance of the method above for training sets of varying sizes, in each case using boosting with decision stumps for 1000 rounds. The figure shows test error rate for boosting with and without prior knowledge, as well as the error rate achieved using the prior model alone with no training examples at all. As can be seen, for fairly small datasets, using prior knowledge gives dramatic improvements over straight boosting, almost halving the error early on, and providing performance equivalent to using two to four times as much data without such knowledge. With a lot of data, as expected, the effect of the prior model is washed out.

7.7.2   Semi-Supervised Learning

In section 5.7.2, we discussed the ubiquitous problem of learning from an abundance of unlabeled examples but a severely limited supply of labeled examples. There, we considered how to make best use of a human annotator through the careful selection of examples for labeling. Whether or not we have the means to obtain additional labels, there sometimes may exist an opportunity to improve classifier accuracy by directly exploiting the unlabeled data, which otherwise is apparently wasted. Intuitively, unlabeled data may provide distributional information that may be helpful for classification (an informal example is given shortly). This problem is often called *semi-supervised learning*. Here, we present one boosting approach based on loss minimization.

In the semi-supervised framework, data is presented in two parts: a set of labeled examples $(x_1, y_1), \ldots, (x_m, y_m)$, together with another, usually much larger, set of unlabeled examples $\tilde{x}_1, \ldots, \tilde{x}_M$. Our approach to handling such mixed data will be to construct an appropriate loss function which can then be optimized using techniques from this chapter. For the labeled examples, we can start with standard AdaBoost, which, as discussed in section 7.1, is based on exponential loss over the labeled examples as in equation (7.3). This loss encourages the construction of a hypothesis F whose sign on labeled examples x_i agrees with their observed labels y_i.

For the unlabeled examples, however, we obviously have no true labels available to match. Nevertheless, in chapter 5 we studied in depth the importance of producing predictions that are highly confident in the sense of having large margins. Moreover, observing the label is not prerequisite to computing such a measure of confidence. This motivates the idea of encouraging F to be large in magnitude, and thus more confident, on the unlabeled examples $\tilde{x}_i$ as well. To do so, we can use a variant of exponential loss, namely,

$$\frac{1}{M} \sum_{i=1}^{M} e^{-|F(\tilde{x}_i)|}, \tag{7.41}$$

an objective whose minimization will have the effect of enlarging the unnormalized absolute margins $|F(\tilde{x}_i)|$. Of course, the theory developed in chapter 5 emphasized the importance of the *normalized* margin (in which the weights of the base hypotheses have been normalized) rather than the unnormalized margin used here, but we also saw that AdaBoost, in minimizing exponential loss, has a tendency to (approximately) maximize the normalized margins as well.

Viewed slightly differently, with respect to a hypothesis F, if we define pseudolabels $\tilde{y}_i = \text{sign}(F(\tilde{x}_i))$, then equation (7.41) can be rewritten as

$$\frac{1}{M} \sum_{i=1}^{M} e^{-\tilde{y}_i F(\tilde{x}_i)}, \tag{7.42}$$

in other words, in the same form as equation (7.3) for labeled pairs $(\tilde{x}_i, \tilde{y}_i)$. Since these are exactly the choices of labels for which equation (7.42) is minimized, this means that the loss in equation (7.41) will tend to be small for those hypotheses F which fit the unlabeled data well for *some* labeling, even if it is not the true, hidden labeling.

For instance, for intuition's sake, we can regard the unlabeled examples geometrically as points in feature space, similar to the setup of section 5.6. Figure 7.10 shows such a set of points. The combined classifier defines a hyperplane in this space defined by the equation $F(x) = 0$. In this example, the line (hyperplane) F_1, which admits a large-margin classification of the data, will clearly be favored by the objective in equation (7.41) over

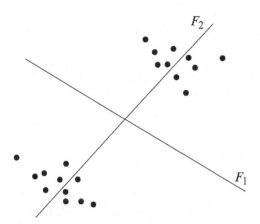

Figure 7.10
A hypothetical set of unlabeled examples in feature space. The linear classifier marked F_1 admits significantly higher margins for some labeling of the points than F_2, and thus will be preferred when using the loss defined by equation (7.41).

F_2, which passes too close to too many examples for this to be possible. This is consistent with our intuition that F_1 divides the data, even if unlabeled, more naturally than F_2.

Combining the loss functions in equations (7.3) and (7.41) yields

$$\frac{1}{m}\sum_{i=1}^{m} e^{-y_i F(x_i)} + \frac{\eta}{M}\sum_{i=1}^{M} e^{-|F(\tilde{x}_i)|}, \tag{7.43}$$

where we have introduced a parameter $\eta > 0$ controlling the relative importance given to the unlabeled examples.

To minimize equation (7.43), we can apply the functional gradient descent approach of section 7.4, specifically, AnyBoost (algorithm 7.3). Using the pseudolabels $\tilde{y}_i$ as in equation (7.42), and differentiating the loss in equation (7.43) to evaluate equation (7.14), this approach prescribes choosing h_t to maximize

$$\frac{1}{m}\sum_{i=1}^{m} y_i h_t(x_i) e^{-y_i F_{t-1}(x_i)} + \frac{\eta}{M}\sum_{i=1}^{M} \tilde{y}_i h_t(x_i) e^{-\tilde{y}_i F_{t-1}(\tilde{x}_i)}.$$

Of course, this has the same form as equation (7.15), meaning that any ordinary base learning algorithm designed for minimization of the weighted classification error on a labeled dataset can be used for this purpose.

Once h_t has been chosen, we need to select $\alpha_t > 0$. To simplify notation, let us for the moment drop subscripts involving t. A line search would choose α to minimize the resulting loss

$$\frac{1}{m} \sum_{i=1}^{m} \exp\left(-y_i(F(x_i) + \alpha h(x_i))\right) + \frac{\eta}{M} \sum_{i=1}^{M} \exp\left(-|F(\tilde{x}_i) + \alpha h(\tilde{x}_i)|\right). \tag{7.44}$$

This could be complicated to compute because of the absolute values in the exponents. Instead, a simpler approach would continue to use the pseudolabels so that α is chosen to minimize

$$\frac{1}{m} \sum_{i=1}^{m} \exp\left(-y_i(F(x_i) + \alpha h(x_i))\right) + \frac{\eta}{M} \sum_{i=1}^{M} \exp\left(-\tilde{y}_i(F(\tilde{x}_i) + \alpha h(\tilde{x}_i))\right). \tag{7.45}$$

In other words, we can use the usual AdaBoost choice of α based on the weighted error on the entire dataset as augmented by the pseudolabels. Note that equation (7.44) is at most equation (7.45), as follows from the simple fact that

$$\tilde{y}_i(F(\tilde{x}_i) + \alpha h(\tilde{x}_i)) \leq |\tilde{y}_i(F(\tilde{x}_i) + \alpha h(\tilde{x}_i))| = |F(\tilde{x}_i) + \alpha h(\tilde{x}_i)|.$$

Therefore, although perhaps not best possible, choosing α in this manner so as to minimize equation (7.45) is guaranteed to effect at least as great a decrease in equation (7.44).

Once h_t and α_t have been selected, F_t is computed as in algorithm 7.3, the pseudolabels are then recomputed with respect to F_t, and the process continues.

This algorithm, called *ASSEMBLE.AdaBoost*, was entered into a competition of semi-supervised learning algorithms in 2001, and took first place among 34 entries. In this case, decision trees were used as base classifiers. Also, the pseudolabel for each unlabeled example $\tilde{x}_i$ was initialized to be the label of its nearest neighbor in the labeled set.

Table 7.3 shows the results on the datasets used in this competition, comparing AS-SEMBLE.AdaBoost's performance with that of AdaBoost trained just on the labeled

Table 7.3
Test results for ASSEMBLE.AdaBoost on seven datasets used in a 2001 competition of semi-supervised learning algorithms

Dataset	# of Features	# of Classes	# Examples			% Error	% Improve
			Labeled	Unlabeled	Test		
P1	13	2	36	92	100	35.0	8.3
P4	192	9	108	108	216	21.3	21.4
P5	1000	2	50	3952	100	24.0	16.9
P6	12	2	530	2120	2710	24.3	0.1
P8	296	4	537	608	211	42.2	16.2
CP2	21	3	300	820	300	49.3	26.7
CP3	10	5	1000	1269	500	58.8	6.7

The last two columns show the test error of ASSEMBLE.AdaBoost, followed by the percent improvement over running AdaBoost just on the labeled data.

examples. In most cases, the improvement in accuracy was very substantial, often in double digits.

Summary

In summary, we have seen that AdaBoost is closely associated with the exponential loss function. Although this connection may not explain how AdaBoost achieves high test accuracy, it does lead to some widely applicable techniques for extending and generalizing it. Specifically, we have explored how, in two different ways, AdaBoost can be viewed as a special case of more general procedures for optimization of an objective function. Also in this chapter, we have explored the close connections between AdaBoost and logistic regression. We have seen how this leads both to a simple modification of AdaBoost for logistic regression and to a method for using AdaBoost to estimate conditional label probabilities. We also explored how regularization can be used as a smoothing technique for avoiding overfitting, as well as the close connections between boosting and regularization using an ℓ_1-norm. Finally, we saw examples of how these general techniques can be applied practically.

Bibliographic Notes

Breiman [36] was the first to interpret AdaBoost as a method for minimizing exponential loss, as in section 7.1, a connection that was later expanded upon by various other authors [87, 98, 168, 178, 186, 205]. The view of boosting as a form of gradient descent, as in section 7.4, is also due to Breiman [36]. The generic AnyBoost procedure, algorithm 7.3, is taken from Mason et al. [168]. A similar generalization was given by Friedman [100], leading to a general procedure based on solving multiple regression problems as in section 7.4.3. When applied to square loss, the resulting procedures are essentially the same as Mallat and Zhang's work on matching pursuit [163].

Friedman, Hastie, and Tibshirani [98] showed how boosting can be understood in the context of a family of statistical techniques called additive modeling. They also provided justification for the use of exponential loss, particularly in terms of its close relationship to logistic loss as discussed somewhat in section 7.5.1. They showed how a function obtained through the minimization of exponential loss can be used to estimate conditional probabilities, as in section 7.5.3. Although they derived a version of AdaBoost for logistic regression called LogitBoost, the AdaBoost.L algorithm presented in section 7.5.2 came in the later work of Collins, Schapire, and Singer [54].

The discussion and experiment in section 7.3 are similar in spirit to work by Mease and Wyner [169] that attempted to expose some of the difficulties with the so-called "statistical view" of boosting, including its interpretation as a method for optimizing a loss as expounded in this chapter. Wyner [232] also gives a variant of AdaBoost that performs well while keeping the exponential loss roughly constant, adding further doubts to this interpretation.

Regularization using an ℓ_1-norm on the weights, as in section 7.6.1, is often called "the lasso," and was proposed in the context of least-squares regression by Tibshirani [218]. The connection to α-Boost with early stopping, as discussed in section 7.6.2, was observed by Hastie, Tibshirani, and Friedman [120], and explored further by Rosset, Zhu, and Hastie [192], who also showed that weak ℓ_1-regularization yields a maximum margin solution, as seen in section 7.6.3. A more advanced and general boosting-like algorithm for tracing the entire ℓ_1-regularized trajectory is given by Zhao and Yu [237].

In addition to those given here, other boosting-like algorithms and methods for regression have been proposed, for instance, by Freund and Schapire [95], Ridgeway, Madigan and Richardson [190], and Duffy and Helmbold [79]. In other work, Duffy and Helmbold [78] discussed conditions under which minimization of a loss function using functional gradient descent can lead to a boosting algorithm in the technical PAC sense of section 2.3.

Further background on many of the statistical topics discussed in this chapter, including regression, logistic regression, and regularization, can be found, for instance, in the text by Hastie, Tibshirani, and Friedman [120]. For additional background on general-purpose optimization methods, including coordinate descent and Gauss-Southwell methods, see, for instance, Luenberger and Ye [160].

The NP-completeness of finding a linear threshold function with minimum classification loss, alluded to in section 7.1, was proved by Höffgen and Simon [124].

The method and experiments in section 7.7.1, including table 7.2 and figure 7.9, are taken from Schapire et al. [203, 204], using a dataset of AP headlines prepared by Lewis and Catlett [151] and Lewis and Gale [152]. The ASSEMBLE.AdaBoost algorithm described in section 7.7.2, including the results adapted in table 7.3, are due to Bennett, Demiriz, and Maclin [18].

Some of the exercises in this chapter are based on material from [98, 233].

Exercises

7.1 Consider the following objective function:

$$L(x, y) \doteq \max\{x - 2y, y - 2x\}.$$

a. Sketch a *contour map* of L. That is, in the $\langle x, y \rangle$-plane, plot the *level set* $\{\langle x, y \rangle : L(x, y) = c\}$ for various values of c.

b. Is L continuous? Convex? Does the gradient of L exist at all values of x and y?

c. What is the minimum (or infimum) of L over all $\langle x, y \rangle$? Where is that minimum value realized?

d. Explain what will happen if we apply coordinate descent to L, starting at any initial point $\langle x, y \rangle$. Is coordinate descent successful in this case (that is, at minimizing the objective function)?

7.2 Continuing exercise 7.1, suppose we approximate L by

$$\tilde{L}(x, y) \doteq \frac{1}{\eta} \ln \left(e^{\eta(x-2y)} + e^{\eta(y-2x)} \right)$$

for some large constant $\eta > 0$.

a. Show that

$$\left| L(x, y) - \tilde{L}(x, y) \right| \leq \frac{\ln 2}{\eta}$$

for all $\langle x, y \rangle$.

b. How would a contour plot of $\tilde{L}$ compare with that of L?

c. Explain what will happen if we apply coordinate descent to $\tilde{L}$, starting at $\langle 0, 0 \rangle$. Give the exact sequence of points $\langle x_t, y_t \rangle$ that will be computed, as well as the resulting loss $\tilde{L}(x_t, y_t)$. Is coordinate descent successful in this case?

7.3 Suppose, as in section 7.3, that instances $\mathbf{x}$ are points in $\mathcal{X} = \{-1, +1\}^N$; that we are using coordinates (and their negations) as base classifiers; and that the label y associated with each instance $\mathbf{x}$ is a simple majority vote of k of the coordinates:

$$y = \text{sign} \left(x_{j_1} + \cdots + x_{j_k} \right)$$

for some (unknown, not necessarily distinct) coordinates $j_1, \ldots, j_k \in \{1, \ldots, N\}$ (where k is odd). Let $(\mathbf{x}_1, y_1), \ldots, (\mathbf{x}_m, y_m)$ be a random training set where the $\mathbf{x}_i$'s are generated according to an arbitrary target distribution $\mathcal{D}$ on $\mathcal{X}$ (and the labels y_i are assigned as just described).

Show that if AdaBoost is run with an exhaustive weak learner for sufficiently many rounds T, then with probability at least $1 - \delta$, the generalization error of the combined classifier H will be at most

$$O\left(\sqrt{\frac{k^2 \ln N}{m} \cdot \ln \left(\frac{m}{k^2 \ln N} \right)} + \frac{\ln(1/\delta)}{m} \right).$$

(An even better bound is also possible.) Thus, m only needs to grow faster than $k^2 \ln N$ for the generalization error to go to zero.

7.4 Continuing exercise 7.3, the exponential loss of equation (7.7), specialized to this setting, has the form

$$L(\lambda) = \frac{1}{m} \sum_{i=1}^{m} \exp(-y_i \lambda \cdot \mathbf{x}_i).$$

a. Compute $\nabla L(\lambda)$, the gradient of L at λ.

b. When using gradient descent, regardless of the learning rate, show that the computed weight vector λ will always be in the span of the training instances, meaning

$$\lambda = \sum_{i=1}^{m} b_i \mathbf{x}_i$$

for some $b_1, \ldots, b_m \in \mathbb{R}$. (Throughout this problem, assume gradient descent is started at $\mathbf{0}$.)

c. An $N \times N$ *Hadamard matrix* has all entries in $\{-1, +1\}$, and all columns are orthogonal to one another. Hadamard matrices $\mathbf{H}_N$ in which N is a power of 2 can be constructed recursively with $\mathbf{H}_1 = (1)$, and

$$\mathbf{H}_{2N} = \begin{pmatrix} \mathbf{H}_N & \mathbf{H}_N \\ \mathbf{H}_N & -\mathbf{H}_N \end{pmatrix}.$$

Verify that matrices constructed in this fashion are indeed Hadamard.

d. For N a power of 2, suppose the target distribution $\mathcal{D}$ on instances is uniform on the columns of the Hadamard matrix $\mathbf{H}_N$. Show that regardless of how instances are labeled, the generalization error of a classifier $H(x) = \text{sign}(\lambda \cdot \mathbf{x})$ computed using gradient descent is at least $1/2 - m/(2N)$. (For the purposes of this exercise, let us count a prediction of 0 as half a mistake.) Thus, when the number of training examples m is small compared to the number of dimensions N, the generalization error is sure to be large.

7.5 For given real values $b_1, \ldots, b_m, c_1, \ldots, c_m$, and nonnegative weights $w_1, \ldots, w_m$, let

$$f(\alpha) = \sum_{i=1}^{m} w_i (\alpha b_i - c_i)^2.$$

Find explicitly the value of α that minimizes f, and also evaluate f at this value.

7.6 Let $\mathcal{H}$ be a class of real-valued base functions that is closed under scaling (so that if $h \in \mathcal{H}$, then ch is also in $\mathcal{H}$ for all $c \in \mathbb{R}$). Show that choosing $h \in \mathcal{H}$ to minimize the squared error criterion in equation (7.17) is equivalent to using AnyBoost (algorithm 7.3) with appropriately normalized base functions from $\mathcal{H}$. Specifically, show that equation (7.17) is minimized (over $\mathcal{H}$) by a function $ch \in \mathcal{H}$ where $c \in \mathbb{R}$, and where h maximizes $-\nabla \mathcal{L}(F_{t-1}) \cdot h$ over all functions in $\mathcal{H}$ with $\|h\|_2 = 1$. (Assume this maximum exists.)

7.7 *GentleAdaBoost* is an algorithm for minimizing exponential loss derived using a form of a numerical technique called Newton's method. The algorithm turns out to be the same as AdaBoost as depicted in algorithm 7.1, except that h_t and α_t are instead found by minimizing the weighted least-squares problem:

$$\sum_{i=1}^{m} e^{-y_i F_{t-1}(x_i)} (\alpha_t h_t(x_i) - y_i)^2. \tag{7.46}$$

Assume all of the base functions in the space $\mathcal{H}$ are classifiers, that is, $\{-1, +1\}$-valued.

a. Under equivalent conditions (that is, the same dataset, same current value of F_{t-1}, etc.), show that GentleAdaBoost selects the same base classifier h_t as AdaBoost (in other words, h_t, together with some value of α_t, minimizes equation (7.46) if and only if it minimizes the corresponding criterion given in algorithm 7.1).

b. Under equivalent conditions (including the same choice of h_t), let α_t^{GB} and α_t^{AB} denote the values of α_t selected by GentleAdaBoost and AdaBoost, respectively. Show that

    i. α_t^{GB} and α_t^{AB} must have the same sign.

    ii. $\alpha_t^{\mathrm{GB}} \in [-1, +1]$.

    iii. $|\alpha_t^{\mathrm{GB}}| \le |\alpha_t^{\mathrm{AB}}|$.

7.8 *LogitBoost* (algorithm 7.5) is an algorithm also derived using Newton's method, but applied to the logistic loss. As in exercise 7.7, assume all of the base functions in $\mathcal{H}$ are classifiers.

a. Under equivalent conditions, show that LogitBoost selects the same base classifier as AdaBoost.L. (Assume the algorithms select α_t and h_t using an exhaustive search.)

b. Under equivalent conditions (including the choice of h_t), let α_t^{LB} and α_t^{ABL} denote the values of α_t selected by LogitBoost and AdaBoost.L, respectively. Give explicit expressions for α_t^{LB} and α_t^{ABL} in terms of the data, h_t, D_t, and Z_t, where D_t and Z_t are as defined in algorithm 7.4.

c. Show that α_t^{LB} and α_t^{ABL} must have the same sign.

d. Prove by example that $|\alpha_t^{\mathrm{LB}}|$ can be strictly smaller or strictly larger than $|\alpha_t^{\mathrm{ABL}}|$.

7.9 Suppose $\mathcal{H}$ consists of a single function $\hbar$ that is identically equal to the constant $+1$. Let the training set consist of $m = 2$ oppositely labeled examples $(x_1, +1)$ and $(x_2, -1)$.

a. For what value of the single parameter λ is the logistic loss in equation (7.20) minimized (where $F_\lambda(x) \doteq \lambda \hbar(x) \equiv \lambda$ for all x)?

b. Suppose LogitBoost is run on this data, but with F_0 initialized to the constant function $F_0 = \lambda_0 \hbar \equiv \lambda_0$, for some $\lambda_0 \in \mathbb{R}$ which is not necessarily zero. Since $h_t = \hbar$ on every round, we can write F_t as $\lambda_t \hbar \equiv \lambda_t$ for some $\lambda_t \in \mathbb{R}$. Write a formula for λ_{t+1} in terms of λ_t. That is, find in closed form the function $U(\lambda)$ which defines the update $\lambda_{t+1} = U(\lambda_t)$.

Algorithm 7.5
LogitBoost, an algorithm based on Newton's method for minimizing logistic loss

---

Given: $(x_1, y_1), \ldots, (x_m, y_m)$ where $x_i \in \mathcal{X}$, $y_i \in \{-1, +1\}$.
Initialize: $F_0 \equiv 0$.
For $t = 1, \ldots, T$:

- For $i = 1, \ldots, m$:

$$p_t(i) = \frac{1}{1 + e^{-F_{t-1}(x_i)}}$$

$$z_t(i) = \begin{cases} \frac{1}{p_t(i)} & \text{if } y_i = +1 \\ -\frac{1}{1 - p_t(i)} & \text{if } y_i = -1 \end{cases}$$

$$w_t(i) = p_t(i)(1 - p_t(i)).$$

- Choose $\alpha_t \in \mathbb{R}$ and $h_t \in \mathcal{H}$ to minimize (or approximately minimize if a heuristic search is used)

$$\sum_{i=1}^{m} w_t(i)(\alpha_t h_t(x_i) - z_t(i))^2.$$

- Update: $F_t = F_{t-1} + \alpha_t h_t$.

Output F_T.

---

c. Show that there exists a constant $C > 0$ such that if $|\lambda_0| \leq C$, then $\lambda_t \to 0$ as $t \to \infty$.

d. Show that if $|\lambda_0| \geq 3$, then $|\lambda_t| \to \infty$ as $t \to \infty$.

e. How would AdaBoost.L handle this same setting (with the same initialization of F_0)?

7.10 Let $L : \mathbb{R}^N \to \mathbb{R}$ be any convex function. Suppose λ is a solution of the constrained optimization problem given in equation (7.34) for some $B > 0$. Show that if $\|\lambda\|_1 < B$, then λ is also a solution of equation (7.34) when B is replaced by any $B' > B$.

7.11 Assume $\mathcal{H}$ consists only of classifiers (that is, base functions with range $\{-1, +1\}$), and that the data is linearly separable with margin $\theta > 0$ (as in equation (7.37)). For any $B > 0$, let λ be a solution of equation (7.34) for the loss $L(\lambda)$ as defined in equation (7.7). Assume also that $\mathcal{H}$ is closed under negation so that $\lambda_j \geq 0$ for all j, without loss of generality.

Let us define the distribution D as $D(i) = \exp(-y_i F_\lambda(x_i))/\mathcal{Z}$ where $\mathcal{Z}$ is a normalization factor, and F_λ is as in equation (7.6). For each $\hbar_j \in \mathcal{H}$, we also define

$$e_j \doteq \sum_{i=1}^{m} D(i) y_i \hbar_j(x_i),$$

which is (twice) the edge of $\hbar_j$ with respect to D.

a. Show how to express $\partial L / \partial \lambda_j$ explicitly in terms of e_j, and possibly other quantities that are independent of j.

b. Show that for some j, $\partial L / \partial \lambda_j$ is strictly negative. Use this to show that $\|\lambda\|_1 = B$. [*Hint:* If this is not the case, show how to modify λ to get strictly lower loss.]

c. We say $\hbar_j$ is *active* if $\lambda_j > 0$. Show that if $\hbar_j$ is active, then it has maximum edge, that is, $e_j \geq e_{j'}$ for all j'.

d. Show that the edges of all active base classifiers are equal, that is, if $\lambda_j > 0$ and $\lambda_{j'} > 0$, then $e_j = e_{j'}$. Furthermore, show that if $\hbar_j$ is active, then $e_j \geq \theta$.

8 Boosting, Convex Optimization, and Information Geometry

In chapter 7, we saw how AdaBoost can be viewed as a special case of more general methods for optimization of an objective function, namely coordinate descent and functional gradient descent. In both of those cases, the emphasis was on construction of a final classifier by manipulating the weights defining it or, equivalently, by iteratively adding multiples of base functions to it. In this chapter, we present a different perspective on the behavior and dynamics of AdaBoost. In this new view, the emphasis will instead be on the distributions D_t, that is, on the weights over examples, which exist in a dual universe to the weights on the weak classifiers that define the final hypothesis.

We will see that AdaBoost is again a special case of a more general and much older algorithm, one based on an approach that combines geometry and information theory in which the distributions D_t are regarded as points in $\mathbb{R}^m$ which are repeatedly projected onto hyperplanes defined by the weak hypotheses. This new perspective will lend geometric intuition to the workings of AdaBoost, revealing a beautiful mathematical structure underlying the workings of the algorithm. We will see that, viewed in terms of optimization, AdaBoost is in fact solving two problems simultaneously, one being the minimization of exponential loss as discussed in section 7.1, and the other being a dual optimization problem involving maximization of the entropy of the distributions over examples subject to constraints. This understanding will enable us to answer basic questions about AdaBoost's dynamics, particularly with regard to the convergence of the example distributions, thus providing the means to prove that the algorithm asymptotically minimizes exponential loss.

The framework we present encompasses logistic regression as well, with only minor modification, thus providing further and deeper unification.

We end this chapter with an application to the problem of modeling the habitats of plant and animal species.

This chapter makes extensive use of notions from mathematical analysis which are reviewed briefly in appendices A.4 and A.5.

8.1   Iterative Projection Algorithms

In this section, we explain how AdaBoost can be seen to be a kind of geometric *iterative projection algorithm*. Although we will eventually use a geometry based on notions from information theory, we begin by considering the analogous setting for ordinary Euclidean geometry.

8.1.1   The Euclidean Analogue

To get an intuitive feeling for such algorithms, consider the following simple geometric problem. Suppose we are given a set of linear constraints on points $\mathbf{x}$ in $\mathbb{R}^m$:

$$\mathbf{a}_1 \cdot \mathbf{x} = b_1$$

$$\mathbf{a}_2 \cdot \mathbf{x} = b_2$$

$$\vdots$$

$$\mathbf{a}_N \cdot \mathbf{x} = b_N. \tag{8.1}$$

These N constraints define a linear subspace of $\mathbb{R}^m$,

$$\mathcal{P} \doteq \{\mathbf{x} \in \mathbb{R}^m : \mathbf{a}_j \cdot \mathbf{x} = b_j \text{ for } j = 1, \dots, N\}, \tag{8.2}$$

which we assume to be nonempty and which we refer to as the *feasible set*. We are also given a *reference point* $\mathbf{x}_0 \in \mathbb{R}^m$. The problem is to find the point $\mathbf{x}$ satisfying the N constraints that is *closest* to $\mathbf{x}_0$. Thus, the problem is to find $\mathbf{x}$ solving the following constrained optimization problem:

minimize: $\|\mathbf{x} - \mathbf{x}_0\|_2^2$

subject to: $\mathbf{a}_j \cdot \mathbf{x} = b_j$ for $j = 1, \dots, N$. \hfill (8.3)

This is the first of several *convex programs* to be presented in this chapter, in each of which the goal is to minimize a convex function subject to linear constraints. Although there are surely many ways of attacking this problem, here is a simple approach that turns out to be rather general. Start at $\mathbf{x} = \mathbf{x}_0$. If all the constraints are satisfied, then we are done. Otherwise, select one unsatisfied constraint, say $\mathbf{a}_j \cdot \mathbf{x} = b_j$, and *project* $\mathbf{x}$ onto the hyperplane defined by this equality; that is, replace $\mathbf{x}$ with the *closest* point satisfying $\mathbf{a}_j \cdot \mathbf{x} = b_j$. Now repeat "until convergence." Pseudocode for this technique is given as algorithm 8.1.

Like many numerical methods, it may be that the procedure never actually reaches a solution of program (8.3) in a finite number of steps. Our intention instead is that the sequence as a whole should converge to a solution so that we can get as close as we like to one in finite time.

Algorithm 8.1
An iterative projection algorithm for finding the closest point, subject to linear constraints

Given: $\mathbf{a}_j \in \mathbb{R}^m, b_j \in \mathbb{R}$ for $j = 1, \ldots, N$
$\qquad \mathbf{x}_0 \in \mathbb{R}^m$.
Goal: find sequence $\mathbf{x}_1, \mathbf{x}_2, \ldots$ converging to the solution of program (8.3).
Initialize: $\mathbf{x}_1 = \mathbf{x}_0$.
For $t = 1, 2, \ldots$

- Choose a constraint j.
- Let $\mathbf{x}_{t+1} = \arg \min\limits_{\mathbf{x}: \mathbf{a}_j \cdot \mathbf{x} = b_j} \|\mathbf{x} - \mathbf{x}_t\|_2^2$

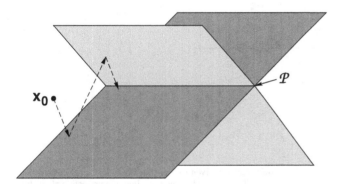

Figure 8.1
An example in $\mathbb{R}^3$ of the input to an iterative projection algorithm. Here, the problem is to find the point at the intersection of the two planes that is closest to the reference point $\mathbf{x}_0$. The dashed arrows depict the first three steps of the algorithm.

A simple three-dimensional example is shown in figure 8.1. Here, there are only two constraints depicted by the two planes. The feasible set $\mathcal{P}$ is the line at their intersection. Beginning at $\mathbf{x}_0$, the algorithm repeatedly projects onto one plane, and then the other, quickly converging to a point in $\mathcal{P}$ which turns out to be the point closest to $\mathbf{x}_0$.

We did not specify how to choose a constraint j on each iteration of algorithm 8.1. One idea is simply to cycle through the constraints in order; this is called *cyclic selection*. Another option is to greedily choose the hyperplane $\mathbf{a}_j \cdot \mathbf{x} = b_j$ that is *farthest* from $\mathbf{x}_t$, with the expectation that bringing $\mathbf{x}_{t+1}$ into line with this most violated constraint will effect the greatest and quickest progress. We will generally focus on this latter option, which we refer to as *greedy selection*. A two-dimensional example is shown in figure 8.2.

It can be proved that with either of these options, as well as a host of others, this algorithm is guaranteed to converge to the (unique) solution, provided the feasible set $\mathcal{P}$ is nonempty.

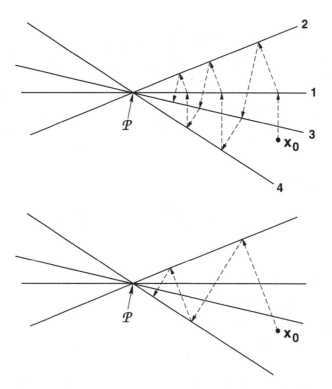

Figure 8.2
In this example, points lie in the plane, and the constraints are given by the four lines so that the feasible set consists of the single point at their common intersection. The arrows show how the iterative projection algorithm would proceed on the first few rounds using *cyclic* selection of constraints (top) in the fixed order given by the numbering of the constraints, versus *greedy* selection (bottom), in which the farthest constraint is always chosen.

When $\mathcal{P}$ is empty, the problem is no longer meaningful, but the iterative projection algorithm can still be executed. The algorithm cannot converge to a single point since there will always remain unsatisfied constraints. Beyond this observation, the dynamics of this simple procedure are not fully understood in this case, especially when using greedy selection.

8.1.2   Information-Theoretic Measures

In the description above, we measured the distance between points in our space in the usual way, using ordinary Euclidean distance. However, other distance measures could be used instead. Indeed, when we soon cast AdaBoost as an iterative projection algorithm, it will be natural to use relative entropy for this purpose, a measure which defines a distance or "divergence" between probability distributions. Although relative entropy was encountered previously in section 6.2.3 and elsewhere, we now take a short detour to comment on its origin and connection to information theory before proceeding in our development.

Suppose we wish to encode each of the m letters of some abstract alphabet $\{\ell_1, \ldots, \ell_m\}$ in bits so that any text written in this alphabet can be encoded in as few bits as possible. The obvious approach is to use a fixed number of bits for each letter of the alphabet; specifically, this requires using $\log m$ bits for each letter, where for now we use base 2 for all logarithms, and where we ignore in this discussion the fact that such quantities are likely to be non-integers. We can do better than this naive encoding, however, because if some letters (such as q in written English) occur much less frequently than others (such as e), then it will be more efficient, in terms of overall code length, to give the more common letters shorter encodings. In fact, if letter ℓ_i of the alphabet occurs with probability $P(i)$, then the optimal encoding of ℓ_i uses $-\log P(i)$ bits. The expected code length of a letter selected randomly under this distribution will then be

$$H(P) \doteq -\sum_{i=1}^{m} P(i) \log P(i). \tag{8.4}$$

This quantity is called the *entropy* of the distribution. It is evidently nonnegative, and it is maximized when P is the uniform distribution, giving a maximum value of $\log m$. Entropy can be regarded as a reasonable measure of the "spread" of the distribution, or its randomness or unpredictability.

Now suppose that the letters of our alphabet are actually distributed according to P, but we believe (incorrectly) that they are distributed according to Q. Then the foregoing will lead us to encode each letter ℓ_i using $-\log Q(i)$ bits, so the expected code length of a random letter under the actual distribution P will be

$$-\sum_{i=1}^{m} P(i) \log Q(i). \tag{8.5}$$

The amount of extra coding effort that results from using Q instead of P is then the difference between equations (8.5) and (8.4), that is,

$$\text{RE}(P \parallel Q) \doteq \left(-\sum_{i=1}^{m} P(i) \log Q(i)\right) - H(P)$$

$$= \sum_{i=1}^{m} P(i) \log \left(\frac{P(i)}{Q(i)}\right). \tag{8.6}$$

This quantity is the *relative entropy*, also known as the *Kullback-Leibler divergence*. As mentioned earlier, it is nonnegative, and equal to zero if and only if $P = Q$. It can be infinite. We sometimes refer to it informally as a "distance," but it lacks the formal properties of a metric; in particular, it is not symmetric and does not satisfy the triangle inequality. Despite these difficulties, it often turns out to be the "right" way to measure distance between probability distributions, arising naturally in many situations.

The *binary* relative entropy, encountered earlier in section 5.4.2, is simply shorthand for relative entropy between two distributions defined on a two-letter alphabet where the probability of one letter determines that of the other. Thus, for $p, q \in [0, 1]$, we define

$$\mathrm{RE}_b \left(p \parallel q \right) \doteq \mathrm{RE} \left((p, 1 - p) \parallel (q, 1 - q) \right)$$

$$= p \log \left(\frac{p}{q} \right) + (1 - p) \log \left(\frac{1 - p}{1 - q} \right). \tag{8.7}$$

Although we used base 2 logarithms above, we will find it mathematically more convenient to use natural logarithm. Thus, throughout this book, we use definitions of entropy and relative entropy in which the logarithms appearing in equations (8.4), (8.6), and (8.7) have been redefined to the natural base.

8.1.3 AdaBoost as an Iterative Projection Algorithm

With this background, we are ready to explain how AdaBoost can be seen to be an iterative projection algorithm that operates in the space of probability distributions over training examples. We will need to spell out the appropriate linear constraints, and, as just discussed, we also will need to modify how we measure distance between points.

As usual, we are given a dataset $(x_1, y_1), \ldots, (x_m, y_m)$, and a space of weak classifiers $\mathcal{H}$ that is assumed, as in chapter 7, to be finite so that we can write

$$\mathcal{H} = \{\hbar_1, \ldots, \hbar_N\}$$

for some indexing of its N elements. For simplicity, we can assume that these are all binary $\{-1, +1\}$-valued, although this is quite unimportant to what follows. We also assume throughout that $\mathcal{H}$ is closed under negation (so $-h \in \mathcal{H}$ if $h \in \mathcal{H}$). We follow the notation of algorithm 1.1 (p. 5).

Unlike earlier parts of the book, our focus now is on probability distributions D over $\{1, \ldots, m\}$, the indices of the m training examples, in other words, the sort of probability distributions D_t used by AdaBoost. What sorts of linear constraints on these distributions does AdaBoost seem to want satisfied? We saw in section 6.4 that in a game-theoretic context, in which the boosting algorithm opposes the weak learning algorithm, the booster's goal is to find a distribution over examples that is as hard as possible for the weak learner. Thus, whereas the weak learner on round t aims to find h_t maximizing the weighted accuracy $\mathbf{Pr}_{i \sim D_t}[y_i = h_t(x_i)]$ or, equivalently, the weighted correlation

$$\sum_{i=1}^{m} D_t(i) y_i h_t(x_i),$$

the boosting algorithm aims to construct distributions D_t for which this correlation (or accuracy) will be small for all weak classifiers.

Moreover, on every round t, the new distribution D_{t+1} is constructed so that this correlation with h_t will be zero. This is because, keeping in mind that

$$D_{t+1}(i) = \frac{D_t(i)e^{-\alpha_t y_i h_t(x_i)}}{Z_t},$$

it follows that

$$\sum_{i=1}^{m} D_{t+1}(i) y_i h_t(x_i) = \frac{1}{Z_t} \sum_{i=1}^{m} D_t(i) e^{-\alpha_t y_i h_t(x_i)} y_i h_t(x_i)$$

$$= -\frac{1}{Z_t} \cdot \frac{dZ_t}{d\alpha_t} = 0, \tag{8.8}$$

where we regard the normalization factor

$$Z_t = \sum_{i=1}^{m} D_t(i) e^{-\alpha_t y_i h_t(x_i)}$$

as a function of α_t. Equation (8.8) follows from the fact that α_t is chosen to minimize Z_t (as shown in section 3.1), so that $dZ_t/d\alpha_t = 0$.

Thus, it would seem that AdaBoost's aim is to pursue a distribution D for which

$$\sum_{i=1}^{m} D(i) y_i \hbar_j(x_i) = 0 \tag{8.9}$$

for every $\hbar_j \in \mathcal{H}$, that is, a distribution D that is so hard that no weak classifier $\hbar_j \in \mathcal{H}$ is at all correlated under D with the labels y_i. Equation (8.9) provides a set of N linear constraints on D corresponding to the constraints in equation (8.1). We use these to define the feasible set $\mathcal{P}$; that is, $\mathcal{P}$ is now defined to be the set of all distributions D satisfying *all* these constraints as in equation (8.9), for all $\hbar_j \in \mathcal{H}$:

$$\mathcal{P} \doteq \left\{ D : \sum_{i=1}^{m} D(i) y_i \hbar_j(x_i) = 0 \text{ for } j = 1, \ldots, N \right\}. \tag{8.10}$$

Having chosen the linear constraints defining $\mathcal{P}$, we next need to choose a reference point analogous to $\mathbf{x}_0$ in section 8.1.1. In the absence of other information, it seems natural to treat all of the training examples equally, and thus to use the uniform distribution U over $\{1, \ldots, m\}$ as our reference point.

Finally, we must choose a distance measure to replace the Euclidean distance used in section 8.1.1. Since we are working in a space of probability distributions, as discussed in section 8.1.2, we now find it appropriate to replace Euclidean geometry with the "information geometry" associated with the relative entropy distance measure. This change affects how points are projected onto hyperplanes as well as what we mean by the "closest" point in $\mathcal{P}$ to the reference point. Otherwise, the basic algorithm given as algorithm 8.1 will remain unchanged.

Putting these ideas together, we arrive at the problem of finding the distribution in $\mathcal{P}$ that is closest to uniform in terms of relative entropy. That is, we reach the following optimization program:

minimize: $\text{RE}\,(D \parallel U)$

subject to: $\displaystyle\sum_{i=1}^{m} D(i)y_i \hbar_j(x_i) = 0$ for $j = 1, \ldots, N$

$D(i) \geq 0$ for $i = 1, \ldots, m$

$\displaystyle\sum_{i=1}^{m} D(i) = 1.$ (8.11)

The program has the same form as program (8.3) except that Euclidean distance has been replaced by relative entropy, and we have added constraints to make explicit the requirement that D has to be a probability distribution.

Note that, by its definition,

$$\text{RE}\,(D \parallel U) = \ln m - H(D) \tag{8.12}$$

where $H(D)$ is the entropy of D as in equation (8.4). Thus, minimization of $\text{RE}\,(D \parallel U)$ is equivalent to maximization of the entropy or spread of the distribution, subject to constraints. This firmly connects this approach to a large and old body of work on *maximum entropy* methods.

To solve program (8.11), the same iterative projection techniques described in section 8.1.1 can be applied. Now, however, our method of projection must be modified and must use relative entropy rather than Euclidean distance. Thus, we begin with $D_1 = U$. Then, on each round, we select a constraint j and compute D_{t+1} to be the projection of D_t onto the hyperplane defined by equation (8.9). That is, D_{t+1} minimizes $\text{RE}\,(D_{t+1} \parallel D_t)$ among all distributions satisfying this equality. The complete algorithm is shown as algorithm 8.2.

This algorithm works just like algorithm 8.1, except for the change in the distance measure. We begin with the reference point, in this case U, and iteratively project onto individual linear constraints. Like algorithm 8.1, this one is known to converge to the (unique) solution

Algorithm 8.2
An iterative projection algorithm corresponding to AdaBoost

Given: $(x_1, y_1), \ldots, (x_m, y_m)$ where $x_i \in \mathcal{X}$, $y_i \in \{-1, +1\}$
      finite, binary hypothesis space $\mathcal{H}$.
Goal: find sequence $D_1, D_2, \ldots$ converging to the solution of program (8.11).
Initialize: $D_1 = U$.
For $t = 1, 2, \ldots$.

- Choose $h_t \in \mathcal{H}$ defining one of the constraints.
- Let $D_{t+1} = \arg \min\limits_{D:\sum_{i=1}^m D(i)y_i h_t(x_i)=0} \mathrm{RE}\,(D \parallel D_t)$.
- Greedy constraint selection: Choose $h_t \in \mathcal{H}$ so that $\mathrm{RE}\,(D_{t+1} \parallel D_t)$ is maximized.

---

of program (8.11), provided that the feasible set $\mathcal{P}$ is nonempty—we will give a proof in section 8.2. From a broader perspective, Euclidean distance (squared) and relative entropy both turn out to be instances of a more general class of distance functions called *Bregman distances* for which it is known that such an iterative projection algorithm will be effective (see exercise 8.5). In the general case, the algorithm is known as *Bregman's algorithm*.

As with our generic description of iterative projection algorithms, we could have left the choice of h_t in algorithm 8.2 unspecified. Instead, from this point forward, we will assume that greedy selection is used in the choice of constraints so that on each round, h_t is chosen to maximize the distance to the violated hyperplane, that is, so that

$$\min_{D:\sum_{i=1}^m D(i)y_i h_t(x_i)=0} \mathrm{RE}\,(D \parallel D_t)$$

will be maximized over all $h_t \in \mathcal{H}$. Because of how D_{t+1} is computed, this is exactly the same as maximizing $\mathrm{RE}\,(D_{t+1} \parallel D_t)$. With this assumption, as already suggested, it can be shown that algorithm 8.2 is simply AdaBoost in disguise, and the assumption of greedy constraint selection is equivalent to using an exhaustive weak learner. In other words, the distributions D_t computed by the two algorithms under these assumptions are identical on every round.

To see this, suppose $h_t \in \mathcal{H}$ is chosen on round t. Then D_{t+1} is chosen to minimize $\mathrm{RE}\,(D \parallel D_t)$ subject to the constraint

$$\sum_{i=1}^m D(i)y_i h_t(x_i) = 0.$$

We can compute this minimization by forming the Lagrangian:

$$\mathcal{L} = \sum_{i=1}^{m} D(i) \ln\left(\frac{D(i)}{D_t(i)}\right) + \alpha \sum_{i=1}^{m} D(i) y_i h_t(x_i) + \mu\left(\sum_{i=1}^{m} D(i) - 1\right). \qquad (8.13)$$

(See appendix A.8 for background.) Here, α and μ are the Lagrange multipliers, and we have explicitly taken into account the constraint that

$$\sum_{i=1}^{m} D(i) = 1. \qquad (8.14)$$

(We do not, however, include the constraints $D(i) \geq 0$ in the Lagrangian since these, it turns out, will be "automatically" satisfied, as will be seen.) Computing derivatives and equating with zero, we get that

$$0 = \frac{\partial \mathcal{L}}{\partial D(i)} = \ln\left(\frac{D(i)}{D_t(i)}\right) + 1 + \alpha y_i h_t(x_i) + \mu.$$

Thus,

$$D(i) = D_t(i) e^{-\alpha y_i h_t(x_i) - 1 - \mu}.$$

Note that μ, an arbitrary constant, will be chosen to enforce equation (8.14), giving

$$D(i) = \frac{D_t(i) e^{-\alpha y_i h_t(x_i)}}{Z}$$

where

$$Z = \sum_{i=1}^{m} D_t(i) e^{-\alpha y_i h_t(x_i)}$$

is a normalization factor. Plugging into equation (8.13) and simplifying gives

$$\mathcal{L} = -\ln Z.$$

Thus, α will be chosen to maximize $\mathcal{L}$ or, equivalently, to minimize Z. This is exactly how α_t is chosen by AdaBoost, as noted in section 3.1. So, identifying D, α, and Z with D_{t+1}, α_t, and Z_t, we see that the two algorithms behave identically for the same choice of h_t.

(Implicitly, we are permitting AdaBoost to choose a negative value of α_t, which is equivalent to our assumption that $\mathcal{H}$ is closed under negation. Further, we are ignoring the degenerate case in which AdaBoost selects α_t to be infinite, which is equivalent to $y_i h(x_i)$

all being of the same sign, for some $h \in \mathcal{H}$, in other words, h itself being a perfect classifier for the dataset.)

The choice of h_t will also be the same as in AdaBoost. Continuing the development above, we have that

$$
\mathrm{RE}\,(D_{t+1} \parallel D_t) = \sum_{i=1}^{m} D_{t+1}(i)\,(-\alpha_t y_i h_t(x_i) - \ln Z_t)
$$

$$
= -\ln Z_t - \alpha_t \sum_{i=1}^{m} D_{t+1}(i)\,y_i h_t(x_i)
$$

$$
= -\ln Z_t \tag{8.15}
$$

where we have used equation (8.8). Thus, algorithm 8.2 chooses h_t to minimize Z_t, which, as shown in section 7.1, is exactly what AdaBoost does as well.

8.1.4 Conditions for a Nonempty Feasible Set

So we conclude that the two algorithms are identical. Later, in section 8.2, we present techniques that can be used to show that the distributions D_t of AdaBoost—that is, algorithm 8.2 when depicted as an iterative projection algorithm—will converge to a distribution that is the unique solution of program (8.11), provided the feasible set $\mathcal{P}$ in equation (8.10) is nonempty.

When is this latter condition satisfied? It turns out that this condition is directly connected to the notion of empirical weak learnability that is so fundamental to boosting. Specifically, we claim the following:

Theorem 8.1 The feasible set $\mathcal{P}$ defined in equation (8.10) is empty if and only if the data is empirically γ-weakly learnable for some $\gamma > 0$.

Proof Let us first assume empirical γ-weak learnability. By definition (as given in section 2.3.3), this means that for every distribution D there exists $\hbar_j \in \mathcal{H}$ such that

$$
\mathbf{Pr}_{i \sim D}\big[y_i = \hbar_j(x_i)\big] \geq \tfrac{1}{2} + \gamma, \tag{8.16}
$$

which is the same as

$$
\sum_{i=1}^{m} D(i)\,y_i \hbar_j(x_i) \geq 2\gamma > 0. \tag{8.17}
$$

This immediately implies that the equations defining the feasible set $\mathcal{P}$ cannot all be simultaneously satisfied, and thus $\mathcal{P}$ is empty.

Conversely, suppose now that $\mathcal{P}$ is empty. Consider the function

$$M(D) \doteq \max_{\hbar_j \in \mathcal{H}} \left| \sum_{i=1}^{m} D(i) y_i \hbar_j(x_i) \right|.$$

This is a continuous, nonnegative function defined over the compact space of all probability distributions D. Therefore, its minimum is attained at some particular distribution $\tilde{D}$. By M's and $\mathcal{P}$'s definitions, if $M(\tilde{D}) = 0$, then $\tilde{D} \in \mathcal{P}$, which we assumed to be empty. Therefore, $M(\tilde{D}) > 0$. Let $\gamma \doteq \frac{1}{2} M(\tilde{D})$. Then, because $\tilde{D}$ minimizes M, for every distribution D,

$$M(D) \geq M(\tilde{D}) = 2\gamma > 0;$$

that is, there exists $\hbar_j \in \mathcal{H}$ for which

$$\left| \sum_{i=1}^{m} D(i) y_i \hbar_j(x_i) \right| \geq 2\gamma.$$

If the sum inside the absolute value happens to be negative, we can replace $\hbar_j$ with $-\hbar_j$, which we assume is also in $\mathcal{H}$. Thus, in either case, equation (8.17) holds, which is equivalent to equation (8.16). That is, we have shown that for every distribution D, there exists $\hbar_j \in \mathcal{H}$ for which equation (8.17) holds, the very definition of the empirical γ-weak learning assumption. ∎

Thus, empirical weak learnability is equivalent to the feasible set $\mathcal{P}$ being empty. Furthermore, from the results of section 5.4.3, both of these conditions are also equivalent to the data being linearly separable with positive margin. So if the data is not weakly learnable, then AdaBoost's distributions converge to the unique solution of program (8.11), as will be seen in section 8.2. But if the data is weakly learnable—which in many respects is the more interesting case from the viewpoint of boosting—then the distributions computed by AdaBoost can never converge to a single distribution since, in this case, the distance between D_t and D_{t+1} must be lower bounded by a constant. This is because, using equation (8.15), as well as the reasoning (and notation) of theorem 3.1, particularly equation (3.9), we have that

$$\begin{aligned}
\mathrm{RE}\,(D_{t+1} \parallel D_t) &= -\ln Z_t \\
&= -\tfrac{1}{2} \ln(1 - 4\gamma_t^2) \\
&\geq -\tfrac{1}{2} \ln(1 - 4\gamma^2) > 0,
\end{aligned}$$

where we used the fact that the empirical γ-weak learning assumption holds in this case for some $\gamma > 0$, so that $\gamma_t \geq \gamma$ for all t. Hence, $\mathrm{RE}\,(D_{t+1} \parallel D_t)$ is at least some positive constant for every t, implying that the distributions can never converge.

The behavior of AdaBoost's distributions in the weakly learnable case is not fully understood. In all closely examined cases, AdaBoost's distributions have been found to converge eventually to a cycle. However, it is not known if this will always be the case, or if AdaBoost's asymptotic behavior can sometimes be chaotic. The dynamics of these distributions can be quite remarkable. Figure 8.3 shows plots over time of AdaBoost's distributions on just two of the training examples. In some cases, convergence to a tight cycle can be quick; in other cases, the behavior may appear chaotic for some time before the algorithm finally converges to a cycle. (An analytic example is given in exercise 8.2.)

8.1.5 Iterative Projection Using Unnormalized Distributions

To alleviate the difficulties posed to algorithm 8.2 by weakly learnable data, we can shift our attention away from the *normalized* distributions used by AdaBoost, and instead consider their form before normalization as *unnormalized* weights on the examples. This will give us an alternative characterization of AdaBoost as an iterative projection algorithm in a way that admits a unified treatment applicable whether or not the data is weakly learnable. We will use this formulation to prove the convergence of AdaBoost's (unnormalized) distributions, as well as the convergence of AdaBoost to the minimum of the exponential loss.

So we will now be working with unnormalized weight vectors. Relative entropy, the distance measure we previously used, is no longer appropriate for such nondistributions. However, as noted earlier, there exists a whole family of distance measures with which iterative projection can be used. *Unnormalized* relative entropy is a natural choice. For two nonnegative vectors $\mathbf{p}, \mathbf{q} \in \mathbb{R}_+^m$, it is defined to be

$$
\mathrm{RE}_u \left(\mathbf{p} \ \| \ \mathbf{q} \right) \doteq \sum_{i=1}^{m} \left[p_i \ln \left(\frac{p_i}{q_i} \right) + q_i - p_i \right]. \tag{8.18}
$$

Like standard (normalized) relative entropy, the unnormalized version is always nonnegative, and is equal to zero if and only if $\mathbf{p} = \mathbf{q}$. When it is clear from context, we write simply RE rather than RE_u.

We can replace relative entropy with unnormalized relative entropy in program (8.11) and algorithm 8.2. We also replace uniform distribution U with the vector $\mathbf{1}$ of all 1's. To emphasize the shift to unnormalized weight vectors, we use lowercase $\mathbf{d}$, $\mathbf{d}_t$, etc. to represent unnormalized weight vectors. Thus, the problem now is to find $\mathbf{d}$ so as to solve:

minimize: $\mathrm{RE}_u \left(\mathbf{d} \ \| \ \mathbf{1} \right)$

subject to: $\displaystyle\sum_{i=1}^{m} d_i y_i \hbar_j(x_i) = 0$ for $j = 1, \ldots, N$

$\qquad\qquad d_i \geq 0$ for $i = 1, \ldots, m.$ \hfill (8.19)

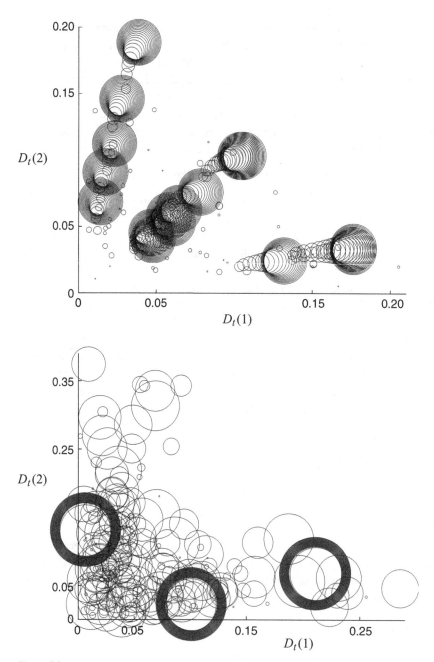

Figure 8.3
(Caption on facing page)

Algorithm 8.3
An iterative projection algorithm corresponding to AdaBoost using unnormalized relative entropy

---

Given: $(x_1, y_1), \ldots, (x_m, y_m)$ where $x_i \in \mathcal{X}$, $y_i \in \{-1, +1\}$
    finite, binary hypothesis space $\mathcal{H}$.
Goal: find sequence $\mathbf{d}_1, \mathbf{d}_2, \ldots$ converging to the solution of program (8.19).
Initialize: $\mathbf{d}_1 = \mathbf{1}$.
For $t = 1, 2, \ldots$

- Choose $h_t \in \mathcal{H}$ defining one of the constraints.
- Let $\mathbf{d}_{t+1} = \arg \min\limits_{\mathbf{d}: \sum_{i=1}^{m} d_i y_i h_t(x_i) = 0} \mathrm{RE}_u (\mathbf{d} \parallel \mathbf{d}_t)$.
- Greedy constraint selection: Choose $h_t \in \mathcal{H}$ so that $\mathrm{RE}_u (\mathbf{d}_{t+1} \parallel \mathbf{d}_t)$ is maximized.

We no longer require that $\mathbf{d}$ be normalized. The feasible set associated with this program is

$$\mathcal{P} \doteq \left\{ \mathbf{d} \in \mathbb{R}_+^m : \sum_{i=1}^{m} d_i y_i \hbar_j(x_i) = 0 \text{ for } j = 1, \ldots, N \right\}. \tag{8.20}$$

Earlier, we faced the problem that there might be no distributions satisfying all the constraints. Now that difficulty is entirely erased: The set $\mathcal{P}$ cannot be empty since all the constraints are trivially satisfied when $\mathbf{d} = \mathbf{0}$, the all 0's vector. This is the key advantage of this shift to unnormalized vectors.

Our iterative projection algorithm is nearly unchanged, and is shown for reference as algorithm 8.3. Of course, we need to emphasize that the relative entropy used in the figure is *unnormalized* relative entropy, that is, $\mathrm{RE}_u (\cdot \parallel \cdot)$. As before, we assume greedy selection of h_t.

We claim first that this procedure is again equivalent to AdaBoost in the sense that on every round, the selected h_t will be the same, and the distributions will be in exact correspondence, after normalization, that is,

Figure 8.3
Examples of AdaBoost's dynamic behavior on two very small artificial learning problems. The plots show a projection onto the first two components of the distribution D_t, that is, $D_t(1)$ on the x-axis and $D_t(2)$ on the y-axis. More specifically, each circle corresponds to one of the rounds t. The *center* of each circle is positioned at the point $\langle D_t(1), D_t(2) \rangle$; that is, the x-coordinate is equal to the value of distribution D_t on the first example in the training set, and the y-coordinate is its value on the second example. The *radius* of each circle is proportional to t, the round number, so that smaller circles indicate earlier rounds and larger circles indicate later rounds. In this way, the entire dynamic time course of the algorithm can be observed at once. In both of the cases shown, the algorithm is apparently converging to a cycle.

$$D_t(i) = \frac{d_{t,i}}{\sum_{i=1}^{m} d_{t,i}}.$$

This can be shown exactly as before. For given $h_t \in \mathcal{H}$, $\mathbf{d}_{t+1}$ is selected to minimize $\mathrm{RE}(\mathbf{d} \parallel \mathbf{d}_t)$ with $\sum_{i=1}^{m} d_i y_i h_t(x_i) = 0$. The Lagrangian now becomes

$$\mathcal{L} = \sum_{i=1}^{m} \left[d_i \ln\left(\frac{d_i}{d_{t,i}}\right) + d_{t,i} - d_i \right] + \alpha \sum_{i=1}^{m} d_i y_i h_t(x_i).$$

Using calculus to minimize with respect to d_i gives

$$d_i = d_{t,i} e^{-\alpha y_i h_t(x_i)}.$$

Plugging into $\mathcal{L}$ gives

$$\mathcal{L} = \sum_{i=1}^{m} d_{t,i} - \sum_{i=1}^{m} d_i$$

$$= \left(\sum_{i=1}^{m} d_{t,i}\right)(1 - Z)$$

where

$$Z = \frac{\sum_{i=1}^{m} d_{t,i} e^{-\alpha y_i h_t(x_i)}}{\sum_{i=1}^{m} d_{t,i}}$$

$$= \sum_{i=1}^{m} D_t(i) e^{-\alpha y_i h_t(x_i)}.$$

So again, α is selected to minimize Z, and again, with $\mathbf{d}$, α, and Z identified with $\mathbf{d}_{t+1}$ α_t, and Z_t, we see an exact correspondence with the computations of AdaBoost. We also see that the same h_t will be selected on each round by the two algorithms since

$$\mathrm{RE}(\mathbf{d}_{t+1} \parallel \mathbf{d}_t) = -\alpha_t \sum_{i=1}^{m} d_{t+1,i}\ y_i h_t(x_i) + \sum_{i=1}^{m} (d_{t,i} - d_{t+1,i})$$

$$= \left(\sum_{i=1}^{m} d_{t,i}\right)(1 - Z_t).$$

So, as for AdaBoost and algorithm 8.2, h_t is selected to minimize Z_t. We conclude that all three algorithms are equivalent.

8.2   Proving the Convergence of AdaBoost

We are now in a position to prove some important convergence properties for AdaBoost. We will show that the unnormalized distributions associated with AdaBoost converge to the unique solution of program (8.19). Further, as a by-product, we will prove that AdaBoost converges asymptotically to the minimum of the exponential loss as discussed, but not proved, in chapter 7.

8.2.1   The Setup

To ease notation, let us define an $m \times N$ matrix $\mathbf{M}$ with entries

$$M_{ij} = y_i \hbar_j(x_i).$$

Note that all of the vectors $\mathbf{d}_t$ computed by our algorithm are exponential in a linear combination of the columns of $\mathbf{M}$. That is, all the $\mathbf{d}_t$'s belong to the set $\mathcal{Q}$, where we define $\mathcal{Q}$ to be the set of all vectors $\mathbf{d}$ of the form

$$d_i = \exp\left(-\sum_{j=1}^{N} \lambda_j M_{ij}\right) \tag{8.21}$$

for some $\lambda \in \mathbb{R}^N$. Since the $\mathbf{d}_t$'s all belong to $\mathcal{Q}$, their limit, if it exists, must be in the closure of $\mathcal{Q}$, denoted $\overline{\mathcal{Q}}$. Moreover, the vector we seek must belong to the feasible set $\mathcal{P}$ defined in equation (8.20). Thus, informally, it would seem that the algorithm, if effective, will converge to a point in both sets, that is, in $\mathcal{P} \cap \overline{\mathcal{Q}}$. We will prove just such convergence, and we will also prove that this is sufficient for all our purposes.

To visualize the sets $\mathcal{P}$ and $\mathcal{Q}$, let us consider a simple example. Suppose the training set consists of only $m = 2$ examples (x_1, y_1) and (x_2, y_2), both labeled positive so that $y_1 = y_2 = +1$. Suppose further that the base hypothesis space $\mathcal{H}$ consists of a single hypothesis $\hbar_1$ where $\hbar_1(x_1) = +1$ and $\hbar_1(x_2) = -1$. Then, by equation (8.20),

$$\mathcal{P} = \left\{\mathbf{d} \in \mathbb{R}_+^2 : d_1 - d_2 = 0\right\},$$

that is, the line $d_2 = d_1$ shown in figure 8.4. And by its definition,

$$\mathcal{Q} = \left\{\mathbf{d} \in \mathbb{R}_+^2 : d_1 = e^{-\lambda_1}, d_2 = e^{\lambda_1}, \lambda_1 \in \mathbb{R}\right\},$$

that is, the hyperbola $d_2 = 1/d_1$ shown in the figure. In this case, $\overline{\mathcal{Q}} = \mathcal{Q}$.

If, as a second example, $\hbar_1$ is redefined so that $\hbar_1(x_1) = \hbar_1(x_2) = +1$, then

$$\mathcal{P} = \left\{\mathbf{d} \in \mathbb{R}_+^2 : d_1 + d_2 = 0\right\},$$

which consists only of the origin $\langle 0, 0 \rangle$, and

$$\mathcal{Q} = \left\{\mathbf{d} \in \mathbb{R}_+^2 : d_1 = e^{-\lambda_1}, d_2 = e^{-\lambda_1}, \lambda_1 \in \mathbb{R}\right\},$$

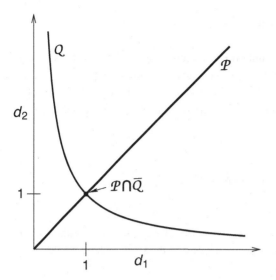

Figure 8.4
A plot of the sets $\mathcal{P}$ and $\mathcal{Q}$ for a tiny dataset consisting of two examples, both positive, and a single base hypothesis with $\hbar_1(x_1) = +1$ and $\hbar_1(x_2) = -1$.

which is the line $d_2 = d_1$, but excluding the origin (since $e^{-\lambda_1} > 0$ for all λ_1). The closure of $\mathcal{Q}$, in this case, is this same line but *including* the origin; that is, $\overline{\mathcal{Q}} = \mathcal{Q} \cup \{\langle 0, 0 \rangle\}$. See figure 8.5.

We return to these examples shortly.

8.2.2 Two Problems in One

We are trying eventually to prove two convergence properties. First, we want to show that the vectors $\mathbf{d}_t$ asymptotically solve program (8.19). That is, written more compactly, we want to show that their limit is equal to

$$\arg \min_{\mathbf{p} \in \mathcal{P}} \mathrm{RE}\left(\mathbf{p} \;\|\; \mathbf{1}\right). \tag{8.22}$$

Our second goal is to show that AdaBoost minimizes exponential loss, which we now rephrase as itself a kind of entropy optimization problem. By unraveling the computation of

$$d_{t+1,i} = d_{t,i} e^{-\alpha_t y_i h_t(x_i)},$$

we see that the sum of these weights after T rounds is

$$\sum_{i=1}^{m} d_{T+1,i} = \sum_{i=1}^{m} \exp\left(-y_i \sum_{t=1}^{T} \alpha_t h_t(x_i)\right),$$

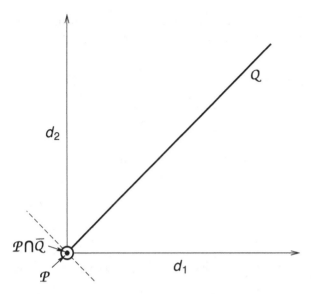

Figure 8.5
A plot of the sets $\mathcal{P}$ and $\mathcal{Q}$ for a second tiny dataset, exactly as in figure 8.4, but with $\hbar_1(x_1) = \hbar_1(x_2) = +1$. The set $\mathcal{P}$ consists only of the origin since the dotted line $d_1 + d_2 = 0$, which defines $\mathcal{P}$, only intersects the nonnegative quadrant at this single point. Note that the origin is omitted from the set $\mathcal{Q}$, but is included in its closure $\overline{\mathcal{Q}}$.

which of course is the exponential loss associated with the combined classifier $\sum_{t=1}^{T} \alpha_t h_t(x)$ as in section 7.1. More generally, any linear combination of weak classifiers $\sum_{j=1}^{N} \lambda_j \hbar_j(x)$ defines a vector $\mathbf{q} \in \mathcal{Q}$ with

$$q_i = \exp\left(-y_i \sum_{j=1}^{N} \lambda_j \hbar_j(x_i)\right).$$

Indeed, the vectors of $\mathcal{Q}$ are in direct correspondence with linear combinations of weak classifiers. The exponential loss associated with this linear combination is again the sum of the components

$$\sum_{i=1}^{m} q_i = \sum_{i=1}^{m} \exp\left(-y_i \sum_{j=1}^{N} \lambda_j \hbar_j(x_i)\right). \tag{8.23}$$

Thus, showing convergence to minimum exponential loss is equivalent to showing that $\sum_{i=1}^{m} d_{t,i}$ converges to

$$\inf_{\mathbf{q} \in \mathcal{Q}} \sum_{i=1}^{m} q_i = \min_{\mathbf{q} \in \overline{\mathcal{Q}}} \sum_{i=1}^{m} q_i.$$

(The minimum must exist since $\overline{\mathcal{Q}}$ is closed, and since we can restrict our attention, for the purposes of the minimum, to a bounded subset of $\overline{\mathcal{Q}}$, such as only those $\mathbf{q}$ for which $\sum_{i=1}^{m} q_i \leq m$; this restricted set is compact.)

Note that

$$\mathrm{RE}\,(\mathbf{0}\,\parallel\,\mathbf{q}) = \sum_{i=1}^{m} q_i.$$

Thus, we can summarize that our second goal is to show that the limit of the vectors $\mathbf{d}_t$ is equal to

$$\arg\min_{\mathbf{q}\in\overline{\mathcal{Q}}} \mathrm{RE}\,(\mathbf{0}\,\parallel\,\mathbf{q}). \tag{8.24}$$

8.2.3   The Proof

We show now that AdaBoost converges to a solution of both equation (8.22) and equation (8.24).

We begin our proof by showing that if $\mathbf{d} \in \mathcal{P} \cap \overline{\mathcal{Q}}$, then a certain equality holds, often referred to as a *Pythagorean theorem* in analogy to the more standard case in which relative entropy is replaced with squared Euclidean distance.

Lemma 8.2   If $\mathbf{d} \in \mathcal{P} \cap \overline{\mathcal{Q}}$, then for all $\mathbf{p} \in \mathcal{P}$ and for all $\mathbf{q} \in \overline{\mathcal{Q}}$,

$$\mathrm{RE}\,(\mathbf{p}\,\parallel\,\mathbf{q}) = \mathrm{RE}\,(\mathbf{p}\,\parallel\,\mathbf{d}) + \mathrm{RE}\,(\mathbf{d}\,\parallel\,\mathbf{q})\,.$$

Proof   We first claim that if $\mathbf{p} \in \mathcal{P}$ and $\mathbf{q} \in \overline{\mathcal{Q}}$, then

$$\sum_{i=1}^{m} p_i \ln q_i = 0.$$

For if $\mathbf{p} \in \mathcal{P}$ and $\mathbf{q} \in \mathcal{Q}$, then there exists $\boldsymbol{\lambda} \in \mathbb{R}^N$ for which

$$q_i = \exp\left(-\sum_{j=1}^{N} \lambda_j M_{ij}\right)$$

for $i = 1, \ldots, m$, and so

$$\sum_{i=1}^{m} p_i \ln q_i = -\sum_{i=1}^{m} p_i \sum_{j=1}^{N} \lambda_j M_{ij}$$

$$= -\sum_{j=1}^{N} \lambda_j \sum_{i=1}^{m} p_i M_{ij} = 0$$

since $\mathbf{p} \in \mathcal{P}$. By continuity,[1] the same holds for $\mathbf{q} \in \overline{\mathcal{Q}}$.

It follows that, for $\mathbf{p} \in \mathcal{P}$ and $\mathbf{q} \in \overline{\mathcal{Q}}$,

$$\text{RE}(\mathbf{p} \parallel \mathbf{q}) = \sum_{i=1}^{m} [p_i \ln p_i - p_i \ln q_i + q_i - p_i]$$

$$= \sum_{i=1}^{m} [p_i \ln p_i + q_i - p_i].$$

Applying this to $\mathbf{d} \in \mathcal{P} \cap \overline{\mathcal{Q}}$, $\mathbf{p} \in \mathcal{P}$, and $\mathbf{q} \in \overline{\mathcal{Q}}$ gives

$$\text{RE}(\mathbf{p} \parallel \mathbf{d}) + \text{RE}(\mathbf{d} \parallel \mathbf{q}) = \sum_{i=1}^{m} [p_i \ln p_i + d_i - p_i] + \sum_{i=1}^{m} [d_i \ln d_i + q_i - d_i]$$

$$= \sum_{i=1}^{m} [p_i \ln p_i + q_i - p_i]$$

$$= \text{RE}(\mathbf{p} \parallel \mathbf{q})$$

since $\sum_{i=1}^{m} d_i \ln d_i = 0$ by the claim above ($\mathbf{d}$ being both in $\mathcal{P}$ and $\overline{\mathcal{Q}}$). ∎

We next prove the following remarkable characterization of the solutions of equations (8.22) and (8.24): If $\mathbf{d}$ is in $\mathcal{P} \cap \overline{\mathcal{Q}}$, then $\mathbf{d}$ *uniquely* solves *both* of the optimization problems of interest.

Theorem 8.3 Suppose $\mathbf{d} \in \mathcal{P} \cap \overline{\mathcal{Q}}$. Then

$$\mathbf{d} = \arg\min_{\mathbf{p} \in \mathcal{P}} \text{RE}(\mathbf{p} \parallel \mathbf{1})$$

and

$$\mathbf{d} = \arg\min_{\mathbf{q} \in \overline{\mathcal{Q}}} \text{RE}(\mathbf{0} \parallel \mathbf{q}).$$

Moreover, $\mathbf{d}$ is the unique minimizer in each case.

Proof By lemma 8.2, since $\mathbf{1} \in \mathcal{Q}$, for any $\mathbf{p} \in \mathcal{P}$,

$$\text{RE}(\mathbf{p} \parallel \mathbf{1}) = \text{RE}(\mathbf{p} \parallel \mathbf{d}) + \text{RE}(\mathbf{d} \parallel \mathbf{1})$$

$$\geq \text{RE}(\mathbf{d} \parallel \mathbf{1})$$

---

1. Technically, we are using the continuity of the function $\mathbf{q} \mapsto \sum_{i=1}^{m} p_i \ln q_i$ when viewed as an extended mapping from $\mathbb{R}_+^m$ to $[-\infty, +\infty)$.

since relative entropy is always nonnegative. Furthermore, $\mathbf{d}$ is the unique minimum since the inequality is strict if $\mathbf{p} \neq \mathbf{d}$. The proof for the other minimization problem is similar.   ∎

This theorem implies that there can be at most one point at the intersection of $\mathcal{P}$ and $\overline{\mathcal{Q}}$. Of course, however, the theorem does not show that $\mathcal{P} \cap \overline{\mathcal{Q}}$ cannot be empty. Nevertheless, this fact will follow from our analysis below of the iterative projection algorithm which will show that the $\mathbf{d}_t$'s must converge to a point in $\mathcal{P} \cap \overline{\mathcal{Q}}$. Thus, in general, $\mathcal{P} \cap \overline{\mathcal{Q}}$ will always consist of exactly one point to which our algorithm, which is equivalent to AdaBoost, necessarily converges.

These facts are illustrated in the examples shown in figures 8.4 and 8.5, and discussed in section 8.2.1. In both cases, we see that $\mathcal{P}$ and $\overline{\mathcal{Q}}$ intersect at a single point (even though $\mathcal{P}$ and $\mathcal{Q}$ do not intersect in the example shown in figure 8.5). Moreover, as claimed generally in theorem 8.3, in both cases this point is evidently the closest point in $\mathcal{P}$ to $\langle 1, 1 \rangle$, and also the closest point in $\overline{\mathcal{Q}}$ to the origin $\langle 0, 0 \rangle$.

We now prove our main convergence result.

Theorem 8.4   The vectors $\mathbf{d}_t$ computed by the iterative projection method of algorithm 8.3 or, equivalently, the unnormalized weight vectors computed by AdaBoost (with exhaustive weak hypothesis selection), converge to the unique point $\mathbf{d}^* \in \mathcal{P} \cap \overline{\mathcal{Q}}$, and therefore to the unique minimum of $\text{RE}\,(\mathbf{p} \parallel \mathbf{1})$ over $\mathbf{p} \in \mathcal{P}$, and the unique minimum of $\text{RE}\,(\mathbf{0} \parallel \mathbf{q})$ over $\mathbf{q} \in \overline{\mathcal{Q}}$. Thus, the exponential loss of the algorithm

$$\sum_{i=1}^{m} d_{t,i}$$

converges to the minimum possible loss

$$\inf_{\lambda \in \mathbb{R}^N} \sum_{i=1}^{m} \exp\left(-y_i \sum_{j=1}^{N} \lambda_j \hbar_j(x_i)\right).$$

Proof   Based on the foregoing, particularly theorem 8.3, it suffices to show that the sequence $\mathbf{d}_1, \mathbf{d}_2, \ldots$ converges to a point $\mathbf{d}^*$ in $\mathcal{P} \cap \overline{\mathcal{Q}}$.

Let

$$L_t \doteq \sum_{i=1}^{m} d_{t,i}$$

be the exponential loss at round t. By our choice of h_t and α_t, which, as discussed in sections 8.1.3 and 8.1.5, are chosen to cause the greatest drop in this loss, we have that

$$L_{t+1} = \min_{j,\alpha} \sum_{i=1}^{m} d_{t,i} e^{-\alpha M_{ij}}. \tag{8.25}$$

In particular, considering the case that $\alpha = 0$, this implies that L_t never increases. By equation (8.25), we can regard the difference $L_{t+1} - L_t$ as a function A of the vector $\mathbf{d}_t$:

$$L_{t+1} - L_t = A(\mathbf{d}_t)$$

where

$$A(\mathbf{d}) \doteq \min_{j,\alpha} \sum_{i=1}^{m} d_i e^{-\alpha M_{ij}} - \sum_{i=1}^{m} d_i. \tag{8.26}$$

Since $L_t \geq 0$ for all t, and since the sequence of L_t's is nonincreasing, it follows that the differences $A(\mathbf{d}_t)$ must converge to zero. This fact, together with the next lemma, will help us prove that the limit of the $\mathbf{d}_t$'s is in $\mathcal{P}$.

Lemma 8.5   If $A(\mathbf{d}) = 0$, then $\mathbf{d} \in \mathcal{P}$. Furthermore, A is a continuous function.

Proof   Recall our assumption that $M_{ij} \in \{-1, +1\}$ for all i, j. Let

$$W_j^+(\mathbf{d}) \doteq \sum_{i:M_{ij}=+1} d_i$$

and

$$W_j^-(\mathbf{d}) \doteq \sum_{i:M_{ij}=-1} d_i.$$

Then, using some calculus,

$$\min_{\alpha} \sum_{i=1}^{m} d_i e^{-\alpha M_{ij}} = \min_{\alpha} \left[W_j^+(\mathbf{d}) \cdot e^{-\alpha} + W_j^-(\mathbf{d}) \cdot e^{\alpha} \right]$$

$$= 2\sqrt{W_j^+(\mathbf{d}) \cdot W_j^-(\mathbf{d})}.$$

Further,

$$\sum_{i=1}^{m} d_i = W_j^+(\mathbf{d}) + W_j^-(\mathbf{d}).$$

Thus,

$$A(\mathbf{d}) = \min_j \left[2\sqrt{W_j^+(\mathbf{d}) \cdot W_j^-(\mathbf{d})} - \left(W_j^+(\mathbf{d}) + W_j^-(\mathbf{d}) \right) \right]$$

$$= -\max_j \left(\sqrt{W_j^+(\mathbf{d})} - \sqrt{W_j^-(\mathbf{d})} \right)^2. \tag{8.27}$$

When written in this form, it is clear that A is continuous since the minimum or maximum of a finite number of continuous functions is continuous.

Suppose now that $A(\mathbf{d}) = 0$. Then for all j, by equation (8.27),

$$0 = -A(\mathbf{d}) \geq \left(\sqrt{W_j^+(\mathbf{d})} - \sqrt{W_j^-(\mathbf{d})} \right)^2 \geq 0,$$

and therefore

$$W_j^+(\mathbf{d}) = W_j^-(\mathbf{d})$$

or, equivalently,

$$0 = W_j^+(\mathbf{d}) - W_j^-(\mathbf{d}) = \sum_{i:M_{ij}=+1} d_i - \sum_{i:M_{ij}=-1} d_i$$

$$= \sum_{i=1}^m d_i M_{ij}.$$

In other words, $\mathbf{d} \in \mathcal{P}$. ∎

Note that the $\mathbf{d}_t$ vectors all lie in a compact space; specifically, because they cannot have negative components, they must all be contained in the compact space $[0, m]^m$, since $0 \leq d_{t,i} \leq \sum_{i=1}^m d_{t,i} \leq \sum_{i=1}^m d_{1,i} = m$. Therefore, there must exist a convergent subsequence $\mathbf{d}_{t_1}, \mathbf{d}_{t_2}, \ldots$ with some limit $\tilde{\mathbf{d}}$; that is,

$$\lim_{k \to \infty} \mathbf{d}_{t_k} = \tilde{\mathbf{d}}.$$

Clearly, each $\mathbf{d}_{t_k} \in \mathcal{Q}$, so the limit $\tilde{\mathbf{d}}$ must be in $\overline{\mathcal{Q}}$. Further, by continuity of A and our earlier observation that $A(\mathbf{d}_t)$ must converge to zero, we have

$$A(\tilde{\mathbf{d}}) = \lim_{k \to \infty} A(\mathbf{d}_{t_k}) = 0.$$

Thus, by lemma 8.5, $\tilde{\mathbf{d}} \in \mathcal{P}$. Therefore, $\tilde{\mathbf{d}} \in \mathcal{P} \cap \overline{\mathcal{Q}}$, and indeed, $\tilde{\mathbf{d}}$ must be the unique member $\mathbf{d}^*$ of $\mathcal{P} \cap \overline{\mathcal{Q}}$.

Finally, we claim that the *entire* sequence $\mathbf{d}_1, \mathbf{d}_2, \ldots$ must converge to $\mathbf{d}^*$. Suppose it does not. Then there exists $\varepsilon > 0$ such that $\|\mathbf{d}^* - \mathbf{d}_t\| \geq \varepsilon$ for infinitely many of the points in the sequence. This infinite set, being in a compact space, must include a convergent subsequence which, by the argument above, must converge to $\mathbf{d}^*$, the only member of $\mathcal{P} \cap \overline{\mathcal{Q}}$ by theorem 8.3. But this is a contradiction since all the points in the subsequence are at least ε away from $\mathbf{d}^*$.

Therefore, the entire sequence $\mathbf{d}_1, \mathbf{d}_2, \ldots$ converges to $\mathbf{d}^* \in \mathcal{P} \cap \overline{\mathcal{Q}}$.   ∎

Theorem 8.4 fully characterizes the convergence properties of the unnormalized weight vectors. However, it tells us what happens to the normalized distributions D_t only when the data is not weakly learnable. In this case, the unnormalized vectors $\mathbf{d}_t$ will converge to a unique $\mathbf{d}^* \in \mathcal{P} \cap \overline{\mathcal{Q}}$, which is also the minimum of the exponential loss in equation (8.23) by theorem 8.4. Since the data is not weakly learnable, it must be linearly inseparable as well (as seen in section 5.4.3), so the exponent in at least one term of this sum must be nonnegative; therefore the entire sum cannot be less than 1. Thus $\mathbf{d}^*$ must be different from $\mathbf{0}$. This means that the normalized distributions D_t will converge to a unique distribution D^* where

$$D^*(i) = \frac{d_i^*}{\sum_{i=1}^{m} d_i^*}.$$

On the other hand, when the data is weakly learnable, the feasible set $\mathcal{P}$ can consist only of the single point $\mathbf{0}$ (as follows from the reasoning used in section 8.1.4). Thus $\mathbf{d}^*$, the only element of $\mathcal{P} \cap \overline{\mathcal{Q}}$, must equal $\mathbf{0}$. So in this case, nothing can be concluded about the convergence of the normalized distributions D_t from the convergence of their unnormalized counterparts; indeed, we have already discussed the fact that they cannot converge to a single point in this case.

Theorem 8.4 only tells us that AdaBoost minimizes exponential loss asymptotically in the limit of a large number of iterations. Later, in section 12.2.4, we will use a different technique to prove bounds on the rate at which this loss is minimized.

8.2.4   Convex Duality

We saw in section 8.2.3 how the same optimization algorithm can be used apparently to solve two seemingly distinct problems simultaneously. That is, the same algorithm both solves program (8.19) and also minimizes the exponential loss. On the surface, this might seem like a rather remarkable coincidence. However, at a deeper level, these two problems are not at all unrelated. Rather, it turns out that one is the *convex dual* of the other, a distinct but in some sense equivalent formulation of the same problem.

Starting with program (8.19), the convex dual can be found by first forming the Lagrangian

$$\mathcal{L} = \sum_{i=1}^{m} (d_i \ln d_i + 1 - d_i) + \sum_{j=1}^{N} \lambda_j \sum_{i=1}^{m} d_i y_i \hbar_j(x_i)$$

where the λ_j's are the Lagrange multipliers. (As usual, we ignore the constraints $d_i \geq 0$ since these will automatically be satisfied.) Computing partial derivatives and setting to zero yields

$$0 = \frac{\partial \mathcal{L}}{\partial d_i} = \ln d_i + \sum_{j=1}^{N} \lambda_j y_i \hbar_j(x_i),$$

so

$$d_i = \exp\left(-y_i \sum_{j=1}^{N} \lambda_j \hbar_j(x_i)\right).$$

Plugging into $\mathcal{L}$ and simplifying gives

$$\mathcal{L} = m - \sum_{i=1}^{m} \exp\left(-y_i \sum_{j=1}^{N} \lambda_j \hbar_j(x_i)\right).$$

Maximization of $\mathcal{L}$ in the λ_j's is the dual problem, which of course is equivalent to minimization of the exponential loss. In general, the solutions of both the original "primal" problem and the dual problem occur at the "saddle point" where the Lagrangian $\mathcal{L}$ is minimized in the "primal variables" d_i and maximized in the "dual variables" λ_j.

Thus, it is because of convex duality that the same algorithm for program (8.19) also minimizes exponential loss.

By a similar calculation, it can be shown that the dual of program (8.11) is also minimization of exponential loss or, more precisely, maximization of

$$\ln m - \ln\left(\sum_{i=1}^{m} \exp\left(-y_i \sum_{j=1}^{N} \lambda_j \hbar_j(x_i)\right)\right).$$

It is not surprising, then, that algorithm 8.2, which computes exactly the normalized equivalents of the vectors in algorithm 8.3, and which also is equivalent to AdaBoost, is a procedure for minimizing the exponential loss as well.

8.3   Unification with Logistic Regression

In section 7.5, we studied logistic regression, an approach that we saw is closely related to the exponential-loss minimization employed by AdaBoost. We will now build on our understanding of this close relationship, using the framework just developed. We will see that the optimization problem solved by AdaBoost is only a slight variant of the one solved by logistic regression in which a single minimization constraint is removed.

For starters, we observe that by slightly changing the distance function used in convex programs (8.11) and (8.19), we arrive at a different convex program that is equivalent via convex duality to logistic regression. In particular, rather than normalized or unnormalized relative entropy, we can use a form of binary relative entropy, specifically,

$$
\text{RE}_b\,(\mathbf{p}\;\|\;\mathbf{q}) = \sum_{i=1}^{m} \left[p_i \ln\left(\frac{p_i}{q_i}\right) + (1 - p_i) \ln\left(\frac{1 - p_i}{1 - q_i}\right) \right]
$$

where $\mathbf{p}$ and $\mathbf{q}$ must be in $[0, 1]^m$. We also change our reference vector from $\mathbf{1}$ to $\frac{1}{2}\mathbf{1}$. The problem now is to find $\mathbf{d} \in [0, 1]^m$ to solve the following:

minimize: $\text{RE}_b\left(\mathbf{d}\;\|\;\frac{1}{2}\mathbf{1}\right)$

subject to: $\displaystyle\sum_{i=1}^{m} d_i y_i \hbar_j(x_i) = 0$ for $j = 1, \ldots, N$

$$
0 \le d_i \le 1 \text{ for } i = 1, \ldots, m. \tag{8.28}
$$

By the same sort of calculation as in section 8.2.4, we find that the dual of this problem is to maximize

$$
m \ln 2 - \sum_{i=1}^{m} \ln\left(1 + \exp\left(-y_i \sum_{j=1}^{N} \lambda_j \hbar_j(x_i)\right)\right) \tag{8.29}
$$

or, equivalently, to minimize the logistic loss of equation (7.20) as studied in section 7.5. An iterative projection algorithm like algorithms 8.2 and 8.3 might easily be derived for program (8.28), and thus for logistic regression. In fact, the algorithm AdaBoost.L (algorithm 7.4 (p. 199)) is an approximate, more analytically tractable version of the algorithm that would be so derived; indeed, the convergence of this algorithm to the minimum of the logistic loss can be proved using the same techniques presented in section 8.2 (see exercise 8.6).

So we see that exponential and logistic loss can be treated in a unified convex-programming framework. Their corresponding programs (8.19) and (8.28) differ only in the choice of distance measure. In fact, these programs can be manipulated further to make the resemblance even more striking. This formulation also addresses the estimation of conditional probabilities as discussed in section 7.5.3.

For notational convenience, let us regard each $\hbar_j$ as a function of both x and y where we define $\hbar_j(x, y) \doteq y\hbar_j(x)$. The empirical average of $\hbar_j$ is of course

$$
\frac{1}{m} \sum_{i=1}^{m} \hbar_j(x_i, y_i). \tag{8.30}
$$

Now suppose $p(y|x)$ is the conditional probability that example x receives label y. Imagine an experiment in which x_i is chosen randomly according to its empirical probability (i.e., uniformly at random from the sample), but then a label y is selected at random according to the true conditional probability distribution $p(\cdot|x_i)$. The expected value of $\hbar_j$ under this "semi-empirical" distribution on pairs (x_i, y) will be

$$\frac{1}{m}\sum_{i=1}^{m}\sum_{y} p(y|x_i)\hbar_j(x_i, y). \tag{8.31}$$

Given enough data, we expect equations (8.30) and (8.31) to be roughly equal since the two are equal in expectation. It therefore may seem natural, in computing an estimate of $p(y|x)$, that we require equality:

$$\frac{1}{m}\sum_{i=1}^{m}\hbar_j(x_i, y_i) = \frac{1}{m}\sum_{i=1}^{m}\sum_{y} p(y|x_i)\hbar_j(x_i, y). \tag{8.32}$$

Naturally, being a conditional probability distribution,

$$\sum_{y} p(y|x) = 1 \tag{8.33}$$

for each x. However, for the purposes of estimating p, we might, in a perverse move, allow this constraint to be dropped. In this case, the left-hand side of equation (8.32) needs to be adjusted to balance the varying weight on different examples x_i. This gives the requirement that

$$\frac{1}{m}\sum_{i=1}^{m}\hbar_j(x_i, y_i)\left(\sum_{y} p(y|x_i)\right) = \frac{1}{m}\sum_{i=1}^{m}\sum_{y} p(y|x_i)\hbar_j(x_i, y). \tag{8.34}$$

So our goal will be to find a set of numbers $p(y|x)$ satisfying equation (8.34); in other words, we will now regard these as unknown variables to be solved for, rather than as true conditional probabilities. Analogous to the maximum-entropy approach taken earlier in this chapter, among all such sets of numbers satisfying the constraints in equation (8.34), we will choose the one that, on average, gives conditional distributions over the labels that are closest to uniform since, a priori, no label should be favored over any other. Moreover, since p might not be normalized, a form of unnormalized relative entropy must be used.

Putting these ideas together yields the following program:

$$\text{minimize:}\ \sum_{i=1}^{m}\text{RE}_u\left(p(\cdot|x_i)\ \|\ \mathbf{1}\right)$$

$$\text{subject to: } \frac{1}{m}\sum_{i=1}^{m}\hbar_j(x_i,y_i)\left(\sum_y p(y|x_i)\right) = \frac{1}{m}\sum_{i=1}^{m}\sum_y p(y|x_i)\hbar_j(x_i,y) \text{ for } j=1,\dots,N$$

$$p(y|x_i) \geq 0 \text{ for } i=1,\dots,m, \text{ and for all } y \tag{8.35}$$

where

$$\text{RE}_u\left(p(\cdot|x_i) \parallel \mathbf{1}\right) = \sum_y \left[p(y|x)\ln p(y|x) + 1 - p(y|x)\right].$$

For simplicity, in this section let us assume that the same example x never appears in the dataset with different labels. Then it can be shown that this program is equivalent to program (8.19). The correspondence is made by setting $d_i = p(-y_i|x_i)$; the variables $p(y_i|x_i)$ turn out always to equal 1 in the solution, and so are irrelevant. Thus, program (8.35) minimizes exponential loss.

Suppose now that we add to program (8.35) a normalization constraint as in equation (8.33). The new program is:

$$\text{minimize: } \sum_{i=1}^{m}\text{RE}_u\left(p(\cdot|x_i) \parallel \mathbf{1}\right)$$

$$\text{subject to: } \frac{1}{m}\sum_{i=1}^{m}\hbar_j(x_i,y_i)\left(\sum_y p(y|x_i)\right) = \frac{1}{m}\sum_{i=1}^{m}\sum_y p(y|x_i)\hbar_j(x_i,y) \text{ for } j=1,\dots,N$$

$$p(y|x_i) \geq 0 \text{ for } i=1,\dots,m, \text{ and for all } y$$

$$\sum_y p(y|x_i) = 1 \text{ for } i=1,\dots,m. \tag{8.36}$$

With this new constraint, it turns out that this program becomes equivalent to program (8.28) for logistic regression. As before, the correspondence can be seen by setting $d_i = p(-y_i|x_i)$, which implies $p(y_i|x_i) = 1 - d_i$ in this case.

Thus, from this perspective, AdaBoost and logistic regression solve identical optimization problems, except that AdaBoost disregards a single normalization constraint.

As for estimation of conditional probabilities as discussed in section 7.5.3, it can be verified that for logistic regression, the values $p(y|x)$ associated with program (8.36) are consistent with those discussed in that section. Further, the estimates $p(y|x)$ for program (8.35), which omits the normalization constraint, also are consistent with those obtained from AdaBoost in section 7.5.3.

8.4 Application to Species Distribution Modeling

As an example of how these ideas can be applied, we consider the problem of modeling the geographic distribution of a given animal or plant species. This is a critical problem in conservation biology: To save a threatened species, one first needs to know where the species prefers to live and what its requirements are for survival, that is, its ecological "niche." As will be seen shortly, such models have important applications, such as in the design of conservation reserves.

The data available for this problem typically consists of a list of geographic coordinates where the species has been observed, such as the set of locations at the top right of figure 8.6. In addition, there is data on a number of environmental variables, such as average temperature, average rainfall, elevation, etc., which have been measured or estimated across a geographic region of interest. Examples are shown on the left side of figure 8.6. The goal is to predict which areas within the region satisfy the requirements of the species' ecological niche, that is, where conditions are suitable for the survival of the species. At the bottom right, figure 8.6 shows such a map produced using the method described below.

It is often the case that only *presence data* is available indicating the occurrence of the species. Museum and herbarium collections constitute the richest source of occurrence localities, but their collections typically have no information about the *failure* to observe the species at any given location. In addition, many locations have not been surveyed at all. This means that we have *only* positive examples, and no negative examples, from which to learn. Moreover, the number of sightings (training examples) will often be very small by machine-learning standards, say 100 or less.

Throughout this book, we have focused on the problem of discriminating positive and negative examples. Now, because we have access only to positive examples, we need to take a different approach. Specifically, in modeling the problem, we will assume that the presence records of where the species has been observed are being chosen randomly from a probability distribution representing the entire population of the species. Our goal, then, is to estimate this distribution based on samples randomly chosen from it. In other words, we treat the problem as one of *density estimation*.

More formally, let $\mathcal{X}$ be the large but finite space we are working over, namely, the set of locations on some discretized map of interest. Let π be a probability distribution over $\mathcal{X}$ representing the distribution of the species across the map. We assume we are given a set of sample locations $x_1, \ldots, x_m$ from $\mathcal{X}$, that is, the observed presence records, each of which we assume has been chosen independently at random from π.

Finally, we are given a set of *base functions* (sometimes also called *features* in this context), $\hbar_1, \ldots, \hbar_N$, which play a role analogous to weak hypotheses in boosting. Each base function $\hbar_j$ provides real-valued information about every point on the map. That is, $\hbar_j : \mathcal{X} \to \mathbb{R}$. For instance, a base function might simply be equal to one of the environmental variables discussed above (such as average temperature). But more generally, it might instead be derived from one or more of these variables. For example, a base function might be equal to the *square* of an environmental variable (such as elevation squared), or to the *product* of two environmental variables (such as elevation times average rainfall). Or, analogous to decision stumps, we might take thresholds of an environmental variable (for

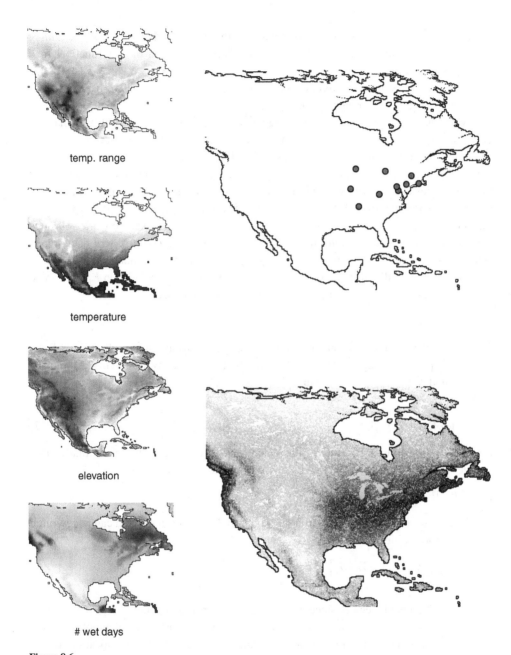

Figure 8.6
Left: some sample environmental variables (with darker areas representing higher values). Top right: a map of the localities where the yellow-throated vireo has been observed. Bottom right: the predicted distribution of the species (darker areas indicating locations most suitable for the species).

instance, 1 if elevation is above 1000 meters, 0 otherwise). In this way, even beginning with a fairly small number of environmental variables, the number of base functions may quickly become quite large.

In all cases, for simplicity we assume without loss of generality that all base functions have been scaled to have range [0, 1].

Given samples and base functions, the goal is to find a distribution P over $\mathcal{X}$ that is a good estimate of π. Such an estimate can be interpreted as approximating a measure of the suitability of every location on the map as habitat for the species.

Our approach will be to construct a convex program of a form similar to those studied throughout this chapter, whose solution can be used as such an estimate. Let $\hat{\pi}$ denote the empirical distribution over $\mathcal{X}$ that places probability $1/m$ on each of the m samples x_i. A first idea is simply to use $\hat{\pi}$ as an estimate of π. However, this is unlikely to work well since we expect m to be much smaller than $\mathcal{X}$, so that nearly all points in $\mathcal{X}$ will be assigned zero probability mass. Nevertheless, even though the empirical distribution is a very poor estimate of the true distribution, the empirical average of any base function $\hbar_j$ is likely to be quite a good estimate of its true expectation. That is, we expect

$$\mathbf{E}_{\hat{\pi}}\left[\hbar_j\right] \approx \mathbf{E}_{\pi}\left[\hbar_j\right]$$

where $\mathbf{E}_{\pi}[\cdot]$ denotes expectation with respect to the true distribution π, and similarly $\mathbf{E}_{\hat{\pi}}[\cdot]$ denotes empirical average. In fact, using Hoeffding's inequality (theorem 2.1) and the union bound, we can compute a value of β (roughly $O(\sqrt{(\ln N)/m})$) such that, with high probability,

$$\left|\mathbf{E}_{\pi}\left[\hbar_j\right] - \mathbf{E}_{\hat{\pi}}\left[\hbar_j\right]\right| \le \beta \tag{8.37}$$

for all base functions $\hbar_j$. It makes sense then, in constructing P, to ensure that it, too, satisfies equation (8.37), that is, that it belongs to the feasible set

$$\mathcal{P} \doteq \left\{P : \left|\mathbf{E}_P\left[\hbar_j\right] - \mathbf{E}_{\hat{\pi}}\left[\hbar_j\right]\right| \le \beta \text{ for } j = 1, \ldots, N\right\}.$$

Note that these constraints are linear in the values of P since each of them can be rewritten as the two inequalities

$$-\beta \le \sum_{x \in \mathcal{X}} P(x)\hbar_j(x) - \mathbf{E}_{\hat{\pi}}\left[\hbar_j\right] \le \beta.$$

Moreover, $\mathcal{P}$ cannot be empty since it always contains $\hat{\pi}$ as a member.

Of the many distributions in $\mathcal{P}$, which one should we pick as our estimate of π? In the absence of data or other information, it seems natural to assume that all the locations on the map are equally likely to be suitable habitat, in other words, that the uniform distribution U over $\mathcal{X}$ is most reasonable, a priori. This suggests that among all distributions in $\mathcal{P}$, we choose the one that is closest to U. If we are using relative entropy as a distance measure as before, then we seek to minimize $\text{RE}\,(P \parallel U)$, which, from equation (8.12), is equivalent to maximizing $H(P)$, the entropy or spread of the distribution P.

Pulling these ideas together, we are proposing to estimate π by selecting the distribution P in $\mathcal{P}$ that has highest entropy or, equivalently, that is closest to uniform in relative entropy. This results in the following optimization problem:

minimize: $\text{RE}\,(P \parallel U)$

subject to: $\left|\mathbf{E}_P\!\left[\hbar_j\right] - \mathbf{E}_{\hat{\pi}}\!\left[\hbar_j\right]\right| \le \beta$ for $j = 1, \ldots, N$

$\qquad\qquad P(x) \ge 0$ for $x \in \mathcal{X}$

$$\sum_{x \in \mathcal{X}} P(x) = 1. \tag{8.38}$$

This program is of nearly the same form as program (8.11) except that the linear constraints are somewhat more complicated, involving inequalities rather than equalities. Still, most of the techniques we have discussed generalize to this case.

At this point, we could adapt the iterative projection method of algorithm 8.2 to handle such inequality constraints. Alternatively, using the techniques of section 8.2.4, it can be shown that the solution of program (8.38) must be of the form

$$Q_\lambda(x) = \frac{1}{\mathcal{Z}_\lambda} \cdot \exp\left(\sum_{j=1}^{N} \lambda_j \hbar_j(x)\right)$$

for some setting of the parameters $\lambda = \langle \lambda_1, \ldots, \lambda_N \rangle$, where $\mathcal{Z}_\lambda$ is a normalization factor. In other words, the solution distribution must be proportional to an exponential in some linear combination of the base functions. The convex dual of program (8.38) turns out to be the problem of finding λ which minimizes

$$-\frac{1}{m} \sum_{i=1}^{m} \ln Q_\lambda(x_i) + \beta \|\lambda\|_1, \tag{8.39}$$

that is, which minimizes the negative log likelihood of the data (the term on the left), plus a penalty or regularization term (on the right) that has the effect of limiting the size of the weights λ_j on the base functions (see section 7.6).

So to solve program (8.38), we only need to find λ minimizing equation (8.39). Even for a very large set of base functions, this can often be done efficiently using the general techniques described in chapter 7 which adjust one parameter at a time to greedily minimize the objective function. That is, although we do not give the details, it is possible to derive a boosting-like algorithm that, on each of a series of rounds, greedily chooses one base function $\hbar_j$ whose associated weight λ_j is adjusted by some value α so as to (approximately) cause the greatest drop in equation (8.39).

This *maxent* approach to species distribution modeling has been used and tested on a wide range of datasets. In one large-scale study, it was compared with 15 other methods on some 226 plant and animal species from six world regions. The median dataset had fewer than 60 presence records. Maxent, on average, performed better than all other methods except for one based on boosted regression trees (see section 7.4.3) which was slightly better.

Maxent was also used as part of a large 2008 study of reserve design in Madagascar. This island nation off the southeastern coast of Africa is a biological "hot spot," one of a small number of areas which together cover just 2.3% of the Earth's land surface, but where half of all plant and three-quarters of all vertebrate species are concentrated.

In 2003, the government of Madagascar announced a commitment to triple protected land areas from 2.9% of the island to 10%. By 2006, protected areas had already expanded to 6.3%, but an opportunity existed to carefully select the remaining 3.7%, while also evaluating the design decisions made up to that point.

For this purpose, data was gathered on some 2315 species from six taxonomic groups. Maxent was then applied to build a distributional model for all species with at least eight presence records. Finally, with a model in hand for each species, a proposed reserve could be constructed using an algorithm called "Zonation" with the purpose of identifying the areas most suitable to the most species based on such models.

The study found that the existing protected areas, covering 6.3% of the island, actually were rather deficient, entirely omitting 28% of the species studied, meaning that these areas were not protecting any significant part of their habitat. It was further found that an alternative design protecting an equivalent amount of land would have protected *all* of the species.

Clearly, of course, it is too late to significantly modify land areas that have already been set aside. Fortunately, however, the study found that it would still be possible to add on to existing conservation areas in a way that protects all species without exceeding the government's target of designating 10% of the land for conservation. These actual and proposed areas are shown on the maps in figure 8.7, where it can be seen, on close inspection, that many areas considered of the highest priority in the study are entirely omitted from the existing conservation areas, but can still be protected without exceeding the government's overall budget.

This study was able to successfully provide detailed recommendations in large part because of the great number of species modeled, and because of the high-resolution models that are possible with maxent.

Summary

In summary, we have provided another powerful perspective on AdaBoost, which turns out to be a special case of a family of iterative projection algorithms. This view provides

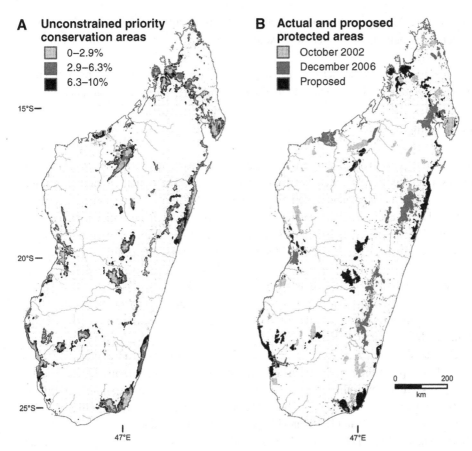

Figure 8.7
On the left, a prioritized map of proposed areas for conservation in Madagascar, unconstrained by previous design decisions. The map shows the top 2.9% of the land that would be chosen as reserve (equivalent in area to what was actually protected in 2002), followed by the next 3.4% (giving an area equivalent to the 6.3% protected in 2006), and finally the last 3.7%, giving total protected area of 10%. On the right, a map showing the actual 2.9% protected in 2002, and the actual additional 3.4% protected through 2006, plus a final proposed expansion of protected areas by 3.7% which would protect all species in the study. (From C. Kremen, A. Cameron, et al., "Aligning conservation priorities across taxa in Madagascar with high-resolution planning tools," *Science*, 320(5873):222–226, April 11, 2008. Reprinted with permission from AAAS.)

geometric intuitions as well as the necessary tools to prove fundamental convergence properties of the algorithm.

With respect to convergence, we have seen that there are two basic cases (assuming exhaustive weak hypothesis selection): If the data satisfies the weak learning assumption, then the distributions D_t computed by AdaBoost cannot converge, but the exponential loss will converge to zero. If the data is not weakly learnable, then the distributions D_t will converge to the unique solution of a certain convex program, and the weak edges will converge to zero. In both cases, the exponential loss is asymptotically minimized.

In addition, this approach provides further unification with logistic regression, showing that convex programs associated with AdaBoost and logistic regression differ only in a single constraint.

Finally, we saw how the ideas in this chapter could be applied to the general problem of density estimation, and specifically to modeling the habitats of plant and animal species.

Bibliographic Notes

An excellent treatment of iterative projection algorithms, as in section 8.1, is given in the text by Censor and Zenios [44]. Early references for the case of orthogonal (Euclidean) projections, as in section 8.1.1, include von Neumann [176], Halperin [116], and Gubin, Polyak, and Raik [113]. Bregman [32] extended this work to more general projections based on Bregman distances, yielding Bregman's algorithm, of which AdaBoost was shown in section 8.1.3 to be a special case. See the references in Censor and Zenios for a more complete history.

Projections based on relative entropy were studied early on by Chentsov [43, 48], and Csiszár [59]. These works included versions of the Pythagorean theorem, given here as lemma 8.2, which forms the foundation of the convergence proof of section 8.2. See also the tutorial by Csiszár and Shields [60].

A classic introduction to information theory is given by Cover and Thomas [57]. The notion of entropy in the context of information theory is due to Shannon [212]. Relative entropy was defined by Kullback and Leibler [144]. The principle of maximum entropy for density estimation was proposed by Jaynes [127], and later generalized by Kullback [145]. See, for instance, Kapur and Kesavan [130] for further background.

Kivinen and Warmuth [135] were the first to point out that AdaBoost computes each successive distribution as an entropy projection onto a hyperplane, as shown in section 8.1.3. Lafferty [147] also, at the same time, made the connection between boosting and information geometry, although his framework did not exactly capture the exponential loss of AdaBoost. The unified treatment given in section 8.1.5, as well as the proof of convergence in section 8.2, are taken principally from Collins, Schapire, and Singer [54]. However, their approach and the one taken here are based directly on the framework and methods of Della Pietra, Della Pietra, and Lafferty [63, 64, 148]. Since AdaBoost is a special case of Bregman's algorithm, a proof of its convergence is also implicit in the earlier work mentioned above on iterative projection algorithms. A different proof is given by Zhang and Yu [236].

Figure 8.3 is adapted from Rudin, Daubechies, and Schapire [194].

For general background on convex analysis and convex optimization, see, for instance, Rockafellar [191], or Boyd and Vandenberghe [31].

In section 8.3, the formulation of logistic regression in program (8.28) and the resulting unification with AdaBoost are from Collins, Schapire, and Singer [54]. The unified view of AdaBoost as logistic regression minus a normalization constraint, as expressed in programs (8.19) and (8.28), is due to Lebanon and Lafferty [149].

The approach to species distribution modeling given in section 8.4 was proposed by Dudík, Phillips, and Schapire [75, 76, 182]. Figure 8.6 is adapted from Dudík [74]. The large-scale comparison study mentioned in section 8.4 was reported by Elith et al. [82]. The application to reserve design in Madagascar is due to Kremen, Cameron, et al. [142]; figure 8.7 is reprinted from that work (with permission), and was converted to black-and-white with the assistance of Cynthia Rudin.

Some of the exercises in this chapter are based on material from [44, 54, 63, 64, 148, 194].

Exercises

8.1 Let $L : \mathbb{R}^N \to \mathbb{R}$ be any function that is convex, nonnegative, continuous, and whose gradient ∇L is also continuous. Furthermore, assume that for all $\lambda_0 \in \mathbb{R}$, the sub-level set $\{\lambda : L(\lambda) \leq L(\lambda_0)\}$ is compact. Suppose coordinate descent as in algorithm 7.2 (p. 181) is used to minimize L. Let λ_t denote the value of λ at the beginning of round t. Let $L_t \doteq L(\lambda_t)$.

a. Create a function $A(\lambda)$ for which $A(\lambda_t) = L_{t+1} - L_t$.

b. Prove that if $A(\lambda) = 0$, then $\nabla L(\lambda) = \mathbf{0}$, and therefore λ is a global minimum of the function L. Also prove that A is continuous.

c. Prove that $L_t \to \min_{\lambda \in \mathbb{R}^N} L(\lambda)$ as $t \to \infty$.

d. Why is this convergence result not generally applicable to exponential loss as defined in equation (7.7)? In other words, which of the properties of L assumed in this exercise might not hold when L is exponential loss?

8.2 Suppose that the training set consists of $m = 3$ positively labeled examples $(x_1, +1)$, $(x_2, +1)$, $(x_3, +1)$, and that $\mathcal{H}$ consists of three base classifiers $\hbar_1, \hbar_2, \hbar_3$ where

$$\hbar_j(x_i) = \begin{cases} -1 & \text{if } i = j \\ +1 & \text{else.} \end{cases}$$

Finally, suppose AdaBoost is used with an exhaustive weak learner which chooses, for any given distribution $\mathcal{D}$, the weak hypothesis $\hbar_j \in \mathcal{H}$ with minimum weighted error and, in case of a tie, chooses that $\hbar_j$ (from among those with minimum weighted error) whose index j is smallest.

a. Give an explicit expression for the distribution D_t computed by AdaBoost on round t. Express your answer in terms of the *Fibonacci sequence*: $f_0 = 0$, $f_1 = 1$, and $f_n = f_{n-1} + f_{n-2}$ for $n \geq 2$. (You might find it easiest to give different answers based on the remainder of t when divided by 3.)

b. Show that the distributions D_t converge to a 3-cycle. That is, find distributions $\tilde{D}_1, \tilde{D}_2, \tilde{D}_3$ such that for $r = 1, 2, 3$, $D_{3k+r} \to \tilde{D}_r$ as k (an integer) grows to ∞. (You can use the fact that $f_n/f_{n-1} \to \phi$ as $n \to \infty$ where $\phi \doteq (1+\sqrt{5})/2$ is the "golden ratio.")

8.3 Continuing the examples in section 8.2.1, suppose the training set consists of $m = 2$ positively labeled examples $(x_1, +1)$ and $(x_2, +1)$, and that $\mathcal{H} = \{\hbar_1, \hbar_2\}$ where $\hbar_1(x_1) = +1$, $\hbar_1(x_2) = -1$, and $\hbar_2(x_1) = \hbar_2(x_2) = +1$. For this case, describe and sketch the sets $\mathcal{P}$ and $\mathcal{Q}$. Also determine $\overline{\mathcal{Q}}$, $\mathcal{P} \cap \mathcal{Q}$, and $\mathcal{P} \cap \overline{\mathcal{Q}}$.

8.4 Assume the same example never appears in the dataset with different labels.

a. Show that if p is a solution of program (8.35), then $p(y_i|x_i) = 1$ for all i.

b. Verify that programs (8.19) and (8.35) are equivalent in the sense that one can be rewritten exactly in the form of the other for an appropriate correspondence of variables.

c. Verify that programs (8.28) and (8.36) are equivalent.

d. Verify that the dual of program (8.28) is the problem of maximizing equation (8.29).

8.5 Let S be a nonempty, convex subset of $\mathbb{R}^m$, and let $\overline{S}$ denote its closure. Let $G : \overline{S} \to \mathbb{R}$ be a strictly convex function that is differentiable at all points in S. The *Bregman distance* associated with G is defined to be

$$B_G\,(\mathbf{p} \parallel \mathbf{q}) \doteq G(\mathbf{p}) - G(\mathbf{q}) - \nabla G(\mathbf{q}) \cdot (\mathbf{p} - \mathbf{q}).$$

It is the distance, at $\mathbf{p}$, between G and a supporting hyperplane at $\mathbf{q}$ (see figure 8.8). It is always nonnegative. This definition applies when $\mathbf{p} \in \overline{S}$ and $\mathbf{q} \in S$. For each $\mathbf{p} \in \overline{S}$,

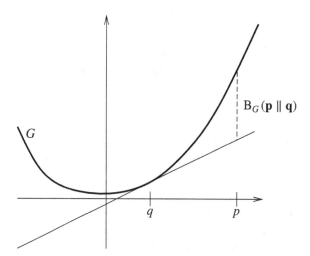

Figure 8.8
An illustration of Bregman distance in $m = 1$ dimensions. In this case, $B_G\,(p \parallel q)$ is the vertical distance at p between G and the line which is tangent to G at q.

we assume that $B_G\,(\mathbf{p} \parallel \cdot)$ can be extended continuously to all $\mathbf{q} \in \overline{\mathcal{S}}$ (with extended range $[0, +\infty]$). We also assume that $B_G\,(\mathbf{p} \parallel \mathbf{q}) = 0$ if and only if $\mathbf{p} = \mathbf{q}$. Both of these assumptions are true in all of the cases that will be of interest to us.

a. Find the Bregman distance for the following cases:

   i. $\mathcal{S} = \mathbb{R}^m$ and $G(\mathbf{p}) = \|\mathbf{p}\|_2^2$.

   ii. $\mathcal{S} = \mathbb{R}_{++}^m$ and $G(\mathbf{p}) = \sum_{i=1}^m p_i \ln p_i$.

   iii. $\mathcal{S} = \left\{\mathbf{p} \in (0, 1]^m : \sum_{i=1}^m p_i = 1\right\}$ and $G(\mathbf{p}) = \sum_{i=1}^m p_i \ln p_i$.

Let $\mathbf{M}$ be an $m \times N$ real matrix, and let $\mathbf{p}_0 \in \overline{\mathcal{S}}$ and $\mathbf{q}_0 \in \mathcal{S}$ be fixed. Let

$$\mathcal{P} \doteq \left\{\mathbf{p} \in \overline{\mathcal{S}} : \mathbf{p}^\top \mathbf{M} = \mathbf{p}_0^\top \mathbf{M}\right\}$$

$$\mathcal{Q} \doteq \left\{\mathbf{q} \in \mathcal{S} : \nabla G(\mathbf{q}) = \nabla G(\mathbf{q}_0) - \mathbf{M}\lambda \text{ for some } \lambda \in \mathbb{R}^N\right\}.$$

b. Show that if $\mathbf{p}_1, \mathbf{p}_2 \in \overline{\mathcal{S}}$ and $\mathbf{q}_1, \mathbf{q}_2 \in \mathcal{S}$, then

$$B_G\,(\mathbf{p}_1 \parallel \mathbf{q}_1) - B_G\,(\mathbf{p}_1 \parallel \mathbf{q}_2) - B_G\,(\mathbf{p}_2 \parallel \mathbf{q}_1) + B_G\,(\mathbf{p}_2 \parallel \mathbf{q}_2)$$

$$= (\nabla G(\mathbf{q}_1) - \nabla G(\mathbf{q}_2)) \cdot (\mathbf{p}_2 - \mathbf{p}_1).$$

c. Show that if $\mathbf{p}_1, \mathbf{p}_2 \in \mathcal{P}$ and $\mathbf{q}_1, \mathbf{q}_2 \in \overline{\mathcal{Q}}$, then

$$B_G\,(\mathbf{p}_1 \parallel \mathbf{q}_1) - B_G\,(\mathbf{p}_1 \parallel \mathbf{q}_2) - B_G\,(\mathbf{p}_2 \parallel \mathbf{q}_1) + B_G\,(\mathbf{p}_2 \parallel \mathbf{q}_2) = 0.$$

(You only need to show this when $\mathbf{q}_1, \mathbf{q}_2 \in \mathcal{Q}$. The case that $\mathbf{q}_1$ or $\mathbf{q}_2$ is in $\overline{\mathcal{Q}}$ then follows by continuity assumptions.)

d. Suppose $\mathbf{d} \in \mathcal{P} \cap \overline{\mathcal{Q}}$. Show that for all $\mathbf{p} \in \mathcal{P}$ and for all $\mathbf{q} \in \overline{\mathcal{Q}}$,

$$B_G\,(\mathbf{p} \parallel \mathbf{q}) = B_G\,(\mathbf{p} \parallel \mathbf{d}) + B_G\,(\mathbf{d} \parallel \mathbf{q}).$$

Therefore,

$$\mathbf{d} = \arg\min_{\mathbf{p} \in \mathcal{P}} B_G\,(\mathbf{p} \parallel \mathbf{q}_0)$$

$$= \arg\min_{\mathbf{q} \in \overline{\mathcal{Q}}} B_G\,(\mathbf{p}_0 \parallel \mathbf{q})$$

and, furthermore, $\mathbf{d}$ is the unique minimizer in each case, by exactly the same proof as in theorem 8.3.

8.6 Continuing exercise 8.5, given our usual training set and hypothesis space, suppose we define $\mathbf{p}_0 = \mathbf{0}$, $\mathbf{q}_0 = \frac{1}{2}\mathbf{1}$, $M_{ij} = y_i \hbar_j(x_i)$, $\mathcal{S} = (0, 1)^m$, and

$$G(\mathbf{d}) = \sum_{i=1}^m (d_i \ln d_i + (1 - d_i) \ln(1 - d_i)).$$

a. Show that

$$
\mathcal{Q} = \left\{ \mathbf{q} \in (0,1)^m : q_i = \frac{1}{1 + e^{y_i F_\lambda(x_i)}} \text{ for } i = 1, \ldots, m, \text{ for some } \lambda \in \mathbb{R}^N \right\},
$$

where F_λ is as in equation (7.6). Also show that $B_G (\mathbf{p}_0 \parallel \mathbf{q}) = -\sum_{i=1}^m \ln(1 - q_i)$.

b. Referring to algorithm 7.4 (p. 199), let $\mathbf{d}_t$ denote the unnormalized weights computed by AdaBoost.L on round t, that is, $d_{t,i} = 1/(1 + e^{y_i F_{t-1}(x_i)})$. Assume an exhaustive choice of α_t and h_t on every round. Show how to modify theorem 8.4 to prove that $\mathbf{d}_t \rightarrow \mathbf{d}^*$, where $\mathbf{d}^*$ is the only point in $\mathcal{P} \cap \overline{\mathcal{Q}}$. [*Hint:* Use the same definition of $A(\mathbf{d})$ as in equation (8.26).]

c. Conclude that AdaBoost.L minimizes the logistic loss, that is,

$$
\mathcal{L}(F_t) \rightarrow \inf_{\lambda \in \mathbb{R}^N} \mathcal{L}(F_\lambda)
$$

where $\mathcal{L}$ is as given in equation (7.21).

8.7 This exercise proves convergence when weak hypotheses are selected in a cyclic, rather than a greedy, fashion. We consider algorithm 8.3 (and adopt its notation), but drop our earlier assumption of greedy constraint selection. For parts (a) and (b), you should not make any assumptions at all about how the h_t's are chosen.

a. Use exercise 8.5(d) to prove that

$$
\text{RE} (\mathbf{0} \parallel \mathbf{d}_t) = \text{RE} (\mathbf{0} \parallel \mathbf{d}_{t+1}) + \text{RE} (\mathbf{d}_{t+1} \parallel \mathbf{d}_t) .
$$

b. Suppose $\mathbf{d}_{t_1}, \mathbf{d}_{t_2}, \ldots$ is a subsequence that converges to $\tilde{\mathbf{d}}$. Show that the subsequence $\mathbf{d}_{t_1+1}, \mathbf{d}_{t_2+1}, \ldots$ also converges to $\tilde{\mathbf{d}}$.

c. Suppose now that weak hypotheses are chosen in cyclic order so that $h_t = \hbar_j$ on round t where $t \equiv j \pmod{N}$. Show that $\mathbf{d}_t \rightarrow \mathbf{d}^*$, where $\mathbf{d}^*$ is as in theorem 8.4.

8.8 Let $\mathcal{P}$ be as in equation (8.20).

a. For any constant $c > 0$, show that the problem of minimizing $\text{RE} (\mathbf{p} \parallel c\mathbf{1})$ over $\mathbf{p} \in \mathcal{P}$ is equivalent to minimizing $\text{RE} (\mathbf{p} \parallel \mathbf{1})$ over $\mathbf{p} \in \mathcal{P}$. In other words, show how to transform a solution of one into a solution of the other.

b. Assume $\mathcal{P}$ includes at least one point $\mathbf{p}$ that is different from $\mathbf{0}$. Under this assumption, show that the problem of minimizing $\text{RE} (\mathbf{p} \parallel \mathbf{1})$ over all $\mathbf{p} \in \mathcal{P}$ is equivalent to minimizing $\text{RE} (P \parallel U)$ over *distributions* $P \in \mathcal{P}$ (where U is uniform distribution).

8.9 Suppose the feasible set $\mathcal{P}$ is now defined by *in*equality constraints:

$$
\mathcal{P} \doteq \left\{ \mathbf{d} \in \mathbb{R}_+^m : \sum_{i=1}^m d_i M_{ij} \leq 0 \text{ for } j = 1, \ldots, N \right\}
$$

where $\mathbf{M}$ is an $m \times N$ matrix with entries in $\{-1, +1\}$. Our goal is to minimize RE $(\mathbf{d} \parallel \mathbf{1})$ over $\mathbf{d} \in \mathcal{P}$.

For any set of indices $R \subseteq \mathcal{I} \doteq \{1, \ldots, N\}$, let

$$\mathcal{P}_R \doteq \left\{ \mathbf{d} \in \mathcal{P} : \sum_{i=1}^{m} d_i M_{ij} = 0 \text{ for } j \in R \right\}.$$

We also define $\mathcal{Q}$ to be all vectors $\mathbf{d}$ of the form given in equation (8.21), but now with the requirement that $\lambda \in \mathbb{R}_+^N$. Finally, let $\mathcal{Q}_R \subseteq \mathcal{Q}$ be all such vectors with the additional condition that $\lambda_j = 0$ for $j \notin R$.

a. Show that if $\mathbf{p} \in \mathcal{P}$ and $\mathbf{q} \in \overline{\mathcal{Q}}$, then $\sum_{i=1}^{m} p_i \ln q_i \geq 0$. If, in addition, $\mathbf{p} \in \mathcal{P}_R$ and $\mathbf{q} \in \overline{\mathcal{Q}}_R$ for some $R \subseteq \mathcal{I}$, show that $\sum_{i=1}^{m} p_i \ln q_i = 0$.

b. Let $R, R' \subseteq \mathcal{I}$, and suppose $\mathbf{d} \in \mathcal{P}_R \cap \overline{\mathcal{Q}}_R$, $\mathbf{p} \in \mathcal{P}_{R'}$, and $\mathbf{q} \in \mathcal{Q}_{R'}$. If, in addition, it is the case that either $\mathbf{p} \in \mathcal{P}_R$ or $\mathbf{q} \in \mathcal{Q}_R$, show that

$$\text{RE} (\mathbf{p} \parallel \mathbf{q}) \geq \text{RE} (\mathbf{p} \parallel \mathbf{d}) + \text{RE} (\mathbf{d} \parallel \mathbf{q}).$$

c. Suppose $\mathbf{d} \in \mathcal{P}_R \cap \overline{\mathcal{Q}}_R$ for some $R \subseteq \mathcal{I}$. Show that

$$\mathbf{d} = \arg \min_{\mathbf{p} \in \mathcal{P}} \text{RE} (\mathbf{p} \parallel \mathbf{1})$$

$$= \arg \min_{\mathbf{q} \in \overline{\mathcal{Q}}} \text{RE} (\mathbf{0} \parallel \mathbf{q}),$$

and that $\mathbf{d}$ is the unique minimizer of each problem.

8.10 Continuing exercise 8.9, suppose we use greedy coordinate descent applied to exponential loss while maintaining the condition that $\lambda_j \geq 0$ for all j at all times. See algorithm 8.4.

a. For each possible choice of $j_t \in \mathcal{I}$, give a simple analytic formula for the value of $\alpha_t \geq -\lambda_{t, j_t}$ that minimizes the expression in the figure.

b. Let $L_t \doteq \sum_{i=1}^{m} d_{t,i}$, and let

$$A(\mathbf{d}) \doteq \min_{j \in \mathcal{I}} \min_{\alpha \geq 0} \sum_{i=1}^{m} d_i e^{-\alpha M_{ij}} - \sum_{i=1}^{m} d_i.$$

(You can use the continuity of A in what follows without proof.) Show that for all t, $L_{t+1} - L_t \leq A(\mathbf{d}_t) \leq 0$. Also show that if $A(\mathbf{d}) = 0$, then $\mathbf{d} \in \mathcal{P}_{R(\mathbf{d})}$ where $R(\mathbf{d}) \doteq \{ j \in \mathcal{I} : \sum_{i=1}^{m} d_i M_{ij} = 0 \}$. [*Hint:* For any j, consider the derivative of the objective $\sum_{i=1}^{m} d_i e^{-\alpha M_{ij}}$ with respect to α, evaluated at $\alpha = 0$.]

Algorithm 8.4
A greedy coordinate-descent algorithm based on minimizing exponential loss subject to the coordinates λ_j never becoming negative

---

Given: matrix $\mathbf{M} \in \{-1, +1\}^{m \times N}$.

Initialize: $\boldsymbol{\lambda}_1 = \mathbf{0}$.

For $t = 1, 2, \ldots$

- $d_{t,i} = \exp\left(-\sum_{j=1}^{N} M_{ij} \lambda_{t,j}\right)$ for $i = 1, \ldots, m$.

- Choose $j_t \in \{1, \ldots, N\}$, $\alpha_t \in \mathbb{R}$ to minimize

$$\sum_{i=1}^{m} d_{t,i} e^{-\alpha_t M_{ij}}$$

  subject to $\alpha_t \geq -\lambda_{t,j_t}$.

- Update $\lambda_{t+1,j} = \begin{cases} \lambda_{t,j} + \alpha_t & \text{if } j = j_t \\ \lambda_{t,j} & \text{else.} \end{cases}$

---

c. Let $\mathbf{d}_{t_1}, \mathbf{d}_{t_2}, \ldots$ be a subsequence that converges to some point $\tilde{\mathbf{d}}$. Show that $\lambda_{t_n,j} \to 0$ as $n \to \infty$ for all $j \notin R(\tilde{\mathbf{d}})$. [*Hint:* If $\lambda_{t_n,j} \not\to 0$, use Taylor's theorem to show that $L_{t+1} - L_t \not\to 0$, a contradiction.]

d. Under the conditions above, show that $\tilde{\mathbf{d}} \in \overline{\mathcal{Q}}_{R(\tilde{\mathbf{d}})}$.

e. Conclude that $\mathbf{d}_t \to \mathbf{d}^*$, where $\mathbf{d}^*$ is the unique solution of both optimization problems given in exercise 8.9(c).

III ALGORITHMIC EXTENSIONS

9 Using Confidence-Rated Weak Predictions

Having studied AdaBoost and boosting theoretically from a variety of perspectives, we turn next to techniques for extending AdaBoost beyond vanilla binary classification using binary base classifiers. Our emphasis now is on algorithm design, beginning in this chapter with techniques involving real-valued base hypotheses.

We have so far taken for granted that the base hypotheses used by AdaBoost always produce predictions that are themselves classifications, either -1 or $+1$. The aim of the base learner in such a setting is to find a base classifier with low weighted classification error, that is, a small number of mistakes on the weighted training set. This setup is simple and natural, and admits the use of off-the-shelf classification learning algorithms as base learners.

In some situations, however, the rigid use of such "hard" predictions can lead to difficulties and significant inefficiencies. For instance, consider the data in figure 9.1, and a simple base classifier whose predictions depend only on which side of the line L a given point falls. Suppose for simplicity that these training examples are equally weighted, as will be the case on the first round of boosting. Here, it would certainly seem natural to classify everything above line L as positive, and this fact should be enough for us to construct a prediction rule that is substantially better than random guessing. But how should this classifier predict on the points below L? In the setup as we have described it up until now, there are only two options: either predict all points below L are positive, or predict they are all negative. Because of the nearly perfect predictions on points above L, either option will yield a classifier that, overall, is significantly better than random, which should be "good enough" for boosting. On the other hand, both options will lead to a very substantial number of mistakes on the points below L. This is a serious problem because in the process of boosting, all of these bad predictions will eventually need to be corrected or "cleaned up" in later rounds of boosting, a process that can add tremendously to the training time.

The problem here is that a "hard" classifier cannot express varying degrees of confidence. Intuitively, the data suggests that we can be highly confident in predicting that points above L are positive. On the other hand, the even split between positives and negatives on examples below L suggests that the best prediction on these points is in fact no prediction at all, but an

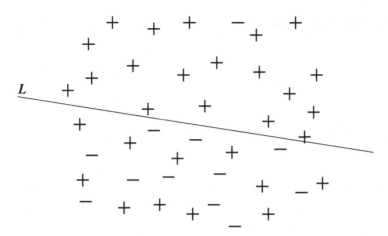

Figure 9.1
A sample dataset.

abstention from prediction expressing a sentiment of absolute uncertainty about the correct label.

Such situations arise naturally with real data as well. For instance, when classifying email as spam or ham, one can easily find somewhat accurate patterns, such as "If *Viagra* occurs in the message, then it is spam." However, it is unclear how such a rule should predict when *Viagra* does not occur in the message and, indeed, whatever prediction is made here should probably have low confidence.

In this chapter, we describe an extension of the boosting framework in which each weak hypothesis generates not only predicted classifications but also *self-rated confidence scores* that estimate the reliability of each of its predictions. Although informally a natural and simple idea, there are two essential questions that arise in its implementation. First, how do we modify AdaBoost—which was designed to handle only simple $\{-1, +1\}$ predictions— to instead use confidence-rated predictions in the most effective manner? And second, how should we design weak learners whose predictions are confidence-rated in the manner described above? In this chapter, we give answers to both of these questions. The result is a powerful set of boosting methods for handling more expressive weak hypotheses, as well as an advanced methodology for designing weak learners appropriate for use with boosting algorithms.

As specific examples, we study techniques for using weak hypotheses that abstain from making predictions on much of the space, as well as for weak hypotheses which partition the instance space into a relatively small number of equivalent prediction regions, such as decision trees and decision stumps. As an application, we demonstrate how this framework can be used as a basis for effectively learning sets of intuitively understandable rules, such as the one given above for detecting spam. We also apply our methodology to derive an algorithm for learning a variant of standard decision trees; the classifiers produced by this algorithm are often both accurate and compact.

In short, this chapter is about techniques for making boosting better. In some cases, the algorithmic improvements we present lead to substantial speedups in training time, while in other cases, we see improvement in accuracy or in the comprehensibility of the learned prediction rules.

9.1   The Framework

The foundation for our framework involving confidence-rated predictions was laid down already in preceding chapters. Indeed, we saw in chapter 5 how the confidence of the predictions made by the *combined* classifier could be measured using the real-valued margin. In the same fashion, we can bundle the predictions and confidences of a *base* classifier into a single real number. In other words, a base hypothesis can now be formulated as a real-valued function $h : \mathcal{X} \to \mathbb{R}$, so that its range is now all of $\mathbb{R}$ rather than just $\{-1, +1\}$. We interpret the sign of the real number $h(x)$ as the predicted label (-1 or $+1$) to be assigned to instance x, while its magnitude $|h(x)|$ is interpreted as the *confidence* in this prediction. Thus, the farther $h(x)$ is from zero, the higher the confidence in the prediction. Although the range of h may generally include all real numbers, we will sometimes restrict this range.

How does this change affect AdaBoost as depicted in algorithm 1.1 (p. 5)? In fact, the required modifications are quite minimal. There is no need to modify the exponential rule for updating D_t:

$$D_{t+1}(i) = \frac{D_t(i)e^{-\alpha_t y_i h_t(x_i)}}{Z_t}.$$

Nor do we need to modify how the combined classifier is computed:

$$H(x) = \text{sign}\left(\sum_{t=1}^{T} \alpha_t h_t(x)\right). \tag{9.1}$$

These are both already consistent with how we interpret real-valued weak hypotheses: Predictions with high confidence, where $h_t(x)$ is large in absolute value, will cause a dramatic change in the distribution D_t, and will have a major influence on the outcome of the final classifier. Conversely, predictions with low confidence, with $h_t(x)$ near zero, will have a correspondingly low effect.

Indeed, the only necessary modification is in the choice of α_t, which earlier depended on the weighted training error

$$\epsilon_t \doteq \mathbf{Pr}_{i \sim D_t}[h_t(x_i) \neq y_i],$$

Algorithm 9.1
A generalized version of AdaBoost with confidence-rated predictions

---

Given: $(x_1, y_1), \ldots, (x_m, y_m)$ where $x_i \in \mathcal{X}$, $y_i \in \{-1, +1\}$.
Initialize: $D_1(i) = 1/m$ for $i = 1, \ldots, m$.
For $t = 1, \ldots, T$:

- Train weak learner using distribution D_t.

- Get weak hypothesis $h_t : \mathcal{X} \to \mathbb{R}$.

- Choose $\alpha_t \in \mathbb{R}$.

- Aim: select h_t and α_t to minimalize the normalization factor

$$Z_t \doteq \sum_{i=1}^{m} D_t(i) \exp(-\alpha_t y_i h_t(x_i)).$$

- Update, for $i = 1, \ldots, m$:

$$D_{t+1}(i) = \frac{D_t(i) \exp(-\alpha_t y_i h_t(x_i))}{Z_t}.$$

Output the final hypothesis:

$$H(x) = \text{sign}\left(\sum_{t=1}^{T} \alpha_t h_t(x)\right).$$

---

a quantity that no longer makes sense when the range of the h_t's extends beyond $\{-1, +1\}$. For the moment, we leave the choice of α_t unspecified, but will return to this issue shortly. The resulting generalized version of AdaBoost is given as algorithm 9.1.

Although α_t is not specified, we can give a bound on the training error of this version of AdaBoost. In fact, the entire first part of our proof of theorem 3.1 remains valid even when α_t is unspecified and h_t is real-valued. Only the final part of that proof where Z_t was computed in terms of ϵ_t is no longer valid. Thus, by the first part of that proof, up through equation (3.5), we have:

Theorem 9.1 Given the notation of algorithm 9.1, the training error of the combined classifier H is at most

$$\prod_{t=1}^{T} Z_t.$$

Theorem 9.1 suggests that in order to minimize overall training error, a reasonable approach might be to greedily minimize the bound given in the theorem by minimizing Z_t on each round of boosting. In other words, the theorem suggests that the boosting algorithm and weak learning algorithm should work in concert to choose α_t and h_t on each round so as to minimalize the normalization factor

$$Z_t \doteq \sum_{i=1}^{m} D_t(i) \exp(-\alpha_t y_i h_t(x_i)), \tag{9.2}$$

as shown in the pseudocode. From the boosting algorithm's perspective, this provides a general principle for choosing α_t. From the weak learner's point of view, we obtain a general criterion for constructing confidence-rated weak hypotheses that replaces the previous goal of minimizing the weighted training error. We will soon see examples of the consequences of both of these points.

Although we focus on minimizing Z_t through the choice of α_t and h_t, it should be noted that this approach is entirely equivalent to the greedy method of minimizing exponential loss (equation (7.3)) via coordinate descent as discussed in sections 7.1 and 7.2. This is because Z_t measures exactly the ratio between the new and old values of the exponential loss so that $\prod_t Z_t$ is its final value. Thus, greedy minimization of the exponential loss on each round is equivalent to minimization of Z_t.

So the approach presented in this chapter is founded on minimization of training error or, alternatively, on minimization of exponential loss on the training set. We do not take up the important question of the impact of such methods on generalization error, although some of the techniques presented in previous chapters can surely be adapted (see exercise 9.2).

9.2 General Methods for Algorithm Design

Next, we develop some general techniques for working in the framework outlined above, especially for choosing α_t, and for designing weak learning algorithms, with particular consideration of efficiency issues. Specific applications of these general methods are described later in sections 9.3 and 9.4.

9.2.1 Choosing α_t in General

As just discussed, given h_t, the boosting algorithm should seek to choose α_t to minimize Z_t. We begin by considering this problem in general.

To simplify notation, when clear from context, we take t to be fixed and omit it as a subscript so that $Z = Z_t$, $D = D_t$, $h = h_t$, $\alpha = \alpha_t$, etc. Also, let $z_i \doteq y_i h_t(x_i)$. In the following discussion, we assume without loss of generality that $D(i) \neq 0$ for all i. Our goal is to find α which minimizes Z as a function of α:

$$Z(\alpha) = Z = \sum_{i=1}^{m} D_t(i)e^{-\alpha z_i}.$$

In general, this quantity can be numerically minimized. The first derivative of Z is

$$Z'(\alpha) = \frac{dZ}{d\alpha} = -\sum_{i=1}^{m} D_t(i)z_i e^{-\alpha z_i}$$

$$= -Z\sum_{i=1}^{m} D_{t+1}(i)z_i$$

by definition of D_{t+1}. Thus, if D_{t+1} is formed using the value of α_t which minimizes Z (so that $Z'(\alpha) = 0$), then we will have that

$$\sum_{i=1}^{m} D_{t+1}(i)z_i = \mathbf{E}_{i \sim D_{t+1}}[y_i h_t(x_i)] = 0.$$

In words, this means that with respect to distribution D_{t+1}, the weak hypothesis h_t will be exactly uncorrelated with the labels y_i.

Moreover,

$$Z''(\alpha) = \frac{d^2 Z}{d\alpha^2} = \sum_{i=1}^{m} D_t(i)z_i^2 e^{-\alpha z_i}$$

is strictly positive for all $\alpha \in \mathbb{R}$ (ignoring the trivial case that $z_i = 0$ for all i), meaning that $Z(\alpha)$ is strictly convex in α. Therefore, $Z'(\alpha)$ can have at most one zero. In addition, if there exists i such that $z_i < 0$, then $Z'(\alpha) \to \infty$ as $\alpha \to \infty$. Similarly, $Z'(\alpha) \to -\infty$ as $\alpha \to -\infty$ if $z_i > 0$ for some i. This means that $Z'(\alpha)$ has at least one root, except in the degenerate case that all nonzero z_i's are of the same sign. Furthermore, because $Z'(\alpha)$ is strictly increasing, we can numerically find the unique minimum of $Z(\alpha)$ by a simple binary search or by more sophisticated numerical methods.

In summary, we have argued the following:

Theorem 9.2 Assume the set $\{y_i h_t(x_i) : i = 1, \ldots, m\}$ includes both positive and negative values. Then there exists a unique choice of α_t which minimizes Z_t. Furthermore, for this choice of α_t, we have that

$$\mathbf{E}_{i \sim D_{t+1}}[y_i h_t(x_i)] = 0 \,. \tag{9.3}$$

Note that, in the language of chapter 8, the condition in equation (9.3), which is essentially the same as equation (8.9), is equivalent to D_{t+1} belonging to the hyperplane associated with the selected weak hypothesis h_t. It can also be shown that D_{t+1} is in fact the projection onto that hyperplane, just as in section 8.1.3.

9.2.2 Binary Predictions

In the very special case of binary predictions in which all predictions $h(x_i)$ are in $\{-1, +1\}$, we let ϵ be the usual weighted error:

$$\epsilon \doteq \sum_{i:y_i \neq h(x_i)} D(i).$$

Then we can rewrite Z as

$$Z = \epsilon e^{\alpha} + (1 - \epsilon)e^{-\alpha},$$

which is minimized when

$$\alpha = \frac{1}{2} \ln \left(\frac{1 - \epsilon}{\epsilon} \right),$$

giving

$$Z = 2\sqrt{\epsilon(1 - \epsilon)}. \tag{9.4}$$

Thus, we immediately recover the original version of AdaBoost for $\{-1, +1\}$-valued base classifiers, as well as the analysis of its training error given in section 3.1 via theorem 9.1. Moreover, as discussed in section 7.1, the expression for Z in equation (9.4) is minimized when ϵ is as far from $\frac{1}{2}$ as possible. If $-h$ can be chosen whenever h can be, then we can assume without loss of generality that $\epsilon < \frac{1}{2}$ so that minimizing Z in equation (9.4) is equivalent to minimizing the weighted training error ϵ. Thus, in this case, we also recover the usual criterion for selecting binary weak hypotheses.

9.2.3 Predictions with Bounded Range

When the predictions of the weak hypotheses lie in some bounded range, say $[-1, +1]$, we cannot in general give analytic expressions for the minimizing choice of α and the resulting value of Z. Nevertheless, we can give useful analytic approximations of these. Since the predictions $h(x_i)$ are in $[-1, +1]$, the z_i's are as well, where, as before, $z_i \doteq y_i h(x_i)$. Thus, we can use the convexity of e^x to upper bound Z as follows:

$$Z = \sum_{i=1}^{m} D(i)e^{-\alpha z_i} \tag{9.5}$$

$$= \sum_{i=1}^{m} D(i) \exp \left(-\alpha \left(\frac{1 + z_i}{2} \right) + \alpha \left(\frac{1 - z_i}{2} \right) \right) \tag{9.6}$$

$$\leq \sum_{i=1}^{m} D(i) \left[\left(\frac{1+z_i}{2} \right) e^{-\alpha} + \left(\frac{1-z_i}{2} \right) e^{\alpha} \right]$$

$$= \frac{e^{\alpha} + e^{-\alpha}}{2} - \frac{e^{\alpha} - e^{-\alpha}}{2} r. \tag{9.7}$$

Here,

$$r = r_t \doteq \sum_{i=1}^{m} D_t(i) y_i h_t(x_i)$$

$$= \mathbf{E}_{i \sim D_t}[y_i h_t(x_i)]$$

is a measure of the correlation between the y_i's and the predictions $h_t(x_i)$ with respect to the distribution D_t. The upper bound given in equation (9.7) is minimized when we set

$$\alpha = \frac{1}{2} \ln \left(\frac{1+r}{1-r} \right), \tag{9.8}$$

which, plugged into equation (9.7), gives

$$Z \leq \sqrt{1 - r^2}. \tag{9.9}$$

Thus, in this case, α_t can be chosen analytically as in equation (9.8), and, to minimize equation (9.9), weak hypotheses can be chosen so as to maximize r_t (or $|r_t|$). Theorem 9.1 and equation (9.9) immediately give a bound of

$$\prod_{t=1}^{T} \sqrt{1 - r_t^2}$$

on the training error of the combined classifier. Of course this approach is approximate, and better results might be possible with more exact calculations.

9.2.4   Weak Hypotheses That Abstain

We next consider a natural special case in which the range of each weak hypothesis h_t is restricted to $\{-1, 0, +1\}$. In other words, a weak hypothesis can make a definitive prediction that the label is -1 or $+1$, or it can "abstain" by predicting 0, effectively saying "I don't know." No other levels of confidence are allowed.

For fixed t, let U_0, U_{-1} and U_{+1} be defined by

$$U_b \doteq \sum_{i:z_i=b} D(i) = \mathbf{Pr}_{i \sim D}[z_i = b]$$

for $b \in \{-1, 0, +1\}$. Also, for readability of notation, we often abbreviate subscripts $+1$ and -1 by the symbols $+$ and $-$ so that U_{+1} is written U_+, and U_{-1} is written U_-. We can calculate Z as

$$Z = \sum_{i=1}^{m} D(i) e^{-\alpha z_i}$$

$$= \sum_{b \in \{-1, 0, +1\}} \sum_{i : z_i = b} D(i) e^{-\alpha b}$$

$$= U_0 + U_- e^{\alpha} + U_+ e^{-\alpha}.$$

Then Z is minimized when

$$\alpha = \frac{1}{2} \ln \left(\frac{U_+}{U_-} \right). \tag{9.10}$$

For this setting of α, we have

$$Z = U_0 + 2\sqrt{U_- U_+}$$

$$= 1 - \left(\sqrt{U_+} - \sqrt{U_-} \right)^2 \tag{9.11}$$

where we have used the fact that $U_0 + U_+ + U_- = 1$. If $U_0 = 0$ (so that h effectively has range $\{-1, +1\}$), then the choices of α and resulting values of Z are identical to those derived in section 9.2.2.

Using abstaining weak hypotheses can sometimes admit a significantly faster implementation, both of the weak learner and of the boosting algorithm. This is especially true when using weak hypotheses that are *sparse* in the sense that they are nonzero on only a relatively small fraction of the training examples. This is because the main operations described above can often be implemented in a way that involves only examples for which a given hypothesis is nonzero. For instance, computing U_+ and U_- clearly involves only such examples, meaning that this will be the case as well for Z as in equation (9.11) and α as in equation (9.10).

Moreover, updating the distribution D_t can also be speeded up by working instead with a set of *unnormalized* weights d_t that are proportional to D_t. In particular, we initialize $d_1(i) = 1$ for $i = 1, \ldots, m$, and then use an unnormalized version of AdaBoost's update rule, namely,

$$d_{t+1}(i) = d_t(i) e^{-\alpha_t y_i h_t(x_i)}. \tag{9.12}$$

It can immediately be seen that $d_t(i)$ will always be off by a fixed multiplicative constant from $D_t(i)$. This constant does not affect the computation of α-values as in equation (9.10) since the constant simply cancels with itself. It also does not affect the choice of the weak hypothesis with the smallest Z-value, or equivalently, from equation (9.11), the largest value of

$$\left| \sqrt{U_+} - \sqrt{U_-} \right|$$

since a computation of this quantity using the unnormalized weights d_t will be off by the same multiplicative constant for every weak hypothesis. Thus, each weak hypothesis can still be evaluated against our criterion for choosing the best in time proportional to the number of examples for which it is nonzero. The key advantage of this technique is that according to the update rule in equation (9.12), only the weights of examples for which the selected weak hypothesis h_t is nonzero need be updated since the weights of all other examples, where h_t is equal to zero, are unchanged.[1]

These ideas are brought together explicitly in algorithm 9.2. For simplicity, we have here assumed a given space $\mathcal{H}$ of N weak hypotheses $\hbar_1, \ldots, \hbar_N$ that is large, but still small enough to search over. As a preprocessing step, this implementation begins by computing, for each weak hypothesis $\hbar_j$, the lists A_+^j and A_-^j of all examples (x_i, y_i) on which $y_i \hbar_j(x_i)$ is $+1$ or -1, respectively. The algorithm also maintains unnormalized weights $d(i)$ as above, where we have dropped the t subscript, emphasizing the fact that only some values change on each iteration. On every round t, for every $\hbar_j$, the values U_-^j and U_+^j are computed corresponding to U_- and U_+ above, though they are off by a multiplicative constant since unnormalized weights $d(i)$ have been used. Next, G_j, our measure of goodness for each $\hbar_j$, is computed and the best j_t is selected along with α_t. Finally, the weights $d(i)$ for which $\hbar_{j_t}(x_i)$ is nonzero are updated. Note that all operations involve only the examples on which the weak hypotheses are nonzero, a substantial savings when these are sparse.

This idea can be carried even further. Rather than recomputing on every round the entire sum defining U_b^j, only some of whose terms may have changed, we can instead update the variables U_b^j just when individual terms change. In other words, whenever some particular $d(i)$ is updated, we can also update all those variables U_b^j whose defining sum includes $d(i)$ as a term; this can be done simply by adding the new value of $d(i)$ and subtracting its old value. To do this efficiently only requires precomputing, for each training example (x_i, y_i), additional "reverse index" lists B_+^i and B_-^i of all weak hypotheses $\hbar_j$ for which $y_i \hbar_j(x_i)$ is $+1$ or -1, respectively, thus making it easy to find all sums affected by an update to $d(i)$. The revised algorithm is shown as algorithm 9.3 with all the required bookkeeping made explicit. Note that the G variables can also be updated only when necessary, and the best chosen efficiently, for instance, by using a priority queue. A simple induction argument shows that the values of U_b^j and G_j are the same at the beginning of each round as in algorithm 9.2. This version of the algorithm can be especially fast when the weak hypotheses are sparse

---

1. On an actual computer, the unnormalized weights d_t may become so small or so large as to cause numerical difficulties. This can be avoided by occasionally renormalizing all of the weights.

Algorithm 9.2
An efficient version of confidence-rated AdaBoost with abstaining weak hypotheses

---

Given: $(x_1, y_1), \ldots, (x_m, y_m)$ where $x_i \in \mathcal{X}$, $y_i \in \{-1, +1\}$
 weak hypotheses $\hbar_1, \ldots, \hbar_N$ with range $\{-1, 0, +1\}$.
Initialize:

- $A_b^j = \{1 \le i \le m : y_i \hbar_j(x_i) = b\}$ for $j = 1, \ldots, N$ and for $b \in \{-1, +1\}$
- $d(i) \leftarrow 1$ for $i = 1, \ldots, m$

For $t = 1, \ldots, T$:

- For $j = 1, \ldots, N$:

   $\circ$ $U_b^j \leftarrow \sum_{i \in A_b^j} d(i)$ for $b \in \{-1, +1\}$.

   $\circ$ $G_j \leftarrow \left| \sqrt{U_+^j} - \sqrt{U_-^j} \right|$.

- $j_t = \arg \max\limits_{1 \le j \le N} G_j$.

- $\alpha_t = \dfrac{1}{2} \ln \left(\dfrac{U_+^{j_t}}{U_-^{j_t}} \right)$.

- for $b \in \{-1, +1\}$, for $i \in A_b^{j_t}$: $d(i) \leftarrow d(i) e^{-\alpha_t b}$.

Output the final hypothesis:

$$H(x) = \mathrm{sign} \left(\sum_{t=1}^{T} \alpha_t \hbar_{j_t}(x) \right).$$

---

in the additional "reverse" sense that only a few are nonzero on a given example x_i so that the sets B_-^i and B_+^i are relatively small.

In section 11.5.1, we give an example of an application in which this technique results in an improvement in computational efficiency by more than three orders of magnitude.

9.2.5   Folding α_t into h_t

As discussed in section 9.1 in our framework, the weak learner should attempt to find a weak hypothesis h that minimizes equation (9.2). Before continuing, we make the small observation that when using confidence-rated weak hypotheses, this expression can be simplified by folding α_t into h_t, in other words, by assuming without loss of generality that the weak learner can freely scale any weak hypothesis h by any constant factor $\alpha \in \mathbb{R}$. Then (dropping t subscripts) the weak learner's goal becomes that of minimizing

Algorithm 9.3
An even more efficient version of algorithm 9.2

Given: $(x_1, y_1), \ldots, (x_m, y_m)$ where $x_i \in \mathcal{X}$, $y_i \in \{-1, +1\}$
$\qquad$ weak hypotheses $\hbar_1, \ldots, \hbar_N$ with range $\{-1, 0, +1\}$.
For $j = 1, \ldots, N$:

- $A_b^j = \{1 \le i \le m : y_i \hbar_j(x_i) = b\}$ for $b \in \{-1, +1\}$.
- $U_b^j \leftarrow \sum_{i \in A_b^j} d(i)$ for $b \in \{-1, +1\}$.
- $G_j \leftarrow \left| \sqrt{U_+^j} - \sqrt{U_-^j} \right|$.

For $i = 1, \ldots, m$:

- $d(i) \leftarrow 1$.
- $B_b^i = \{1 \le j \le N : y_i \hbar_j(x_i) = b\}$ for $b \in \{-1, +1\}$.

For $t = 1, \ldots, T$:

- $j_t = \arg \max_{1 \le j \le N} G_j$.
- $\alpha_t = \dfrac{1}{2} \ln \left(\dfrac{U_+^{j_t}}{U_-^{j_t}} \right)$.
- For $b \in \{-1, +1\}$, for $i \in A_b^{j_t}$:

  $\circ$ $\Delta \leftarrow d(i) \left(e^{-\alpha_t b} - 1 \right)$.

  $\circ$ $d(i) \leftarrow d(i) e^{-\alpha_t b}$.

  $\circ$ $U_b^j \leftarrow U_b^j + \Delta$ for $b \in \{-1, +1\}$ and for $j \in B_b^i$.

- Recompute G_j for all j for which U_+^j or U_-^j has changed.

Output the final hypothesis:

$$H(x) = \mathrm{sign} \left(\sum_{t=1}^{T} \alpha_t \hbar_{j_t}(x) \right).$$

$$Z = \sum_{i=1}^{m} D(i) \exp(-y_i h(x_i)). \tag{9.13}$$

The technique presented in section 9.2.6 makes use of this simplified criterion. In addition, for some algorithms, it may be possible to make appropriate modifications to handle such a loss function directly. For instance, gradient-based algorithms, such as those used for training neural networks, can easily be modified to minimize equation (9.13) rather than the more traditional mean squared error.

9.2.6   Domain-Partitioning Weak Hypotheses

We focus next on weak hypotheses that make their predictions based on a *partitioning* of the domain $\mathcal{X}$. To be more specific, each such weak hypothesis h is associated with a partition of $\mathcal{X}$ into disjoint blocks $X_1, \ldots, X_J$ which cover all of $\mathcal{X}$ and for which $h(x) = h(x')$ for all $x, x' \in X_j$. In other words, h's prediction depends only on which block X_j a given instance falls into. A prime example of such a hypothesis is a decision tree (or stump) whose leaves define a partition of the domain.

Suppose that we have already found a partition $X_1, \ldots, X_J$ of the space. What predictions should be made for each block of the partition? In other words, how do we find a function $h : \mathcal{X} \to \mathbb{R}$ which respects the given partition, and which minimizes equation (9.13) for the given distribution $D = D_t$?

For all x within each block X_j, $h(x)$ will be equal to some fixed value c_j, so our goal is simply to find appropriate choices for c_j. For each j and for $b \in \{-1, +1\}$, let

$$W_b^j \doteq \sum_{i:x_i \in X_j \wedge y_i = b} D(i) = \mathbf{Pr}_{i \sim D}\left[x_i \in X_j \wedge y_i = b\right]$$

be the weighted fraction of examples which fall in block j and which are labeled b. Then equation (9.13) can be rewritten as

$$Z = \sum_{j=1}^{J} \sum_{i:x_i \in X_j} D(i) \exp(-y_i c_j)$$

$$= \sum_{j=1}^{J} \left(W_+^j e^{-c_j} + W_-^j e^{c_j} \right). \tag{9.14}$$

Using standard calculus, we see that this is minimized when

$$c_j = \frac{1}{2} \ln \left(\frac{W_+^j}{W_-^j} \right). \tag{9.15}$$

Plugging into equation (9.14), this choice gives

$$Z = 2 \sum_{j=1}^{J} \sqrt{W_+^j W_-^j}. \tag{9.16}$$

Equation (9.15) provides the best choice of c_j according to our criterion. Note that the sign of c_j is equal to the (weighted) majority class within block j. Moreover, c_j will be close to zero (a low-confidence prediction) if there is a roughly equal split of positive and negative examples in block j; likewise, c_j will be far from zero if one label strongly predominates.

Further, equation (9.16) provides a criterion for selecting among domain-partitioning base classifiers: The base learning algorithm should seek a base classifier from a given family that minimizes this quantity. Once found, the real-valued predictions for each block are given by equation (9.15).

For example, if using decision stumps as base classifiers, we can search through the space of all possible splits of the data based on the given features or attributes in a manner nearly identical to that given in section 3.4.2. In fact, the only necessary changes are in the criterion for choosing the best split, and in the values at the leaves of the stump. For instance, when considering a J-way split as in equation (3.21), rather than using the weighted error computed in equation (3.22) as the selection criterion, we would instead use the corresponding Z-value, which in this case, by the arguments above, would be exactly as given in equation (9.16). Likewise, c_j, rather than being set as in equation (3.20), would instead be set as in equation (9.15).

In general, each candidate split creates a partition of the domain from which W_+^j and W_-^j—and thus also Z as in equation (9.16)—can be computed. Once the split with the smallest Z has been determined, the actual real-valued prediction for each branch of the split can be computed using equation (9.15).

The criterion given by equation (9.16) can also be used as a splitting criterion in growing a decision tree for use as a weak hypothesis, rather than the more traditional Gini index or entropic function. In other words, the decision tree could be built by greedily choosing at each decision node the split which causes the greatest drop in the value of the function given in equation (9.16). (See exercises 9.5 and 9.6.) In this fashion, during boosting, each tree can be built using the splitting criterion given by equation (9.16) while the predictions at the leaves of the boosted trees are given by equation (9.15). An alternative approach for combining boosting with decision trees is given in section 9.4.

The scheme presented above requires that we predict as in equation (9.15) on block j. It may well happen that W_-^j or W_+^j is very small or even zero, in which case c_j will be very large or infinite in magnitude. In practice, such large predictions may cause numerical problems. In addition, there may be theoretical reasons to suspect that large, overly confident predictions will increase the tendency to overfit.

To limit the magnitudes of the predictions, we can instead use the "smoothed" values

$$c_j = \frac{1}{2} \ln \left(\frac{W_+^j + \varepsilon}{W_-^j + \varepsilon} \right) \tag{9.17}$$

in lieu of equation (9.15) for some appropriately small positive value of ε. Because W_-^j and W_+^j are both bounded between 0 and 1, this has the effect of bounding $|c_j|$ by

$$\frac{1}{2} \ln \left(\frac{1 + \varepsilon}{\varepsilon} \right) \approx \frac{1}{2} \ln \left(\frac{1}{\varepsilon} \right).$$

Moreover, this smoothing only slightly weakens the value of Z since plugging into equation (9.14) gives

$$Z = \sum_{j=1}^{J} \left(W_+^j \sqrt{\frac{W_-^j + \varepsilon}{W_+^j + \varepsilon}} + W_-^j \sqrt{\frac{W_+^j + \varepsilon}{W_-^j + \varepsilon}} \right)$$

$$\leq \sum_{j=1}^{J} \left(\sqrt{(W_-^j + \varepsilon) W_+^j} + \sqrt{(W_+^j + \varepsilon) W_-^j} \right)$$

$$\leq \sum_{j=1}^{J} \left(2\sqrt{W_-^j W_+^j} + \sqrt{\varepsilon W_+^j} + \sqrt{\varepsilon W_-^j} \right) \tag{9.18}$$

$$\leq 2 \sum_{j=1}^{J} \sqrt{W_-^j W_+^j} + \sqrt{2J\varepsilon}. \tag{9.19}$$

In equation (9.18), we used the inequality $\sqrt{x+y} \leq \sqrt{x} + \sqrt{y}$ for nonnegative x and y. In equation (9.19), we used the fact that

$$\sum_{j=1}^{J} (W_-^j + W_+^j) = 1,$$

which implies

$$\sum_{j=1}^{J} \left(\sqrt{W_-^j} + \sqrt{W_+^j} \right) \leq \sqrt{2J}.$$

(Recall that J is the number of blocks in the partition.) Thus, comparing equations (9.19) and (9.16), we see that Z will not be greatly degraded by smoothing if we choose $\varepsilon \ll 1/(2J)$. In practice, ε is typically chosen to be on the order of $1/m$.

Practically, the use of confidence-rated predictions can lead to very dramatic improvements in performance. For instance, figure 9.2 shows the results of one experiment demonstrating this effect. Here, the problem is to classify titles of newspaper articles by their broad topic, as in section 7.7.1. The base classifiers are decision stumps which test for the presence or absence of a word or short phrase, and predict accordingly. When AdaBoost is run with $\{-1, +1\}$-valued base classifiers (that is, without confidence-rated predictions), the slow convergence described at the beginning of this chapter is observed, and for the very reason that was earlier given.

When confidence-rated predictions are employed (using the method above for constructing domain-partitioning base classifiers), the improvement in efficiency is spectacular. Table 9.1 shows the number of iterations needed to achieve various test error rates. For

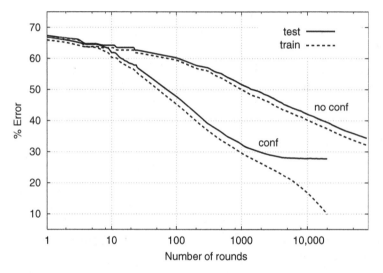

Figure 9.2
Train and test error curves for boosting on decision stumps on a text-categorization task with confidence-rated base hypotheses (bottom curves), or without (top curves).

Table 9.1
A comparison of the number of rounds needed to achieve various test accuracies both with and without confidence-rated predictions for the same learning task as in figure 9.2

| % Error | Round First Reached | | Speedup |
	Conf.	No conf.	
40	268	16,938	63.2
35	598	65,292	109.2
30	1,888	>80,000	–

The speedup column shows how many times faster boosting is with confidence-rated predictions than without.

instance, in this case the number of iterations to achieve a test error of 35% has been slashed by a factor of more than 100.

9.3 Learning Rule-Sets

We look next at two learning algorithms based on the general framework and methods developed above. The first of these is for learning sets of *rules*, simple "if-then" statements for formulating a prediction. For instance, in classifying email as spam or ham, one could easily imagine many plausible rules:

If *Viagra* occurs in the message,   then predict *spam*.
If message is from my wife,   then predict *ham*.
If message contains corrupted html links, then predict *spam*.
$\vdots$

Such rules are generally considered to be intuitive, and easy for people to understand. Indeed, some early spam-filtering systems asked users to formulate their *own* rules for identifying spam, and such rule-sets have also been utilized in the past, for instance, in so-called expert systems for medical diagnosis. A variety of learning algorithms, such as RIPPER, have been devised for inferring a good rule-set from data.

Rules are in fact a special form of abstaining hypotheses. For instance, in our formalism, the first rule above could be reformulated as the following:

$$h(x) = \begin{cases} +1 & \text{if } \textit{Viagra} \text{ occurs in message } x \\ 0 & \text{else.} \end{cases}$$

In general, rules output -1 or $+1$ when some condition holds (in this case, *Viagra* occurring in the message), and 0 otherwise. Examples which satisfy the condition are said to be *covered* by the rule.

Viewed in isolation, the problem of finding a good rule-set presents many challenges: How do we balance the natural tension that exists between the competing goals of selecting rules that cover as many examples as possible, versus choosing rules that are as accurate as possible on the examples that they do cover? (These goals are typically in competition, because usually it is easier for more specialized rules to be more accurate.) What do we do if two rules in the set contradict one another in their predictions (one predicting positive and the other negative on an example covered by both)? How much overlap should there be between rules in terms of the examples that they cover? And how do we construct a concise set of rules that will be as accurate as possible in its overall predictions?

In fact, we can provide a boosting-based answer to all these challenges by directly applying confidence-rated boosting techniques using rules as (abstaining) weak hypotheses. Doing so will result in a combined hypothesis with the following form as a set of weighted rules:

If C_1, then predict s_1 with confidence α_1.

$$\vdots \tag{9.20}$$

If C_T then predict s_T with confidence α_T.

Here, each rule (weak hypothesis) has an associated condition C_t, prediction $s_t \in \{-1, +1\}$, and confidence α_t. To evaluate such a rule-set (combined hypothesis) on a new example x, we simply add up, for each rule covering x, the predictions s_t weighted by α_t, and then take the sign of the computed sum. That is,

$$H(x) = \text{sign}\left(\sum_{t:C_t \text{ holds on } x} \alpha_t s_t\right). \tag{9.21}$$

This description is nothing more than an equivalent reformulation of equation (9.1) for the present setting. Note that contradictory rules are handled simply by assigning each a weight or confidence, and evaluating the prediction of the entire rule-set by taking a weighted sum of the predictions of all covering rules.

The rule-set itself can be constructed using the usual boosting mechanism of repeatedly assigning weights to examples, and then searching through some space of conditions for the rule (weak hypothesis) that optimizes some criterion. This mechanism automatically focuses the construction of each subsequent rule on parts of the domain where accuracy or coverage is poor. We can directly apply the results of section 9.2.4 to set the value of each α_t, and to provide a criterion for choosing the best rule on each round. Note that this criterion, as given in equation (9.11), provides a concrete and principled means of balancing the trade-off between the competing goals of finding a rule with both high coverage and high accuracy.

In addition to their intuitive interpretability, we note that rules, like abstaining weak hypotheses in general, can sometimes admit significant efficiency improvements since, using the techniques described in section 9.2.4, operations which might naively require time proportional to the total number of training examples can usually be done instead in time proportional just to the number of examples actually covered by the selected rule, which might be much smaller.

So far, we have left unspecified the form of the condition used in defining each rule. Here, as is so often the case, there exist myriad possibilities, of which we discuss just a few.

For concreteness, let us assume that instances are described by features or attributes as in section 3.4.2. Along the lines of the decision stumps explored in that section, we might consider using the same sorts of simple conditions that can naturally be defined using such features. For instance, this leads to rules such as these:

If (eye-color = blue) then predict $+1$.
If (sex = female)   then predict -1.

If (height $\geq$ 60)   then predict -1.
If (age $\leq$ 30)   then predict $+1$.

$\vdots$

Finding rules with conditions of these forms and optimizing the criterion in equation (9.11) can be done efficiently using a search technique very similar to what was described in section 3.4.2 for finding decision stumps, but using this modified criterion. Such rules are really just a one-sided, confidence-rated version of decision stumps, and thus are rather weak.

In some settings, it may be advantageous to use rules whose conditions are more expressive, leading to rules that are more specialized but potentially more accurate on the examples that they do cover. Conditions which are *conjunctions* of other base conditions are often considered natural for this purpose. For instance, this leads to rules like this one:

If (sex $=$ male) $\wedge$ (age $\geq$ 40) $\wedge$ (blood-pressure $\geq$ 135)
then predict $+1$.

In general, these conditions have the form $B_1 \wedge \cdots \wedge B_\ell$ where each B_j is a base condition chosen from some set that is presumably easy to search, such as conditions of the forms given above.

Finding the optimal conjunctive condition will often be computationally infeasible. Nevertheless, there are natural greedy search techniques that can be used. Specifically, starting with an empty conjunction, we can iteratively add one conjunct at a time on each iteration, choosing the conjunct that causes the greatest improvement in our search criterion given in equation (9.11).

These ideas form the core of a program called SLIPPER for learning rule-sets, although SLIPPER also incorporates the following variations: First, the greedy approach just described tends to find overly specialized rules which also tend to overfit. To prevent this, on each round of boosting, the training data is randomly split into a growing set and a pruning set. A conjunction is grown as above using the growing set, but then this conjunction is pruned back by choosing the pruning (truncation of the conjunction) that optimizes our usual criterion on the pruning set. Second, for enhanced interpretability, SLIPPER uses only conjunctive rules which predict $+1$, that is, for the positive class; in other words, in the notation of equation (9.20), s_t is equal to $+1$ for all rules. The exceptions are the constant-value rules which can predict $+1$ on all instances or -1 on all instances (such rules are equivalent to the condition C_t always being equal to **true**). Third, SLIPPER uses a cross-validation technique to choose the number of rules in the set (or equivalently, the number of rounds of boosting). In rough terms, this means the given dataset is repeatedly split into a training set and a validation set. After training on the training set, the best number of rounds is selected based on performance on the validation set. Training is then repeated on the entire dataset for the selected number of rounds.

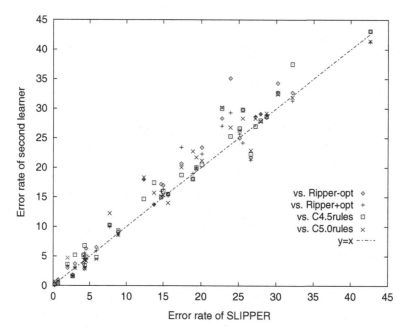

Figure 9.3
Summary of experimental results comparing SLIPPER with some other methods for learning rule-sets. Each point in the plot represents a comparison of SLIPPER's percent test error (x-coordinate) versus a competing algorithm's percent test error (y-coordinate) on a single benchmark dataset. (Copyright ©1999 Association for the Advancement of Artificial Intelligence. Reprinted, with permission, from [50].)

Figure 9.3 compares the test accuracy of SLIPPER on 32 benchmark datasets with a number of other well-established algorithms for learning rule-sets, namely C4.5rules, C5.0rules, and two variants of RIPPER (see the bibliographic notes for further reading on these). The comparison is evidently quite favorable. Moreover, the rule-sets that are found tend to be reasonably compact compared to most of the other methods, and of a form that is often understandable to humans.

9.4   Alternating Decision Trees

We turn next to a second application of the confidence-rated framework.

Some of the best performance results for boosting have been obtained using decision trees as base hypotheses. However, when this approach is taken, the resulting combined hypothesis may be quite big, being the weighted majority vote (or thresholded sum) of a possibly large forest of trees which themselves may individually be rather sizable. In many cases, the size and complexity of such a combined hypothesis is justified by its high accuracy. But sometimes, it is important to find a classifier that is not only accurate but also somewhat more compact and understandable. We saw in section 9.3 how rule-sets can be learned for this purpose. Here, we describe an alternative method in which boosting is used to learn a *single*, though nonstandard, decision tree that can often be reasonably compact and comprehensible while still giving accurate predictions. The basic idea is to use weak hypotheses that roughly correspond to *paths* through a tree, rather than an *entire* tree, and to select them in a manner that makes it possible for the combined hypothesis to be arranged conveniently in the form of a tree.

The particular kind of tree that is found in this way is called an *alternating decision tree (ADT)*. Figure 9.4 shows an example of such a tree which resembles, but clearly is also quite distinct from, an ordinary decision tree. An ADT consists of levels that alternate between two types of nodes: *Splitter nodes*, drawn as rectangles in the figure, are each labeled with a test or condition as in ordinary decision trees, while *prediction nodes*, drawn as ellipses, are associated with a real-valued (confidence-rated) prediction. In an ordinary decision tree, any instance defines a *single* path from the root to a leaf. In contrast, in an ADT, an instance

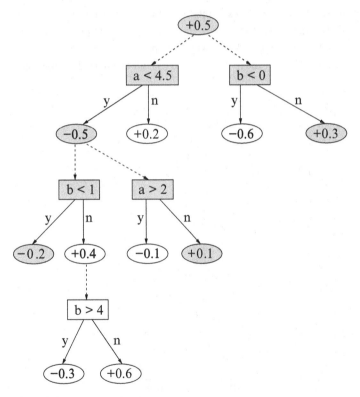

Figure 9.4
An alternating decision tree. Nodes have been shaded along all paths defined by an instance in which $a = 1$ and $b = 0.5$.

defines *multiple* paths through the tree. For instance, in figure 9.4, we have shaded the nodes along all of the paths defined by an instance in which $a = 1$ and $b = 0.5$. These paths are determined by starting at the root and working our way down. When a splitter node is reached, we branch next to just one child based on the result of the test associated with the node, just as in an ordinary decision tree. But when a prediction node is reached, we need to traverse to *all* of its children.

The real-valued prediction associated with an ADT on a particular instance is the sum of the values at the prediction nodes along *all* of the paths defined by that instance. For instance, in the example above, this prediction would be

$$0.5 - 0.5 + 0.3 - 0.2 + 0.1 = +0.2.$$

As usual, taking the sign of this value provides the predicted classification, in this case $+1$.

In form, ADTs generalize both ordinary decision trees and boosted decision stumps, while preserving much of the comprehensibility of both.

To learn an ADT, we can use boosting with appropriately defined weak hypotheses. To see this, we note that any ADT can be decomposed into a sum of simpler hypotheses, one for each splitter node (as well as the root), and each in the form of a single path or branch through the tree. For instance, the tree in figure 9.4 can be decomposed into six such *branch predictors*, as shown in figure 9.5. Each of these is evaluated like an ordinary decision tree,

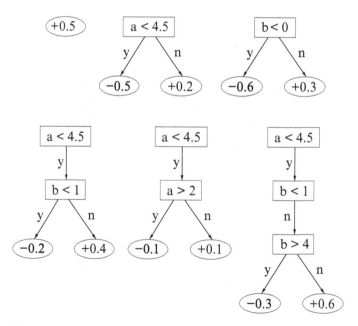

Figure 9.5
A decomposition of the alternating decision tree in figure 9.4 into six branch predictors.

but with the stipulation that if an evaluation "falls off" the branch, then the result is 0. Thus, the bottom-right branch predictor in the figure evaluates to $+0.6$ on an instance in which $a = 1$ and $b = 2$, but evaluates to 0 on any instance in which $a \geq 4.5$ or $b < 1$. The top-left branch predictor always evaluates to the constant $+0.5$. By the manner in which ADTs are evaluated, it can be seen that the ADT in figure 9.4 is functionally equivalent, in terms of its predictions, to the sum of the branch predictors in figure 9.5. Moreover, any ADT can be decomposed in this way.

(Note that there is no ordering associated with these branch predictors. The point is simply that the ADT can be decomposed into an unordered sum of branch predictors. And although the boosting technique described below constructs a set of branch predictors one by one, there will still be considerable variation in the order in which they are added.)

So our approach to learning an ADT is to use boosting with weak hypotheses which are branch predictors as above, but which are appropriately constrained so that the final, resulting set of branch predictors can be arranged as an ADT.

Every branch predictor is defined by a *condition B* given by the test at the last splitter node along the branch, together with a *precondition P* which holds if and only if all the tests along the path to that last splitter node hold. For instance, the bottom-right branch predictor in figure 9.5 has the condition "$b > 4$" and precondition "$(a < 4.5) \wedge (b \geq 1)$." In general, the branch predictor computes a function of the form

$$
h(x) = \begin{cases} 0 & \text{if } P \text{ does not hold on } x \\ c_1 & \text{if } P \text{ holds and } B \text{ holds on } x \\ c_2 & \text{if } P \text{ holds but } B \text{ does not hold on } x, \end{cases} \tag{9.22}
$$

where c_1 and c_2 are the real-valued predictions at its leaves.

Thus, branch predictors are *both* abstaining and domain-partitioning. Learning such weak hypotheses can be accomplished by straightforwardly combining the techniques of sections 9.2.4 and 9.2.6. In general, an abstaining domain-partitioning hypothesis h is associated with a partition of the domain into disjoint blocks $X_0, X_1, \ldots, X_J$ as in section 9.2.6, but with the added restriction that h abstain on X_0 (so that $h(x) = 0$ for all $x \in X_0$). Then it can be shown, as before, that the best c_j (prediction for h on X_j) for $j = 1, \ldots, J$ is computed as in equation (9.15), but for this choice, we have

$$
Z = W^0 + 2 \sum_{j=1}^{J} \sqrt{W_+^j W_-^j} \tag{9.23}
$$

where

$$
W^0 \doteq \sum_{i:x_i \in X_0} D(i) = \mathbf{Pr}_{i \sim D}[x_i \in X_0].
$$

(For simplicity, we are ignoring issues regarding the smoothing of predictions as in section 9.2.6; these could also be applied here.)

These ideas immediately provide a means of choosing a branch predictor on each round of boosting for a given set $\mathcal{P}$ of candidate preconditions, and set $\mathcal{B}$ of candidate conditions. In particular, for each $P \in \mathcal{P}$ and $B \in \mathcal{B}$, we consider the corresponding branch predictor (equation (9.22)) and compute its Z-value as in equation (9.23), selecting the one for which this value is minimized. Then the real-valued predictions c_1 and c_2 are given by equation (9.15).

What should we use for the sets $\mathcal{P}$ and $\mathcal{B}$? The set of conditions $\mathcal{B}$ can be some set of fixed base conditions, such as those used for decision stumps. As for the set of preconditions, in order that the resulting set of branch predictors be equivalent to an ADT, we need to use preconditions corresponding to paths to splitter nodes that have already been added to the tree. Thus, this set will grow from round to round. In particular, initially the tree is empty and we let $\mathcal{P} = \{\mathbf{true}\}$ where **true** is a condition that always holds. When a new branch predictor defined by precondition P and condition B is found on round t, both $P \wedge B$ and $P \wedge \neg B$, corresponding to the two splits of this branch, are added to $\mathcal{P}$.

Finally, for the root node, we initialize the ADT using a weak hypothesis that predicts a constant real value, where this value is set using the methods of section 9.2. Putting these ideas together leads to algorithm 9.4. Here, on round t, we write $W_t(C)$ for the sum of the weights of examples for which condition C holds, and among these we write $W_t^+(C)$ and $W_t^-(C)$ for the total weights of just the positive and negative examples (respectively). These implicitly depend on the current distribution D_t. Thus,

$$W_t^b(C) \doteq \mathbf{Pr}_{i \sim D_t}[C \text{ holds on } x_i \ \wedge \ y_i = b] \tag{9.24}$$

for $b \in \{-1, +1\}$, and

$$W_t(C) \doteq \mathbf{Pr}_{i \sim D_t}[C \text{ holds on } x_i] \,. \tag{9.25}$$

Although the output of this pseudocode is the (thresholded) sum of branch predictors, this sum can immediately be put in the form of an ADT as previously discussed, a data structure that might also provide the basis for the most convenient and efficient implementation. Various other techniques might also be employed for improved efficiency, such as the use of unnormalized weights as discussed in section 9.2.4.

Because the base hypotheses used by ADTs tend to be rather weak, there is a tendency for the algorithm to overfit; in practice, this typically must be controlled using some form of cross-validation.

As an illustration of how ADTs can be interpreted, figure 9.6 shows the tree constructed by this algorithm when run for six rounds on the heart-disease dataset described in section 1.2.3, where "healthy" and "sick" classes have been identified with labels $+1$ and -1, respectively. For this dataset, ADTs achieve a test error of about 17%, roughly the same as decision

Algorithm 9.4
The alternating decision tree algorithm

Given: $(x_1, y_1), \ldots, (x_m, y_m)$ where $x_i \in \mathcal{X}$, $y_i \in \{-1, +1\}$
  set $\mathcal{B}$ of base conditions.

Initialize:

- $h_0(x) = \frac{1}{2} \ln((1 + r_0)/(1 - r_0))$ for all x where $r_0 = \frac{1}{m} \sum_{i=1}^{m} y_i$.

- $\mathcal{P} \leftarrow \{\textbf{true}\}$.

- For $i = 1, \ldots, m$, let $D_1(i) = \begin{cases} 1/(1 + r_0) & \text{if } y_i = +1 \\ 1/(1 - r_0) & \text{if } y_i = -1. \end{cases}$

For $t = 1, \ldots, T$:

- Find $P \in \mathcal{P}$ and $B \in \mathcal{B}$ that minimize

$$Z_t = W_t(\neg P) + 2\sqrt{W_t^+(P \wedge B) W_t^-(P \wedge B)} + 2\sqrt{W_t^+(P \wedge \neg B) W_t^-(P \wedge \neg B)}$$

where W_t^+, W_t^-, and W_t are defined as in equations (9.24) and (9.25).

- Let h_t be the corresponding branch predictor:

$$h_t(x) = \begin{cases} 0 & \text{if } P \text{ does not hold on } x \\ \frac{1}{2} \ln\left(\frac{W_t^+(P \wedge B)}{W_t^-(P \wedge B)}\right) & \text{if } P \text{ holds and } B \text{ holds on } x \\ \frac{1}{2} \ln\left(\frac{W_t^+(P \wedge \neg B)}{W_t^-(P \wedge \neg B)}\right) & \text{if } P \text{ holds but } B \text{ does not hold on } x. \end{cases}$$

- $\mathcal{P} \leftarrow \mathcal{P} \cup \{P \wedge B, P \wedge \neg B\}$.

- Update, for $i = 1, \ldots, m$:

$$D_{t+1}(i) = \frac{D_t(i) \exp(-\alpha_t y_i h_t(x_i))}{Z_t}.$$

Output the final hypothesis:

$$H(x) = \text{sign}\left(\sum_{t=0}^{T} h_t(x)\right).$$

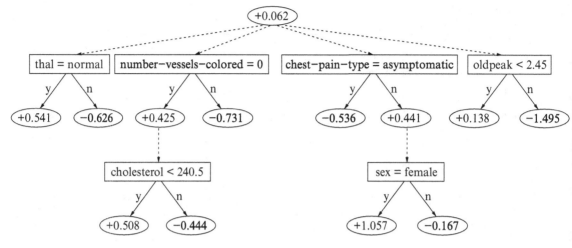

Figure 9.6
The alternating decision tree constructed for the heart disease dataset.

stumps, and better than boosting on decision trees, which gives an error around 20% while using a combined hypothesis that may be two orders of magnitude larger. This smaller size already makes ADTs more interpretable, but so does their structure, as we now discuss.

To begin, we note that the meaning of splitter nodes can largely be understood in isolation. For instance, from the figure, we can infer that a cholesterol level above 240.5 and asymptomatic chest pain are both predictors of heart problems, as indicated by the fact that they both generate negative contributions to the prediction sum. We also can analyze the interactions of the nodes. Parallel splitter nodes, such as the four nodes in the first level, represent little or no interaction. For instance, the fact that the "thal" test is normal increases the likelihood that the person is healthy, irrespective of the "number of vessels colored" or the type of chest pain. In contrast, the significance of the two decision nodes in the second level depends on the evaluation of their ancestral decision nodes. Specifically, regarding the node "sex = female," the fact that a patient is a male appears to be more predictive of a heart problem when chest pain is symptomatic than in the population in general. This implies that only when the chest pain is symptomatic is it worthwhile to consider the patient's gender. The root of the tree is associated with the fixed (unconditional) contribution of +0.062, a small positive number indicating that (according to this training set) there are slightly more healthy people than sick people.

Summary

This chapter has explored a general framework for boosting using confidence-rated weak hypotheses. This framework provides general principles for the selection and construction of weak hypotheses, as well as the modification of AdaBoost. Within this framework, we have seen how old algorithms can be adjusted and new algorithms derived, leading to substantial improvements in speed, accuracy, and interpretability.

Bibliographic Notes

The overall approach taken in this chapter is due to Schapire and Singer [205]. This includes the framework and almost all of the results of sections 9.1 and 9.2, as well as algorithm 9.1. However, the highly efficient technique for handling sparse weak hypotheses given in section 9.2.4 and leading to algorithms 9.2 and 9.3 is an adaptation of work by Collins [52] (see also Collins and Koo [53]). The experiments in section 9.2.6, including table 9.1 and figure 9.2, are based on results reported by Schapire and Singer [206].

The splitting criterion given in equation (9.16) for generating domain-partitioning base hypotheses, including decision trees, was also proposed by Kearns and Mansour [132], although their motivation was rather different. The techniques used for assigning confidences as in equation (9.15) to the individual predictions of such base hypotheses, and also for smoothing these predictions as in equation (9.17), are closely related to those suggested earlier by Quinlan [183].

In allowing weak hypotheses which can abstain to various degrees, the framework given here is analogous to Blum's "specialist" model of online learning [25].

The SLIPPER algorithm and experiments described in section 9.3, including figure 9.3, are due to Cohen and Singer [50]. SLIPPER's method for building rules (that is, the weak learner) is similar to that of previous methods for learning rule-sets, particularly Cohen's RIPPER [49] and Fürnkranz and Widmer's IREP [104]. The C4.5rules and C5.0rules algorithms for rule-set induction use decision-tree techniques as developed by Quinlan [184].

The alternating decision tree algorithm of section 9.4 is due to Freund and Mason [91], including the adapted figure 9.6. ADTs are similar to the option trees of Buntine [41], developed further by Kohavi and Kunz [137].

Some of the exercises in this chapter are based on material from [54, 132, 205].

Exercises

9.1 Given the notation and assumptions of section 9.2.3, let $\tilde{\alpha}$ be the value of α given in equation (9.8), and let $\hat{\alpha}$ be the value of α which exactly minimizes equation (9.5). Show that $\tilde{\alpha}$ and $\hat{\alpha}$ have the same sign, and that $|\tilde{\alpha}| \leq |\hat{\alpha}|$.

9.2 Suppose the base functions h in $\mathcal{H}$ are confidence-rated with range $[-1, +1]$, that is, $h : \mathcal{X} \to [-1, +1]$. Most of the definitions of margin, convex hull, etc. from sections 5.1 and 5.2 carry over immediately to this setting without modification. For any $h \in \mathcal{H}$ and any value $\nu \in [-1, +1]$, let

$$h'_{h,v}(x) \doteq \begin{cases} +1 & \text{if } h(x) \geq v \\ -1 & \text{else,} \end{cases}$$

and let

$$\mathcal{H}' \doteq \left\{ h'_{h,v} : h \in \mathcal{H}, v \in [-1, +1] \right\}$$

be the space of all such functions.

a. For fixed h and x, suppose v is chosen uniformly at random from $[-1, +1]$. Compute the expected value of $h'_{h,v}(x)$.

b. Let d' be the VC-dimension of $\mathcal{H}'$. Show that the bound given in theorem 5.5 holds in this setting with probability at least $1 - \delta$ for all $f \in \text{co}(\mathcal{H})$, but with d replaced by d'.

9.3 Let $\mathcal{H}$ and $\mathcal{H}'$ be as in exercise 9.2.

a. Show that if a training set is linearly separable with margin $\theta > 0$, using functions from $\mathcal{H}$ (so that equation (3.10) holds for some $g_1, \ldots, g_k \in \mathcal{H}$), then the data is γ-empirically weakly learnable by classifiers in $\mathcal{H}'$ (using an exhaustive weak learner) for some $\gamma > 0$.

b. Prove or disprove that the converse holds in general.

9.4 Let $\mathcal{H} = \{\hbar_1, \ldots, \hbar_N\}$ be a space of weak classifiers, each with range $\{-1, +1\}$. Suppose the sets $P \doteq \{1 \leq i \leq m : y_i = +1\}$ and $C_j \doteq \{1 \leq i \leq m : \hbar_j(x_i) = +1\}$ have been precomputed, and that they are quite small compared to m (so that most examples are negative, and the weak classifiers predict -1 on most examples). Show how to implement AdaBoost using an exhaustive weak learner over $\mathcal{H}$ in such a way that:

1. evaluating the weighted error (with respect to distribution D_t) of any particular weak classifier $\hbar_j$ takes time $O\big(|C_j| + |P|\big)$, so that an exhaustive weak learner can be implemented in time $O\big(\sum_{j=1}^{N}(|C_j| + |P|)\big)$;

2. given the currently selected weak classifier $h_t = \hbar_{j_t}$, the running time of the boosting algorithm (*not* including the call to the weak learner) is $O\big(|C_{j_t}| + |P|\big)$.

In other words, the running time should depend only on the number of positive examples, and the number of examples predicted positive by the weak classifiers.

9.5 Given our usual dataset $(x_1, y_1), \ldots, (x_m, y_m)$, a decision tree can be constructed using a greedy, top-down algorithm. Specifically, let $\mathcal{H}$ be a set of binary functions $h : \mathcal{X} \to \{-1, +1\}$ representing a class of possible splits for the internal nodes of the tree. Initially, the tree consists only of a leaf at its root. Then, on each of a sequence of iterations, one leaf ℓ of the current tree T is selected and replaced by an internal node associated with some split h, leading to two new leaves depending on the outcome of that split. We write $T_{\ell \to h}$ to represent the newly formed tree. An example is shown in figure 9.7.

To describe how ℓ and h are chosen, let $I : [0, 1] \to \mathbb{R}_+$ be an *impurity function* for which $I(p) = I(1 - p)$, and which is increasing on $\left[0, \frac{1}{2}\right]$. For $b \in \{-1, +1\}$, and for ℓ a

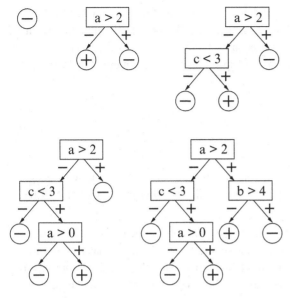

Figure 9.7
Several steps in the construction of a decision tree using decision stumps as splitting functions (with the construction progressing from left to right, and then from top to bottom). At each step, one leaf is replaced by a new internal node and two new leaves.

leaf of a tree, let $n^b(\ell)$ denote the number of training examples (x_i, y_i) such that x_i reaches leaf ℓ, and $y_i = b$. Also, let $n(\ell) = n^-(\ell) + n^+(\ell)$. Overloading notation, we define the impurity of a leaf ℓ to be $I(\ell) \doteq I(n^+(\ell)/n(\ell))$, and the impurity of the entire tree $\mathcal{T}$ to be

$$I(\mathcal{T}) \doteq \frac{1}{m} \sum_{\ell \in \mathcal{T}} n(\ell) \cdot I(\ell),$$

where summation is over all leaves ℓ of the tree $\mathcal{T}$.

To grow the tree as above, on each iteration the leaf ℓ and the split h are chosen that effect the greatest drop in impurity

$$\Delta I(\ell, h) \doteq \frac{n(\ell)}{m} \cdot \left[I(\ell) - \left(\frac{n(\ell_+^h)}{n(\ell)} \cdot I(\ell_+^h) + \frac{n(\ell_-^h)}{n(\ell)} \cdot I(\ell_-^h) \right) \right]$$

where ℓ_+^h and ℓ_-^h are the two leaves that would be created if ℓ were replaced by an internal node with split h.

a. Show that $\Delta I(\ell, h) = I(\mathcal{T}) - I(\mathcal{T}_{\ell \to h})$.

A decision tree can be viewed as defining a domain-partitioning hypothesis since the sets of examples reaching each leaf are disjoint from one another. Suppose a *real-valued* prediction is assigned to each leaf so that the tree defines a real-valued function F whose value, on any instance x, is given by the leaf that is reached by x. Suppose further that these values are chosen to minimize the exponential loss on the training set (as in equation (9.3)) over all real-valued functions of the particular form specified by the given tree. Let $L(\mathcal{T})$ be the resulting loss for a tree $\mathcal{T}$.

b. Show that if

$$I(p) \doteq 2\sqrt{p(1-p)}, \tag{9.26}$$

then $L(\mathcal{T}) = I(\mathcal{T})$.

c. For this same choice of impurity function, and for any tree $\mathcal{T}$, show how to assign a binary label in $\{-1, +1\}$ to each leaf ℓ so that the resulting tree-classifier will have training error at most $I(\mathcal{T})$.

d. Consider using each of the losses listed below in place of exponential loss. In each case, determine how the impurity function $I(p)$ should be redefined so that $L(\mathcal{T}) = I(\mathcal{T})$ (where $L(\mathcal{T})$, as above, is the minimum loss of any real-valued function of the form given by the tree $\mathcal{T}$). Also in each case, explain how to assign a binary label to each leaf, as in part (c), so that the resulting tree-classifier's training error is at most $I(\mathcal{T})$.

  i. Logistic loss (using base-2 logarithm): $\frac{1}{m}\sum_{i=1}^{m} \lg(1 + \exp(-y_i F(x_i)))$.

  ii. Square loss: $\frac{1}{m}\sum_{i=1}^{m}(y_i - F(x_i))^2$.

9.6 Continuing exercise 9.5, assume henceforth that we are using exponential loss and the impurity function in equation (9.26). Also, let us assume the data is empirically γ-weakly learnable by $\mathcal{H}$ (as defined in section 2.3.3).

a. Let $\mathcal{T}_{*\to h}$ denote the tree that would result if *every* leaf of the tree $\mathcal{T}$ were replaced by an internal node that splits on h, with each new node leading to two new leaves (so that h appears many times in the tree). For any tree $\mathcal{T}$, show that there exists a split $h \in \mathcal{H}$ such that $L(\mathcal{T}_{*\to h}) \leq L(\mathcal{T})\sqrt{1 - 4\gamma^2}$.

b. For any tree $\mathcal{T}$ with t leaves, show that there exists a leaf ℓ of $\mathcal{T}$ and a split $h \in \mathcal{H}$ such that

$$\Delta I(\ell, h) \geq \frac{1 - \sqrt{1 - 4\gamma^2}}{t} \cdot I(\mathcal{T}) \geq \frac{2\gamma^2}{t} \cdot I(\mathcal{T}).$$

[*Hint:* For the second inequality, first argue that $\sqrt{1 - x} \leq 1 - \frac{1}{2}x$ for $x \in [0, 1]$.]

c. Show that after T rounds of the greedy algorithm described in exercise 9.5, the resulting tree $\mathcal{T}$ (with binary leaf predictions chosen as in exercise 9.5(c)) will have training error at most $\exp(-2\gamma^2 H_T)$ where $H_T \doteq \sum_{t=1}^{T}(1/t)$ is the T-th harmonic number. (Since $\ln(T + 1) \leq H_T \leq 1 + \ln T$ for $T \geq 1$, this bound is at most $(T + 1)^{-2\gamma^2}$.)

9.7 Let $\mathcal{H} = \{\hbar_1, \ldots, \hbar_N\}$ be a space of real-valued base hypotheses, each with range $[-1, +1]$.

a. Suppose on each round that the base hypothesis $h_t \in \mathcal{H}$ which maximizes $|r_t|$ as in section 9.2.3 is selected, and that α_t is chosen as in equation (9.8). Show how to modify the proof of section 8.2 to prove that this algorithm asymptotically minimizes exponential loss (in the same sense as in theorem 8.4).

b. Prove the same result when h_t and α_t are instead selected on each round to exactly minimize Z_t (equation (9.2)).

10 Multiclass Classification Problems

Until now, we have focused only on using boosting for binary classification problems in which the goal is to categorize each example into one of only two categories. In practice, however, we are often faced with *multiclass* problems in which the number of categories is more than two. For instance, in letter recognition, we need to categorize images into 26 categories for the letters $A, B, C, \ldots, Z$.

Although AdaBoost was designed explicitly for two-class problems, one might expect the generalization to the multiclass case to be natural and straightforward. In fact, there turn out to be many ways of extending boosting for multiclass learning, as will be seen in this chapter.

We begin with the most direct generalization of AdaBoost. This version, called AdaBoost.M1, has the advantage of simplicity and ease of implementation, but requires that the base classifiers be much better than random guessing, a condition that for many natural base learners cannot be fulfilled. For weaker base learners, this can be an insurmountable problem requiring a fundamentally different approach.

Aside from AdaBoost.M1, most multiclass versions of AdaBoost are based in some way on a reduction from the multiclass case to the simpler binary case. In other words, the problem of making a multi-way classification is replaced by multiple yes-no questions. For instance, if we are classifying images by the letter they represent, we might replace the question "What letter is this?" which has 26 possible answers, with 26 binary questions:

"Is it an A or not?"
"Is it a B or not?"
"Is it a C or not?"
$\vdots$

Clearly, if we can learn to answer these 26 questions accurately, then we can also answer the original classification question. This simple "one-against-all" approach is the basis of the multiclass AdaBoost.MH algorithm.

Asking so many questions might seem rather inefficient and, more importantly, one might notice that only one or two wrong answers to these binary questions are enough to cause an incorrect answer in the final classification. To alleviate this difficulty, we might consider asking more complex binary questions, such as:

"Is it a vowel or a consonant?"

"Is it in the first half of the alphabet?"

"Is it one of the letters in the word MACHINE?"

Given predicted answers to such binary questions for a particular instance, we can formulate a final classification by choosing the label that is "most consistent" with the binary responses. Even if many of these are erroneous, we still stand a reasonable chance of producing an overall prediction that is correct since the answers to the questions are more informative and overlap one another in the information they provide. Thus, such a scheme may be both more efficient and more robust.

Of course, the number of binary questions of this type grows extremely quickly, which means that the number of ways of reducing multiclass to binary is still more vast. Fortunately, as we will see, it turns out to be possible to study this problem in a general setting, and to derive and analyze an algorithm called AdaBoost.MO that can be applied to an entire family of reductions.

This general approach of reducing a more complicated learning problem to a simple binary classification problem can be applied in other situations as well. In particular, as we will see in chapter 11, we can use this method for ranking problems where the goal is to learn to rank a set of objects. For instance, we might want to rank documents by their relevance to a given search query. Once reduced to binary, an application of AdaBoost leads to a ranking algorithm called RankBoost. We can further view multiclass classification as a ranking problem, leading to yet another multiclass algorithm called AdaBoost.MR whose purpose is to rank the correct label higher than the incorrect ones.

Moreover, although we focus only on their combination with boosting, the reduction techniques that we present are quite general, and can certainly be applied to other learning methods as well, such as support-vector machines.

The ability of the algorithms in this chapter to generalize beyond the provided training set is clearly an issue of considerable importance. Nevertheless, we limit our scope in this chapter only to the study of performance on the training set. We note, however, that the techniques for analyzing generalization error given in previous chapters can certainly be applied to the multiclass setting as well (see exercises 10.3 and 10.4).

As an illustration, this chapter also includes an application of the presented techniques to the classification of caller utterances according to their meaning, a key component of spoken-dialogue systems.

10.1   A Direct Extension to the Multiclass Case

Our setup for multiclass learning is essentially the same as in the binary case, except that each label y_i is now assumed to belong to a set $\mathcal{Y}$ of all possible labels where the cardinality of $\mathcal{Y}$ may be greater than 2. For instance, in the letter recognition example above, $\mathcal{Y}$ would be the set $\{A, B, \ldots, Z\}$. Throughout this chapter, we denote this cardinality $|\mathcal{Y}|$ by K.

The first multiclass version of AdaBoost is called *AdaBoost.M1*—the *M* stands for multiclass, and the *1* distinguishes this extension as the first and most direct. As is natural, the weak learner in this setting generates hypotheses h which assign to each instance exactly one of the K possible labels so that $h : \mathcal{X} \rightarrow \mathcal{Y}$. Pseudocode for AdaBoost.M1 is shown as algorithm 10.1, and differs only slightly from binary AdaBoost (algorithm 1.1 (p. 5)). The goal of the weak learner is to generate on round t a base classifier h_t with low classification error

$$\epsilon_t \doteq \mathbf{Pr}_{i \sim D_t}[h_t(x_i) \neq y_i],$$

just as for binary AdaBoost. The update to the distribution D_t is also the same as for AdaBoost, as given in the first form of the update from algorithm 1.1. The final hypothesis H is only slightly different: For a given instance x, H now outputs the label y that maximizes the sum of the weights of the weak hypotheses predicting that label. In other words, rather than computing a weighted majority vote as in binary classification, H computes the weighted *plurality* of the predictions of the base hypotheses.

In analyzing the training error of AdaBoost.M1, we require the same weak learning assumption as in the binary case, namely, that each weak hypothesis h_t have weighted error ϵ_t below $\frac{1}{2}$. When this condition is satisfied, theorem 10.1 (below) proves the same bound on the training error as for binary AdaBoost, showing that the error of the combined final hypothesis decreases exponentially, as in the binary case. This is of course good news for base learners that are able to meet this condition. Unfortunately, this requirement on the performance of the weak learner is much stronger than might be desired. In the binary case, when $K = 2$, a random guess will be correct with probability $\frac{1}{2}$, so the weak learning assumption posits performance only a little better than random. However, when $K > 2$, the probability of a correct random prediction is only $1/K$, which is less than $\frac{1}{2}$. Thus, our requirement that the accuracy of the weak hypothesis be greater than $\frac{1}{2}$ is significantly stronger than simply requiring that the weak hypothesis perform better than random guessing. For instance, with $K = 10$ classes, guessing randomly will give accuracy of 10%, which is far less than the 50% requirement.

Moreover, in the case of binary classification, a weak hypothesis h_t with error significantly *larger* than $\frac{1}{2}$ is of equal value to one with error significantly *less* than $\frac{1}{2}$ since h_t can be replaced by its negation $-h_t$ (an effect that happens "automatically" in AdaBoost, which chooses $\alpha_t < 0$ in such a case). However, for $K > 2$, a hypothesis h_t with error ϵ_t above

Algorithm 10.1
AdaBoost.M1: A first multiclass extension of AdaBoost

Given: $(x_1, y_1), \ldots, (x_m, y_m)$ where $x_i \in \mathcal{X}$, $y_i \in \mathcal{Y}$.
Initialize: $D_1(i) = 1/m$ for $i = 1, \ldots, m$.
For $t = 1, \ldots, T$:

- Train weak learner using distribution D_t.

- Get weak hypothesis $h_t : \mathcal{X} \to \mathcal{Y}$.

- Aim: select h_t to minimalize the weighted error:

$$\epsilon_t \doteq \mathbf{Pr}_{i \sim D_t}[h_t(x_i) \neq y_i].$$

- If $\epsilon_t \geq \frac{1}{2}$, then set $T = t - 1$ and exit loop.

- Choose $\alpha_t = \dfrac{1}{2} \ln\left(\dfrac{1 - \epsilon_t}{\epsilon_t}\right).$

- Update, for $i = 1, \ldots, m$:

$$D_{t+1}(i) = \frac{D_t(i)}{Z_t} \times \begin{cases} e^{-\alpha_t} & \text{if } h_t(x_i) = y_i \\ e^{\alpha_t} & \text{if } h_t(x_i) \neq y_i \end{cases}$$

where Z_t is a normalization factor (chosen so that D_{t+1} will be a distribution).

Output the final hypothesis:

$$H(x) = \arg\max_{y \in \mathcal{Y}} \sum_{t=1}^{T} \alpha_t \mathbf{1}\{h_t(x) = y\}.$$

$\frac{1}{2}$ is useless to the boosting algorithm, and generally cannot be converted into one with error below $\frac{1}{2}$. This is a significant difficulty. If such a weak hypothesis is returned by the weak learner, AdaBoost.M1, as we have presented it, simply halts, using only the weak hypotheses that were already computed (although there are other ways one might imagine for dealing with this).

In proving a bound on the training error, as in theorem 3.1, we give a slightly more general proof for the weighted training error with respect to an arbitrary initial distribution D_1.

Theorem 10.1 Given the notation of algorithm 10.1, assume that $\epsilon_t < \frac{1}{2}$ for all t, and let $\gamma_t \doteq \frac{1}{2} - \epsilon_t$. Let D_1 be an arbitrary initial distribution over the training set. Then the weighted training error of AdaBoost.M1's combined classifier H with respect to D_1 is bounded as

$$\mathbf{Pr}_{i \sim D_1}[H(x_i) \neq y_i] \leq \prod_{t=1}^{T} \sqrt{1 - 4\gamma_t^2} \leq \exp\left(-2\sum_{t=1}^{T}\gamma_t^2\right).$$

Proof The proof follows the same outline as in theorem 3.1, so we focus only on the differences from that proof.

First, let

$$F(x, y) \doteq \sum_{t=1}^{T} \alpha_t \left(\mathbf{1}\{y = h_t(x)\} - \mathbf{1}\{y \neq h_t(x)\}\right).$$

Noticing that

$$D_{t+1}(i) = \frac{D_t(i) \exp\left(-\alpha_t \left(\mathbf{1}\{y = h_t(x)\} - \mathbf{1}\{y \neq h_t(x)\}\right)\right)}{Z_t},$$

we can unravel this recurrence to obtain

$$D_{T+1}(i) = \frac{D_1(i)e^{-F(x_i, y_i)}}{\prod_{t=1}^{T} Z_t}.$$

If $H(x) \neq y$, then there exists a label $\ell \neq y$ such that

$$\sum_{t=1}^{T} \alpha_t \mathbf{1}\{y = h_t(x)\} \leq \sum_{t=1}^{T} \alpha_t \mathbf{1}\{\ell = h_t(x)\} \leq \sum_{t=1}^{T} \alpha_t \mathbf{1}\{y \neq h_t(x)\}.$$

The last inequality uses the fact that $\alpha_t \geq 0$ since $\epsilon_t < \frac{1}{2}$. Thus, $H(x) \neq y$ implies that $F(x, y) \leq 0$. Therefore, in general,

$$\mathbf{1}\{H(x) \neq y\} \leq e^{-F(x, y)}.$$

Now the same argument as in equation (3.5) gives that the (weighted) training error is

$$\sum_{i=1}^{m} D_1(i)\mathbf{1}\{H(x_i) \neq y_i\} \leq \prod_{t=1}^{T} Z_t.$$

Finally, the computation of Z_t beginning with equation (3.6) and leading to equation (3.9) is unchanged. ∎

It is disappointing, in the multiclass case, that we need to require such high accuracy, exceeding $\frac{1}{2}$, in order to analyze AdaBoost.M1. In fact, this difficulty turns out to be provably unavoidable when the performance of the weak learner is measured only in terms of error rate. This means that, in a sense, AdaBoost.M1 is the best we can hope for in a multiclass boosting algorithm. To be more precise, we know that in the binary case, a base learner that performs slightly better than random on any distribution can always be used in conjunction with a boosting algorithm to achieve perfect training accuracy (and also arbitrarily good generalization accuracy, given sufficient data). Unfortunately, when $K > 2$, this is simply not possible, in general. We show this next with an example of a weak learner that consistently returns weak classifiers with accuracy significantly better than the random guessing rate of $1/K$, but for which no boosting algorithm can exist that uses such weak classifiers to compute a combined classifier with perfect (training) accuracy.

In this simple three-class example, we suppose that $\mathcal{X} = \{a, b, c\}$, $\mathcal{Y} = \{1, 2, 3\}$, and the training set consists of the three labeled examples $(a, 1)$, $(b, 2)$, and $(c, 3)$. Further, we suppose that we are using a base learner which chooses base classifiers that never distinguish between a and b. In particular, the base learner always chooses one of the following two base classifiers:

$$\hbar_1(x) = \begin{cases} 1 & \text{if } x = a \text{ or } x = b \\ 3 & \text{if } x = c, \end{cases}$$

or

$$\hbar_2(x) = \begin{cases} 2 & \text{if } x = a \text{ or } x = b \\ 3 & \text{if } x = c. \end{cases}$$

Then for any distribution over the training set, since a and b cannot both have weight exceeding $\frac{1}{2}$, it can be argued that either $\hbar_1$ or $\hbar_2$ will have accuracy at least $\frac{1}{2}$ (though not necessarily *exceeding* $\frac{1}{2}$, as would be necessary for theorem 10.1 to be of value here). This is substantially more than the accuracy of $\frac{1}{3}$ which would be achieved by pure random guessing among the three labels of $\mathcal{Y}$. However, regardless of how the training distributions are selected, and regardless of how the collected base classifiers are combined, a final classifier H that bases its predictions only on those of the base hypotheses will necessarily classify a and b in exactly the same way, and therefore will misclassify at least one of them. Thus, the training accuracy of H on the three examples can never exceed $\frac{2}{3}$, so perfect accuracy cannot be achieved by any boosting method. (This argument is somewhat informal in its treatment of the notion of a general boosting algorithm; a more rigorous proof could be devised along the lines of the lower bound proved later in section 13.2.2. See exercise 13.10.)

Despite this limitation, in practice AdaBoost.M1 works quite effectively when using fairly strong base classifiers, such as decision trees and neural networks, which typically are able to find base classifiers with accuracy surpassing $\frac{1}{2}$, even on the difficult distributions constructed by boosting. For instance, in section 1.2.2, we looked at how AdaBoost performs on a range of benchmark datasets using C4.5, the decision-tree learning algorithm, as a base learner. Eleven of the datasets that were used were multiclass, ranging from

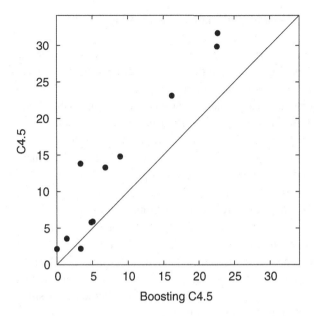

Figure 10.1
A comparison of C4.5 with and without boosting on 11 multiclass benchmark datasets. See figure 1.3 (p. 12) for further explanation.

3 up to 26 classes. Figure 10.1 shows the subset of the results in figure 1.3 that involve these 11 multiclass datasets. From these experiments, we see that AdaBoost.M1, when used in combination with C4.5 (which itself handles multiclass problems directly), gives performance that is strong overall, and apparently is not adversely affected by the 50%-accuracy requirement.

On the other hand, when using the much weaker decision stumps as base hypotheses (which also can be modified directly for multiclass problems), AdaBoost.M1 is not even able to get off the ground on the nine datasets with four or more classes—on each one of these, the best decision stump found on the very first round of boosting already has an error exceeding 50% (which is why AdaBoost.M1 was not used in the experiments reported in section 1.2.2). For the two datasets with exactly three classes, AdaBoost.M1 successfully improves the test error, from 35.2% to 4.7% in one case, and from 37.0% to 9.2% in the other; however, in the second case, a different multiclass method does significantly better, achieving a test error of 4.4%.

Thus, when using weak base classifiers, AdaBoost.M1 is inadequate for multiclass problems. In the remainder of this chapter, as well as in section 11.4, we develop multiclass boosting techniques that place far less stringent demands on the weak learning algorithm (including the method that was actually used in the decision-stump experiments reported in section 1.2.2).

10.2 The One-against-All Reduction and Multi-label Classification

To make boosting possible even with a very weak base learner, in one way or another, the communication between the boosting algorithm and the base learner must be augmented. We will shortly see several examples of how this can be done. As discussed earlier, the multiclass algorithms that we now focus on are generally based on reductions to the binary case. The first of these, called AdaBoost.MH, is based on a "one-against-all" reduction in which the multi-way classification problem is reduced to several binary problems, each asking if a given instance is or is not an example of a particular class. Each of these binary problems could be treated independently, training a separate copy of AdaBoost for each. Here, instead, we pursue a more unified approach in which the binary problems are all handled together and simultaneously in a single run of the boosting algorithm.

Furthermore, in this section, we consider the more general *multi-label* setting in which each example may be assigned more than one class. Such problems arise naturally, for instance, in text categorization problems where the same document (say, a news article) may easily be relevant to more than one general topic; for example, an article about a presidential candidate who throws out the first ball at a major-league baseball game should be classified as belonging to both the "politics" and the "sports" categories.

10.2.1 Multi-label Classification

As before, $\mathcal{Y}$ is a finite set of labels or classes of cardinality K. In the standard single-label classification setting considered up to this point, each example $x \in \mathcal{X}$ is assigned a single class $y \in \mathcal{Y}$ so that labeled examples are pairs (x, y). The goal then, typically, is to find a hypothesis $H : \mathcal{X} \to \mathcal{Y}$ that minimizes the probability that $y \neq H(x)$ on a newly observed example (x, y). In contrast, in the multi-label case, each instance $x \in \mathcal{X}$ may belong to *multiple* labels in $\mathcal{Y}$. Thus, a labeled example is a pair (x, Y) where $Y \subseteq \mathcal{Y}$ is the *set* of labels assigned to x. The single-label case is clearly a special case in which $|Y| = 1$ for all observations.

It is unclear in this setting precisely how to formalize the goal of a learning algorithm and, in general, the "right" formalization may well depend on the problem at hand. One possibility is to seek a hypothesis that attempts to predict just one of the labels assigned to an example. In other words, the goal is to find $H : \mathcal{X} \to \mathcal{Y}$ which minimizes the probability that $H(x) \notin Y$ on a new observation (x, Y). We call this measure the *one-error* of hypothesis H since it measures the probability of not getting even one of the labels correct. We denote the one-error of a hypothesis h with respect to a distribution D over observations (x, Y) by one-err$_D(H)$. That is,

$$\text{one-err}_D(H) \doteq \mathbf{Pr}_{(x,Y) \sim D}[H(x) \notin Y].$$

Note that for single-label classification problems, the one-error is identical to ordinary classification error. In what follows, and in chapter 11, we introduce other loss measures that can be used in the multi-label setting. We begin with one of these called the Hamming loss, and we show how its minimization also leads to an algorithm for the standard single-label multiclass case.

10.2.2 Hamming Loss

Rather than predicting just one label correctly, the goal might instead be to predict all and only all of the correct labels. In this case, the learning algorithm generates a hypothesis that predicts *sets* of labels, and the loss depends on how this predicted set differs from the one that was observed. Thus, $H : \mathcal{X} \to 2^{\mathcal{Y}}$ and, with respect to a distribution D, the loss is

$$\frac{1}{K} \cdot \mathbf{E}_{(x,Y) \sim D}[\ |H(x) \bigtriangleup Y|\ ] \tag{10.1}$$

where $A \bigtriangleup B$ denotes the *symmetric difference* between two sets A and B, that is, the set of elements in exactly one of the two sets. (The $1/K$ appearing in equation (10.1) is meant merely to ensure a value in $[0, 1]$.) We call this measure the *Hamming loss* of H, and we denote it by $\mathrm{hloss}_D(H)$.

When D is the empirical distribution (that is, the uniform distribution over the m training examples), we denote this empirical Hamming loss by $\widehat{\mathrm{hloss}}(H)$. Similarly, empirical one-error is denoted $\widehat{\mathrm{one\text{-}err}}(H)$.

To minimize Hamming loss, we can, in a natural way, decompose the problem into K orthogonal binary classification problems following the intuitive one-against-all approach that was described earlier. That is, we can think of Y as specifying K binary labels, each depending on whether some label y is or is not included in Y. Similarly, $H(x)$ can be viewed as K binary predictions. The Hamming loss then can be regarded as an average of the error rate of H on these K binary problems.

For $Y \subseteq \mathcal{Y}$, let us define $Y[\ell]$ for $\ell \in \mathcal{Y}$ to indicate ℓ's inclusion in Y:

$$Y[\ell] \doteq \begin{cases} +1 & \text{if } \ell \in Y \\ -1 & \text{if } \ell \notin Y. \end{cases} \tag{10.2}$$

Thus, we can identify any subset Y with a vector in $\{-1, +1\}^K$ or, equivalently, a function mapping $\mathcal{Y}$ to $\{-1, +1\}$. Throughout this chapter, we will move fluidly between these two equivalent representations of Y either as a subset or as a binary vector/function. To simplify notation, we also identify any function $H : \mathcal{X} \to 2^{\mathcal{Y}}$ with a corresponding two-argument function $H : \mathcal{X} \times \mathcal{Y} \to \{-1, +1\}$ defined by

$$H(x, \ell) \doteq H(x)[\ell] = \begin{cases} +1 & \text{if } \ell \in H(x) \\ -1 & \text{if } \ell \notin H(x). \end{cases}$$

The Hamming loss given in equation (10.1) can then be rewritten as

Algorithm 10.2
AdaBoost.MH: A multiclass, multi-label version of AdaBoost based on Hamming loss

---

Given: $(x_1, Y_1), \ldots, (x_m, Y_m)$ where $x_i \in \mathcal{X}$, $Y_i \subseteq \mathcal{Y}$.
Initialize: $D_1(i, \ell) = 1/(mK)$ for $i = 1, \ldots, m$ and $\ell \in \mathcal{Y}$ (where $K = |\mathcal{Y}|$).
For $t = 1, \ldots, T$:

- Train weak learner using distribution D_t.

- Get weak hypothesis $h_t : \mathcal{X} \times \mathcal{Y} \to \mathbb{R}$.

- Choose $\alpha_t \in \mathbb{R}$.

- Aim: select h_t and α_t to minimalize the normalization factor

$$Z_t \doteq \sum_{i=1}^{m} \sum_{\ell \in \mathcal{Y}} D_t(i, \ell) \exp(-\alpha_t \, Y_i[\ell] \, h_t(x_i, \ell)).$$

- Update, for $i = 1, \ldots, m$ and for $\ell \in \mathcal{Y}$:

$$D_{t+1}(i, \ell) = \frac{D_t(i, \ell) \exp(-\alpha_t \, Y_i[\ell] \, h_t(x_i, \ell))}{Z_t}.$$

Output the final hypothesis:

$$H(x, \ell) = \mathrm{sign}\left(\sum_{t=1}^{T} \alpha_t h_t(x, \ell) \right).$$

$$\frac{1}{K} \sum_{\ell \in \mathcal{Y}} \mathbf{Pr}_{(x,Y) \sim D}[\, H(x, \ell) \neq Y[\ell]\,].$$

(Technically, we sometimes allow H to output a prediction of 0 which, in this definition, is always counted as an error.)

With the above reduction to binary classification in mind, it is rather straightforward to see how to use boosting to minimize Hamming loss. The main idea of the reduction is simply to replace each training example (x_i, Y_i) by K examples $((x_i, \ell), Y_i[\ell])$ for $\ell \in \mathcal{Y}$. In other words, each instance is actually a pair of the form (x_i, ℓ) whose binary label is $+1$ if $\ell \in Y_i$, and -1 otherwise. The result is the boosting algorithm called *AdaBoost.MH—M* for multiclass, H for Hamming. As shown in algorithm 10.2, the procedure maintains a distribution D_t over examples i and labels ℓ. On round t, the weak learner accepts the distribution D_t (as well as the training set), and generates a weak hypothesis $h_t : \mathcal{X} \times \mathcal{Y} \to \mathbb{R}$. In this way, the communication between the booster and the weak learner is significantly richer than in Ada-Boost.M1, where both D_t and h_t were of a much simpler form. We can interpret $h_t(x, \ell)$ as a confidence-rated prediction of whether label ℓ should or should not be assigned to example x, as indicated by the sign of the prediction (with the magnitude measuring confidence). Our reduction also leads to the choice of final hypothesis shown in the algorithm.

Note that we have adopted a general approach that admits the use of confidence-rated predictions as in chapter 9. As such, we have left α_t unspecified. Continuing with this approach, we can see that the analysis for the binary case given by theorem 9.1 can be combined with the reduction used to derive this algorithm, yielding the following bound on the Hamming loss of the final hypothesis:

Theorem 10.2 Assuming the notation of algorithm 10.2, the empirical Hamming loss of AdaBoost.MH's final hypothesis H is at most

$$\widehat{\mathrm{hloss}}(H) \le \prod_{t=1}^{T} Z_t.$$

We can immediately adapt ideas from chapter 9 to this binary classification problem. As before, theorem 10.2 suggests that our goal, in the choice of both h_t and α_t, should be to minimalize

$$Z_t \doteq \sum_{i=1}^{m} \sum_{\ell \in \mathcal{Y}} D_t(i, \ell) \exp(-\alpha_t \, Y_i[\ell] \, h_t(x_i, \ell)) \tag{10.3}$$

on each round. For instance, if we require that each h_t have range $\{-1, +1\}$, then we should choose

$$\alpha_t = \frac{1}{2} \ln \left(\frac{1 - \epsilon_t}{\epsilon_t} \right) \tag{10.4}$$

where

$$\epsilon_t \doteq \mathbf{Pr}_{(i,\ell) \sim D_t}[h_t(x_i, \ell) \ne Y_i[\ell]]$$

can be thought of as a weighted Hamming loss with respect to D_t. As before, this choice gives

$$Z_t = 2\sqrt{\epsilon_t(1 - \epsilon_t)}.$$

So, to minimize Z_t, the weak learning algorithm should choose ϵ_t as far from $\frac{1}{2}$ as possible; in other words, it should seek to minimize the Hamming loss weighted by D_t. Note that, as in the binary case, if the base classifier guesses randomly, then ϵ_t will be equal to $\frac{1}{2}$; moreover, any value of ϵ_t that is bounded away from $\frac{1}{2}$ will give Z_t that is strictly less than 1, thus ensuring eventual perfect training accuracy. Thus, whereas AdaBoost.M1 required a weak learning algorithm that must be very substantially better than random, we see that AdaBoost.MH can be used with any weak learner that is just slightly better than random guessing.

We also can combine these ideas with those in section 9.2.6 on domain-partitioning weak hypotheses. As in that section, suppose that h is associated with a partition $X_1, \ldots, X_J$ of the space $\mathcal{X}$. It is natural then to create a partition of the set $\mathcal{X} \times \mathcal{Y}$ consisting of all sets $X_j \times \{\ell\}$ for $j = 1, \ldots, J$ and $\ell \in \mathcal{Y}$. An appropriate hypothesis h can then be formed which predicts $h(x, \ell) = c_{j\ell}$ for $x \in X_j$. Applied to the current setting, equation (9.15) implies that we should choose

$$c_{j\ell} = \frac{1}{2} \ln \left(\frac{W_+^{j\ell}}{W_-^{j\ell}} \right) \tag{10.5}$$

where

$$W_b^{j\ell} \doteq \sum_{i=1}^{m} D(i, \ell) \mathbf{1}\{x_i \in X_j \wedge Y_i[\ell] = b\}.$$

(In this case, as in section 9.2.6, the α_t's are fixed to be 1.) By equation (9.16), this choice of $c_{j\ell}$ gives

$$Z_t = 2 \sum_{j=1}^{J} \sum_{\ell \in \mathcal{Y}} \sqrt{W_+^{j\ell} W_-^{j\ell}}. \tag{10.6}$$

So, in a manner similar to that described in section 9.2.6 for the binary case, we can design base learners that seek domain-partitioning base classifiers, such as (multi-label) decision stumps, based on the criterion in equation (10.6), and giving real-valued predictions as in equation (10.5).

10.2.3   Relation to One-Error and Single-Label Classification

We can use AdaBoost.MH even when the goal is to minimize one-error. Perhaps the most natural way to do this is to define a classifier H^1 that predicts the label y for which the weighted sum of the weak-hypothesis predictions in favor of y is greatest; that is,

$$H^1(x) = \arg\max_{y \in \mathcal{Y}} \sum_{t=1}^{T} \alpha_t h_t(x, y). \tag{10.7}$$

The next simple theorem relates the one-error of H^1 and the Hamming loss of H.

Theorem 10.3 With respect to any distribution D over observations (x, Y) with $\emptyset \neq Y \subseteq \mathcal{Y}$,

$$\text{one-err}_D(H^1) \leq K \, \text{hloss}_D(H)$$

(where $K = |\mathcal{Y}|$).

Proof Assume $Y \neq \emptyset$ and suppose $H^1(x) \notin Y$. We argue that this implies that $H(x, \ell) \neq Y[\ell]$ for some $\ell \in \mathcal{Y}$. First, suppose the maximum in equation (10.7) is strictly positive, and let $\ell = H^1(x)$ realize the maximum. Then $H(x, \ell) = +1$ (since the maximum is positive), but $Y[\ell] = -1$ since $\ell \notin Y$. On the other hand, if the maximum in equation (10.7) is non-positive, then $H(x, \ell)$ is 0 or -1 for all $\ell \in \mathcal{Y}$, but $Y[\ell] = +1$ for some $\ell \in \mathcal{Y}$ since Y is not empty.

Thus, in either case, if $H^1(x) \notin Y$, then $H(x, \ell) \neq Y[\ell]$ for some $\ell \in \mathcal{Y}$. This implies that

$$\mathbf{1}\{H^1(x) \notin Y\} \leq \sum_{\ell \in \mathcal{Y}} \mathbf{1}\{H(x, \ell) \neq Y[\ell]\},$$

which, taking expectations of both sides with respect to $(x, Y) \sim D$, yields the theorem. ∎

In particular, this means that AdaBoost.MH can be applied to single-label multiclass classification problems. Combining theorems 10.2 and 10.3 results in a bound on the training error of the final hypothesis H^1 that is at most

$$K \prod_{t=1}^{T} Z_t \tag{10.8}$$

where Z_t is as in equation (10.3). In fact, theorem 10.4 below will imply a better bound of

$$\frac{K}{2} \prod_{t=1}^{T} Z_t \tag{10.9}$$

for the one-error of AdaBoost.MH when applied to single-label problems. Moreover, the leading constant $K/2$ can be improved somewhat by assuming without loss of generality that, prior to examining any of the data, a 0-th weak hypothesis is chosen that predicts -1 on all example-label pairs; that is, $h_0 \equiv -1$. For this weak hypothesis, $\epsilon_0 = 1/K$, and Z_0 is minimized by setting $\alpha_0 = \frac{1}{2} \ln(K-1)$, which gives $Z_0 = 2\sqrt{K-1}/K$. Plugging into the bound of equation (10.9), we therefore get an improved bound of

$$\frac{K}{2} \prod_{t=0}^{T} Z_t = \sqrt{K-1} \prod_{t=1}^{T} Z_t.$$

This hack is equivalent to modifying algorithm 10.2 only in the manner in which D_1 is initialized. Specifically, D_1 should be chosen so that

$$D_1(i, \ell) = \begin{cases} 1/(2m) & \text{if } \ell = y_i \\ 1/[2m(K-1)] & \text{else.} \end{cases}$$

Note that H^1 is unaffected.

An alternative to the approach taken in equation (10.7) would choose any label y for which $H(x, y) = +1$. This approach has the advantage of being less specific to the representation used by the learning algorithm but, on the other hand, fails to take into account the strength of the predictions for each class, which we expect to be highly informative. It will be possible to obtain an analysis of this alternate approach for single-label problems as a special case of theorem 10.4.

10.3 Application to Semantic Classification

As a typical example of how these ideas can be applied, consider the problem of categorizing the type of call requested by a phone customer of the telecommunications company AT&T. Some examples of spoken customer utterances and their correct classifications are shown in table 10.2. In this problem, there are 15 predefined categories, shown in table 10.1, intended to capture the caller's intention. Most of these are requests for information or specific services, or instructions on how a call is to be billed. Note that this is in fact a multi-label problem—the same utterance may have multiple labels.

To apply boosting, we can use AdaBoost.MH since it is designed for such multiclass, multi-label problems. We next need to select or design a base learning algorithm. Here, we choose the very simple decision stumps mentioned above. Specifically, each such classifier first tests a given document for the presence or absence of a particular term. A "term" can be a single word (such as *collect*), a pair of adjacent words (such as *my home*), or a possibly sparse triple of adjacent words (such as *person ? person*, which will match any word in place of the question mark, such as in the phrase "person to person"). The presence or absence of a term partitions the domain of all possible documents into two disjoint sets, so

Table 10.1
The classes in the call classification task

AC	AreaCode	CM	Competitor	RA	Rate
AS	AttService	DM	DialForMe	3N	ThirdNumber
BC	BillingCredit	DI	Directory	TI	Time
CC	CallingCard	HO	HowToDial	TC	TimeCharge
CO	Collect	PP	PersonToPerson	OT	Other

Table 10.2
Some typical example utterances and their classifications in the call classification task

yes I'd like to place a collect call long distance please	Collect
operator I need to make a call but I need to bill it to my office	ThirdNumber
yes I'd like to place a call on my master card please	CallingCard
I'm trying to make a calling card call to five five five one two one two in chicago	CallingCard, DialForMe
I just called a number in sioux city and I musta rang the wrong number because I got the wrong party and I would like to have that taken off of my bill	BillingCredit
yeah I need to make a collect call to bob	Collect, PersonToPerson

we can apply the techniques of section 10.2.2 to define a criterion for selecting the "best" base classifier on each round (equation (10.6)), and also for selecting a set of values for every label which will be output by the base classifier, depending on whether or not the term is present.

This leads to base classifiers of the form given in figures 10.2 and 10.3, which show the first several base classifiers found by boosting on the actual dataset. For instance, the second one says roughly in words:

If the word *card* appears in what was said, then predict positively for the class CallingCard with high confidence, and negatively (with varying degrees of confidence) for each of the other classes; otherwise, if *card* does not appear, then predict negatively for the CallingCard class, and abstain on each of the other classes.

Many of the terms found seem natural for this task, such as *collect*, *card*, *my home*, and *person ? person*. This suggests boosting's usefulness for selecting "features" from a very large space of candidates. It is curious, however, that on many rounds, terms that seem unimportant are chosen, such as *I*, *how*, and *and*. In such cases, it may be that these words are more useful than might be guessed, perhaps because they are used or not used in typical phrasings of these sorts of requests. In the case of *and* on round 13, we see in fact that all of the predictions are low confidence, suggesting that this term, although selected, is rather unimportant.

As can be seen on this dataset, boosting can also be used as a method for identifying outliers. This is because such mislabeled or highly ambiguous examples tend to receive the most weight under the distributions computed by boosting. For example, table 10.3 is a list of some of the examples with the highest weight under the final distribution computed by boosting. Most of these examples are indeed outliers, many of which are clearly mislabeled. In practice, once identified, such examples could either be removed entirely from the dataset, or their labels corrected by hand.

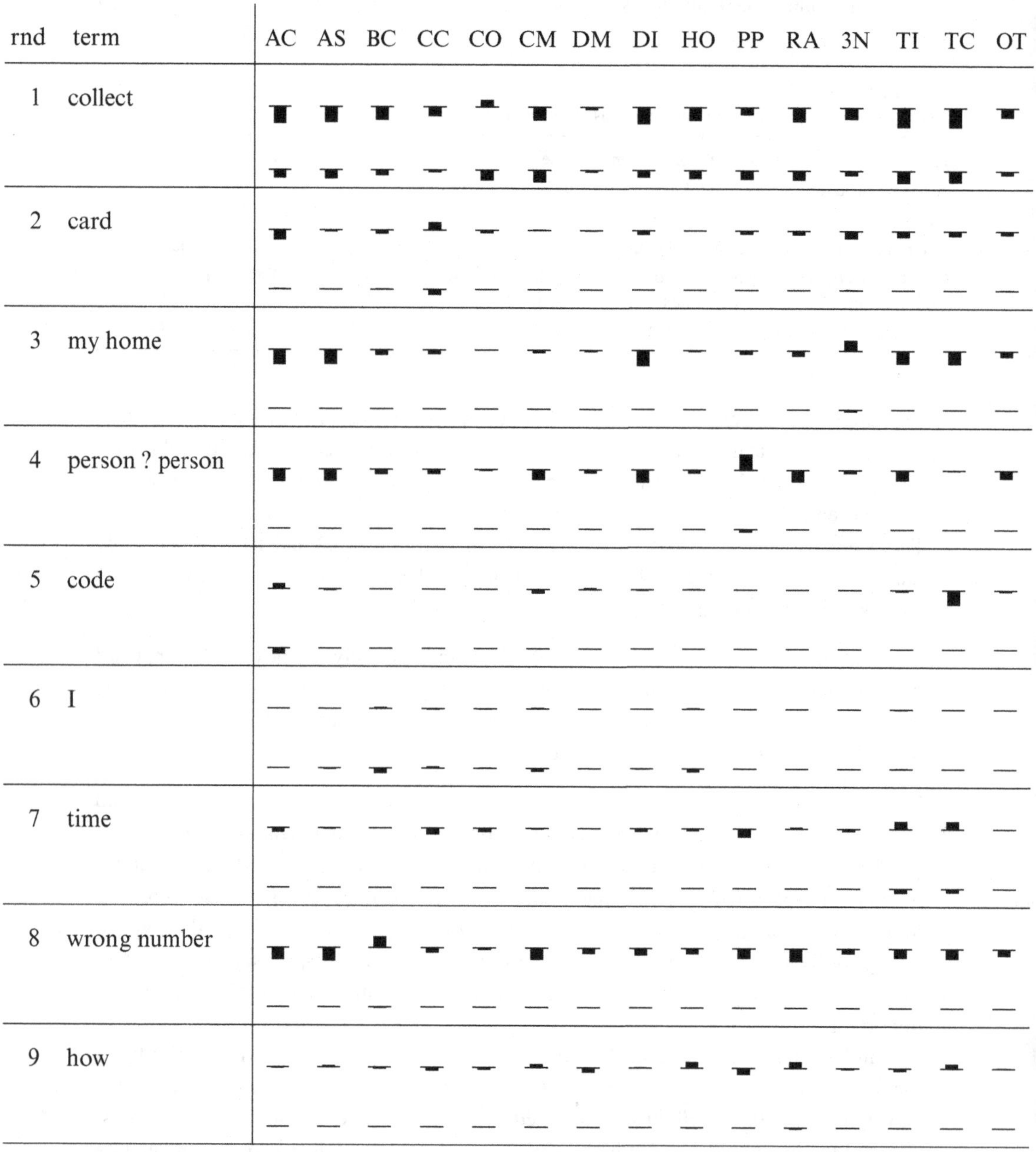

rnd	term	AC	AS	BC	CC	CO	CM	DM	DI	HO	PP	RA	3N	TI	TC	OT

Figure 10.2
The first nine weak hypotheses found when confidence-rated AdaBoost.MH is run on the call classification task using the weak learning algorithm described in the text. Each weak hypothesis has the following form and interpretation: If the term associated with the weak hypothesis occurs in the given document, then output the first row of values; otherwise, output the second row of values. Here, each value, represented graphically as a bar, gives the output of the weak hypothesis for one of the classes, which may be positive or negative.

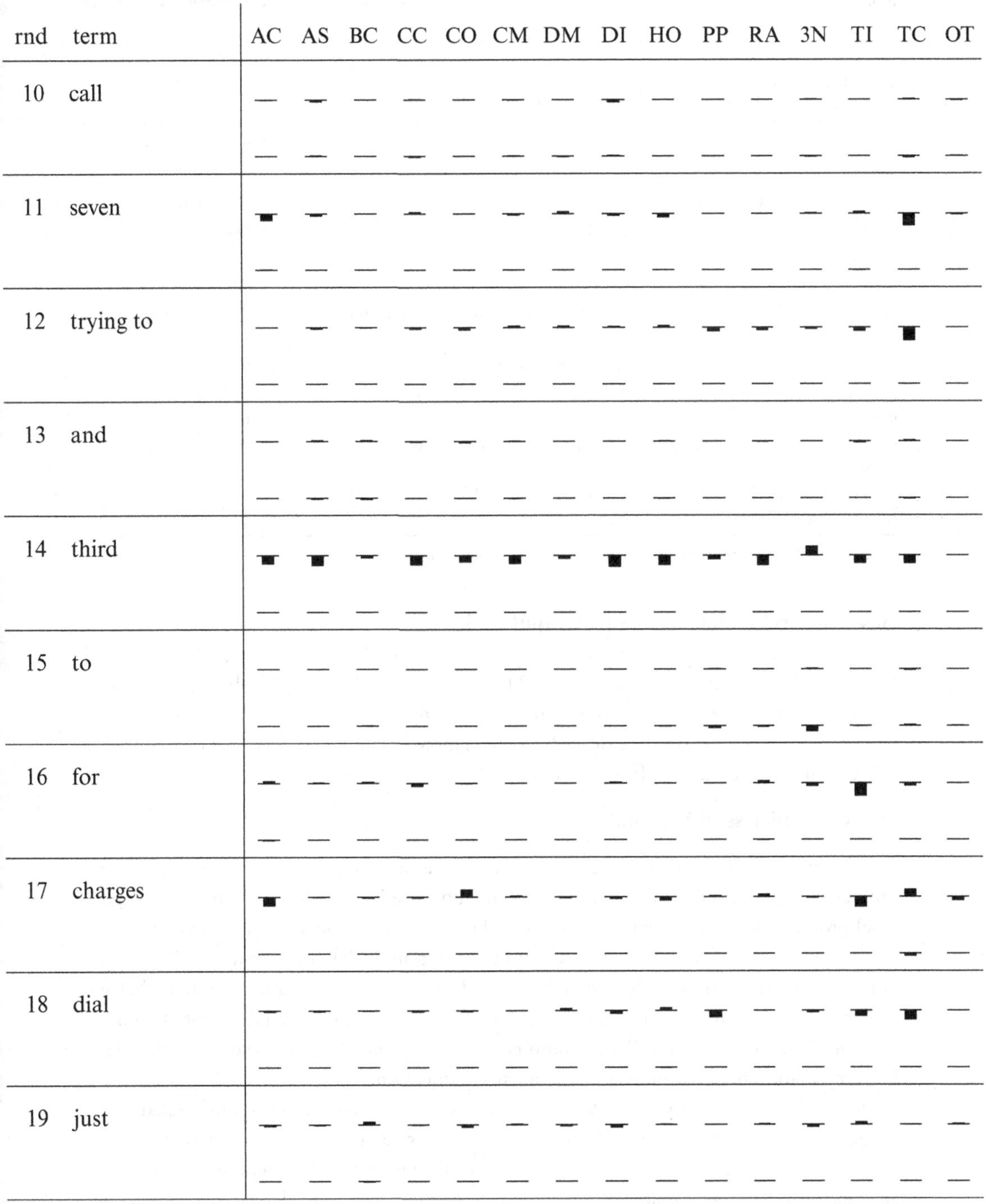

rnd	term	AC	AS	BC	CC	CO	CM	DM	DI	HO	PP	RA	3N	TI	TC	OT
10	call															
11	seven															
12	trying to															
13	and															
14	third															
15	to															
16	for															
17	charges															
18	dial															
19	just															

Figure 10.3
The next ten weak hypotheses (continuing figure 10.2).

Table 10.3
Examples with the highest final weight on the call classification task

I'm trying to make a credit card call	Collect
hello	Rate
yes I'd like to make a long distance collect call please	CallingCard
calling card please	Collect
yeah I'd like to use my calling card number	Collect
can I get a collect call	CallingCard
yes I would like to make a long distant telephone call and have the charges billed to another number	CallingCard, DialForMe
yeah I can not stand it this morning I did oversea call is so bad	BillingCredit
yeah special offers going on for long distance	AttService, Rate
mister xxxxx please william xxxxx	PersonToPerson
yes ma'am I I'm trying to make a long distance call to a non dialable point in san miguel philippines	AttService, Other
yes I like to make a long distance call and charge it to my home phone that's where I'm calling at my home	DialForMe

Many of the labels supplied by human annotators are obviously incorrect.

10.4   General Reductions Using Output Codes

As described in section 10.2, AdaBoost.MH solves multiclass single-label classification problems by reducing to a set of binary problems using a very straightforward one-against-all approach. In this section, we describe a much more general technique that encompasses a large family of reductions from multiclass to binary.

10.4.1   Multiclass to Multi-label

In fact, we can think about these reductions formally as mappings from the given single-label problem to a multi-label formulation. The method used in section 10.2 maps a single-label problem into a multi-label problem in the simplest and most obvious way, namely, by mapping each single-label observation (x, y) to a multi-label observation $(x, \{y\})$. In other words, an example with label y is mapped to a multi-label example with a label set consisting of the singleton $\{y\}$, meaning that y is the one and only label that should be associated with this instance. When combined with AdaBoost.MH, the result is a multiclass boosting algorithm based on this one-against-all reduction.

However, it is generally possible, and often desirable, to use a more sophisticated mapping corresponding to some other multiclass-to-binary reduction. In general, we can use any injective (one-to-one) mapping $\Omega : \mathcal{Y} \to 2^{\overline{\mathcal{Y}}}$ for this purpose. This mapping specifies how each example should be relabeled or "coded" to create a new multi-label example. In particular, each example (x, y) gets mapped to $(x, \Omega(y))$; that is, every label y is replaced by multi-label set $\Omega(y)$. Note that Ω maps to subsets of an unspecified label set $\overline{\mathcal{Y}}$ of cardinality

$\overline{K} = |\overline{\mathcal{Y}}|$ which typically is not the same as $\mathcal{Y}$. Intuitively, each element $\overline{y}$ of $\overline{\mathcal{Y}}$ is a binary question or dichotomy. Examples (x, y) (in the original problem) for which $\overline{y} \in \Omega(y)$ are positive examples for class $\overline{y}$, while those for which $\overline{y} \notin \Omega(y)$ are the negative examples of $\overline{y}$. Equivalently, we can identify Ω with a $K \times \overline{K}$ $\{-1, +1\}$-valued *coding matrix* where

$$\Omega(y, \overline{y}) \doteq \Omega(y)[\overline{y}] = \begin{cases} +1 & \text{if } \overline{y} \in \Omega(y) \\ -1 & \text{else,} \end{cases}$$

and where we continue to identify $\Omega(y)$, a subset, with a vector in $\{-1, +1\}^{\overline{K}}$. Each $\overline{y} \in \overline{\mathcal{Y}}$ corresponds, then, to a binary question in which each example (x, y) (in the original problem) is given the binary label $\Omega(y, \overline{y})$.

For example, the reduction of section 10.2 is obtained simply by setting $\overline{\mathcal{Y}} = \mathcal{Y}$ and $\Omega(y) = \{y\}$ for all y. A more interesting example is given in table 10.4. At the top is a sample coding matrix Ω mapping the original label set $\mathcal{Y} = \{a, b, c, d\}$ to the mapped label set $\overline{\mathcal{Y}} = \{1, 2, 3\}$. According to this coding, label 1 in $\overline{\mathcal{Y}}$ asks if an example's label is in $\{a, d\}$ or if it is in the complement $\{b, c\}$; label 2 asks if it is in $\{a, b\}$ or $\{c, d\}$; and label 3 asks if it is in $\{b, c, d\}$ or $\{a\}$. So columns of this matrix can be viewed as binary problems or dichotomies between one set of labels and another. The rows, on the other hand, can be viewed as binary "codewords" that encode the original set of labels: a as $\langle +1, +1, -1 \rangle$, b as $\langle -1, +1, +1 \rangle$, and so on. The bottom of the figure shows how a small dataset would be relabeled by Ω. We can regard the mapped labels either as multi-label sets or as the

Table 10.4
A sample coding matrix (top) and its effect on a sample dataset (bottom)

Ω	1	2	3
a	+1	+1	−1
b	−1	+1	+1
c	−1	−1	+1
d	+1	−1	+1

	Dichotomies			
original	1	2	3	multi-label
$(x_1, a) \rightarrow$	$(x_1, +1)$	$(x_1, +1)$	$(x_1, -1)$	$= (x_1, \{1, 2\})$
$(x_2, c) \rightarrow$	$(x_2, -1)$	$(x_2, -1)$	$(x_2, +1)$	$= (x_2, \{3\})$
$(x_3, a) \rightarrow$	$(x_3, +1)$	$(x_3, +1)$	$(x_3, -1)$	$= (x_3, \{1, 2\})$
$(x_4, d) \rightarrow$	$(x_4, +1)$	$(x_4, -1)$	$(x_4, +1)$	$= (x_4, \{1, 3\})$
$(x_5, b) \rightarrow$	$(x_5, -1)$	$(x_5, +1)$	$(x_5, +1)$	$= (x_5, \{2, 3\})$

A multiclass, single-label example in the original dataset (on the left of the bottom table) gets mapped to three binary examples, one for each of the three dichotomies associated with this code (middle columns) or, equivalently, to a single, multi-label example (right column).

binary labels of the three dichotomies defined by the columns of Ω. For instance, (x_3, a) gets mapped to the multi-labeled example $(x_3, \{1, 2\})$ or, equivalently, it can be viewed as a positive example for dichotomies 1 and 2, and a negative example for dichotomy 3.

Once such a multi-label formulation Ω has been chosen, we can apply AdaBoost.MH directly to the transformed, multi-labeled training set. The result is a learning method that attempts to solve all of the binary problems associated with Ω simultaneously. Because this mapping is arbitrary, the technique and analysis that we now describe are quite general, and can be applied to any multiclass-to-binary reduction.

After applying AdaBoost.MH to the transformed data, how should we classify a new instance x? The most direct idea is to evaluate AdaBoost.MH's final classifier H on x, and then to choose the label $y \in \mathcal{Y}$ for which the mapped codeword $\Omega(y)$ is closest in Hamming distance (that is, the number of coordinates where two binary vectors disagree) to $H(x, \cdot)$. In other words, we predict the label y which minimizes

$$\sum_{\overline{y} \in \overline{\mathcal{Y}}} \mathbf{1}\{\Omega(y, \overline{y}) \neq H(x, \overline{y})\}.$$

This is called *Hamming decoding*.

A weakness of this approach is that it ignores the confidence with which each label was included or not included in the label set predicted by H. An alternative approach is to predict that label y which, if it had been paired with x in the training set, would have caused (x, y) to be given the smallest total weight under the final distribution for the reduction induced by Ω, and thus most closely fits the learned combined hypothesis. In other words, the idea is to predict the label y which minimizes

$$\sum_{\overline{y} \in \overline{\mathcal{Y}}} \exp(-\Omega(y, \overline{y}) \, F(x, \overline{y}))$$

where $F(x, \overline{y}) \doteq \sum_{t=1}^{T} \alpha_t h_t(x, \overline{y})$ is the weighted sum of weak hypotheses output by Ada-Boost.MH. This expression also represents the exponential loss (see section 7.1) associated with example (x, y) for this reduction. We therefore call this approach *loss-based decoding*. The resulting algorithm is called *AdaBoost.MO*—*M* for multiclass, *O* for output coding. Pseudocode is given as algorithm 10.3, including both Hamming and loss-based decoding variants.

How should we choose the code Ω? The one-against-all reduction corresponds to a square matrix with $+1$ on the diagonal and -1 in all other entries, as shown at the top of table 10.5 for a four-class problem. Intuitively, however, it is often desirable to map different labels to sets or codewords which are far from one another, say, in terms of their symmetric difference, or Hamming distance. Such a reduction will be richly redundant, and thus robust in the information that each binary problem provides. The idea is that if all of the codewords are far apart, then even if $H(x, \cdot)$ is incorrect in its predictions on many of the mapped labels, the codeword corresponding to the correct label will remain the closest, so that the overall prediction will still be correct.

Algorithm 10.3
AdaBoost.MO: A multiclass version of AdaBoost based on output codes

---

Given: $(x_1, y_1), \ldots, (x_m, y_m)$ where $x_i \in \mathcal{X}$, $y_i \in \mathcal{Y}$
    output code $\Omega : \mathcal{Y} \to 2^{\overline{\mathcal{Y}}}$.

- Run AdaBoost.MH on relabeled data: $(x_1, \Omega(y_1)), \ldots, (x_m, \Omega(y_m))$.
- Get back final hypothesis H of form $H(x, \overline{y}) = \mathrm{sign}(F(x, \overline{y}))$
    where $F(x, \overline{y}) \doteq \sum_{t=1}^{T} \alpha_t h_t(x, \overline{y})$.
- Output modified final hypothesis:

$$H^{ham}(x) = \arg\min_{y \in \mathcal{Y}} \sum_{\overline{y} \in \overline{\mathcal{Y}}} \mathbf{1}\{\Omega(y, \overline{y}) \neq H(x, \overline{y})\} \quad \text{(Hamming decoding)}$$

or

$$H^{lb}(x) = \arg\min_{y \in \mathcal{Y}} \sum_{\overline{y} \in \overline{\mathcal{Y}}} \exp\left(-\Omega(y, \overline{y}) F(x, \overline{y})\right) \quad \text{(loss-based decoding)}.$$

This is the essence of an approach known as *error-correcting output coding* which uses codes that have been designed with exactly such an error-correcting property. Note that when $\overline{K}$ is not too small, even an entirely random code Ω is likely to have this property. Alternatively, when K is not too large, we can use a *complete* code consisting of all possible dichotomies of the labels, as shown at the bottom of table 10.5. In all such codes, the Hamming distance between any pair of rows will be roughly $\overline{K}/2$ (or better), compared to just 2 for the one-against-all code.

In some domains, a binary coding of the labels may already be naturally defined by the nature of the problem. For instance, if classifying phonemes, each class (phoneme) may be naturally described by a set of binary features: voiced or unvoiced, vowel or consonant, fricative or not, and so on. The code Ω then can correspond to the values of each of these binary output features for each phoneme.

Theorem 10.4 formalizes the intuitions above, giving a bound on the training error in terms of the quality of the code as measured by the minimum distance (or symmetric difference) between any pair of codewords. We do not give a proof of the theorem because it will follow as an immediate special case of theorem 10.5 below.

Theorem 10.4 Assuming the notation of algorithm 10.3 and algorithm 10.2 (viewed as a subroutine), let

$$\rho = \min_{\ell_1, \ell_2 \in \mathcal{Y} : \ell_1 \neq \ell_2} |\Omega(\ell_1) \triangle \Omega(\ell_2)| . \tag{10.10}$$

Table 10.5
The one-against-all (top) and complete (bottom) coding matrices for a four-class problem

Ω				
a	+1	−1	−1	−1
b	−1	+1	−1	−1
c	−1	−1	+1	−1
d	−1	−1	−1	+1

Ω							
a	+1	−1	−1	−1	+1	+1	−1
b	−1	+1	−1	−1	+1	−1	+1
c	−1	−1	+1	−1	−1	+1	+1
d	−1	−1	−1	+1	−1	−1	−1

Names for the columns or dichotomies have been omitted. The complete code omits degenerate dichotomies which are all +1 or all −1, and also any dichotomy which is the negation of one that has already been included.

When run with this choice of Ω, the training error of AdaBoost.MO is upper bounded by

$$\frac{2\overline{K}}{\rho} \cdot \widehat{\text{hloss}}(H) \le \frac{2\overline{K}}{\rho} \prod_{t=1}^{T} Z_t$$

for Hamming decoding, and by

$$\frac{\overline{K}}{\rho} \prod_{t=1}^{T} Z_t$$

for loss-based decoding (where $\overline{K} = |\overline{\mathcal{Y}}|$).

We can use theorem 10.4 to improve the bound in equation (10.8) for AdaBoost.MH to that in equation (10.9) when applied to single-label multiclass problems. We apply theorem 10.4 to the code defined by $\Omega(y) = \{y\}$ for all $y \in \mathcal{Y}$. Clearly, $\rho = 2$ in this case. Moreover, we claim that H^1, as defined in equation (10.7), produces predictions identical to those generated by H^{lb} when using loss-based decoding in AdaBoost.MO. This is because

$$\sum_{\overline{y} \in \mathcal{Y}} \exp\left(-\Omega(y, \overline{y})\, F(x, \overline{y})\right) = e^{-F(x,y)} - e^{F(x,y)} + \sum_{\overline{y} \in \mathcal{Y}} e^{F(x,\overline{y})},$$

so that the minimum over y is attained when $F(x, y)$ is maximized. Applying theorem 10.4 now gives the bound in equation (10.9).

Although an improvement, these bounds for AdaBoost.MH are still rather poor in the sense that they depend strongly on the number of classes K, and thus will be weak on problems with a large number of classes. In fact, when using codes with strong error-correcting properties, theorem 10.4 indicates that there does not need to be an explicit dependence on the number of classes. For instance, if the code Ω is chosen at random (uniformly among all possible codes), then, for large $\overline{K}$, we expect $\rho/\overline{K}$ to approach $\frac{1}{2}$. In this case, the leading coefficients in the bounds of theorem 10.4 approach 4 for Hamming decoding, and 2 for loss-based decoding, independent of the number of classes K in the original label set $\mathcal{Y}$. This suggests that the method may be highly effective on problems with a large number of classes. However, there is an important trade-off here: When a random code Ω is used, the resulting binary problems, which are defined by a random partition of the classes, may be highly unnatural, making it difficult to learn these underlying binary problems.

10.4.2   More General Codes

The output-coding approach described so far requires that every dichotomy of the classes to be learned must involve *all* of the classes. This is potentially a limitation since such binary problems can be exceedingly difficult to learn due to their unnaturalness. For instance, if attempting to optically recognize handwritten digits, it may be very hard to learn to distinguish digits belonging to the set $\{0, 1, 5, 6, 9\}$ from those belonging to $\{2, 3, 4, 7, 8\}$. The problem is that such unnatural, disjunctive concepts are highly complex and difficult to characterize.

For this reason, it is sometimes advantageous to use dichotomies that involve only a *subset* of the classes. For instance, in the example above, we might attempt to learn to distinguish digits in the set $\{1, 7\}$ from those in the set $\{0, 6\}$. A classifier trained for this task would be expected to give accurate predictions only when presented with examples from one of the target classes, in this case, 0, 1, 6, or 7; nothing would be expected of its performance on examples belonging to other classes.

Such a dichotomy involving just a few of the classes is likely to be much simpler, and thus easier to learn. At an extreme, we can consider distinguishing just one class from one other, for instance, distinguishing 3's from 7's, a problem that surely should be easier than the complex dichotomy above involving all 10 classes. When one binary problem is solved for each of the $\binom{K}{2}$ pairs of classes, this leads to the *all-pairs* approach discussed further below.

The output-coding framework outlined above can be extended to accommodate dichotomies involving only a subset of the classes. We saw earlier that the code Ω can be viewed as a matrix of $\{-1, +1\}$ values, an interpretation that we adopt henceforth, abandoning our earlier alternative view of Ω as a mapping to multi-label sets. Furthermore, we now allow entries of Ω to take the value 0 so that as a function, Ω maps $\mathcal{Y} \times \overline{\mathcal{Y}}$ to $\{-1, 0, +1\}$. We interpret the value 0 for entry $\Omega(y, \overline{y})$ to be an indication that class y is irrelevant for dichotomy $\overline{y}$, and thus that a classifier's predictions on examples with this label are immaterial. Such examples are simply ignored during training.

For instance, Ω may be a matrix such as the one at the top of table 10.6. Here, dichotomy 1 asks if an example's class belongs to the set $\{a\}$ or if it belongs to $\{b, d\}$, with examples in

Table 10.6
Another sample coding matrix (top), and its effect on a sample dataset (bottom)

Ω	1	2	3
a	+1	−1	−1
b	−1	0	+1
c	0	+1	−1
d	−1	0	−1

	Dichotomies		
Original	1	2	3
$(x_1, a) \rightarrow$	$(x_1, +1)$	$(x_1, -1)$	$(x_1, -1)$
$(x_2, c) \rightarrow$		$(x_2, +1)$	$(x_2, -1)$
$(x_3, a) \rightarrow$	$(x_3, +1)$	$(x_3, -1)$	$(x_3, -1)$
$(x_4, d) \rightarrow$	$(x_4, -1)$		$(x_4, -1)$
$(x_5, b) \rightarrow$	$(x_5, -1)$		$(x_5, +1)$

Similar to table 10.4, each multiclass, single-label example in the original dataset is mapped to binary examples
in the three dichotomies of this code. Now, however, some of these are omitted from some of the resulting binary
datasets.

Table 10.7
The all-pairs coding matrix for a four-class problem

Ω						
a	+1	+1	+1	0	0	0
b	−1	0	0	+1	+1	0
c	0	−1	0	−1	0	+1
d	0	0	−1	0	−1	−1

class c being of no relevance; dichotomy 2 asks if the example's class is in $\{c\}$ or in $\{a\}$,
with classes b and d being irrelevant; and dichotomy 3 asks if it is in $\{b\}$ or in $\{a, c, d\}$.
The bottom of the figure shows how a multiclass dataset gets mapped to the three binary
problems using this code. Note that examples with label c are omitted from the first binary
problem, as are examples with label b or d from the second. For instance, example (x_5, b)
becomes a negative example for binary problem 1, a positive example for binary problem 3,
and is omitted from binary problem 2.

Table 10.7 shows the matrix Ω for the all-pairs code mentioned above for a four-class
problem. This code consists of one dichotomy for every pair of classes. Intuitively, such
dichotomies should be the easiest and most natural binary problems one could extract from
a multiclass problem. On the other hand, when the number of classes is large, the number
of dichotomies will be quadratically larger, although the training set for each dichotomy
will be relatively small. Also, the error-correcting properties of this code are not so strong.

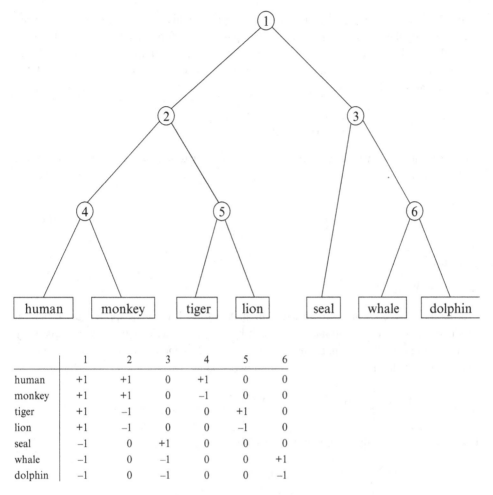

	1	2	3	4	5	6
human	+1	+1	0	+1	0	0
monkey	+1	+1	0	−1	0	0
tiger	+1	−1	0	0	+1	0
lion	+1	−1	0	0	−1	0
seal	−1	0	+1	0	0	0
whale	−1	0	−1	0	0	+1
dolphin	−1	0	−1	0	0	−1

Figure 10.4
Seven classes arranged naturally in a hierarchy, and a corresponding code based on this hierarchy.

We can sometimes derive codes using known structure among the classes. For instance, it may be that the classes form a natural hierarchy as shown in figure 10.4. In such a case, a code corresponding exactly to this tree structure can be created in which each dichotomy corresponds to an internal node pitting the classes in its left subtree against those in its right subtree, ignoring all others, as shown in the figure.

We can modify AdaBoost.MO to handle such $\{-1, 0, +1\}$-valued codes by ignoring some examples on some of the dichotomies as dictated by the code. In other words, we saw earlier that AdaBoost.MO is a reduction to a binary classification problem in which there is one training instance for each of the $\overline{K}m$ pairs $(x_i, \overline{y})$ for each (x_i, y_i) in the original training set and each $\overline{y} \in \overline{\mathcal{Y}}$; the binary label assigned to this pair is $\Omega(y_i, \overline{y})$. Now we can follow exactly the same reduction but omit all pairs $(x_i, \overline{y})$ for which $\Omega(y_i, \overline{y}) = 0$. This is equivalent in the context of boosting to setting the initial distribution of such examples to be zero. Thus, mathematically, the only needed modification is in the initialization of D_1. In particular, we let

$$D_1(i, \overline{y}) = \frac{|\Omega(y_i, \overline{y})|}{sm} = \begin{cases} 0 & \text{if } \Omega(y_i, \overline{y}) = 0 \\ 1/(sm) & \text{else,} \end{cases}$$

where s is the *sparsity* measuring the number of non-zeros in the output code when applied to the dataset:

$$s \doteq \frac{1}{m} \sum_{i=1}^{m} \sum_{\overline{y} \in \overline{\mathcal{Y}}} |\Omega(y_i, \overline{y})| = \frac{1}{m} \sum_{i=1}^{m} |S_{y_i}|, \tag{10.11}$$

and where

$$S_y \doteq \{\overline{y} \in \overline{\mathcal{Y}} : \Omega(y, \overline{y}) \neq 0\}.$$

After initializing D_1 in this modified fashion, AdaBoost.MH can be applied just as before, producing a weighted combination of weak hypotheses $F(x, \overline{y})$ whose sign is given by $H(x, \overline{y})$. The decoding methods described above can be generalized to ignore zero entries in the output code. In particular, for Hamming decoding, we redefine H^{ham} to be

$$H^{ham}(x) = \arg\min_{y \in \mathcal{Y}} \sum_{\overline{y} \in S_y} \mathbf{1}\{H(x, \overline{y}) \neq \Omega(y, \overline{y})\}.$$

Likewise, for loss-based decoding, we now have

$$H^{lb}(x) = \arg\min_{y \in \mathcal{Y}} \sum_{\overline{y} \in S_y} \exp(-\Omega(y, \overline{y}) F(x, \overline{y})).$$

Algorithm 10.4 shows such a generalized version of AdaBoost.MO in which the subroutine call to AdaBoost.MH has been "compiled out." Note that, because we have modified only the distributions D_t, we can continue to use all of the preceding techniques for choosing α_t and for finding weak hypotheses h_t. On the other hand, in many cases it may be possible to implement this same algorithm more efficiently by taking advantage of codes which are very sparse, or which have special structure.

Our analysis of the training error of this method, a direct generalization of theorem 10.4, uses a generalized measure ρ of the minimum Hamming distance between two rows of the code Ω in which entries are ignored if they are 0 in either (or both) of the rows. That is, for distinct rows ℓ_1 and ℓ_2, we first define

Algorithm 10.4
A generalized version of AdaBoost.MO

Given: $(x_1, y_1), \ldots, (x_m, y_m)$ where $x_i \in \mathcal{X}$, $y_i \in \mathcal{Y}$
      output code $\Omega : \mathcal{Y} \times \overline{\mathcal{Y}} \to \{-1, 0, +1\}$.
Initialize:
      $D_1(i, \overline{y}) = |\Omega(y_i, \overline{y})|/(sm)$ for $i = 1, \ldots, m$ and $\overline{y} \in \overline{\mathcal{Y}}$,
      where s is as in equation (10.11).
For $t = 1, \ldots, T$:

- Train weak learner using distribution D_t.
- Get weak hypothesis $h_t : \mathcal{X} \times \overline{\mathcal{Y}} \to \mathbb{R}$.
- Choose $\alpha_t \in \mathbb{R}$.
- Aim: select h_t and α_t to minimalize the normalization factor

$$
Z_t \doteq \sum_{i=1}^{m} \sum_{\overline{y} \in \overline{\mathcal{Y}}} D_t(i, \overline{y}) \exp(-\alpha_t \, \Omega(y_i, \overline{y}) \, h_t(x_i, \overline{y})).
$$

- Update, for $i = 1, \ldots, m$ and $\overline{y} \in \overline{\mathcal{Y}}$:

$$
D_{t+1}(i, \overline{y}) = \frac{D_t(i, \overline{y}) \exp(-\alpha_t \, \Omega(y_i, \overline{y}) \, h_t(x_i, \overline{y}))}{Z_t}.
$$

Let

$$
F(x, \overline{y}) = \sum_{t=1}^{T} \alpha_t h_t(x, \overline{y})
$$

$$
H(x, \overline{y}) = \text{sign}(F(x, \overline{y})).
$$

Output final hypothesis:

$$
H^{ham}(x) = \arg\min_{y \in \mathcal{Y}} \sum_{\overline{y} : \Omega(y, \overline{y}) \neq 0} \mathbf{1}\{H(x, \overline{y}) \neq \Omega(y, \overline{y})\} \quad \text{(Hamming decoding)}
$$

or

$$
H^{lb}(x) = \arg\min_{y \in \mathcal{Y}} \sum_{\overline{y} : \Omega(y, \overline{y}) \neq 0} \exp(-\Omega(y, \overline{y}) \, F(x, \overline{y})) \quad \text{(loss-based decoding)}.
$$

$$T_{\ell_1, \ell_2} \doteq \{\bar{y} \in S_{\ell_1} \cap S_{\ell_2} : \Omega(\ell_1, \bar{y}) \neq \Omega(\ell_2, \bar{y})\}$$

to be the set of nonzero entries where ℓ_1 and ℓ_2 differ. Then ρ is the minimum cardinality of any such set. Also, the empirical Hamming error, specialized to this setting and ignoring zero entries, becomes

$$\widehat{\text{hloss}}(H) \doteq \frac{1}{sm} \sum_{i=1}^{m} \sum_{\bar{y} \in S_{y_i}} \mathbf{1}\{H(x_i, \bar{y}) \neq \Omega(y_i, \bar{y})\}.$$

Note that by the same arguments used in theorem 10.2 applied to this modified reduction to binary, this loss is upper bounded by the exponential loss

$$\frac{1}{sm} \sum_{i=1}^{m} \sum_{\bar{y} \in S_{y_i}} \exp(-\Omega(y, \bar{y}) \, F(x, \bar{y})) = \prod_{t=1}^{T} Z_t.$$

Theorem 10.5 Assuming the notation of algorithm 10.4, and given the definitions above, let

$$\rho \doteq \min_{\ell_1, \ell_2 \in \mathcal{Y} : \ell_1 \neq \ell_2} |T_{\ell_1, \ell_2}|.$$

When run with this choice of Ω, the training error of generalized AdaBoost.MO is upper bounded by

$$\frac{2s}{\rho} \widehat{\text{hloss}}(H) \leq \frac{2s}{\rho} \prod_{t=1}^{T} Z_t$$

for Hamming decoding, and by

$$\frac{s}{\rho} \prod_{t=1}^{T} Z_t$$

for loss-based decoding.

Proof We give a unified proof for both Hamming and loss-based decoding. In either case, for a fixed example, let $L(x, y, \bar{y})$ be the relevant loss that would be suffered on example x if the correct label were y on dichotomy (or mapped label) $\bar{y} \in S_y$. Thus, for Hamming decoding, where the relevant loss is Hamming (or misclassification) error,

$$L(x, y, \bar{y}) = \mathbf{1}\{H(x, \bar{y}) \neq \Omega(y, \bar{y})\},$$

and for loss-based decoding, based on exponential loss,

$$L(x, y, \overline{y}) = \exp(-\Omega(y, \overline{y}) \, F(x, \overline{y})).$$

Suppose the actual correct label for x is y. Then for either coding scheme, the final classifier H^{ham} or H^{lb} makes a mistake only if

$$\sum_{\overline{y} \in S_\ell} L(x, \ell, \overline{y}) \leq \sum_{\overline{y} \in S_y} L(x, y, \overline{y})$$

for some $\ell \neq y$. This implies that

$$\sum_{\overline{y} \in S_y} L(x, y, \overline{y}) \geq \tfrac{1}{2} \sum_{\overline{y} \in S_y} L(x, y, \overline{y}) + \tfrac{1}{2} \sum_{\overline{y} \in S_\ell} L(x, \ell, \overline{y})$$

$$\geq \tfrac{1}{2} \sum_{\overline{y} \in S_y \cap S_\ell} (L(x, y, \overline{y}) + L(x, \ell, \overline{y}))$$

$$\geq \tfrac{1}{2} \sum_{\overline{y} \in T_{y,\ell}} (L(x, y, \overline{y}) + L(x, \ell, \overline{y})), \qquad (10.12)$$

where in the second and third inequalities, we have simply dropped some nonnegative terms.

If $\overline{y} \in T_{y,\ell}$, then $\Omega(\ell, \overline{y}) = -\Omega(y, \overline{y})$. Thus, for Hamming decoding, at least one of $L(x, y, \overline{y})$ or $L(x, \ell, \overline{y})$ will be equal to 1 in this case, which implies that equation (10.12) is at least

$$\frac{|T_{y,\ell}|}{2} \geq \frac{\rho}{2}.$$

Therefore, if M^{ham} is the number of training errors made by H^{ham}, then this argument shows that

$$M^{ham} \cdot \frac{\rho}{2} \leq \sum_{i=1}^{m} \sum_{\overline{y} \in S_{y_i}} L(x_i, y_i, \overline{y})$$

$$= sm \, \widehat{\mathrm{hloss}}(H)$$

$$\leq sm \prod_{t=1}^{T} Z_t,$$

which is equivalent to the bound for Hamming decoding stated in the theorem.

For loss-based decoding, because $\Omega(\ell, \overline{y}) = -\Omega(y, \overline{y})$ for $\overline{y} \in T_{y,\ell}$, and because we are using exponential loss, equation (10.12) becomes

$$\frac{1}{2} \sum_{\overline{y} \in T_{y,\ell}} \left(L(x, y, \overline{y}) + \frac{1}{L(x, y, \overline{y})} \right),$$

which is at least $|T_{y,\ell}| \geq \rho$ since $z + 1/z \geq 2$ for all $z > 0$. So again, if M^{lb} is the number of training errors made by H^{lb}, then

$$M^{lb} \rho \leq \sum_{i=1}^{m} \sum_{\overline{y} \in S_{y_i}} L(x_i, y_i, \overline{y})$$

$$= sm \prod_{t=1}^{T} Z_t,$$

giving the bound for loss-based decoding.   ∎

Theorem 10.4 can be obtained as an immediate corollary simply by applying theorem 10.5 to an output code Ω with no zero entries. The theorem again formalizes the trade-off between codes in which the codewords are far apart, as measured by ρ/s, against the difficulty of learning the various dichotomies, as measured by the Z_t's.

For the all-pairs reduction, $\rho = 1$ and $s = K - 1$, so that with loss-based decoding, the overall training error is at most

$$(K - 1) \prod_{t=1}^{T} Z_t.$$

For a code based on a hierarchy as in figure 10.4, $\rho = 1$ and s is at most the depth of the tree.

Experimentally, loss-based decoding seems to nearly always perform at least as well as Hamming decoding, consistent with the theory. However, the code giving best performance on a particular dataset seems to depend very much on the problem at hand. One-against-all is often satisfactory, but not always the best. For instance, on the 26-class "letter" benchmark dataset used elsewhere in this book (such as in section 1.3), the test error rates shown in table 10.8 were obtained using decision stumps as weak hypotheses. On this dataset, all-pairs is far superior to one-against-all, while a random code (with no zero entries) does

Table 10.8
Percent test error rates for various coding and decoding schemes on two benchmark datasets

	Letter		Soybean-Large	
	Hamming	Loss-based	Hamming	Loss-based
One-against-All	27.7	14.6	8.2	7.2
All-Pairs	7.8	7.1	9.0	8.8
Random	30.9	28.3	5.6	4.8

worse than either. On the other hand, on the "soybean-large" benchmark dataset, which has 19 classes, the best results are obtained using a random code, and the worst with the all-pairs reduction.

Summary

In summary, we have seen in this chapter that there are many ways of extending binary AdaBoost when confronting a multiclass learning task. When using a relatively strong base learner, the most straightforward extension, AdaBoost.M1, can be used. For weaker base learners, the multiclass problem must be reduced to multiple binary problems. There are numerous ways of devising such a reduction, and we have discussed several specific and general strategies and analyses. These include AdaBoost.MH, which can be used not only for multiclass but also for multi-label data, as well as AdaBoost.MO, which can be used across a very broad range of reductions or codes.

Bibliographic Notes

The AdaBoost.M1 algorithm and analysis of section 10.1 are due to Freund and Schapire [95], as are the experiments reported at the end of that section and in figure 10.1 [93]. The AdaBoost.MH algorithm and analysis of section 10.2 are due to Schapire and Singer [205]. The experiments in section 10.3 were conducted by Schapire and Singer [206] on a task and with data developed by Gorin and others [109, 110, 189].

The results and methods in section 10.4.1 are from Schapire and Singer [205], and are based directly on the error-correcting output coding technique of Dietterich and Bakiri [70]. The generalization in section 10.4.2 is essentially from Allwein, Schapire, and Singer [6], although here we have included somewhat improved versions of AdaBoost.MO and its analysis in theorem 10.5. Some similar, though more specialized, results were given earlier by Guruswami and Sahai [114]. The all-pairs approach was studied previously by Friedman [99] and Hastie and Tibshirani [119]. The results in table 10.8 are excerpted from far more extensive experiments reported by Allwein, Schapire, and Singer [6], who also gave results on the generalization error of some of the methods studied in this chapter. More general decoding schemes and improved analyses are given, for instance, by Klautau, Jevtić, and Orlitsky [136], and Escalera, Pujol, and Radeva [83].

Other approaches for extending boosting to the multiclass setting have been proposed, for instance, by Schapire [200], Abe, Zadrozny, and Langford [2], Eibl and Pfeiffer [81], Zhu et al. [238], and Mukherjee and Schapire [173]. See also Beygelzimer, Langford, and Ravikumar's [19] more general work on reducing multiclass to binary.

Some of the exercises in this chapter are based on material from [6].

Exercises

10.1 Consider a modification of AdaBoost.M1 (algorithm 10.1) in which the algorithm is *not* forced to halt when $\epsilon_t \geq \frac{1}{2}$, but is simply allowed to proceed. Assume the weak learner is exhaustive, returning on each round the weak classifier $h \in \mathcal{H}$ with minimum weighted error. Suppose on some round t that $\epsilon_t > \frac{1}{2}$.

a. For this modified version of AdaBoost.M1, explain what will happen on all subsequent rounds $t+1, t+2, \ldots$.

b. Under these conditions, how will the resulting combined classifiers differ for the modified and unmodified versions?

10.2 AdaBoost.Mk (algorithm 10.5) is a generalization of AdaBoost.M1 that relaxes the requirement that the weighted errors of the weak classifiers be smaller than $\frac{1}{2}$, but that provides correspondingly weaker guarantees on performance. The algorithm takes an integer parameter $k \geq 1$ (with $k = 1$ corresponding to AdaBoost.M1). The setting of α_t will be discussed shortly. For a real-valued function $f : \mathcal{Y} \rightarrow \mathbb{R}$, we use in the algorithm the notation arg k-$\max_{y \in \mathcal{Y}} f(y)$ to stand for the top k elements of $\mathcal{Y}$ when ordered by f, that is, a set $A \subseteq \mathcal{Y}$ with $|A| = k$ and for which $f(y) \geq f(y')$ for all $y \in A$ and $y' \notin A$. (If more than one set A satisfies this condition, we allow one to be chosen arbitrarily.) Thus, $H(x)$ returns the top k labels as ordered by the weighted votes of the weak classifiers.

a. Show that

$$\frac{1}{m}\sum_{i=1}^{m}\mathbf{1}\{y_i \notin H(x_i)\} \leq \prod_{t=1}^{T}Z_t.$$

b. Assume that $\epsilon_t < k/(k+1)$ for all t. Show how to choose α_t so that the fraction of training examples for which $y_i \notin H(x_i)$ is at most

$$\exp\left(-\sum_{t=1}^{T}\mathrm{RE}_b\left(\frac{k}{k+1}\ \|\ \epsilon_t\right)\right).$$

c. Conclude that if the weighted accuracy of each weak classifier is at least $1/(k+1)+\gamma$, then after T rounds, at least a fraction $1 - e^{-2\gamma^2 T}$ of the training examples i will have the correct label y_i ranked among the top k, that is, included in the set $H(x_i)$.

10.3 In this exercise and exercise 10.4, we will see one way of generalizing the margins analysis of chapter 5 to the current multiclass setting, specifically, to AdaBoost.MO using loss-based decoding as in algorithm 10.4. For simplicity, assume the weak hypotheses h_t are chosen from a finite space $\mathcal{H}$, and all have range $\{-1, +1\}$. We also assume Ω includes no zero entries, and that (without loss of generality) $\alpha_t \geq 0$ for all t. The convex hull of $\mathcal{H}$,

Algorithm 10.5
AdaBoost.Mk, a generalization of AdaBoost.M1

Given: $(x_1, y_1), \ldots, (x_m, y_m)$ where $x_i \in \mathcal{X}, y_i \in \mathcal{Y}$
  parameter $k \geq 1$.
Initialize: $D_1(i) = 1/m$ for $i = 1, \ldots, m$.
For $t = 1, \ldots, T$:

- Train weak learner using distribution D_t.

- Get weak hypothesis $h_t : \mathcal{X} \to \mathcal{Y}$.

- Aim: select h_t to minimalize the weighted error:

$$\epsilon_t \doteq \mathbf{Pr}_{i \sim D_t}[h_t(x_i) \neq y_i].$$

- If $\epsilon_t \geq k/(k+1)$, then set $T = t - 1$, and exit loop.

- Choose $\alpha_t > 0$.

- Update, for $i = 1, \ldots, m$:

$$D_{t+1}(i) = \frac{D_t(i)}{Z_t} \times \begin{cases} e^{-k\alpha_t} & \text{if } h_t(x_i) = y_i \\ e^{\alpha_t} & \text{if } h_t(x_i) \neq y_i \end{cases}$$

  where Z_t is a normalization factor (chosen so that D_{t+1} will be a distribution).

Output the final hypothesis:

$$H(x) = \arg\,k\text{-}\max_{y \in \mathcal{Y}} \sum_{t=1}^{T} \alpha_t \mathbf{1}\{h_t(x) = y\}.$$

$\mathrm{co}(\mathcal{H})$, is the same as in equation (5.4), except that the functions involved are defined on the domain $\mathcal{X} \times \overline{\mathcal{Y}}$ rather than $\mathcal{X}$.

For $f \in \mathrm{co}(\mathcal{H})$, $\eta > 0$, and $(x, y) \in \mathcal{X} \times \mathcal{Y}$, let

$$v_{f,\eta}(x, y) \doteq -\frac{1}{\eta} \ln \left(\frac{1}{K} \sum_{\overline{y} \in \overline{\mathcal{Y}}} \exp\left(-\eta \Omega(y, \overline{y}) f(x, \overline{y})\right) \right).$$

We define the margin of labeled example (x, y) with respect to f, η to be

$$\mathcal{M}_{f,\eta}(x, y) \doteq \frac{1}{2} \left(v_{f,\eta}(x, y) - \max_{\ell \neq y} v_{f,\eta}(x, \ell) \right).$$

a. Show that $\mathcal{M}_{f,\eta}(x, y) \in [-1, +1]$. Also, for an appropriate choice of f and η, show that $\mathcal{M}_{f,\eta}(x, y) \le 0$ if and only if H^{lb} misclassifies (x, y) (where, as usual, we count a tie in the "arg min" used to compute H^{lb} as a misclassification).

Let $f \in \mathrm{co}(\mathcal{H})$ and let $\theta > 0$ be fixed. Let n be a (fixed) positive integer, and let $\mathcal{A}_n, \tilde{f}, \tilde{h}_1, \ldots, \tilde{h}_n$ be as in the proof of theorem 5.1 (but with modified domain $\mathcal{X} \times \overline{\mathcal{Y}}$). We also adopt the notation $\mathbf{Pr}_S[\cdot]$, $\mathbf{Pr}_\mathcal{D}[\cdot]$, $\mathbf{Pr}_{\tilde{f}}[\cdot]$, and so on from that proof, where S is the training set and $\mathcal{D}$ is the true distribution over $\mathcal{X} \times \mathcal{Y}$.

b. For fixed $x \in \mathcal{X}$, show that

$$\mathbf{Pr}_{\tilde{f}}\left[\exists \overline{y} \in \overline{\mathcal{Y}} : \left|f(x, y) - \tilde{f}(x, y)\right| \ge \frac{\theta}{4}\right] \le \beta_n$$

where $\beta_n \doteq 2\overline{K} e^{-n\theta^2/32}$.

In what follows, you can use (without proof) the following technical fact: Let

$$\mathcal{E}_\theta \doteq \left\{\frac{4\ln\overline{K}}{i\theta} : i = 1, \ldots, \left\lceil\frac{8\ln\overline{K}}{\theta^2}\right\rceil\right\}.$$

For any $\eta > 0$, let $\hat{\eta}$ be the closest value in $\mathcal{E}_\theta$ to η. Then for all $f \in \mathrm{co}(\mathcal{H})$ and for all $(x, y) \in \mathcal{X} \times \mathcal{Y}$,

$$\left|v_{f,\eta}(x, y) - v_{f,\hat{\eta}}(x, y)\right| \le \frac{\theta}{4}.$$

c. Let $\eta > 0$, and let $\hat{\eta} \in \mathcal{E}_\theta$ be as above. Suppose for some $x \in \mathcal{X}$ that $|f(x, \overline{y}) - \tilde{f}(x, \overline{y})| \le \theta/4$ for all $\overline{y} \in \overline{\mathcal{Y}}$. Show the following for all $y \in \mathcal{Y}$:

   i. $\left|v_{f,\eta}(x, y) - v_{\tilde{f},\eta}(x, y)\right| \le \theta/4$.

   ii. $\left|v_{f,\eta}(x, y) - v_{\tilde{f},\hat{\eta}}(x, y)\right| \le \theta/2$.

   [*Hint:* Prove and then use the fact that $\left(\sum_i a_i\right) / \left(\sum_i b_i\right) \le \max_i (a_i/b_i)$ for any positive numbers $a_1, \ldots, a_n; b_1, \ldots, b_n$.]

d. For any distribution P over pairs (x, y), show that

$$\mathbf{Pr}_{P,\tilde{f}}\left[\left|\mathcal{M}_{f,\eta}(x, y) - \mathcal{M}_{\tilde{f},\hat{\eta}}(x, y)\right| \ge \frac{\theta}{2}\right] \le \beta_n.$$

e. Let

$$\varepsilon_n \doteq \sqrt{\frac{\ln\left[|\mathcal{E}_\theta| \cdot |\mathcal{H}|^n / \delta\right]}{2m}}.$$

Show that with probability at least $1 - \delta$ over the choice of the random training set, for all $\tilde{f} \in \mathcal{A}_n$, and for all $\hat{\eta} \in \mathcal{E}_\theta$,

$$\mathbf{Pr}_\mathcal{D}\left[\mathcal{M}_{\tilde{f},\hat{\eta}}(x, y) \le \frac{\theta}{2}\right] \le \mathbf{Pr}_S\left[\mathcal{M}_{\tilde{f},\hat{\eta}}(x, y) \le \frac{\theta}{2}\right] + \varepsilon_n.$$

(Note that θ and n are *fixed*.)

f. Show that with probability at least $1 - \delta$, for all $f \in \text{co}(\mathcal{H})$, and for all $\eta > 0$,

$$\mathbf{Pr}_\mathcal{D}\left[\mathcal{M}_{f,\eta}(x, y) \le 0\right] \le \mathbf{Pr}_S\left[\mathcal{M}_{f,\eta}(x, y) \le \theta\right] + 2\beta_n + \varepsilon_n.$$

For an appropriate choice of n, we can now obtain a result analogous to theorem 5.1 (you do not need to show this).

10.4 Continuing exercise 10.3, let

$$\epsilon_t \doteq \mathbf{Pr}_{(i,\overline{y})\sim D_t}[h_t(x_i, \overline{y}) \ne \Omega(y_i, \overline{y})]$$

be the weighted error of h_t, which we assume without loss of generality is at most $\frac{1}{2}$, and let α_t be chosen as in equation (10.4). Let f and η be chosen as in exercise 10.3(a), and let $\theta > 0$.

a. Suppose, for some $(x, y) \in \mathcal{X} \times \mathcal{Y}$, that $\mathcal{M}_{f,\eta}(x, y) \le \theta$. For $\overline{y} \in \overline{\mathcal{Y}}$ and $\ell \in \mathcal{Y}$, let

$$z(\overline{y}) \doteq \eta\Omega(y, \overline{y})f(x, \overline{y}) - \eta\theta$$

$$z_\ell(\overline{y}) \doteq \eta\Omega(\ell, \overline{y})f(x, \overline{y}) + \eta\theta.$$

Show that

i. $\displaystyle\sum_{\overline{y} \in \overline{\mathcal{Y}}} e^{-z(\overline{y})} \ge \sum_{\overline{y} \in \overline{\mathcal{Y}}} e^{-z_\ell(\overline{y})}$ for some $\ell \ne y$.

ii. $\displaystyle\sum_{\overline{y} \in \overline{\mathcal{Y}}} e^{-z(\overline{y})} \ge \rho$ where ρ is as in equation (10.10).

b. Let $\gamma_t \doteq \frac{1}{2} - \epsilon_t$. Prove that the fraction of training examples i for which $\mathcal{M}_{f,\eta}(x_i, y_i) \le \theta$ is at most

$$\frac{\overline{K}}{\rho} \cdot \prod_{t=1}^{T} \sqrt{(1 + 2\gamma_t)^{1+\theta}(1 - 2\gamma_t)^{1-\theta}}.$$

10.5 When using AdaBoost.MO with the all-pairs coding matrix, each dichotomy $\overline{y}$ is identified with an unordered pair of distinct labels, that is,

$$\overline{\mathcal{Y}} = \{\{\ell_1, \ell_2\} : \ell_1, \ell_2 \in \mathcal{Y}, \ell_1 \ne \ell_2\}.$$

Suppose each weak hypothesis $h_t : \mathcal{X} \times \overline{\mathcal{Y}} \to \mathbb{R}$ can be written in the form

$$h_t(x, \{\ell_1, \ell_2\}) = \frac{\Omega(\ell_1, \{\ell_1, \ell_2\})}{2} \cdot \left(\tilde{h}_t(x, \ell_1) - \tilde{h}_t(x, \ell_2)\right) \tag{10.13}$$

for some $\tilde{h}_t : \mathcal{X} \times \mathcal{Y} \to \mathbb{R}$.

a. In equation (10.13), ℓ_1 and ℓ_2 are treated symmetrically on the left, but appear not to be so treated on the right. Show that the right-hand side of equation (10.13) is in fact equal to the same expression if ℓ_1 and ℓ_2 are swapped.

b. Show that if loss-based decoding is used, then

$$H^{lb}(x) = \arg\max_{y \in \mathcal{Y}} \sum_{t=1}^{T} \alpha_t \tilde{h}_t(x, y).$$

10.6 Suppose the label set $\mathcal{Y} = \{0, \ldots, K-1\}$, and that we apply AdaBoost.MO with $\overline{\mathcal{Y}} \doteq \{1, \ldots, K-1\}$ and

$$\Omega(y, \overline{y}) \doteq \begin{cases} +1 & \text{if } \overline{y} \le y \\ -1 & \text{else.} \end{cases}$$

Using the notation from algorithm 10.3, suppose it happens that the computed function F is monotone in the sense that $F(x, \overline{y}_1) \ge F(x, \overline{y}_2)$ if $\overline{y}_1 \le \overline{y}_2$.

a. Show that the two decoding methods are equivalent in this case, that is, $H^{ham} \equiv H^{lb}$ (assuming ties in their respective arg mins are broken in the same way).

b. Show that

$$\frac{1}{m} \sum_{i=1}^{m} \frac{H^{lb}(x_i) - y_i}{K-1} \le \prod_{t=1}^{T} Z_t.$$

c. Suppose each h_t has the form

$$h_t(x, \overline{y}) = \begin{cases} +1 & \text{if } \overline{y} \le \tilde{h}_t(x) \\ -1 & \text{else} \end{cases}$$

for some $\tilde{h}_t : \mathcal{X} \to \mathcal{Y}$, and assume also that $\alpha_t \ge 0$ for all t. Show that $H^{lb}(x)$ is a *weighted median* of the $\tilde{h}_t(x)$ values with weights α_t. (A weighted median of real numbers $v_1, \ldots, v_n$ with nonnegative weights $w_1, \ldots, w_n$ is any number v for which $\sum_{i : v_i < v} w_i \le \frac{1}{2} \sum_{i=1}^{n} w_i$ and $\sum_{i : v_i > v} w_i \le \frac{1}{2} \sum_{i=1}^{n} w_i$.)

10.7 AdaBoost.MO is designed to find F to minimize $\frac{1}{m} \sum_{i=1}^{m} L(F, (x_i, y_i))$ where

$$L(F, (x, y)) \doteq \sum_{\overline{y} \in S_y} \exp\left(-\Omega(y, \overline{y}) F(x, \overline{y})\right).$$

a. Let Ω be any code (possibly with zero entries), and let p be any distribution on $\mathcal{X} \times \mathcal{Y}$. For simplicity, assume $p(y|x) > 0$ for all x, y. Among *all* functions $F : \mathcal{X} \times \overline{\mathcal{Y}} \to \mathbb{R}$, find one that minimizes the expected loss $\mathbf{E}_{(x,y) \sim p}[L(F, (x, y))]$.

b. Let $\mathcal{Y}$, $\overline{\mathcal{Y}}$, Ω, and F be as in exercise 10.6. For any x, find a conditional probability distribution $p(y|x)$ such that $F(x, \cdot)$ minimizes the conditional expected loss

$$\mathbf{E}_{y \sim p(\cdot|x)}[L(F, (x, y))].$$

Your answer should be in closed form, and expressed in terms of F.

11 Learning to Rank

We consider next how to learn to rank a set of objects, a problem that arises naturally in a variety of domains. For instance, web search engines seek to rank documents or web pages according to their relevance to a given query. Similarly, the purpose of a recommendation system may be to rank movies according to the chance that a particular viewer will like them. Indeed, problems that may seem on the surface to be classification problems often turn out, when viewed in practical terms, instead to be ranking problems. For instance, in bioinformatics, one may wish to learn to identify all the proteins with a given property. This would seem to be a classification problem, but in practice, one is often actually seeking a ranking of the proteins by their probability of having this property so that the ones at the top of the ranking can be verified in a physical laboratory. And as previously mentioned, any multiclass, multi-label classification problem can be viewed as a ranking problem in which the goal is to rank the categories that a given instance is most likely to belong to.

In this chapter, we present a boosting-based technique for handling such ranking problems, which we study in a general framework. The main algorithm, RankBoost, is based on a straightforward reduction from ranking to binary classification, specifically, to a set of binary questions asking, for each pair of instances, which is to be ranked higher than the other. Alternatively, RankBoost can be viewed as an algorithm for minimizing a particular loss function analogous to the exponential loss function minimized by AdaBoost as discussed in chapter 7. Moreover, although distinct, these two loss functions present minimization problems that turn out to be closely related, indicating that ordinary binary AdaBoost may itself have unintended properties as a ranking method.

RankBoost takes advantage of techniques developed earlier, particularly for making use of confidence-rated base hypotheses as in chapter 9. Some of these methods can provide significant practical improvements in efficiency. Superficially, RankBoost would seem to be an inherently inefficient approach (compared, for instance, to AdaBoost) because of its design as an algorithm based on the handling of *pairs* of instances. Nevertheless, as will be seen, when the ranking problem has a particular natural form, the algorithm can be implemented in a way that is especially efficient.

When RankBoost is applied to solve multiclass, multi-label classification problems, the resulting algorithm is called AdaBoost.MR, an alternative to the AdaBoost.MH algorithm of section 10.2, and one that can be implemented with equivalent efficiency using the techniques mentioned above.

At the end of this chapter, we present two applications of RankBoost, one for the problem of parsing English sentences, and the other for finding genes which may be relevant to particular forms of cancer.

11.1 A Formal Framework for Ranking Problems

We begin with a formal description of the problem of learning to rank some collection of objects. In this setting, the objects that we are interested in ranking are called *instances*. For example, in the movie-ranking task, each movie is an instance. As usual, the set of all instances is called the *domain* or *instance space*, and is denoted by $\mathcal{X}$. The goal of learning is to compute a "good" ranking of all the instances in $\mathcal{X}$—for example, a ranking of all movies from most to least likely to be enjoyed by a particular movie-viewer.

Every learning process must begin with data. In classification learning, it is assumed that this training data takes the form of a set of training instances, each paired with its presumably correct label or classification. In a similar fashion, a learning algorithm in the ranking setting must also be provided with some kind of training data. What should we assume about its form?

Certainly, the learner must be provided with a set of *training instances*, that is, a relatively small and finite subset of the domain $\mathcal{X}$, which we denote by V. For instance, in movie ranking, these training instances might comprise all the movies seen and ranked by the target user. Of course, in addition to this sampling of instances, the learner, whose goal is to infer a good ranking, must also be given some information about how these instances should be properly ranked relative to one another. Ideally, we might wish to assume that the learner is provided with a total ordering of all of these training instances, that is, a complete ranking of every one of the training instances relative to every other instance. In the movie-ranking setting, this would mean that the user would need to specify his favorite movie, followed by his second favorite, his third favorite, and so on for all of the movies seen. In practice, this might be too much to ask.

More typically, in an actual system, the user might be asked to rate each movie with, say, 1 to 5 stars. Such ratings are really providing ranking information: 5-star movies are preferred to 4-star movies, which are preferred to 3-star movies, and so on. However, this ranking is not a total order since no preference is expressed between two movies receiving the same number of stars. Furthermore, there may be reason to discount comparisons between movies of different genres; for instance, the scale used to rate children's movies might not be comparable to the scale used for action thrillers.

These considerations are indicative of the need to accommodate ranking information that is as general in form as possible. To this end, we assume only that the learner is provided with information about the relative ranking of individual pairs of instances. That is, for various pairs of instances (u, v), the learner is informed as to whether v should be ranked above or below u. In the movie setting, this means converting rating information provided by the user into a list of pairs of movies in which one is preferred to the other by virtue of receiving more stars. However, the list would omit pairs in which both movies receive the same number of stars and, if appropriate, could also omit other pairs, such as pairs of movies of different genres.

Thus, we can think of the training feedback provided to the learning algorithm as a set of pairs of training instances indicating that one should be ranked higher than the other. The goal of the learning algorithm then is to use this ranking feedback to infer a good ranking of the entire domain, typically by finding a ranking that is maximally consistent with the feedback.

Formally, then, the input to the learning algorithm is a set V of training instances from $\mathcal{X}$, together with a set E of ordered pairs of distinct training instances (u, v). We interpret the inclusion of such a pair to mean that v should correctly be ranked above u. Members of the set E are called *preference pairs*. We assume without loss of generality that every training instance in V occurs in at least one preference pair.

Note that this feedback is equivalent to a directed graph, called the *feedback graph*, in which the vertices are the training instances in V, and the edges are exactly the preference pairs in E. Figure 11.1 shows examples of typical graphs that might be provided as feedback. Graph (a) shows feedback that amounts to a total order over all of the training instances. Graph (b) gives an example of *bipartite feedback* in which one set of instances should all be ranked above all others, as would be the case, for example, if all movies were simply rated as either "good" or "bad." Graph (c) shows *layered feedback* in which the feedback is arranged in layers (for instance, using a 3-star rating system). Note that both bipartite feedback and feedback representing a total order are special cases of layered feedback.

Graph (d) emphasizes the point that the feedback can be entirely arbitrary, and may be inconsistent in various senses. In particular, it might seem logical that if (u, v) and (v, w) are preference pairs, then (u, w) should be as well; that is, if w is preferred to v, and v is preferred to u, then it seems to follow that w should be preferred to u. Nevertheless, in the formalism that we adopt, we do *not* require that the feedback satisfy any such transitivity condition. We also allow the feedback graph to contain cycles. However, we do assume that E contains no "self-loops," that is, pairs of the form (u, u), since these do not make sense in our setting, and there is nothing to be learned from them.

As an example of where such inconsistencies might arise, the instances could be sports teams with each preference pair (u, v) representing the outcome of a single game in which team v beat team u. In such a setting, there is no guarantee of any kind of transitivity: It is entirely possible for team w to beat team v, and v to beat u, but for u later to beat team w.

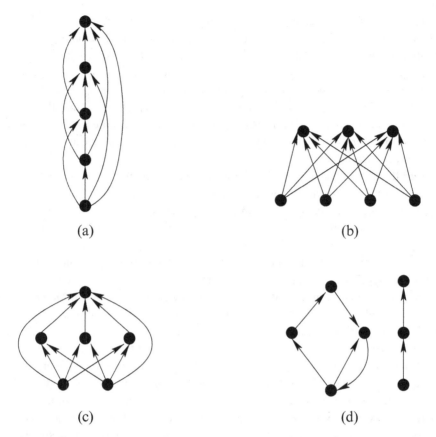

Figure 11.1
Four sample feedback graphs. The vertices are instances, and the edges are the preference pairs indicating that one instance should be ranked above the other.

Such inconsistent feedback is analogous to receiving the same example with contradictory labels in the classification setting.

As noted earlier, the aim of the learning algorithm is to find a good ranking over the entire domain $\mathcal{X}$. Formally, we represent such a ranking by a real-valued function $F : \mathcal{X} \to \mathbb{R}$ with the interpretation that F ranks v above u if $F(v) > F(u)$. Note that the actual numerical values of F are immaterial; only the relative ordering that they define is of interest (although the algorithms that we describe shortly will in fact use these numerical values as part of the training process).

To quantify the "goodness" of a ranking F with respect to the given feedback, we compute the fraction of preference-pair misorderings:

$$\frac{1}{|E|} \sum_{(u,v) \in E} \mathbf{1}\{F(v) \le F(u)\}.$$

In other words, using our interpretation of the ranking of $\mathcal{X}$ defined by F, we simply compute the extent to which F agrees or disagrees with the pair-by-pair ordering provided by the given set E of preference pairs. This quantity is called the *empirical ranking loss*, and is denoted $\widehat{\mathrm{rloss}}(F)$.

More generally, we can compute such a loss measure with respect to any distribution D over a finite set of preference pairs. Thus, formally, suppose D is a distribution over $\mathcal{X} \times \mathcal{X}$ with finite support (that is, zero on all but a finite set of pairs). Then the *ranking loss of F with respect to D*, denoted $\mathrm{rloss}_D(F)$, is the weighted fraction of misorderings:

$$\mathrm{rloss}_D(F) \doteq \sum_{u,v} D(u, v)\mathbf{1}\{F(v) \leq F(u)\} = \mathbf{Pr}_{(u,v)\sim D}[F(v) \leq F(u)] .$$

(Throughout this chapter, when a specific range is not specified on a sum, we always assume summation over just those elements of $\mathcal{X}$ for which the summand is not zero.)

Of course, the real purpose of learning is to produce a ranking that performs well even on instances not observed in training. For instance, for the movie task, we would like to find a ranking of all movies that accurately predicts which ones a movie-viewer will like more or less than others; obviously, this ranking is of value only if it includes movies that the viewer has not already seen. As in other learning settings, how well the learning system performs on unseen data depends on many factors, such as the number of instances covered in training and the representational complexity of the ranking produced by the learner. These issues go beyond the scope of this chapter, although many of the methods for classification described in other parts of this book are certainly applicable here as well. We instead focus on algorithms simply for minimizing ranking loss with respect to the given feedback.

11.2   A Boosting Algorithm for the Ranking Task

In this section, we describe an approach to the ranking problem based on boosting. We focus on the *RankBoost* algorithm, its analysis, and its interpretation.

11.2.1   RankBoost

Pseudocode for RankBoost is shown as algorithm 11.1. The algorithm is very similar to confidence-rated AdaBoost, but with some key modifications. Like AdaBoost, RankBoost operates in rounds. On each round t, a distribution D_t is computed, and a weak learner is called to find h_t. Unlike AdaBoost, however, in RankBoost, D_t is a distribution over *pairs* of instances, conceptually over all of $V \times V$ (or even $\mathcal{X} \times \mathcal{X}$), though in fact concentrated just on the given set E of preference pairs. The initial distribution D_1 is simply the uniform distribution over E, and for each subsequent distribution, $D_t(u, v)$ indicates the importance on round t of h_t ranking v above u. Also, h_t is now called a *weak ranker*; as a real-valued function on $\mathcal{X}$, we interpret h_t as providing a ranking of all instances in $\mathcal{X}$ in much the same way as the (final) ranking F.

Algorithm 11.1
The RankBoost algorithm, using a pair-based weak learner

Given: finite set $V \subseteq \mathcal{X}$ of training instances
    set $E \subseteq V \times V$ of preference pairs.

Initialize: for all u, v, let $D_1(u, v) = \begin{cases} 1/|E| & \text{if } (u, v) \in E \\ 0 & \text{else.} \end{cases}$

For $t = 1, \ldots, T$:

- Train weak learner using distribution D_t.
- Get weak ranking $h_t : \mathcal{X} \to \mathbb{R}$.
- Choose $\alpha_t \in \mathbb{R}$.
- Aim: select h_t and α_t to minimalize the normalization factor

$$Z_t \doteq \sum_{u,v} D_t(u, v) \exp\left(\tfrac{1}{2}\alpha_t(h_t(u) - h_t(v))\right).$$

- Update, for all u, v: $D_{t+1}(u, v) = \dfrac{D_t(u, v) \exp\left(\tfrac{1}{2}\alpha_t(h_t(u) - h_t(v))\right)}{Z_t}$.

Output the final ranking: $F(x) = \tfrac{1}{2} \sum_{t=1}^{T} \alpha_t h_t(x)$.

RankBoost uses the weak rankings to update the distribution as shown in the algorithm. Suppose that (u, v) is a preference pair so that we want v to be ranked higher than u (in all other cases, $D_t(u, v)$ will be zero). Assuming for the moment that the parameter $\alpha_t > 0$ (as it usually will be), this rule decreases the weight $D_t(u, v)$ if h_t gives a correct ranking ($h_t(v) > h_t(u)$), and increases the weight otherwise. Thus, D_t will tend to concentrate on the pairs whose relative ranking is hardest to determine correctly. The actual setting of α_t will be discussed shortly. The final ranking F is simply a weighted sum of the weak rankings.

The RankBoost algorithm can in fact be derived directly from AdaBoost, using an appropriate reduction to binary classification. In particular, we can regard each preference pair (u, v) as providing a binary question of the form "Should v be ranked above or below u?" Moreover, weak hypotheses in the reduced binary setting are assumed to have a particular form, namely, as a scaled difference $h(u, v) = \tfrac{1}{2}(h(v) - h(u))$. The final hypothesis, which is a linear combination of weak hypotheses, then inherits this same form "automatically," yielding a function that can be used to rank instances. When AdaBoost is applied, the resulting algorithm is exactly RankBoost. (The scaling factors of $\tfrac{1}{2}$ appearing above and in the algorithm have no significance, and are included only for later mathematical convenience.)

Although a bound on the ranking loss falls out from the reduction, we choose to prove such a bound directly. This theorem also provides the criterion given in the algorithm for choosing α_t and for designing the weak learner, as we discuss below. As in the proof of theorem 3.1, we give a general result for any initial distribution D_1.

Theorem 11.1 Assuming the notation of algorithm 11.1, the empirical ranking loss of F or, more generally, the ranking loss of F with respect to any initial distribution D_1, is at most

$$\text{rloss}_{D_1}(F) \leq \prod_{t=1}^{T} Z_t.$$

Proof Unraveling the update rule, we have that

$$D_{T+1}(u, v) = \frac{D_1(u, v) \exp(F(u) - F(v))}{\prod_{t=1}^{T} Z_t}.$$

Using the fact that $1\{x \geq 0\} \leq e^x$ for all real x, we thus have that the ranking loss with respect to initial distribution D_1 is

$$\sum_{u,v} D_1(u, v) \mathbf{1}\{F(u) \geq F(v)\} \leq \sum_{u,v} D_1(u, v) \exp(F(u) - F(v))$$

$$= \sum_{u,v} D_{T+1}(u, v) \prod_{t=1}^{T} Z_t = \prod_{t=1}^{T} Z_t.$$

This proves the theorem. ∎

11.2.2 Choosing α_t and Criteria for Weak Learners

In view of the bound established in theorem 11.1, we are guaranteed to produce a combined ranking with low ranking loss if on each round t, we choose α_t and the weak learner constructs h_t so as to (approximately) minimize

$$Z_t \doteq \sum_{u,v} D_t(u, v) \exp\left(\tfrac{1}{2}\alpha_t(h_t(u) - h_t(v))\right). \tag{11.1}$$

This is the rationale for the objective shown in algorithm 11.1. Thus, analogous to the approach taken in chapter 9, minimization of Z_t can again be used as a guide both in the choice of α_t and in the design of the weak learner. Several of the techniques from chapter 9 for working with confidence-rated weak hypotheses can be applied here directly, as we now sketch. To simplify notation, we here fix t and drop all t subscripts when they are clear from the context.

First and most generally, for any given weak ranking h, as in section 9.2.1, Z can be viewed as a convex function of α with a unique minimum that can be found numerically, for instance via a simple binary search (except in trivial degenerate cases).

A second method of minimizing Z can be applied in the special case that h has range $\{-1, +1\}$. Such binary weak rankers arise naturally, and are especially easy to work with in many domains. They can be used to divide the instance space into two sets, one of which is generally to be preferred to the other. For instance, in movie ranking, a weak ranker that is $+1$ on foreign films and -1 on all others can be used to express the sentiment that foreign films are generally preferable to nonforeign films.

For such weak rankers, the scaled difference $\frac{1}{2}(h(v) - h(u))$ appearing in equation (11.1) in the exponent has range $\{-1, 0, +1\}$. Thus, we can minimize Z analytically in terms of α using techniques from section 9.2.4. Specifically, for $b \in \{-1, 0, +1\}$, let

$$U_b \doteq \sum_{u,v} D(u, v)\mathbf{1}\{h(v) - h(u) = 2b\} = \mathbf{Pr}_{(u,v)\sim D}[h(v) - h(u) = 2b].$$

Also, abbreviate U_{+1} by U_+, and U_{-1} by U_-. Then

$$Z = U_0 + U_- e^\alpha + U_+ e^{-\alpha}.$$

As in section 9.2.4, it can be verified that Z is minimized by setting

$$\alpha = \frac{1}{2} \ln\left(\frac{U_+}{U_-}\right), \tag{11.2}$$

which yields

$$Z = U_0 + 2\sqrt{U_- U_+}. \tag{11.3}$$

Thus, if we are using weak rankings with range restricted to $\{-1, +1\}$, we should attempt to find h minimizing equation (11.3), and we should then set α as in equation (11.2). For instance, if using decision stumps, then the search technique described in sections 3.4.2 and 9.2.6 can be straightforwardly modified for this purpose.

Later, in section 11.3.1, we will describe further general techniques for finding weak rankings and selecting α. Although inexact, we will see how these methods can effect substantial computational savings by reducing the problem of finding a weak ranking to an ordinary binary-classification problem.

11.2.3   RankBoost and AdaBoost's Loss Functions

In chapter 7, we saw that AdaBoost naturally minimizes a particular loss function, namely, the exponential loss. Specifically, given examples $(x_1, y_1), \ldots, (x_m, y_m)$, with labels $y_i \in \{-1, +1\}$, AdaBoost seeks a function F_λ which minimizes

$$\sum_{i=1}^{m} \exp\left(-y_i F_\lambda(x_i)\right) \tag{11.4}$$

where

$$F_\lambda(x) \doteq \sum_{j=1}^{N} \lambda_j \hbar_j(x)$$

is a linear combination over the given family of all base classifiers $\hbar_1, \ldots, \hbar_N$ (assumed, as before, to be finite).

In a similar fashion, RankBoost also can be understood as a method for minimizing a particular loss function. By arguments similar to those in section 7.1, it can be shown that RankBoost greedily minimizes

$$\sum_{(u,v)\in E} \exp(F_\lambda(u) - F_\lambda(v)) \tag{11.5}$$

where F_λ and the $\hbar_j$'s are defined just as before. We refer to the loss in equation (11.5) as the *ranking exponential loss* and, to avoid possible confusion, we here refer to the ordinary exponential loss in equation (11.4) as the *classification* exponential loss.

As in chapter 7, it can be seen that RankBoost on each round t updates a single parameter λ_j corresponding to h_t by adding $\frac{1}{2}\alpha_t$ to it. Then theorem 11.1 follows from the simple observation that ranking loss is upper bounded by ranking exponential loss, which turns out to equal $\prod_{t=1}^{T} Z_t$ in the notation of that theorem.

Although the AdaBoost and RankBoost loss functions are somewhat different, they turn out to be closely related, a connection that we pause now to spell out. In particular, under a quite benign assumption about the family of base functions, it can be shown that any process that minimizes AdaBoost's classification exponential loss will simultaneously minimize RankBoost's ranking exponential loss for corresponding bipartite feedback. This suggests that although AdaBoost is intended for use as a classification algorithm, it may inadvertently be producing good rankings of the data as well.

To be more precise, suppose we are given binary labeled data as above, and assume for simplicity that the data includes no duplicate instances. Given data and a family of base functions, we could run AdaBoost on the data, as suggested above. Alternatively, we could regard this same data as providing bipartite feedback which ranks all of the positive examples in the dataset above all of the negative examples. Formally, this means that the set of preference pairs E is equal to $V_- \times V_+$ where

$$V_- \doteq \{x_i : y_i = -1\}$$

$$V_+ \doteq \{x_i : y_i = +1\}. \tag{11.6}$$

With these definitions, we could now apply RankBoost. In this case, the ranking exponential loss given in equation (11.5) is equal to

$$\sum_{u \in V_-} \sum_{v \in V_+} \exp\left(F_\lambda(u) - F_\lambda(v)\right).$$ (11.7)

By factoring, it can be seen that equation (11.7) is equal to

$$\left(\sum_{u \in V_-} e^{F_\lambda(u)}\right) \left(\sum_{v \in V_+} e^{-F_\lambda(v)}\right) = L^-(\lambda) \cdot L^+(\lambda)$$ (11.8)

where we define

$$L^b(\lambda) \doteq \sum_{i:y_i=b} e^{-bF_\lambda(x_i)}$$

for $b \in \{-1, +1\}$, and where we abbreviate L^{-1} and L^{+1} by L^- and L^+.

In comparison, AdaBoost minimizes equation (11.4), which can be written in the form

$$L^-(\lambda) + L^+(\lambda).$$ (11.9)

We now make the very benign assumption that the base function class includes one function that is identically equal to $+1$; that is, one base function, say, $\hbar_1$, is such that $\hbar_1(x) = +1$ for all x. Under this assumption, it can be shown that any process, such as AdaBoost, that minimizes classification exponential loss as in equation (11.9) also simultaneously minimizes ranking exponential loss as in equation (11.8).

We will not prove this here in full generality. However, to give some intuition, consider the special case in which a process like AdaBoost converges to some finite vector of parameters $\lambda^* \in \mathbb{R}^N$ which minimizes the classification exponential loss in equation (11.9). Then each partial derivative is equal to zero; that is,

$$0 = \frac{\partial(L^- + L^+)(\lambda^*)}{\partial \lambda_j} = \frac{\partial L^-(\lambda^*)}{\partial \lambda_j} + \frac{\partial L^+(\lambda^*)}{\partial \lambda_j}$$ (11.10)

for all j. In particular, when $j = 1$, since $\hbar_1$ is identically equal to $+1$, we have that

$$\frac{\partial L^b(\lambda^*)}{\partial \lambda_1} = \sum_{i:y_i=b} -be^{-bF_\lambda(x_i)} = -bL^b(\lambda^*)$$

for $b \in \{-1, +1\}$, so equation (11.10) becomes

$$L^-(\lambda^*) - L^+(\lambda^*) = 0.$$ (11.11)

On the other hand, the partial derivatives of the ranking exponential loss in equation (11.8) at λ^* are

$$\frac{\partial (L^- \cdot L^+)(\boldsymbol{\lambda}^*)}{\partial \lambda_j} = L^-(\boldsymbol{\lambda}^*) \cdot \frac{\partial L^+(\boldsymbol{\lambda}^*)}{\partial \lambda_j} + L^+(\boldsymbol{\lambda}^*) \cdot \frac{\partial L^-(\boldsymbol{\lambda}^*)}{\partial \lambda_j}$$

$$= L^+(\boldsymbol{\lambda}^*) \left[\frac{\partial L^+(\boldsymbol{\lambda}^*)}{\partial \lambda_j} + \frac{\partial L^-(\boldsymbol{\lambda}^*)}{\partial \lambda_j} \right] \tag{11.12}$$

$$= 0. \tag{11.13}$$

Here, equations (11.12) and (11.13) follow from equations (11.11) and (11.10), respectively. Thus, $\boldsymbol{\lambda}^*$ is also a minimum of the ranking exponential loss.

This suggests that AdaBoost, though not designed for such a purpose, may be reasonable as a method for producing a ranking. On the other hand, RankBoost, which has ranking as its explicit design goal, might do a better and faster job. Moreover, as earlier noted in section 7.3, these loss functions only partially capture the essence of the associated algorithms, and say little or nothing about their dynamics or ability to generalize.

11.3   Methods for Improving Efficiency

RankBoost would appear to be an inherently slow algorithm on large datasets since the main operations take $O(|E|)$ time, which is often quadratic in the number of training instances $|V|$. Nevertheless, in many natural cases, this running time can be improved very substantially, as we show in this section.

11.3.1   Reducing to Binary Classification

In section 11.2.2, we studied methods for finding weak rankings h_t and selecting α_t based on minimization of Z_t as in equation (11.1). Although these methods are exact, we will see now that working instead with an approximation of Z_t can make it possible to combine RankBoost with much more efficient weak learners designed for binary classification rather than ranking. In other words, we show that ranking problems can in principle be solved using a weak learning algorithm intended instead for ordinary binary classification. This approach will also pave the way for the other efficiency improvements given in the sections that follow.

As before, we fix t and omit it from subscripts when clear from context. Our approximation of Z is based on the convexity of $e^{\alpha x}$ as a function of x, which implies that

$$\exp\left(\tfrac{1}{2}\alpha(h(u) - h(v))\right) \le \tfrac{1}{2}\left(e^{\alpha h(u)} + e^{-\alpha h(v)}\right)$$

for any α and for any values of $h(u)$ and $h(v)$. Applied to Z as in equation (11.1), this gives

$$Z \le \tfrac{1}{2} \sum_{u,v} D(u, v) \left(e^{\alpha h(u)} + e^{-\alpha h(v)}\right)$$

$$= \sum_u \left(\tfrac{1}{2} \sum_v D(u, v)\right) e^{\alpha h(u)} + \sum_v \left(\tfrac{1}{2} \sum_u D(u, v)\right) e^{-\alpha h(v)}. \tag{11.14}$$

Motivated by the parenthesized expressions that appear here, let us now define $\tilde{D}(x, y)$ as follows, for all instances $x \in \mathcal{X}$ and for $y \in \{-1, +1\}$:

$$\tilde{D}(x, -1) \doteq \frac{1}{2} \sum_{x'} D(x, x')$$

$$\tilde{D}(x, +1) \doteq \frac{1}{2} \sum_{x'} D(x', x). \tag{11.15}$$

Note that $\tilde{D}$ is in fact a distribution since

$$\sum_{x} \sum_{y \in \{-1, +1\}} \tilde{D}(x, y) = \sum_{x} \left(\tilde{D}(x, -1) + \tilde{D}(x, +1) \right)$$

$$= \sum_{x} \left(\left(\frac{1}{2} \sum_{x'} D(x, x') \right) + \left(\frac{1}{2} \sum_{x'} D(x', x) \right) \right)$$

$$= \frac{1}{2} \sum_{x, x'} D(x, x') + \frac{1}{2} \sum_{x, x'} D(x', x) = 1.$$

Since the definitions in equation (11.15) are exactly the parenthesized quantities appearing in equation (11.14), we can rewrite this bound on Z as

$$Z \leq \sum_{x} \tilde{D}(x, -1) \, e^{\alpha h(x)} + \sum_{x} \tilde{D}(x, +1) \, e^{-\alpha h(x)}$$

$$= \sum_{x} \sum_{y \in \{-1, +1\}} \tilde{D}(x, y) \, e^{-\alpha y h(x)}. \tag{11.16}$$

This expression has precisely the same form as the weighted exponential loss encountered in chapter 9, such as in equation (9.2), which the booster and weak learner aim to minimize on each round of boosting in the context of ordinary binary classification, using confidence-rated predictions. Thus, rather than working directly with Z and the possibly large set of preference pairs given in E, the approximation in equation (11.16) suggests an alternative approach: On each round t, we construct a binary-classification training set in which each training instance x is replaced by two oppositely labeled examples, $(x, -1)$ and $(x, +1)$. Then, using the distribution $D = D_t$ over pairs of instances, we compute the distribution $\tilde{D} = \tilde{D}_t$ over labeled examples (x, y) as in equation (11.15). Finally, using the various techniques outlined in chapter 9, we apply a binary-classification weak learning algorithm to this data and distribution to find a (possibly confidence-rated) weak hypothesis h, and also to select α, with the objective of minimizing equation (11.16).

As an example, for weak rankings with bounded range, say, $[-1, +1]$, we can set α using the approximation of Z given in section 9.2.3. Specifically, applying equation (9.7) to equation (11.16) gives the upper bound

$$Z \leq \frac{e^{\alpha} + e^{-\alpha}}{2} - \frac{e^{\alpha} - e^{-\alpha}}{2} r, \tag{11.17}$$

where now

$$r \doteq \sum_{x} \sum_{y \in \{-1, +1\}} \tilde{D}(x, y) y h(x)$$

$$= \sum_{x} h(x) \left(\tilde{D}(x, +1) - \tilde{D}(x, -1) \right). \tag{11.18}$$

As seen earlier, the right-hand side of equation (11.17) is minimized when

$$\alpha = \frac{1}{2} \ln \left(\frac{1 + r}{1 - r} \right), \tag{11.19}$$

which, plugging back into equation (11.17), yields $Z \leq \sqrt{1 - r^2}$. Thus, to approximately minimize Z using weak rankings with range $[-1, +1]$, we can attempt to maximize $|r|$ as defined in equation (11.18), and then set α as in equation (11.19). If the range of the weak rankings is further restricted to $\{-1, +1\}$, then it can be checked that

$$r = 1 - 2 \mathbf{Pr}_{(x,y) \sim \tilde{D}} [h(x) \neq y],$$

so that, in this case, maximizing r is equivalent to finding a weak ranking (really a classifier) h having small classification error with respect to the weighted binary-classification dataset constructed as above.

Compared to working with preference pairs, this approach of reducing to a binary-classification problem may be much more efficient, though inexact. RankBoost, in the general form given in algorithm 11.1, uses a *pair-based* weak learner that aims to minimize Z_t, given a distribution over preference pairs. Now, however, we see that RankBoost can instead be used with an *instance-based* weak learner that attempts to minimize the approximation in equation (11.16) with respect to a distribution on binary labeled examples. Even in this latter case, we are still left with the difficulty of maintaining and computing D_t and $\tilde{D}_t$ efficiently. We will see next how this can be done when the feedback is well structured.

11.3.2 Layered Feedback

We begin by describing a more efficient implementation of RankBoost for feedback that is *layered*. Such feedback is defined by disjoint subsets $V_1, \ldots, V_J$ of $\mathcal{X}$ such that, for $j < k$, all instances in V_k are ranked above all instances in V_j. Formally, this means that the set of preference pairs is exactly

$$E = \bigcup_{1 \leq j < k \leq J} V_j \times V_k. \tag{11.20}$$

For example, layered feedback arises in the movie-ranking task, mentioned earlier, in which each movie is rated with 1 to J stars. For that matter, the feedback will be layered in any application in which individual instances are assigned a grade or rating along an ordered scale.

When there are just $J = 2$ layers, the feedback is said to be *bipartite* since in this case, the edges $V_1 \times V_2$ define a complete bipartite feedback graph. Feedback of this special form arises naturally, for instance, in document rank-retrieval tasks common in the field of information retrieval. Here, a set of documents may have each been judged to be relevant or irrelevant to some topic or query. Although predicting such judgments can be viewed as a classification task, it is generally more desirable to produce a ranked list of all documents with the relevant ones near the top—in other words, an ordering in which the relevant documents are preferred to irrelevant ones. Feedback that encodes such preferences is evidently bipartite. In fact, as we have already discussed, any binary-classification problem can instead be treated as a bipartite ranking problem in a similar fashion.

If RankBoost is implemented naively as in section 11.2, then the space and time-per-round requirements will be $O(|E|)$, that is, on the order of the number of preference pairs $|E|$, where in this case,

$$|E| = \sum_{j<k} |V_j| \cdot |V_k|.$$

Typically, this will be quadratic in the number of training instances. To a degree, such complexity is inevitable when working with a pair-based weak learner whose input is a distribution D_t on E. However, in section 11.3.1, we saw that RankBoost can also be used with an instance-based weak learner whose input is instead a distribution $\tilde{D}_t$ on the (usually) much smaller set $V \times \{-1, +1\}$. This presents an opening for improving the efficiency of RankBoost in the latter setting. Rather than maintaining D_t and using it to compute $\tilde{D}_t$ as in equation (11.15), operations which require $O(|E|)$ time and space, we will see now that $\tilde{D}_t$ can be computed directly and much more efficiently by exploiting the special structure of the layered feedback without first finding D_t explicitly.

Let F_t denote the combined hypothesis accumulated through round t:

$$F_t(x) \doteq \frac{1}{2} \sum_{t'=1}^{t} \alpha_{t'} h_{t'}(x).$$

By unraveling the recurrence for D_t used by RankBoost, it can be verified that

$$D_t(u, v) = \frac{1}{\mathcal{Z}_t} \cdot \exp\left(F_{t-1}(u) - F_{t-1}(v)\right) \tag{11.21}$$

for $(u, v) \in E$ (and zero for all other pairs), where $\mathcal{Z}_t$ is a normalization factor. Now suppose $x \in V_j$. Then plugging equation (11.21) into equation (11.15) gives

$$\tilde{D}_t(x, -1) \doteq \frac{1}{2} \sum_{x'} D_t(x, x')$$

$$= \frac{1}{2\mathcal{Z}_t} \cdot \sum_{k=j+1}^{J} \sum_{x' \in V_k} \exp\left(F_{t-1}(x) - F_{t-1}(x')\right) \tag{11.22}$$

$$= \frac{1}{2\mathcal{Z}_t} \exp\left(F_{t-1}(x)\right) \sum_{k=j+1}^{J} \sum_{x' \in V_k} \exp\left(-F_{t-1}(x')\right). \tag{11.23}$$

Equation (11.22) uses equation (11.21) along with the fact that $(x, x') \in E$ if and only if $x' \in V_{j+1} \cup V_{j+2} \cup \cdots \cup V_J$ by definition of the layered feedback. The double sum appearing in equation (11.23) may seem fairly expensive to compute for each x separately. However, because these sums do not depend on x specifically, but only on its layer j, they can be computed just once for each layer, and then used repeatedly. More specifically, to represent these sums, we define, for $j = 1, \ldots, J$,

$$S_{t,j}(-1) \doteq \sum_{x \in V_j} \exp\left(-F_{t-1}(x)\right)$$

and

$$C_{t,j}(-1) \doteq \sum_{k=j+1}^{J} S_{t,k}(-1).$$

Notice that $S_{t,j}(-1)$ can be computed for *all* j simultaneously with a single scan through the training instances, and thus in time $O(|V|)$ (where, as usual, V is the set of all training instances, in this case, the union of all J disjoint layers). Further, once these have been found, we can also compute $C_{t,j}(-1)$, for all j, using the simple relation $C_{t,j}(-1) = C_{t,j+1}(-1) + S_{t,j}(-1)$ in a pass that takes just $O(J) = O(|V|)$ time.

With these definitions, equation (11.23) can be rewritten as

$$\tilde{D}_t(x, -1) = \frac{1}{2\mathcal{Z}_t} \cdot \exp\left(F_{t-1}(x)\right) \cdot C_{t,j}(-1)$$

for all $x \in V_j$. Similarly, $\tilde{D}_t(x, +1)$ can be computed using analogous quantities $S_{t,j}(+1)$ and $C_{t,j}(+1)$. The normalization factor $\mathcal{Z}_t$ can also be found in $O(|V|)$ time (see exercise 11.6).

This approach to computing $\tilde{D}_t$ is summarized in algorithm 11.2, a more efficient version of RankBoost that we call *RankBoost.L*. The derivations above show that the computation of $\tilde{D}_t$ by RankBoost.L is equivalent to finding $\tilde{D}_t$ as in equation (11.15) based on RankBoost's computation of D_t. Furthermore, we have argued that this implementation requires space and time per round that are just $O(|V|)$, regardless of the number of layers J.

Algorithm 11.2
RankBoost.L, a more efficient version of RankBoost for layered feedback using an instance-based weak learner

Given: nonempty, disjoint subsets $V_1, \ldots, V_J$ of $\mathcal{X}$ representing preference pairs

$$E = \bigcup_{1 \le j < k \le J} V_j \times V_k.$$

Initialize: $F_0 \equiv 0$.
For $t = 1, \ldots, T$:

- For $j = 1, \ldots, J$ and $y \in \{-1, +1\}$, let

$$S_{t,j}(y) = \sum_{x \in V_j} \exp\left(y F_{t-1}(x)\right)$$

  and let

$$C_{t,j}(+1) = \sum_{k=1}^{j-1} S_{t,k}(+1), \qquad C_{t,j}(-1) = \sum_{k=j+1}^{J} S_{t,k}(-1).$$

- Train instance-based weak learner using distribution $\tilde{D}_t$ where, for $x \in V_j$, $j = 1, \ldots, J$, and $y \in \{-1, +1\}$,

$$\tilde{D}_t(x, y) = \frac{1}{2\mathcal{Z}_t} \cdot \exp(-y F_{t-1}(x)) \cdot C_{t,j}(y),$$

  and where $\mathcal{Z}_t$ is a normalization factor (chosen so that $\tilde{D}_t$ is a distribution).
- Get weak ranking $h_t : \mathcal{X} \to \mathbb{R}$.
- Choose $\alpha_t \in \mathbb{R}$.
- Aim: select h_t and α_t to minimize $\displaystyle\sum_x \sum_{y \in \{-1, +1\}} \tilde{D}_t(x, y)\, e^{-\alpha_t y h_t(x)}$.
- Update: $F_t = F_{t-1} + \frac{1}{2}\alpha_t h_t$.

Output the final ranking: $\displaystyle F(x) = F_T(x) = \frac{1}{2} \sum_{t=1}^{T} \alpha_t h_t(x)$.

11.3.3 Quasi-layered Feedback

So RankBoost can be implemented particularly efficiently when the feedback is layered. This technique can be generalized to a much broader class of problems in which the feedback is not layered per se, but can be decomposed, vaguely speaking, into a kind of union or sum in which each component is layered.

To make this notion of decomposition precise, we will first need to generalize RankBoost and our formalism to handle *weighted* feedback. We have assumed until now that all preference pairs are given equal importance; sometimes, however, we may wish to give some pairs greater weight than others. For instance, in movie ranking, we might wish to give pairs representing the preference for a 5-star movie over a 1-star movie greater weight than a pair that represents a 3-star movie that is preferred to a 2-star movie.

Formally, this amounts to providing the learning algorithm with a nonnegative, real-valued *feedback function* φ, where the weight $\varphi(u, v) \geq 0$ represents the relative importance of pair (u, v), with $\varphi(u, v)$ strictly positive if and only if (u, v) is a preference pair. Conceptually, φ is defined over all of $\mathcal{X} \times \mathcal{X}$, but is in fact zero everywhere except on the finite preference-pair set E. We also can assume without loss of generality that φ sums to 1 so that

$$\sum_{u,v} \varphi(u, v) = 1. \tag{11.24}$$

For instance, the (unweighted) feedback function used until now is defined by

$$\varphi(u, v) = \begin{cases} 1/|E| & \text{if } (u, v) \in E \\ 0 & \text{else.} \end{cases} \tag{11.25}$$

RankBoost can easily be modified for more general feedback functions φ simply by using φ as the initial distribution D_1. Theorem 11.1 then provides a bound on the empirical ranking loss relative to φ, that is, $\text{rloss}_\varphi(F)$.

With this extended formalism, we can now focus on *quasi-layered feedback*, that is, feedback given by a function φ that can be decomposed as a weighted sum of layered feedback functions. Thus, such feedback can be written in the form

$$\varphi(u, v) = \sum_{i=1}^{m} w_i \varphi_i(u, v) \tag{11.26}$$

for some set of positive weights w_i that sum to 1, and for some sequence of layered feedback functions φ_i. The weights w_i encode the relative importance assigned to each function φ_i. Each of these, in turn, is associated with layered feedback over a subset V^i of the training instances. That is, V^i is partitioned into disjoint layers $V_1^i, \ldots, V_{J_i}^i$ which define the set E^i of preference pairs just as in equation (11.20). The feedback φ_i is then defined exactly as in equation (11.25), but with E replaced by E^i. In the special case that $J_i = 2$ for all i so that each component feedback function is bipartite, we say that the combined feedback function φ is *quasi-bipartite*.

Of course, any feedback function can be written in quasi-bipartite form (and, therefore, in quasi-layered form) by choosing the sets V_1^i and V_2^i to be singletons, with one component for each edge. Here, however, we focus on natural cases in which the sets defining the layers are fairly sizable.

For instance, in a different formulation of the ranked-retrieval task, our goal might be to learn to rank documents by their relevance to a range of possible queries. In other words, given a query q (say, a search term), we want the system to rank all of the documents in its database by their relevance to q. To train such a system, we provide it with a set of queries $q_1, \ldots, q_m$, and for each query, we also provide a set of documents, each of which has been judged relevant or irrelevant to that particular query. To formulate such data as a ranking problem, we define the domain $\mathcal{X}$ to be the set of all pairs (q, d) of queries q and documents d. The feedback is naturally quasi-bipartite. In particular, for each training query q_i, we define one bipartite feedback function φ_i in which V_2^i (respectively, V_1^i) consists of all pairs (q_i, d) where d is a training document for q_i that has been judged relevant (respectively, irrelevant). Thus, φ_i encodes the fact that (q_i, d_2) should be ranked above (q_i, d_1) if d_2 is relevant for q_i but d_1 is irrelevant for q_i. Assuming the queries have equal importance, we can then let $w_i = 1/m$.

If the documents have instead been graded along a scale of relevance (for instance, very relevant, somewhat relevant, barely relevant, not at all relevant), then a similar formulation leads to feedback that is quasi-layered in general, even if not quasi-bipartite.

RankBoost.L (algorithm 11.2) can be directly generalized for quasi-layered feedback simply by treating each component separately and combining the results linearly. More specifically, as in section 11.3.2, the main computational challenge is in computing $\tilde{D}_t$ on each round t. As before, using the recurrent definition of D_t computed by RankBoost as in algorithm 11.1 together with the decomposition of $D_1 = \varphi$ in equation (11.26), we can write

$$D_t(u, v) = \frac{1}{\mathcal{Z}_t} \cdot D_1(u, v) \exp\left(F_{t-1}(u) - F_{t-1}(v)\right)$$

$$= \frac{1}{\mathcal{Z}_t} \sum_{i=1}^{m} w_i \varphi_i(u, v) \exp\left(F_{t-1}(u) - F_{t-1}(v)\right)$$

$$= \frac{1}{\mathcal{Z}_t} \sum_{i=1}^{m} w_i d_t^i(u, v)$$

where $\mathcal{Z}_t$ is a normalization factor, and where we define

$$d_t^i(u, v) \doteq \varphi_i(u, v) \exp\left(F_{t-1}(u) - F_{t-1}(v)\right).$$

Although d_t^i is not a distribution, we can nevertheless apply equation (11.15) to it, thus defining

$$\tilde{d}_t^i(x, -1) \doteq \frac{1}{2} \sum_{x'} d_t^i(x, x')$$

$$\tilde{d}_t^i(x, +1) \doteq \frac{1}{2} \sum_{x'} d_t^i(x', x).$$

With these definitions, along with equation (11.15), we get that

$$\tilde{D}_t(x, -1) = \frac{1}{2} \sum_{x'} D_t(x, x')$$

$$= \frac{1}{2Z_t} \sum_{x'} \sum_{i=1}^m w_i d_t^i(x, x')$$

$$= \frac{1}{Z_t} \sum_{i=1}^m w_i \left(\frac{1}{2} \sum_{x'} d_t^i(x, x') \right)$$

$$= \frac{1}{Z_t} \sum_{i=1}^m w_i \tilde{d}_t^i(x, -1).$$

A similar calculation holds for $\tilde{D}_t(x, +1)$ so that, in general,

$$\tilde{D}_t(x, y) = \frac{1}{Z_t} \sum_{i=1}^m w_i \tilde{d}_t^i(x, y)$$

for $y \in \{-1, +1\}$. Further, $\tilde{d}_t^i(x, y)$ can be computed for each i separately exactly as in section 11.3.2.

Combining these ideas leads to the algorithm *RankBoost.qL*, shown as algorithm 11.3. The space and time per round needed to compute $\tilde{d}_t^i$, for each i, is $O(|V^i|)$ by our earlier arguments. Thus, the total time and space is

$$O\left(\sum_{i=1}^m |V^i| \right),$$

a dramatic improvement (in most cases) over a direct implementation of RankBoost, which could be as bad as

$$O\left(\sum_{i=1}^m |E^i| \right).$$

Algorithm 11.3
RankBoost.qL, an efficient version of RankBoost for quasi-layered feedback using an instance-based weak learner

---

Given:

- for $i = 1, \ldots, m$, nonempty, disjoint subsets $V_1^i, \ldots, V_{J_i}^i$ of $\mathcal{X}$ representing preference pairs $E^i = \bigcup_{1 \le j < k \le J_i} V_j^i \times V_k^i$

- positive weights w_i such that $\sum_{i=1}^m w_i = 1$.

Initialize: $F_0 \equiv 0$.
For $t = 1, \ldots, T$:

- For $i = 1, \ldots, m$, $j = 1, \ldots, J_i$, and $y \in \{-1, +1\}$, let

$$S_{t,j}^i(y) = \sum_{x \in V_j^i} \exp\left(y F_{t-1}(x)\right),$$

  and let

$$C_{t,j}^i(+1) = \sum_{k=1}^{j-1} S_{t,k}^i(+1), \qquad C_{t,j}^i(-1) = \sum_{k=j+1}^{J_i} S_{t,k}^i(-1).$$

- For $i = 1, \ldots, m$, $x \in \mathcal{X}$, and $y \in \{-1, +1\}$, let

$$\tilde{d}_t^i(x, y) = \frac{\exp\left(-y F_{t-1}(x)\right) C_{t,j}^i(y)}{2|E^i|}$$

  for $x \in V_j^i$ (and 0 for all $x \notin V_1^i \cup \cdots \cup V_{J_i}^i$).

- Train instance-based weak learner using distribution $\tilde{D}_t$ where, for $x \in \mathcal{X}$ and $y \in \{-1, +1\}$,

$$\tilde{D}_t(x, y) = \frac{1}{\mathcal{Z}_t} \sum_{i=1}^m w_i \tilde{d}_t^i(x, y),$$

  and where $\mathcal{Z}_t$ is a normalization factor (chosen so that $\tilde{D}_t$ is a distribution).

- Get weak ranking $h_t : \mathcal{X} \to \mathbb{R}$.

- Choose $\alpha_t \in \mathbb{R}$.

- Aim: select h_t and α_t to minimize $\sum_x \sum_{y \in \{-1, +1\}} \tilde{D}_t(x, y) \, e^{-\alpha_t y h_t(x)}$.

- Update: $F_t = F_{t-1} + \frac{1}{2} \alpha_t h_t$.

Output the final ranking: $F(x) = F_T(x) = \frac{1}{2} \sum_{t=1}^T \alpha_t h_t(x)$.

11.4   Multiclass, Multi-label Classification

These techniques for learning to rank provide a different approach to multiclass, multi-label classification as studied in chapter 10. The idea is to treat any such problem as a ranking task in which the goal is to learn to rank the labels from most to least likely to be assigned to a particular instance. As in chapter 10, each training example is a pair (x_i, Y_i) where $x_i \in \mathcal{X}$ and $Y_i \subseteq \mathcal{Y}$, and where $\mathcal{Y}$ is a set of K labels. We continue to use the notation $Y[\ell]$ defined in equation (10.2). We view each example (x_i, Y_i) as providing feedback indicating that for instance x_i, each of the labels in Y_i should be ranked higher than each of the remaining labels in $\mathcal{Y} - Y_i$. Such feedback is naturally quasi-bipartite. Thus, the domain for the ranking problem is the set of all instance-label pairs $\mathcal{X} \times \mathcal{Y}$, and we can define φ, as described in section 11.3.3, with $w_i = 1/m$, $J_i = 2$, and each φ_i defined by the sets

$$
\begin{aligned}
V_1^i &= \{x_i\} \times (\mathcal{Y} - Y_i) &= \{(x_i, \overline{y}) : \overline{y} \notin Y_i\} \\
V_2^i &= \{x_i\} \times Y_i &= \{(x_i, y) : y \in Y_i\}.
\end{aligned}
$$

(Here, we are assuming implicitly that the x_i's are unique, although the algorithm we give shortly will be valid even when this is not the case.)

When RankBoost.qL is applied using this reduction, we obtain a multiclass, multi-label version of AdaBoost based on ranking. This algorithm is shown as algorithm 11.4, and is called *AdaBoost.MR—M* for multiclass, *R* for ranking. Here, we have streamlined the pseudocode, collapsing many of the computations of RankBoost.qL in specializing it to the current setting. We also have simplified some of the notation, writing $C_t^i(+1)$ for $C_{t,2}^i(+1) = S_{t,2}^i(+1)$; $C_t^i(-1)$ for $C_{t,1}^i(-1) = S_{t,1}^i(-1)$; and $\tilde{D}_t(i, \ell)$ for $\tilde{D}_t((x_i, \ell), Y_i[\ell])$. (We can ignore $C_{t,1}^i(+1)$, $C_{t,2}^i(-1)$, and $\tilde{D}_t((x_i, \ell), -Y_i[\ell])$ since all of these are always zero under this reduction. See exercise 11.3.)

The final output of the algorithm is a real-valued function F on $\mathcal{X} \times \mathcal{Y}$ with the interpretation that $F(x, \cdot)$ provides a predicted ranking of the labels to be assigned to given instance x (so that label ℓ_1 is ranked higher than ℓ_0 if $F(x, \ell_1) > F(x, \ell_0)$). The function F can be used for classification simply by choosing a single best label, as in equation (10.7), yielding the classifier

$$
H^1(x) = \arg \max_{y \in \mathcal{Y}} F(x, y).
$$

Similar to the analysis in section 10.2.3, we can then compute an upper bound on the one-error of H^1 (that is, the probability of H^1 missing all of the correct labels) in terms of the ranking loss. We state and prove this result only with respect to the empirical distribution defined by the training set, although a more general result with respect to any distribution over pairs (x, Y) holds as well.

Algorithm 11.4
The AdaBoost.MR algorithm for multiclass, multi-label classification problems

---

Given: $(x_1, Y_1), \ldots, (x_m, Y_m)$ where $x_i \in \mathcal{X}, Y_i \subseteq \mathcal{Y}$.
Initialize: $F_0 \equiv 0$.
For $t = 1, \ldots, T$:

- For $i = 1, \ldots, m$, let

$$C_t^i(+1) = \sum_{\ell \in \mathcal{Y} - Y_i} \exp\left(F_{t-1}(x_i, \ell)\right)$$

$$C_t^i(-1) = \sum_{\ell \in Y_i} \exp\left(-F_{t-1}(x_i, \ell)\right).$$

- Train weak learner using distribution $\tilde{D}_t$ where

$$\tilde{D}_t(i, \ell) = \frac{\exp\left(-Y_i[\ell] \cdot F_{t-1}(x_i, \ell)\right) \cdot C_t^i(Y_i[\ell])}{2 \mathcal{Z}_t |Y_i| \cdot |\mathcal{Y} - Y_i|}$$

  for $i = 1, \ldots, m$ and $\ell \in \mathcal{Y}$, where $\mathcal{Z}_t$ is a normalization factor (chosen so that $\tilde{D}_t$ will be a distribution on $\{1, \ldots, m\} \times \mathcal{Y}$).

- Get weak hypothesis $h_t : \mathcal{X} \times \mathcal{Y} \to \mathbb{R}$.

- Choose $\alpha_t \in \mathbb{R}$.

- Aim: select h_t and α_t to minimalize

$$\tilde{Z}_t \doteq \sum_{i=1}^{m} \sum_{\ell \in \mathcal{Y}} \tilde{D}_t(i, \ell) \exp\left(-\alpha_t \, Y_i[\ell] \, h_t(x_i, \ell)\right).$$

- Update: $F_t = F_{t-1} + \frac{1}{2} \alpha_t h_t$.

Output the final hypothesis:

$$F(x, \ell) = F_T(x, \ell) = \frac{1}{2} \sum_{t=1}^{T} \alpha_t h_t(x, \ell).$$

Theorem 11.2 Using the notation of algorithm 11.4 and the definition of φ above, assume $Y_i \neq \emptyset$ for all i. Then

$$\widehat{\text{one-err}}(H^1) \leq (K-1)\,\text{rloss}_\varphi(F)$$

$$\leq (K-1)\prod_{t=1}^{T}\tilde{Z}_t$$

(where $K = |\mathcal{Y}|$).

Proof Let $\hat{y}_i = H^1(x_i)$. If, for some i, $\hat{y}_i \notin Y_i$, then $F(x_i, y) \leq F(x_i, \hat{y}_i)$ for all $y \in Y_i$. Thus, in general,

$$\mathbf{1}\{\hat{y}_i \notin Y_i\} \leq \frac{1}{|Y_i|}\sum_{y \in Y_i}\sum_{\bar{y} \notin Y_i}\mathbf{1}\{F(x_i, y) \leq F(x_i, \bar{y})\}.$$

Therefore,

$$\frac{1}{K-1}\widehat{\text{one-err}}(H^1) = \frac{1}{m(K-1)}\sum_{i=1}^{m}\mathbf{1}\{H^1(x_i) \notin Y_i\}$$

$$\leq \frac{1}{m}\sum_{i=1}^{m}\left[\frac{1}{|\mathcal{Y} - Y_i|}\mathbf{1}\{\hat{y}_i \notin Y_i\}\right]$$

$$\leq \frac{1}{m}\sum_{i=1}^{m}\left[\frac{1}{|Y_i|\,|\mathcal{Y} - Y_i|}\sum_{y \in Y_i}\sum_{\bar{y} \notin Y_i}\mathbf{1}\{F(x_i, y) \leq F(x_i, \bar{y})\}\right]$$

$$= \text{rloss}_\varphi(F).$$

This proves the first inequality given in the theorem. The second inequality follows from theorem 11.1 and equation (11.16). ∎

Thus, in the case of single-label, multiclass classification, theorem 11.2 immediately yields a bound on the training error of the classifier H^1 derived from AdaBoost.MR.

Note that the space and time-per-round requirements of AdaBoost.MR are $O(mK)$, the same as AdaBoost.MH. Furthermore, the criteria for choosing a weak hypothesis h_t are identical for the two algorithms. Thus, AdaBoost.MR is entirely comparable to AdaBoost.MH, both in complexity and in compatibility with weak learners. The difference is that Ada-Boost.MR aims to produce good rankings of the labels for individual instances, while AdaBoost.MH is designed to minimize Hamming loss. In practice, the two algorithms are quite comparable in performance, both giving decent results when using a weak base learning algorithm such as decision stumps; for instance, the multiclass results in section 1.2.2 were obtained with AdaBoost.MR.

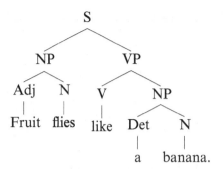

Figure 11.2
A sample parse tree. The terminal nodes of the tree are labeled with words of the sentence being parsed. Nonterminal nodes are labeled with syntactic units (S = sentence, NP = noun phrase, VP = verb phrase, etc.).

11.5 Applications

We end this chapter with a description of two example applications of RankBoost.

11.5.1 Parsing English Sentences

We first describe how RankBoost has been used to improve the performance of a state-of-the-art parser. Parsing is a fundamental problem in natural language processing. Given a sentence in English (or any other language), the problem is to compute the sentence's associated *parse tree*. For instance, the sentence

Fruit flies like a banana.

might get mapped to the tree shown in figure 11.2. Such a tree provides a wealth of information about the sentence, including the part of speech of each word; the overall structure of the sentence, including its hierarchical decomposition into syntactically relevant phrases; and the grammatical relationships between these words and phrases.

Because of the ambiguity and imprecision of natural languages, there will typically be more than one plausible parse for any given sentence. For instance, the sentence above has (at least) two meanings—either it can be an observation about drosophila enjoying bananas, or it can be a comparison of the aerodynamics of fruit generally with bananas in particular. These two meanings correspond to two distinct, syntactic parses of the sentence, one shown in figure 11.2 and the other in figure 11.3. (Indeed, the full Groucho Marx quote—"Time flies like an arrow; fruit flies like a banana"—derives its humor from exactly this syntactic ambiguity.)

When the meaning of the sentence is disregarded and only its syntactic structure is considered, ambiguity becomes truly ubiquitous, yielding multiple plausible parses for a great many English sentences. For this reason, parsers are often designed to output a ranking of the parses that seem to be the most promising. For instance, a probabilistic parser might

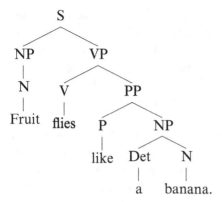

Figure 11.3
A different parse tree for the same sentence as in figure 11.2.

attempt to estimate the probability of each tree being associated with the given sentence, and then output a ranking, according to this probability, of the most probable trees.

This is where there exists an opportunity to apply RankBoost, specifically, as a kind of post-processing tool for improving the rankings produced by an existing parser. Here is one specific scheme that has been proposed. We begin with a training set of sentence-tree pairs (s_i, t_i) where, for sentence s_i, the parse tree t_i represents the "gold standard" selected by a human expert. During training, each sentence s_i is fed to a given parser which generates k candidate parse trees $\hat{t}_{i1}, \ldots, \hat{t}_{ik}$, where k is perhaps 20. The gold standard tree t_i may or may not be included in this group, but in either case, the candidate that is closest to it (for some reasonable definition of "close") can be identified; without loss of generality, let $\hat{t}_{i1}$ be this best tree among the candidates. To apply RankBoost, we can now provide feedback encoding the fact that $\hat{t}_{i1}$ is considered better than the other candidates. Thus, the instances are all pairs $(s_i, \hat{t}_{ij})$, and the preference pairs are defined so as to place $(s_i, \hat{t}_{i1})$ above $(s_i, \hat{t}_{ij})$ for all $j > 1$. This feedback is quasi-bipartite, each sentence s_i defining its own bipartite feedback function. Even so, RankBoost.qL provides no advantage since the number of preference pairs is nearly equal to (actually, slightly smaller than) the number of training instances.

For weak rankings, we can use binary rankings defined by a large set of linguistically informed "features." Such a ranking is a $\{-1, +1\}$-valued function on sentence-tree pairs that is $+1$ if and only if the corresponding feature is present. For instance, one such weak ranking might be $+1$ if the given tree contains an instance of the rule $\langle S \rightarrow NP\ VP \rangle$ (meaning a sentence can consist of a noun phrase followed by a verb phrase), and -1 otherwise. A full listing of the types of features used goes beyond the scope of this book.

This setup has many advantages. First of all, since we are using binary weak rankings, we can use the exact method given in equations (11.2) and (11.3) for setting α_t and computing

Z_t. More importantly, because the weak rankings h_t are $\{-1, +1\}$-valued, their scaled differences $\frac{1}{2}(h_t(v) - h_t(u))$, as used by RankBoost, will be $\{-1, 0, +1\}$-valued, just like the abstaining weak hypotheses in section 9.2.4. Moreover, these differences are likely to be quite sparse. This means that we can dramatically improve efficiency by applying the techniques described in that section for exploiting sparsity to substantially minimize the number of weights updated on each round, and to make each round's search for the best feature very fast.

To get the best performance, we note that the parser we start with may already do a decent job of ranking based on its own score, often a (log) probability as mentioned above. It makes sense to use this information, rather than starting from scratch. Thus, on round 0, we can use the scores given by the parser as a weak ranking of the candidates, and then select all subsequent rankings as described above.

After training RankBoost in this fashion, we obtain a ranking function F. To use it on a new test sentence s, we first run the parser to obtain a set of k candidate trees which are then re-ranked using F. This technique can significantly improve the quality of the rankings produced by the parser. For instance, on a corpus of *Wall Street Journal* articles, re-ranking using RankBoost resulted in a 13% relative decrease in one standard error measure. In these experiments, the efficiency techniques described in section 9.2.4 were especially helpful, yielding an implementation that was faster than a naive version of the algorithm by roughly a factor of 2600, and making it reasonable to run RankBoost for 100,000 rounds on a very large dataset of around a million parse trees and 500,000 features (weak rankings).

11.5.2 Finding Cancer Genes

As a second example application, we describe how RankBoost has been used in a bioinformatics setting to identify genes which may potentially be relevant to various forms of cancer. By training on examples of genes already known to be relevant or irrelevant, the idea is to learn a ranking of all genes that places those related to cancer at the top of the list, hopefully including some whose connection to cancer is not already known.

This problem fits neatly into the ranking framework described in section 11.1. The genes are the instances. Those with known relevance or irrelevance are the training instances. The feedback is naturally bipartite, with all genes that are relevant to cancer "preferred" to all those that are irrelevant (since we want them to be ranked higher). Our goal is to infer from these training instances a ranking of all the instances (genes) in which those related to cancer are ranked higher than those that are not.

Thus, we can apply RankBoost. First, however, we need to choose a weak learning algorithm for finding weak rankers. As is common for such research, each gene was described here by microarray expression levels, that is, by a vector of N real numbers, each measuring the degree to which the gene was measured to be expressed, or activated, in particular tissue samples collected from various patients or under varying experimental conditions. Clearly, we have many options in the design of a weak learner for such data. In this study, very simple weak rankers were used, each identified with individual samples, that is, specific coordinates of the expression vectors. In other words, each weak ranker was selected from a family $\{\hbar_1, \ldots, \hbar_N\}$ where, for every gene represented by a vector $\mathbf{x} \in \mathbb{R}^N$ of expression levels, the output of weak ranker $\hbar_j$ is defined simply to be the j-th coordinate $\hbar_j(\mathbf{x}) = x_j$. Although the data is bipartite, the RankBoost algorithm shown as algorithm 11.1 was used in combination with an exhaustive, pair-based weak learning algorithm so that, on each round t, the weak ranker $h_t = \hbar_{j_t}$ and the value $\alpha_t \in \mathbb{R}$ were chosen together to minimize Z_t, as defined in the algorithm, over all choices of j_t and α_t.

One of the datasets used was for leukemia, and consisted of 7129 genes whose expression levels had been measured on $N = 72$ samples. For training, just 10 of the genes were used as instances known to be relevant, and 157 were selected as instances known to be irrelevant. RankBoost was then trained on these 167 training instances as described above, resulting in a ranking of all 7129 genes.

Table 11.1 shows the top 25 genes identified in this manner. For each of these genes, an attempt was made to determine its relevance to leukemia based on a search of the scientific literature and using assorted online tools. As can be seen from the summary given in the table, many of these genes are already known either to be a target for possible drug therapy in treating leukemia, or to be a marker that may be useful in its diagnosis. Many other highly ranked genes in the table are not known at this time to be markers or targets, but show potential to have these properties. For example, the top-ranked gene KIAA0220 encodes a protein whose function is not currently known, but that shows strong similarity to another protein that is known to be involved in various forms of cancer, and thus that may be useful as a target in the treatment of leukemia. Of course, further experimental testing will be needed to determine if these genes actually are related to leukemia, but finding such potentially useful genes whose properties are currently unknown is precisely the goal of this research. These results thus seem very promising.

The table also shows how these genes are ranked using two other standard statistical methods. As can be seen, the ranking produced by RankBoost is very different from that of these other methods, suggesting that the techniques might give results that can be used in a complementary fashion for finding relevant genes.

Summary

In this chapter, we examined a framework for studying ranking problems, as well as a boosting algorithm for ranking. This algorithm is based on a reduction to binary classification involving the relative ordering of pairs of instances. This makes it flexible in terms of the feedback with which it can be applied, but potentially can lead to a quadratic running time if the feedback is dense. Nevertheless, even in such cases, we saw how the algorithm can be implemented very efficiently in the special but natural case of layered or quasi-layered feedback. Further, we saw how RankBoost and its variants can be used with weak learning algorithms intended for ordinary binary classification, possibly with confidence-rated predictions. Treating multi-label, multiclass classification as a ranking problem leads to the AdaBoost.MR algorithm. Finally, we looked at applications of RankBoost to parsing and finding cancer-related genes.

Table 11.1
The top 25 genes ranked using RankBoost on the leukemia dataset

	Gene	Relevance Summary	t-Statistic Rank	Pearson Rank
1.	KIAA0220	□	6628	2461
2.	G-gamma globin	◆	3578	3567
3.	Delta-globin	◆	3663	3532
4.	Brain-expressed HHCPA78 homolog	□	6734	2390
5.	Myeloperoxidase	◆	139	6573
6.	Probable protein disulfide isomerase ER-60 precursor	□	6650	575
7.	NPM1 Nucleophosmin	◆	405	1115
8.	CD34	◆	6732	643
9.	Elongation factor-1-beta	×	4460	3413
10.	CD24	◆	81	1
11.	60S ribosomal protein L23	□	1950	73
12.	5-aminolevulinic acid synthase	□	4750	3351
13.	HLA class II histocompatibility antigen	◆	5114	298
14.	Epstein-Barr virus small RNA-associated protein	□	6388	1650
15.	HNRPA1 Heterogeneous nuclear ribonucleoprotein A1	□	4188	1791
16.	Azurocidin	◆	162	6789
17.	Red cell anion exchanger (EPB3, AE1, Band 3)	□	3853	4926
18.	Topoisomerase II beta	■	17	3
19.	HLA class I histocompatibility antigen	×	265	34
20.	Probable G protein-coupled receptor LCR1 homolog	□	30	62
21.	HLA-SB alpha gene (class II antigen)	×	6374	317
22.	Int-6	◇	3878	912
23.	Alpha-tubulin	□	5506	1367
24.	Terminal transferase	◆	6	9
25.	Glycophorin B precursor	□	3045	5668

For each gene, the relevance has been labeled as follows: ■ = known therapeutic target; □ = potential therapeutic target; ◆ = known marker; ◇ = potential marker; × = no link found. The table also indicates the rank of each gene according to two other standard statistical methods.

Bibliographic Notes

The approach to ranking adopted in section 11.1, as well as the RankBoost algorithm of section 11.2.1 and techniques of section 11.2.2, are all taken from Freund et al. [90]. Minimization of the ranking loss is essentially equivalent to optimization of other standard measures, specifically, the area under the receiver-operating-characteristic curve and the Wilcoxon-Mann-Whitney statistic; see, for instance, Cortes and Mohri [55].

The results of section 11.2.3 are due to Rudin et al. [193] (see also Rudin and Schapire [195]), who give a more rigorous treatment.

The techniques described in section 11.3 significantly generalize the work of Freund et al. [90], who had given such efficiency improvements only in the bipartite case. These generalizations arose as part of an unpublished collaborative project with Olivier Chapelle and Taesup Moon. Layered feedback is sometimes also called k-partite, as studied, for instance, by Rajaram and Agarwal [185].

The AdaBoost.MR algorithm of section 11.4 is due to Schapire and Singer [205], and is a generalization of the single-label version, called AdaBoost.M2, given earlier by Freund and Schapire [95].

The application of RankBoost to parsing given in section 11.5.1 is work by Collins [52] (see also Collins and Koo [53]). The cancer-gene study of section 11.5.2, including table 11.1 (reprinted with permission), is taken from Agarwal and Sengupta [5].

Numerous other techniques have been proposed for learning to rank; see, for instance, the survey by Liu [156]. An alternative boosting-based approach to ranking is given by Xu and Li [234]. Analyses of the generalization capabilities of ranking algorithms have been given in various works including [3, 4, 90, 185, 193, 195].

Some of the exercises in this chapter are based on material from [90].

Exercises

11.1 Let $(x_1, y_1), \ldots, (x_m, y_m)$ be a multiclass training set with $x_i \in \mathcal{X}$ and $y_i \in \mathcal{Y}$, where $|\mathcal{Y}| = K > 2$. Assume for simplicity that the x_i's are all unique. Consider two approaches to this problem, one based on AdaBoost.MO (algorithm 10.4 (p. 329)) using an all-pairs coding matrix Ω (see exercise 10.5), and the other based on RankBoost (algorithm 11.1). Under appropriate conditions, we will see in this exercise that these two approaches are equivalent.

To avoid confusion, we sometimes add superscripts to the variables appearing in algorithms 10.4 and 11.1—MO for the former, RB for the latter. In the all-pairs approach, we assume each weak hypothesis h_t^{MO} can be decomposed as in equation (10.13) for some $\tilde{h}_t$ which, for clarity, we write here as $\tilde{h}_t^{\mathrm{MO}}$. We also assume that loss-based decoding is used (so that H^{MO} refers to H^{lb} in algorithm 10.4).

In the RankBoost approach, the domain $\mathcal{X}^{\mathrm{RB}}$ is $\mathcal{X} \times \mathcal{Y}$, and the set E of preference pairs consists of all pairs $((x_i, \ell), (x_i, y_i))$ for $\ell \in \mathcal{Y} - \{y_i\}$, and for $i = 1, \ldots, m$. Given $x \in \mathcal{X}$, we use the final ranking F^{RB} to predict a label using the rule

$$H^{RB}(x) = \arg\max_{y \in \mathcal{Y}} F^{RB}(x, y).$$

a. Suppose $\tilde{h}_{t'}^{MO} \equiv h_{t'}^{RB}$ and $\alpha_{t'}^{MO} = \alpha_{t'}^{RB}$ for all $t' < t$. Show that:

   i. $D_t^{MO}(i, \{y_i, \ell\}) = D_t^{RB}((x_i, \ell), (x_i, y_i))$ for all i and for $\ell \neq y_i$.

   ii. The criteria for selecting α_t and h_t are the same for the two methods, that is, if $\tilde{h}_t^{MO} \equiv h_t^{RB}$ and $\alpha_t^{MO} = \alpha_t^{RB}$ then $Z_t^{MO} = Z_t^{RB}$.

b. Show that if $\tilde{h}_t^{MO} \equiv h_t^{RB}$ and $\alpha_t^{MO} = \alpha_t^{RB}$ for $t = 1, \ldots, T$, then $H^{MO}(x) = H^{RB}(x)$ for all x (assuming ties are broken in the same way).

11.2 Let $(x_1, y_1), \ldots, (x_m, y_m) \in \mathcal{X} \times \{-1, +1\}$ be binary labeled training examples with the x_i's all unique. Suppose we apply RankBoost.L with domain $\mathcal{X}$ and preference pairs $E = V_1 \times V_2$ where

$$V_1 = \{x_i : y_i = -1\}$$

$$V_2 = \{x_i : y_i = +1\}.$$

a. In the notation of algorithm 11.2, show that $\tilde{D}_t(x, y) = 0$ for all $(x, y) \in \mathcal{X} \times \{-1, +1\}$, except for the training pairs (x_i, y_i).

b. Show that $\tilde{D}_t(x_i, y_i) = e^{-y_i F_{t-1}(x_i)}/(2Z_t(y_i))$ where we here define $Z_t(b) \doteq \sum_{i:y_i=b} e^{-bF_{t-1}(x_i)}$ for $b \in \{-1, +1\}$.

11.3 Give details verifying that AdaBoost.MR is the algorithm obtained from Rank-Boost.qL under the reduction given at the beginning of section 11.4.

11.4 Let $(x_1, y_1), \ldots, (x_m, y_m) \in \mathcal{X} \times \{-1, +1\}$ be binary labeled training examples with the x_i's all unique. Consider algorithm 11.5, a variant of confidence-rated AdaBoost (algorithm 9.1 (p. 274)). Here, on each round t, rather than adding $\alpha_t h_t$ to the combined classifier, we add $\frac{1}{2}(\alpha_t h_t + \beta_t)$ where α_t and β_t are together tuned to minimize Z_t. (The factor of $\frac{1}{2}$ is unimportant, and is included only for later mathematical convenience.)

We compare this algorithm with RankBoost (algorithm 11.1) with domain $\mathcal{X}$ and $E = V_- \times V_+$, where V_- and V_+ are as in equation (11.6). To avoid confusion, we sometimes add superscripts to the variables in algorithms 11.5 and 11.1 (AB for the former, RB for the latter). Assume that α_t^{AB}, β_t^{AB}, and α_t^{RB} are chosen numerically to exactly minimize the respective criteria Z_t^{AB} and Z_t^{RB}.

Show that these two algorithms are equivalent in the sense that if $h_{t'}^{AB} = h_{t'}^{RB}$ for $t' < t$, then Z_t^{AB} and Z_t^{RB} are minimized by the same choices of α_t and h_t (over any space $\mathcal{H}$). Thus, if $h_t^{AB} \equiv h_t^{RB}$ for $t = 1, \ldots, T$, then for some $C \in \mathbb{R}$, $F^{AB}(x) = F^{RB}(x) + C$ for all $x \in \mathcal{X}$. [*Hint:* For any given h_t^{AB} and α_t^{AB}, consider the value of Z_t^{AB} when minimized over $\beta_t^{AB} \in \mathbb{R}$.]

11.5 Let $V_1, \ldots, V_J$ be a disjoint collection of nonempty subsets of $\mathcal{X}$, let $V = V_1 \cup \cdots \cup V_J$, and let E be as in equation (11.20).

Algorithm 11.5
A variant of confidence-rated AdaBoost

Given: $(x_1, y_1), \ldots, (x_m, y_m)$ where $x_i \in \mathcal{X}$, $y_i \in \{-1, +1\}$.
Initialize: $D_1(i) = 1/m$ for $i = 1, \ldots, m$.
For $t = 1, \ldots, T$:

- Train weak learner using distribution D_t.
- Get weak hypothesis $h_t : \mathcal{X} \to \mathbb{R}$.
- Choose $\alpha_t, \beta_t \in \mathbb{R}$.
- Aim: select α_t, β_t and h_t to minimalize the normalization factor

$$Z_t \doteq \sum_{i=1}^{m} D_t(i) \exp\left(-\tfrac{1}{2} y_i (\alpha_t h_t(x_i) + \beta_t)\right).$$

- Update, for $i = 1, \ldots, m$:

$$D_{t+1}(i) = \frac{D_t(i) \exp\left(-\tfrac{1}{2} y_i (\alpha_t h_t(x_i) + \beta_t)\right)}{Z_t}.$$

Output the final hypothesis:

$$H(x) = \text{sign}(F(x)) \text{ where } F(x) = \tfrac{1}{2} \sum_{t=1}^{T} (\alpha_t h_t(x) + \beta_t).$$

---

a. Suppose, for given real numbers $g_1 < \cdots < g_J$, that we apply RankBoost with initial distribution $D_1 = \varphi$ where

$$\varphi(u, v) = c(g_k - g_j) \tag{11.27}$$

for all $(u, v) \in V_j \times V_k$ with $j < k$ (and $\varphi(u, v) = 0$ for $(u, v) \notin E$), and where $c > 0$ is chosen so that equation (11.24) is satisfied. Given F_{t-1}, show how to compute the entire distribution $\tilde{D}_t$ in time $O(|V|)$.

b. Suppose, more generally, that we are instead given arbitrary positive real numbers g_{jk}, for $1 \le j < k \le J$, and that $g_k - g_j$ is replaced by g_{jk} in equation (11.27). Given F_{t-1}, show how to compute the entire distribution $\tilde{D}_t$ in time $O(|V| + J^2)$.

11.6 In RankBoost.L (algorithm 11.2), assume that all values of $C_{t,j}(y)$ and $S_{t,j}(y)$ have already been computed. Show how to compute $\mathcal{Z}_t$ in time $O(J)$.

11.7 Suppose we are given bipartite feedback, that is, disjoint nonempty sets V_1 and V_2 with $V = V_1 \cup V_2$ and $E = V_1 \times V_2$. Describe how to exactly implement RankBoost (algorithm 11.1) subject to the following specifications:

- On round t, $h_t \in \mathcal{H}$ and $\alpha_t \in \mathbb{R}$ are selected to exactly minimize Z_t, where $\mathcal{H}$ is a given finite set of N binary classifiers (each with range $\{-1, +1\}$).

- The total space required is $O(|V| + T)$ (not including storage of $\mathcal{H}$, which we assume is given).

- On each round, the running time for all computations, other than the choice of h_t, is $O(|V|)$.

- For any candidate hypothesis $h_t \in \mathcal{H}$, the time to evaluate h_t (that is, the time to compute Z_t for this choice of h_t and a corresponding choice of α_t) is $O(|V|)$. Thus, the best h_t can be found on each round in $O(N \cdot |V|)$ time.

11.8 In a multiclass version of logistic regression (section 7.5.1), we posit that there is some function $F : \mathcal{X} \times \mathcal{Y} \to \mathbb{R}$ (perhaps of a particular parametric form) for which the probability of y given x is proportional to $e^{F(x,y)}$, that is,

$$\mathbf{Pr}[y \mid x; F] = \frac{e^{F(x,y)}}{\sum_{\ell \in \mathcal{Y}} e^{F(x,\ell)}}.$$

Let $(x_1, y_1), \ldots, (x_m, y_m)$ be a set of training examples in $\mathcal{X} \times \mathcal{Y}$, and let $\mathcal{L}(F)$ denote the negative conditional log likelihood of the data under F:

$$\mathcal{L}(F) \doteq -\sum_{i=1}^{m} \ln(\mathbf{Pr}[y_i \mid x_i; F]).$$

A function F that minimizes this expression can be constructed by initializing $F_0 \equiv 0$, and then iteratively setting $F_t = F_{t-1} + \alpha_t h_t$ for some appropriate choice of $\alpha_t \in \mathbb{R}$ and $h_t : \mathcal{X} \times \mathcal{Y} \to \mathbb{R}$. In what follows, let us fix t and write $F = F_{t-1}$, $\alpha = \alpha_t$, $h = h_t$, etc.

a. Show that

$$\mathcal{L}\left(F + \tfrac{1}{2}\alpha h\right) - \mathcal{L}(F)$$

$$\leq C + \sum_{i=1}^{m} \sum_{\ell \neq y_i} A_i \exp\left(F(x_i, \ell) - F(x_i, y_i) + \tfrac{1}{2}\alpha(h(x_i, \ell) - h(x_i, y_i))\right) \qquad (11.28)$$

where

$$A_i = \frac{1}{1 + \sum_{\ell \neq y_i} \exp\left(F(x_i, \ell) - F(x_i, y_i)\right)}$$

and

$$C = -\sum_{i=1}^{m} A_i \sum_{\ell \neq y_i} \exp\left(F(x_i, \ell) - F(x_i, y_i)\right).$$

Also, explain why minimizing equation (11.28) over α and h is the same as minimizing

$$\sum_{i=1}^{m} \sum_{\ell \neq y_i} D(i, \ell) \exp\left(\tfrac{1}{2}\alpha(h(x_i, \ell) - h(x_i, y_i))\right) \tag{11.29}$$

where D is a distribution of the form

$$D(i, \ell) = \frac{A_i \exp\left(F(x_i, \ell) - F(x_i, y_i)\right)}{\mathcal{Z}}, \tag{11.30}$$

and $\mathcal{Z}$ is a normalization factor.

Thus, on each iteration, we can attempt to approximately minimize $\mathcal{L}$ by choosing α and h to minimalize equation (11.29).

b. Show that RankBoost, if used as in exercise 11.1, chooses α_t and h_t on each round to minimalize an expression of the same form as equation (11.29), using a distribution of the same form as equation (11.30), but for different choices of the A_i's.

c. Alternatively, we can attempt to minimalize

$$\tfrac{1}{2}\sum_{i=1}^{m} \sum_{\ell \neq y_i} D(i, \ell) \left(e^{\alpha h(x_i, \ell)} + e^{-\alpha h(x_i, y_i)}\right), \tag{11.31}$$

which is an upper bound on equation (11.29), by convexity. Show that if $Y_i = \{y_i\}$ for all i, then AdaBoost.MR chooses α_t and h_t to minimalize an expression of the same form as equation (11.31), using a distribution of the same form as equation (11.30), but with different choices of the A_i's.

Thus, both RankBoost and AdaBoost.MR can be modified for logistic regression by changing only how the relevant distributions are computed.

IV ADVANCED THEORY

12 Attaining the Best Possible Accuracy

In this last part of the book, we study a number of advanced theoretical topics with a continuing focus on fundamental properties and limitations of boosting and AdaBoost, as well as techniques and principles for the design of improved algorithms.

We begin, in this chapter, with a return to the central problem of understanding AdaBoost's ability to generalize. Previously, in chapters 4 and 5, we provided analyses of AdaBoost's generalization error where, as in our study of boosting generally, we took as our starting point the weak learning assumption, that is, the premise that the classifiers generated by the weak learning algorithm are reliably better than random guessing. Naively, this assumption did indeed seem weak, but we have now come to see that its consequences are actually quite strong. Not only does it imply that eventually boosting will perfectly fit any training set, but the results of chapters 4 and 5 show that it also implies that the generalization error can be driven arbitrarily close to zero with sufficient training data. This is an excellent property—the very one that defines boosting.

On the other hand, we know that it cannot always be possible to attain perfect generalization accuracy. Typically, we expect real data to be corrupted with some form of noise, randomness, or mislabeling that makes it impossible to perfectly predict the labels of nearly all test examples, even with unlimited training and computation. Instead, we are faced with a fundamental limit on how much the test error can be minimized due to intrinsic randomness in the data itself. This minimum possible error rate is called the *Bayes error*.

Thus, our earlier analyses superficially appear to be inapplicable when the Bayes error is strictly positive. However, this is not necessarily the case. Even if the weak learning assumption does not hold so that the weighted errors of the weak hypotheses are converging to $\frac{1}{2}$, these analyses can still be applied, depending as they do on the edges of all the weak hypotheses. Moreover, in practice the weak learning assumption may in fact continue to hold, even when perfect generalization is unachievable. This is because the weak hypothesis space typically is not fixed, but grows in complexity with the size of the training set; for instance, this happens "automatically" when using decision trees as base classifiers since the generated trees will usually be bigger if trained with more data. This presents the usual delicate balance between complexity and fit to the data, but one that leaves open the possibility, according to our analysis, for very good generalization, as is often seen in practice.

Nevertheless, these analyses do not explicitly provide absolute guarantees on the performance of AdaBoost relative to the optimal Bayes error (other than when it is zero). In other words, they do not specify conditions under which AdaBoost's generalization error will necessarily converge to the best possible error rate; rather, they provide generalization bounds which are in terms of statistics that can be measured only after training is complete.

In this chapter, we give an alternative analysis in which we prove that a slight variation of AdaBoost does indeed produce a combined classifier whose accuracy is very close to the optimum attainable by any classifier whatsoever, provided the base classifiers are sufficiently but not overly expressive, and provided the training set is sufficiently large. In this sense, the algorithm is said to be *universally consistent*. (Note that this notion of consistency is entirely unrelated to and distinct from the one studied, for instance, in section 2.2.5.)

This analysis pulls together many of the topics studied earlier in this book, particularly the view of AdaBoost as an algorithm for minimizing exponential loss. The analysis shows first that AdaBoost quickly minimizes the true expected exponential loss relative to the minimum possible, and then shows how this directly implies good classification accuracy compared to the Bayes optimal.

Although these results are strong, they are limited by their underlying assumptions, especially with regard to the expressiveness of the base hypotheses. To emphasize this point, we also give a simple example in which minimization of exponential loss provably fails to generate a classifier close to the Bayes optimal, even when the noise affecting the data is of a particularly simple form.

12.1 Optimality in Classification and Risk Minimization

We begin with a discussion of optimality in classification and its relation to minimization of exponential loss. We return to the simple problem of binary classification with $\mathcal{X}$ denoting the instance space, and the set of possible labels consisting only of $\mathcal{Y} = \{-1, +1\}$. We let $\mathcal{D}$ denote the true distribution over labeled pairs in $\mathcal{X} \times \mathcal{Y}$. Unless specified otherwise, in this chapter probabilities and expectations denoted $\mathbf{Pr}[\cdot]$ and $\mathbf{E}[\cdot]$ are with respect to a random pair (x, y) generated according to $\mathcal{D}$.

In general, for such a random pair, the label y will not necessarily be determined by the instance x. In other words, the conditional probability that x is labeled positive, denoted

$$\pi(x) \doteq \mathbf{Pr}[y = +1 \mid x], \tag{12.1}$$

need not be equal to 0 or 1. When $\pi(x) \in (0, 1)$, it becomes inherently impossible to predict y perfectly from x, even with full knowledge of $\mathcal{D}$. Nevertheless, we can still characterize the best that is possible in minimizing the chance of an incorrect prediction. In particular, if y is predicted to be $+1$, then the probability of being incorrect is $1 - \pi(x)$; and if y is predicted to be -1, then an error occurs with probability $\pi(x)$. Thus, to minimize the chance of a mistake, we should predict using the rule

$$h_{\text{opt}}(x) = \begin{cases} +1 & \text{if } \pi(x) > \frac{1}{2} \\ -1 & \text{if } \pi(x) < \frac{1}{2}. \end{cases}$$

(It makes no difference how we predict if $\pi(x) = \frac{1}{2}$.) This rule is called the *Bayes optimal classifier*. Its error, called the *Bayes (optimal) error*, is exactly

$$\text{err}^* \doteq \text{err}(h_{\text{opt}}) = \mathbf{E}[\min\{\pi(x), 1 - \pi(x)\}].$$

This is the minimum error achievable by *any* classifier, regardless of any considerations of learning or computation. (Here, as usual, $\text{err}(h)$ denotes the generalization error of a classifier h as in equation (2.3).)

Thus, the best we can hope for in a learning procedure is that its error will converge to the Bayes error. The purpose of this chapter is to give general conditions under which AdaBoost has this property.

As seen in section 7.1, AdaBoost can be interpreted as an algorithm for minimizing exponential loss. That is, given a training set $S = \langle (x_1, y_1), \ldots, (x_m, y_m) \rangle$, AdaBoost minimizes the *empirical risk* (or loss)

$$\widehat{\text{risk}}(F) \doteq \frac{1}{m} \sum_{i=1}^{m} e^{-y_i F(x_i)}$$

over all linear combinations F of base classifiers in the given space $\mathcal{H}$. (We assume an exhaustive weak learner that, on every round, returns the best weak hypothesis.) The empirical risk can itself be viewed as an estimate or proxy for the *true risk*, that is, the expected loss with respect to the true distribution $\mathcal{D}$:

$$\text{risk}(F) \doteq \mathbf{E}\left[e^{-yF(x)}\right]. \tag{12.2}$$

As seen in section 7.5.3, this expectation can be broken down using marginalization as

$$\mathbf{E}\left[\mathbf{E}\left[e^{-yF(x)} \mid x\right]\right] = \mathbf{E}\left[\pi(x)e^{-F(x)} + (1 - \pi(x))e^{F(x)}\right], \tag{12.3}$$

where the outer expectations are only with respect to x, and the inner expectation on the left is with respect to y conditioned on x. As with classification error, we can now compute the minimum possible value of this risk by optimizing on each instance x separately. This can be done by setting to zero the first derivative of the expression inside the expectation (taken with respect to $F(x)$). Doing so gives the optimal predictor

$$F_{\text{opt}}(x) = \frac{1}{2} \ln \left(\frac{\pi(x)}{1 - \pi(x)} \right) \tag{12.4}$$

where we allow this function to include $\pm\infty$ in its range in case $\pi(x)$ is 0 or 1. With respect to exponential loss, this is the optimal predictor over *all* real-valued functions F, not only those that are linear combinations of the base classifiers. Plugging back into equation (12.3) gives the *optimal (exponential) risk*

$$\text{risk}^* \doteq \text{risk}(F_{\text{opt}}) = 2\mathbf{E}\left[\sqrt{\pi(x)(1 - \pi(x))} \right].$$

Note that

$$\text{sign}(F_{\text{opt}}(x)) = \begin{cases} +1 & \text{if } \pi(x) > \frac{1}{2} \\ -1 & \text{if } \pi(x) < \frac{1}{2}. \end{cases}$$

Thus, the sign of F_{opt}, the minimizer of the exponential risk, is exactly equal to the Bayes optimal classifier h_{opt} (ignoring the case $\pi(x) = \frac{1}{2}$). This means that if we can minimize the exponential loss—not only on the training set, but also over the entire distribution—then we can trivially convert it into a classifier that is optimal with respect to classification accuracy.

Of course, finding F_{opt} exactly is sure to be infeasible since we are working only with a finite training sample from $\mathcal{D}$, and also because our learning algorithms are restricted to use functions F of a particular form. Nevertheless, we will see that it is sufficient to find a function F whose risk is *close* to optimal. That is, if F's true risk is close to risk*, then the generalization error of $\text{sign}(F)$ will also be close to the Bayes error. This is the first part of our analysis.

In the second part, we bound the risk of the predictor F generated by AdaBoost relative to the optimal risk, thus also obtaining a bound on the generalization error of its combined classifier $H = \text{sign}(F)$ relative to the Bayes error. (Here, we are using $f(g)$ as shorthand for the function obtained by composing f with g.)

Beginning with the first part of the analysis, the next theorem shows generally that closeness to the optimal risk also implies closeness to the Bayes error.

Theorem 12.1   In the notation above, suppose the function $F : \mathcal{X} \to \mathbb{R}$ is such that

$$\text{risk}(F) \leq \text{risk}^* + \varepsilon. \tag{12.5}$$

Let $h(x) = \text{sign}(F(x))$ if $F(x) \neq 0$, and let $h(x)$ be chosen arbitrarily from $\{-1, +1\}$ otherwise. Then

$$\text{err}(h) \leq \text{err}^* + \sqrt{2\varepsilon - \varepsilon^2} \leq \text{err}^* + \sqrt{2\varepsilon}.$$

Proof   Let us focus first on a single instance $x \in \mathcal{X}$. Let $\nu(x)$ denote the conditional probability that h misclassifies x relative to the conditional probability of h_{opt} doing the same. That is,

$$v(x) \doteq \mathbf{Pr}[h(x) \neq y \mid x] - \mathbf{Pr}[h_{\text{opt}}(x) \neq y \mid x].$$

Our eventual goal is to bound

$$\mathbf{E}[v(x)] = \text{err}(h) - \text{err}(h_{\text{opt}}) = \text{err}(h) - \text{err}^*.$$

Clearly, $v(x) = 0$ if $h(x) = h_{\text{opt}}(x)$. Otherwise, suppose $h_{\text{opt}}(x) = -1$ (so that $\pi(x) \leq \frac{1}{2}$) but $h(x) = +1$. Then we can compute directly that

$$v(x) = (1 - \pi(x)) - \pi(x) = 1 - 2\pi(x).$$

Similarly, $v(x) = 2\pi(x) - 1$ if $h_{\text{opt}}(x) = +1$ and $h(x) = -1$. Thus, in general,

$$v(x) = \begin{cases} 0 & \text{if } h(x) = h_{\text{opt}}(x) \\ |1 - 2\pi(x)| & \text{else.} \end{cases} \tag{12.6}$$

Likewise, let $\rho(x)$ be the corresponding quantity for the risk:

$$\rho(x) \doteq \mathbf{E}\left[e^{-yF(x)} \mid x\right] - \mathbf{E}\left[e^{-yF_{\text{opt}}(x)} \mid x\right].$$

This quantity is always nonnegative since the risk is minimized pointwise for every x by F_{opt}. By assumption,

$$\mathbf{E}[\rho(x)] = \text{risk}(F) - \text{risk}(F_{\text{opt}}) = \text{risk}(F) - \text{risk}^* \leq \varepsilon.$$

If $h(x) = +1$ but $h_{\text{opt}}(x) = -1$, then $F(x) \geq 0$ but $\pi(x) \leq \frac{1}{2}$. Under these circumstances, the conditional risk

$$\mathbf{E}\left[e^{-yF(x)} \mid x\right] = \pi(x)e^{-F(x)} + (1 - \pi(x))e^{F(x)}, \tag{12.7}$$

as a function of $F(x)$, is convex with a single minimum at $F_{\text{opt}}(x) \leq 0$. This means that its minimum on the restricted range $F(x) \geq 0$ is realized at the point closest to $F_{\text{opt}}(x)$, namely, $F(x) = 0$. Thus, equation (12.7) is at least 1 in this case. A symmetric argument shows that the same holds when $h(x) = -1$ but $h_{\text{opt}}(x) = +1$. Therefore, by equation (12.4),

$$\rho(x) \geq \begin{cases} 0 & \text{if } h(x) = h_{\text{opt}}(x) \\ 1 - 2\sqrt{\pi(x)(1 - \pi(x))} & \text{else.} \end{cases} \tag{12.8}$$

Let $\phi : [0, 1] \to [0, 1]$ be defined by

$$\phi(z) \doteq 1 - \sqrt{1 - z^2}.$$

Then equations (12.6) and (12.8) imply that

$$\rho(x) \geq \phi(v(x)) \tag{12.9}$$

for all x. This is because if $h(x) = h_{\text{opt}}(x)$, then $\phi(v(x)) = \phi(0) = 0 \leq \rho(x)$. And if $h(x) \neq h_{\text{opt}}(x)$, then

$$\phi(\nu(x)) = 1 - \sqrt{1 - |1 - 2\pi(x)|^2} = 1 - 2\sqrt{\pi(x)(1 - \pi(x))} \leq \rho(x).$$

It can be verified (by taking derivatives) that ϕ is convex. Thus, by equation (12.9) and Jensen's inequality (equation (A.4)),

$$\mathbf{E}[\rho(x)] \geq \mathbf{E}[\phi(\nu(x))] \geq \phi\left(\mathbf{E}[\nu(x)]\right).$$

Since ϕ is strictly increasing, it has a well-defined inverse that is also increasing, namely,

$$\phi^{-1}(z) = \sqrt{2z - z^2}. \tag{12.10}$$

Pulling everything together gives

$$
\begin{aligned}
\mathrm{err}(h) - \mathrm{err}(h_{\mathrm{opt}}) &= \mathbf{E}[\nu(x)] \\
&\leq \phi^{-1}\left(\mathbf{E}[\rho(x)]\right) \\
&= \phi^{-1}\left(\mathrm{risk}(F) - \mathrm{risk}(F_{\mathrm{opt}})\right) \\
&\leq \phi^{-1}(\varepsilon) = \sqrt{2\varepsilon - \varepsilon^2}. \qquad \blacksquare
\end{aligned}
$$

12.2   Approaching the Optimal Risk

Theorem 12.1 shows that we can find a classifier that is close in accuracy to the Bayes optimal if we can approximately minimize the expected exponential loss relative to the best possible among all real-valued functions. We know that AdaBoost minimizes exponential loss; specifically, in section 8.2 we proved that AdaBoost asymptotically (that is, in the limit of a large number of rounds) minimizes the exponential loss on the training set relative to the best linear combination of base classifiers. Unfortunately, this is inadequate for our current purposes because, to apply theorem 12.1 to AdaBoost, we will need to extend this analysis along several dimensions: First, we will need nonasymptotic results that give explicit rates of convergence (unlike the analysis of section 8.2); second, we now need to analyze the true, rather than the empirical, risk; and third, we now require convergence to the optimal among *all* functions, not just those that are linear combinations of base classifiers.

12.2.1   Expressiveness of the Base Hypotheses

We will eventually need to address all of these, but we start with the last point, which regards the expressiveness of the weak hypotheses in the space $\mathcal{H}$. Let us denote the *span* of $\mathcal{H}$, that is, the set of all linear combinations of weak hypotheses in $\mathcal{H}$, by

$$\mathrm{span}(\mathcal{H}) \doteq \left\{ F : x \mapsto \sum_{t=1}^{T} \alpha_t h_t(x) \,\middle|\, \alpha_1, \ldots, \alpha_T \in \mathbb{R}; h_1, \ldots, h_T \in \mathcal{H}; T \geq 1 \right\}.$$

For simplicity, we assume $\mathcal{H}$ consists only of binary classifiers with range $\{-1, +1\}$, and we also assume $\mathcal{H}$ is closed under negation so that $-h \in \mathcal{H}$ whenever $h \in \mathcal{H}$.

To apply theorem 12.1 to AdaBoost, the algorithm must at least have the potential opportunity to choose a function F whose true risk is close to the best possible. Since such algorithms output functions only in the span of $\mathcal{H}$, this means that we must assume that there exist functions in $\text{span}(\mathcal{H})$ which have close to minimum risk. In other words, for any $\varepsilon > 0$, we need to assume that there exists some F in $\text{span}(\mathcal{H})$ which satisfies equation (12.5). This is equivalent to assuming that

$$\inf_{F \in \text{span}(\mathcal{H})} \text{risk}(F) = \text{risk}^*. \tag{12.11}$$

This is our strongest and most important assumption. In section 12.3, we will explore what happens when it does not hold.

If F_{opt} is actually in $\text{span}(\mathcal{H})$, then equation (12.11) clearly holds. However, here we are making the slightly weaker assumption that F_{opt}'s risk can only be approached, not necessarily attained, by functions in $\text{span}(\mathcal{H})$. This assumption can be relaxed a bit further by assuming that the smallest risk of functions in $\text{span}(\mathcal{H})$ is close to, rather than equal to, the optimal (so that equation (12.11) holds only approximately). Our analysis can be applied in this case, yielding asymptotic error bounds that will be correspondingly close to, but different from, the Bayes error.

To simplify the analysis, we regard $\mathcal{H}$ as a fixed space. However, as noted earlier, larger training sets sometimes warrant richer hypothesis spaces. Our analysis will be applicable in this case as well, and will quantify how quickly the hypotheses can increase in complexity as a function of the number of training examples while still admitting convergence to the Bayes optimal.

12.2.2 Proof Overview

Our goal is to show that $\text{risk}(F_T)$, the true risk of the function generated by AdaBoost after T rounds, converges to the optimal risk, $\text{risk}^* = \text{risk}(F_{\text{opt}})$. Since F_{opt} may not itself belong to the span of $\mathcal{H}$, we instead focus on comparing F_T's risk with that of a fixed *reference function* $\check{F}$ that is in the span. This will be sufficient for our purposes since, by equation (12.11), $\check{F}$ can itself be chosen to have risk arbitrarily close to risk^*.

Our analysis will require that we take into account the norm, or overall magnitude, of the weights defining functions in the span of $\mathcal{H}$, especially the reference functions. If F is in $\text{span}(\mathcal{H})$, then it can be written in the form

$$F(x) = \sum_{t=1}^{T} \alpha_t h_t(x).$$

We define its *norm*, written $|F|$, to be

$$\sum_{t=1}^{T} |\alpha_t|. \tag{12.12}$$

If the function F can be written in more than one way as a linear combination of base hypotheses, then we define the norm to be the minimum (or infimum) value of equation (12.12) among all such equivalent representations.

Equation (12.11) then implies that there exist, for each $B > 0$, reference functions $\check{F}_B$ in the span of $\mathcal{H}$ such that $|\check{F}_B| < B$, and such that

$$\text{risk}(\check{F}_B) \to \text{risk}^* \tag{12.13}$$

as $B \to \infty$. Thus, if we can show that the function F_T produced by AdaBoost has risk close to that of $\check{F}_B$, then this will also imply risk close to optimal, for an appropriately large choice of B.

An annoyance of working with exponential loss is its unboundedness, that is, the property that $e^{-yF(x)}$ can be unboundedly large. This is particularly a problem when trying to relate the exponential loss on the training set to its true expectation, since a random variable with a very large range is also likely to have high variance, making the estimation of its expectation infeasible from a small sample. This difficulty is reflected, for instance, by Hoeffding's inequality (theorem 2.1), which requires that the random variables be bounded. (An extreme example illustrating the problem is a lottery ticket that pays a million dollars with probability 10^{-6}, and otherwise results in the loss of one dollar. Its expected value is very close to zero, but any sample of reasonable size will almost certainly consist only of losing tickets with an empirical average of -1. The variance of this random variable is about 10^6.)

To sidestep this problem, we will restrict the range of the functions generated by AdaBoost by "clamping" them within a fixed range, thus also limiting the magnitude of the exponential loss. Specifically, for $C > 0$, let us define the function

$$\text{clamp}_C(z) \doteq \begin{cases} C & \text{if } z \geq C \\ z & \text{if } -C \leq z \leq C \\ -C & \text{if } z \leq -C, \end{cases}$$

which simply clamps its argument to the range $[-C, C]$. Next, let us define $\overline{F}_T$ to be the clamped version of F_T:

$$\overline{F}_T(x) \doteq \text{clamp}_C(F_T(x)).$$

Note that the classifications induced by $\overline{F}_T$ are the same as for F_T since

$$\text{sign}(\overline{F}_T(x)) = \text{sign}(F_T(x))$$

always. Therefore, if $\text{sign}(\overline{F}_T)$ converges to the Bayes optimal, then $\text{sign}(F_T)$ does as well. By theorem 12.1, this means that it is sufficient to show that the risk of $\overline{F}_T$ converges to the optimal risk. This, in turn, can be proved using the fact that, on the one hand, $\overline{F}_T$ is bounded, so its empirical risk is close to its true risk; and, on the other hand, the empirical risk of $\overline{F}_T$ is not much worse than that of F_T, which is minimized by the learning algorithm.

So we can now summarize our entire argument in four parts. We will show each of the following, where we use the notation $\lesssim$ to indicate informal, approximate inequality:

1. The empirical exponential loss of the function F_T generated by AdaBoost, an algorithm that provably minimizes this loss, rapidly converges to a value not much worse than that of the reference function $\check{F}_B$; that is,

$$\widehat{\text{risk}}(F_T) \lesssim \widehat{\text{risk}}(\check{F}_B).$$

2. Clamping does not significantly increase risk, so that

$$\widehat{\text{risk}}(\overline{F}_T) \lesssim \widehat{\text{risk}}(F_T).$$

3. The empirical risk of the clamped versions of all functions of the form generated by AdaBoost will be close to their true risk, so that

$$\text{risk}(\overline{F}_T) \lesssim \widehat{\text{risk}}(\overline{F}_T).$$

   This is essentially a uniform-convergence result of the sort seen in chapters 2 and 4.

4. Similarly, the empirical risk of the fixed reference function $\check{F}_B$ will be close to its true risk, so that

$$\widehat{\text{risk}}(\check{F}_B) \lesssim \text{risk}(\check{F}_B).$$

Combining all four parts along with equation (12.13) will allow us to conclude that

$$\text{risk}(\overline{F}_T) \lesssim \widehat{\text{risk}}(\overline{F}_T) \lesssim \widehat{\text{risk}}(F_T) \lesssim \widehat{\text{risk}}(\check{F}_B) \lesssim \text{risk}(\check{F}_B) \lesssim \text{risk}^*,$$

so that, by theorem 12.1, the error of the corresponding classifier $\text{sign}(\overline{F}_T) = \text{sign}(F_T)$ is also close to the Bayes optimal.

12.2.3 Formal Proofs

In more precise terms, we prove the following theorem which provides a bound on Ada-Boost's risk in terms of the risk of the reference function, the number of rounds T, the number of training examples m, and the complexity of the base hypothesis space $\mathcal{H}$ as measured by its VC-dimension d (see section 2.2.3). Note that both the reference function $\check{F}_B$ and the clamping parameter C are used only for the sake of the mathematical argument, and need not be known by the algorithm.

Theorem 12.2 Suppose AdaBoost is run on m random examples from distribution $\mathcal{D}$ for T rounds, producing output F_T, using an exhaustive weak learner and a negation-closed base hypothesis space $\mathcal{H}$ of VC-dimension d. Let $\check{F}_B$ be a reference function as above. Then for a suitable choice of C defining $\overline{F}_T = \text{clamp}_C(F_T)$, with probability at least $1 - \delta$,

$$\text{risk}(\overline{F}_T) \le \text{risk}(\check{F}_B) + \frac{2B^{6/5}}{T^{1/5}}$$

$$+ 2\left(\frac{32}{m}\left((T+1)\ln\left(\frac{me}{T+1}\right) + dT\ln\left(\frac{me}{d}\right) + \ln\left(\frac{16}{\delta}\right)\right)\right)^{1/4}$$

$$+ e^B\sqrt{\frac{\ln(4/\delta)}{m}}. \tag{12.14}$$

As shown in the next corollary, this immediately implies convergence to the Bayes optimal as the sample size m gets large, for a suitable number of rounds T. Here, for the moment we add subscripts or superscripts, as in F_T^m, B_m, T_m, etc., to emphasize explicitly the dependence on m. Also, as used in the corollary, an infinite sequence of random variables $X_1, X_2, \ldots$ is said to *converge almost surely* (or *with probability* 1) to some other random variable X, written $X_m \xrightarrow{a.s.} X$, if

$$\mathbf{Pr}\left[\lim_{m\to\infty} X_m = X\right] = 1. \tag{12.15}$$

Corollary 12.3   If, under the conditions of theorem 12.2, we run AdaBoost for $T = T_m = \theta(m^a)$ rounds, where a is any constant in $(0, 1)$, then as $m \to \infty$,

$$\text{risk}(\overline{F}_{T_m}^m) \xrightarrow{a.s.} \text{risk}^*, \tag{12.16}$$

and therefore,

$$\text{err}(H_m) \xrightarrow{a.s.} \text{err}^* \tag{12.17}$$

where $H_m(x) = \text{sign}(F_{T_m}^m(x)) = \text{sign}(\overline{F}_{T_m}^m(x))$.

Proof   Before proving the corollary, we make some general remarks concerning the convergence of random variables. Almost sure convergence, as defined in equation (12.15), is equivalent to the condition that for all $\varepsilon > 0$, with probability 1, all of the X_m's come within ε of X, for m sufficiently large; that is,

$$\mathbf{Pr}[\exists n \ge 1, \forall m \ge n : |X_m - X| < \varepsilon] = 1. \tag{12.18}$$

A commonly used tool for proving such convergence is the *Borel-Cantelli lemma*, which states that if $e_1, e_2, \ldots$ is a sequence of events for which

$$\sum_{m=1}^{\infty} \mathbf{Pr}[e_m \text{ does } not \text{ hold}] < \infty,$$

then

$\mathbf{Pr}[\exists n \geq 1, \forall m \geq n : e_m \text{ holds}] = 1.$

In other words, with probability 1, all of the events e_m hold for m sufficiently large, provided that the sum of the individual probabilities of the events not holding converges to any finite value. Thus, setting e_m to the event that $|X_m - X| < \varepsilon$, we see that to prove equation (12.18), it suffices to show that

$$\sum_{m=1}^{\infty} \mathbf{Pr}[|X_m - X| \geq \varepsilon] < \infty. \tag{12.19}$$

And therefore, to show $X_m \xrightarrow{a.s.} X$, it suffices to show that equation (12.19) holds for all $\varepsilon > 0$. We will apply this technique shortly.

To prove the corollary, we set $B = B_m = (\ln m)/4$, and $\delta = \delta_m = 1/m^2$. With these choices, for every $\varepsilon > 0$, we can choose m so large that

1. the excess risk appearing in equation (12.14)—that is, the amount by which $\text{risk}(\overline{F}_{T_m}^m)$ can exceed $\text{risk}(\check{F}_{B_m})$—is smaller than $\varepsilon/2$;

2. $\text{risk}(\check{F}_{B_m})$ is within $\varepsilon/2$ of risk^*.

Together, these imply that for m sufficiently large, the probability that

$$\text{risk}(\overline{F}_{T_m}^m) < \text{risk}^* + \varepsilon$$

is at least $1 - \delta_m$. Since $\text{risk}^* \leq \text{risk}(\overline{F}_{T_m}^m)$ always, and since $\sum_{m=1}^{\infty} \delta_m < \infty$, the Borel-Cantelli lemma now implies, by the argument above, that $\text{risk}(\overline{F}_{T_m}^m)$ converges almost surely to risk^*, proving equation (12.16). From this, equation (12.17) now follows by a direct application of theorem 12.1. ∎

These results can be generalized to the case in which the complexity of the base hypotheses depends on the number of training examples m simply by regarding the VC-dimension d as a (not too fast-growing) function of m, and adjusting T appropriately.

12.2.4 Bounding How Fast AdaBoost Minimizes Empirical Risk

We now prove theorem 12.2 following the four-part outline given above. We begin with part 1, in which we bound the rate at which AdaBoost minimizes the exponential loss.

Lemma 12.4 After T rounds, the exponential loss of the function F_T generated by AdaBoost satisfies

$$\widehat{\text{risk}}(F_T) \leq \widehat{\text{risk}}(\check{F}_B) + \frac{2B^{6/5}}{T^{1/5}}.$$

Proof   We adopt the notation of both algorithms 1.1 (p. 5) and 7.1 (p. 178). Our approach will be to focus on three key quantities, how they relate to one another, and how they evolve over time. The first of these is

$$R_t \doteq \ln\left(\widehat{\mathrm{risk}}(F_t)\right) - \ln\left(\widehat{\mathrm{risk}}(\check{F}_B)\right), \tag{12.20}$$

that is, the difference between the logarithm of the exponential loss attained by AdaBoost after T rounds, and that of the reference function $\check{F}_B$. Our aim is to show that R_t gets small quickly. Note that R_t never increases.

The second quantity of interest is

$$S_t \doteq B + \sum_{t'=1}^{t} \alpha_{t'}, \tag{12.21}$$

which will provide an upper bound on the norms $|\check{F}_B| + |F_t|$. Here and throughout, we assume without loss of generality that the α_t's are all nonnegative (or equivalently, that $\epsilon_t \leq \frac{1}{2}$ for all t), so that S_t never decreases.

And the third quantity that we focus on is the edge $\gamma_t \doteq \frac{1}{2} - \epsilon_t$.

Roughly speaking, our first claim shows that if AdaBoost's exponential loss is large relative to its associated norm, then the edge γ_t must also be large.

Claim 12.5   For $t \geq 1$,

$$R_{t-1} \leq 2\gamma_t S_{t-1}.$$

Proof   As usual, D_t is the distribution computed by AdaBoost on round t. Thus, in the present notation,

$$D_t(i) = \frac{\exp\left(-y_i F_{t-1}(x_i)\right)}{m \cdot \widehat{\mathrm{risk}}(F_{t-1})}. \tag{12.22}$$

Let us also define the analogous distribution $\check{D}$ for $\check{F}_B$:

$$\check{D}(i) \doteq \frac{\exp\left(-y_i \check{F}_B(x_i)\right)}{m \cdot \widehat{\mathrm{risk}}(\check{F}_B)}.$$

Since relative entropy, as defined in equations (6.11) and (8.6) and discussed in section 8.1.2, is never negative, we have

$$0 \leq \mathrm{RE}\left(D_t \parallel \check{D}\right)$$

$$= \sum_{i=1}^{m} D_t(i) \ln\left(\frac{D_t(i)}{\check{D}(i)}\right)$$

$$= \ln \left(\widehat{\mathrm{risk}}(\check{F}_B) \right) - \ln \left(\widehat{\mathrm{risk}}(F_{t-1}) \right) - \sum_{i=1}^{m} D_t(i) y_i F_{t-1}(x_i) + \sum_{i=1}^{m} D_t(i) y_i \check{F}_B(x_i).$$

That is,

$$R_{t-1} \le -\sum_{i=1}^{m} D_t(i) y_i F_{t-1}(x_i) + \sum_{i=1}^{m} D_t(i) y_i \check{F}_B(x_i). \tag{12.23}$$

To prove the claim, we bound the two terms on the right.

We have that

$$2\gamma_t = (1 - \epsilon_t) - \epsilon_t$$

$$= \sum_{i=1}^{m} D_t(i) y_i h_t(x_i)$$

$$= \max_{h \in \mathcal{H}} \sum_{i=1}^{m} D_t(i) y_i h(x_i),$$

where the last equality uses our assumptions that the weak learner is exhaustive, and that $\mathcal{H}$ is closed under negation. Thus,

$$\left| \sum_{i=1}^{m} D_t(i) y_i F_{t-1}(x_i) \right| = \left| \sum_{i=1}^{m} D_t(i) y_i \sum_{t'=1}^{t-1} \alpha_{t'} h_{t'}(x_i) \right|$$

$$= \left| \sum_{t'=1}^{t-1} \alpha_{t'} \sum_{i=1}^{m} D_t(i) y_i h_{t'}(x_i) \right|$$

$$\le \left(\sum_{t'=1}^{t-1} \alpha_{t'} \right) \max_{h \in \mathcal{H}} \left| \sum_{i=1}^{m} D_t(i) y_i h(x_i) \right|$$

$$= 2\gamma_t \cdot \sum_{t'=1}^{t-1} \alpha_{t'}. \tag{12.24}$$

Furthermore, we can write $\check{F}_B$ in the form

$$\check{F}_B(x) = \sum_{j=1}^{n} b_j \hat{h}_j(x)$$

where

$$\sum_{j=1}^{n} |b_j| \le B, \tag{12.25}$$

and $\hat{h}_1, \ldots, \hat{h}_n$ are in $\mathcal{H}$. Then by a similar argument,

$$\left| \sum_{i=1}^{m} D_t(i) y_i \check{F}_B(x_i) \right| \le 2\gamma_t \cdot B. \tag{12.26}$$

Combining equations (12.23), (12.24), and (12.26), together with the definition of S_{t-1} in equation (12.21), yields

$$R_{t-1} \le \left| \sum_{i=1}^{m} D_t(i) y_i F_{t-1}(x_i) \right| + \left| \sum_{i=1}^{m} D_t(i) y_i \check{F}_B(x_i) \right| \le 2\gamma_t S_{t-1},$$

as claimed.   ∎

Next, let us define

$$\Delta R_t \doteq R_{t-1} - R_t, \tag{12.27}$$

$$\Delta S_t \doteq S_t - S_{t-1},$$

the amounts by which R_t *decreases* and S_t *increases* on round t. Note that these are both nonnegative. The next claim shows how these are related and, specifically, how their ratio is controlled by the edge γ_t.

Claim 12.6   For $t \ge 1$,

$$\frac{\Delta R_t}{\Delta S_t} \ge \gamma_t.$$

Proof   We can compute ΔR_t exactly as follows:

$$\Delta R_t = \ln\left(\widehat{\mathrm{risk}}(F_{t-1}) \right) - \ln\left(\widehat{\mathrm{risk}}(F_t) \right)$$

$$= -\ln\left(\frac{\frac{1}{m} \sum_{i=1}^{m} \exp\left(-y_i F_t(x_i) \right)}{\widehat{\mathrm{risk}}(F_{t-1})} \right)$$

$$= -\ln\left(\frac{\frac{1}{m} \sum_{i=1}^{m} \exp\left(-y_i (F_{t-1}(x_i) + \alpha_t h_t(x_i)) \right)}{\widehat{\mathrm{risk}}(F_{t-1})} \right)$$

$$= -\ln\left(\sum_{i=1}^{m} D_t(i) \exp\left(-\alpha_t y_i h_t(x_i) \right) \right)$$

$$= -\frac{1}{2} \ln(1 - 4\gamma_t^2), \tag{12.28}$$

where the last equality uses equation (3.9) from the analysis of AdaBoost's training error given in theorem 3.1.

We can also obtain an exact expression for ΔS_t from the definition of α_t given in algorithm 1.1:

$$\Delta S_t = \alpha_t = \frac{1}{2} \ln \left(\frac{1+2\gamma_t}{1-2\gamma_t} \right).$$

Combining yields

$$\frac{\Delta R_t}{\Delta S_t} = \frac{-\ln(1-4\gamma_t^2)}{\ln \left(\frac{1+2\gamma_t}{1-2\gamma_t} \right)} \doteq \Upsilon(\gamma_t)$$

where Υ is the same function encountered in section 5.4.1 and defined in equation (5.32). The claim now follows from the fact that $\Upsilon(\gamma) \geq \gamma$ for all $0 \leq \gamma \leq \frac{1}{2}$ (see figure 5.4 (p. 113)). ∎

Together, these claims imply that the quantity $R_t^2 S_t$ never increases, as we show next, which will allow us in turn to relate R_t and S_t directly.

Claim 12.7 For $t \geq 1$, if $R_t \geq 0$, then

$$R_t^2 S_t \leq R_{t-1}^2 S_{t-1}.$$

Proof Combining claims 12.5 and 12.6 gives

$$\frac{2\Delta R_t}{R_{t-1}} \geq \frac{\Delta S_t}{S_{t-1}}. \tag{12.29}$$

Thus,

$$R_t^2 S_t = (R_{t-1} - \Delta R_t)^2 (S_{t-1} + \Delta S_t)$$

$$= R_{t-1}^2 S_{t-1} \left(1 - \frac{\Delta R_t}{R_{t-1}} \right)^2 \left(1 + \frac{\Delta S_t}{S_{t-1}} \right)$$

$$\leq R_{t-1}^2 S_{t-1} \cdot \exp \left(-\frac{2\Delta R_t}{R_{t-1}} + \frac{\Delta S_t}{S_{t-1}} \right) \tag{12.30}$$

$$\leq R_{t-1}^2 S_{t-1} \tag{12.31}$$

where equation (12.30) uses $1 + x \leq e^x$ for all $x \in \mathbb{R}$, and equation (12.31) follows from equation (12.29). ∎

Applying claim 12.7 repeatedly yields (when $R_{t-1} \geq 0$)

$$R_{t-1}^2 S_{t-1} \leq R_0^2 S_0 \leq B^3, \tag{12.32}$$

since $S_0 = B$, and

$$R_0 = -\ln\left(\widehat{\mathrm{risk}}(\check{F}_B)\right) \leq |\check{F}_B| \leq B.$$

Combining equations (12.28) and (12.32), along with claim 12.5, now implies that

$$\Delta R_t = -\frac{1}{2}\ln(1 - 4\gamma_t^2) \geq 2\gamma_t^2 \geq \frac{1}{2}\left(\frac{R_{t-1}}{S_{t-1}}\right)^2 \geq \frac{1}{2}\left(\frac{R_{t-1}}{B^3/R_{t-1}^2}\right)^2 = \frac{R_{t-1}^6}{2B^6}. \tag{12.33}$$

This shows that if the relative loss is large, then the progress that is made in reducing it will be large as well. The next and last claim shows how this implies an inductive bound on R_t:

Claim 12.8 Let $c = 1/(2B^6)$. If $R_t > 0$, then

$$\frac{1}{R_t^5} \geq \frac{1}{R_{t-1}^5} + 5c. \tag{12.34}$$

Proof Multiplying both sides by R_{t-1}^5 and rearranging terms, equation (12.34) can be rewritten as

$$\left(\frac{R_{t-1}}{R_t}\right)^5 \geq 1 + 5cR_{t-1}^5. \tag{12.35}$$

We have that

$$\left(\frac{R_t}{R_{t-1}}\right)^5\left(1 + 5cR_{t-1}^5\right) = \left(1 - \frac{\Delta R_t}{R_{t-1}}\right)^5\left(1 + 5cR_{t-1}^5\right)$$

$$\leq \exp\left(-\frac{5\Delta R_t}{R_{t-1}} + 5cR_{t-1}^5\right) \tag{12.36}$$

$$\leq 1, \tag{12.37}$$

where equation (12.36) uses $1 + x \leq e^x$ for all x, and equation (12.37) follows from equation (12.33). This implies equation (12.35) and the claim. ∎

We can now prove lemma 12.4. If either $R_T \leq 0$ or $T \leq B^6$, then the lemma holds trivially (since $\widehat{\mathrm{risk}}(F_T) \leq 1$), so we assume $R_T > 0$ and $T > B^6$ in what follows. Repeatedly applying claim 12.8 yields

$$\frac{1}{R_T^5} \geq \frac{1}{R_0^5} + 5cT \geq 5cT.$$

Thus,

$$R_T \leq \left(\frac{2B^6}{5T}\right)^{1/5} \leq \frac{B^{6/5}}{T^{1/5}}.$$

That is,

$$
\widehat{\mathrm{risk}}(F_T) \le \widehat{\mathrm{risk}}(\check{F}_B) \cdot \exp\left(\frac{B^{6/5}}{T^{1/5}}\right)
$$

$$
\le \widehat{\mathrm{risk}}(\check{F}_B) \cdot \left(1 + \frac{2B^{6/5}}{T^{1/5}}\right)
$$

$$
\le \widehat{\mathrm{risk}}(\check{F}_B) + \frac{2B^{6/5}}{T^{1/5}}
$$

since $e^x \le 1 + 2x$ for $x \in [0, 1]$, and since $\widehat{\mathrm{risk}}(\check{F}_B) \le 1$. ∎

12.2.5 Bounding the Effect of Clamping

Moving on to part 2 of the proof, we show next that the degradation in exponential loss caused by clamping is limited.

Lemma 12.9 For any $F : \mathcal{X} \to \mathbb{R}$ and $C > 0$, let $\overline{F}(x) \doteq \mathrm{clamp}_C(F(x))$. Then

$$
\widehat{\mathrm{risk}}(\overline{F}) \le \widehat{\mathrm{risk}}(F) + e^{-C}.
$$

Proof Let (x, y) be any labeled pair. If $yF(x) \le C$, then

$$
y\overline{F}(x) = \mathrm{clamp}_C(yF(x)) \ge yF(x),
$$

so $e^{-y\overline{F}(x)} \le e^{-yF(x)}$. Otherwise, if $yF(x) > C$, then $y\overline{F}(x) = C$, so $e^{-y\overline{F}(x)} = e^{-C}$. In either case, we conclude that

$$
e^{-y\overline{F}(x)} \le e^{-yF(x)} + e^{-C}.
$$

Therefore,

$$
\frac{1}{m}\sum_{i=1}^{m} e^{-y_i \overline{F}(x_i)} \le \frac{1}{m}\sum_{i=1}^{m} e^{-y_i F(x_i)} + e^{-C}
$$

as claimed. ∎

12.2.6 Relating Empirical and True Risks

For part 3, we relate the empirical risk to the true risk for all clamped functions of the form produced by AdaBoost. Let $\mathrm{span}_T(\mathcal{H})$ be the subset of $\mathrm{span}(\mathcal{H})$ consisting of all linear combinations of *exactly* T base hypotheses:

$$
\mathrm{span}_T(\mathcal{H}) \doteq \left\{ F : x \mapsto \sum_{t=1}^{T} \alpha_t h_t(x) \;\middle|\; \alpha_1, \ldots, \alpha_T \in \mathbb{R}; h_1, \ldots, h_T \in \mathcal{H} \right\}.
$$

We wish to show that

$$\text{risk}(\text{clamp}_C(F)) \lesssim \widehat{\text{risk}}(\text{clamp}_C(F)) \tag{12.38}$$

uniformly for all F in $\text{span}_T(\mathcal{H})$, and so in particular for F_T generated by AdaBoost. We prove this in two steps. First, we use techniques developed in chapters 2 and 4 to show that the empirical probability of choosing an example (x, y) for which $yF(x) \leq \theta$ will very likely be close to its true probability, for all F in $\text{span}_T(\mathcal{H})$ and all real θ. We then apply this result to show equation (12.38).

Below, $\mathbf{Pr}_{\mathcal{D}}[\cdot]$ and $\mathbf{E}_{\mathcal{D}}[\cdot]$ denote true probability and expectation, and $\mathbf{Pr}_S[\cdot]$ and $\mathbf{E}_S[\cdot]$ denote empirical probability and expectation.

Lemma 12.10 Assume $m \geq \max\{d, T+1\}$. Then with probability at least $1 - \delta$, for all $F \in \text{span}_T(\mathcal{H})$ and for all $\theta \in \mathbb{R}$,

$$\mathbf{Pr}_{\mathcal{D}}[yF(x) \leq \theta] \leq \mathbf{Pr}_S[yF(x) \leq \theta] + \varepsilon \tag{12.39}$$

where

$$\varepsilon = \sqrt{\frac{32}{m}\left((T+1)\ln\left(\frac{me}{T+1}\right) + dT\ln\left(\frac{me}{d}\right) + \ln\left(\frac{8}{\delta}\right)\right)}. \tag{12.40}$$

Proof We apply the general-purpose uniform-convergence results outlined in section 2.2. For each $F \in \text{span}_T(\mathcal{H})$ and each $\theta \in \mathbb{R}$, let us define the subset $A_{F,\theta}$ of $\mathcal{Z} \doteq \mathcal{X} \times \{-1, +1\}$ to be

$$A_{F,\theta} \doteq \{(x, y) \in \mathcal{Z} : yF(x) \leq \theta\}.$$

Let $\mathcal{A}$ be the set of all such subsets:

$$\mathcal{A} \doteq \left\{A_{F,\theta} : F \in \text{span}_T(\mathcal{H}), \theta \in \mathbb{R}\right\}.$$

Proving the lemma then is equivalent to showing that

$$\mathbf{Pr}_{\mathcal{D}}[(x, y) \in A] \leq \mathbf{Pr}_S[(x, y) \in A] + \varepsilon$$

for all $A \in \mathcal{A}$, with high probability. Theorem 2.6 provides a direct means of proving this. To apply the theorem, we need to count the number of "in-out behaviors" induced by sets $A \in \mathcal{A}$, that is, we need to bound the size of

$$\Pi_{\mathcal{A}}(S) \doteq \{\{(x_1, y_1), \ldots, (x_m, y_m)\} \cap A : A \in \mathcal{A}\}$$

for any finite sample $S = \langle (x_1, y_1), \ldots, (x_m, y_m) \rangle$.

Suppose that $\theta \in \mathbb{R}$ and that F is a function of the form

$$F(x) = \sum_{t=1}^{T} \alpha_t h_t(x). \tag{12.41}$$

Then clearly an example (x, y) is in $A_{F,\theta}$ if and only if $yF(x) \le \theta$, that is, if and only if $G_{F,\theta}(x, y) = -1$ where

$$G_{F,\theta}(x, y) \doteq \text{sign}(yF(x) - \theta) = \text{sign}\left(\sum_{t=1}^{T} \alpha_t y h_t(x) - \theta\right).$$
(12.42)

(For this proof, we temporarily redefine $\text{sign}(0) \doteq -1$.) This means that each induced subset

$$\{(x_1, y_1), \ldots, (x_m, y_m)\} \cap A_{F,\theta}$$

is in exact one-to-one correspondence with the dichotomies induced by the space $\mathcal{G}$ of all functions $G_{F,\theta}$ of the form given in equation (12.42). (Recall that a dichotomy refers to the behavior, or labeling, induced by a function on the sample S—see section 2.2.3.) Thus, there must be the same number of subsets in $\Pi_A(S)$ as dichotomies on S induced by functions in $\mathcal{G}$. Therefore, we focus now on counting the latter.

Similar to the proof of lemma 4.2, let us fix $h_1, \ldots, h_T$ and define the $(T+1)$-dimensional vectors

$$\mathbf{x}'_i = \langle y_i h_1(x_i), \ldots, y_i h_T(x_i); -1\rangle.$$

Then for any function F as in equation (12.41) and any θ, there must exist a linear threshold function σ on $\mathbb{R}^{T+1}$ such that $G_{F,\theta}(x_i, y_i) = \sigma(\mathbf{x}'_i)$ for all i. (Specifically, the coefficients defining σ are $\langle \alpha_1, \ldots, \alpha_T; \theta\rangle$, whose inner product with $\mathbf{x}'_i$ is exactly $y_i F(x_i) - \theta$.) Lemma 4.1 shows that the class Σ_{T+1} of all such linear threshold functions has VC-dimension $T+1$, which means, by Sauer's lemma (lemma 2.4) and equation (2.12), that the number of dichotomies induced by Σ_{T+1} on the m points $\mathbf{x}'_1, \ldots, \mathbf{x}'_m$ (and thus by $\mathcal{G}$ on S when $h_1, \ldots, h_T$ are fixed) is at most

$$\left(\frac{me}{T+1}\right)^{T+1}.$$

Since $\mathcal{H}$ has VC-dimension d, the number of behaviors of base classifiers $h \in \mathcal{H}$ on S is at most $(me/d)^d$. Therefore, by the same argument used in the proof of lemma 4.5, the number of dichotomies induced by $\mathcal{G}$, and thus $|\Pi_A(S)|$, is at most

$$\left(\frac{me}{T+1}\right)^{T+1} \left(\frac{me}{d}\right)^{dT}.$$

Therefore, this is also a bound on $\Pi_A(m)$, the largest value of $|\Pi_A(S)|$ on any sample S of size m.

Plugging into theorem 2.6 now gives the claimed result. ∎

We can now prove equation (12.38).

Lemma 12.11   Let $C > 0$, and assume $m \geq \max\{d, T+1\}$. With probability at least $1 - \delta$, for all $F \in \mathrm{span}_T(\mathcal{H})$,

$$\mathrm{risk}(\mathrm{clamp}_C(F)) \leq \widehat{\mathrm{risk}}(\mathrm{clamp}_C(F)) + e^C \cdot \varepsilon$$

where ε is as in equation (12.40).

Proof   We assume equation (12.39) holds for all $F \in \mathrm{span}_T(\mathcal{H})$ and all $\theta \in \mathbb{R}$. By lemma 12.10, this will be so with probability at least $1 - \delta$. Let $\overline{F}(x) \doteq \mathrm{clamp}_C(F(x))$.

Mapping equation (12.39) to the loss function of interest, we claim first that

$$\mathbf{Pr}_{\mathcal{D}}\left[e^{-y\overline{F}(x)} \geq \theta\right] \leq \mathbf{Pr}_S\left[e^{-y\overline{F}(x)} \geq \theta\right] + \varepsilon \tag{12.43}$$

for all θ. For if $e^{-C} \leq \theta \leq e^C$, then $e^{-y\overline{F}(x)} \geq \theta$ if and only if $yF(x) \leq \ln \theta$, so that equation (12.43) follows from equation (12.39). If $\theta > e^C$, then both the true and the empirical probabilities appearing in equation (12.43) are equal to zero; likewise, if $\theta < e^{-C}$, then they are both equal to 1. In either case, equation (12.43) holds trivially.

It is known that the expected value of any random variable X with range $[0, M]$ can be computed by integrating the complement of its cumulative distribution function. That is,

$$\mathbf{E}[X] = \int_0^M \mathbf{Pr}[X \geq \theta]\, d\theta.$$

Thus, applying equation (12.43) and the fact that $e^{-y\overline{F}(x)}$ cannot exceed e^C gives

$$\mathrm{risk}(\overline{F}) = \mathbf{E}_{\mathcal{D}}\left[e^{-y\overline{F}(x)}\right]$$

$$= \int_0^{e^C} \mathbf{Pr}_{\mathcal{D}}\left[e^{-y\overline{F}(x)} \geq \theta\right] d\theta$$

$$\leq \int_0^{e^C} \left(\mathbf{Pr}_S\left[e^{-y\overline{F}(x)} \geq \theta\right] + \varepsilon\right) d\theta$$

$$= \mathbf{E}_S\left[e^{-y\overline{F}(x)}\right] + e^C \cdot \varepsilon$$

$$= \widehat{\mathrm{risk}}(\overline{F}) + e^C \cdot \varepsilon,$$

as claimed.   ∎

Part 4 of the proof is comparatively simple since we only need to show that the single function $\check{F}_B$ is likely to have empirical risk close to its true risk.

Lemma 12.12 With probability at least $1 - \delta$,

$$\widehat{\text{risk}}(\check{F}_B) \leq \text{risk}(\check{F}_B) + e^B \sqrt{\frac{\ln(2/\delta)}{m}}.$$

Proof Consider the random variables $\exp(-y_i \check{F}_B(x_i) - B)$, whose average is $e^{-B} \widehat{\text{risk}}(\check{F}_B)$, and whose expectation is $e^{-B} \text{risk}(\check{F}_B)$. Because $|\check{F}_B| \leq B$ and the hypotheses in $\mathcal{H}$ are binary, $|y_i \check{F}_B(x_i)| \leq B$, so that these random variables are in $[0, 1]$. Applying Hoeffding's inequality (theorem 2.1) now gives

$$e^{-B} \widehat{\text{risk}}(\check{F}_B) \leq e^{-B} \text{risk}(\check{F}_B) + \sqrt{\frac{\ln(2/\delta)}{m}}$$

with probability at least $1 - \delta$.   ∎

12.2.7 Finishing the Proof

We can now complete the proof of theorem 12.2 by combining lemmas 12.4 and 12.9 (applied to F_T) as well as lemmas 12.11 and 12.12. Together with the union bound, these give, with probability at least $1 - 2\delta$, that

$$\text{risk}(\overline{F}_T) \leq \text{risk}(\check{F}_B) + B\sqrt{\frac{\ln T}{T}} + e^{-C} + e^C \cdot \varepsilon + e^B \sqrt{\frac{\ln(2/\delta)}{m}} \tag{12.44}$$

where ε is as in equation (12.40). Replacing δ with $\delta/2$, and choosing C to minimize equation (12.44), completes the proof of theorem 12.2.

12.2.8 Comparison to Margin-Based Bounds

As the amount of training data increases, the foregoing shows that the classification accuracy of AdaBoost converges to optimality, provided the base hypotheses possess the right degree of expressiveness. This guarantee is absolute, in contrast to the generalization-error bounds given in section 5.2, which are in terms of the margins as measured on the dataset *following* training. Moreover, the current analysis does not depend on the weak learning assumption, and so is applicable even if the edges of the weak hypotheses are rapidly approaching zero.

On the other hand, the analysis given in this chapter, as in chapter 4, requires that the number of rounds T be controlled and kept significantly smaller than the training set size m (but also large enough for the algorithm to approach minimal exponential loss). In other words, the analysis predicts overfitting if the algorithm is run for too long. In this way, the analysis fails to explain the cases in which AdaBoost manages to avoid overfitting, unlike the margins analysis whose bounds are entirely independent of T.

In short, the margins theory seems to better capture AdaBoost's behavior when the weak learning assumption holds, for instance, when using a reasonably strong base learner, like a decision-tree algorithm, that does indeed generate base hypotheses that are consistently and significantly better than random. In this case, by the results of section 5.4.1, we can expect large margins and an accompanying resistance to overfitting. When, due to noise or randomness in the data, the weak learning assumption does not hold without an inordinate blowup in the complexity of the base hypotheses, the current analysis shows that boosting can still be used—though in a mode requiring somewhat greater control—to deliver results comparable to the best possible.

The analysis of the generalization error given in this chapter was based on minimization of exponential loss. On the other hand, in section 7.3 we saw that this property alone is not sufficient to guarantee good generalization, and that any analysis must also take into account *how* the algorithm minimizes loss, as is done in the margins-based analysis of AdaBoost. These results are not in contradiction. On the contrary, the current analysis is very much based on the manner in which AdaBoost is able to generate a predictor with nearly minimal exponential loss by combining a relatively small number of base hypotheses.

12.3   How Minimizing Risk Can Lead to Poor Accuracy

Corollary 12.3 depends crucially on the key assumption that the minimum exponential loss can be realized or approached by linear combinations of base hypotheses as stated formally in equation (12.11). When this assumption does not hold, AdaBoost may produce a combined classifier whose performance is extremely poor relative to the Bayes optimal. This is true even though the base hypotheses may be rich enough to represent the Bayes optimal classifier as a linear threshold function, and even with unlimited training data, and even if the noise affecting the data is of a very simple form. Moreover, the difficulty applies to any algorithm that minimizes exponential loss, including AdaBoost.

To see this, we construct a simple example of a distribution $\mathcal{D}$ over labeled pairs, and a base hypothesis space $\mathcal{H}$ for which the linear combination of base hypotheses with minimum exponential loss induces a classifier with accuracy as bad as random guessing, even though the Bayes optimal classifier can be represented by just such a linear combination.

12.3.1   A Construction Using Confidence-Rated Hypotheses

In this construction, the instance space $\mathcal{X}$ consists of just three instances: the "large-margin" example, x_{lm}; the "puller," x_{pu}; and the "penalizer," x_{pe}. (The meaning of the names will become apparent later.) To generate a labeled example (x, y) according to $\mathcal{D}$, we first randomly choose x to be equal to x_{lm} with probability $\frac{1}{4}$; x_{pu} with probability $\frac{1}{4}$; and x_{pe} with probability $\frac{1}{2}$. The label y is chosen independently of x to be $+1$ with probability $1 - \eta$, and -1 with probability η, where $0 < \eta < \frac{1}{2}$ is the fixed noise rate. Thus, it is as if the "true" label of each example, which in this case is always $+1$, is flipped to its opposite value -1 with probability η prior to being observed by the learner. Such a *uniform noise* model, which affects the true labels of all examples with equal probability, is perhaps the simplest possible model of noise.

The hypothesis space $\mathcal{H}$ consists of just two hypotheses: $\hbar_1$ and $\hbar_2$. Here, as in chapter 9, we allow these to be real-valued or confidence-rated. Later, we show how the same construction can be modified for binary classifiers. The hypotheses $\hbar_1$ and $\hbar_2$ are defined as follows:

x	$\hbar_1(x)$	$\hbar_2(x)$
x_{lm}	1	0
x_{pe}	c	$-\frac{1}{5}$
x_{pu}	c	1

where $c > 0$ is a small constant to be chosen later. In fact, our argument will hold for all sufficiently small (but positive) values of c. The hypotheses in $\mathcal{H}$ can be plotted geometrically as in figure 12.1.

Note that the Bayes optimal classifier for the distribution $\mathcal{D}$ predicts that all instances are positive, incurring a Bayes error rate of exactly η. This classifier can be represented as the sign of a (trivial) linear combination of base hypotheses, namely, $\mathrm{sign}(\hbar_1(x))$.

In minimizing exponential loss, we aim to find a linear combination of $\hbar_1$ and $\hbar_2$,

$$F_\lambda(x) \doteq \lambda_1 \hbar_1(x) + \lambda_2 \hbar_2(x),$$

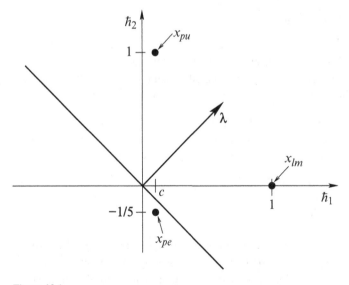

Figure 12.1
A plot of the hypotheses $\hbar_1$ and $\hbar_2$ on the instances x_{lm}, x_{pe}, and x_{pu}. Each instance x is represented by the point $\langle \hbar_1(x), \hbar_2(x) \rangle$. The vector λ schematically depicts the coefficients on $\hbar_1$ and $\hbar_2$ obtained by minimizing the exponential loss. The line perpendicular to λ represents the resulting decision boundary, which, in this case, predicts x_{pe} to be negative, and the other two instances to be positive.

that minimizes risk(F_λ) as defined in equation (12.2). We consider an ideal situation in which the true risk with respect to $\mathcal{D}$ is minimized directly, as will be the case in the limit of a very large training set for an algorithm like AdaBoost (if run for enough rounds). Our aim now is to show that the resulting classifier sign(F_λ) will have very poor accuracy.

Let us define

$$K(z) \doteq (1 - \eta)e^{-z} + \eta e^z. \tag{12.45}$$

Then by construction of $\mathcal{D}$ and $\mathcal{H}$, we can write out the risk of F_λ explicitly as

$$L(\lambda, c) \doteq \text{risk}(F_\lambda) = \tfrac{1}{4} K(\lambda_1) + \tfrac{1}{2} K\left(c\lambda_1 - \tfrac{1}{5}\lambda_2\right) + \tfrac{1}{4} K\left(c\lambda_1 + \lambda_2\right), \tag{12.46}$$

where the three terms on the right correspond, respectively, to the expected loss associated with x_{lm}, x_{pe}, and x_{pu}. With c fixed, the vector λ is chosen to minimize this expression. Intuitively, when c is small, λ_1 is controlled almost entirely by x_{lm}, while λ_2 is controlled by the other two instances. In particular, the puller will tend to pull λ_2 in a strongly positive direction since it turns out that $\hbar_2$'s higher-confidence prediction on the puller more than offsets the higher weight assigned to the penalizer under the distribution $\mathcal{D}$. As a result, the penalizer will be predicted negative, as seen in figure 12.1. If this happens, then the overall error of the resulting classifier will be at least $\tfrac{1}{2}$ because of the penalizer's large weight under $\mathcal{D}$.

More formally, we prove the following:

Theorem 12.13   Given the construction described above, let $\lambda^*(c)$ be any value of λ that minimizes the exponential loss $L(\lambda, c)$. Then for any sufficiently small value of $c > 0$, the classification error of sign$(F_{\lambda^*(c)})$ is at least $\tfrac{1}{2}$. On the other hand, for some other choice of λ, the classification error of sign(F_λ) is equal to the Bayes error rate of η.

Proof   Because $K(z)$ is convex and unbounded as z tends to $\pm\infty$, and because $L(\lambda^*(c), c) \leq L(\mathbf{0}, c) = 1$, it can be argued that the vectors $\lambda^*(c)$, for all $c \in [0, 1]$, must all lie in a bounded subset of $\mathbb{R}^2$; without loss of generality, this subset is also closed, and therefore compact.

When $c = 0$,

$$L(\lambda, 0) = \tfrac{1}{4} K(\lambda_1) + \tfrac{1}{2} K\left(-\tfrac{1}{5}\lambda_2\right) + \tfrac{1}{4} K(\lambda_2).$$

By the results of section 9.2.1, the minimizer $\lambda^*(0)$ of this expression is unique. Moreover, because its derivative with respect to λ_2, $\partial L(\lambda, 0)/\partial\lambda_2$, is strictly negative when $\lambda_2 = 0$, and because L (as a function only of λ_2) is convex, the minimizing value $\lambda_2^*(0)$ must be strictly positive.

We claim that $\lambda^*(c)$ converges to $\lambda^*(0)$ as c converges to 0 (from the right). If it does not, then there exist $\varepsilon > 0$ and a sequence $c_1, c_2, \ldots$ such that $0 < c_n < 1/n$, and

$$\|\lambda^*(c_n) - \lambda^*(0)\| > \varepsilon \tag{12.47}$$

for all n. Because the $\lambda^*(c_n)$'s lie in a compact space, the sequence must have a convergent subsequence; without loss of generality, let that subsequence be the entire sequence so that $\lambda^*(c_n) \to \tilde{\lambda}$ for some $\tilde{\lambda}$. By definition of $\lambda^*(c_n)$ as a minimizer,

$$L(\lambda^*(c_n), c_n) \le L(\lambda^*(0), c_n)$$

for all n. Taking limits, this implies by the continuity of L that

$$L(\tilde{\lambda}, 0) = \lim_{n \to \infty} L(\lambda^*(c_n), c_n) \le \lim_{n \to \infty} L(\lambda^*(0), c_n) = L(\lambda^*(0), 0).$$

But because $\lambda^*(0)$ is the unique minimizer of $L(\lambda, 0)$, this means that $\tilde{\lambda} = \lambda^*(0)$, which contradicts equation (12.47). Therefore, $\lambda^*(c) \to \lambda^*(0)$, as claimed.

For any c, the resulting prediction on the penalizer x_{pe} will be the sign of

$$F_{\lambda^*(c)}(x_{pe}) = c\lambda_1^*(c) - \tfrac{1}{5}\lambda_2^*(c),$$

which, in the limit $c \to 0$, is equal to $-\tfrac{1}{5}\lambda_2^*(0) < 0$ by the arguments above. Thus, for c sufficiently small, x_{pe} will be predicted to be negative, giving an overall error with respect to $\mathcal{D}$ of at least $\tfrac{1}{2}$. This is as bad as random guessing, and much worse than the Bayes error of η, which, as observed earlier, is realized by a trivial combination of the two base hypotheses. ∎

12.3.2 A Modified Construction Using Binary Classifiers

This construction can be modified so that all of the weak hypotheses are in fact binary classifiers with range $\{-1, +1\}$. In other words, for some distribution $\mathcal{D}$ over examples, and for some space of binary base classifiers, minimizing exponential loss over linear combinations of classifiers from this hypothesis space results in a classifier with accuracy as poor as random guessing, despite the existence of another linear combination of these same base classifiers whose performance matches the Bayes optimal.

To show this, we now represent instances by binary vectors $\mathbf{x}$ in $\mathcal{X} \doteq \{-1, +1\}^N$, where $N \doteq 2n + 11$, and where $n > 0$ will be chosen shortly. The base classifiers in $\mathcal{H}$ are each identified with a component of $\mathbf{x}$; that is, for each component j, there is a base classifier $\hbar_j$ for which $\hbar_j(\mathbf{x}) = x_j$ for every instance $\mathbf{x}$.

We will find it convenient to decompose every instance $\mathbf{x}$ into its first $2n + 1$ components, denoted $\mathbf{x}^{[1]}$, and its remaining 10 components, denoted $\mathbf{x}^{[2]}$. Thus, $\mathbf{x} = \langle \mathbf{x}^{[1]}; \mathbf{x}^{[2]} \rangle$ where $\mathbf{x}^{[1]} \in \{-1, +1\}^{2n+1}$ and $\mathbf{x}^{[2]} \in \{-1, +1\}^{10}$. Roughly speaking, this decomposition will correspond to the two base hypotheses $\hbar_1$ and $\hbar_2$ used in the construction of section 12.3.1.

Let $\mathcal{S}_k^p$ denote the set of p-dimensional binary vectors whose components add up to exactly k:

$$\mathcal{S}_k^p \doteq \left\{ \mathbf{u} \in \{-1, +1\}^p : \sum_{j=1}^p u_j = k \right\}.$$

For instance, $\mathcal{S}_p^p$ consists only of the all $+1$'s vector, while $\mathcal{S}_0^p$ consists of all p-dimensional vectors with an exactly equal number of $+1$'s and -1's.

The distribution $\mathcal{D}$ can now be described in terms of these sets. Specifically, a random instance $\mathbf{x} = \langle \mathbf{x}^{[1]}; \mathbf{x}^{[2]} \rangle$ is generated under $\mathcal{D}$ as follows:

- With probability $\frac{1}{4}$, a "large-margin" instance is chosen by selecting $\mathbf{x}^{[1]}$ uniformly at random from $\mathcal{S}_{2n+1}^{2n+1}$ and $\mathbf{x}^{[2]}$ uniformly from $\mathcal{S}_0^{10}$.

- With probability $\frac{1}{2}$, a "penalizer" instance is chosen with $\mathbf{x}^{[1]}$ selected uniformly from $\mathcal{S}_1^{2n+1}$ and $\mathbf{x}^{[2]}$ from $\mathcal{S}_{-2}^{10}$.

- With probability $\frac{1}{4}$, a "puller" instance is chosen with $\mathbf{x}^{[1]}$ selected uniformly from $\mathcal{S}_1^{2n+1}$ and $\mathbf{x}^{[2]}$ from $\mathcal{S}_{10}^{10}$.

The label y is selected just as before to be $+1$ with probability $1 - \eta$ and -1 otherwise. Thus, as before, the Bayes error is η, and now the Bayes optimal classifier can be represented by the majority vote of the components of $\mathbf{x}^{[1]}$.

As was done for instances, we also decompose every weight vector $\boldsymbol{\lambda} \in \mathbb{R}^N$ into $\langle \boldsymbol{\lambda}^{[1]}; \boldsymbol{\lambda}^{[2]} \rangle$, where $\boldsymbol{\lambda}^{[1]} \in \mathbb{R}^{2n+1}$ and $\boldsymbol{\lambda}^{[2]} \in \mathbb{R}^{10}$. A linear combination of weak classifiers thus has the form

$$F_{\boldsymbol{\lambda}}(\mathbf{x}) \doteq \sum_{j=1}^N \lambda_j x_j = \sum_{j=1}^{2n+1} \lambda_j^{[1]} x_j^{[1]} + \sum_{j=1}^{10} \lambda_j^{[2]} x_j^{[2]}. \tag{12.48}$$

Its risk with respect to $\mathcal{D}$ is

$$\text{risk}(F_{\boldsymbol{\lambda}}) \doteq \mathbf{E}_{\mathcal{D}}[\exp(-y F_{\boldsymbol{\lambda}}(\mathbf{x}))]$$

$$= \sum_{\mathbf{x}, y} \mathcal{D}(\mathbf{x}, y) \exp\left(-y\left(\sum_{j=1}^{2n+1} \lambda_j^{[1]} x_j^{[1]} + \sum_{j=1}^{10} \lambda_j^{[2]} x_j^{[2]}\right)\right) \tag{12.49}$$

where the outer sum is over all labeled pairs $(\mathbf{x}, y)$ in $\mathcal{X} \times \{-1, +1\}$.

We claim that when this risk is minimized, all of the $\lambda_j^{[1]}$'s are necessarily equal to one another, as are all of the $\lambda_j^{[2]}$'s. Suppose this is not the case, and that $\boldsymbol{\lambda} = \langle \boldsymbol{\lambda}^{[1]}; \boldsymbol{\lambda}^{[2]} \rangle$ minimizes equation (12.49) with $\lambda_1^{[1]} \neq \lambda_2^{[1]}$. Holding all of the other parameters $\lambda_3^{[1]}, \lambda_4^{[1]}, \ldots, \lambda_{2n+1}^{[1]}$, and $\boldsymbol{\lambda}^{[2]}$ fixed, and treating these as constants, we see that every term appearing in the sum in equation (12.49) has the form

$$a \exp\left(b_1 \lambda_1^{[1]} + b_2 \lambda_2^{[1]}\right)$$

for some $b_1, b_2 \in \{-1, +1\}$, and some $a \geq 0$. Combining terms with the same exponent, the risk, as a function of $\lambda_1^{[1]}$ and $\lambda_2^{[1]}$, thus must have the form

$$A e^{\lambda_1^{[1]} - \lambda_2^{[1]}} + A' e^{\lambda_2^{[1]} - \lambda_1^{[1]}} + B e^{\lambda_1^{[1]} + \lambda_2^{[1]}} + C e^{-\lambda_1^{[1]} - \lambda_2^{[1]}} \tag{12.50}$$

where A, A', B, and C are nonnegative, and do not depend on $\lambda_1^{[1]}$ or $\lambda_2^{[1]}$; in fact, by the manner in which the distribution $\mathcal{D}$ was constructed, all four of these must be strictly positive. Moreover, because of the natural symmetry of the distribution, the probability of a labeled example $(\mathbf{x}, y)$ under $\mathcal{D}$ is unchanged by swapping the values of $x_1^{[1]}$ and $x_2^{[1]}$. This implies that $A = A'$. But then replacing $\lambda_1^{[1]}$ and $\lambda_2^{[1]}$ with their average $(\lambda_1^{[1]} + \lambda_2^{[1]})/2$ in equation (12.50) leads to a strictly smaller risk since $\lambda_1^{[1]} \neq \lambda_2^{[1]}$ (and since $e^z + e^{-z}$ is minimized uniquely when $z = 0$). This is a contradiction.

By similar arguments, at the minimizer of the risk, $\lambda_1^{[1]} = \lambda_j^{[1]}$ and $\lambda_1^{[2]} = \lambda_j^{[2]}$ for every component j; that is,

$$\lambda_1^{[1]} = \lambda_2^{[1]} = \cdots = \lambda_{2n+1}^{[1]} = \lambda^{[1]}$$

and

$$\lambda_1^{[2]} = \lambda_2^{[2]} = \cdots = \lambda_{10}^{[2]} = \lambda^{[2]}$$

for some common values $\lambda^{[1]}$ and $\lambda^{[2]}$. Thus, henceforth, we need consider vectors $\boldsymbol{\lambda}^{[1]}$ and $\boldsymbol{\lambda}^{[2]}$ of only this form.

Note that if $\mathbf{x}^{[1]} \in \mathcal{S}_{k_1}^{2n+1}$ and $\mathbf{x}^{[2]} \in \mathcal{S}_{k_2}^{10}$, then by equation (12.48),

$$F_{\boldsymbol{\lambda}}(\mathbf{x}) = \lambda^{[1]} k_1 + \lambda^{[2]} k_2.$$

Thus, by the construction of $\mathcal{D}$, equation (12.49) now simplifies to

$$\tfrac{1}{4} K\big((2n+1)\lambda^{[1]}\big) + \tfrac{1}{2} K\big(\lambda^{[1]} - 2\lambda^{[2]}\big) + \tfrac{1}{4} K\big(\lambda^{[1]} + 10\lambda^{[2]}\big) \tag{12.51}$$

where the three terms correspond to large-margin, penalizer, and puller instances, respectively, and where K was defined in equation (12.45). If we now define

$$\tilde{\lambda}_1 \doteq (2n+1)\lambda^{[1]},$$

$$\tilde{\lambda}_2 \doteq 10\lambda^{[2]},$$

$$\tilde{c} \doteq \frac{1}{2n+1},$$

then equation (12.51) can be written

$$\tfrac{1}{4} K\left(\tilde{\lambda}_1\right) + \tfrac{1}{2} K\left(\tilde{c}\tilde{\lambda}_1 - \tfrac{1}{5}\tilde{\lambda}_2\right) + \tfrac{1}{4} K\left(\tilde{c}\tilde{\lambda}_1 + \tilde{\lambda}_2\right),$$

which has the identical form as equation (12.46), the risk for the construction of section 12.3.1. In other words, we have reduced the minimization problem involving binary classifiers to our previous, simpler construction involving real-valued base hypotheses. Thus, we can now proceed exactly as before to show that for n sufficiently large (so that $\tilde{c}$ is sufficiently small), all of the penalizer examples will be classified -1 by the classifier induced by minimizing the risk, which therefore will have generalization error at least $\tfrac{1}{2}$.

So we conclude that AdaBoost's classification error can be much worse than optimal if the weak hypothesis space is not adequately expressive. In addition, in section 7.5.3, we described a technique for estimating the conditional probability of an instance being positive or negative. As pointed out in that section, this method relies on essentially the same assumption of expressiveness as given in equation (12.11). The example given above shows that this assumption is indispensable, and that the technique can fail badly without it. With suitable modifications, the same argument can be applied to logistic regression as well (see exercise 12.9).

Experiments based on the construction above are reported in section 14.4.

12.3.3 The Difficulty of Uniform Noise

In the preceding example, we utilized the simple uniform-noise model in which all labels of all instances are corrupted with the same probability $\eta > 0$. The results show that even a small positive value of η will cause the generalization error to be as bad as random guessing, despite the fact that with no noise ($\eta = 0$), an algorithm like AdaBoost will provably generate a classifier with perfect generalization accuracy (given enough training data). So from $\eta = 0$ to $\eta > 0$, the generalization error jumps abruptly from 0 to 50%.

Although contrived, this suggests that AdaBoost may be quite susceptible to such uniform noise. Indeed, experiments have shown this to be the case. For instance, in one empirical study, boosting was compared with bagging (another method of generating and combining base classifiers—see section 5.5) using a decision-tree algorithm as base learner. Among nine real-world benchmark datasets, boosting outperformed bagging significantly on five, while bagging did not beat boosting on even one (on the other four, there was no statistically significant difference). However, when artificial uniform-noise was added at a rate of 10%, the results were reversed: bagging performed better than boosting on six of the datasets, while boosting did better on just one (with a statistical tie occurring on the other two).

While we expect any algorithm to do worse on noisy data, these results show that the degradation in performance for boosting is faster than for other algorithms. Intuitively, this poor performance seems to be a consequence of AdaBoost's deliberate concentration on "hard" examples, a propensity that leads the algorithm to pile ever more weight onto the corrupted examples in a futile effort to match the noisy labels. An example is shown in figure 12.2. This was seen also in section 10.3, where this tendency was exploited beneficially as a means of identifying outliers.

The example constructed above suggests that a second factor affecting performance on noisy data may be an inability to represent the function minimizing the exponential loss using a linear combination of base classifiers of limited complexity.

Although AdaBoost degrades disappointingly with the addition of uniform noise in such semi-artificial experiments, it has also been observed that AdaBoost performs quite well on a wide array of real-world datasets. Such data is almost never "clean," having been corrupted

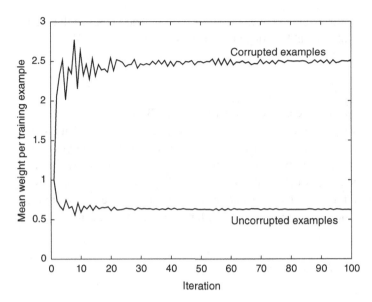

Figure 12.2
In this experiment, prior to training, 20% of the 2800 examples comprising this benchmark dataset were selected at random and their labels artificially corrupted. AdaBoost was then run using a decision-tree algorithm as the base learner. The graph shows the average weight, on each round, placed on the corrupted examples, compared with the weight placed on those that were left uncorrupted. (Copyright ©2000 Kluwer Academic Publishers (now Springer). Reprinted from figure 9 of [68] with permission from Springer Science and Business Media, LLC.)

in one way or another by measurement or recording errors, mislabelings, deletions, and so on. This paradox suggests that perhaps *uniform* noise is a poor model of the real-world influences that lead to the corruption of data. Perhaps, in real datasets, noise does not affect all instances equally, but instead affects instances close to the boundary that separates positives from negatives more strongly than those that are far from this boundary. Indeed, as discussed in section 7.5.1, logistic regression, a close relative of AdaBoost, posits just such a noise model, further hinting at the poor fit between such methods and uniform noise.

On the other hand, there may be an opportunity here to substantially improve AdaBoost's ability to handle noise. Indeed, a number of such algorithms have been suggested. Of those that are provably resistant to uniform noise, most are based on the construction of a very different kind of combined classifier; rather than assembling a final classifier that computes a (weighted) majority vote of the base classifiers, these methods instead construct a *branching program*, a computational structure that is much like a decision tree (see section 1.3), but in which two or more outgoing edges can lead to the same node. Thus, rather than forming a tree, the graph structure of a branching program forms a directed acyclic graph. A full description of such methods is beyond the scope of this book.

An alternative approach for making boosting resistant to noise and outliers will emerge from the theoretical study of optimal boosting given in chapter 13.

Summary

In this chapter, we have identified conditions under which AdaBoost provably converges to the best possible accuracy. This was proved using the algorithm's ability to minimize exponential loss, together with a proof that nearly minimal exponential loss implies nearly optimal classification accuracy. But we also saw in this chapter that AdaBoost's performance can be very poor when the weak hypotheses are insufficiently expressive, even with effectively unlimited training data. The uniform noise assumed in this example, though perhaps not entirely realistic, seems to be a problem for boosting, both theoretically and empirically.

Bibliographic Notes

Results on the consistency of AdaBoost and its variants have been studied under various conditions by a number of authors, including Breiman [38], Mannor, Meir, and Zhang [164], Jiang [128], Lugosi and Vayatis [161], Zhang [235], Zhang and Yu [236], and Bickel, Ritov, and Zakai [20]. The development given in sections 12.1 and 12.2 directly follows the proof of Bartlett and Traskin [14], with some modifications, the most significant being the improved rate of convergence given in lemma 12.4 which is due to Mukherjee, Rudin, and Schapire [172]. Theorem 12.1 was essentially proved by Zhang [235] and, in the slightly more refined form given here, by Bartlett, Jordan, and McAuliffe [12].

The example and proof given in section 12.3.1 are due to Long and Servedio [159], with some modifications and simplifications. Figure 12.1 is adapted from their paper as well. Their results show further that boosting with exponential loss will fail even when using certain forms of regularization, or when boosting is stopped early after only a limited number of rounds. The example in section 12.3.2 was inspired by one that they had used in their paper, but only experimentally and without proof.

Most of the works from the literature mentioned up to this point are applicable to broad and general classes of loss functions, not just exponential loss as presented here.

The experiments mentioned in section 12.3.3 that compare boosting and bagging with noisy data were reported by Dietterich [68]. Figure 12.2 was reprinted, with permission, from this work. See also Maclin and Opitz [162].

Algorithms for boosting in the presence of noise are given by Kalai and Servedio [129], and by Long and Servedio [157, 158]. These utilize an approach to boosting originally due to Mansour and McAllester [165], based on a branching-program representation. Other practical and theoretical research on boosting with various kinds of noise include [9, 17, 106, 141, 143, 186, 210].

Some of the exercises in this chapter are based on material from [12, 38, 159, 161, 172, 236].

Exercises

12.1 Regarding the proof of theorem 12.1, verify that:

a. ϕ is convex.

b. ϕ is strictly increasing.

c. $\phi^{-1}(z)$ is as given in equation (12.10), and is increasing.

12.2 This exercise generalizes theorem 12.1. Let $\ell : \mathbb{R} \to \mathbb{R}_+$ be a margin-based loss function with the following properties: (1) ℓ is convex; and (2) the derivative ℓ' of ℓ exists at 0 and is negative, that is, $\ell'(0) < 0$. Note that these properties together imply that ℓ is decreasing on $(-\infty, 0]$.

We use the notation in section 12.1, but redefine certain key quantities in terms of ℓ. In particular, h_{opt} and err* are exactly as before, but for $F : \mathcal{X} \to \mathbb{R}$, we redefine

$$\text{risk}(F) \doteq \mathbf{E}[\ell(yF(x))]$$

and

$$\text{risk}^* \doteq \inf_F \text{risk}(F),$$

where the infimum is taken over all possible functions F. Further, for $p \in [0, 1]$ and $z \in \mathbb{R}$, let

$$C(p, z) \doteq p\ell(z) + (1 - p)\ell(-z),$$

and let $C_{\min}(p) \doteq \inf_{z \in \mathbb{R}} C(p, z)$.

As in theorem 12.1, we now let $F : \mathcal{X} \to \mathbb{R}$ be a given, fixed function, and let h be a corresponding thresholded classifier. Finally, we redefine $\rho(x) \doteq C(\pi(x), F(x)) - C_{\min}(\pi(x))$.

a. Show that

$$\rho(x) \geq \begin{cases} 0 & \text{if } h(x) = h_{\text{opt}}(x) \\ \ell(0) - C_{\min}(\pi(x)) & \text{else.} \end{cases}$$

b. For $r \in [-1, +1]$, we redefine

$$\phi(r) \doteq \ell(0) - C_{\min}\left(\frac{1+r}{2}\right).$$

Prove that ϕ has the following properties:

i. $\phi(r) = \phi(-r)$ for $r \in [-1, +1]$.

ii. ϕ is convex. [*Hint:* First prove and then apply the fact that if $\mathcal{F}$ is a family of convex, real-valued functions, then the function g defined by $g(x) = \sup_{f \in \mathcal{F}} f(x)$ is also convex.]

iii. $\phi(0) = 0$ and $\phi(r) > 0$ for $r \neq 0$. [*Hint:* For fixed $r \neq 0$, consider the values of $C((1 + r)/2, z)$ in a small neighborhood of $z = 0$.]

iv. ϕ is strictly increasing on $[0, 1]$.

c. Prove that

$$\phi(\text{err}(h) - \text{err}^*) \leq \text{risk}(F) - \text{risk}^*.$$

d. Let $F_1, F_2, \ldots$ be a sequence of functions, and $h_1, h_2, \ldots$ a corresponding sequence of thresholded classifiers (that is, $h_n(x) = \text{sign}(F_n(x))$ whenever $F_n(x) \neq 0$). Prove that, as $n \to \infty$, if $\text{risk}(F_n) \to \text{risk}^*$, then $\text{err}(h_n) \to \text{err}^*$.

12.3 We continue exercise 12.2.

a. Suppose the loss $\ell(z) = \ln(1 + e^{-z})$. Show that

$$\phi(r) = \text{RE}_b\left(\frac{1+r}{2} \,\Big\|\, \frac{1}{2}\right).$$

Also, show that if $\text{risk}(F) \leq \text{risk}^* + \varepsilon$, then

$$\text{err}(\text{sign}(F)) \leq \text{err}^* + \sqrt{2\varepsilon}.$$

b. Compute $\phi(r)$ for each of the following loss functions. Express your answers in as simple a form as possible.

i. $\ell(z) = (1 - z)^2$.

ii. $\ell(z) = (\max\{1 - z, 0\})^2$.

iii. $\ell(z) = \max\{1 - z, 0\}$.

Exercises 12.4 and 12.5 outline alternative methods for obtaining rates of convergence of the exponential loss to its minimum for two different variants of AdaBoost. Aside from the changes described below, we adopt the setup and notation of section 12.2. In particular, $\check{F}_B$ is a reference function with $|\check{F}_B| < B$.

12.4 *AdaBoost.S* is the same as AdaBoost, except that at the end of each round, the current combination of weak hypotheses is *scaled back*, that is, multiplied by a scalar in $[0, 1]$ if doing so will further reduce the exponential loss. Pseudocode is shown as algorithm 12.1, using the formulation of AdaBoost as a greedy algorithm for minimizing exponential loss

Algorithm 12.1
AdaBoost.S, a modified version of AdaBoost

Given: $(x_1, y_1), \ldots, (x_m, y_m)$ where $x_i \in \mathcal{X}$, $y_i \in \{-1, +1\}$.
Initialize $F_0 \equiv 0$.
For $t = 1, \ldots, T$:

- Choose $h_t \in \mathcal{H}$, $\alpha_t \in \mathbb{R}$ to minimize

$$\frac{1}{m} \sum_{i=1}^m \exp(-y_i(F_{t-1}(x_i) + \alpha_t h_t(x_i)))$$

  (over all choices of α_t and h_t).
- Update:

$$\tilde{F}_t = F_{t-1} + \alpha_t h_t$$

  and scale back:

$$F_t = s_t \tilde{F}_t$$

  where $s_t \in [0, 1]$ minimizes

$$\frac{1}{m} \sum_{i=1}^m \exp(-y_i s_t \tilde{F}_t).$$

Output F_T.

---

as presented in section 7.1. The code is largely the same as in algorithm 7.1 (p. 178), maintaining a combination F_t of weak hypotheses, and greedily choosing α_t and h_t on each round to effect the greatest drop in the empirical exponential loss. However, at the end of the round, after creating the new combination $\tilde{F}_t = F_{t-1} + \alpha_t h_t$, the result is multiplied by the value s_t in $[0, 1]$ that causes the greatest decrease in the exponential loss.

Below, D_t, R_t, and ΔR_t are defined as in equations (12.22), (12.20), and (12.27), but with F_t as redefined above.

a. Prove that

$$\sum_{i=1}^m D_t(i) y_i F_{t-1}(x_i) \geq 0.$$

[*Hint:* Consider the first derivative of $\widehat{\mathrm{risk}}(s\tilde{F}_{t-1})$ when viewed as a function of s.]

b. Prove that if $R_{t-1} \geq 0$, then

$$\Delta R_t \geq \frac{R_{t-1}^2}{2B^2}.$$

[*Hint:* Prove an upper bound on R_{t-1} and a lower bound on ΔR_t, both in terms of γ_t (appropriately redefined for AdaBoost.S).]

c. Prove that if $R_t > 0$, then

$$\frac{1}{R_t} \geq \frac{1}{R_{t-1}} + \frac{1}{2B^2}.$$

d. Finally, show that

$$\widehat{\text{risk}}(F_T) \leq \widehat{\text{risk}}(\check{F}_B) + \frac{4B^2}{T}$$

(a much better bound than the one given for AdaBoost in lemma 12.4).

12.5 Consider a variant of AdaBoost that is the same as algorithm 7.1 (p. 178) except that α_t is restricted to the set $[-c_t, c_t]$; that is, on each round, $F_t = F_{t-1} + \alpha_t h_t$ where α_t and h_t are chosen together to greedily minimize the exponential loss over all choices of $h_t \in \mathcal{H}$ and over all choices of α_t in the restricted set $[-c_t, c_t]$ (rather than over all $\alpha_t \in \mathbb{R}$, as in algorithm 7.1). Here, $c_1, c_2, \ldots$ is a prespecified, nonincreasing sequence of positive numbers for which we assume that $\sum_{t=1}^{\infty} c_t = \infty$, but $\sum_{t=1}^{\infty} c_t^2 < \infty$. (For instance, $c_t = t^{-a}$, where $\frac{1}{2} < a \leq 1$, satisfies these conditions.) We assume $B > c_1$.

In what follows, R_t and D_t are as defined in equations (12.20) and (12.22) (with F_t as redefined above). However, we here redefine $S_t \doteq B + \sum_{t'=1}^{t} c_{t'}$.

a. For any $\alpha \in \mathbb{R}$ and $h \in \mathcal{H}$, use Taylor's theorem (theorem A.1) to show that

$$\ln\left(\widehat{\text{risk}}(F_{t-1} + \alpha h)\right) \leq \ln\left(\widehat{\text{risk}}(F_{t-1})\right) - \alpha \sum_{i=1}^{m} D_t(i) y_i h(x_i) + \frac{\alpha^2}{2}.$$

b. Let $\hat{h}_1, \ldots, \hat{h}_n \in \mathcal{H}$, and let $w_1, \ldots, w_n \in \mathbb{R}$ with $\sum_{j=1}^{n} |w_j| = 1$. Show that

$$\ln\left(\widehat{\text{risk}}(F_t)\right) \leq \ln\left(\widehat{\text{risk}}(F_{t-1})\right) - c_t \sum_{i=1}^{m} \sum_{j=1}^{n} w_j D_t(i) y_i \hat{h}_j(x_i) + \frac{c_t^2}{2}.$$

[*Hint:* Prove upper and lower bounds on $\sum_{j=1}^{n} |w_j| \ln\left(\widehat{\text{risk}}(F_{t-1} + c_t \text{sign}(w_j)\hat{h}_j)\right)$.]

c. On a particular round t, show that there exist a finite set of hypotheses $\hat{h}_1, \ldots, \hat{h}_n \in \mathcal{H}$, and real numbers $a_1, \ldots, a_n$ and $b_1, \ldots, b_n$ such that F_{t-1} and $\check{F}_B$ can be written in the form

$$F_{t-1}(x) = \sum_{j=1}^{n} a_j \hat{h}_j(x) \quad \text{and} \quad \check{F}_B(x) = \sum_{j=1}^{n} b_j \hat{h}_j(x),$$

and for which

$$\sum_{j=1}^{n} \left(|a_j| + |b_j| \right) \leq S_{t-1}.$$

(Keep in mind that $\mathcal{H}$ need not be finite.)

d. By setting $w_j = (b_j - a_j)/W$ in part (b), where $W \doteq \sum_{j=1}^{n} |b_j - a_j|$, show that

$$R_t \leq R_{t-1} \left(1 - \frac{c_t}{S_{t-1}} \right) + \frac{c_t^2}{2}.$$

[*Hint:* Use equation (12.23).]

e. Show that

$$1 - \frac{c_t}{S_{t-1}} \leq \frac{S_{t-1}}{S_t}.$$

f. Show that

$$R_T \leq \frac{B^2}{S_T} + \frac{1}{2} \sum_{t=1}^{T} \frac{S_t}{S_T} \cdot c_t^2.$$

g. Let $\sigma(1), \sigma(2), \dots$ be a sequence of positive integers such that $1 \leq \sigma(t) \leq t$ for all t, and as $t \to \infty$, $\sigma(t) \to \infty$ but $S_{\sigma(t)}/S_t \to 0$. Show that such a sequence must exist.

h. Show that

$$R_T \leq \frac{B^2}{S_T} + \frac{1}{2} \left[\frac{S_{\sigma(T)}}{S_T} \sum_{t=1}^{\sigma(T)} c_t^2 + \sum_{t=\sigma(T)+1}^{T} c_t^2 \right], \tag{12.52}$$

and that the right-hand side of this inequality approaches 0 as $T \to \infty$. This shows that $\lim_{T \to \infty} \widehat{\text{risk}}(F_T) \leq \widehat{\text{risk}}(\check{F}_B)$, with rates of convergence in terms of B and the c_t's that can be obtained using equation (12.52).

12.6 Rather than using AdaBoost for a bounded number of rounds, consider applying regularization to the exponential loss. To be specific, given the setup and assumptions of theorem 12.2, and for $B > 0$, let $\hat{F}_B$ be any function which minimizes $\widehat{\text{risk}}(F)$ over all $F \in \text{span}(\mathcal{H})$ with $|F| \leq B$. (For simplicity, assume such a minimizing function exists.) As usual, $\check{F}_B$ is a reference function from this same space.

a. Prove that, with probability at least $1 - \delta$,

$$\text{risk}(\hat{F}_B) \leq \text{risk}(\check{F}_B) + O\left(e^B \cdot B \cdot \sqrt{\frac{d \ln(m/d)}{m}} + e^B \sqrt{\frac{\ln(1/\delta)}{m}}\right).$$

[*Hint:* Use the techniques of section 5.3.]

b. Conclude that $\text{risk}(\hat{F}_B)$ converges almost surely to risk* as $m \to \infty$, for an appropriate choice of B as a function of m.

12.7 Let the domain $\mathcal{X} = [0, 1]^n$, and let us assume that the conditional probability function π given in equation (12.1) is Lipschitz, meaning that for some constant $k > 0$, and for all $\mathbf{x}, \mathbf{x}' \in \mathcal{X}$,

$$\left|\pi(\mathbf{x}) - \pi(\mathbf{x}')\right| \leq k \|\mathbf{x} - \mathbf{x}'\|_2.$$

Let $\mathcal{H}$ be the space of all decision trees with at most cn internal nodes where each test at each node is of the form $x_j \leq v$, for some $j \in \{1, \ldots, n\}$ and some $v \in \mathbb{R}$. Here, $c > 0$ is an absolute constant of your choosing (not dependent on n, k, or π).

a. Show that equation (12.11) holds in this case.

b. Show that the VC-dimension of $\mathcal{H}$ is upper bounded by a polynomial in n.

12.8 Verify the following details, which were omitted from the proof of theorem 12.13:

a. The vectors $\boldsymbol{\lambda}^*(c)$, for all $c \in [0, 1]$, are included in some compact subset of $\mathbb{R}^2$.

b. The minimizer of $\boldsymbol{\lambda}^*(0)$ is unique.

c. The partial derivative $\partial L(\boldsymbol{\lambda}, 0)/\partial \lambda_2$ is strictly negative when $\lambda_2 = 0$.

d. $\lambda_2^*(0) > 0$.

12.9 Let $\ell : \mathbb{R} \to \mathbb{R}_+$ be a margin-based loss function satisfying exactly the same properties described at the beginning of exercise 12.2. Note that these properties imply that ℓ is continuous. Suppose that in the construction of section 12.3.1 exponential loss is replaced by ℓ. In particular, this means redefining

$$K(z) \doteq (1 - \eta)\ell(z) + \eta\ell(-z).$$

In this exercise, we will see how to modify theorem 12.13 to prove a more general result that holds when any loss function ℓ with the stated properties is minimized in place of exponential loss.

a. Prove that $\lim_{s \to -\infty} \ell(s) = \infty$. [*Hint:* Use equation (A.3).]

b. Show that there exists a compact set $C \subseteq \mathbb{R}^2$ such that if $\boldsymbol{\lambda}$ minimizes $L(\boldsymbol{\lambda}, c)$ for any $c \in [0, 1]$, then $\boldsymbol{\lambda} \in C$.

c. Show that if ℓ is strictly convex, then $L(\boldsymbol{\lambda}, 0)$ has a unique minimum. Also, give an example showing that the minimum of $L(\boldsymbol{\lambda}, 0)$ need *not* be unique without this additional assumption. (You should not assume ℓ is strictly convex in the remaining parts of this exercise.)

d. Let $M \subseteq \mathbb{R}^2$ be the set of *all* minima of $L(\lambda, 0)$. Show that if $\lambda \in M$, then $\lambda_2 > 0$.

e. Let $\lambda^*(c)$ be as in theorem 12.13 (but for loss ℓ), and let $c_1, c_2, \ldots$ be any sequence converging to 0. Prove that if the sequence $\lambda^*(c_1), \lambda^*(c_2), \ldots$ converges, then its limit is in M.

f. Show that there exists $c_0 > 0$ such that for all $c \in (0, c_0]$, $F_{\lambda^*(c)}(x_{pe}) < 0$.

12.10 Throughout this exercise, assume that instances $\mathbf{x}$ are binary vectors in $\{-1, +1\}^N$. We consider weighted combinations of the components of such vectors which now include a constant term. In other words, weight vectors now have the form $\lambda = \langle \lambda_0, \lambda_1, \ldots, \lambda_N \rangle \in \mathbb{R}^{N+1}$, and (re)define the combination

$$F_\lambda(\mathbf{x}) \doteq \lambda_0 + \sum_{j=1}^{N} \lambda_j x_j.$$

a. Suppose the weak learner produces confidence-rated decision stumps of the form

$$h(\mathbf{x}) = \begin{cases} c_+ & \text{if } x_j = +1 \\ c_- & \text{if } x_j = -1 \end{cases}$$

for some $c_+, c_- \in \mathbb{R}$ and some index $j \in \{1, \ldots, N\}$. Show that if $h_1, \ldots, h_T$ all have this form, and $\alpha_1, \ldots, \alpha_T \in \mathbb{R}$, then there exists $\lambda \in \mathbb{R}^{N+1}$ for which $\sum_{t=1}^{T} \alpha_t h_t(\mathbf{x}) = F_\lambda(\mathbf{x})$ for all $\mathbf{x} \in \{-1, +1\}^N$.

b. Suppose $\mathcal{D}$ is the distribution in section 12.3.2, and that $\lambda \in \mathbb{R}^{N+1}$ minimizes the risk $\mathbb{E}_{\mathcal{D}}\left[e^{-yF_\lambda(\mathbf{x})}\right]$. What will be the classification error (with respect to $\mathcal{D}$) of the induced classifier, $\text{sign}(F_\lambda)$? How does this compare to the Bayes optimal?

c. For any noise rate $\eta \in \left(0, \frac{1}{2}\right)$, show how to construct a modified distribution $\mathcal{D}$ so that if λ minimizes the risk (with respect to this new distribution), then the induced classifier, $\text{sign}(F_\lambda)$, will have classification error at least $\frac{1}{2}$, even though the Bayes error can be achieved by some other combination of the same form.

13 Optimally Efficient Boosting

Much of this book has been concerned with the efficiency of boosting, especially of Ada-Boost. In section 3.1, we proved a bound on how quickly AdaBoost drives down the training error in terms of the edges of the weak classifiers. In chapters 4 and 5, we proved an assortment of bounds on the generalization error that in one way or another made use of the training-error analysis. These bounds on AdaBoost's performance are quite good in many respects, indicating, for instance, that AdaBoost's training error drops exponentially fast when the weak learning assumption holds. However, they also leave us wondering if it might be possible to do even better, perhaps with a different algorithm. In other words, these results raise basic questions about the nature of "optimal" boosting: Is AdaBoost the best possible algorithm? If not, what algorithm is, and how close does AdaBoost come? These questions concern the fundamental resource requirements that are necessary for boosting to be possible.

To find answers, we begin by studying how to optimally minimize the training error when allowed up to T calls to a weak learning algorithm for which the empirical γ-weak learning assumption is guaranteed to hold. Here, as in chapter 6, the interaction between the booster and the weak learner is viewed as a game. However, whereas in chapter 6 we regarded each *round* of boosting as a complete game that is repeated T times, now we regard the *entire sequence* of T rounds of boosting as a single game that is played just once.

Using this formulation, we derive an algorithm called *boost-by-majority* (BBM) which is very nearly optimal for this game. In terms of γ and T, its training error turns out to be exactly the tail of a certain binomial distribution, whereas the bound for AdaBoost given in theorem 3.1 is precisely the upper bound on this same tail that would be obtained by applying Hoeffding's inequality (theorem 2.1). Thus, in terms of the training error, the gap between AdaBoost and optimality is the same as the difference between Hoeffding's inequality and the true probability that it is used to approximate—a gap that, in a certain sense, vanishes asymptotically.

We next consider the generalization error, whose minimization is of course the true purpose of boosting. Not surprisingly, the results of chapter 4 can be immediately applied to derive an upper bound on the generalization error of BBM. More interestingly, the bounds so obtained turn out to be exactly the best possible for *any* boosting algorithm. In other words, in terms of T and γ, there exist learning problems for which any boosting algorithm will have generalization error at least as large as that given by the upper bound for BBM (up to an additive difference which vanishes as the number of training examples gets large). Equivalently, this lower bound provides a floor on the minimum number of rounds of boosting needed to achieve a desired accuracy. Thus, in these terms, BBM is essentially optimal, and AdaBoost is close behind.

Besides being optimal in the senses discussed above, BBM may have another potential advantage over AdaBoost, namely, in its handling of outliers. As seen in sections 10.3 and 12.3.3, when some of the data are mislabeled or ambiguous, AdaBoost piles more and more weight on such difficult examples, sometimes substantially degrading performance. BBM also concentrates on harder examples but, in contrast to AdaBoost, actually puts *less* weight on the *very* hardest examples, effectively "giving up" on the outliers. This may be an important benefit on noisy datasets.

Unfortunately, BBM also has an important disadvantage. Unlike AdaBoost, it is non-adaptive, meaning that the minimum edge γ must be provided before boosting begins. This property seriously hinders its use in practical applications. In chapter 14, we describe a technique for making BBM adaptive.

13.1 The Boost-by-Majority Algorithm

We begin by considering how to optimally minimize the training error. This will lead to a derivation of the boost-by-majority algorithm.

13.1.1 The Voting Game

As usual, we assume we have been given m training examples $(x_1, y_1), \ldots, (x_m, y_m)$. We also assume access to a weak learning algorithm satisfying the empirical γ-weak learning assumption, meaning that, for any distribution D over the sample, the weak learner is guaranteed to return a weak hypothesis h whose weighted error with respect to D is at most $\frac{1}{2} - \gamma$. Finally, we assume that the booster is allowed to access the weak learner T times. Under these conditions, our goal is to determine the minimum training error that can be guaranteed by any boosting algorithm. Note that this is essentially equivalent to asking for the minimum number of rounds of boosting necessary to achieve some desired accuracy.

For now, we further restrict our attention to boosting algorithms whose combined classifier takes the form of a simple (unweighted) majority vote over the weak hypotheses. This restriction may slightly limit what is possible for the booster. Even so, the results of section 13.2 will show that no boosting algorithm can do significantly better, even without this limitation.

We can regard the boosting process as a game between the two interacting players, the booster and the weak learner. The game is played as follows: On each of a sequence of rounds $t = 1, \ldots, T$:

1. the booster chooses a distribution D_t over the training set;

2. the weak learner chooses a hypothesis h_t such that

$$\mathbf{Pr}_{i \sim D_t}[h_t(x_i) \neq y_i] \leq \tfrac{1}{2} - \gamma. \tag{13.1}$$

At the end of T rounds, the final hypothesis is formed as a simple majority vote of the weak hypotheses:

$$H(x) = \mathrm{sign}\left(\sum_{t=1}^{T} h_t(x)\right). \tag{13.2}$$

The loss of the booster in this game is the training error

$$\frac{1}{m}\sum_{i=1}^{m} \mathbf{1}\{H(x_i) \neq y_i\} = \frac{1}{m}\sum_{i=1}^{m} \mathbf{1}\left\{y_i \sum_{t=1}^{T} h_t(x_i) \leq 0\right\}. \tag{13.3}$$

The booster's goal is to minimize this loss, while the weak learner's goal is to maximize it.

When compared with our earlier game-theoretic formulation of boosting given in section 6.4, elements of the game described above may seem odd, or even incorrect. Indeed, there do exist very significant differences between the two formulations, each capturing different aspects of the boosting problem and thereby yielding different insights.

To be specific, in the formulation of section 6.4, the game of interest is played *repeatedly*, once on every round, with loss suffered at the end of *each* round. Also, this game was defined by a matrix over training examples and a *fixed space* of weak hypotheses. In the current setup, we instead regard the *entire* sequence of T rounds as a *single* game. Although in principle it might be possible to describe this game by a matrix, it is more natural to define it in terms of sequential play that alternates between the two players with loss incurred only at the end of the sequence. Further, we make no restrictions on the weak hypotheses other than that they satisfy the γ-weak learning assumption.

A final, more subtle difference between the two games is in the apparent goals of the two players, especially the weak learner: In the setup of section 6.4, the weak learner wishes to *minimize* the weighted error of its weak hypotheses, while the booster tries to make this difficult by choosing a hard distribution. Now, instead, the weak learner has a diametrically opposite interest in choosing weak hypotheses with the *largest* weighted error possible (though not exceeding $\tfrac{1}{2} - \gamma$), since these are intuitively more likely to make it difficult for the booster to achieve its goal of producing a combined hypothesis with low error. Thus, the weak learner's goal is exactly reversed in the two game-theoretic models of boosting.

Nevertheless, despite this seeming contradiction, both formulations lead to sensible insights and algorithms.

To get some intuition for the game, let us consider some simple cases. First, consider a "lazy booster" that chooses the uniform distribution over the training set on every round. The response of the weak learner to this strategy is likely to be simple: Choose some weak hypothesis h that is correct on $\frac{1}{2} + \gamma$ of the training examples, and output this same weak hypothesis on every round. The final majority-vote classifier will then be equivalent to h, so that its training error is exactly as large as h's. Clearly, and unsurprisingly, the booster has to change the distribution in order to prevent the weak learner from always outputting the same weak hypothesis.

As a second example, and one which will play a key role in the following, consider an *oblivious weak learner* that entirely ignores the distributions D_t. Instead, on every round, a random weak hypothesis is chosen by this weak learner whose prediction on every training example x_i is selected independently to match the correct label y_i with probability $\frac{1}{2} + \gamma$, and otherwise is equal to its opposite $-y_i$ (with probability $\frac{1}{2} - \gamma$). In other words, conditional on the correct label, the predictions of the weak hypotheses on the examples are independent of one another, and each is correct with probability $\frac{1}{2} + \gamma$. Regardless of the distributions provided by the booster, the expected weighted error of such a weak hypothesis will be exactly $\frac{1}{2} - \gamma$. Strictly speaking, this leaves open the possibility of the randomly chosen weak hypothesis having an *actual* weighted error that exceeds $\frac{1}{2} - \gamma$. Nevertheless, for the moment, for the purposes of this informal discussion, we ignore this complication and allow such a weak learner, even though it does not technically satisfy the requirements of the game.

If the weak learner uses this oblivious strategy, then the booster's final training error is likely to be very small. This is because each example is correctly classified independently by each weak hypothesis with probability $\frac{1}{2} + \gamma$, and it is correctly classified by the final hypothesis if and only if more than half of the weak hypotheses are correct. Thus, the chance that it is misclassified is the same as the probability of at most $T/2$ heads in a sequence of T coin flips when the probability of heads on each flip is $\frac{1}{2} + \gamma$. This probability is exactly

$$\sum_{j=0}^{\lfloor T/2 \rfloor} \binom{T}{j} \left(\tfrac{1}{2}+\gamma\right)^j \left(\tfrac{1}{2}-\gamma\right)^{T-j}. \tag{13.4}$$

Since this holds for each training example, the expected training error will also be exactly equal to this quantity, which, by Hoeffding's inequality (theorem 2.1), is at most $e^{-2\gamma^2 T}$. As informally suggested here, when made rigorous, this argument shows that for any booster, the oblivious weak learner (with some technical modifications) can force the training error to be very close to the quantity in equation (13.4) when the number of training examples is large.

One option for playing this game, of course, is to apply AdaBoost or, rather, the α-Boost version given in section 6.4.3, in which, on every round, the hypothesis weight α_t in algorithm 1.1 is fixed to the constant

$$\alpha = \frac{1}{2} \ln \left(\frac{1+2\gamma}{1-2\gamma} \right) \tag{13.5}$$

so that the final hypothesis will be a simple majority vote as required in this game. We refer to this algorithm, with this setting of α, as *NonAdaBoost* since it is a nonadaptive boosting algorithm. A straightforward modification of theorem 3.1 then shows that the loss of this boosting algorithm will be at most

$$(1-4\gamma^2)^{T/2} \le e^{-2\gamma^2 T},$$

which exactly matches the upper bound on equation (13.4) provided by Hoeffding's inequality. Thus, already we can see that the gap between AdaBoost and optimality for this game is not large, though perhaps not the best possible.

In fact, as we will see, the boost-by-majority algorithm achieves an upper bound on the training error that is *exactly* equal to equation (13.4) for any weak learner. This will show that both BBM and the oblivious weak learner are essentially optimal for their respective roles in the game.

13.1.2   A Chip Game

To simplify the presentation, let us define, for example i and round t, the variable

$$z_{t,i} \doteq y_i h_t(x_i),$$

which is $+1$ if h_t correctly classifies (x_i, y_i), and -1 otherwise. We also define the variable

$$s_{t,i} \doteq y_i \sum_{t'=1}^{t} h_{t'}(x_i) = \sum_{t'=1}^{t} z_{t',i},$$

which is the unnormalized margin of the classifier constructed through round t. We write $\mathbf{s}_t$ and $\mathbf{z}_t$ for the corresponding vectors with components as above.

In terms of these variables, the voting game we are studying can be redescribed more visually as a "chip game." Here, each training example is identified with a *chip*, and each of the m chips has an integer *position*; specifically, the position of chip i at the end of round t is $s_{t,i}$. Initially, all chips are at position 0 so that $\mathbf{s}_0 = \mathbf{0}$. On every round t, the booster chooses a distribution D_t over the chips. In general, chips at the same position need not be assigned the same weight under D_t, although this will usually happen naturally. Given D_t, the weak learner next chooses to increment (move up by 1) the positions of some of the

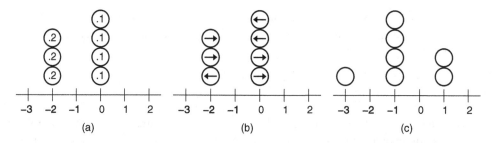

Figure 13.1
One round of the chip game: (a) The booster selects a distribution over the chips, indicated by the numbers appearing in each chip; (b) the weak learner chooses some of the chips to be incremented (moved right one position), and the rest to be decremented (moved left one position), as indicated by the arrows; (c) the chips are moved to their new positions, as specified by the weak learner.

chips, and to decrement (move down by 1) the positions of all the rest. In other words, the weak learner chooses a vector $\mathbf{z}_t \in \{-1, +1\}^m$ and updates the chip positions:

$$\mathbf{s}_t = \mathbf{s}_{t-1} + \mathbf{z}_t. \tag{13.6}$$

See figure 13.1 for an example of a single round of the game.

Importantly, the weak learner is required to increment the positions of at least $\frac{1}{2} + \gamma$ of the chips, as weighted by D_t; that is, the weak learner must choose $\mathbf{z}_t$ so that

$$\mathbf{Pr}_{i \sim D_t}\left[z_{t,i} = +1\right] \geq \tfrac{1}{2} + \gamma \tag{13.7}$$

or, equivalently,

$$\mathbf{E}_{i \sim D_t}\left[z_{t,i}\right] \geq 2\gamma. \tag{13.8}$$

The choice of $\mathbf{z}_t$ of course corresponds to the choice of h_t, and the condition in equation (13.7) is then simply the γ-weak learning assumption.

After T rounds, the loss suffered by the booster is the fraction of chips at nonpositive positions:

$$L(\mathbf{s}_T) \doteq \frac{1}{m}\sum_{i=1}^{m}\mathbf{1}\{s_{T,i} \leq 0\}, \tag{13.9}$$

a direct translation of equation (13.3).

13.1.3 Deriving Optimal Play

How, then, should this game be played optimally? In section 6.1.2, we saw the benefit of analyzing a sequentially played game from the end of the game backward to its beginning. We can apply the same idea here.

Suppose at the beginning of the final round T that the chip positions are given by the vector $\mathbf{s}_{T-1}$, and that the booster chooses distribution D_T over the chips. How would an optimal weak learner respond? The weak learner's goal is to choose $\mathbf{z}_T \in \{-1, +1\}^m$ so as to maximize the resulting loss for the final chip positions, namely,

$$L(\mathbf{s}_T) = L(\mathbf{s}_{T-1} + \mathbf{z}_T).$$

However, $\mathbf{z}_T$ must satisfy the constraint in equation (13.8), that is, it must belong to the set $\mathcal{Z}(D_T)$ where

$$\mathcal{Z}(D) \doteq \left\{ \mathbf{z} \in \{-1, +1\}^m : \mathbf{E}_{i \sim D}[z_i] \geq 2\gamma \right\}.$$

So if the booster chooses D_T, then its final loss will be

$$\max_{\mathbf{z}_T \in \mathcal{Z}(D_T)} L(\mathbf{s}_{T-1} + \mathbf{z}_T). \tag{13.10}$$

Therefore, when the chips are in positions $\mathbf{s}_{T-1}$ on round T, an optimal booster will select D_T which minimizes equation (13.10), giving a loss of

$$\min_{D_T} \max_{\mathbf{z}_T \in \mathcal{Z}(D_T)} L(\mathbf{s}_{T-1} + \mathbf{z}_T)$$

(where such a minimum will always be understood to be taken over all distributions on $\{1, \ldots, m\}$). This expression is a function of the chip positions $\mathbf{s}_{T-1}$. Given these positions, it computes the loss that will result if both players play optimally for the rest of the game. It also specifically prescribes that the optimal booster use the distribution D_T that realizes the minimum.

To continue this argument, let us define for each round t a function $\Lambda_t(\mathbf{s}_t)$ that is equal to the loss that would result if the chips are in positions given by vector $\mathbf{s}_t$ at the end of round t, and given that both players play optimally for the part of the game that remains after this round. Note that after round T, the game is over and the loss suffered is already determined. Thus,

$$\Lambda_T(\mathbf{s}_T) = L(\mathbf{s}_T). \tag{13.11}$$

For earlier rounds $t \leq T$, we can use the same reasoning as above. The chips begin the round in positions $\mathbf{s}_{t-1}$. If the booster chooses D_t, an optimal weak learner will respond with $\mathbf{z}_t \in \mathcal{Z}(D_t)$ to maximize the loss for the remainder of the game $\Lambda_t(\mathbf{s}_{t-1} + \mathbf{z}_t)$. Thus, the booster should select D_t to minimize

$$\max_{\mathbf{z}_t \in \mathcal{Z}(D_t)} \Lambda_t(\mathbf{s}_{t-1} + \mathbf{z}_t),$$

so that the loss suffered under optimal play beginning after round $t - 1$ is

$$\Lambda_{t-1}(\mathbf{s}_{t-1}) = \min_{D_t} \max_{\mathbf{z}_t \in \mathcal{Z}(D_t)} \Lambda_t(\mathbf{s}_{t-1} + \mathbf{z}_t). \tag{13.12}$$

This recurrence, in principle, allows us to compute the optimal loss under optimal play and, furthermore, provides the optimal strategy for both players—the booster should play the distribution D_t that realizes the minimum and, given D_t, the weak learner should play the vector $\mathbf{z}_t$ that realizes the maximum. On the other hand, these strategies do not lend themselves easily to analysis or implementation.

At the beginning of the game, under optimal play, the loss suffered by the booster with all chips starting at position 0 at time 0 is $\Lambda_0(\mathbf{0})$. Thus, unraveling the recurrence in equation (13.12) gives an explicit expression for the value of the game, that is, the loss for the entire game under optimal play:

$$\Lambda_0(\mathbf{0}) = \min_{D_1} \max_{\mathbf{z}_1 \in \mathcal{Z}(D_1)} \cdots \min_{D_T} \max_{\mathbf{z}_T \in \mathcal{Z}(D_T)} L\left(\sum_{t=1}^{T} \mathbf{z}_t\right).$$

Needless to say, this is a rather unwieldy formula.

13.1.4 A Tractable Approximation

The function Λ_t characterizes optimality exactly, but is difficult to compute and work with mathematically, as are the optimal strategies that it implicitly defines. Fortunately, as we show next, Λ_t can be usefully approximated in a way that admits both a closed-form analysis of the game and the derivation of the BBM algorithm, a strategy for the booster that is close to optimal and straightforward to implement. This approximation will eventually be stated in terms of a "potential function," a concept at the heart of BBM and its analysis. Although this algorithm can perhaps be stated and analyzed without giving a full derivation of Λ_t's approximation, we provide one anyway with the purpose of revealing where the potential function and the algorithm itself are coming from, while also illustrating a more general approach.

The basic recurrence in equation (13.12) is especially unpleasant for two reasons: first, because the maximum is constrained to the set $\mathcal{Z}(D_t)$, making it more complicated to handle than if there were no constraint on $\mathbf{z}_t$; and second, because the optimization requires consideration of all m chips at once. The next important lemma eliminates both of these difficulties. By making a slight approximation, the lemma will allow us to rewrite equation (13.12) in such a way that the maximum is unconstrained and, moreover, the optimization will decompose so that each chip can be considered separately and independently from all the rest of the chips. Indeed, these simplifications will make it possible to solve the (approximated) recurrence exactly.

Lemma 13.1 Let $G : \{-1, +1\}^m \to \mathbb{R}$, and assume

$$G(\mathbf{z}) \leq \sum_{i=1}^{m} g_i(z_i) \tag{13.13}$$

for all $\mathbf{z} \in \{-1, +1\}^m$, and some sequence of functions $g_i : \{-1, +1\} \to \mathbb{R}$. Then

$$\min_{D} \max_{\mathbf{z} \in \mathcal{Z}(D)} G(\mathbf{z}) \leq \sum_{i=1}^{m} \inf_{w_i \geq 0} \max_{z_i \in \{-1,+1\}} [g_i(z_i) + w_i \cdot (z_i - 2\gamma)]. \tag{13.14}$$

Note that the right-hand side of equation (13.12) has exactly the form given on the left of equation (13.14) for any fixed $\mathbf{s}_{t-1}$ since we can take

$$G(\mathbf{z}) = \Lambda_t(\mathbf{s}_{t-1} + \mathbf{z}).$$

The lemma says that if such a function G can be (approximately) decomposed chip by chip, then the entire min-max expression can be as well. And, moreover, the resulting optimization problems involve only individual chips.

At the heart of the proof is a reversal in the order of taking a minimum or a maximum as seen in section 6.1.3.

Proof   We first eliminate the restriction on the choice of $\mathbf{z}$ by introducing a new variable λ and modifying the quantity being maximized. Specifically, for any D,

$$\max_{\mathbf{z} \in \mathcal{Z}(D)} G(\mathbf{z}) = \max_{\mathbf{z} \in \{-1,+1\}^m} \inf_{\lambda \geq 0} \left[G(\mathbf{z}) + \lambda \left(\sum_{i=1}^{m} D(i) z_i - 2\gamma \right) \right]. \tag{13.15}$$

This is because if $\mathbf{z} \in \mathcal{Z}(D)$, so that

$$\sum_{i=1}^{m} D(i) z_i \geq 2\gamma, \tag{13.16}$$

then the infimum appearing in equation (13.15), taken over all $\lambda \geq 0$, will be realized when $\lambda = 0$, and so will be equal to $G(\mathbf{z})$. On the other hand, if $\mathbf{z} \notin \mathcal{Z}(D)$, so that equation (13.16) does not hold, then the infimum will be $-\infty$, as can be seen by setting λ to be arbitrarily large.

We now introduce an approximation based on the fact, pointed out in section 6.1.3, that the "max min" of any function taken over any set is always upper bounded by its "min max" (and likewise when using infima or suprema). In other words, for any function $f : U \times V \to \mathbb{R}$ defined over sets U and V,

$$\sup_{u \in U} \inf_{v \in V} f(u, v) \leq \inf_{v \in V} \sup_{u \in U} f(u, v).$$

Applied here, this shows that the right-hand side of equation (13.15) is at most

$$\inf_{\lambda \geq 0} \max_{\mathbf{z} \in \{-1,+1\}^m} \left[G(\mathbf{z}) + \lambda \left(\sum_{i=1}^{m} D(i) z_i - 2\gamma \right) \right].$$

Thus,

$$\min_{D} \max_{\mathbf{z} \in \mathcal{Z}(D)} G(\mathbf{z}) \leq \min_{D} \inf_{\lambda \geq 0} \max_{\mathbf{z} \in \{-1,+1\}^m} \left[G(\mathbf{z}) + \lambda \left(\sum_{i=1}^{m} D(i) z_i - 2\gamma \right) \right]$$

$$= \min_{D} \inf_{\lambda \geq 0} \max_{\mathbf{z} \in \{-1,+1\}^m} \left[G(\mathbf{z}) + \sum_{i=1}^{m} \lambda D(i)(z_i - 2\gamma) \right] \tag{13.17}$$

since D is a distribution. Note that by setting

$$w_i = \lambda D(i), \tag{13.18}$$

the minimum over D and the infimum over λ can be collapsed into a single infimum over a vector $\mathbf{w}$ with all nonnegative components (which do not necessarily sum to 1). In this way, equation (13.17) can be rewritten as

$$\inf_{\mathbf{w} \in \mathbb{R}_+^m} \max_{\mathbf{z} \in \{-1,+1\}^m} \left[G(\mathbf{z}) + \sum_{i=1}^{m} w_i \cdot (z_i - 2\gamma) \right]. \tag{13.19}$$

As a final simplification, equation (13.13) implies that equation (13.19) is at most

$$\inf_{\mathbf{w} \in \mathbb{R}_+^m} \max_{\mathbf{z} \in \{-1,+1\}^m} \sum_{i=1}^{m} [g_i(z_i) + w_i \cdot (z_i - 2\gamma)]$$

$$= \inf_{\mathbf{w} \in \mathbb{R}_+^m} \sum_{i=1}^{m} \max_{z_i \in \{-1,+1\}} [g_i(z_i) + w_i \cdot (z_i - 2\gamma)]$$

$$= \sum_{i=1}^{m} \inf_{w_i \geq 0} \max_{z_i \in \{-1,+1\}} [g_i(z_i) + w_i \cdot (z_i - 2\gamma)] \tag{13.20}$$

since each maximum and each infimum can be evaluated independently for each component. This completes the proof. ∎

In fact, the simplified optimization problem appearing on the right-hand side of equation (13.14) can easily be solved separately for each chip using the following:

Lemma 13.2 If $g(+1) \leq g(-1)$, then

$$\inf_{w \geq 0} \max_{z \in \{-1,+1\}} [g(z) + w \cdot (z - 2\gamma)] = \left(\tfrac{1}{2} + \gamma \right) g(+1) + \left(\tfrac{1}{2} - \gamma \right) g(-1). \tag{13.21}$$

Moreover, the infimum on the left is realized when

$$w = \frac{g(-1) - g(+1)}{2}. \tag{13.22}$$

Proof   Writing out the maximum gives

$$\max_{z\in\{-1,+1\}} [g(z) + w \cdot (z - 2\gamma)] = \max \{ g(-1) + w \cdot (-1 - 2\gamma), \; g(+1) + w \cdot (1 - 2\gamma) \}.$$

(13.23)

As a function of w, this is the maximum of two lines, one with negative slope and the other with positive slope; moreover, the y-intercept of the latter line is below that of the former. Thus, the function is as plotted in figure 13.2. Evidently, the minimum occurs where the two lines intersect, that is, at the value given in equation (13.22). Plugging in this value for w gives equation (13.21).   ∎

Armed with these lemmas, we can recursively derive a good, decomposable upper bound on Λ_t. Specifically, we will find a bound of the form

$$\Lambda_t(\mathbf{s}) \leq \frac{1}{m} \sum_{i=1}^{m} \Phi_t(s_i)$$

(13.24)

for all rounds t and all position vectors $\mathbf{s}$. To do so, we first let

$$\Phi_T(s) \doteq \mathbf{1}\{s \leq 0\}$$

(13.25)

so that equation (13.24) holds with equality when $t = T$ (by equations (13.9) and (13.11)). Next, for $t = 1, \ldots, T$, we define

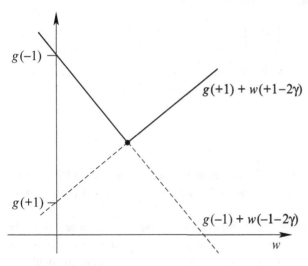

Figure 13.2
A plot of equation (13.23) as a function of w.

$$\Phi_{t-1}(s) \doteq \inf_{w \geq 0} \max_{z \in \{-1,+1\}} [\Phi_t(s+z) + w \cdot (z - 2\gamma)].$$ (13.26)

Then equation (13.24) will hold by backwards induction since, by the recursive expression for Λ_t given in equation (13.12) (multiplied on both sides by m), we have

$$m \Lambda_{t-1}(\mathbf{s}) = \min_{D} \max_{\mathbf{z} \in \mathcal{Z}(D)} m \Lambda_t(\mathbf{s} + \mathbf{z})$$

$$\leq \sum_{i=1}^{m} \inf_{w \geq 0} \max_{z \in \{-1,+1\}} [\Phi_t(s_i + z) + w \cdot (z - 2\gamma)]$$

$$= \sum_{i=1}^{m} \Phi_{t-1}(s_i).$$

Here, we used equation (13.24) inductively and applied lemma 13.1 with

$$G(\mathbf{z}) = m \Lambda_t(\mathbf{s} + \mathbf{z})$$ (13.27)

and

$$g_i(z) = \Phi_t(s_i + z).$$ (13.28)

Moreover, lemma 13.2 gives

$$\Phi_{t-1}(s) = \left(\tfrac{1}{2} + \gamma\right) \Phi_t(s+1) + \left(\tfrac{1}{2} - \gamma\right) \Phi_t(s-1),$$ (13.29)

which, with equation (13.25), can be solved in closed form to give

$$\Phi_t(s) = \text{Binom}\left(T - t, \frac{T - t - s}{2}, \frac{1}{2} + \gamma\right)$$ (13.30)

where $\text{Binom}(n, k, p)$ denotes the probability of at most k heads (k not necessarily an integer) in n flips of a coin whose probability of heads is p:

$$\text{Binom}(n, k, p) \doteq \sum_{j=0}^{\lfloor k \rfloor} \binom{n}{j} p^j (1 - p)^{n-j}.$$

Equation (13.30) can be verified by backwards induction using equation (13.29), while simultaneously verifying that the conditions of lemma 13.2 are satisfied (see exercise 13.3).

The function $\Phi_t(s)$ is called the *potential function*. As we have seen, it can be intuitively interpreted as the potential loss associated with a single chip at position s at the end of round t. This is discussed further in section 13.1.7. Note that $\Phi_t(s)$ depends implicitly on both the total number of rounds T and the edge γ.

13.1.5   Algorithm

Based on this development, we can now state a bound on the loss suffered by an optimal boosting algorithm, which we saw earlier is $\Lambda_0(\mathbf{0})$. In particular, setting $t = 0$, and noting that all chips begin at position 0, we have shown that this optimal loss is bounded as

$$\Lambda_0(\mathbf{0}) \le \frac{1}{m}\sum_{i=1}^{m}\Phi_0(0) = \Phi_0(0) = \text{Binom}\left(T, \frac{T}{2}, \frac{1}{2}+\gamma\right) \tag{13.31}$$

by equations (13.24) and (13.30). This is exactly equal to equation (13.4), our earlier lower bound for the oblivious weak learner.

   This optimal algorithm, according to the argument above, selects on round t that distribution D_t which realizes the minimum in equation (13.12). It is unclear how to compute this distribution tractably. However, we can instead use the distribution given by our approximation. In particular, the proof of lemma 13.1, specifically equation (13.18), suggests that this distribution should be set proportionally to the values w_i, where, tracing through the proof, we see that w_i realizes the infimum on the right-hand side of equation (13.14).

   In our case, on round t with the chips at position $\mathbf{s}$, lemma 13.1 is applied with G and g_i as in equations (13.27) and (13.28). The foregoing discussion then prescribes that we first choose a weight w_i for each chip i in the manner described above. Specifically, by our choice of g_i, we should choose $w_i = w_t(s_i)$ where w_t is the *weighting function*

$$w_t(s) \doteq \arg\min_{w\ge 0}\ \max_{z\in\{-1,+1\}}\ [\Phi_t(s+z)+w\cdot(z-2\gamma)]. \tag{13.32}$$

Like the potential function, the weighting function is central to our development. As for $\Phi_t(s)$, the notation $w_t(s)$ hides implicit dependence on T and γ.

   Using lemma 13.2 and equation (13.30), the expression appearing in equation (13.32) can be put in closed form as

$$w_t(s) = \frac{\Phi_t(s-1)-\Phi_t(s+1)}{2} \tag{13.33}$$

$$= \frac{1}{2}\binom{T-t}{\left\lfloor\frac{T-t-s+1}{2}\right\rfloor}\left(\frac{1}{2}+\gamma\right)^{\lfloor(T-t-s+1)/2\rfloor}\left(\frac{1}{2}-\gamma\right)^{\lceil(T-t+s-1)/2\rceil} \tag{13.34}$$

(see exercise 13.3). Finally, having computed the weights w_i, we can choose a distribution for round t that is proportional to these weights:

$$D_t(i) \propto w_t(s_i).$$

Pulling all of these ideas together, we can finally see the boost-by-majority algorithm emerging, as in algorithm 13.1, where we have reverted to a description in terms of the original boosting problem rather than the chip-game abstraction. The algorithm proceeds like

Algorithm 13.1
The boost-by-majority algorithm

Given: $(x_1, y_1), \ldots, (x_m, y_m)$ where $x_i \in \mathcal{X}$, $y_i \in \{-1, +1\}$
      edge $\gamma > 0$ and number of rounds T.
Initialize: $s_{0,i} = 0$ for $i = 1, \ldots, m$.
For $t = 1, \ldots, T$:

- $D_t(i) = \dfrac{w_t(s_{t-1,i})}{\mathcal{Z}_t}$ for $i = 1, \ldots, m$
  where $\mathcal{Z}_t$ is a normalization factor and

$$w_t(s) \doteq \frac{1}{2} \binom{T-t}{\lfloor \frac{T-t-s+1}{2} \rfloor} \left(\frac{1}{2} + \gamma \right)^{\lfloor (T-t-s+1)/2 \rfloor} \left(\frac{1}{2} - \gamma \right)^{\lceil (T-t+s-1)/2 \rceil}.$$

- Train weak learner using distribution D_t.
- Get weak hypothesis $h_t : \mathcal{X} \to \{-1, +1\}$ with sufficiently small error:

$$\mathbf{Pr}_{i \sim D_t}[h_t(x_i) \neq y_i] \leq \tfrac{1}{2} - \gamma.$$

- Update, for $i = 1, \ldots, m$:

$$s_{t,i} = s_{t-1,i} + y_i h_t(x_i).$$

Output the final hypothesis:

$$H(x) = \mathrm{sign}\left(\sum_{t=1}^{T} h_t(x) \right).$$

AdaBoost, on each round constructing a distribution and training a given weak learning algorithm. Here, of course, we require that each weak hypothesis have weighted error at most $\frac{1}{2} - \gamma$. The principal difference from AdaBoost is in the choice of distribution. BBM chooses $D_t(i)$, as described above, proportional to the weighting function w_t given in equation (13.34) evaluated at the current unnormalized margin (chip position) $s_{t-1,i}$ of example i. The final hypothesis is an unweighted majority vote of all the weak hypotheses.

NonAdaBoost, the nonadaptive version of AdaBoost described in section 13.1.1, is identical except that we instead would use $w_t(s) = e^{-\alpha s}$ where α is as set in equation (13.5).

13.1.6 Analysis

We also have everything in place to analyze this algorithm. The key to this analysis is a proof that the total potential of all the chips (training examples) together can never increase from one round to the next. This will immediately yield a bound on BBM's training error, which is exactly equal to the average potential at the end of the game.

Theorem 13.3 Using the notation above and in algorithm 13.1, the total potential of all training examples in BBM can never increase. That is, for $t = 1, \ldots, T$:

$$\sum_{i=1}^{m} \Phi_{t-1}(s_{t-1,i}) \geq \sum_{i=1}^{m} \Phi_t(s_{t,i}).$$

Proof From equations (13.32) and (13.26), we have that for any s,

$$\Phi_{t-1}(s) = \max_{z \in \{-1,+1\}} [\Phi_t(s+z) + w_t(s) \cdot (z - 2\gamma)].$$

Therefore, letting $z_{t,i} \doteq y_i h_t(x_i)$ and plugging in $s = s_{t-1,i}$, we see that

$$\Phi_{t-1}(s_{t-1,i}) \geq \Phi_t(s_{t-1,i} + z_{t,i}) + w_t(s_{t-1,i}) \cdot (z_{t,i} - 2\gamma) \tag{13.35}$$

$$= \Phi_t(s_{t,i}) + w_t(s_{t-1,i}) \cdot (z_{t,i} - 2\gamma). \tag{13.36}$$

(Actually, it can be shown that equation (13.35) must always hold with equality, but this stronger fact is not needed for the proof.) Since we assumed empirical γ-weak learnability, h_t must have edge γ as in equation (13.1) or, equivalently, equation (13.8). These conditions can be rewritten as

$$\frac{\displaystyle\sum_{i=1}^{m} w_t(s_{t-1,i}) z_{t,i}}{\displaystyle\sum_{i=1}^{m} w_t(s_{t-1,i})} \geq 2\gamma$$

by definition of D_t. That is,

$$\sum_{i=1}^{m} w_t(s_{t-1,i}) \cdot (z_{t,i} - 2\gamma) \geq 0.$$

Combining with equation (13.36) gives

$$\sum_{i=1}^{m} \Phi_{t-1}(s_{t-1,i}) \geq \sum_{i=1}^{m} \left[\Phi_t(s_{t,i}) + w_t(s_{t-1,i}) \cdot (z_{t,i} - 2\gamma) \right]$$

$$= \sum_{i=1}^{m} \Phi_t(s_{t,i}) + \sum_{i=1}^{m} w_t(s_{t-1,i}) \cdot (z_{t,i} - 2\gamma)$$

$$\geq \sum_{i=1}^{m} \Phi_t(s_{t,i}),$$

as claimed.   ∎

A bound on the training error now follows immediately. The optimality that the bound implies for BBM is discussed below.

Corollary 13.4   Using the notation of algorithm 13.1, the training error of BBM's final classifier H is at most

$$\mathrm{Binom}\left(T, \frac{T}{2}, \frac{1}{2}+\gamma\right) \doteq \sum_{j=0}^{\lfloor T/2 \rfloor} \binom{T}{j} \left(\tfrac{1}{2}+\gamma\right)^{j} \left(\tfrac{1}{2}-\gamma\right)^{T-j}. \tag{13.37}$$

Proof   Repeatedly applying theorem 13.3 gives that

$$\Phi_0(0) = \frac{1}{m}\sum_{i=1}^{m} \Phi_0(s_{0,i}) \geq \frac{1}{m}\sum_{i=1}^{m} \Phi_T(s_{T,i}).$$

The expression on the right is, by definition, exactly the training error of the final hypothesis H. And by the general formula for $\Phi_t(s)$ in equation (13.30), the expression on the left, $\Phi_0(0)$, is equal to equation (13.37).   ∎

13.1.7 Game-Theoretic Optimality

In section 13.1.1, we saw that when the number of chips is large, a version of the oblivious weak learner forces any booster to have training error approaching equation (13.37). Thus, corollary 13.4 shows that BBM and the oblivious weak learner are essentially optimal for their respective roles in the game.

Recall that the oblivious weak learner treats each chip independently of the other chips, as well as the history of the game. In the boosting setting, this corresponds to weak hypotheses whose predictions are independent of one another. Such a case would intuitively seem to be especially favorable to learning. However, we now see that this case is actually (close to) the worst possible in our current adversarial setting. Furthermore, we see that when the weak hypotheses are not independent, BBM is able to effectively force them to behave as if they were, achieving exactly the same training error as if in the case of full independence.

The near optimality of the oblivious weak learner is also helpful in interpreting the potential function $\Phi_t(s)$ and its relationship to BBM. Indeed, as can be seen from the expression for $\Phi_t(s)$ in equation (13.30) or, alternatively, from its recursive formulation in equations (13.29) and (13.25), $\Phi_t(s)$ is exactly the probability that a chip at position s will end up at a nonpositive position at the end of the game when the remaining $T - t$ rounds of the game are played against the oblivious weak learner. That is,

$$\Phi_t(s) = \mathbf{Pr}[s + z_{t+1} + \cdots + z_T \le 0], \tag{13.38}$$

where $z_{t+1}, \ldots, z_T$ are independent random variables, each equal to $+1$ with probability $\frac{1}{2} + \gamma$, and -1 otherwise. Thus, the average potential of all the training examples, which is the key quantity used in the analysis of section 13.1.6, is exactly the expected training error under the same assumption. In other words, theorem 13.3 can be understood as a proof that the expected training error never increases from one round to the next, where expectation is over imagined random play of all future rounds by an oblivious weak learner. And corollary 13.4 then follows by observing that the training error at the end of the game, when there are no more rounds to be played, is therefore at most the expected training error before the game begins.

Regarding the weights $w_t(s)$, note that a chip that begins round t at position s will either end the round at position $s + 1$ with potential $\Phi_t(s + 1)$, or at position $s - 1$ with potential $\Phi_t(s - 1)$. Thus, the relative impact of decrementing rather than incrementing the position of that chip is proportional to $\Phi_t(s - 1) - \Phi_t(s + 1)$, which intuitively helps explain the choice of weights $w_t(s)$ that BBM places on the chip as in equation (13.33).

As we have formulated the chip game, the optimality of BBM and the oblivious weak learner is not entirely satisfying since the latter is technically not even a valid weak learner for this game, and the former only approximates the optimal player of section 13.1.3. We can, however, modify the game in such a way that the two players are both valid and optimal. We briefly sketch two such modifications.

In the first of these, we allow the weak learner to make *randomized* choices in its predictions for the individual examples, and thus in the movement of the chips. In other words, the weak learner must now choose on every round a random weak hypothesis h_t whose *expected* error cannot exceed $\frac{1}{2} - \gamma$. In terms of the chip game, this is equivalent to the weak learner selecting a distribution over vectors $\mathbf{z}_t \in \{-1, +1\}^m$ with the requirement that equations (13.7) and (13.8) hold *in expectation* over the random choice of $\mathbf{z}_t$ when chosen according to the selected distribution. The loss of the game can then be computed in expectation with respect to all of the randomized choices of the weak learner. Note that the oblivious weak learner, as described in section 13.1.1, is now a valid weak learner under this relaxed reformulation of the game. Moreover, our analysis of BBM can be shown to hold for this relaxed game as well, thus yielding matching upper and lower bounds on the (expected) loss, and so implying that both BBM and the oblivious weak learner are exactly optimal for their respective roles. (See exercise 13.9.)

In an alternative but closely related relaxation of the game, we do not allow the weak learner to make randomized choices, but instead endow the weak learner with the additional power to split or divide chips. In other words, rather than having to increment or decrement each chip as a single, indivisible unit, the weak learner may choose to split the chip into two parts—not necessarily of equal size—one which is incremented and one which is decremented. Thus, the chips behave more like globs of Jell-O which can be cut arbitrarily into smaller globs. These split globs can in turn be split again on future rounds. As before, the weak learner must on each round increment at least a fraction $\frac{1}{2} + \gamma$ of the Jell-O, as weighted by the distribution chosen by the booster; and the final loss is the fraction of the initial quantity of Jell-O at a final position of zero or below.

For this modified game, the counterpart of the oblivious weak learner can be implemented exactly as the strategy that divides every glob into unequal halves, incrementing a fraction $\frac{1}{2} + \gamma$ of the glob, and decrementing the remaining fraction. For this strategy, the fraction of all the Jell-O at nonpositive positions after T rounds will be exactly as given in equation (13.4) by a similar argument.

Furthermore, BBM can be shown to be exactly optimal for this relaxed game as well. The algorithm can be derived just as before, where now it can be shown that the central approximation proved in lemma 13.1 holds with equality. Thus, the optimal game-theoretic algorithm, which turns out to be BBM (suitably modified for globs rather than chips), can be obtained exactly in this case. The argument leading to corollary 13.4 can also be modified and shown to hold for this game. Since, as before, the upper and lower bounds match exactly, we see that BBM and the oblivious weak learner are the game-theoretic optimal players for this game as well.

All this suggests a different, though closely related, approach to the derivation of tractable, nearly optimal players. To approximate the optimal player for the original game, we first relax the game itself in a way that increases the power of the adversary (weak learner), and then compute the optimal player for the modified game, which in this case yields BBM.

13.2 Optimal Generalization Error

Having analyzed BBM's training error and its near optimality for the voting game, we turn next to a study of the generalization error, whose minimization is the object of learning. We continue to focus in this section on the case that the boosting algorithm is permitted to make T calls to a weak learning algorithm satisfying the empirical γ-weak learning condition. Under this assumption, we will see that BBM's generalization error is *exactly* the best possible for *any* boosting algorithm when the number of training examples becomes large (with T and γ held fixed).

13.2.1 An Upper Bound for BBM

Not surprisingly, the results of chapter 4 can be immediately and directly applied to derive bounds on the generalization error of BBM. (In fact, in most cases an even simpler analysis could have been used since BBM always outputs a combined classifier that is an *unweighted* majority vote of the base hypotheses.) Specifically, theorems 4.3 and 4.6, applied to BBM, show that the generalization error $\mathrm{err}(H)$ of the combined hypothesis H can be bounded in terms of the training error $\widehat{\mathrm{err}}(H)$ as

$$\mathrm{err}(H) \leq \widehat{\mathrm{err}}(H) + \tilde{O}\left(\sqrt{\frac{TC}{m}}\right) \tag{13.39}$$

where m is the number of training examples, T is the number of rounds, and C is a measure of the complexity of the base hypothesis space $\mathcal{H}$, either $\ln|\mathcal{H}|$ or its VC-dimension d.

Likewise, similar to the discussion in section 4.2, when boosting by resampling is used, we can represent H by a sequence of Tm_0 training examples, where m_0 is the number of examples required by the weak learner. In other words, BBM can be viewed as a compression scheme of size Tm_0. Applying theorem 2.8 with $\kappa = Tm_0$ then gives again a bound of the form in equation (13.39), where the complexity C is now replaced by the weak learning sample size m_0.

Thus, assuming either a bound on the number of examples needed for weak learning or a bound on the complexity of the base hypothesis space $\mathcal{H}$, we see that the generalization error of BBM can be upper bounded as in equation (13.39). Moreover, applying corollary 13.4 immediately gives us a bound of the form

$$\mathrm{err}(H) \leq \mathrm{Binom}\left(T, \frac{T}{2}, \frac{1}{2}+\gamma\right) + \tilde{O}\left(\sqrt{\frac{TC}{m}}\right).$$

This means that as m becomes large with T and γ fixed, the rightmost term becomes negligible, and we obtain an upper bound on the generalization error that approaches the bound given in corollary 13.4. As we show next, this latter bound is exactly the best achievable by any boosting algorithm, meaning that BBM is, in this sense, optimal.

13.2.2 A General Lower Bound

To prove such a lower bound on the generalization error, we need to begin by defining what we mean by a boosting algorithm. Here, we will return to the formal definitions given in section 2.3. Recall that a weak learning algorithm A in the PAC model for target class $\mathcal{C}$ has the property that for some $\gamma > 0$, for all $c \in \mathcal{C}$, and for all distributions $\mathcal{D}$ over the domain $\mathcal{X}$, if given $\delta > 0$ and $m_0 = m_0(\delta)$ examples $(x_1, c(x_1)), \ldots, (x_{m_0}, c(x_{m_0}))$ where each x_i is independently distributed according to $\mathcal{D}$, the algorithm will, with probability at least $1 - \delta$, output a hypothesis h with error at most $\frac{1}{2} - \gamma$ with respect to $\mathcal{D}$. In this context, we refer to γ as A's edge.

A boosting algorithm B is one which, when provided with access to a weak PAC learning algorithm A for $\mathcal{C}$, as well as $\epsilon > 0$, $\delta > 0$, and $m = m(\epsilon, \delta)$ examples labeled according to any $c \in \mathcal{C}$, and drawn according to any distribution $\mathcal{D}$, will with probability at least $1 - \delta$, output a hypothesis H with error at most ϵ with respect to $\mathcal{D}$. Note, importantly, that a boosting algorithm should be general in the sense of *not* requiring knowledge of the target class $\mathcal{C}$ (although we do allow it to have other information about the weak learner, such as the required sample size m_0, the associated edge γ, etc.). We also require that B's sample size m be polynomial in the appropriate parameters. Aside from this requirement, B is entirely unrestricted and is allowed, for instance, to have a superpolynomial running time, or to output a combined hypothesis of any form whatsoever.

We will prove a lower bound on the generalization error that can be achieved by a boosting algorithm for a fixed number of calls T to the weak learner, and with fixed edge $\gamma > 0$. Alternatively, such a bound can be inverted to give a sharp lower bound on the number of rounds that are necessary for any boosting algorithm to achieve a given target generalization error ϵ (still with fixed edge γ). Thus, these bounds characterize the optimal efficiency of any boosting algorithm in terms of how the number of rounds must depend on the desired accuracy.

The intuitive idea for the proof of the lower bound is the same as in section 13.1.1, namely, to use a variant of the oblivious weak learner which produces a random hypothesis that is correct on each example with probability $\frac{1}{2} + \gamma$. Such a hypothesis will, in expectation, have error $\frac{1}{2} - \gamma$ for any distribution. Moreover, no matter how such weak hypotheses are combined for making predictions on new data, there will always linger some chance of a mistake; this probability, which happens to match the upper bound for BBM given in corollary 13.4, will provide the lower bound we seek.

Formally, we will prove the following:

Theorem 13.5 Let B be any boosting algorithm as defined above, let $0 < \gamma < \frac{1}{2}$, and let T be a positive odd integer. Then for any $\nu > 0$, there exist a target class $\mathcal{C}$, a distribution $\mathcal{D}$, a target function $c \in \mathcal{C}$, and a weak learning algorithm A for $\mathcal{C}$ with edge γ such that if B makes T calls to A, then the generalization error of its combined classifier will be at least

$$\text{Binom}\left(T, \frac{T}{2}, \frac{1}{2} + \gamma\right) - \nu \tag{13.40}$$

with probability at least $1 - \nu$ (where the probability is taken with respect to the random sample provided to B and any internal randomization used by A and B).

The theorem says that it is nearly certain that B's generalization error will be at least equation (13.40). In other words, if B's confidence parameter δ is chosen to be smaller than $1 - \nu$, then its error parameter ϵ cannot be made smaller than equation (13.40) without increasing T.

The proof will occupy the remainder of this section. Although the intuitive idea outlined above is simple, there are many subtle but technical details that will need to be worked out to ensure that all of the formal requirements of the learning model are satisfied, especially with respect to the definition of a weak learning algorithm. This proof is not crucial to understanding the other material in this chapter.

13.2.3 The Construction

We begin the proof with the construction of the target class $\mathcal{C}$ and the weak learning algorithm A, and later prove that the generalization error will be as given in the theorem when A is used as a weak learner for B.

Let the domain $\mathcal{X} = \{0, 1\}^n$, the set of all n-bit strings, and let the target distribution $\mathcal{D}$ be uniform over $\mathcal{X}$. The positive integer n will act as a "complexity parameter"—instances are all of length n; the hypotheses that A constructs will be representable using strings of length polynomial in n; and A will have time and sample complexity polynomial in n. We will also allow B to use any number of examples m that can be bounded by a polynomial in n. Since ϵ, γ, δ, and T are all effectively fixed, this will be the case for any boosting algorithm whose sample complexity is polynomial either in the sample complexity or in the hypothesis complexity of the weak learner.

We will use the *probabilistic method* to construct both $\mathcal{C}$ and the base hypothesis space $\mathcal{H}$ used by A. This means that we will imagine that $\mathcal{C}$ and $\mathcal{H}$ are chosen *randomly* according to some appropriately constructed probability distribution. We will then show that, in expectation over the choice of the classes $\mathcal{C}$ and $\mathcal{H}$, the conclusion of the theorem is satisfied, which clearly implies the *existence* of such classes.

To construct the target class $\mathcal{C}$, we first select a random function $c : \mathcal{X} \to \{-1, +1\}$ by independently, for each $x \in \mathcal{X}$, choosing $c(x)$ to be -1 or $+1$ with equal probability. Then the class $\mathcal{C}$ is chosen simply to consist of this single function: $\mathcal{C} = \{c\}$. This class is obviously very small and trivial. In fact, with knowledge of $\mathcal{C}$, the target c can be "learned" with no data at all since c is the only function in the class. However, as pointed out earlier, the boosting algorithm does *not* know $\mathcal{C}$, even though the weak learner does.

We next construct the weak learning algorithm A. Of course, since A knows c, it might simply output the hypothesis $h = c$, but this would make the learning process rather trivial for the booster, whereas our purpose in this construction is just the opposite—that is, for A to release as little information about c as possible while still satisfying the γ-weak learning condition.

As suggested informally above, we would ideally like to use the notion of an oblivious weak learner that randomly chooses a hypothesis h such that, for each x, $h(x)$ is chosen randomly to be $c(x)$ with probability $\frac{1}{2} + \gamma$ and $-c(x)$ otherwise. However, there are a number of technicalities that need to be addressed. First, although the *expected* error of such a hypothesis is exactly $\frac{1}{2} - \gamma$, weak learning demands that the error *actually* be at most $\frac{1}{2} - \gamma$ with high probability. This difficulty can first be addressed by choosing $h(x)$ to be correct with slightly higher probability than $\frac{1}{2} + \gamma$, say $\frac{1}{2} + \gamma'$ for some $\gamma' > \gamma$. It turns out that this will be sufficient to ensure an error of $\frac{1}{2} - \gamma$ (with high probability), provided that the target distribution D generating examples for the weak learner is "smooth" in the sense of no examples having "large" weight under the distribution. (This distribution should not be confused with the distribution $\mathcal{D}$ that generates examples for the booster. The target distribution D, from the weak learner's perspective, is one that will be constructed by the booster.)

However, when substantial probability mass is concentrated on one or more examples, we face a further difficulty. At an extreme, when D is concentrated entirely on a single example x_0, choosing h randomly as above will result, with respect to D, in an error below $\frac{1}{2} - \gamma$

exactly when $h(x_0) = c(x_0)$, which happens with probability $\frac{1}{2} + \gamma'$. Thus, in this case, there is no way to guarantee that the weak learning condition will hold *with high probability*, that is, with probability close to 1.

We can address this problem by designing a weak learner that identifies the examples with large mass under the target distribution D, and then augments the random oblivious hypothesis with an *exception list* that includes the correct classifications of all of the large-mass examples. In other words, such a hypothesis predicts $h(x) = c(x)$ if x has large mass, and otherwise chooses $h(x)$ randomly as before. Since the number of large-mass examples in any distribution is necessarily small, the exception lists will also always be short.

Finally, we note that the hypotheses we have so far discussed have very long descriptions: every function mapping $\mathcal{X}$ to $\{-1, +1\}$ has a nonzero probability of being generated, which means each hypothesis requires 2^n bits to specify, and that the size of the entire hypothesis space is 2^{2^n}, far too large to admit learning. To alleviate this difficulty, before learning begins, we will construct a much smaller hypothesis space consisting of a relatively small number of "ground" hypotheses, each produced using the random, oblivious process above, together with all possible hypotheses that can be obtained by adding exception lists. The weak learner can then choose from this preselected space of hypotheses.

Having sketched the main ideas of the construction, we turn now to the details. The hypothesis space $\mathcal{H}$ used by the weak learner is constructed as follows. First, a set of *ground hypotheses* is selected:

$$\mathcal{G} \doteq \left\{ \overline{g}_r : r \in \{0, 1\}^n \right\}.$$

Each of the 2^n ground hypotheses is indexed by an n-bit string r called the *seed*. The classifier $\overline{g}_r$ is constructed randomly by letting

$$\overline{g}_r(x) = \begin{cases} c(x) & \text{with probability } \frac{1}{2} + \gamma' \\ -c(x) & \text{with probability } \frac{1}{2} - \gamma' \end{cases} \tag{13.41}$$

independently for each x where we define

$$\gamma' \doteq \gamma + 2\Delta,$$

and

$$\Delta \doteq \frac{1}{\sqrt{n}}.$$

The weak hypotheses in $\mathcal{H}$ include all ground hypotheses augmented with all possible exception lists of length at most n^2. That is, each hypothesis in $\mathcal{H}$ has the form $\hbar_{r,E}$ where r is a seed, and E is the exception list, a set of at most n^2 examples:

$$\mathcal{H} \doteq \left\{ \hbar_{r,E} : r \in \{0, 1\}^n, E \subseteq \mathcal{X}, |E| \leq n^2 \right\}.$$

Algorithm 13.2
The weak learning algorithm A', designed for boosting by reweighting

---

Given: distribution D over $\mathcal{X}$ (and built-in knowledge of $\mathcal{C}$, $\mathcal{H}$, γ, and Δ).

- Choose an n-bit seed r uniformly at random.
- Let E be the set of all examples with probability mass at least $1/n^2$:

$$E = \left\{ x \in \mathcal{X} : D(x) \geq \frac{1}{n^2} \right\}.$$

- If the error of $\hbar_{r,E}$ with respect to D is at most $\frac{1}{2} - \gamma - \Delta$,
  then output $\hbar_{r,E}$; otherwise, abort by outputting c.

Such a hypothesis correctly classifies all examples in E, and classifies all other examples using the ground hypothesis $\overline{g}_r$:

$$\hbar_{r,E}(x) = \begin{cases} c(x) & \text{if } x \in E \\ \overline{g}_r(x) & \text{else.} \end{cases}$$

Finally, we are ready to describe the weak learning algorithm. For simplicity, we first describe a weak learner A' designed for boosting by reweighting. As discussed in section 3.4.1, such a weak learner receives as input an actual distribution D over a set of training examples (though here treated formally as a distribution over the entire domain $\mathcal{X}$), and must produce a weak hypothesis with error at most $\frac{1}{2} - \gamma$ with respect to the given distribution D. Such a weak learning algorithm does not satisfy the formal definition reviewed in section 13.2.2, although boosting is commonly combined with such weak learners, as discussed in section 3.4.1. Later, we describe a boosting-by-resampling version as formally required. Thus, the proof will actually apply to either form of boosting.

The algorithm A', shown as algorithm 13.2, pulls together the informal ideas presented earlier, identifying high-mass examples (with probability at least $1/n^2$) which are placed on an exception list, and classifying all other examples using a randomly chosen ground hypothesis. Note that $|E| \leq n^2$ since D is a distribution. If the resulting hypothesis $\hbar_{r,E}$ still has unacceptably high error, we say that an *abort* occurs, and in this case the target c is used as the output hypothesis (its error always being zero). This guarantees that the generated weak hypothesis will always have error below $\frac{1}{2} - \gamma$ (actually, even slightly better than this). The next lemma shows, moreover, that aborts occur only very rarely:

Lemma 13.6 Let c be fixed, and suppose A' is run on distribution D. Let r be the seed chosen on the first step, and assume that $\overline{g}_r$, as a random variable, is independent of D. Then the probability of an abort, that is, the probability that $\hbar_{r,E}$ has error exceeding $\frac{1}{2} - \gamma - \Delta$ with respect to D, is at most e^{-2n}.

Proof   The error of $\hbar_{r,E}$ can be written as

$$\text{err}(\hbar_{r,E}) = \sum_{x \in \mathcal{X} - E} D(x)\mathbf{1}\{\overline{g}_r(x) \neq c(x)\} = \sum_{x \in \mathcal{X} - E} D(x)I_x$$

where each I_x is an independent random variable that is equal to 1 with probability $\frac{1}{2} - \gamma'$ and 0 otherwise. To bound this weighted sum, we use a generalized form of Hoeffding's inequality (theorem 2.1) which states the following:

Theorem 13.7   Let $X_1, \ldots, X_m$ be independent random variables such that $X_i \in [0, 1]$. Let $w_1, \ldots, w_m$ be a set of nonnegative weights. Denote the weighted sum of the random variables by $S_m = \sum_{i=1}^m w_i X_i$. Then for any $\varepsilon > 0$ we have

$$\mathbf{Pr}[S_m \geq \mathbf{E}[S_m] + \varepsilon] \leq \exp\left(-\frac{2\varepsilon^2}{\sum_{i=1}^m w_i^2}\right)$$

and

$$\mathbf{Pr}[S_m \leq \mathbf{E}[S_m] - \varepsilon] \leq \exp\left(-\frac{2\varepsilon^2}{\sum_{i=1}^m w_i^2}\right).$$

The expected error of $\hbar_{r,E}$ is

$$\mathbf{E}\left[\text{err}(\hbar_{r,E})\right] = \left(\tfrac{1}{2} - \gamma'\right) \sum_{x \in \mathcal{X} - E} D(x) \leq \tfrac{1}{2} - \gamma'.$$

So applying theorem 13.7 gives

$$\mathbf{Pr}\left[\text{err}(\hbar_{r,E}) > \tfrac{1}{2} - \gamma' + \Delta\right] \leq \mathbf{Pr}\left[\text{err}(\hbar_{r,E}) > \mathbf{E}\left[\text{err}(\hbar_{r,E})\right] + \Delta\right]$$

$$\leq \exp\left(-\frac{2\Delta^2}{\sum_{x \in \mathcal{X} - E} D(x)^2}\right). \tag{13.42}$$

Since $D(x) < 1/n^2$ for every x not in E,

$$\sum_{x \in \mathcal{X} - E} D(x)^2 \leq \frac{1}{n^2} \sum_{x \in \mathcal{X} - E} D(x) \leq \frac{1}{n^2}.$$

Thus, equation (13.42) is at most e^{-2n} by our choice of Δ.   ∎

We can now build a boost-by-resampling weak learner A which uses A' as a subroutine. Such a weak learner, when provided with $m_0(\delta)$ labeled examples chosen independently

Algorithm 13.3
The weak learning algorithm A, designed for boosting by resampling

---

Given: $(x_1, c(x_1)), \ldots, (x_{m_0}, c(x_{m_0}))$.

- Let $\hat{D}$ be the empirical distribution on the sample:

$$\hat{D}(x) \doteq \frac{1}{m_0} \sum_{i=1}^{m_0} \mathbf{1}\{x_i = x\}.$$

- Run A' on distribution $\hat{D}$, and output the returned hypothesis.

---

from an unknown distribution D, must, with probability at least $1 - \delta$, output a hypothesis with error at most $\frac{1}{2} - \gamma$ with respect to D. Our algorithm A, shown as algorithm 13.3, simply forms the empirical distribution $\hat{D}$ in which each of the given m_0 examples is assigned probability $1/m_0$, and then runs A' on this distribution, outputting the hypothesis so obtained.

By our construction of the algorithm A', this returned hypothesis h will always have training error (which is the same as the error measured with respect to $\hat{D}$) at most $\frac{1}{2} - \gamma - \Delta$. Thus, in order that this hypothesis have error at most $\frac{1}{2} - \gamma$ with respect to the distribution D that generated the training set, it suffices to show that this true error $\mathrm{err}(h)$ exceeds its training error by at most Δ with high probability. If we are in the case $h = c$, this is trivially true since both errors are exactly zero. In all other cases, we can apply the results of section 2.2.2. In particular, each hypothesis $\hbar_{r,E}$ can be represented using n bits for the seed r, and n bits for each of up to n^2 examples on the exception list. Thus,

$$\lg |\mathcal{H}| = O(n^3).$$

Plugging into theorem 2.2, we can then calculate that a sample of size

$$m_0 = \left\lceil \frac{\ln |\mathcal{H}| + \ln(1/\delta)}{2\Delta^2} \right\rceil = O(n^4 + n \ln(1/\delta)) \tag{13.43}$$

is sufficient to guarantee that

$$\mathrm{err}(\hbar_{r,E}) \le \widehat{\mathrm{err}}(\hbar_{r,E}) + \Delta$$

for all $\hbar_{r,E} \in \mathcal{H}$ with probability at least $1 - \delta$. Thus, in particular, for the h output by A, we will have

$$\mathrm{err}(h) \le \widehat{\mathrm{err}}(h) + \Delta \le \left(\tfrac{1}{2} - \gamma - \Delta\right) + \Delta = \tfrac{1}{2} - \gamma.$$

We conclude that A satisfies the definition of a weak learning algorithm for $\mathcal{C}$ with edge γ, and that its sample complexity is as given in equation (13.43).

13.2.4 Overview of the Analysis

Having finally completed our construction of the weak learner, we are ready to analyze the generalization error of the boosting algorithm B when it is used with this weak learner. Note that A' gets called on every round, whether directly by B (if using boosting by reweighting) or as a subroutine of A.

There are many sources of randomness that are part of either the learning process or of our construction, namely:

- the randomly constructed target function c;
- the randomly constructed weak hypothesis space $\mathcal{H}$;
- the training set S consisting of a sequence of m random training instances (but not their labels, which are determined by c);
- the random seeds $\mathbf{r} = \langle r_1, \dots, r_T \rangle$ selected on the T calls to A';
- the boosting algorithm's own internal randomization, denoted by the random variable $\mathcal{R}$. (This randomization might be used for various purposes, such as random resampling of the training set when calling the weak learner. Concretely, $\mathcal{R}$ might take the form, for instance, of an infinite sequence of random bits, although such details are of no concern to us.)

To prove theorem 13.5, we will show that with respect to *all* of the sources of randomness, B's error is likely to be at least $\beta^* - \nu$, for n sufficiently large, where

$$\beta^* \doteq \mathrm{Binom}\left(T, \frac{T}{2}, \frac{1}{2} + \gamma\right). \tag{13.44}$$

That is, we will show that

$$\mathbf{Pr}_{c, \mathcal{H}, S, \mathbf{r}, \mathcal{R}}\left[\mathrm{err}(H, c) \geq \beta^* - \nu\right] \geq 1 - \nu, \tag{13.45}$$

where $\mathrm{err}(H, c)$ denotes the true error of the final hypothesis H output by B relative to the target c. Here and throughout this proof, we often add subscripts to probabilities in order to emphasize which random quantities the probability is taken over. Equation (13.45) is sufficient for the proof since it is equivalent, by marginalization, to

$$\mathbf{E}_{c, \mathcal{H}}\left[\mathbf{Pr}_{S, \mathbf{r}, \mathcal{R}}\left[\mathrm{err}(H, c) \geq \beta^* - \nu \mid c, \mathcal{H}\right]\right] \geq 1 - \nu,$$

which, in turn, implies that there exist a *particular* target c and hypothesis space $\mathcal{H}$ for which

$$\mathbf{Pr}_{S, \mathbf{r}, \mathcal{R}}\left[\mathrm{err}(H, c) \geq \beta^* - \nu \mid c, \mathcal{H}\right] \geq 1 - \nu,$$

exactly the statement of the theorem.

Here is a rough outline of how we will prove equation (13.45). The notation used here is somewhat informal and will be made more precise shortly.

First, since they have no influence on the computation of H, we can regard the choice of labels c on instances not in S as if they were still random, even after H has been computed. We can then compare the error of H with respect to the actual choice of c to its expectation. By Hoeffding's inequality, these will be close, allowing us to show that

$$\mathbf{E}_c[\text{err}(H, c)] \lesssim \text{err}(H, c) \tag{13.46}$$

with high probability. (As used elsewhere in this book, we write $\lesssim$ to denote informal, approximate inequality.)

Next, we will argue that with full knowledge of the random process generating c and $\mathcal{H}$, there is an optimal rule *opt* for predicting the label of a test instance, given the predictions of the weak hypotheses. Since it is optimal, we will have

$$\mathbf{E}_c[\text{err}(opt, c)] \leq \mathbf{E}_c[\text{err}(H, c)]. \tag{13.47}$$

The quantity on the left-hand side of equation (13.47) depends on the particular predictions of the weak hypotheses, which are fixed in this expression. By Hoeffding's inequality, applied a second time, this expression will be close to its expectation under the random choice of $\mathcal{H}$, so that

$$\mathbf{E}_{c,\mathcal{H}}[\text{err}(opt, c)] \lesssim \mathbf{E}_c[\text{err}(opt, c)] \tag{13.48}$$

with high probability.

Finally, this quantity on the left, in which both c and $\mathcal{H}$ are random according to the process used in our construction, turns out to converge to exactly β^* as in equation (13.44) as n gets large. Combined with equations (13.46), (13.47), and (13.48), we will thus obtain

$$\beta^* \approx \mathbf{E}_{c,\mathcal{H}}[\text{err}(opt, c)] \lesssim \mathbf{E}_c[\text{err}(opt, c)] \leq \mathbf{E}_c[\text{err}(H, c)] \lesssim \text{err}(H, c)$$

with high probability, a rough equivalent of equation (13.45), whose proof is our goal.

13.2.5 Viewing the Booster as a Fixed Function

In more detail, we begin by formulating a mathematical view of the boosting algorithm as a *fixed* function, a perspective that is crucial to the proof. The boosting algorithm B computes its final hypothesis H on the basis of the training sample and the weak hypotheses it receives from the weak learner. And although B may be randomized, we can regard its randomization $\mathcal{R}$ as itself an input to the algorithm. In this way, B's computation of a final hypothesis can be viewed as a *fixed and deterministic* function of:

- the training sample S;
- the labels (values of c) on the training instances in S, denoted $c_{|S}$;
- the weak hypotheses $h_1, \ldots, h_T$ returned on the T calls to A', including their values on *all* instances in $\mathcal{X}$;
- B's internal randomization $\mathcal{R}$.

As a function, B maps these inputs to a final hypothesis H which, for simplicity, we assume does not use randomization in formulating its predictions (although our argument can be generalized to handle this case as well).

We can take this understanding of B's computation a step deeper so that we are working directly with the ground hypotheses $\overline{g}_r$, rather than the actual weak hypotheses h_t returned by A'. This will simplify the analysis since the weak hypotheses may be muddled by exception lists or aborts. Let r_t and E_t denote the random seed and exception list selected by A' on the t-th call. Let $g_t \doteq \overline{g}_{r_t}$ be the corresponding ground hypothesis, and let us further define the function

$$g'_t \doteq \begin{cases} c & \text{if abort occurs on } t\text{-th call to } A' \\ g_t & \text{else.} \end{cases}$$

This definition allows us to write h_t in the unified form

$$h_t(x) = \begin{cases} c(x) & \text{if } x \in E_t \\ g'_t(x) & \text{else,} \end{cases} \tag{13.49}$$

which holds whether or not an abort occurs.

We claim that the boosting algorithm can now be viewed instead as a fixed and deterministic function of:

- the modified ground hypotheses $g'_1, \ldots, g'_T$ (rather than $h_1, \ldots, h_T$);
- the training sample S, the training labels $c_{|S}$, and B's randomization $\mathcal{R}$, just as before.

In other words, in addition to the latter items, we claim that we can view B's computation as a function of $\mathbf{g}'$ rather than $\mathbf{h}$ (where we use vector notation $\mathbf{h}$ to stand for all of the weak hypotheses $\langle h_1, \ldots, h_T \rangle$ together, and similarly for $\mathbf{g}$ and $\mathbf{g}'$). This is because equation (13.49) shows that each h_t is itself a function only of g'_t, E_t, and the labels $c(x)$ on the instances in E_t. But because each exception list is a subset of the sample S, the labels of instances appearing on such lists are actually included in $c_{|S}$. Furthermore, the exception list E_t is determined by the distribution received by A', or the sample received by A, that is, by the history up to the point at which the weak learner was invoked. Therefore, E_t is itself a fixed function of the other elements which determine B's computation. Thus, B's computation of its final hypothesis H can be viewed as a deterministic function only of S, $c_{|S}$, $\mathcal{R}$, and $\mathbf{g}'$.

Let us now *fix* several of the sources of randomness, namely, the sample S, its labeling $c_{|S}$, and the randomization $\mathcal{R}$ and $\mathbf{r}$ used by B and A'. Later, we will take expectation over these to obtain equation (13.45). For now, these can all be arbitrary, except that we assume that all of the seeds $r_1, \ldots, r_T$ are distinct.

With all of these variables held fixed and treated as constants, by the above argument the boosting algorithm can be viewed as a deterministic function only of $\mathbf{g}'$ so that its final hypothesis H is computed as

$$H = \mathcal{B}(\mathbf{g}')$$

for some fixed, deterministic function $\mathcal{B}$. We also write

$$\mathcal{B}(\mathbf{g}', x) \doteq \mathcal{B}(\mathbf{g}')(x)$$

to denote its (fixed and deterministic) prediction on a test instance x.

We assume without loss of generality that $\mathcal{B}$ is a total function in the sense of being defined for *all* inputs of the correct syntactic form (that is, functions g'_t that map $\mathcal{X}$ to $\{-1, +1\}$, and test instances $x \in \mathcal{X}$). Although $\mathcal{B}$ should properly be applied only to $\mathbf{g}'$, this assumption allows us to consider its application to $\mathbf{g}$ instead, as in $\mathcal{B}(\mathbf{g})$ or $\mathcal{B}(\mathbf{g}, x)$. Essentially, this means always using the ground hypotheses g_t on each round, ignoring the possibility of an abort condition. Mathematically, this substitution will be very convenient since although aborts are rare (by lemma 13.6), they are still a nuisance. Later, of course, we will have to account for aborts as well.

13.2.6 Analyzing the Error

Given the fixed function $\mathcal{B}$, our goal now is to analyze the error of the resulting final hypothesis $\mathcal{B}(\mathbf{g})$ relative to the target c, where c and the g_t's are generated according to the random process described in section 13.2.3 (but with S and $c_{|S}$ fixed). In particular, since all of the seeds r_t are distinct, the g_t's are generated independently of one another (conditional on c) as in equation (13.41).

As before, we denote the error, for any given H and c, by

$$\mathrm{err}(H, c) \doteq \mathbf{Pr}_{x \sim \mathcal{D}}[H(x) \neq c(x)] = 2^{-n} \cdot \sum_{x \in \mathcal{X}} \mathbf{1}\{H(x) \neq c(x)\}.$$

Also, since we are interested primarily in what happens off the training set, let us define $\overline{\mathcal{X}}$ to be the set of all instances in $\mathcal{X}$ *not* included in the sample S; let $\overline{c}$ be the restriction of c to $\overline{\mathcal{X}}$ (that is, the labels on all the points in $\overline{\mathcal{X}}$); and let

$$\overline{\mathrm{err}}(H, \overline{c}) \doteq \mathbf{Pr}_{x \sim \mathcal{D}}\big[H(x) \neq c(x) \mid x \in \overline{\mathcal{X}}\big] = \frac{1}{|\overline{\mathcal{X}}|} \cdot \sum_{x \in \overline{\mathcal{X}}} \mathbf{1}\{H(x) \neq c(x)\}$$

denote the error just on $\overline{\mathcal{X}}$.

Following the outline above, we first show that for any $\mathbf{g}$, the error of $\mathcal{B}(\mathbf{g})$ is likely to be close to its expectation under the random choice of $\overline{c}$.

Lemma 13.8 Let $\mathbf{g}$ be fixed, and let $\overline{c}$ be chosen at random, conditional on $\mathbf{g}$. Then with probability at least $1 - e^{-2n}$,

$$\overline{\mathrm{err}}(\mathcal{B}(\mathbf{g}), \overline{c}) \geq \mathbf{E}_{\overline{c}}[\overline{\mathrm{err}}(\mathcal{B}(\mathbf{g}), \overline{c}) \mid \mathbf{g}] - \sqrt{\frac{n}{|\overline{\mathcal{X}}|}}.$$

Proof   Given $\mathbf{g}$, the $c(x)$'s remain independent of one another. Therefore, the random variables

$$M_x \doteq \mathbf{1}\{\mathcal{B}(\mathbf{g}, x) \neq c(x)\},$$

for $x \in \overline{\mathcal{X}}$, are independent of one another. Applying Hoeffding's inequality (theorem 2.1) to their average

$$\overline{\mathrm{err}}(\mathcal{B}(\mathbf{g}), \overline{c}) = \frac{1}{|\mathcal{X}|} \cdot \sum_{x \in \overline{\mathcal{X}}} M_x$$

now gives the result.   ∎

Let us consider a single example x in $\overline{\mathcal{X}}$. Given $\mathbf{g}$, the probability of misclassifying x depends only on $c(x)$, and can be computed to be

$$\mathbf{Pr}_{c(x)}[c(x) \neq \mathcal{B}(\mathbf{g}, x) \mid \mathbf{g}].$$

Clearly, this is at least

$$\min_{y \in \{-1,+1\}} \mathbf{Pr}_{c(x)}[c(x) \neq y \mid \mathbf{g}].$$

And since $c(x)$ is conditionally independent, given $\mathbf{g}(x)$, of all the values of $\mathbf{g}$ on instances other than x, this is simply equal to

$$\min_{y \in \{-1,+1\}} \mathbf{Pr}_{c(x)}[c(x) \neq y \mid \mathbf{g}(x)]. \tag{13.50}$$

Let $opt(\mathbf{g}, x)$ denote the value of y that minimizes this expression, and let $opt(\mathbf{g})$ denote the prediction function $opt(\mathbf{g}, \cdot)$. This is the *Bayes optimal* classifier encountered in section 12.1.

By taking into account the manner in which $c(x)$ and $\mathbf{g}(x)$ are generated, we can determine $opt(\mathbf{g}, x)$ explicitly as follows. For $y \in \{-1, +1\}$, we have

$$\mathbf{Pr}[c(x) = y \mid \mathbf{g}(x)] = \frac{\mathbf{Pr}[\mathbf{g}(x) \mid c(x) = y] \cdot \mathbf{Pr}[c(x) = y]}{\mathbf{Pr}[\mathbf{g}(x)]} \tag{13.51}$$

$$\propto \mathbf{Pr}[\mathbf{g}(x) \mid c(x) = y] \tag{13.52}$$

$$= \prod_{t=1}^{T} \left[\left(\tfrac{1}{2} + \gamma'\right)^{\mathbf{1}\{g_t(x) = y\}} \left(\tfrac{1}{2} - \gamma'\right)^{\mathbf{1}\{g_t(x) \neq y\}} \right] \tag{13.53}$$

$$= \prod_{t=1}^{T} \left[\left(\tfrac{1}{2} + \gamma'\right)^{(1 + y g_t(x))/2} \left(\tfrac{1}{2} - \gamma'\right)^{(1 - y g_t(x))/2} \right]$$

$$\propto \prod_{t=1}^{T} \left(\frac{1 + 2\gamma'}{1 - 2\gamma'} \right)^{y g_t(x)/2}.$$

(In this context, we write $f \propto g$ to mean f is equal to g times a positive value that does not depend on y.) Here, equation (13.51) is exactly Bayes rule. Equation (13.52) uses the fact that $c(x)$ is equally likely to be each label. Equation (13.53) follows from the random process of generating ground hypotheses as in equation (13.41). And the last two lines are straightforward manipulations.

Thus, taking the logarithm of the ratio of this final expression when $y = +1$ or $y = -1$ gives

$$\ln \left(\frac{\mathbf{Pr}[c(x) = +1 \mid \mathbf{g}(x)]}{\mathbf{Pr}[c(x) = -1 \mid \mathbf{g}(x)]} \right) = \ln \left(\frac{1 + 2\gamma'}{1 - 2\gamma'} \right) \cdot \sum_{t=1}^{T} g_t(x).$$

The sign of the quantity on the left tells us which value of $c(x)$ is more likely, and thus which should be chosen by $opt(\mathbf{g}, x)$ to realize the minimum of equation (13.50). It follows, therefore, that

$$opt(\mathbf{g}, x) = \mathrm{sign} \left(\sum_{t=1}^{T} g_t(x) \right). \tag{13.54}$$

(Recall that we are assuming that T is odd, so that a tie, in which the sign function receives an argument of zero, can never occur.) In other words, taking a majority vote of the T ground hypotheses is the best possible prediction in this setting.

Since it is optimal for every $\mathbf{g}$ and every x, the expected error of $opt(\mathbf{g})$ is a lower bound on that of $\mathcal{B}(\mathbf{g})$:

$$\mathbf{E}_{\overline{c}}[\overline{\mathrm{err}}(\mathcal{B}(\mathbf{g}), \overline{c})] = \frac{1}{|\mathcal{X}|} \cdot \sum_{x \in \mathcal{X}} \mathbf{Pr}_{c(x)}[\mathcal{B}(\mathbf{g}, x) \neq c(x) \mid \mathbf{g}]$$

$$\geq \frac{1}{|\mathcal{X}|} \cdot \sum_{x \in \mathcal{X}} \mathbf{Pr}_{c(x)}[opt(\mathbf{g}, x) \neq c(x) \mid \mathbf{g}]$$

$$= \mathbf{E}_{\overline{c}}[\overline{\mathrm{err}}(opt(\mathbf{g}), \overline{c})]. \tag{13.55}$$

Note that for random $\mathbf{g}$, the expected optimal error appearing in this expression can be computed directly. This is because, for any $x \in \mathcal{X}$,

$$\mathbf{E}_{\mathbf{g}(x)}\left[\mathbf{Pr}_{c(x)}[opt(\mathbf{g}, x) \neq c(x) \mid \mathbf{g}]\right] = \mathbf{Pr}_{c(x), \mathbf{g}(x)}[opt(\mathbf{g}, x) \neq c(x)]$$

$$= \mathbf{Pr}_{c(x), \mathbf{g}(x)}\left[c(x) \neq \mathrm{sign} \left(\sum_{t=1}^{T} g_t(x) \right) \right]$$

$$= \mathrm{Binom}\left(T, \frac{T}{2}, \frac{1}{2} + \gamma' \right) \doteq \mathrm{err}^*, \tag{13.56}$$

that is, the chance of fewer than half the random g_t's correctly classifying x. Call this probability err*.

Using Hoeffding's inequality again, we can further show that equation (13.55) is very likely to be close to its expectation err*.

Lemma 13.9 With probability at least $1 - e^{-2n}$ over the random choice of $\mathbf{g}$,

$$\mathbf{E}_{\overline{c}}[\overline{\mathrm{err}}(opt(\mathbf{g}), \overline{c})] \geq \mathrm{err}^* - \sqrt{\frac{n}{|\mathcal{X}|}}.$$

Proof Let us define the random variables

$$O_x \doteq \mathbf{Pr}_{c(x)}[opt(\mathbf{g}, x) \neq c(x) \mid \mathbf{g}(x)]$$

for $x \in \overline{\mathcal{X}}$. Note that $\mathbf{E_g}[O_x] = \mathrm{err}^*$ by equation (13.56). Thus, applying Hoeffding's inequality (theorem 2.1) to their average

$$\mathbf{E}_{\overline{c}}[\overline{\mathrm{err}}(opt(\mathbf{g}), \overline{c})] = \frac{1}{|\mathcal{X}|} \cdot \sum_{x \in \overline{\mathcal{X}}} O_x$$

gives the result.   ∎

Combining lemma 13.8, equation (13.55), and lemma 13.9, along with the union bound, we thus have shown that with probability at least $1 - 2e^{-2n}$,

$$\overline{\mathrm{err}}(\mathcal{B}(\mathbf{g}), \overline{c}) \geq \mathbf{E}_{\overline{c}}[\overline{\mathrm{err}}(\mathcal{B}(\mathbf{g}), \overline{c}) \mid \mathbf{g}] - \sqrt{\frac{n}{|\mathcal{X}|}}$$

$$\geq \mathbf{E}_{\overline{c}}[\overline{\mathrm{err}}(opt(\mathbf{g}), \overline{c}) \mid \mathbf{g}] - \sqrt{\frac{n}{|\mathcal{X}|}}$$

$$\geq \mathrm{err}^* - 2\sqrt{\frac{n}{|\mathcal{X}|}}.$$

This implies that

$$\mathrm{err}(\mathcal{B}(\mathbf{g}), c) \geq 2^{-n} \sum_{x \in \overline{\mathcal{X}}} \mathbf{1}\{\mathcal{B}(\mathbf{g}, x) \neq c(x)\}$$

$$= \frac{|\mathcal{X}|}{2^n} \cdot \overline{\mathrm{err}}(\mathcal{B}(\mathbf{g}), \overline{c})$$

$$\geq \frac{|\mathcal{X}|}{2^n} \cdot \left[\mathrm{err}^* - 2\sqrt{\frac{n}{|\mathcal{X}|}} \right]$$

$$\geq \left(1 - \frac{m}{2^n}\right) \mathrm{err}^* - 2\sqrt{\frac{n}{2^n}} \doteq \beta_n \tag{13.57}$$

with probability at least $1 - 2e^{-2n}$, where, in the last line, we used $2^n - m \leq |\overline{\mathcal{X}}| \leq 2^n$ since S is a sample of m (not necessarily distinct) instances. We denote the quantity in equation (13.57) by β_n.

13.2.7 Bringing Everything Together

We can now use lemma 13.6 to factor in the possibility of an abort when $\mathcal{B}$ is applied, more properly, to $\mathbf{g}'$ rather than $\mathbf{g}$. In particular, we have that

$$\mathbf{Pr}_{\bar{c},\mathcal{H}}\big[\mathrm{err}(\mathcal{B}(\mathbf{g}'), c) < \beta_n\big] \leq \mathbf{Pr}_{\bar{c},\mathcal{H}}\big[\mathrm{err}(\mathcal{B}(\mathbf{g}), c) < \beta_n \vee \mathbf{g} \neq \mathbf{g}'\big] \tag{13.58}$$

$$\leq \mathbf{Pr}_{\bar{c},\mathcal{H}}[\mathrm{err}(\mathcal{B}(\mathbf{g}), c) < \beta_n] + \mathbf{Pr}_{\bar{c},\mathcal{H}}\big[\exists t : g_t \neq g_t'\big]$$

$$\leq 2e^{-2n} + Te^{-2n}$$

where the last two lines use the union bound (repeatedly) together with equation (13.57) and lemma 13.6 (which implies that $g_t \neq g_t'$ with probability at most e^{-2n}).

We can now take expectation with respect to S, $c_{|S}$, $\mathbf{r}$, and $\mathcal{R}$, which, until this point, had been fixed. Let H denote the final hypothesis. To handle the possibility of $\mathbf{r}$ including two identical seeds, we use the fact that for any two events a and b,

$$\mathbf{Pr}[a] = \mathbf{Pr}[a, b] + \mathbf{Pr}[a, \neg b]$$

$$\leq \mathbf{Pr}[a|b] + \mathbf{Pr}[\neg b].$$

Thus,

$$\mathbf{Pr}_{S,c,\mathcal{H},\mathbf{r},\mathcal{R}}[\mathrm{err}(H, c) < \beta_n] \leq \mathbf{Pr}_{S,c,\mathcal{H},\mathbf{r},\mathcal{R}}[\mathrm{err}(H, c) < \beta_n \mid r_1, \ldots, r_T \text{ distinct}]$$

$$+ \mathbf{Pr}_{S,c,\mathcal{H},\mathbf{r},\mathcal{R}}[r_1, \ldots, r_T \text{ not all distinct}] . \tag{13.59}$$

The first term on the right is at most $(T + 2)e^{-2n}$ since it is the (conditional) expectation of the probability appearing on the left-hand side of equation (13.58). As for the second term on the right of equation (13.59), the chance that two particular random seeds are identical is exactly 2^{-n}. Therefore, by the union bound, the chance that T seeds are not all distinct is at most $\binom{T}{2} \cdot 2^{-n}$. Therefore,

$$\mathbf{Pr}_{S,c,\mathcal{H},\mathbf{r},\mathcal{R}}[\mathrm{err}(H, c) < \beta_n] \leq (T + 2)e^{-2n} + \binom{T}{2} \cdot 2^{-n}. \tag{13.60}$$

Clearly, the right-hand side of equation (13.60) can be made smaller than $\nu > 0$ for n sufficiently large. Furthermore, keeping in mind that m, γ' and err^* all depend implicitly on n, we see that for n large, $\beta_n \to \beta^*$ (where β^* is as in equation (13.44)) since $\gamma' \to \gamma$ and since we assume that m, the sample size, is bounded by a polynomial in n. Therefore, $\beta_n \geq \beta^* - \nu$ for n sufficiently large. Thus, we have proved eqution (13.45), completing the proof of theorem 13.5. ∎

13.3   Relation to AdaBoost

We next consider the relationship between BBM and the more familiar AdaBoost algorithm. Not only are their error bounds related, but we will further see that a nonadaptive version of AdaBoost can be derived as a special case of BBM. On the other hand, there also exist some fundamental differences between the algorithms.

13.3.1   Comparison of Error Bounds

We have already seen that BBM's error, as a function of T and γ, takes the form of the tail of a binomial distribution as given in equation (13.37). This bound applies to the training error, as proved in corollary 13.4, as well as to the generalization error, when the number of training examples is large, as seen in section 13.2.1. Furthermore, in section 13.2.2, we showed that this bound is the best possible for any boosting algorithm. So BBM is essentially optimal when T and γ are known and fixed.

As already noted, when AdaBoost or NonAdaBoost is used, theorem 3.1 implies that the training error will be at most $e^{-2\gamma^2 T}$, a bound that also holds for the generalization error in the limit of large training sets. As earlier noted, this is exactly the bound Hoeffding's inequality (theorem 2.1) gives for the tail of the binomial in equation (13.37).

In fact, the better bound implied by theorem 3.1 for AdaBoost's training error of

$$\left(\sqrt{1-4\gamma^2}\right)^T \tag{13.61}$$

for this case is also a Chernoff bound. In particular, it can be proved (see exercise 5.4) that the chance of at most qn heads in n flips of a coin with bias p, where $q < p$, is bounded as

$$\mathrm{Binom}\,(n, qn, p) \le \exp\left(-n \cdot \mathrm{RE}_b\,(q \parallel p)\right), \tag{13.62}$$

where $\mathrm{RE}_b\,(\cdot \parallel \cdot)$ is the binary relative entropy given in equation (5.36). Thus, in the case of the bound for BBM, we get

$$\mathrm{Binom}\left(T, \frac{T}{2}, \frac{1}{2}+\gamma\right) \le \exp\left(-T \cdot \mathrm{RE}_b\left(\frac{1}{2} \parallel \frac{1}{2}+\gamma\right)\right), \tag{13.63}$$

which is exactly equal to equation (13.61). Furthermore, it can be shown that

$$\mathrm{Binom}\left(T, \frac{T}{2}, \frac{1}{2}+\gamma\right) \ge \exp\left(-T \cdot \left[\mathrm{RE}_b\left(\frac{1}{2} \parallel \frac{1}{2}+\gamma\right) + O\left(\frac{\ln T}{T}\right)\right]\right). \tag{13.64}$$

Since $(\ln T)/T$ becomes negligible as T becomes large, this means that the approximation in equation (13.63) is tight for a large number of rounds. Thus, AdaBoost's error bounds are quite close to the optimal bounds enjoyed by BBM.

Figure 13.3 shows a plot of the bounds for BBM and AdaBoost as a function of T. As T grows, we know that the bounds must exhibit the same exponential behavior, as can be

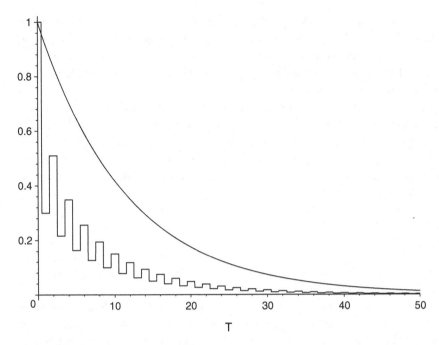

Figure 13.3
A comparison of the error bounds for nonadaptive AdaBoost (top curve, from equation (13.61)) and BBM (bottom curve, from equation (13.37)) as a function of T with $\gamma = 0.2$. The BBM bound is defined only at integral values of T, and appears jagged because the bound is generally worse when T is even (see exercise 13.8).

seen in the figure. On the other hand, for small T, there is clearly a big numerical difference between them.

13.3.2   Deriving AdaBoost from BBM

In addition to the close relationship between their error bounds, AdaBoost and BBM turn out also to be strongly connected as algorithms, with NonAdaBoost, the nonadaptive version of AdaBoost discussed in section 13.1.1, a kind of limiting special case of BBM.

In particular, when the number of rounds T is chosen to be very large, the first T_0 rounds of BBM, for any fixed T_0, will behave nearly exactly like NonAdaBoost. In this sense, nonadaptive AdaBoost can be regarded as the limit of BBM that is obtained by letting $T \to \infty$ with γ fixed. (In chapter 14, we will look at a different limit that will yield a different algorithm.)

To see this, we show that the weights used by BBM on round t converge, up to an irrelevant constant factor, to those for NonAdaBoost when t is smaller than any fixed T_0, and T is increased without bound. For this, we also need to assume that the same weak hypotheses were computed on the preceding rounds as for NonAdaBoost. Since the weights on all the preceding rounds of BBM are converging as $T \to \infty$ to the same weights as for NonAdaBoost, this is likely to be the case. However, this cannot be proven to always be true in general since some weak learning algorithms are numerically unstable, meaning that even tiny changes in the distribution selected on a given round can cause significant changes in the computed weak hypothesis.

In this section, we write $w_t^T(s)$, rather than $w_t(s)$, to make explicit the dependence of the weighting function on the number of rounds T. Referring to algorithm 13.1, each training example i begins round t with unnormalized margin $s_{t-1,i}$ and is assigned weight $w_t^T(s_{t-1,i})$. Thus, to prove the claim above, it suffices to show that as $T \to \infty$, the weights $w_t^T(s)$, suitably scaled, converge to the weights used by NonAdaBoost (with α as in equation (13.5)), namely

$$e^{-\alpha s} = \left(\frac{1 - 2\gamma}{1 + 2\gamma} \right)^{s/2} \tag{13.65}$$

for $|s| \le t \le T_0$. (Multiplicative constants can be ignored because the weights are normalized in forming the distribution D_t.)

For simplicity of presentation, we consider only the case that T is odd and s is even. The other cases can be handled similarly. Note that because all the training examples begin at position 0, and all are incremented or decremented on every round, their parities will always remain in agreement and, furthermore, will always be opposite to the parity of t. Let $\overline{T} \doteq T - t$, which, by the preceding discussion and assumptions, must be even.

From equation (13.34), the weight $w_t^T(s)$ used by BBM can be rewritten as

$$\frac{1}{2} \left(\frac{1 - 2\gamma}{1 + 2\gamma} \right)^{s/2} \cdot \left(\frac{\overline{T}}{\frac{\overline{T}}{2} - \frac{s}{2}} \right) \left(\frac{1}{2} + \gamma \right)^{\overline{T}/2} \left(\frac{1}{2} - \gamma \right)^{\overline{T}/2}. \tag{13.66}$$

To deal with the binomial coefficient, we note that for any integers $n \ge k \ge 1$,

$$\frac{\binom{2n}{n}}{\binom{2n}{n+k}} = \frac{\binom{2n}{n}}{\binom{2n}{n-k}} = \frac{(n+k)(n+k-1) \cdots (n+1)}{n(n-1) \cdots (n-k+1)}$$

$$= \prod_{j=0}^{k-1} \left(1 + \frac{k}{n-j} \right).$$

In the limit $n \to \infty$ with k fixed, each of the k terms in the product converges to 1; therefore, the entire product converges to 1 as well.

Thus, taking $n = \overline{T}/2$ and $k = |s|/2$ in equation (13.66), and defining the constant

$$C_{\overline{T}} = \frac{1}{2} \left(\frac{\overline{T}}{\overline{T}/2} \right) \left(\frac{1}{2} + \gamma \right)^{\overline{T}/2} \left(\frac{1}{2} - \gamma \right)^{\overline{T}/2},$$

we see that for fixed s and t, $w_t^T(s)/C_{T-t}$ converges to equation (13.65) as T (odd) grows to infinity, proving the claim (for this case).

It follows by an inductive argument that the behavior of BBM with large T will be essentially indistinguishable from NonAdaBoost on the first T_0 rounds, for any fixed T_0 (modulo the technical numerical caveats mentioned above concerning the weak learning algorithm).

13.3.3   Comparison of Weights

Although their behavior is very similar on the first several rounds when T is large, there exist important differences between AdaBoost and BBM at later stages of the algorithm, particularly with respect to the weighting functions that differentiate the two algorithms.

We have seen that NonAdaBoost weights examples with unnormalized margin s proportionally to equation (13.65). Such a weighting function is shown at the top of figure 13.4. Note that this weighting function is fixed, and does not change with additional rounds of boosting.

In stark contrast, at the bottom, figure 13.4 shows the weighting function $w_t(s)$ used by BBM for various values of t. Note first that this function changes significantly over time: As t, the round number, increases, its peak value shifts steadily rightward. Moreover, the weights become much more concentrated as the end of boosting approaches. Indeed, on the very last round, all of the weight will be concentrated solely on the examples exactly on the boundary between a correct or incorrect prediction since, at this point, the fate of all other examples has already been decided.

Perhaps the most striking difference from AdaBoost is the non-monotonicity of BBM's weighting function. This means that whereas AdaBoost piles ever more weight on examples which are continually misclassified by the weak hypotheses, BBM will do the same, but only up to a point. Eventually, examples that are misclassified too many times will see their weight actually *decrease* with further misclassifications. In other words, BBM is actually giving up on these very hard examples.

This could potentially be an important advantage. AdaBoost is known to sometimes "spin its wheels" on outliers—examples that may be hard due to labeling errors or inherent ambiguity (see sections 10.3 and 12.3.3). The shape of BBM's weighting function suggests that this algorithm may instead abandon such examples for the greater good of the overall learning process.

On the other hand, BBM is not a practical algorithm because, unlike AdaBoost, it is not adaptive. To use it, we need to choose T and to anticipate a lower bound γ on all of the edges of the forthcoming weak hypotheses *before* boosting begins. In practice, guessing the right values for these parameters can be very difficult. To address this issue, in chapter 14 we describe a technique for making BBM adaptive.

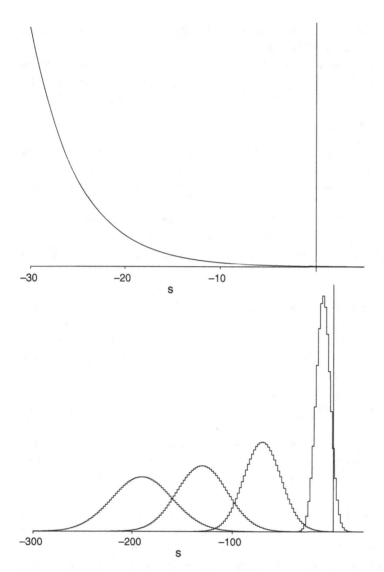

Figure 13.4
A comparison of the weighting function used by nonadaptive AdaBoost (top) and BBM (bottom) when $T = 1000$ and $\gamma = 0.1$. The BBM curves are plotted, from left to right, for rounds $t = 50, 350, 650,$ and 950. (These curves appear jagged because they are defined only at integer values.)

Summary

In this chapter, we took a close look at the nature of optimality in boosting, leading to the boost-by-majority algorithm, which we derived in an abstract framework based on a chip game. BBM is nearly optimal in terms of minimizing both the training error and the generalization error, as was seen, in both cases, by matching its performance to lower bounds based on an oblivious weak learner.

We also studied the close relationship between AdaBoost and BBM, and noted that the previously proved bounds for AdaBoost indicate that it is not far behind optimal BBM in performance. On the other hand, the behavior of the two algorithms may be very different on outliers. In any case, AdaBoost is much more practical than BBM because of its adaptiveness. To overcome this limitation, in chapter 14 we consider a technique for making BBM adaptive.

Bibliographic Notes

The boost-by-majority algorithm and analysis of section 13.1, including the voting-game formulation, are due to Freund [88]. The derivation given in section 13.1.4 is based on ideas from Schapire's [201] work on "drifting games," a framework that generalizes BBM and its analysis. The proof of lemma 13.1 incorporates some key (unpublished) insights that are due to Indraneel Mukherjee.

The lower bound given in section 13.2.2 is a substantial elaboration of one originally given by Freund [88].

Theorem 13.7 and equation (13.62) are due to Hoeffding [123]. Equation (13.64) is based on known lower bounds on the tail of a binomial distribution which can be found, for instance, in section 12.1 of Cover and Thomas [57], and the references therein.

Some of the exercises in this chapter are based on material from [46, 201].

Exercises

13.1 All of the boosting algorithms we have considered in this book compute the distribution D_t in a strongly sequential fashion, with each D_t depending on the preceding weak hypotheses $h_1, \ldots, h_{t-1}$. Is this kind of adaptiveness truly necessary? Can there exist "universal" distributions which are effective for boosting against any weak learner without adjustment based on the weak hypotheses actually received?

To formalize this question, consider a variant of the voting game given in section 13.1.1 that proceeds as follows:

1. the booster chooses T distributions $D_1, \ldots, D_T$ over a given and fixed training set of m examples;

2. the weak learner chooses T hypotheses $h_1, \ldots, h_T$ such that equation (13.1) holds for $t = 1, \ldots, T$.

The final hypothesis is then formed as a simple majority vote as in equation (13.2). Let us say that the booster wins the game if H has training error zero; otherwise, the weak learner wins.

Show *either* that there exists a strategy for the booster that wins the game always against any weak learner, for some appropriate choice of T; *or* prove that no such winning strategy can exist.

13.2 Give an example showing that the inequality given in equation (13.31) can be strict, that is, showing that it is possible that $\Lambda_0(\mathbf{0}) < \Phi_0(\mathbf{0})$.

13.3 Verify that equation (13.30) satisfies both equations (13.25) and (13.29). Also verify equation (13.34).

13.4 Suppose in the construction given in section 13.1 that abstaining weak hypotheses are used with range $\{-1, 0, +1\}$. Now, in place of equation (13.1), we require $\mathbf{E}_{i \sim D_t}[y_i h_t(x_i)] \geq 2\gamma$. And in terms of the chip game, this means that chip i's position is increased on round t by $z_{t,i} \in \{-1, 0, +1\}$ with the requirement that equation (13.8) hold. The derivation leading to equations (13.24), (13.25), and (13.26) (*except* lemma 13.2) can be straightforwardly modified for this case simply by replacing $\{-1, +1\}$ with $\{-1, 0, +1\}$. Thus, the potential $\Phi_T(s)$ is as in equation (13.25), but for $t = 1, \ldots, T$, is now redefined to be

$$\Phi_{t-1}(s) \doteq \inf_{w \geq 0} \max_{z \in \{-1,0,+1\}} [\Phi_t(s+z) + w \cdot (z - 2\gamma)]. \tag{13.67}$$

Likewise, BBM can be modified for this case simply by plugging in a different definition of $w_t(s)$. The rest of this exercise refers to these modified definitions.

a. Show that $\Phi_t(s)$ is nonincreasing for all t, that is, $\Phi_t(s) \geq \Phi_t(s')$ if $s < s'$.

b. For $t = 1, \ldots, T$, show that

$$\Phi_{t-1}(s) = \max\left\{(\tfrac{1}{2} + \gamma)\Phi_t(s+1) + (\tfrac{1}{2} - \gamma)\Phi_t(s-1),\right.$$
$$\left.(1 - 2\gamma)\Phi_t(s) + 2\gamma\ \Phi_t(s+1)\right\}.$$

Also, find $w_t(s)$, the value of $w \geq 0$ which realizes the infimum in equation (13.67), in terms of $\Phi_t(s-1)$, $\Phi_t(s)$, and $\Phi_t(s+1)$. (Your answer should give $w_t(s)$ explicitly, not using an "arg min".)

13.5 Let $\theta > 0$ be a desired minimum normalized margin that is given and known in advance. As in BBM, assume the γ-weak learning condition holds, where $\gamma > 0$ is also known.

a. Show how to modify BBM and its analysis so that the fraction of training examples with normalized margin at most θ is guaranteed not to exceed

$$\text{Binom}\left(T, \left(\frac{1+\theta}{2}\right)T, \frac{1}{2} + \gamma\right).$$

b. For what (fixed) values of θ and γ does this bound approach zero as $T \to \infty$?

13.6 Suppose in equation (13.25) that we instead defined $\Phi_T(s) \doteq e^{-\alpha s}$ for some $\alpha > 0$, thus also redefining $\Phi_t(s)$, for $t < T$, via equation (13.26), as well as $w_t(s)$ via equation (13.32).

a. Explain why equation (13.24) holds for this redefined version of Φ_t.

b. Compute the new versions of $\Phi_t(s)$ and $w_t(s)$ in closed form.

c. Show how to choose α to optimize $\Phi_0(0)$, which bounds the training error.

d. Verify that the resulting bound on the training error is the same as can be obtained for NonAdaBoost from theorem 3.1. Also verify that if the new version of $w_t(s)$ is substituted in BBM (with the optimized choice of α), then the resulting algorithm is exactly equivalent to NonAdaBoost.

13.7 Consider the following online prediction problem, similar to the one studied in section 6.3. There are m experts. On each round t, expert i predicts $x_{t,i} \in \{-1, +1\}$, and the learner makes its own prediction $\hat{y}_t$ as a weighted majority vote of the expert predictions. The true label y_t is then revealed. Thus, formally, on each round $t = 1, \ldots, T$:

- the learner chooses a weight vector $\mathbf{v}_t \in \mathbb{R}_+^m$;
- the expert predictions $\mathbf{x}_t \in \{-1, +1\}^m$ are revealed;
- the learner predicts $\hat{y}_t = \text{sign}(\mathbf{v}_t \cdot \mathbf{x}_t)$;
- nature reveals $y_t \in \{-1, +1\}$.

The learner makes a mistake if $\hat{y}_t \neq y_t$; likewise, expert i makes a mistake if $x_{t,i} \neq y_t$.

In this problem, we assume that one of the experts makes at most k mistakes, where k is known ahead of time. We also assume that the learner is *conservative*, meaning that rounds on which $\hat{y}_t = y_t$ are entirely ignored in the sense that the state of the algorithm does not change. For such algorithms, we can assume without loss of generality that a mistake occurs on *every* round (since other rounds are ignored). Thus, t is actually counting the number of mistakes of the learner, rather than the number of rounds.

This can be formulated as a chip game in which the chips are now identified with experts. In particular, we make the following redefinitions of the variables and quantities appearing in section 13.1.2:

- $z_{t,i} \doteq -y_t x_{t,i}$;
- $D_t(i) = v_{t,i}/\mathcal{Z}_t$, where $\mathcal{Z}_t$ is a normalization factor;
- $\gamma = 0$;
- $L(\mathbf{s}_T) \doteq \frac{1}{m}\sum_{i=1}^{m} \mathbf{1}\{s_{T,i} \leq 2k - T\}$.

All of the following are with respect to these new definitions, which of course also impact $\mathbf{s}_t$, Φ_t, etc.

a. Show that equation (13.8) holds for all t.

b. If the game is played for a full T rounds, show that $L(\mathbf{s}_T) \geq 1/m$.

c. Calculate $\Phi_t(s)$ and $w_t(s)$ in closed form.

d. Suppose the learner chooses the weight vector $\mathbf{v}_t$ by setting $v_{t,i} = w_t(s_{t-1,i})$. Further-more, suppose we let $T = 1 + T_0$ where T_0 is the largest positive integer for which

$$2^{T_0} \leq m \cdot \sum_{j=0}^{k} \binom{T_0}{j}.$$

Prove that the number of mistakes made by such a learner cannot exceed T_0. (It can be shown that $T_0 \leq 2k + 2\sqrt{k \ln m} + \lg m$.)

13.8 As seen in figure 13.3, the bound on BBM's training error is significantly worse for an even number of rounds than for an odd number of rounds. This is largely the result of our convention of counting a tied vote among the weak hypotheses as a full mistake. This exercise considers an alternative in which such a tie counts as only half a mistake, as is natural if ties result in random-guess predictions.

More specifically, suppose $T > 0$ is even, and that the loss or training error of the booster in equation (13.3), as well as the corresponding loss $L(\mathbf{s}_T)$ of the chips in equation (13.9), are replaced by

$$\frac{1}{m} \sum_{i=1}^{m} \ell\left(y_i \sum_{t=1}^{T} h_t(x_i)\right) = \frac{1}{m} \sum_{i=1}^{m} \ell(s_{T,i})$$

where

$$\ell(s) \doteq \begin{cases} 1 & \text{if } s < 0 \\ \frac{1}{2} & \text{if } s = 0 \\ 0 & \text{if } s > 0. \end{cases}$$

Note that our treatment for an odd number of rounds is unchanged since, in this case, $s_{T,i}$ will never be 0.

In this problem, we write $\Phi_t^T(s)$ and $w_t^T(s)$ with superscripts to make explicit the dependence of the potential and weighting functions on the total number of rounds T. These functions are still defined by equations (13.26) and (13.32), although equation (13.25) naturally requires appropriate modification. By the same analysis, if this modified weighting function is used in BBM, then the training error will be at most the (modified) initial potential $\Phi_0^T(0)$.

a. Show, under this revised definition, that

$$\Phi_t^T(s) = \frac{1}{2}\left(\Phi_{t+1}^{T+1}(s-1) + \Phi_{t+1}^{T+1}(s+1)\right).$$

(Keep in mind our assumption that T is even.)

b. Find an analogous expression for $w_t^T(s)$.

c. Prove that

$$\Phi_0^{T+1}(0) \le \Phi_0^T(0) = \Phi_0^{T-1}(0).$$

This shows that the bound on the (modified) training error is nonincreasing as a function of T, and also that there is no advantage to using T rounds, rather than $T-1$, if T is even.

d. Sketch how to modify the proof of theorem 13.5 so that it applies when T is even where, in this case, equation (13.40) is replaced by $\Phi_0^T(0) - v$, that is,

$$\frac{1}{2}\left[\mathrm{Binom}\left(T, \frac{T-1}{2}, \frac{1}{2}+\gamma\right) + \mathrm{Binom}\left(T, \frac{T+1}{2}, \frac{1}{2}+\gamma\right)\right] - v.$$

13.9 Section 13.1.7 briefly discusses a relaxed game in which weak hypotheses—or, equivalently, chip movements $\mathbf{z}_t$—are selected in a randomized fashion. More formally, the game is played as follows. On each round t, the booster chooses a distribution D_t over chips, and the weak learner responds with a distribution Q_t over $\{-1, +1\}^m$, the set of possible chip movements. The vector $\mathbf{z}_t$ is then selected at random according to Q_t, and the chips are then moved as usual as in equation (13.6). Rather than equations (13.7) and (13.8), we instead require that these hold in expectation, that is,

$$\mathbf{E}_{\mathbf{z}_t \sim Q_t, i \sim D_t}\left[z_{t,i}\right] \ge 2\gamma.$$

The goal is to minimize the expected loss

$$\mathbf{E}_{\mathbf{z}_1 \sim Q_1, \dots, \mathbf{z}_T \sim Q_T}\left[L\left(\sum_{t=1}^{T} \mathbf{z}_t\right)\right].$$

(Technically, we assume that the booster and weak learner map the preceding history of events to a decision (D_t or Q_t) in a deterministic fashion so that the only source of randomness is in the choice of $\mathbf{z}_t$'s.)

As before, let $\Lambda_t(\mathbf{s}_t)$ be the expected loss that will be incurred if the chips are in position $\mathbf{s}_t$ on round t, and if the game is henceforth played optimally by both players.

a. Analogous to equations (13.11) and (13.12), for this relaxed version of the game, give an expression for Λ_T, and also a recursive expression for Λ_{t-1} in terms of Λ_t. Justify your answers.

b. Prove that

$$\Lambda_t(\mathbf{s}) = \frac{1}{m}\sum_{i=1}^{m}\Phi_t(s_i)$$

for all **s** and t (where the definition of Φ_t is unchanged). In particular, conclude that the value of the game is exactly as given in equation (13.37).

c. Suppose now that the weak learner (deterministically) chooses on each round t a distribution Q_t over weak hypotheses, and that h_t is then selected at random from Q_t. Rather than equation (13.1), we now assume

$$\mathbf{E}_{h_t \sim Q_t}\big[\mathbf{Pr}_{i \sim D_t}[h_t(x_i) \neq y_i]\big] \leq \tfrac{1}{2} - \gamma.$$

Under this modified assumption, show that the expected training error of the final hypothesis H generated by BBM is at most that given in equation (13.37).

13.10 Consider boosting in a multiclass setting when the number of classes is $K > 2$. For the purposes of this exercise, we modify the definition of a weak learning algorithm, as reviewed in section 13.2.2, replacing the requirement that h's error be at most $\tfrac{1}{2} - \gamma$ with the weaker condition that h's error be at most $1 - 1/K - \gamma$.

Prove formally that for any boosting algorithm B, and for any $\nu > 0$, there exist a target class $\mathcal{C}$, a distribution $\mathcal{D}$, a target function $c \in \mathcal{C}$, and a weak learning algorithm for $\mathcal{C}$ such that, regardless of the number of times that B calls A, the generalization error of its combined classifier will be at least

$$1 - \frac{1}{K - 1} - \nu$$

with probability at least $1 - \nu$ (where the probability is taken with respect to the same quantities as in theorem 13.5). In other words, show that boosting, as formally defined, is not possible when $\epsilon < 1 - 1/(K - 1)$.

14 Boosting in Continuous Time

AdaBoost owes much of its practicality as a boosting algorithm to its adaptiveness, its ability to automatically adjust to weak hypotheses with varying accuracies, thus alleviating the need for knowledge prior to the start of the boosting process of a minimum edge γ, or even the total number of rounds T that will be run. The boost-by-majority algorithm, studied in chapter 13, is not adaptive. Still, it may have other advantages over AdaBoost: It is theoretically more efficient (in terms of the number of rounds to achieve some accuracy) and, perhaps more importantly, it may be better at handling outliers. In this companion chapter, we study a method for making BBM adaptive while, hopefully, retaining its other positive qualities.

BBM is actually nonadaptive in two senses. First, it requires knowledge of a value $\gamma > 0$ for which the γ-weak learning assumption holds so that all weak hypotheses have edge at least γ. And second, it is nonadaptive in its inability to fully exploit weak hypotheses which happen to have edges significantly better than γ. We will see that this latter form of non-adaptiveness can be overcome by adjusting the weights on the weak hypotheses and allowing the algorithm's "clock" to advance by more than one "tick" on each round. However, the resulting algorithm still requires knowledge of the minimum edge γ. To handle this difficulty, we imagine allowing γ to become very small, while simultaneously increasing the total number of rounds T. In the limit $\gamma \to 0$, the number of rounds becomes infinite. If the total time of the entire boosting process is nevertheless squeezed into a finite interval, then in the limit, boosting is conceptually proceeding in *continuous* time. The result is a continuous-time version of BBM called BrownBoost that, like AdaBoost, can adapt to varying edges among the weak hypotheses.

In section 13.3.2, we saw that NonAdaBoost, a nonadaptive version of AdaBoost, can be derived from BBM. Correspondingly, we will see in this chapter that AdaBoost, in its usual, adaptive form, is itself a special case of BrownBoost. Or, in other words, BrownBoost is a generalization of AdaBoost. As will be seen, this generalization explicitly incorporates an anticipated *in*ability to drive the training error to zero, as is to be expected with noisy data, or data containing outliers.

We end this chapter with some experiments comparing BrownBoost and AdaBoost on noisy data.

14.1   Adaptiveness in the Limit of Continuous Time

Our goal is to make BBM adaptive. As noted above, its non-adaptiveness takes two forms, namely, required prior knowledge of a minimum edge γ, together with an inability to fully exploit weak hypotheses with edges much better than γ. We begin with an informal overview of the main ideas for overcoming each of these.

14.1.1   Main Ideas

Suppose on some round t that a weak hypothesis h is received from the weak learner with weighted error substantially below $\frac{1}{2} - \gamma$, in other words, with edge much larger than the minimum requirement of γ. Even when this happens, BBM will treat h like any other weak hypothesis, essentially ignoring its relative strength. Thus, h will be used just once, and an entirely new weak hypothesis will be sought on the following round.

There is, however, a natural alternative. Under the conditions above, it may well happen that h's error continues to be smaller than $\frac{1}{2} - \gamma$ when measured with respect to the *new* distribution D_{t+1}. In this case, h can be used a second time on round $t + 1$, just as if it had been received fresh from the weak learner. This may happen yet again on the following round, so that h can be used a third time. And continuing in this way, the same weak hypothesis h may be used many times until at last its error exceeds $\frac{1}{2} - \gamma$. At this point, a new weak hypothesis must be obtained from the weak learner, and the process begins again. In the end, weak hypotheses with edges significantly exceeding γ will be included many times in the majority-vote classifier formed by BBM so that this final hypothesis will actually be a *weighted* majority over the weak hypotheses, with the most weight assigned to weak hypotheses with the lowest weighted error, just like AdaBoost. This already can be seen to be a form of adaptiveness.

This idea can be understood and generalized by considering the potential function $\Phi_t(s)$ at the heart of BBM, as studied in detail in section 13.1. Recall that the essence of our analysis of BBM's training error was theorem 13.3, a proof that the total (or average) potential of the m chips (or training examples) never increases from round to round. Since the final average potential is exactly the training error, this implied an immediate bound on the training error in terms of the initial potential $\Phi_0(0)$, as seen in corollary 13.4. Thus, a given desired training error of $\epsilon > 0$ can be attained simply by choosing the number of rounds T large enough that $\Phi_0(0) \le \epsilon$.

In fact, this proof technique permits great freedom in how we use a given weak hypothesis, provided that the total potential is not allowed to increase. Given a weak hypothesis h, BBM simply increments the "clock" t:

$$t \leftarrow t + 1,$$

and advances the position s_i of each chip i by $z_i \doteq y_i h(x_i)$:

$$s_i \leftarrow s_i + z_i.$$

But there are other possibilities in how these might be updated. As seen above, we can use the same weak hypothesis h many times, say for k consecutive rounds. This is equivalent to advancing the clock t by k:

$$t \leftarrow t + k,$$

and advancing the chips by k times their usual increment of z_i:

$$s_i \leftarrow s_i + kz_i.$$

Under the assumption that h has weighted error at most $\frac{1}{2} - \gamma$ on each of the k time steps, theorem 13.3 implies that the total potential at the end of these k steps will be no larger than at the beginning. The point, however, is that this is the *only* property we care about for the analysis.

This observation opens the door to immediate generalization. As a start, we can decouple the amount by which the clock and the chips are advanced so that the clock is advanced, say, by some positive integer ξ:

$$t \leftarrow t + \xi,$$

and the chips by some integer increment α:

$$s_i \leftarrow s_i + \alpha z_i,$$

where we no longer require $\xi = \alpha$. In fact, we can allow any choice of ξ and α, so long as the total potential does not increase. We do not here specify particular choices, but intuitively, we may wish to choose ξ large to speed the entire process which must end when the clock t reaches T.

Suppose, on the r-th round of this process, that a weak hypothesis h_r is received, and the clock and chips are advanced by ξ_r and α_r as above. Then the final hypothesis will be the weighted majority vote

$$H(x) \doteq \text{sign}\left(\sum_{r=1}^{R} \alpha_r h_r(x)\right),$$

where R is the total number of rounds until the clock reaches T (and where we now carefully distinguish between "rounds" r and "time steps" t). Under this definition, an example (x_i, y_i) is misclassified by H if and only if the corresponding chip has been moved by the process described above to a final position z_i that is not positive. Thus, by exactly the same proof as in corollary 13.4, the training error of H can be shown to be at most the initial potential $\Phi_0(0)$, provided we respect the requirement that the total potential must never increase.

In this way, BBM can be modified to exploit weak hypotheses with varying edges, provided they are all at least γ. This latter condition, of course, remains a serious obstacle. A natural idea to get around it is simply to choose γ so small that it is almost sure to fall below the edges of all the weak hypotheses. In the limit $\gamma \rightarrow 0$, this is certain to be the case. Of course, according to our analysis of BBM, to achieve the same accuracy in the final classifier with smaller values of γ requires a correspondingly larger number of time steps T. Thus, as $\gamma \rightarrow 0$, T becomes infinite. If we rescale our notion of time, holding it fixed within some finite interval, this will mean in the limit that time is advancing *continuously* rather than in discrete steps.

So, to summarize, to remove the assumption of γ-weak learnability, we consider the continuous-time limit of BBM obtained by letting $\gamma \rightarrow 0$, combined with the technique given above for handling weak hypotheses with varying edges. To implement these ideas, we will first need to derive the continuous-time limits of both the potential function $\Phi_t(s)$ and the weighting function $w_t(s)$. Furthermore, we will need a technique for computing how much the clock and the chips should be advanced so as to maximize the progress that can be wrung from each weak hypothesis, subject to the condition that the average potential should never increase.

We turn now to a detailed treatment.

14.1.2   The Continuous-Time Limit

Our initial goal is to understand how the various elements of BBM behave in the limit as $\gamma \rightarrow 0$, and as the number of time steps T simultaneously grows to infinity. In the usual setting for BBM, "time" is indexed by integers $t = 0, 1, \ldots, T$, and similarly, "space"— that is, the positions of the chips—is indexed by integers $s \in \mathbb{Z}$. Thus, both time and space are discrete, and the potential function $\Phi_t(s)$ and the weighting function $w_t(s)$ are defined in terms of these discrete quantities.

Now, as we let T get large, it will be natural to focus not on the *actual* number of time steps t of BBM that have elapsed, but rather on the *fraction* of the T time steps that have passed, which we denote by

$$\tau = \frac{t}{T}. \tag{14.1}$$

In other words, it makes sense to rescale our notion of time so that boosting begins at time $\tau = 0$ and ends at time $\tau = 1$. Each discrete time step of BBM then takes, after rescaling, time $1/T$. As T increases, this tiny increment approaches zero, at which point boosting is conceptually proceeding in continuous time.

We will see shortly that our notion of space also will become continuous so that at each (continuous) moment in time $\tau \in [0, 1]$, each chip will occupy a continuously valued position $\psi \in \mathbb{R}$. The potential function $\Phi_t(s)$, which measures the potential at each chip position at each moment in time, must thus be correspondingly replaced by a function $\Phi(\psi, \tau)$ that

Table 14.1
Some key quantities used in the (discrete-time) derivation of BBM, and their continuous-time analogues

	BBM	Continuous Time
time	t	τ
margin/chip position	s	ψ
potential function	$\Phi_t(s)$	$\Phi(\psi, \tau)$
weighting function	$w_t(s)$	$w(\psi, \tau)$

is defined in terms of these continuous variables, and that is itself the limit, after appropriate rescaling, of $\Phi_t(s)$. Similarly for the weighting function. (For notational reference, table 14.1 summarizes some key quantities for BBM and their continuous-time analogues.)

We have already noted that we require a limit in which $\gamma \to 0$ as $T \to \infty$. In fact, for this limit to be meaningful, it will be necessary that the values of T and γ be coupled appropriately to one another. Specifically, we have seen that the training error of BBM is at most the tail of the binomial distribution given in equation (13.37), which is approximately $e^{-2\gamma^2 T}$ by Hoeffding's inequality. Thus, for this bound to have a meaningful finite limit, we need the product $\gamma^2 T$ to be held fixed. To do this, we let $T \to \infty$, and set

$$\gamma = \frac{1}{2}\sqrt{\frac{\beta}{T}} \tag{14.2}$$

where β is a constant whose value we discuss later. (The factor of $\frac{1}{2}$ has no real impact since β is an arbitrary constant.) Clearly, this choice of γ converges to zero, while $\gamma^2 T$ is held to the fixed constant $\beta/4$.

The next step is to determine the limits of the weighting and potential functions which are at the foundation of BBM. The weighting functions plotted in figure 13.4 (p. 452) strongly resemble normal distributions. This is because they are binomial distributions which are well known to converge to normal distributions. To compute their limits precisely, recall from equation (13.38) that the potential $\Phi_t(s)$ turns out to be exactly equal to the probability that a particular random walk on the set of integers $\mathbb{Z}$, beginning at s, will end at a nonpositive value. Specifically, equation (13.38) can be rewritten as

$$\Phi_t(s) = \mathbf{Pr}\big[s + Y_{\overline{T}} \leq 0\big] = \mathbf{Pr}\big[Y_{\overline{T}} \leq -s\big] \tag{14.3}$$

where

$$\overline{T} \doteq T - t = T(1 - \tau), \tag{14.4}$$

and where

$$Y_{\overline{T}} = \sum_{j=1}^{\overline{T}} X_j$$

is a sum of independent random variables X_j, each of which is $+1$ with probability $\frac{1}{2} + \gamma$, and -1 otherwise. The central limit theorem tells us that such a sum of independent random variables, if appropriately scaled and translated, will converge in distribution to a normal distribution as $\overline{T} \to \infty$. (See appendix A.9 for further background.) In this case, the mean of the sum $Y_{\overline{T}}$ is $2\gamma\overline{T}$, and its variance is $(1 - 4\gamma^2)\overline{T}$. Thus, subtracting the mean and dividing by the standard deviation gives the standardized sum

$$
\frac{Y_{\overline{T}} - 2\gamma\overline{T}}{\sqrt{(1 - 4\gamma^2)\overline{T}}},
\tag{14.5}
$$

which, by the central limit theorem, converges as $\overline{T} \to \infty$ to a standard normal distribution with mean 0 and unit variance.

As γ gets very small, its appearance in the denominator of equation (14.5) becomes negligible. Thus, for $\overline{T}$ large, equation (14.5) can be approximated by

$$
\tilde{Y}_{\overline{T},\gamma} \doteq \frac{Y_{\overline{T}} - 2\gamma\overline{T}}{\sqrt{\overline{T}}} = \frac{Y_{\overline{T}}}{\sqrt{T(1 - \tau)}} - \sqrt{\beta(1 - \tau)}
$$

by equations (14.2) and (14.4). Since this random variable is asymptotically the same as equation (14.5) (each differing from the other by a factor that converges to 1), its distribution also converges to standard normal.

The event $Y_{\overline{T}} \le -s$ appearing in equation (14.3) holds if and only if

$$
\tilde{Y}_{\overline{T},\gamma} \le -\frac{s}{\sqrt{T(1 - \tau)}} - \sqrt{\beta(1 - \tau)}.
\tag{14.6}
$$

We would like the quantity on the right not to depend explicitly on T so that its limit will be meaningful. This can be achieved in the way that the discrete positions s of chips are replaced by continuous positions ψ, an operation we alluded to earlier but did not specify. Now we can be precise and define the linear mapping from discrete to continuous positions that we will use:

$$
\psi = s\sqrt{\frac{\beta}{T}}.
\tag{14.7}
$$

Here, a scaling factor proportional to $1/\sqrt{T}$ has been chosen for the purpose of "absorbing" the appearance of this same factor on the right-hand side of equation (14.6); in particular, this definition causes the quantity $s/\sqrt{T}$ which appears in that expression now to be replaced simply by $\psi/\sqrt{\beta}$. (The constant $\sqrt{\beta}$ in equation (14.7) is arbitrary, and was chosen for mathematical convenience in what follows.) Thus, with ψ defined as above, the right-hand side of equation (14.6) can now be written as

$$
-\frac{\psi}{\sqrt{\beta(1 - \tau)}} - \sqrt{\beta(1 - \tau)} = -\frac{\psi + \beta(1 - \tau)}{\sqrt{\beta(1 - \tau)}}.
\tag{14.8}
$$

Let Y^* be a standard normal random variable (with zero mean and unit variance). By the argument given above, $\Phi_t(s)$ is equal to the probability that $\tilde{Y}_{T,\gamma}$ is at most equation (14.8), which converges to

$$\Phi(\psi,\,\tau) \doteq \mathbf{Pr}\left[Y^* \le -\frac{\psi + \beta(1-\tau)}{\sqrt{\beta(1-\tau)}}\right].$$

To summarize, we have shown that for any ψ and τ, if s and t are chosen to satisfy the scaling given in equations (14.1) and (14.7) (or to nearly satisfy these equations, given that they must be integers), and if γ is chosen as in equation (14.2), then as $T \to \infty$, the potential function $\Phi_t(s)$, which depends implicitly on T and γ, converges to $\Phi(\psi,\,\tau)$. In other words, $\Phi(\psi,\,\tau)$, under appropriate rescaling of the relevant variables, is the limit of BBM's potential function.

By the definition of the normal distribution, $\Phi(\psi,\,\tau)$ can be defined equivalently in a form that does not reference the random variable Y^*, namely,

$$\Phi(\psi,\,\tau) \doteq \frac{1}{2}\mathrm{erfc}\left(\frac{\psi + \beta(1-\tau)}{\sqrt{2\beta(1-\tau)}}\right) \tag{14.9}$$

where $\mathrm{erfc}(u)$ is the *complementary error function*

$$\mathrm{erfc}(u) \doteq \frac{2}{\sqrt{\pi}}\int_u^\infty e^{-x^2}dx, \tag{14.10}$$

which is plotted in figure 14.1. Thus, we have arrived at a closed-form expression for the limit of the potential function.

14.1.3   An Alternative Derivation

Although this derivation is complete, we here present a rather different method for deriving the potential function $\Phi(\psi,\,\tau)$, one based on setting up and solving a partial differential equation. We start from scratch with equation (13.29), the recursive formulation of the potential function, which, by direct substitution, implies that

$$\Phi_t(s) - \Phi_{t-1}(s) = \Phi_t(s) - \left[\left(\tfrac{1}{2}+\gamma\right)\Phi_t(s+1) + \left(\tfrac{1}{2}-\gamma\right)\Phi_t(s-1)\right]$$

$$= -\tfrac{1}{2}\left(\Phi_t(s+1) - 2\Phi_t(s) + \Phi_t(s-1)\right)$$

$$\quad - \gamma\left(\Phi_t(s+1) - \Phi_t(s-1)\right). \tag{14.11}$$

Next, we rewrite this equation in the continuous domain in terms of $\Phi(\psi,\,\tau)$. For the moment, we identify $\Phi(\psi,\,\tau)$ with $\Phi_t(s)$, where $\tau = t/T$ and $\psi = s\sqrt{\beta/T}$ as before, so that $\Phi(\psi,\,\tau)$ depends implicitly on T, a dependence that will vanish when the limit $T \to \infty$ is taken. As noted earlier, every step of BBM causes τ to increase by $\Delta\tau \doteq 1/T$.

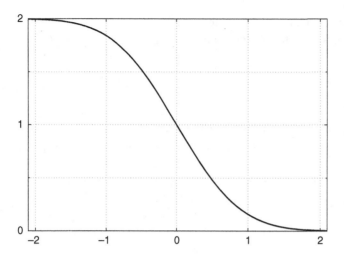

Figure 14.1
A plot of the function erfc(u) as given in equation (14.10).

In addition, when s is incremented or decremented by 1, ψ, by its definition in terms of s, is incremented or decremented by

$$\Delta\psi \doteq \sqrt{\frac{\beta}{T}} = \sqrt{\beta\Delta\tau} = 2\gamma$$

by equation (14.2). Plugging in these notational changes, equation (14.11) becomes

$$\Phi(\psi, \tau) - \Phi(\psi, \tau - \Delta\tau) = -\tfrac{1}{2}\left[\Phi(\psi + \Delta\psi, \tau) - 2\Phi(\psi, \tau) + \Phi(\psi - \Delta\psi, \tau)\right]$$
$$- \gamma\left[\Phi(\psi + \Delta\psi, \tau) - \Phi(\psi - \Delta\psi, \tau)\right].$$

Dividing both sides by

$$-\beta\Delta\tau = -(\Delta\psi)^2 = -2\gamma\Delta\psi,$$

we arrive at the following difference equation:

$$-\frac{1}{\beta}\cdot\frac{\Phi(\psi, \tau) - \Phi(\psi, \tau - \Delta\tau)}{\Delta\tau} = \frac{1}{2}\cdot\frac{\Phi(\psi + \Delta\psi, \tau) - 2\Phi(\psi, \tau) + \Phi(\psi - \Delta\psi, \tau)}{(\Delta\psi)^2}$$
$$+ \frac{\Phi(\psi + \Delta\psi, \tau) - \Phi(\psi - \Delta\psi, \tau)}{2\Delta\psi}. \tag{14.12}$$

Taking the limit as $T \to \infty$, so that $\Delta\tau \to 0$ and $\Delta\psi \to 0$, gives the following partial differential equation:

$$-\frac{1}{\beta}\cdot\frac{\partial\Phi(\psi, \tau)}{\partial\tau} = \frac{1}{2}\cdot\frac{\partial^2\Phi(\psi, \tau)}{\partial\psi^2} + \frac{\partial\Phi(\psi, \tau)}{\partial\psi}. \tag{14.13}$$

To derive this, we used the fact that for any differentiable function $f : \mathbb{R} \to \mathbb{R}$,

$$\frac{f(x + \Delta x) - f(x)}{\Delta x}$$

converges, in the limit $\Delta x \to 0$, to $f'(x)$, the derivative of f at x, by definition. We also used the fact that

$$\frac{f(x + \Delta x) - 2f(x) + f(x - \Delta x)}{(\Delta x)^2} = \frac{\frac{f(x+\Delta x)-f(x)}{\Delta x} - \frac{f(x)-f(x-\Delta x)}{\Delta x}}{\Delta x}$$

converges to $f''(x)$, the second derivative of f, as $\Delta x \to 0$.

Thus, in the limit, $\Phi(\psi, \tau)$ must satisfy equation (14.13). This equation turns out to be well known: It describes the time evolution of a so-called Brownian process, which is the continuous-time limit of a random walk.

Recall that at the end of a run of BBM, at time T, the potential function $\Phi_T(s)$ is defined to be an indicator function that counts training mistakes as in equation (13.25). Therefore, in the continuous-time limit, the potential function at the end of the boosting process, $\tau = 1$, should satisfy

$$\Phi(\psi, 1) = \mathbf{1}\{\psi \leq 0\}. \tag{14.14}$$

This equation acts as a kind of "boundary condition." Solving the partial differential equation in equation (14.13) subject to equation (14.14) gives exactly equation (14.9), as can be verified by plugging the solution into the equation (see exercise 14.1). Thus, we have obtained the same limiting potential function as before.

As a technical point, we note that $\Phi(\psi, \tau)$ is continuous on its entire range, except at the point $\psi = 0, \tau = 1$. A discontinuity at this point is inevitable. And although equation (14.14) defines $\Phi(0, 1)$ to be 1, it could perhaps more reasonably be defined to be $\frac{1}{2}$. We discuss this annoying discontinuity further below, including how to stay away from it.

The weighting function $w_t(s)$ also gets replaced by a function $w(\psi, \tau)$ in terms of the new continuous variables. Since multiplying the weights by a positive constant has no effect, due to normalization, we divide the formula for $w_t(s)$ given in equation (13.33) by $\Delta \psi = \sqrt{\beta/T}$, so that $\sqrt{T/\beta} \cdot w_t(s)$ becomes

$$\sqrt{\frac{T}{\beta}} \cdot \frac{\Phi_t(s-1) - \Phi_t(s+1)}{2} = \frac{\Phi(\psi - \Delta\psi, \tau) - \Phi(\psi + \Delta\psi, \tau)}{2\Delta\psi}.$$

In the limit $\Delta\psi \to 0$, this gives the weighting function

$$w(\psi, \tau) = -\frac{\partial \Phi(\psi, \tau)}{\partial \psi} \propto \exp\left(-\frac{(\psi + \beta(1 - \tau))^2}{2\beta(1 - \tau)}\right), \tag{14.15}$$

where we write $f \propto g$ to mean that f is equal to g times a positive constant that does not depend on ψ.

Both the potential function $\Phi(\psi, \tau)$ and the weighting function $w(\psi, \tau)$ are plotted for sample values of τ in figure 14.2. Since these are the limits of the corresponding functions for BBM, it is not surprising that the weighting function in this figure is almost identical to the one shown in figure 13.4 for BBM with $T = 1000$ (other than being a lot smoother).

14.2 BrownBoost

Having computed the limit of the potential and weighting functions, we can return to our earlier ideas for the design of an adaptive boost-by-majority algorithm.

14.2.1 Algorithm

Given our usual dataset of m training examples, the state of the continuous-time algorithm can be described by the current time $\tau \in [0, 1]$, and by the position ψ_i of each chip/training example i. From the derivation above, we can compute weights $w(\psi_i, \tau)$ for each of these which, when normalized, define a distribution D. The weak learning algorithm can be used to obtain a weak hypothesis h whose error with respect to D is less than $\frac{1}{2}$, as usual. What, then, do we do with h?

According to the outline of ideas presented in section 14.1.1, the clock and chip positions should now be advanced by some amounts, subject to various conditions. Specifically, applying these earlier ideas to the newly derived continuous-time domain, the clock should be advanced by some amount $\xi > 0$ from τ to $\tau' = \tau + \xi$, and each chip i should be moved in the direction $y_i h(x_i)$ by some amount α to the new position

$$\psi_i' = \psi_i + \alpha y_i h(x_i).$$

As in section 14.1.1, we treat ξ and α as distinct variables. To find values for them, we define two conditions, or equations, that they must satisfy, and then solve the equations simultaneously.

First, recall that in our intuitive description of the algorithm, h is used repeatedly for many subsequent time steps of BBM until its edge has been "used up." Thus, at the new time τ', and in the new chip positions ψ_i', it should be the case that h's weighted error is exactly $\frac{1}{2}$, so that its edge has been reduced to zero. This condition means that

$$\frac{\sum_{i=1}^{m} w(\psi_i', \tau') \mathbf{1}\{h(x_i) \neq y_i\}}{\sum_{i=1}^{m} w(\psi_i', \tau')} = \frac{1}{2},$$

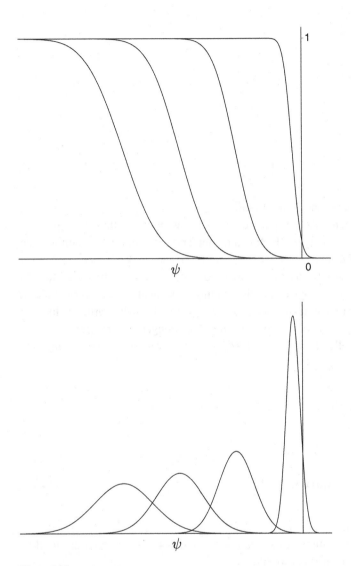

Figure 14.2
A plot of the potential function (top) and weighting function (bottom) when $\beta = 40$, as given in equations (14.9) and (14.15). In each figure, the curves are plotted, from left to right, with $\tau = 0.05, 0.35, 0.65$, and 0.95. (The four potential functions, although distinct, quickly become visually indistinguishable as they approach the limits of their range.) Based on the derivation in the text, the values for β and τ given here correspond to the variable settings for the plot of BBM's weighting function given in figure 13.4, which very closely resembles the smooth weighting function shown here.

which is equivalent to

$$\sum_{i=1}^{m} w(\psi_i', \ \tau') \ y_i h(x_i) = 0$$

or

$$\sum_{i=1}^{m} w(\psi_i + \alpha y_i h(x_i), \ \tau + \xi) \ y_i h(x_i) = 0. \tag{14.16}$$

This is the first equation that α and ξ should satisfy.

For the second condition, as discussed in section 14.1.1, we must continue to respect the key property that was used to analyze BBM: that the total potential of all the examples can never increase. In fact, in the continuous domain, if the chips and clock advance to a point at which the total potential has strictly *decreased*, then it turns out, by continuity of the potential function $\Phi(\psi, \ \tau)$, that it will always be possible to move the clock slightly further ahead while still ensuring that the total potential does not increase, relative to its starting value (see exercise 14.4). This means that here we can make an even stronger requirement, and insist that the total potential actually remain *unchanged*—neither increasing nor decreasing—so that

$$\sum_{i=1}^{m} \Phi(\psi_i, \ \tau) = \sum_{i=1}^{m} \Phi(\psi_i', \ \tau'),$$

or

$$\sum_{i=1}^{m} \Phi(\psi_i, \ \tau) = \sum_{i=1}^{m} \Phi(\psi_i + \alpha y_i h(x_i), \ \tau + \xi). \tag{14.17}$$

This is the second equation.

So α and ξ are chosen to satisfy equations (14.16) and (14.17), and then are used to update the clock and chip positions accordingly.

This entire process of finding weak hypotheses and solving for the appropriate updates to τ and the chip positions ψ_i repeats iteratively, and finally terminates when the clock τ reaches 1. Or, to avoid difficulties arising from the discontinuity in the potential function Φ when $\tau = 1$, we may wish to terminate when τ reaches some earlier cutoff $1 - c$, for some small $c > 0$. Upon termination, the final combined classifier is formed by taking a weighted majority vote of the weak hypotheses where each is assigned its associated weight α. The complete algorithm, called *BrownBoost* because of its connection to Brownian motion, is shown as algorithm 14.1. The procedure works in iterations which we index by r, rather than t as in the rest of the book, to avoid confusion with the time steps of the BBM algorithm that conceptually is at its underpinning. We discuss the choice of β below.

14.2.2 Analysis

Because of the discontinuity in the potential function at $\tau = 1$, it is possible that no simultaneous solution will exist to BrownBoost's two equations (see exercise 14.6). However, if the algorithm is permitted to terminate when the clock τ reaches or exceeds $1 - c$, for some small $c > 0$, then the next theorem shows that a solution must always exist. (We do not discuss computational methods for actually finding a solution, but in practice, standard numerical methods can be applied.)

Theorem 14.1 Let Φ and w be defined as in equations (14.9) and (14.15). For any $\psi_1, \ldots, \psi_m \in \mathbb{R}$, $z_1, \ldots, z_m \in \{-1, +1\}$, $c > 0$, and $\tau \in [0, 1 - c)$, there exist $\alpha \in \mathbb{R}$ and $\tau' \in [\tau, 1]$ such that

$$\sum_{i=1}^{m} \Phi(\psi_i, \tau) = \sum_{i=1}^{m} \Phi(\psi_i + \alpha z_i, \tau'), \tag{14.18}$$

and either $\tau' \geq 1 - c$, or

$$\sum_{i=1}^{m} w(\psi_i + \alpha z_i, \tau') z_i = 0. \tag{14.19}$$

Proof We refer to a pair $\langle \alpha, \tau' \rangle$ with the properties stated in the theorem as a *BrownBoost solution*; our goal is to show that such a pair exists.

Let

$$\Pi(\alpha, \tau') \doteq \sum_{i=1}^{m} \Phi(\psi_i + \alpha z_i, \tau') \tag{14.20}$$

be the total potential of all chips after adjusting their positions by α, and after advancing the clock to τ'. In this notation, equation (14.18) holds if and only if

$$\Pi(0, \tau) = \Pi(\alpha, \tau').$$

Let

$$\mathcal{L} \doteq \left\{ \langle \alpha, \tau' \rangle : \Pi(\alpha, \tau') = \Pi(0, \tau), \alpha \in \mathbb{R}, \tau' \in [\tau, 1 - c] \right\} \tag{14.21}$$

be the *level set* of all pairs $\langle \alpha, \tau' \rangle$ satisfying equation (14.18), and with $\tau \leq \tau' \leq 1 - c$. To prove the theorem, it is sufficient (but not necessary) to find such a pair for which

Algorithm 14.1
The BrownBoost algorithm. The potential function $\Phi(\psi, \tau)$ and weighting function $w(\psi, \tau)$ are given in equations (14.9) and (14.15), respectively

---

Given: $(x_1, y_1), \ldots, (x_m, y_m)$ where $x_i \in \mathcal{X}$, $y_i \in \{-1, +1\}$
      target error $\epsilon \in \left(0, \frac{1}{2}\right)$
      clock cutoff $c \in [0, 1)$.
Initialize:

- Set β so that $\Phi(0, 0) = \epsilon$.

- Let $\tau_1 = 0$ and $\psi_{1,i} = 0$ for $i = 1, \ldots, m$.

For $r = 1, 2, \ldots$ until $\tau_r \geq 1 - c$:

- $D_r(i) = \dfrac{w(\psi_{r,i}, \tau_r)}{\mathcal{Z}_r}$ for $i = 1, \ldots, m$,
  where $\mathcal{Z}_r$ is a normalization factor.

- Train weak learner using distribution D_r.

- Get weak hypothesis $h_r : \mathcal{X} \to \{-1, +1\}$.

- Aim: select h_r to minimalize the weighted error:

$$\mathbf{Pr}_{i \sim D_r}[h_r(x_i) \neq y_i].$$

- Find $\xi_r \geq 0$ and $\alpha_r \in \mathbb{R}$ such that $\tau_r + \xi_r \leq 1$,

$$\sum_{i=1}^{m} \Phi(\psi_{r,i}, \tau_r) = \sum_{i=1}^{m} \Phi(\psi_{r,i} + \alpha_r y_i h_r(x_i), \tau_r + \xi_r),$$

and either $\tau_r + \xi_r \geq 1 - c$ or

$$\sum_{i=1}^{m} w(\psi_{r,i} + \alpha_r y_i h_r(x_i), \tau_r + \xi_r) \, y_i h_r(x_i) = 0.$$

- Update:

$$\tau_{r+1} = \tau_r + \xi_r$$

$$\psi_{r+1,i} = \psi_{r,i} + \alpha_r y_i h_r(x_i) \ \text{ for } i = 1, \ldots, m.$$

Output the final hypothesis:

$$H(x) = \text{sign}\left(\sum_{r=1}^{R} \alpha_r h_r(x)\right)$$

where R is the total number of iterations completed.

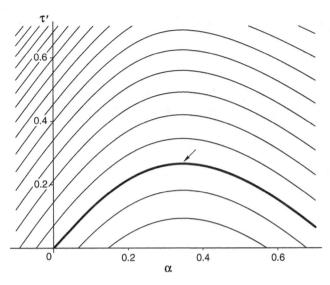

Figure 14.3
A typical contour plot for the function Π of equation (14.20), plotted on the very first round when $\tau = 0$ and $\psi_i = 0$ for all i. In this case, there are $m = 3$ training examples, one of which is misclassified (so $z_1 = z_2 = +1$ and $z_3 = -1$). The parameter β was chosen so that $\Phi(0, 0) = 1/4$. The level curves in the figure represent sets of points for which the value of Π is held constant. The level set $\mathcal{L}$ of interest (equation (14.21)) is the dark curve passing through $\langle 0, \tau \rangle$. The condition $\partial\Pi/\partial\alpha = 0$, which is the same as equation (14.19), is equivalent to the level curve becoming exactly horizontal; thus, in this case, a BrownBoost solution would exist at the very top of the dark curve, as indicated by the arrow.

either $\tau' = 1 - c$ or equation (14.19) holds, since these conditions imply that the pair is a BrownBoost solution. An example is shown in figure 14.3.

Note that, letting $\psi_i' = \psi_i + \alpha z_i$, we have by the chain rule from calculus that

$$\frac{\partial\Pi(\alpha, \tau')}{\partial\alpha} = \sum_{i=1}^{m} \frac{\partial\Phi(\psi_i', \tau')}{\partial\psi_i'} \cdot \frac{d\psi_i'}{d\alpha}$$

$$= -\sum_{i=1}^{m} w(\psi_i', \tau')z_i \tag{14.22}$$

by equation (14.15). Therefore, the left-hand side of equation (14.19), which is identical to the right-hand side of equation (14.22), always is equal to $-\partial\Pi/\partial\alpha$. So equation (14.19) is equivalent to the condition that $\partial\Pi/\partial\alpha = 0$.

In terms of a contour plot as in figure 14.3, this condition is equivalent to the level curve of interest becoming perfectly horizontal, as indicated in the figure. If this never happens, then intuitively the curve should eventually reach $\tau' = 1 - c$. In either case, we obtain the needed solution. Unfortunately, there are numerous potential complications; for instance, in principle, the level set might not be connected, or could asymptote without either of the conditions above being satisfied.

To prove the theorem rigorously, we show first that if the α values of pairs in $\mathcal{L}$ are not bounded (so that they extend to $\pm\infty$), then a solution to equation (14.18) must exist at $\tau' = 1$, satisfying the theorem. Otherwise, when the α values are bounded, we argue that $\mathcal{L}$ is compact, and thus includes a pair with a maximal τ' value. Finally, we show that this pair is a BrownBoost solution.

Following this outline, suppose that the set of α-values occurring in $\mathcal{L}$, that is,

$$\mathcal{L}_1 \doteq \left\{ \alpha : \langle \alpha, \tau' \rangle \in \mathcal{L} \text{ for some } \tau' \right\},$$

is unbounded. If

$$\sup \mathcal{L}_1 = \infty,$$

then there exists $\langle \alpha_1, \tau_1' \rangle, \langle \alpha_2, \tau_2' \rangle, \ldots$ such that $\langle \alpha_n, \tau_n' \rangle \in \mathcal{L}$ and $\alpha_n \to \infty$. This implies that as $\alpha_n \to \infty$,

$$\Phi(\psi_i + \alpha_n z_i, \ \tau_n') = \frac{1}{2}\mathrm{erfc}\left(\frac{\psi_i + \alpha_n z_i + \beta(1 - \tau_n')}{\sqrt{2\beta(1 - \tau_n')}} \right)$$

is approaching 0 if $z_i = +1$, and 1 if $z_i = -1$, since the argument to the erfc is approaching $+\infty$ or $-\infty$, depending on z_i. This value of 0 or 1 is the same as $\Phi(\psi_i + \tilde{\alpha}z_i, \ 1)$ for some sufficiently large value of $\tilde{\alpha}$. Thus,

$$\Pi(0, \ \tau) = \Pi(\alpha_n, \ \tau_n') \to \Pi(\tilde{\alpha}, \ 1).$$

It follows that the pair $\tilde{\alpha}$ and $\tilde{\tau}' = 1$ is a BrownBoost solution with $\Pi(0, \ \tau) = \Pi(\tilde{\alpha}, \ \tilde{\tau}')$, and $\tilde{\tau}' \geq 1 - c$. (The case $\inf \mathcal{L}_1 = -\infty$ is handled symmetrically.)

Thus, we can assume henceforth that $\mathcal{L}_1$ is bounded and, therefore, that $\mathcal{L}$ is bounded as well. Furthermore, $\mathcal{L}$ is closed. For if $\langle \alpha_1, \tau_1' \rangle, \langle \alpha_2, \tau_2' \rangle, \ldots$ is a sequence of pairs in $\mathcal{L}$ converging to $\langle \hat{\alpha}, \hat{\tau}' \rangle$, then because Π is continuous on the region of interest,

$$\Pi(\alpha_n, \ \tau_n') \to \Pi(\hat{\alpha}, \ \hat{\tau}').$$

Since the left-hand side is equal to the fixed value $\Pi(0, \ \tau)$ for all n, $\Pi(\hat{\alpha}, \ \hat{\tau}')$ is as well. Further, since each τ_n' is in the closed set $[\tau, 1 - c]$, $\hat{\tau}'$ must be also. Therefore, $\langle \hat{\alpha}, \hat{\tau}' \rangle \in \mathcal{L}$.

So $\mathcal{L}$ is compact, being both closed and bounded, and is also nonempty, since it includes $\langle 0, \tau \rangle$. These properties imply that there exists a pair $\langle \tilde{\alpha}, \tilde{\tau}' \rangle \in \mathcal{L}$ with maximum τ'-value, so that $\tilde{\tau}' \geq \tau'$ for all $\langle \alpha, \tau' \rangle \in \mathcal{L}$. We claim that $\langle \tilde{\alpha}, \tilde{\tau}' \rangle$ is the desired solution. Suppose, by way of reaching a contradiction, that it is not. Since it is in $\mathcal{L}$, this means that $\tilde{\tau}' < 1 - c$ and that $\partial\Pi/\partial\alpha$, evaluated at $\langle \tilde{\alpha}, \tilde{\tau}' \rangle$, is different from zero, by equation (14.22). Suppose $\partial\Pi/\partial\alpha$ is positive at this point (the argument when it is negative is symmetric). Then increasing $\tilde{\alpha}$ slightly causes Π to increase. That is, there exists $\varepsilon_+ > 0$ such that

$$\Pi(\tilde{\alpha} + \varepsilon_+, \ \tilde{\tau}') > \Pi(\tilde{\alpha}, \ \tilde{\tau}') = \Pi(0, \ \tau). \tag{14.23}$$

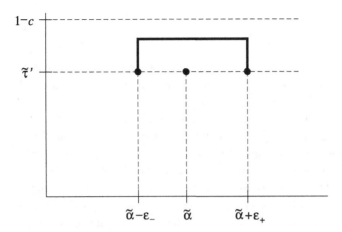

Figure 14.4
Construction of a path from $\langle \tilde{\alpha} - \varepsilon_-, \tilde{\tau}' \rangle$ to $\langle \tilde{\alpha} + \varepsilon_+, \tilde{\tau}' \rangle$ as used in the proof of theorem 14.1.

Likewise, there exists $\varepsilon_- > 0$ such that

$$\Pi(\tilde{\alpha} - \varepsilon_-, \tilde{\tau}') < \Pi(0, \tau). \tag{14.24}$$

We can now create a continuous path in the $\langle \alpha, \tau' \rangle$-plane from $\langle \tilde{\alpha} - \varepsilon_-, \tilde{\tau}' \rangle$ to $\langle \tilde{\alpha} + \varepsilon_+, \tilde{\tau}' \rangle$ in such a way that all of the points on the path, other than the endpoints, have τ' values smaller than $1 - c$ and strictly larger than $\tilde{\tau}'$. (See figure 14.4.) Because Π is continuous, equations (14.23) and (14.24) imply that there must be an intermediate point $\langle \hat{\alpha}, \hat{\tau}' \rangle$ on the path with $\Pi(\hat{\alpha}, \hat{\tau}') = \Pi(0, \tau)$, that is, in the level set $\mathcal{L}$. However, $\hat{\tau}'$, being on the selected path, must be strictly larger than $\tilde{\tau}'$; this is a contradiction since $\tilde{\tau}'$ was itself chosen as the maximum among points in $\mathcal{L}$.

Thus, as claimed, $\langle \tilde{\alpha}, \tilde{\tau}' \rangle$ is the BrownBoost solution we seek, completing the proof. ∎

There is no guarantee that BrownBoost's termination condition $\tau = 1$ (or even an earlier cutoff) will ever be reached. But suppose that it does terminate, and let us momentarily drop subscripts so that τ and ψ_i represent, respectively, the final time on the clock and the final position of chip i just before termination. If the algorithm halts with $\tau = 1$, then the training error of its final hypothesis H is simple to analyze using the same idea as in corollary 13.4: At time $\tau = 1$, the average potential

$$\frac{1}{m} \sum_{i=1}^{m} \Phi(\psi_i, 1)$$

is exactly equal to the training error by equation (14.14) and by H's definition. Since this average potential never changed throughout the algorithm's execution, it must be equal to the average initial potential, which is

$$\Phi(0,\ 0) = \frac{1}{2}\mathrm{erfc}\left(\sqrt{\frac{\beta}{2}}\right). \tag{14.25}$$

Thus, the algorithm takes as input a parameter $\epsilon > 0$, which is the target error, and sets β so that equation (14.25) will be equal to ϵ. Note that this ensures that the final error at $\tau = 1$ will be *exactly* ϵ.

If, as discussed in section 14.1.3, $\Phi(0,\ 1)$ is instead defined to be $\frac{1}{2}$, we still obtain an exact result for the training error at $\tau = 1$, but slightly redefined so that a prediction of 0 counts as only half a mistake. This alternative definition is reasonable since such a prediction can be regarded as a random guess that is correct with probability exactly $\frac{1}{2}$.

If the algorithm is permitted to terminate at some time $\tau < 1$, we can also obtain training error bounds. If the final hypothesis H makes a mistake on some training example i, so that $\psi_i \leq 0$, then because $\Phi(\psi,\ \tau)$ is decreasing in ψ (since the erfc function is decreasing), we must have $\Phi(\psi_i,\ \tau) \geq \Phi(0,\ \tau)$. Since Φ is never negative, we thus have, in general,

$$\Phi(0,\ \tau) \cdot \mathbf{1}\{\psi_i \leq 0\} \leq \Phi(\psi_i,\ \tau).$$

Averaging both sides over all examples gives

$$\Phi(0,\ \tau) \cdot \frac{1}{m}\sum_{i=1}^{m}\mathbf{1}\{\psi_i \leq 0\} \leq \frac{1}{m}\sum_{i=1}^{m}\Phi(\psi_i,\ \tau).$$

The left-hand side is $\Phi(0,\ \tau)$ times the training error. The right-hand side is the average potential at time τ, which, as noted above, is equal to the initial potential $\Phi(0,\ 0) = \epsilon$. Therefore, using Φ's definition in equation (14.9), if $\tau \geq 1 - c$, then the training error is at most

$$\frac{2\epsilon}{\mathrm{erfc}\left(\sqrt{\beta c/2}\right)}. \tag{14.26}$$

Since the denominator approaches 1 as $c \to 0$, this bound can be made arbitrarily close to 2ϵ by choosing c sufficiently small. (For a technique that instead approaches ϵ, see exercise 14.7.)

14.3   AdaBoost as a Special Case of BrownBoost

In section 13.3.2, we saw that the behavior of BBM on the initial rounds converges to that of NonAdaBoost, a nonadaptive version of AdaBoost, as T becomes large. Correspondingly, in this section, we will see that AdaBoost, in its usual adaptive form, can be derived from BrownBoost, an adaptive version of BBM, by taking an appropriate limit, namely, the limit as the error parameter ϵ is taken to zero. Thus, AdaBoost can be viewed as a special case of BrownBoost in which a final training error of zero is anticipated. Or, turning this statement around, BrownBoost can be viewed as a generalization of AdaBoost in which a positive final training error is expected.

To show this, we need to argue that, under this limit, the distribution over examples computed by BrownBoost on every round converges to that for AdaBoost, and that the weighted-majority combined classifiers are the same for the two algorithms. We presume here that the same sequence of weak classifiers is returned by the weak learning algorithm for either boosting algorithm, a reasonable assumption since the distributions on which they are trained will be nearly the same; however, as pointed out in section 13.3.2, the assumption is unprovable in general for reasons of numerical instability. Thus, under this assumption, to show that the combined hypotheses are the same, it suffices to show that the coefficients α_r computed by the two algorithms are the same, in the limit.

Although we are interested in what happens when $\epsilon \to 0$, we will find it more convenient in what follows to frame the discussion in terms of the limit $\beta \to \infty$. Because of how BrownBoost chooses β as a function of ϵ (so that equation (14.25) is equal to ϵ), these two cases are exactly equivalent.

To clarify the notation, let us write $\psi_{r,i}^{\beta}, D_r^{\beta}, \alpha_r^{\beta}$, etc. for the variables used by BrownBoost (algorithm 14.1) when run with parameter β (for some corresponding choice of ϵ), and let D_r^*, α_r^*, etc. denote the variables used by AdaBoost (algorithm 1.1 (p. 5)), where we now use r rather than t to index the round number for both algorithms. For BrownBoost, we assume that the clock cutoff has been fixed to an arbitrary positive constant $c \in (0, 1)$. Further, we assume that BrownBoost is run *lingeringly*, meaning that it never halts unless forced to do so; that is, on every round r, it chooses a solution to its equations with $\tau_{r+1} < 1 - c$, unless no such solution exists.

In precise terms, we prove the following concerning BrownBoost's behavior under the limit $\beta \to \infty$ (which, as just noted, is equivalent to $\epsilon \to 0$).

Theorem 14.2 Suppose BrownBoost (with fixed cutoff $c \in (0, 1)$) and AdaBoost are run on the same dataset and are provided with the same round-by-round sequence of weak hypotheses $h_1, h_2, \ldots$, none of which are perfectly accurate or perfectly inaccurate on the entire dataset. Assume the notation above, and that BrownBoost is run lingeringly. Let r be any positive integer. Then for all sufficiently large β, BrownBoost will not halt before reaching round r. Furthermore, as $\beta \to \infty$, BrownBoost's distribution and hypothesis weights on round r converge to those for AdaBoost; that is,

$$D_r^{\beta} \to D_r^* \tag{14.27}$$

and

$$\alpha_r^{\beta} \to \alpha_r^*. \tag{14.28}$$

Note that, because we assume the same sequence of weak classifiers $h_1, h_2, \ldots$ is received by both algorithms, equation (14.28) implies that

$$\sum_{r=1}^{R}\alpha_r^{\beta}h_r(x) \;\rightarrow\; \sum_{r=1}^{R}\alpha_r^{*}h_r(x)$$

for any R and x, so that the weighted-majority combined classifiers will also be the same for AdaBoost and BrownBoost in the limit (except possibly in the degenerate case that the sum on the right is exactly zero).

Proof   Assume inductively that equation (14.28) holds on rounds $1, \ldots, r-1$. We wish to show that equations (14.27) and (14.28) hold on the current round r. We also must show that the time τ does not reach the cutoff of $1-c$ within r rounds. Thus, for β sufficiently large, we assume inductively that

$$\tau_r^{\beta} < 1 - c, \tag{14.29}$$

and will show that the same holds for τ_{r+1}^{β}, ensuring that the algorithm does not terminate.

Let us fix r, and drop it from the notation when it is clear from context so that $\tau^{\beta} = \tau_r^{\beta}$, $\psi_i^{\beta} = \psi_{r,i}^{\beta}$, and so on. We also define $\psi_i^{*} = \psi_{r,i}^{*}$ to be the unnormalized margin computed by AdaBoost:

$$\psi_i^{*} \doteq y_i \sum_{r'=1}^{r-1}\alpha_{r'}^{*}h_{r'}(x_i).$$

Note that by our inductive hypothesis on equation (14.28),

$$\psi_i^{\beta} \rightarrow \psi_i^{*} \tag{14.30}$$

as $\beta \rightarrow \infty$ since

$$\psi_i^{\beta} = y_i \sum_{r'=1}^{r-1}\alpha_{r'}^{\beta}h_{r'}(x_i).$$

Finally, we will sometimes write w^{β} and Φ^{β} to make explicit the dependence of Brown-Boost's weighting and potential functions on the parameter β.

So, to summarize, given our inductive assumptions, we need to prove equations (14.27) and (14.28), and that BrownBoost does not halt. We prove each of these three in turn.

Lemma 14.3   Under the assumptions and notation above,

$$D_r^{\beta} \rightarrow D_r^{*}.$$

Proof   We can rewrite the weighting function of equation (14.15) as follows:

$$w^{\beta}(\psi,\,\tau) \propto \exp\left(-\frac{\psi^2 + 2\psi\beta(1-\tau) + \beta^2(1-\tau)^2}{2\beta(1-\tau)}\right)$$

$$= \exp\left(-\frac{\psi^2}{2\beta(1-\tau)} - \psi - \frac{\beta(1-\tau)}{2}\right)$$

$$\propto \exp\left(-\frac{\psi^2}{2\beta(1-\tau)} - \psi\right)$$

$$= \exp\left(-\psi\left(1 + \frac{\psi}{2\beta(1-\tau)}\right)\right) \tag{14.31}$$

(where $f \propto g$ means f is equal to g times a positive factor that does not depend on ψ). Thus,

$$w^\beta(\psi_i^\beta, \tau^\beta) \propto \exp\left(-\psi_i^\beta\left(1 + \frac{\psi_i^\beta}{2\beta(1-\tau^\beta)}\right)\right). \tag{14.32}$$

By equations (14.29) and (14.30), it follows that the expression on the right converges to $\exp(-\psi_i^*)$, which is exactly proportional to $D_r^*(i)$, the normalized weight assigned by AdaBoost to training example i (see, for instance, equation (3.2)). Since $D_r^\beta(i)$ is proportional to equation (14.32), equation (14.27) follows immediately. ∎

Let $z_i \doteq y_i h(x_i)$. As in the proof of theorem 14.1, let

$$\Pi^\beta(\alpha, \tau') \doteq \sum_{i=1}^m \Phi^\beta(\psi_i^\beta + \alpha z_i, \tau')$$

be the total potential of all the training examples after adjusting their positions by α and advancing the clock to τ'. At the solution $\langle \alpha^\beta, \tau'^\beta \rangle$ found by BrownBoost, where $\tau'^\beta \doteq \tau_{r+1}^\beta$, we will have

$$\Pi^\beta(\alpha^\beta, \tau'^\beta) = \Pi^\beta(0, \tau^\beta). \tag{14.33}$$

Further, the solution either will have $\tau'^\beta \geq 1 - c$, or will satisfy

$$\sum_{i=1}^m w^\beta(\psi_i^\beta + \alpha^\beta z_i, \tau'^\beta) z_i = 0. \tag{14.34}$$

To show that BrownBoost does not halt on the current round, we apply theorem 14.1, where we proved that such a solution must exist, and we show that, for β large, the cutoff $1 - c$ cannot be attained by the solution guaranteed by this theorem.

Lemma 14.4 Under the assumptions and notation above,

$$\tau'^\beta < 1 - c.$$

Proof   The proof of theorem 14.1 shows specifically that a solution to BrownBoost's equations will exist with $\tau'^{\beta} = 1$ or $\tau'^{\beta} \leq 1 - c$. To prove the lemma, we show that the cases $\tau'^{\beta} = 1$ and $\tau'^{\beta} = 1 - c$ are not possible, for β large, so that a solution with $\tau'^{\beta} < 1 - c$ must necessarily exist and be chosen by BrownBoost, which we assume is being run lingeringly.

First, note that $\Phi^{\beta}(\psi, 1)$ is always in $\{0, 1\}$, so if $\tau'^{\beta} = 1$, then $\Pi^{\beta}(\alpha^{\beta}, \tau'^{\beta})$ must be an integer. But because the potential remains constant throughout the execution of BrownBoost,

$$\Pi^{\beta}(\alpha^{\beta}, \tau'^{\beta}) = m \cdot \Phi^{\beta}(0, 0) = m\epsilon, \tag{14.35}$$

which is not an integer for β large and ϵ correspondingly small but positive. Thus, $\tau'^{\beta} \neq 1$. (This argument assumes $\Phi(0, 1) \doteq 1$, but can be straightforwardly modified if instead $\Phi(0, 1) \doteq \frac{1}{2}$.)

Suppose next that $\tau'^{\beta} = 1 - c$. We show that this leads to a contradiction, for β large. Let b be any constant for which $c < b < 1$, and let

$$d \doteq \sqrt{bc} - c > 0. \tag{14.36}$$

Since the current weak hypothesis h is neither perfectly accurate nor perfectly inaccurate, there must exist i and i' for which $z_i = -z_{i'}$. Further, for β sufficiently large,

$$\psi_i^{\beta} + \psi_{i'}^{\beta} \leq 2\beta d$$

since, by equation (14.30), the left-hand side is converging to a fixed value while the right-hand side is growing to infinity. Because $z_i + z_{i'} = 0$, this implies that

$$(\psi_i^{\beta} + \alpha^{\beta} z_i) + (\psi_{i'}^{\beta} + \alpha^{\beta} z_{i'}) \leq 2\beta d,$$

which means at least one of the parenthesized expressions on the left, say the first, is at most βd, that is,

$$\psi_i^{\beta} + \alpha^{\beta} z_i \leq \beta d.$$

Rewriting, using equation (14.36), this gives

$$\frac{\psi_i^{\beta} + \alpha^{\beta} z_i + \beta c}{\sqrt{2\beta c}} \leq \sqrt{\frac{\beta b}{2}}.$$

Thus,

$$\Pi^{\beta}(\alpha^{\beta}, \tau'^{\beta}) \geq \Phi^{\beta}(\psi_i^{\beta} + \alpha^{\beta} z_i, 1 - c)$$

$$= \frac{1}{2}\text{erfc}\left(\frac{\psi_i^{\beta} + \alpha^{\beta} z_i + \beta c}{\sqrt{2\beta c}}\right)$$

$$\geq \frac{1}{2}\text{erfc}\left(\sqrt{\frac{\beta b}{2}}\right) \tag{14.37}$$

by Φ's definition in equation (14.9), and because the erfc function is decreasing. Using a standard approximation to the erfc function,

$$\frac{2}{\sqrt{\pi}} \cdot \frac{e^{-u^2}}{u + \sqrt{u^2 + 2}} \leq \mathrm{erfc}(u) \leq \frac{2}{\sqrt{\pi}} \cdot \frac{e^{-u^2}}{u + \sqrt{u^2 + 4/\pi}}, \tag{14.38}$$

which holds for all $u > 0$, it follows from equation (14.37) that

$$\Pi^\beta(\alpha^\beta, \tau'^\beta) \geq \exp\left(-\beta\left(\frac{b}{2} + o(1)\right)\right) \tag{14.39}$$

(where $o(1)$ represents a quantity that approaches zero as $\beta \to \infty$). On the other hand, as argued earlier,

$$\Pi^\beta(\alpha^\beta, \tau'^\beta) = m \cdot \Phi^\beta(0, 0) = \frac{m}{2}\mathrm{erfc}\left(\sqrt{\frac{\beta}{2}}\right) \leq \exp\left(-\beta\left(\frac{1}{2} - o(1)\right)\right) \tag{14.40}$$

where we have again applied equation (14.38). Since $b < 1$, when β is large, equations (14.39) and (14.40) are in contradiction. ∎

It remains only to show that $\alpha^\beta \to \alpha^*$. In very rough terms, this can be seen as follows: By lemma 14.4, $\tau'^\beta < 1 - c$, and therefore equation (14.34) must hold at the solution $\langle \alpha^\beta, \tau'^\beta \rangle$. Approximating $w^\beta(\psi, \tau)$ by $\exp(-\psi)$ based on the proof of lemma 14.3, this equation becomes

$$\sum_{i=1}^{m} \exp\left(-(\psi_i^\beta + \alpha^\beta z_i)\right) z_i = 0. \tag{14.41}$$

Recall from section 7.1 that α^* is chosen by AdaBoost to minimize

$$\sum_{i=1}^{m} \exp\left(-(\psi_i^* + \alpha^* z_i)\right),$$

in other words, to have derivative with respect to α^* equal to zero:

$$\sum_{i=1}^{m} \exp\left(-(\psi_i^* + \alpha^* z_i)\right) z_i = 0. \tag{14.42}$$

Since $\psi_i^\beta \to \psi_i^*$, the matching equations (14.41) and (14.42) imply that $\alpha^\beta \to \alpha^*$. The next lemma provides a more rigorous proof of equation (14.28) based on this idea.

Lemma 14.5 Let $\delta > 0$. Under the assumptions and notation above, for β sufficiently large,

$$|\alpha^\beta - \alpha^*| < \delta.$$

Proof   For all i, we must have

$$\psi_i^\beta + \alpha^\beta z_i + \beta(1 - \tau'^\beta) > 0 \tag{14.43}$$

for β large. Otherwise, if this were not the case for some i, then

$$\Pi^\beta(\alpha^\beta, \tau'^\beta) \geq \Phi^\beta(\psi_i^\beta + \alpha^\beta z_i, \tau'^\beta)$$

$$= \frac{1}{2}\text{erfc}\left(\frac{\psi_i^\beta + \alpha^\beta z_i + \beta(1 - \tau'^\beta)}{\sqrt{2\beta(1 - \tau'^\beta)}}\right)$$

$$\geq \tfrac{1}{2}\text{erfc}(0) = \tfrac{1}{2}$$

by Φ's definition in equation (14.9). This contradicts equation (14.35) for β large (and ϵ therefore small). Thus, equation (14.43) holds for all i, which is equivalent to saying that

$$\alpha^\beta \in (M_-^\beta, M_+^\beta)$$

where

$$M_-^\beta \doteq \max_{i:z_i=+1}\left[-\psi_i^\beta - \beta(1 - \tau'^\beta)\right]$$

$$M_+^\beta \doteq \min_{i:z_i=-1}\left[\psi_i^\beta + \beta(1 - \tau'^\beta)\right]. \tag{14.44}$$

Let

$$W^\beta(\alpha, \tau') \doteq \sum_{i=1}^m \exp\left(-(\psi_i^\beta + \alpha z_i)\left(1 + \frac{\psi_i^\beta + \alpha z_i}{2\beta(1 - \tau')}\right)\right) z_i.$$

By equations (14.31) and (14.22),

$$W^\beta(\alpha, \tau') \propto \sum_{i=1}^m w^\beta(\psi_i^\beta + \alpha z_i, \tau') z_i = -\frac{\partial \Pi^\beta(\alpha, \tau')}{\partial \alpha}. \tag{14.45}$$

Therefore, equation (14.34), which must be satisfied at the solution $\langle \alpha^\beta, \tau'^\beta \rangle$, is equivalent to the condition

$$W^\beta(\alpha^\beta, \tau'^\beta) = 0. \tag{14.46}$$

Further, for β sufficiently large, we claim that $W^\beta(\alpha, \tau')$ is decreasing in α for $\alpha \in (M_-^\beta, M_+^\beta)$. To see this, note first that $\text{erfc}(u)$ is convex for $u > 0$, as can be seen in figure 14.1. Thus, $\Phi^\beta(\psi_i^\beta + \alpha z_i, \tau')$—which, by its definition in equation (14.9), is equal to erfc evaluated at a linear function of α—is convex in α for α satisfying equation (14.43). In turn, this implies that $\Pi^\beta(\alpha, \tau')$, being the sum of several convex functions, is also convex in α, for $\alpha \in (M_-^\beta, M_+^\beta)$. Therefore, $\partial \Pi^\beta(\alpha, \tau')/\partial \alpha$ is increasing in α, which means, by equation (14.45), that $W^\beta(\alpha, \tau')$ is decreasing in α, for α in this interval.

For any α and $\tau < 1$, it is clear, using equation (14.30), that

$$W^\beta(\alpha, \tau) \to W^*(\alpha)$$

as $\beta \to \infty$, where

$$W^*(\alpha) \doteq \sum_{i=1}^m \exp\left(-(\psi_i^* + \alpha z_i)\right) z_i,$$

the corresponding function for AdaBoost. Moreover, this convergence is uniform for $\tau \in [0, 1-c]$, meaning that the convergence happens simultaneously for all values of τ so that

$$\sup_{0 \le \tau \le 1-c} \left| W^\beta(\alpha, \tau) - W^*(\alpha) \right| \to 0.$$

From their definition in equation (14.44), it can be seen that $M_-^\beta \to -\infty$ and $M_+^\beta \to +\infty$ as $\beta \to \infty$, by equation (14.30), and since $0 \le \tau'^\beta < 1 - c$. Thus, $\alpha^* \in (M_-^\beta, M_+^\beta)$ for β sufficiently large.

It also can be checked that W^* is strictly decreasing and, by equation (14.42), is equal to zero at α^*. This implies that $W^*(\alpha^* + \delta) < 0$, so for β sufficiently large,

$$W^\beta(\alpha^* + \delta, \tau') < 0$$

for all $\tau' \in [0, 1-c]$. Since $W^\beta(\alpha, \tau'^\beta)$ is decreasing in α for $\alpha \in (M_-^\beta, M_+^\beta)$, and since $\alpha^* > M_-^\beta$, it follows that $W^\beta(\alpha, \tau'^\beta) < 0$ for $\alpha^* + \delta \le \alpha < M_+^\beta$, precluding a solution to equation (14.46) in this interval. And we have already argued that the solution cannot happen for any $\alpha \ge M_+^\beta$. Thus, we have eliminated all possibilities for the solution α^β to be at least $\alpha^* + \delta$.

Therefore, $\alpha^\beta < \alpha^* + \delta$. A similar argument shows that $\alpha^\beta > \alpha^* - \delta$, completing the proof. ∎

Thus, we have also completed the proof of theorem 14.2, having shown that as $\beta \to \infty$, which is the same as $\epsilon \to 0$, the behavior of BrownBoost converges exactly to that of AdaBoost for any finite number of rounds. ∎

14.4 Experiments with Noisy Data

Theorem 14.2 suggests AdaBoost may be best matched with a setting in which the training error can be driven to zero. This agrees with the training-error analysis of section 3.1, where we saw how the weak learning assumption suffices to assure perfect training accuracy in a very small number of rounds. But this view is also consistent with AdaBoost's susceptibility to noise, discussed in section 12.3.3, and its general propensity to direct inordinate attention to the hardest examples, which might well have been corrupted or mislabeled.

BrownBoost, on the other hand, may have a better chance of handling such noisy settings. First, the algorithm explicitly anticipates a nonzero training error of $\epsilon > 0$, as seen in section 14.2.2. And furthermore, as was the case for BBM, as discussed in section 13.3.3, BrownBoost's weighting function causes it to deliberately "give up" on the hardest examples, focusing instead on those examples that still have a reasonable chance of eventually being correctly classified.

As an illustration of the improvement in performance that might be possible, BrownBoost was compared experimentally with AdaBoost on the noisy, synthetic learning problem described in section 12.3.2, which we showed in that section will ultimately cause AdaBoost to perform very poorly under appropriate limits. As earlier explained, examples in this setting are binary vectors of length $N = 2n + 11$ with weak hypotheses identified with individual coordinates; here, the cases $n = 5$ and $n = 20$ were tested. The "clean" label associated with each example can be computed as a simple majority vote over a subset of its coordinates. The actual observed labels, however, are noisy versions of the clean labels which have been corrupted (that is, negated) with a noise rate of η; noise rates of 0% (no noise), 5%, and 20% were considered in the experiments.

BrownBoost was run with various values of ϵ, and the one giving lowest training error was selected for use during testing. AdaBoost.L, the version of AdaBoost based on logistic loss from section 7.5.2, was also compared, since its more moderate weighting function suggests that it might handle noise and outliers better than AdaBoost. (Note, however, that AdaBoost.L must also eventually perform very poorly on this data, by arguments similar to those in section 12.3.2; see also exercise 12.9.)

Training sets of $m = 1000$ and 10,000 examples were used. Each algorithm was run for a maximum of 1000 rounds but, as in algorithm 14.1, BrownBoost can stop early if the clock τ reaches $1 - c$, where a cutoff of $c = 0.01$ was used throughout.

Table 14.2 reports the error for each algorithm on a separate test set of 5000 *uncorrupted* examples, that is, with labels that are clean. Consistent with what was proved in section 12.3.2, AdaBoost does quite poorly on this problem. AdaBoost.L does better in the easiest case that $n = 5$ and $\eta = 5$%, but otherwise performs almost as badly as AdaBoost. (Observe, incidentally, that when $n = 20$, performance actually gets *worse* for both algorithms when given *more* data.) BrownBoost, on the other hand, performs very well, attaining almost perfect test accuracy in most cases when $n = 5$, and giving far better accuracy than either AdaBoost or AdaBoost.L in the harder case that $n = 20$.

These same algorithms were also tested on real-world, benchmark datasets, artificially corrupted with additional label noise at rates of 0%, 10% and 20%. Here, each boosting method was combined with the alternating decision tree algorithm of section 9.4. Also, a variant of BrownBoost was used in which the "boundary condition" of equation (14.14) is replaced by

Table 14.2
The results of running AdaBoost, AdaBoost.L, and BrownBoost on the noisy, synthetic learning problem of section 12.3.2 with various settings of n, m, and η

		$m = 1000$			$m = 10,000$		
n	η	AdaBoost	AdaBoost.L	BrownBoost	AdaBoost	AdaBoost.L	BrownBoost
5	0%	0.0	0.0	0.0	0.0	0.0	0.0
	5%	19.4	2.7	0.4	8.5	0.0	0.0
	20%	23.1	22.0	2.2	21.0	17.4	0.0
20	0%	0.0	3.7	0.8	0.0	0.0	0.1
	5%	31.1	29.9	10.7	41.3	36.8	5.4
	20%	30.4	30.2	21.1	36.9	36.1	12.0

Each entry shows percent error on *clean* (uncorrupted) test examples. All results are averaged over ten random repetitions of the experiment.

Table 14.3
The results of running AdaBoost, AdaBoost.L, and BrownBoost on the "letter" and "satimage" benchmark datasets

Dataset	η	AdaBoost	AdaBoost.L	BrownBoost
letter	0%	3.7	3.7	4.2
	10%	10.8	9.4	7.0
	20%	15.7	13.9	10.5
satimage	0%	4.9	5.0	5.2
	10%	12.1	11.9	6.2
	20%	21.3	20.9	7.4

After converting to binary by combining the classes into two arbitrary groups, each dataset was split randomly into training and test sets, and corrupted for training with artificial noise at rate η. The entries of the table show percent error on *uncorrupted* test examples. All results are averaged over 50 random repetitions of the experiment.

$$\Phi(\psi, 1) = \mathbf{1}\{\psi \leq \vartheta\}, \tag{14.47}$$

for some parameter $\vartheta \geq 0$; see exercise 14.2. Both ϵ and ϑ were chosen by training on 75% of the training data using various settings of these parameters, and then choosing the single setting that performed best on the remaining, held-out training examples.

Table 14.3 shows percent error on clean, uncorrupted test examples. Again, BrownBoost performs much better than the other algorithms in the presence of noise.

Summary

In this chapter, we have described a technique for making BBM adaptive by porting it to a continuous-time setting. We saw that BrownBoost, the resulting algorithm, is a generalization of AdaBoost, but one which may have favorable properties in its handling of noisy data and outliers.

Bibliographic Notes

The results of sections 14.1, 14.2, and 14.3 are an elaboration and extension of the work of Freund [89] on the original version of BrownBoost, as well as later work by Freund and Opper [92] which connected the continuous-time framework with drifting games [201], and also introduced an approach based on differential equations similar to that given in section 14.1.3.

The experiments summarized in section 14.4 were conducted jointly with Evan Ettinger and Sunsern Cheamanunkul.

Further background on the central limit theorem and the convergence of distributions can be found in any standard text on probability, such as [21, 33, 84, 215]. More about Brownian motion and stochastic differential equations can be found, for instance, in [61, 131, 177, 216]. Equation (14.38) appears in Gautschi [105].

Some of the exercises in this chapter are based on material from [92].

Exercises

14.1 Let $\Phi(\psi, \tau)$ be defined as in equation (14.9), for some $\beta > 0$.

a. Verify that the partial differential equation given in equation (14.13) is satisfied for all $\psi \in \mathbb{R}$ and $\tau \in [0, 1)$.

b. Verify that the boundary condition given in equation (14.14) is satisfied away from $\psi = 0$. More specifically, let $\langle \psi_n, \tau_n \rangle$ be any sequence of pairs in $\mathbb{R} \times [0, 1)$. Show that if $\langle \psi_n, \tau_n \rangle \to \langle \psi, 1 \rangle$ as $n \to \infty$, where $\psi \neq 0$, then $\Phi(\psi_n, \tau_n) \to \mathbf{1}\{\psi \leq 0\}$.

c. For all $v \in [0, 1]$, show there exists a sequence $\langle \psi_n, \tau_n \rangle$ in $\mathbb{R} \times [0, 1)$ such that $\langle \psi_n, \tau_n \rangle \to \langle 0, 1 \rangle$ and $\Phi(\psi_n, \tau_n) \to v$ as $n \to \infty$.

14.2 Let $\vartheta > 0$ be a fixed value representing a desired margin. Suppose equation (14.14) is replaced with the modified boundary condition given in equation (14.47).

a. Find an expression for $\Phi(\psi, \tau)$ which satisfies equations (14.13) and (14.47) in the sense of exercise 14.1.

b. Find an expression for the weighting function $w(\psi, \tau)$ that corresponds to this modified potential function.

Note that if BrownBoost is used with these modified versions of Φ and w (for given values of $\epsilon > 0$ and $\vartheta > 0$), and if the algorithm stops at time $\tau = 1$, then the fraction of training examples i with margin $\psi_i \leq \vartheta$ will be exactly ϵ.

c. Show how this potential function could alternatively be derived in the limit $T \to \infty$ from the potential associated with the version of BBM given in exercise 13.5 (for an appropriate choice of θ in terms of T, β, and ϑ).

14.3 Suppose that $\Phi_t(s)$ and $w_t(s)$ are redefined as in exercise 13.6, with α hardwired using the value derived in part (c) of that exercise. We saw earlier that these choices, in BBM, lead to NonAdaBoost. Here, we explore what happens in the continuous-time limit.

a. For fixed $\beta > 0$, $\psi \in \mathbb{R}$, and $\tau \in [0, 1]$, let s, t, and γ be chosen, as functions of T, to satisfy equations (14.1), (14.2), and (14.7) (or to satisfy them as nearly as possible, subject to s and t being integers). Compute $\Phi(\psi, \tau)$, the limit of $\Phi_t(s)$ as $T \to \infty$. Also, use equation (14.15) to compute $w(\psi, \tau)$. Your final answers should be in terms of β, ψ, and τ only. [*Hint:* Use the fact that for any $a \in \mathbb{R}$, $\lim_{x \to \infty}(1 + a/x)^x = e^a$.]

b. Explain why we expect that your answer in part (a) for $\Phi(\psi, \tau)$ should satisfy equation (14.13). Then verify that it does.

In the remainder of this exercise, we consider a variant of BrownBoost (algorithm 14.1) in which the potential and weighting functions have been replaced by those in part (a). We use a cutoff of $c = 0$, and assume $\beta > 0$ throughout.

c. For this modified version of BrownBoost, show that there always exists a solution to the algorithm's two main equations. That is, for any $\psi_1, \ldots, \psi_m \in \mathbb{R}$, $z_1, \ldots, z_m \in \{-1, +1\}$, and $\tau \in [0, 1)$, prove that there exist $\alpha \in \mathbb{R}$ and $\tau' \in [\tau, 1]$ such that equation (14.18) holds, and either $\tau' = 1$ or equation (14.19) holds (using the revised definition of Φ, of course). You can assume that the z_i's are not all the same sign. Also show that this solution is unique, except possibly when $\tau' = 1$.

d. Suppose, for some integer $R > 0$, that $\tau_{R+1} < 1$ (so that the clock has not run out within R rounds). Show that modified BrownBoost's behavior on these first R rounds is identical to that of AdaBoost (algorithm 1.1). That is, assuming the same sequence of weak hypotheses $h_1, \ldots, h_R$ is provided to both algorithms, prove that $D_r^{\mathrm{AB}} = D_r^{\mathrm{BB}}$ and $\alpha_r^{\mathrm{AB}} = \alpha_r^{\mathrm{BB}}$ for $r = 1, \ldots, R$, where we use superscripts AB and BB to distinguish the variables of AdaBoost and (modified) BrownBoost, respectively (and where we use r instead of t to denote round number).

e. Let $R > 0$ be a fixed integer. Show that for β sufficiently large, $\tau_{R+1} < 1$. (You can assume that the sequence of weak hypotheses is fixed and independent of β.)

f. Given $\epsilon \in \left(0, \frac{1}{2}\right)$, explain how a stopping criterion could be added to AdaBoost which would be equivalent to the stopping criterion $\tau_r = 1$ used in modified BrownBoost. If the empirical γ-weak learning assumption holds, for some $\gamma > 0$, must (modified) BrownBoost necessarily halt within a finite number of rounds? Why or why not?

Exercises 14.4, 14.5, and 14.6 explore the nature of BrownBoost solutions in greater detail. For all of these, we adopt the setup and notation of theorem 14.1, including the definition of $\Pi(\alpha, \tau')$ given in equation (14.20). Also, we let $\epsilon \doteq \Pi(0, \tau)/m$, and we assume $\epsilon \in \left(0, \frac{1}{2}\right)$, and that $\beta > 0$ is given and fixed.

14.4 Suppose there exist $\alpha \in \mathbb{R}$ and $\tau' \in [\tau, 1-c)$ which satisfy equation (14.19), but for which $\Pi(\alpha, \tau') < \Pi(0, \tau)$. Show that there exists a BrownBoost solution $\langle \tilde{\alpha}, \tilde{\tau}' \rangle$ with $\tilde{\tau}' > \tau'$.

14.5 Let $\delta \doteq \frac{1}{2} - \frac{1}{2m}\sum_{i=1}^{m} z_i$, and assume $\delta \in \left(0, \frac{1}{2}\right)$.

a. Show that if ϵ is not an integer multiple of $1/m$, then there cannot exist a BrownBoost solution $\langle \alpha, \tau' \rangle$ with $\tau' = 1$. Also, show that if $\epsilon \neq \delta$, then there must exist a BrownBoost solution with $\tau' \leq 1-c$.

b. Consider the function

$$G(u) \doteq A \, \mathrm{erfc}(u+a) - B \, \mathrm{erfc}(u+b)$$

for real constants A, B, a, and b, where $A > B > 0$. Let G' be its derivative. Prove the following:

i. If $a \leq b$, then $G(u) > 0$ for all $u \in \mathbb{R}$.

ii. If $a > b$, then there exist unique values u_0 and u_1 such that $G(u_0) = 0$ and $G'(u_1) = 0$; furthermore, $u_0 \neq u_1$. [*Hint:* Sketch G, taking into consideration its limit as $u \to \pm\infty$, as well as the sign of $G'(u)$ at all values of u.]

c. Consider the special case in which there exist values s_- and s_+ such that, for all i,

$$\psi_i = \begin{cases} s_- & \text{if } z_i = -1 \\ s_+ & \text{if } z_i = +1. \end{cases}$$

Find a number τ_0, as a function of s_-, s_+, and β, such that the following hold for all $\tau' < 1$:

i. If $\tau' \geq \tau_0$, then for all α, $\Pi(\alpha, \tau') \neq \delta m$.

ii. If $\tau' < \tau_0$, then there exists a unique α such that $\Pi(\alpha, \tau') = \delta m$. However, the pair $\langle \alpha, \tau' \rangle$ does not satisfy equation (14.19).

d. Let $z_1, \ldots, z_m$ and δ be given as above. Find values for $\psi_1, \ldots, \psi_m$, $c > 0$, and $\tau \in [0, 1-c)$ for which the *only* BrownBoost solutions are when $\tau' = 1$.

14.6 Prove that theorem 14.1 is false when $c = 0$ in the following general sense: Let $z_1, \ldots, z_m$ and $\delta \in \left(0, \frac{1}{2}\right)$ be as in exercise 14.5, and let $c = 0$. Find values for $\psi_1, \ldots, \psi_m$ and $\tau \in [0, 1)$ for which *no* BrownBoost solution exists.

14.7 In section 14.2.2, we saw that if BrownBoost terminates at some time $\tau \geq 1-c$, then the training error of H is bounded by equation (14.26). In this exercise, we will prove a better bound when a randomized version of H is used instead.

Suppose BrownBoost halts, and in addition to the notation of algorithm 14.1, let us write τ and ψ_i for the values of these variables upon termination. Given x, we redefine H to make a random prediction that is $+1$ with probability

$$\frac{\Phi(-F(x),\,\tau)}{\Phi(F(x),\,\tau)+\Phi(-F(x),\,\tau)},$$

and -1 otherwise, where $F(x) \doteq \sum_{r=1}^{R}\alpha_r h_r(x)$.

a. Give an exact expression for the expected training error of H in terms of the potentials of the chips, where expectation is with respect to the randomized predictions of H.

b. For all $\psi \in \mathbb{R}$, show that $\Phi(\psi,\,\tau)+\Phi(-\psi,\,\tau) \geq 2\Phi(0,\,\tau)$.

c. Show that the expected training error of H is at most

$$\frac{\epsilon}{\mathrm{erfc}\left(\sqrt{\beta c/2}\right)},$$

which approaches ϵ as $c \to 0$.

14.8 Using the notation and assumptions of theorem 14.2 and its proof, this exercise explores what happens if BrownBoost is *not* run lingeringly. We suppose that this happens for the first time on round r, meaning that the preceding $r-1$ rounds were run lingeringly. In particular, this implies that equations (14.29) and (14.30) are still valid. We assume further that $\psi_i^* > 0$ for all i.

a. For $a \in (0, c)$ and $\beta > 0$, let

$$\mathcal{L}_a^\beta \doteq \left\{\langle \alpha, \tau'\rangle : \Pi^\beta(\alpha,\,\tau') = \Pi^\beta(0,\,\tau^\beta),\, 1-c \leq \tau' \leq 1-a\right\}.$$

Show that for all β sufficiently large, there exists $a \in (0, c)$ for which $\mathcal{L}_a^\beta$ is nonempty and compact. [*Hint:* To show non-emptiness, first argue that $\Pi^\beta(0, 1) < m\epsilon$, but $\Pi^\beta(0, 1-c) > m\epsilon$.]

b. Using part (a), show that for β sufficiently large, there exists a pair $\langle \alpha^\beta, \tau'^\beta\rangle$ which satisfies both equations (14.33) and (14.34), and where $1-c < \tau'^\beta < 1$.

c. We assume henceforth that $\langle \alpha^\beta, \tau'^\beta\rangle$ are chosen as in part (b). Let q be any constant in $(0, 1)$. For β sufficiently large, show that $\tau'^\beta > 1 - \beta^{q-2}$. [*Hint:* Adapt the proof of lemma 14.4.]

d. Let

$$\mu_+ \doteq \min_{i:z_i=+1} \psi_i^*, \quad \mu_- \doteq \min_{i:z_i=-1} \psi_i^*,$$

and let $\tilde{\alpha} \doteq (\mu_- - \mu_+)/2$. Show that $\alpha^\beta \to \tilde{\alpha}$ as $\beta \to \infty$. Is this limit $\tilde{\alpha}$ necessarily equal to α^*? Justify your answer. [*Hint:* For all $\delta > 0$ and for β large, show that if $|\alpha^\beta - \tilde{\alpha}| \geq \delta$, then equation (14.34) cannot be satisfied.]

Appendix: Some Notation, Definitions, and Mathematical Background

In this appendix, we describe some of the notation and definitions used in the book, and briefly outline some general mathematical background. For a more in-depth treatment, refer to standard texts, such as those cited, on real analysis [197]; convex analysis and optimization [31, 191]; and probability [21, 33, 84, 215].

A.1 General Notation

If a is an event, its probability is denoted $\mathbf{Pr}[a]$. The expected value of a real-valued random variable X is written $\mathbf{E}[X]$. Often, these are subscripted to clarify what sources of randomness the probability or expectation is with respect to.

The set of all real numbers is written $\mathbb{R}$, while $\mathbb{R}_+$ denotes the set of all nonnegative real numbers, and $\mathbb{R}_{++}$ the set of all strictly positive real numbers. The set of all integers is written $\mathbb{Z}$.

The *union* of sets $A_1, \ldots, A_n$ is denoted $A_1 \cup \cdots \cup A_n$ or, occasionally, $\bigcup_{i=1}^n A_i$. Their *intersection* is written $A_1 \cap \cdots \cap A_n$. Their *Cartesian product* (that is, the set of all *tuples* of the form $\langle a_1, \ldots, a_n \rangle$, where $a_i \in A_i$ for $i = 1, \ldots, n$) is written $A_1 \times \cdots \times A_n$. When all n sets are equal to the same set A, this is abbreviated A^n. The *set difference* of two sets A and B (that is, the set of elements in A that are not also in B) is written $A - B$. We write $A \subseteq B$ to indicate that A is a (not necessarily proper) subset of B. The *power set* of a set A (that is, the set of all its subsets) is denoted 2^A. The *empty set* is written $\emptyset$.

The symbol $\doteq$ means "equal by definition." For $x \in \mathbb{R}$, we define

$$
\mathrm{sign}(x) \doteq \begin{cases} +1 & \text{if } x > 0 \\ 0 & \text{if } x = 0 \\ -1 & \text{if } x < 0. \end{cases}
$$

However, in some sections of the book, we temporarily redefine $\mathrm{sign}(0)$, as explained in the text.

We define the *indicator function* $\mathbf{1}\{\cdot\}$ to be 1 if its argument is true, and 0 otherwise.

Natural logarithm is written $\ln x$, and its base is denoted by $e \approx 2.71828$. Logarithm base 2 is written $\lg x$. When the base is unimportant or clear from context, we sometimes write $\log x$ generically with no base. By convention, $0 \log 0$ is defined to be 0. For readability, we often write e^x as $\exp(x)$.

An *ordered pair* (or 2-tuple) is written (x, y), or $\langle x, y \rangle$. *Vectors* are usually written in bold; for instance, $\mathbf{x}$. The components of such a vector $\mathbf{x} \in \mathbb{R}^n$ are denoted $x_1, \ldots, x_n$. The *inner product* of two vectors $\mathbf{x}, \mathbf{y} \in \mathbb{R}^n$ is written $\mathbf{x} \cdot \mathbf{y}$; thus,

$$\mathbf{x} \cdot \mathbf{y} \doteq \sum_{i=1}^{n} x_i y_i.$$

When in a linear-algebraic context, a vector $\mathbf{x} \in \mathbb{R}^n$ is treated as a column vector. More often, however, $\mathbf{x}$ is simply identified with the tuple $\langle x_1, \ldots, x_n \rangle$.

Matrices are also usually in bold, such as $\mathbf{M}$, with entries M_{ij}. The *transpose* of matrix $\mathbf{M}$ is denoted $\mathbf{M}^\top$.

We use "big Oh" notation in a not entirely formal manner to hide constants and low-order terms in complicated formulas. If f and g are real-valued functions on n real values, we say that $f(\mathbf{x})$ is $O(g(\mathbf{x}))$ if $f(\mathbf{x})$ is at most a positive constant times larger than $g(\mathbf{x})$ under "appropriate" limits. Often, this will be a limit in which all of the variables are getting large, but sometimes we are interested in the case that one or more of the variables is approaching 0. The "right" limit is usually clear from the context. For instance, $3x^3 + 2x + x^2 \ln x + 9$ is $O(x^3)$ under the limit $x \to \infty$; it is also $O(x^4)$.

Analogously, $f(\mathbf{x})$ is $\Omega(g(\mathbf{x}))$ if it is *at least* a positive constant times $g(\mathbf{x})$ under appropriate limits. We also use the "soft Oh" notation $\tilde{O}(g(\mathbf{x}))$ to hide logarithmic factors in a similar manner. For instance, $2x^2 \ln x + x^{1.5} + 17$ is $\tilde{O}(x^2)$. Finally, we say that $f(\mathbf{x})$ is $\theta(g(\mathbf{x}))$ if $f(\mathbf{x})$ is both $O(g(\mathbf{x}))$ and $\Omega(g(\mathbf{x}))$.

A.2 Norms

For $p \geq 1$, the ℓ_p-*norm* of a vector $\mathbf{x} \in \mathbb{R}^n$, written $\|\mathbf{x}\|_p$, is defined to be

$$\|\mathbf{x}\|_p \doteq \left(\sum_{i=1}^{n} |x_i|^p \right)^{1/p}.$$

Letting p grow to ∞ yields the ℓ_∞-norm:

$$\|\mathbf{x}\|_\infty \doteq \max_{1 \leq i \leq n} |x_i|.$$

These norms naturally occur in pairs, called *duals*. In particular, the norms ℓ_p and ℓ_q form a dual pair if

$$\frac{1}{p} + \frac{1}{q} = 1.$$

This means that ℓ_1 and ℓ_∞ are duals, while the usual Euclidean norm, ℓ_2, is dual with itself.

We sometimes write $\|\mathbf{x}\|$ when the norm ℓ_p is either unimportant or clear from context.

A.3 Maxima, Minima, Suprema, and Infima

Let $A \subseteq \mathbb{R}$. We write $\max A$ for the largest element of A. Often, we work with elements referenced by some index ι in some set I. We then write

$$\max_{\iota \in I} a_\iota$$

as shorthand for

$$\max\{a_\iota : \iota \in I\},$$

and similarly for the other concepts described below. We also define

$$\arg\max_{\iota \in I} a_\iota \tag{A.1}$$

to be any index $\tilde{\iota} \in I$ which realizes the maximum, that is, for which $a_{\tilde{\iota}} \geq a_\iota$ for all $\iota \in I$. If more than one index has this property, then equation (A.1) is equal to any such index, breaking ties arbitrarily (and not necessarily in a way that is "favorable" in any sense).

In general, for $A \subseteq \mathbb{R}$, $\max A$ need not exist since A might not have a largest element (for instance, if A is the set of all negative real numbers). In such cases, we can instead work with the *supremum* of A, written $\sup A$, which is defined to be the least upper bound on A, that is, the smallest number $s \in \mathbb{R}$ such that $a \leq s$ for all $a \in A$. If no such number exists, as happens if A includes unboundedly large elements, then $\sup A = +\infty$. And if A is empty, then $\sup A = -\infty$. For instance, if A is the set of all negative numbers, then $\sup A = 0$. In all cases, $\sup A$ is defined and exists for all $A \subseteq \mathbb{R}$, and is equal to $\max A$ whenever the maximum exists.

The notions of min, arg min, and infimum are defined analogously. Specifically, $\inf A$, the *infimum* of $A \subseteq \mathbb{R}$, is the greatest lower bound on A, that is, the largest number s for which $s \leq a$ for all $a \in A$.

A.4 Limits

Let $\mathbf{x}_1, \mathbf{x}_2, \ldots$ be a *sequence* of points in $\mathbb{R}^n$. We say the sequence *converges* to $\tilde{\mathbf{x}} \in \mathbb{R}^n$, written $\mathbf{x}_t \to \tilde{\mathbf{x}}$ as $t \to \infty$, or

$$\lim_{t \to \infty} \mathbf{x}_t = \tilde{\mathbf{x}},$$

if for all $\varepsilon > 0$, there exists $t_0 > 0$ such that

$$\|\mathbf{x}_t - \tilde{\mathbf{x}}\| < \varepsilon$$

for all $t \geq t_0$.

Similarly, if $x_1, x_2, \ldots$ is a sequence in $\mathbb{R}$, then $x_t \to +\infty$ if for all $B > 0$, there exists $t_0 > 0$ such that $x_t > B$ for all $t \geq t_0$. The limit $x_t \to -\infty$ is defined analogously.

For any such sequence, we also define the following one-sided *upper limit* or *limit superior*:

$$\limsup_{t \to \infty} x_t \doteq \lim_{t_0 \to \infty} \sup_{t \geq t_0} x_t.$$

In words, if this expression is equal to s, then for all $\varepsilon > 0$, there exists $t_0 > 0$ such that $x_t < s + \varepsilon$ for all $t \geq t_0$. Moreover, s is the smallest number with this property. Thus, s can be viewed as a limiting best upper bound on the sequence. Analogously, the *lower limit* or *limit inferior* is

$$\liminf_{t \to \infty} x_t \doteq \lim_{t_0 \to \infty} \inf_{t \geq t_0} x_t.$$

Note that $\limsup x_t$ and $\liminf x_t$ exist for all sequences, although either can be infinite. These two quantities are equal to one another if and only if the entire sequence has a limit (which must equal their common value).

If $\mathbf{f} : A \to \mathbb{R}^m$, where $A \subseteq \mathbb{R}^n$, and $\tilde{\mathbf{x}} \in A$, then the limit

$$\lim_{\mathbf{x} \to \tilde{\mathbf{x}}} \mathbf{f}(\mathbf{x})$$

exists and is equal to $\mathbf{y}$ (also written $\mathbf{f}(\mathbf{x}) \to \mathbf{y}$ as $\mathbf{x} \to \tilde{\mathbf{x}}$) if for all sequences $\mathbf{x}_1, \mathbf{x}_2, \ldots$ in A, none of whose elements are equal to $\tilde{\mathbf{x}}$, if $\mathbf{x}_t \to \tilde{\mathbf{x}}$, then $\mathbf{f}(\mathbf{x}_t) \to \mathbf{y}$ (provided at least one such sequence exists). If $A \subseteq \mathbb{R}$, then the limit as $x \to \pm\infty$ is defined analogously.

A.5   Continuity, Closed Sets, and Compactness

Let $f : A \to \mathbb{R}$ where $A \subseteq \mathbb{R}^n$. Then f is *continuous at* $\tilde{\mathbf{x}}$ if for every sequence $\mathbf{x}_1, \mathbf{x}_2, \ldots$ in A, if $\mathbf{x}_t \to \tilde{\mathbf{x}}$, then $f(\mathbf{x}_t) \to f(\tilde{\mathbf{x}})$. The function f is *continuous* if it is continuous at every point in its domain A. Occasionally, we also consider functions with a range that includes $\pm\infty$. Continuity is defined for such extended real-valued functions in exactly the same way. For instance, the familiar functions x^2, e^x, and $\cos x$ are all continuous on $\mathbb{R}$. The function $\text{sign}(x)$ is not continuous. The function $\ln x$ is continuous as a real-valued function on $\mathbb{R}_{++}$; if we define $\ln 0 = -\infty$, then it also becomes a continuous extended real-valued function on $\mathbb{R}_+$.

By the *intermediate value theorem*, if $f : [a, b] \to \mathbb{R}$ is continuous, then for any value u between $f(a)$ and $f(b)$, there must exist $x \in [a, b]$ for which $f(x) = u$.

We say that the set $A \subseteq \mathbb{R}^n$ is *closed* if every convergent sequence of points in A converges to a point that is actually in A. That is, A is closed if for every sequence $\mathbf{x}_1, \mathbf{x}_2, \ldots$ in A, if $\mathbf{x}_t \to \tilde{\mathbf{x}}$, then $\tilde{\mathbf{x}} \in A$. For instance, in $\mathbb{R}$, the sets $[0, 1]$, $\mathbb{Z}$, and $\mathbb{R}$ are all closed, but the set $(0, 1)$ is not.

The *closure* of a set $A \subseteq \mathbb{R}^n$, written $\overline{A}$, is the smallest closed set that includes A. Said differently, $\overline{A}$ consists exactly of those points $\tilde{\mathbf{x}} \in \mathbb{R}^n$ for which there exists a sequence of points in A that converges to $\tilde{\mathbf{x}}$. For instance, the closure of $(0, 1)$ is $[0, 1]$.

A set $A \subseteq \mathbb{R}^n$ is *bounded* if there exists $B > 0$ such that $\|\mathbf{x}\| < B$ for all $\mathbf{x} \in A$. The set A is *compact* if it is both closed and bounded. For instance, $[0, 1]$ is compact, but neither $(0, 1)$ nor $\mathbb{R}$ is. Compact sets have a number of important properties:

First, if $A \subseteq \mathbb{R}^n$ is compact and nonempty, and if $f : A \to \mathbb{R}$ is continuous, then f actually attains its maximum at a point in A. In other words,

$$\max_{\mathbf{x} \in A} f(\mathbf{x})$$

exists, meaning that there exists $\mathbf{x}_0 \in A$ such that $f(\mathbf{x}) \leq f(\mathbf{x}_0)$ for all $\mathbf{x} \in A$.

Second, if $A \subseteq \mathbb{R}^n$ is compact, and if $\mathbf{x}_1, \mathbf{x}_2, \ldots$ is any (not necessarily convergent) sequence of points in A, then this sequence must have a *convergent subsequence*. That is, there must exist indices $i_1 < i_2 < \cdots$ such that the subsequence $\mathbf{x}_{i_1}, \mathbf{x}_{i_2}, \ldots$ converges, and therefore has a limit in A.

A.6 Derivatives, Gradients, and Taylor's Theorem

Let $f : \mathbb{R} \to \mathbb{R}$. Then the first *derivative* of f is denoted either f' or df/dx, with $f'(\tilde{x})$ and $df(\tilde{x})/dx$ both denoting its value when evaluated at a particular value $\tilde{x}$. Similarly, f'' (or $d^2 f/dx^2$) and $f^{(k)}$ denote second and k-th derivatives, respectively.

A form of *Taylor's theorem* can be stated as follows:

Theorem A.1 Let $f : [a, b] \to \mathbb{R}$ be $k + 1$ times continuously differentiable. Then for all $x_0, x \in [a, b]$, there exists $\hat{x}$ between x_0 and x such that

$$f(x) = f(x_0) + (x - x_0)f'(x_0) + \cdots + \frac{(x - x_0)^k}{k!} f^{(k)}(x_0) + \frac{(x - x_0)^{k+1}}{(k+1)!} f^{(k+1)}(\hat{x}).$$

Now let $f : \mathbb{R}^n \to \mathbb{R}$ be a function defined on variables $x_1, \ldots, x_n$. Then $\partial f/\partial x_i$ denotes the *partial derivative* of f with respect to x_i, and $\partial f(\tilde{\mathbf{x}})/\partial x_i$ gives its value at a particular point $\tilde{\mathbf{x}}$. The *gradient* of f, denoted ∇f, is a vector consisting of its partial derivatives:

$$\nabla f = \left\langle \frac{\partial f}{\partial x_1}, \ldots, \frac{\partial f}{\partial x_n} \right\rangle,$$

with $\nabla f(\tilde{\mathbf{x}})$ denoting its value at $\tilde{\mathbf{x}}$. If $\mathbf{d}$ is a unit-length vector specifying a direction, then the slope of f at $\tilde{\mathbf{x}}$ in direction $\mathbf{d}$ is $\nabla f(\tilde{\mathbf{x}}) \cdot \mathbf{d}$. In other words, if we let $g(u) \doteq f(\tilde{\mathbf{x}} + u\mathbf{d})$, then

$$g'(0) = \nabla f(\tilde{\mathbf{x}}) \cdot \mathbf{d}. \tag{A.2}$$

This means that f is locally increasing most rapidly in the direction of the gradient, and decreasing most rapidly in the direction of the negative gradient.

The *chain rule* states that if the variables $x_1, \ldots, x_n$ of a function $f(x_1, \ldots, x_n)$ are themselves functions of a single variable u, so that

$$f(x_1, \ldots, x_n) = f(x_1(u), \ldots, x_n(u))$$

is actually itself a function of u, then its derivative can be computed by the rule

$$\frac{df}{du} = \sum_{i=1}^{n} \frac{\partial f}{\partial x_i} \cdot \frac{dx_i}{du}.$$

For instance, equation (A.2) follows by letting $x_i(u) = \tilde{x}_i + ud_i$.

A.7 Convexity

A set $A \subseteq \mathbb{R}^n$ is a *convex set* if for all $\mathbf{u}, \mathbf{v} \in A$, and for all $p \in [0, 1]$, the point $p\mathbf{u} + (1 - p)\mathbf{v}$ is also in A. For such a convex set A, we say that $f : A \to \mathbb{R}$ is a *convex function* if for all $\mathbf{u}, \mathbf{v} \in A$, and for all $p \in [0, 1]$,

$$f(p\mathbf{u} + (1 - p)\mathbf{v}) \leq pf(\mathbf{u}) + (1 - p)f(\mathbf{v}).$$

The function f is *strictly convex* if this condition holds with *strict* inequality whenever $\mathbf{u} \neq \mathbf{v}$ and $p \in (0, 1)$. For instance, the functions $1 - 2x$, x^2, e^x, and $-\ln x$ are all convex on their respective domains, and all strictly convex except for the first one.

The property of convexity is closed under various natural operations. For instance, the sum of two or more convex functions is convex, as is the composition of a convex function with a linear function. A convex function has no local minima. A strictly convex function can have at most one global minimum. If a real-valued function $f : \mathbb{R}^n \to \mathbb{R}$ defined on all of $\mathbb{R}^n$ is convex, then it also must be continuous.

Suppose f is a function of only one variable, that is, with domain a (convex) subset of $\mathbb{R}$. If f is twice differentiable, then it is convex if and only if f'' is nonnegative. Further, if f'' is strictly positive everywhere, then f is strictly convex (but the converse does not necessarily hold). A convex function f must lie entirely above any tangent line at any point x_0. If f is differentiable at x_0, this means

$$f(x) \geq f(x_0) + f'(x_0)\,(x - x_0) \tag{A.3}$$

for all x in the domain.

Jensen's inequality states that if f is convex, and X is any real-valued random variable, then

$$f(\mathbf{E}[X]) \leq \mathbf{E}[f(X)]. \tag{A.4}$$

A.8 The Method of Lagrange Multipliers

Suppose we wish to find the solution, over $\mathbf{x} \in \mathbb{R}^n$, of a convex optimization problem of the form

minimize: $f(\mathbf{x})$

subject to: $g_i(\mathbf{x}) \leq 0$ for $i = 1, \dots, m$

$$\mathbf{a}_j \cdot \mathbf{x} = b_j \text{ for } j = 1, \dots, \ell$$

where $f, g_1, \dots, g_m$ are all convex; $\mathbf{a}_1, \dots, \mathbf{a}_\ell \in \mathbb{R}^n$; and $b_1, \dots, b_\ell \in \mathbb{R}$. We refer to this as the *primal* problem. A commonly used technique for handling such problems is first to form the *Lagrangian*:

$$L(\mathbf{x}, \boldsymbol{\alpha}, \boldsymbol{\beta}) \doteq f(\mathbf{x}) + \sum_{i=1}^{m} \alpha_i g_i(\mathbf{x}) + \sum_{j=1}^{\ell} \beta_j (\mathbf{a}_j \cdot \mathbf{x} - b_j).$$

This is a function of the original, "primal" variables $\mathbf{x}$ and the new "dual" variables, called *Lagrange multipliers*, $\alpha_1, \dots, \alpha_m$ and $\beta_1, \dots, \beta_\ell$. The β_j's are unconstrained, but we restrict the α_i's to be nonnegative.

Next, for each choice of $\boldsymbol{\alpha}$ and $\boldsymbol{\beta}$, this method prescribes finding $\mathbf{x}$ which minimizes L, and plugging the result back into L. In other words, we compute

$$h(\boldsymbol{\alpha}, \boldsymbol{\beta}) \doteq \inf_{\mathbf{x} \in \mathbb{R}^n} L(\mathbf{x}, \boldsymbol{\alpha}, \boldsymbol{\beta}).$$

We then obtain the *dual* optimization problem:

maximize: $h(\boldsymbol{\alpha}, \boldsymbol{\beta})$

subject to: $\alpha_i \geq 0$ for $i = 1, \dots, m$.

Under suitable conditions, it can be shown that this optimization problem will have the same value as the original, primal problem. When this is the case, we can solve the dual problem for $\boldsymbol{\alpha}$ and $\boldsymbol{\beta}$, and then obtain a solution to the primal by finding $\mathbf{x}$ which minimizes L for these values.

An example is given in section 8.1.3.

A.9   Some Distributions and the Central Limit Theorem

The *binomial coefficient* $\binom{n}{k}$ counts the number of ways of choosing a subset of size k from a set of n elements. Thus,

$$\binom{n}{k} \doteq \frac{n!}{k!\,(n-k)!},$$

and by convention, $\binom{n}{k} \doteq 0$ if $k < 0$ or $k > n$.

Suppose $X_1, \ldots, X_n$ are n independent random variables, each equal to 1 with probability p, and 0 otherwise. Then the distribution of the random variable

$$Y \doteq \sum_{i=1}^{n} X_i,$$

which counts the total number of 1's, is called the *binomial distribution*. Specifically, we have

$$\mathbf{Pr}[Y = k] = \binom{n}{k} p^k (1 - p)^{n-k}.$$

The *variance* of a real-valued random variable X is defined to be

$$\operatorname{Var} X \doteq \mathbf{E}\!\left[(X - \mathbf{E}[X])^2\right].$$

For instance, in the example above, $\operatorname{Var} X_i = p(1 - p)$, and $\operatorname{Var} Y = np(1 - p)$. The *standard deviation* of X is $\sqrt{\operatorname{Var} X}$, and is a standard measure of the "spread" of the distribution.

In one dimension, a random variable X obeys a *normal* or *Gaussian distribution* with mean μ and standard deviation σ if its *probability density function* is given by

$$p(x; \mu, \sigma) = \frac{1}{\sigma \sqrt{2\pi}} \exp\left(-\frac{(x - \mu)^2}{2\sigma^2}\right),$$

meaning that for all $z \in \mathbb{R}$,

$$\mathbf{Pr}[X \le z] = \int_{-\infty}^{z} p(x; \mu, \sigma)\,dx.$$

Standard normal refers to the normal distribution with $\mu = 0$ and $\sigma = 1$.

The *central limit theorem* states that the sum of a large number of independent random variables, when properly standardized, will converge to a normal distribution. More precisely, let $X_1, X_2, \ldots$ be independent, identically distributed random variables, each with mean μ and standard deviation σ. Let

$$Y_n \doteq \sum_{i=1}^{n} X_i$$

be the sum of the first n variables, and let

$$Z_n \doteq \frac{Y_n - n\mu}{\sigma \sqrt{n}}$$

be a standardized version of the sum with mean 0 and standard deviation 1. Then the central limit theorem states that Z_n *converges in distribution* to standard normal, meaning that for all $z \in \mathbb{R}$,

$$\lim_{n \to \infty} \mathbf{Pr}[Z_n \leq z] = \mathbf{Pr}\left[Z^* \leq z\right],$$

where Z^* is a standard normal random variable.

Bibliography

[1] Naoki Abe and Hiroshi Mamitsuka. Query learning strategies using boosting and bagging. In *Machine Learning: Proceedings of the Fifteenth International Conference*, pages 1–9, 1998.

[2] Naoki Abe, Bianca Zadrozny, and John Langford. An iterative method for multi-class cost-sensitive learning. In *Proceedings of the Tenth ACM SIGKDD International Conference on Knowledge Discovery and Data Mining*, pages 3–11, 2004.

[3] Shivani Agarwal, Thore Graepel, Ralf Herbrich, Sariel Har-Peled, and Dan Roth. Generalization bounds for the area under the ROC curve. *Journal of Machine Learning Research*, 6:393–425, April 2005.

[4] Shivani Agarwal and Dan Roth. Learnability of bipartite ranking functions. In *Learning Theory: 18th Annual Conference on Learning Theory*, pages 16–31, 2005.

[5] Shivani Agarwal and Shiladitya Sengupta. Ranking genes by relevance to a disease. In *8th Annual International Conference on Computational Systems Bioinformatics*, 2009.

[6] Erin L. Allwein, Robert E. Schapire, and Yoram Singer. Reducing multiclass to binary: A unifying approach for margin classifiers. *Journal of Machine Learning Research*, 1:113–141, December 2000.

[7] Ethem Alpaydin. *Introduction to Machine Learning*. MIT Press, 2004.

[8] Martin Anthony and Peter L. Bartlett. *Neural Network Learning: Theoretical Foundations*. Cambridge University Press, 1999.

[9] Javed A. Aslam and Scott E. Decatur. General bounds on statistical query learning and PAC learning with noise via hypothesis boosting. *Information and Computation*, 141(2):85–118, March 1998.

[10] Maria-Florina Balcan and Avrim Blum. A discriminative model for semi-supervised learning. *Journal of the ACM*, 57(3), March 2010.

[11] Peter L. Bartlett. The sample complexity of pattern classification with neural networks: The size of the weights is more important than the size of the network. *IEEE Transactions on Information Theory*, 44(2):525–536, March 1998.

[12] Peter L. Bartlett, Michael I. Jordan, and Jon D. McAuliffe. Convexity, classification, and risk bounds. *Journal of the American Statistical Association*, 101(473):138–156, March 2006.

[13] Peter L. Bartlett and Shahar Mendelson. Rademacher and Gaussian complexities: Risk bounds and structural results. *Journal of Machine Learning Research*, 3:463–482, November 2002.

[14] Peter L. Bartlett and Mikhail Traskin. AdaBoost is consistent. *Journal of Machine Learning Research*, 8:2347–2368, 2007.

[15] Eric Bauer and Ron Kohavi. An empirical comparison of voting classification algorithms: Bagging, boosting, and variants. *Machine Learning*, 36(1/2):105–139, 1999.

[16] Eric B. Baum and David Haussler. What size net gives valid generalization? *Neural Computation*, 1(1):151–160, 1989.

[17] Shai Ben-David, Philip M. Long, and Yishay Mansour. Agnostic boosting. In *Proceedings 14th Annual Conference on Computational Learning Theory and 5th European Conference on Computational Learning Theory*, pages 507–516, 2001.

[18] Kristin P. Bennett, Ayhan Demiriz, and Richard Maclin. Exploiting unlabeled data in ensemble methods. In *Proceedings of the Eighth ACM SIGKDD International Conference on Knowledge Discovery and Data Mining*, pages 289–296, 2002.

[19] Alina Beygelzimer, John Langford, and Pradeep Ravikumar. Error-correcting tournaments. In *Algorithmic Learning Theory: 20th International Conference*, pages 247–262, 2009.

[20] Peter J. Bickel, Ya'acov Ritov, and Alon Zakai. Some theory for generalized boosting algorithms. *Journal of Machine Learning Research*, 7:705–732, 2006.

[21] Patrick Billingsley. *Probability and Measure*, third edition. Wiley, 1995.

[22] Christopher M. Bishop. *Pattern Recognition and Machine Learning*. Springer, 2006.

[23] David Blackwell. An analog of the minimax theorem for vector payoffs. *Pacific Journal of Mathematics*, 6(1):1–8, Spring 1956.

[24] David Blackwell. Controlled random walks. In *Proceedings of the International Congress of Mathematicians, 1954*, volume 3, pages 336–338. North-Holland, 1956.

[25] Avrim Blum. Empirical support for Winnow and Weighted-Majority algorithms: Results on a calendar scheduling domain. *Machine Learning*, 26(1):5–23, 1997.

[26] Avrim Blum. Random projection, margins, kernels, and feature-selection. In *Subspace, Latent Structure and Feature Selection*, pages 52–68. Springer, 2005.

[27] Anselm Blumer, Andrzej Ehrenfeucht, David Haussler, and Manfred K. Warmuth. Occam's razor. *Information Processing Letters*, 24(6):377–380, April 1987.

[28] Anselm Blumer, Andrzej Ehrenfeucht, David Haussler, and Manfred K. Warmuth. Learnability and the Vapnik-Chervonenkis dimension. *Journal of the Association for Computing Machinery*, 36(4):929–965, October 1989.

[29] Bernhard E. Boser, Isabelle M. Guyon, and Vladimir N. Vapnik. A training algorithm for optimal margin classifiers. In *Proceedings of the Fifth Annual ACM Workshop on Computational Learning Theory*, pages 144–152, 1992.

[30] Stéphane Boucheron, Olivier Bousquet, and Gábor Lugosi. Theory of classification: A survey of some recent advances. *ESAIM: Probability and Statistics*, 9:323–375, 2005.

[31] Stephen Boyd and Lieven Vandenberghe. *Convex Optimization*. Cambridge University Press, 2004.

[32] L. M. Bregman. The relaxation method of finding the common point of convex sets and its application to the solution of problems in convex programming. *USSR Computational Mathematics and Mathematical Physics*, 7(3):200–217, 1967.

[33] Leo Breiman. *Probability*. SIAM, 1992. (Originally Addison-Wesley, 1962.)

[34] Leo Breiman. Bagging predictors. *Machine Learning*, 24(2):123–140, 1996.

[35] Leo Breiman. Arcing classifiers. *Annals of Statistics*, 26(3):801–849, 1998.

[36] Leo Breiman. Prediction games and arcing classifiers. *Neural Computation*, 11(7):1493–1517, 1999.

[37] Leo Breiman. Random forests. *Machine Learning*, 45(1):5–32, 2001.

[38] Leo Breiman. Population theory for boosting ensembles. *Annals of Statistics*, 32(1):1–11, 2004.

[39] Leo Breiman, Jerome H. Friedman, Richard A. Olshen, and Charles J. Stone. *Classification and Regression Trees*. Chapman & Hall/CRC, 1984.

[40] Peter Bühlmann and Torsten Hothorn. Boosting algorithms: Regularization, prediction and model fitting. *Statistical Science*, 22(4):477–505, 2007.

[41] Wray Buntine. Learning classification trees. *Statistics and Computing*, 2:63–73, 1992.

[42] Rich Caruana and Alexandru Niculescu-Mizil. An empirical comparison of supervised learning algorithms. In *Proceedings of the 23rd International Conference on Machine Learning*, pages 161–168, 2006.

[43] N. N. Čencov. *Statistical Decision Rules and Optimal Inference*. American Mathematical Society, 1982.

[44] Yair Censor and Stavros A. Zenios. *Parallel Optimization: Theory, Algorithms, and Applications*. Oxford University Press, 1997.

[45] Nicolò Cesa-Bianchi, Yoav Freund, David Haussler, David P. Helmbold, Robert E. Schapire, and Manfred K. Warmuth. How to use expert advice. *Journal of the ACM*, 44(3):427–485, May 1997.

[46] Nicolò Cesa-Bianchi, Yoav Freund, David P. Helmbold, and Manfred K. Warmuth. On-line prediction and conversion strategies. *Machine Learning*, 25:71–110, 1996.

[47] Nicolò Cesa-Bianchi and Gábor Lugosi. *Prediction, Learning, and Games*. Cambridge University Press, 2006.

[48] N. N. Chentsov. Nonsymmetrical distance between probability distributions, entropy and the theorem of Pythagoras. *Mathematical Notes*, 4:686–691, September 1968.

[49] William W. Cohen. Fast effective rule induction. In *Proceedings of the Twelfth International Conference on Machine Learning*, pages 115–123, 1995.

[50] William W. Cohen and Yoram Singer. A simple, fast, and effective rule learner. In *Proceedings of the Sixteenth National Conference on Artificial Intelligence*, pages 335–342, 1999.

[51] David Cohn, Les Atlas, and Richard Ladner. Improving generalization with active learning. *Machine Learning*, 15(2):201–221, 1994.

[52] Michael Collins. Discriminative reranking for natural language parsing. In *Proceedings of the Seventeenth International Conference on Machine Learning*, pages 175–182, 2000.

[53] Michael Collins and Terry Koo. Discriminative reranking for natural language parsing. *Computational Linguistics*, 31(1):25–70, March 2005.

[54] Michael Collins, Robert E. Schapire, and Yoram Singer. Logistic regression, AdaBoost and Bregman distances. *Machine Learning*, 48(1/2/3): 253–285, 2002.

[55] Corinna Cortes and Mehryar Mohri. AUC optimization vs. error rate minimization. In *Advances in Neural Information Processing Systems 16*, 2004.

[56] Corinna Cortes and Vladimir Vapnik. Support-vector networks. *Machine Learning*, 20(3):273–297, September 1995.

[57] Thomas M. Cover and Joy A. Thomas. *Elements of Information Theory*. Wiley, 1991.

[58] Nello Cristianini and John Shawe-Taylor. *An Introduction to Support Vector Machines and Other Kernel-based Learning Methods*. Cambridge University Press, 2000.

[59] I. Csiszár. I-divergence geometry of probability distributions and minimization problems. *Annals of Probability*, 3(1):146–158, 1975.

[60] Imre Csiszár and Paul C. Shields. Information theory and statistics: A tutorial. *Foundations and Trends in Communications and Information Theory*, 1(4):417–528, 2004.

[61] Sasha Cyganowski, Peter Kloeden, and Jerzy Ombach. *From Elementary Probability to Stochastic Differential Equations with MAPLE*. Springer, 2002.

[62] George B. Dantzig. A proof of the equivalence of the programming problem and the game problem. In *Activity Analysis of Production and Allocation: Proceedings of a Conference*, pages 330–335. John Wiley & Sons, 1951.

[63] Stephen Della Pietra, Vincent Della Pietra, and John Lafferty. Inducing features of random fields. *IEEE Transactions on Pattern Analysis and Machine Intelligence*, 19(4):380–393, April 1997.

[64] Stephen Della Pietra, Vincent Della Pietra, and John Lafferty. Duality and auxiliary functions for Bregman distances. Technical Report CMU-CS-01-109, School of Computer Science, Carnegie Mellon University, 2001.

[65] Ayhan Demiriz, Kristin P. Bennett, and John Shawe-Taylor. Linear programming boosting via column generation. *Machine Learning*, 46(1/2/3):225–254, 2002.

[66] Robert Detrano, Andras Janosi, Walter Steinbrunn, Matthias Pfisterer, Johann-Jakob Schmid, Sarbjit Sandhu, Kern H. Guppy, Stella Lee, and Victor Froelicher. International application of a new probability algorithm for the diagnosis of coronary artery disease. *American Journal of Cardiology*, 64(5):304–310, August 1989.

[67] Luc Devroye, Lázló Györfi, and Gábor Lugosi. *A Probabilistic Theory of Pattern Recognition*. Springer, 1996.

[68] Thomas G. Dietterich. An experimental comparison of three methods for constructing ensembles of decision trees: Bagging, boosting, and randomization. *Machine Learning*, 40(2):139–158, 2000.

[69] Thomas G. Dietterich. Ensemble learning. In Michael A. Arbib, editor, *The Handbook of Brain Theory and Neural Networks*, pages 405–408, second edition, MIT Press, 2002.

[70] Thomas G. Dietterich and Ghulum Bakiri. Solving multiclass learning problems via error-correcting output codes. *Journal of Artificial Intelligence Research*, 2:263–286, January 1995.

[71] Harris Drucker and Corinna Cortes. Boosting decision trees. In *Advances in Neural Information Processing Systems 8*, pages 479–485. MIT Press, 1996.

[72] Harris Drucker, Robert Schapire, and Patrice Simard. Boosting performance in neural networks. *International Journal of Pattern Recognition and Artificial Intelligence*, 7(4):705–719, 1993.

[73] Richard O. Duda, Peter E. Hart, and David G. Stork. *Pattern Classification*, second edition. Wiley, 2001.

[74] Miroslav Dudík. *Maximum Entropy Density Estimation and Modeling Geographic Distributions of Species*. Ph.D. thesis, Princeton University, 2007.

[75] Miroslav Dudík, Steven J. Phillips, and Robert E. Schapire. Performance guarantees for regularized maximum entropy density estimation. In *Learning Theory: 17th Annual Conference on Learning Theory*, pages 472–486, 2004.

[76] Miroslav Dudík, Steven J. Phillips, and Robert E. Schapire. Maximum entropy density estimation with generalized regularization and an application to species distribution modeling. *Journal of Machine Learning Research*, 8:1217–1260, 2007.

[77] R. M. Dudley. Central limit theorems for empirical measures. *Annals of Probability*, 6(6):899–929, 1978.

[78] Nigel Duffy and David Helmbold. Potential boosters? In *Advances in Neural Information Processing Systems 12*, pages 258–264. MIT Press, 2000.

[79] Nigel Duffy and David Helmbold. Boosting methods for regression. *Machine Learning*, 47(2/3):153–200. 2002.

[80] Andrzej Ehrenfeucht, David Haussler, Michael Kearns, and Leslie Valiant. A general lower bound on the number of examples needed for learning. *Information and Computation*, 82(3):247–261, September 1989.

[81] Günther Eibl and Karl-Peter Pfeiffer. Multiclass boosting for weak classifiers. *Journal of Machine Learning Research*, 6:189–210, 2005.

[82] Jane Elith, Catherine H. Graham, Robert P. Anderson, Miroslav Dudík, Simon Ferrier, Antoine Guisan, Robert J. Hijmans, Falk Huettmann, John R. Leathwick, Anthony Lehmann, Jin Li, Lucia G. Lohmann, Bette A. Loiselle, Glenn Manion, Craig Moritz, Miguel Nakamura, Yoshinori Nakazawa, Jacob McC. M. Overton, A. Townsend Peterson, Steven J. Phillips, Karen Richardson, Ricardo Scachetti-Pereira, Robert E. Schapire, Jorge Soberón, Stephen Williams, Mary S. Wisz, and Niklaus E. Zimmermann. Novel methods improve prediction of species' distributions from occurrence data. *Ecography*, 29:129–151, 2006.

[83] Sergio Escalera, Oriol Pujol, and Petia Radeva. On the decoding process in ternary error-correcting output codes. *IEEE Transactions on Pattern Analysis and Machine Intelligence*, 32(1):120–134, January 2010.

[84] William Feller. *An Introduction to Probability Theory and Its Applications*, volume 2, second edition. Wiley, 1971.

[85] Sally Floyd and Manfred Warmuth. Sample compression, learnability, and the Vapnik-Chervonenkis dimension. *Machine Learning*, 21(3):269–304, 1995.

[86] Dean P. Foster and Rakesh Vohra. Regret in the on-line decision problem. *Games and Economic Behavior*, 29:7–35, 1999.

[87] Marcus Frean and Tom Downs. A simple cost function for boosting. Technical report, Department of Computer Science and Electrical Engineering, University of Queensland, 1998.

[88] Yoav Freund. Boosting a weak learning algorithm by majority. *Information and Computation*, 121(2):256–285, 1995.

[89] Yoav Freund. An adaptive version of the boost by majority algorithm. *Machine Learning*, 43(3):293–318, June 2001.

[90] Yoav Freund, Raj Iyer, Robert E. Schapire, and Yoram Singer. An efficient boosting algorithm for combining preferences. *Journal of Machine Learning Research*, 4:933–969, 2003.

[91] Yoav Freund and Llew Mason. The alternating decision tree learning algorithm. In *Proceedings of the Sixteenth International Conference on Machine Learning*, pages 124–133, 1999.

[92] Yoav Freund and Manfred Opper. Drifting games and Brownian motion. *Journal of Computer and System Sciences*, 64:113–132, 2002.

[93] Yoav Freund and Robert E. Schapire. Experiments with a new boosting algorithm. In *Machine Learning: Proceedings of the Thirteenth International Conference*, pages 148–156, 1996.

[94] Yoav Freund and Robert E. Schapire. Game theory, on-line prediction and boosting. In *Proceedings of the Ninth Annual Conference on Computational Learning Theory*, pages 325–332, 1996.

[95] Yoav Freund and Robert E. Schapire. A decision-theoretic generalization of on-line learning and an application to boosting. *Journal of Computer and System Sciences*, 55(1):119–139, August 1997.

[96] Yoav Freund and Robert E. Schapire. Adaptive game playing using multiplicative weights. *Games and Economic Behavior*, 29:79–103, 1999.

[97] Peter W. Frey and David J. Slate. Letter recognition using Holland-style adaptive classifiers. *Machine Learning*, 6(2):161–182, 1991.

[98] Jerome Friedman, Trevor Hastie, and Robert Tibshirani. Additive logistic regression: A statistical view of boosting. *Annals of Statistics*, 28(2):337–407, April 2000.

[99] Jerome H. Friedman. Another approach to polychotomous classification. Technical report, Stanford University, 1996.

[100] Jerome H. Friedman. Greedy function approximation: A gradient boosting machine. *Annals of Statistics*, 29(5):1189–1232, October 2001.

[101] Drew Fudenberg and David K. Levine. Consistency and cautious fictitious play. *Journal of Economic Dynamics and Control*, 19(5–7):1065–1089, 1995.

[102] Drew Fudenberg and David K. Levine. *The Theory of Learning in Games*. MIT Press, 1998.

[103] Drew Fudenberg and Jean Tirole. *Game Theory*. MIT Press, 1991.

[104] Johannes Fürnkranz and Gerhard Widmer. Incremental reduced error pruning. In *Machine Learning: Proceedings of the Eleventh International Conference*, pages 70–77, 1994.

[105] Walter Gautschi. Error function and Fresnel integrals. In Milton Abramowitz and Irene A. Stegun, editors, *Handbook of Mathematical Functions with Formulas, Graphs, and Mathematical Tables*, pages 295–329. U.S. Department of Commerce, 1972.

[106] Dmitry Gavinsky. Optimally-smooth adaptive boosting and application to agnostic learning. *Journal of Machine Learning Research*, 4:101–117, 2003.

[107] Claudio Gentile and David P. Helmbold. Improved lower bounds for learning from noisy examples: An information-theoretic approach. *Information and Computation*, 166(2):133–155, May 2001.

[108] Mikael Goldmann, Johan Håstad, and Alexander Razborov. Majority gates vs. general weighted threshold gates. *Computational Complexity*, 2:277–300, 1992.

[109] A. L. Gorin, B. A. Parker, R. M. Sachs, and J. G. Wilpon. How may I help you? In *Proceedings Third IEEE Workshop on Interactive Voice Technology for Telecommunications Applications*, pages 57–60, 1996.

[110] A. L. Gorin, G. Riccardi, and J. H. Wright. How may I help you? *Speech Communication*, 23(1–2):113–127, October 1997.

[111] Adam J. Grove and Dale Schuurmans. Boosting in the limit: Maximizing the margin of learned ensembles. In *Proceedings of the Fifteenth National Conference on Artificial Intelligence*, pages 692–699, 1998.

[112] Peter D. Grünwald. *The Minimum Description Length Principle*. MIT Press, 2007.

[113] L. G. Gubin, B. T. Polyak, and E. V. Raik. The method of projections for finding the common point of convex sets. *USSR Computational Mathematics and Mathematical Physics*, 7(6):1–24, 1967.

[114] Venkatesan Guruswami and Amit Sahai. Multiclass learning, boosting, and error-correcting codes. In *Proceedings of the Twelfth Annual Conference on Computational Learning Theory*, pages 145–155, 1999.

[115] D. W. Hagelbarger. SEER, A SEquence Extrapolating Robot. *IRE Transactions on Electronic Computers*, EC-5(1):1–7, March 1956.

[116] I. Halperin. The product of projection operators. *Acta Scientiarum Mathematicarum*, 23:96–99, 1962.

[117] James Hannan. Approximation to Bayes risk in repeated play. In M. Dresher, A. W. Tucker, and P. Wolfe, editors, *Contributions to the Theory of Games*, volume 3, pages 97–139. Princeton University Press, 1957.

[118] Sergiu Hart and Andreu Mas-Colell. A general class of adaptive strategies. *Journal of Economic Theory*, 98(1):26–54, 2001.

[119] Trevor Hastie and Robert Tibshirani. Classification by pairwise coupling. *Annals of Statistics*, 26(2):451–471, 1998.

[120] Trevor Hastie, Robert Tibshirani, and Jerome Friedman. *The Elements of Statistical Learning: Data Mining, Inference, and Prediction*, second edition. Springer, 2009.

[121] David Haussler, Michael Kearns, Nick Littlestone, and Manfred K. Warmuth. Equivalence of models for polynomial learnability. *Information and Computation*, 95(2):129–161, December 1991.

[122] David P. Helmbold and Robert E. Schapire. Predicting nearly as well as the best pruning of a decision tree. *Machine Learning*, 27(1):51–68, April 1997.

[123] Wassily Hoeffding. Probability inequalities for sums of bounded random variables. *Journal of the American Statistical Association*, 58(301):13–30, March 1963.

[124] Klaus-U. Höffgen and Hans-U. Simon. Robust trainability of single neurons. In *Proceedings of the Fifth Annual ACM Workshop on Computational Learning Theory*, pages 428–439, 1992.

[125] Robert C. Holte. Very simple classification rules perform well on most commonly used datasets. *Machine Learning*, 11(1):63–90, 1993.

[126] Jeffrey C. Jackson and Mark W. Craven. Learning sparse perceptrons. In *Advances in Neural Information Processing Systems 8*, pages 654–660. MIT Press, 1996.

[127] E. T. Jaynes. Information theory and statistical mechanics. *Physical Review*, 106(4):620–630, May 15, 1957.

[128] Wenxin Jiang. Process consistency for AdaBoost. *Annals of Statistics*, 32(1):13–29, 2004.

[129] Adam Tauman Kalai and Rocco A. Servedio. Boosting in the presence of noise. *Journal of Computer and System Sciences*, 71(3):266–290, 2005.

[130] J. N. Kapur and H. K. Kesavan. *Entropy Optimization Principles with Applications*. Academic Press, 1992.

[131] Ioannis Karatzas and Steven E. Shreve. *Brownian Motion and Stochastic Calculus*, second edition. Springer, 1991.

[132] Michael Kearns and Yishay Mansour. On the boosting ability of top-down decision tree learning algorithms. In *Proceedings of the Twenty-Eighth Annual ACM Symposium on the Theory of Computing*, pages 459–468, 1996.

[133] Michael Kearns and Leslie G. Valiant. Cryptographic limitations on learning Boolean formulae and finite automata. *Journal of the Association for Computing Machinery*, 41(1):67–95, January 1994.

[134] Michael J. Kearns and Umesh V. Vazirani. *An Introduction to Computational Learning Theory*. MIT Press, 1994.

[135] Jyrki Kivinen and Manfred K. Warmuth. Boosting as entropy projection. In *Proceedings of the Twelfth Annual Conference on Computational Learning Theory*, pages 134–144, 1999.

[136] Aldebaro Klautau, Nikola Jevtić, and Alon Orlitsky. On nearest-neighbor error-correcting output codes with application to all-pairs multiclass support vector machines. *Journal of Machine Learning Research*, 4:1–15, April 2003.

[137] Ron Kohavi and Clayton Kunz. Option decision trees with majority votes. In *Machine Learning: Proceedings of the Fourteenth International Conference*, pages 161–169, 1997.

[138] Ron Kohavi and David H. Wolpert. Bias plus variance decomposition for zero-one loss functions. In *Machine Learning: Proceedings of the Thirteenth International Conference*, pages 275–283, 1996.

[139] V. Koltchinskii and D. Panchenko. Empirical margin distributions and bounding the generalization error of combined classifiers. *Annals of Statistics*, 30(1):1–50, February 2002.

[140] Eun Bae Kong and Thomas G. Dietterich. Error-correcting output coding corrects bias and variance. In *Proceedings of the Twelfth International Conference on Machine Learning*, pages 313–321, 1995.

[141] Nir Krause and Yoram Singer. Leveraging the margin more carefully. In *Proceedings of the Twenty-First International Conference on Machine Learning*, pages 496–503, 2004.

[142] C. Kremen, A. Cameron, A. Moilanen, S. J. Phillips, C. D. Thomas, H. Beentje, J. Dransfield, B. L. Fisher, F. Glaw, T. C. Good, G. J. Harper, R. J. Hijmans, D. C. Lees, E. Louis Jr., R. A. Nussbaum, C. J. Raxworthy,

A. Razafimpahanana, G. E. Schatz, M. Vences, D. R. Vieites, P. C. Wright, and M. L. Zjhra. Aligning conservation priorities across taxa in Madagascar with high-resolution planning tools. *Science*, 320(5873):222–226, April 11, 2008.

[143] Abba Krieger, Chuan Long, and Abraham Wyner. Boosting noisy data. In *Proceedings of the Eighteenth International Conference on Machine Learning*, pages 274–281, 2001.

[144] S. Kullback and R. A. Leibler. On information and sufficiency. *Annals of Mathematical Statistics*, 22(1):79–86, 1951.

[145] Solomon Kullback. *Information Theory and Statistics*. Wiley, 1959.

[146] Ludmila I. Kuncheva. *Combining Pattern Classifiers: Methods and Algorithms*. Wiley, 2004.

[147] John Lafferty. Additive models, boosting and inference for generalized divergences. In *Proceedings of the Twelfth Annual Conference on Computational Learning Theory*, pages 125–133, 1999.

[148] John D. Lafferty, Stephen Della Pietra, and Vincent Della Pietra. Statistical learning algorithms based on Bregman distances. In *Proceedings of the Canadian Workshop on Information Theory*, pages 77–80, 1997.

[149] Guy Lebanon and John Lafferty. Boosting and maximum likelihood for exponential models. In *Advances in Neural Information Processing Systems 14*, pages 447–454. MIT Press, 2002.

[150] Michel Ledoux and Michel Talagrand. *Probability in Banach Spaces: Isoperimetry and Processes*. Springer-Verlag, 1991.

[151] David D. Lewis and Jason Catlett. Heterogeneous uncertainty sampling for supervised learning. In *Machine Learning: Proceedings of the Eleventh International Conference*, pages 148–156, 1994.

[152] David D. Lewis and William A. Gale. A sequential algorithm for training text classifiers. In *Proceedings of the 17th Annual International ACM SIGIR Conference on Research and Development in Information Retrieval*, pages 3–12, 1994.

[153] Nick Littlestone. Learning quickly when irrelevant attributes abound: A new linear-threshold algorithm. *Machine Learning*, 2(4):285–318, 1988.

[154] Nick Littlestone and Manfred Warmuth. Relating data compression and learnability. Unpublished manuscript, November 1987.

[155] Nick Littlestone and Manfred K. Warmuth. The weighted majority algorithm. *Information and Computation*, 108(2):212–261, 1994.

[156] Tie-Yan Liu. Learning to rank for information retrieval. *Foundations and Trends in Information Retrieval*, 3(3):225–331, 2009.

[157] Philip M. Long and Rocco A. Servedio. Martingale boosting. In *Learning Theory: 18th Annual Conference on Learning Theory*, pages 79–94, 2005.

[158] Philip M. Long and Rocco A. Servedio. Adaptive martingale boosting. In *Advances in Neural Information Processing Systems 21*, pages 977–984. 2009.

[159] Philip M. Long and Rocco A. Servedio. Random classification noise defeats all convex potential boosters. *Machine Learning*, 78(3):287–304, 2010.

[160] David G. Luenberger and Yinyu Ye. *Linear and Nonlinear Programming*, third edition. Springer, 2008.

[161] Gábor Lugosi and Nicolas Vayatis. On the Bayes-risk consistency of regularized boosting methods. *Annals of Statistics*, 32(1):30–55, 2004.

[162] Richard Maclin and David Opitz. An empirical evaluation of bagging and boosting. In *Proceedings of the Fourteenth National Conference on Artificial Intelligence*, pages 546–551, 1997.

[163] Stéphane G. Mallat and Zhifeng Zhang. Matching pursuits with time-frequency dictionaries. *IEEE Transactions on Signal Processing*, 41(12):3397–3415, December 1993.

[164] Shie Mannor, Ron Meir, and Tong Zhang. Greedy algorithms for classification—consistency, convergence rates, and adaptivity. *Journal of Machine Learning Research*, 4:713–742, October 2003.

[165] Yishay Mansour and David McAllester. Boosting using branching programs. *Journal of Computer and System Sciences*, 64(1):103–112, 2002.

[166] Stephen Marsland. *Machine Learning: An Algorithmic Perspective*. Chapman & Hall/CRC, 2009.

[167] Llew Mason, Peter Bartlett, and Jonathan Baxter. Direct optimization of margins improves generalization in combined classifiers. In *Advances in Neural Information Processing Systems 11*, pages 288–294. MIT Press, 1999.

[168] Llew Mason, Jonathan Baxter, Peter Bartlett, and Marcus Frean. Functional gradient techniques for combining hypotheses. In A. J. Smola, P. L. Bartlett, B. Schölkopf, and D. Schuurmans, editors, *Advances in Large Margin Classifiers*, pages 221–246. MIT Press, 2000.

[169] David Mease and Abraham Wyner. Evidence contrary to the statistical view of boosting. *Journal of Machine Learning Research*, 9:131–156, February 2008.

[170] Ron Meir and Gunnar Rätsch. An introduction to boosting and leveraging. In S. Mendelson and A. Smola, editors, *Advanced Lectures on Machine Learning*, pages 119–184. Springer, 2003.

[171] Tom M. Mitchell. *Machine Learning*. McGraw Hill, 1997.

[172] Indraneel Mukherjee, Cynthia Rudin, and Robert E. Schapire. The rate of convergence of AdaBoost. In *Proceedings of the 24th Annual Conference on Learning Theory*, 2011.

[173] Indraneel Mukherjee and Robert E. Schapire. A theory of multiclass boosting. In *Advances in Neural Information Processing Systems 23*, 2011.

[174] Roger B. Myerson. *Game Theory: Analysis of Conflict*. Harvard University Press, 1997.

[175] J. von Neumann. Zur theorie der gesellschaftsspiele. *Mathematische Annalen*, 100:295–320, 1928.

[176] John von Neumann. *Functional Operators, Volume II: The Geometry of Orthogonal Spaces*. Princeton University Press, 1950.

[177] Bernt Øksendal. *Stochastic Differential Equations: An Introduction with Applications*, sixth edition. Springer, 2003.

[178] T. Onoda, G. Rätsch, and K.-R. Müller. An asymptotic analysis of AdaBoost in the binary classification case. In *Proceedings of the 8th International Conference on Artificial Neural Networks*, pages 195–200, 1998.

[179] Martin J. Osborne and Ariel Rubinstein. *A Course in Game Theory*. MIT Press, 1994.

[180] Guillermo Owen. *Game Theory*, third edition. Academic Press, 1995.

[181] Nikunj C. Oza and Stuart Russell. Online bagging and boosting. In *Proceedings of the Eighth International Workshop on Artificial Intelligence and Statistics*, pages 105–112, 2001.

[182] Steven J. Phillips, Miroslav Dudík, and Robert E. Schapire. A maximum entropy approach to species distribution modeling. In *Proceedings of the Twenty-First International Conference on Machine Learning*, 2004.

[183] J. R. Quinlan. Bagging, boosting, and C4.5. In *Proceedings of the Thirteenth National Conference on Artificial Intelligence*, pages 725–730, 1996.

[184] J. Ross Quinlan. *C4.5: Programs for Machine Learning*. Morgan Kaufmann, 1993.

[185] Shyamsundar Rajaram and Shivani Agarwal. Generalization bounds for k-partite ranking. In *Proceedings of the NIPS-2005 Workshop on Learning to Rank*, 2005.

[186] G. Rätsch, T. Onoda, and K.-R. Müller. Soft margins for AdaBoost. *Machine Learning*, 42(3):287–320, 2001.

[187] Gunnar Rätsch and Manfred K. Warmuth. Efficient margin maximizing with boosting. *Journal of Machine Learning Research*, 6:2131–2152, December 2005.

[188] Lev Reyzin and Robert E. Schapire. How boosting the margin can also boost classifier complexity. In *Proceedings of the 23rd International Conference on Machine Learning*, pages 753–760, 2006.

[189] G. Riccardi, A. L. Gorin, A. Ljolje, and M. Riley. Spoken language understanding for automated call routing. In *Proceedings of the 1997 IEEE International Conference on Acoustics, Speech, and Signal Processing*, volume 2, pages 1143–1146, 1997.

[190] Greg Ridgeway, David Madigan, and Thomas Richardson. Boosting methodology for regression problems. In *Proceedings of the Seventh International Workshop on Artificial Intelligence and Statistics*, pages 152–161, 1999.

[191] R. Tyrrell Rockafellar. *Convex Analysis*. Princeton University Press, 1970.

[192] Saharon Rosset, Ji Zhu, and Trevor Hastie. Boosting as a regularized path to a maximum margin classifier. *Journal of Machine Learning Research*, 5:941–973, 2004.

[193] Cynthia Rudin, Corinna Cortes, Mehryar Mohri, and Robert E. Schapire. Margin-based ranking meets boosting in the middle. In *Learning Theory: 18th Annual Conference on Learning Theory*, pages 63–78, 2005.

[194] Cynthia Rudin, Ingrid Daubechies, and Robert E. Schapire. The dynamics of AdaBoost: Cyclic behavior and convergence of margins. *Journal of Machine Learning Research*, 5:1557–1595, December 2004.

[195] Cynthia Rudin and Robert E. Schapire. Margin-based ranking and an equivalence between AdaBoost and RankBoost. *Journal of Machine Learning Research*, 10:2193–2232, 2009.

[196] Cynthia Rudin, Robert E. Schapire, and Ingrid Daubechies. Analysis of boosting algorithms using the smooth margin function. *Annals of Statistics*, 35(6):2723–2768, 2007.

[197] Walter Rudin. *Principles of Mathematical Analysis*, third edition. McGraw-Hill, 1976.

[198] N. Sauer. On the density of families of sets. *Journal of Combinatorial Theory*, series A, 13:145–147, 1972.

[199] Robert E. Schapire. The strength of weak learnability. *Machine Learning*, 5(2):197–227, 1990.

[200] Robert E. Schapire. Using output codes to boost multiclass learning problems. In *Machine Learning: Proceedings of the Fourteenth International Conference*, pages 313–321, 1997.

[201] Robert E. Schapire. Drifting games. *Machine Learning*, 43(3):265–291, June 2001.

[202] Robert E. Schapire, Yoav Freund, Peter Bartlett, and Wee Sun Lee. Boosting the margin: A new explanation for the effectiveness of voting methods. *Annals of Statistics*, 26(5):1651–1686, October 1998.

[203] Robert E. Schapire, Marie Rochery, Mazin Rahim, and Narendra Gupta. Incorporating prior knowledge into boosting. In *Proceedings of the Nineteenth International Conference on Machine Learning*, 2002.

[204] Robert E. Schapire, Marie Rochery, Mazin Rahim, and Narendra Gupta. Boosting with prior knowledge for call classification. *IEEE Transactions on Speech and Audio Processing*, 13(2):174–181, March 2005.

[205] Robert E. Schapire and Yoram Singer. Improved boosting algorithms using confidence-rated predictions. *Machine Learning*, 37(3):297–336, December 1999.

[206] Robert E. Schapire and Yoram Singer. BoosTexter: A boosting-based system for text categorization. *Machine Learning*, 39(2/3):135–168, May/June 2000.

[207] Greg Schohn and David Cohn. Less is more: Active learning with support vector machines. In *Proceedings of the Seventeenth International Conference on Machine Learning*, pages 839–846, 2000.

[208] Bernhard Schölkopf and Alex Smola. *Learning with Kernels*. MIT Press, 2002.

[209] Holger Schwenk and Yoshua Bengio. Training methods for adaptive boosting of neural networks. In *Advances in Neural Information Processing Systems 10*, pages 647–653. MIT Press, 1998.

[210] Rocco A. Servedio. Smooth boosting and learning with malicious noise. *Journal of Machine Learning Research*, 4:633–648, September 2003.

[211] Shai Shalev-Shwartz and Yoram Singer. On the equivalence of weak learnability and linear separability: New relaxations and efficient boosting algorithms. *Machine Learning*, 80(2–3):141–163, 2010.

[212] C. E. Shannon. A mathematical theory of communication. *The Bell System Technical Journal*, 27:379–423, July 1948, and 623–656, October 1948.

[213] Claude E. Shannon. A mind-reading (?) machine. Technical report, Bell Laboratories, 1953.

[214] Amanda J. C. Sharkey, editor. *Combining Artificial Neural Nets: Ensemble and Modular Multi-Net Systems*. Springer, 1999.

[215] A. N. Shiryaev. *Probability*, second edition. Springer, 1996.

[216] S. K. Srinivasan and R. Vasudevan. *Introduction to Random Differential Equations and Their Applications*. Elsevier, 1971.

[217] Robert Tibshirani. Bias, variance and prediction error for classification rules. Technical report. Department of Statistics, University of Toronto, November 1996.

[218] Robert Tibshirani. Regression shrinkage and selection via the lasso. *Journal of the Royal Statistical Society*, series B (Methodological), 58(1):267–288, 1996.

[219] Gokhan Tur, Dilek Hakkani-Tür, and Robert E. Schapire. Combining active and semi-supervised learning for spoken language understanding. *Speech Communication*, 45(2):171–186, 2005.

[220] Gokhan Tur, Robert E. Schapire, and Dilek Hakkani-Tür. Active learning for spoken language understanding. In *Proceedings of the 2003 IEEE International Conference on Acoustics, Speech, and Signal Processing*, volume 1, pages 276–279, 2003.

[221] L. G. Valiant. A theory of the learnable. *Communications of the ACM*, 27(11):1134–1142, November 1984.

[222] Vladimir Vapnik. *Estimation of Dependences Based on Empirical Data*. Springer-Verlag, 1982.

[223] Vladimir N. Vapnik. *The Nature of Statistical Learning Theory*. Springer, 1995.

[224] Vladimir N. Vapnik. *Statistical Learning Theory*. Wiley, 1998.

[225] V. N. Vapnik and A. Ya. Chervonenkis. On the uniform convergence of relative frequencies of events to their probabilities. *Theory of Probability and Its Applications*, 16(2):264–280, 1971.

[226] V. N. Vapnik and A. Ya. Chervonenkis. *Theory of Pattern Recognition*. Nauka, 1974. (In Russian.)

[227] Paul Viola and Michael Jones. Rapid object detection using a boosted cascade of simple features. In *Proceedings of the 2001 IEEE Computer Society Conference on Computer Vision and Pattern Recognition*, volume 1, pages 511–518, 2001.

[228] Paul Viola and Michael Jones. Robust real-time object detection. In *Proceeding of IEEE Workshop on Statistical and Computational Theories of Vision*, 2001.

[229] Volodimir G. Vovk. Aggregating strategies. In *Proceedings of the Third Annual Workshop on Computational Learning Theory*, pages 371–383, 1990.

[230] Liwei Wang, Masashi Sugiyama, Zhaoxiang Jing, Cheng Yang, Zhi-Hua Zhou, and Jufu Feng. A refined margin analysis for boosting algorithms via equilibrium margin. *Journal of Machine Learning Research*, 12:1835–1863, June 2011.

[231] Frans M. J. Willems, Yuri M. Shtarkov, and Tjalling J. Tjalkens. The context tree weighting method: Basic properties. *IEEE Transactions on Information Theory*, 41(3):653–664, 1995.

[232] Abraham J. Wyner. On boosting and the exponential loss. In *Proceedings of the Ninth International Workshop on Artificial Intelligence and Statistics*, 2003.

[233] Yongxin Taylor Xi, Zhen James Xiang, Peter J. Ramadge, and Robert E. Schapire. Speed and sparsity of regularized boosting. In *Proceedings of the Twelfth International Conference on Artificial Intelligence and Statistics*, pages 615–622, 2009.

[234] Jun Xu and Hang Li. AdaRank: A boosting algorithm for information retrieval. In *Proceedings of the 30th Annual International ACM SIGIR Conference on Research and Development in Information Retrieval*, pages 391–398, 2007.

[235] Tong Zhang. Statistical behavior and consistency of classification methods based on convex risk minimization. *Annals of Statistics*, 32(1):56–134, 2004.

[236] Tong Zhang and Bin Yu. Boosting with early stopping: Convergence and consistency. *Annals of Statistics*, 33(4):1538–1579, 2005.

[237] Peng Zhao and Bin Yu. Stagewise Lasso. *Journal of Machine Learning Research*, 8:2701–2726, December 2007.

[238] Ji Zhu, Hui Zou, Saharon Rosset, and Trevor Hastie. Multi-class AdaBoost. *Statistics and Its Interface*, 2:349–360, 2009.

Index of Algorithms, Figures, and Tables

Subject and Author Index

Note: Numbers, symbols, Greek letters, etc. are alphabetized as if spelled out in words. Page listings tagged with "n" refer to footnotes; those tagged with "x" refer to exercises.

Adaptive Computation and Machine Learning

Thomas Dietterich, Editor

Christopher Bishop, David Heckerman, Michael Jordan,
and Michael Kearns, Associate Editors

Printed in the United States
by Baker & Taylor Publisher Services

Printed in the United States
by Baker & Taylor Publisher Services